AQA Psychology A

A2

Exclusively endorsed by AQA

James Bailey
Nick Lund
Julia Willerton
Jane Willson

Series editor
Simon Green

Nelson Thornes

Published in 2009 by:
Nelson Thornes Ltd
Delta Place
27 Bath Road
CHELTENHAM
GL53 7TH
United Kingdom

10 11 12 13 / 10 9 8 7 6 5 4 3

A catalogue record for this book is available from the British Library

ISBN 978 0 7487 9825 4

Cover photograph: Getty/Katrina Wittkamp
Illustrations by Wearset Ltd; additional illustrations by Dave Russell Illustrations and Paul McCaffrey

Page make-up by Wearset Ltd, Boldon, Tyne and Wear

Printed in China by 1010 Printing International Ltd

Contents

Unit 3
Topics in psychology

References and other supporting documentation available online
www.nelsonthornes.com/psychology_answers

AQA introduction

Nelson Thornes has worked in partnership with AQA to ensure this book and the accompanying online resources offer you the best support for your A Level course.

All resources have been approved by senior AQA examiners so you can feel assured that they closely match the specification for this subject and provide you with everything you need to prepare successfully for your exams.

These print and online resources together **unlock blended learning**; this means that the links between the activities in the book and the activities online blend together to maximise your understanding of a topic and help you achieve your potential.

These online resources are available on **kerboodle!** which can be accessed via the internet at www.kerboodle.com/live, anytime, anywhere. If your school or college subscribes to this service you will be provided with your own personal login details. Once logged in, access your course and locate the required activity.

For more information and help visit **www.kerboodle.com**

The electronic resources support all the topics of the book regardless of which you choose to study for Units 3 and 4 (see the Introduction to this book for more details on options available). When in **kerboodle!** you will see a variety of worksheets, teacher notes and interactive resources such as:

🔲 Learning activity

These resources include a variety of interactive and non-interactive activities to support your learning.

✓ Progress tracking

These resources include a variety of tests that you can use to check your knowledge on particular topics (Test yourself) and a range of resources that enable you to analyse and understand examination questions (On your marks …).

🔲 Research support

These resources include WebQuests, in which you are assigned a task and provided with a range of web links to use as source material for research.

🎧 Audio stimulus

Each chapter has a podcast summarising the important points.

🔲 How to use this book

This book covers the specification for your course and is arranged in a sequence approved by AQA. The book content is divided into two units – Unit 3 and Unit 4 – which match the units of the AQA Psychology A A2 specification. It is then divided into sections matched to the eight sections of the specification. For Unit 3: Biological rhythms and sleep; Perception; Relationships; Aggression; Eating behaviour; Gender; Intelligence; Cognition and development. Unit 4 covers A, B and C; part A has sections for Psychopathology, part B Psychology in action, which contains the sections on media, addictive behaviour and anomalistic psychology, and part C is Psychological research and scientific method. Each section introduction contains a table that maps to the section content in the specification so you can see at a glance where to find the information you need. Sections are then further divided into chapters, and then topics, making them clear and easy to use. Each section ends with a 'How science works' practical activity and further reading suggestions. The content of the book is designed to meet the requirements of 'How science works' by giving you the necessary skills and information to plan your own psychological investigations and through the use of margin features highlighting the skills needed.

The features in this book include:

Learning objectives

At the beginning of each topic you will find a list of learning objectives that are linked to the requirements of the specification.

 Key terms

Terms that you will need to be able to define and understand.

 Hint

Hints to aid your understanding of the content.

 Links

This highlights any key areas where sections relate to one another.

There are also special versions of the Hint and Link features which have been developed specifically for the A2 book. These address the need for reference to relevant approaches issues and debates in your answers to questions in the exams, and to emphasise 'How science works' in psychology.

 Hint

How science works

These bring out elements of 'How science works' in psychology and some contain the letters A to L in brackets to show how they relate specifically to in the specification.

 Links

Approaches, issues and debates

These offer links to the introductory chapter on approaches issues and debates and support you to provide coverage for those relevant to your answers.

 Research study

Certain studies are described in more detail. These research studies are designed to represent the research methods and findings typical of a particular area of psychological research. They also act as a focus for discussing methodological and ethical issues in psychological research, and there are links from them to the Research methods chapters. You will need to know details of studies and concepts specifically mentioned in the specification, but you should also know additional studies and concepts in outline to use in discussion and evaluation.

How science works: practical activity

At the end of each section there is a practical activity for you to undertake. Actually designing investigations, collecting data and analysing and interpreting the findings of your own research will bring the subject to life and will help you to develop a more thorough understanding of how science works.

■ Summary questions

Short questions that test your understanding of the subject and allow you to apply the skills you develop to different scenarios. The final question in each set is designed to be a stretch and challenge question and to require more thought. Answers are supplied free at **www.nelsonthornes.com/psychology_answers**.

This link is also where you will find the extensive reference list for the book, the glossary of key terms, a table summarising types of sampling, a suggested information sheet and consent form for participants, tables with summary information on measures of dispersion and central tendency, and research studies for the Addictive behaviour section. Nelson Thornes is responsible for the solution(s) given and they may not constitute the only possible solution(s).

 AQA Examiner's tip

Hints from AQA examiners to help you with your study and to prepare for your exam.

AQA Examination-style questions

Questions in the style that you can expect in your exam. These can be found at the end of each unit with guidance on how to answer them. AQA examination questions are reproduced by permission of the Assessment and Qualifications Alliance.

Key points

A bulleted list at the end of each topic summarising the content in an easy-to-understand way.

▦ Weblinks in the book

As Nelson Thornes is not responsible for third party content online, there may be some changes to this material that are beyond our control. In order for us to ensure that the links referred to in the book are as up-to-date and stable as possible, the websites are usually homepages with supporting instructions on how to reach the relevant pages if necessary.

Please let us know at **kerboodle@nelsonthornes.com.** if you find a link that doesn't work and we will do our best to redirect the link, or to find an alternative site.

Introduction to this book

Congratulations on successfully completing your AS studies in psychology! You are now moving on to A2 Psychology, and this textbook contains all the information that you will need to be equally successful at this level.

Much of the material will be familiar to you from AS. You have been introduced to the various approaches within psychology, and covered topics such as cognitive, developmental, biological and social psychology, individual differences and research methods. In A2 you will have the opportunity to study some of these in more depth, but you will also meet some new and exciting areas.

The AQA Psychology Specification A divides A2 into two units. In Unit 3 you are required to study three topics from a choice of eight. The topics have been chosen to represent a wide range of research areas within psychology. They range from sleep and biological rhythms, through perception, relationships and aggression, to eating behaviour, gender, intelligence and cognitive development. Your teacher will help you choose the three you will study. The examination for Unit 3 will assess your knowledge and understanding of these three topic areas. It will also assess your awareness of approaches, issues and debates in psychology. You have already met these in your AS studies. Approaches include biological, behavioural and psychodynamic models of behaviour, including their strengths and weaknesses. Issues and debates include gender and cultural bias, reductionism, psychology as a science, free will and determinism, and the use of non-human animals in research. For each of the topics you study you will be expected to show awareness and understanding of relevant approaches, issues and debates.

Unit 4 is divided into three sections. In the first, Psychopathology, you will study one out of schizophrenia, depression, or anxiety disorders. You will need to show your understanding of diagnosis and classification, and be able to describe and evaluate alternative explanations for your chosen disorder. Finally, you will study the appropriateness and effectiveness of biological and psychological therapies.

The second section, Psychology in action, focuses on psychology in the real world. You will study one out of media psychology, the psychology of addictive behaviour, or anomalistic psychology. Media psychology covers psychological explanations for the effects of the media on social behaviour, attitudes and how they can be changed, and the psychology of celebrity. The psychology of addictive behaviour is concerned with explanations for the initiation and maintenance of addictions, in particular smoking and gambling. It also covers other factors in addiction, such as personality and the media, and methods of reducing addictive behaviour. Anomalistic psychology is the study of unusual beliefs and experiences, such as belief in psychic healing, psychokinesis and ESP. This is a key area for the application of rigorous scientific methods to test the validity of these beliefs and experiences. In many cases it turns out that we can explain observations using well-established psychological principles.

The third section of Unit 4 covers Psychological research and the scientific method. It builds on your studies at AS to develop your understanding of the scientific method as it is applied in psychology.

Areas covered include the major features of the scientific process, designing psychological investigations, analysing data, and reporting on investigations.

As the scientific study of behaviour, an underlying aim of the Psychology AS and A2 specification is the development of an awareness of how science works. Besides the material covered in the research methods section of the specification, you will be introduced to wider aspects of how science works. These include evaluating methodology, how scientists communicate information, the applications of scientific findings, ethical issues in the scientific process, and the way society uses science to inform decision making.

The content of this book mirrors the Psychology A2 Specification A, closely following the order of topics. Each topic begins with a table showing that part of the specification and the relevant page numbers for each aspect of the topic. Margin features include a glossary and AQA Examiner's tips, links to other sections of the book and, most importantly, guidance on the use of approaches, issues and debates in relation to that particular topic. Other margin features emphasise how material in the text illustrates features of how science works. Although coursework is not formally assessed as part of Psychology A2, it is the most effective way of learning research methods. Each topic, therefore, ends with a suggestion for a related practical activity, as well as key points and summary questions. Finally, at the end of the Unit 3 chapters and the end of the Unit 4 chapters there are examination-style questions for you to practise on.

There is a great deal of material in this book, but don't forget that you will only be studying three topics for Unit 3, one disorder in Psychopathology, and one of the three Psychology in action topics. You will still have to work hard, but we hope that you will find psychology at A2 exciting and stimulating.

Introductory chapter on approaches, issues and debates

Approaches

As psychology has developed as a science, it has incorporated a number of alternative approaches that you will have come across in your studies at AS. Your understanding of these will be further developed as you study the topics you have selected in A2 Units 3 and 4. Different approaches emphasise different factors in behaviour. For instance the biological approach looks at brain structure and function, while a behaviourist focuses on learning experiences and the role of conditioning. The development of approaches and methods is a key aspect of psychology. It is important that you appreciate the strengths and weaknesses of those approaches.

The topics you have chosen to study in Unit 3 will involve different approaches. For example, cognition and development involves cognitive and biological approaches. To explain eating behaviour we might use biological, cognitive, behavioural and psychodynamic approaches. The key features of the main approaches are outlined below. The section on psychopathology in Unit 4 uses the various approaches in explaining psychological disorders.

The biological approach

This emphasises the role of brain structure and function in behaviour, and makes several key assumptions:

- By measuring various aspects of brain function we can relate behaviour to changes in the brain. These aspects might involve electrical activity of neurons, or the use of modern scanning techniques to detect changes in patterns of activity in different brain areas. In the study of psychological disorders we are especially interested in brain neurotransmitters.

- The biological approach also emphasises the role of genetics in behaviour. It does not assume that all behaviour is genetically determined, but a popular biological model of many behaviours is that genetic factors interact with the environment.

- Although the focus is on brain function, the biological approach can also involve the measurement of other physiological functions such as heart rate and blood hormone levels.

- It is scientific and uses modern methods such as fMRI (functional magnetic resonance imaging) and genetic analysis of an individual's DNA. Results are objective and can be replicated.

- This approach is reductionist (see page xi). It might ignore psychological and social factors.

The behavioural approach

In contrast to the biological approach the behavioural approach emphasises the role of learning and the environment. There are several key assumptions:

- All behaviour, including psychological disorders, is learned through early experience. There is no place for genetic (inherited) factors.

- Learning occurs through different types of conditioning, such as operant and classical (see page 239). Social learning can involve observation and imitation of others; social learning theory has played an important part in explaining child development.

- Rewards and punishment play important roles in learning. Behaviour that is rewarded is likely to be learned and repeated, while behaviour that is punished is less likely to be learned.

- It is based on scientific experiments, especially the early work of Thorndike and Skinner using cats, rats and pigeons.

- The approach is reductionist, in that behaviour is reduced to simple associations between behaviour and the environment. It largely ignores the cognitive factors that have been shown to be important in behaviour. Social learning theory was developed to help overcome these limitations.

The cognitive approach

This approach emphasises the scientific study of human cognitive processes. These include memory, perception, attention, and also thoughts and feelings. There are several key assumptions:

- Cognitive processes can be studied in the laboratory using carefully controlled scientific experiments. These can identify the psychological processes involved in, for instance, memory, attention and perception (see page 44).

- This approach often uses the way computers work to model human cognitive processes. It also uses computer terminology. For example, another term for the approach is 'information processing'.

- A major area of research that has developed over the last 10 years combines the cognitive and biological approaches. Known as *cognitive neuroscience*, it explores the brain systems involved in human cognitive processes.

- The *cognitive-behavioural* approach explains the causes of psychological disorders and leads to particular treatments using a combination of cognitive and behavioural techniques.

The cognitive approach can be reductionist, as it tries to break down cognitive processes into basic information-processing units. There is little emphasis on social and cultural factors.

The psychodynamic approach

There are many psychodynamic approaches, but Freud's psychoanalytic model has been the most influential. This is a complex approach with several key assumptions:

Our behaviour is influenced not just by our conscious experience but by experiences and processes buried in our unconscious.

Our personality is made of three components. The conscious ego balances the competing demands of the id and the superego. The id is a reservoir of basic inherited instincts such as sex and aggression, while the superego represents our moral conscience, that develops during childhood.

During childhood we pass through various stages of psychosexual development. At each stage id energy is focused on a different part of the body, such as mouth (oral stage), anus and genitals. Unsuccessful negotiation of these stages leads to conflicts and anxieties.

The ego tries to protect us from these anxieties using defence mechanisms such as repression into the unconscious.

The approach treats people as complex, and although Freud over-estimated sexual development's role he was the first to emphasise the importance of early experience and the unconscious.

Many of the ideas and concepts used in the psychodynamic approach are impossible to test using controlled experiments, and its place in modern scientific psychology is hotly debated. This does not mean the ideas are wrong, only that they cannot be objectively confirmed. The approach is particularly relevant to the study of psychological disorders (page 317).

Issues and debates

An important part of the specification for Unit 3, Topics in psychology, requires you to develop an appreciation of issues and debates in psychology. So what are issues and debates? You will already have come across lots of specific theories, approaches and research studies. These may come from different areas of psychology, for example, cognitive, developmental or biological psychology. You will have already developed some of the skills needed to evaluate particular theories and studies. For example, whether theories are supported or challenged by research evidence or a study has ecological validity.

However, part of the background to all psychological research is a number of issues and debates that can apply to many theories and studies, regardless of the area of psychology they relate to. In comparison to the critical evaluative skills that you already have, these issues and debates represent a more general level of analysis and commentary.

Not all issues and debates are relevant to all areas of psychology. You will be expected to show an understanding of why an issue is important for a particular topic, and why it might influence our thinking about particular approaches and studies.

The main issues and debates are briefly reviewed below. In the book relevant issues and debates are discussed using examples.

Psychology as science

Science is a particular approach to studying the world that emphasises *objectivity*, i.e. the experimenter is clearly separated from whatever they are studying. The biologist deals with physiological processes, the chemist with compounds, the astronomer planets and stars. In science we identify variables to be studied and measured. Controlled experiments are used to investigate relationships between variables, and findings are used to test hypotheses and develop theories. Psychology has adopted the framework of science and during your course you will gain an understanding of how science works. However, there are still issues over whether psychology can be called a science in the same way as biology and chemistry.

Objectivity: psychologists are people doing experiments usually on other people. The psychologist may have beliefs and expectations about the experiment, while the participant may react to the presence of the experimenter in unexpected ways, e.g. demand characteristics. Some people would argue that this means that psychology can never be purely objective.

Falsifiability: theories lead to predictions or hypotheses that are tested in experiments. If they are not supported by results, the theory is wrong. This is falsifiability and a critical part of science. But some theories are not falsifiable, e.g. some of Freud's ideas are so complex it is impossible to produce a testable hypothesis.

Sciences such as biology and chemistry have a single *paradigm*, which is 'a shared set of assumptions, methods, and terminology about what should be studied and why and how' (Kuhn, 1962). In contrast, psychology has approaches, such as biological, psychoanalytic, behavioural, etc. These approaches use different paradigms, partly because human behaviour is so complex and varied.

Many experimental studies in psychology have led to reliable, replicable results. Different researchers doing the same experiment get the same results, key to the scientific approach.

Reductionism in psychology

Reductionism is a scientific approach that tries to explain phenomena in terms of basic elements. For example, think about the behaviour of a group of friends. We might want to explain why one of them begins a violent argument with one of the others. To explain this we could look at the group dynamics involved. The argument may be the result of jealousy. Or we could look at the individual themselves; perhaps they have a particularly aggressive personality. A psychobiologist might be interested in the patterns of brain activity associated with this behaviour. We could even investigate the activity of single brain neurons. These accounts represent different *levels of explanation*. As we move from looking at the social group, then the individual, then patterns of brain activity and finally the activity of single neurons, the accounts are becoming more *reductionist*.

You can immediately see that some approaches are more reductionist than others. A psychobiologist investigates behaviour by looking at brain activity. This is a reductionist approach as it may ignore psychological and cultural variables. There are other forms of reductionism in psychology:

- Evolutionary reductionism attempts to explain human behaviour in terms of evolutionary theory. This means that it looks at behaviour and assumes it must at some time have been adaptive and therefore inherited. This approach may ignore the fact that cultures and societies develop in ways that do not involve evolutionary processes. This might involve cultural transmission of ideas and technology from generation to generation.

- Environmental reductionism relates specifically to the behaviourist approach. This tries to explain all human behaviour in terms of simple conditioning, i.e. learned associations between stimuli and responses. This ignores the role of cognitive processes in complex human learning.

- Methodological reductionism. This relates to the scientific approach in psychology in which certain variables are identified and then studied in a carefully controlled experiment. This approach is very successful in biology and chemistry which work with far simpler systems. Human behaviour has so many variables that they cannot all be identified and operationalised.

Returning to levels of explanation, it may be that no particular approach is right or wrong. A sensible view would be that a full description of aggressive behaviour requires all of the levels mentioned above – group dynamics, individual characteristics, and activity in the brain and neurons.

Free will and determinism

This is a complex issue and much of the debate is beyond the scope of Psychology A-level. However, there are some basic features which you should be aware of. Humans have a sense that they can choose which of several courses of action to take. We have a strong sense of free will. However, most of the approaches in psychology are trying to identify the causes of behaviour, i.e. what *determines* our behaviour. In this sense most approaches in psychology are 'deterministic'. If we can explain someone's behaviour fully then there is no room for free will.

If this were true it would have important consequences for society. We assume that individuals take responsibility for their actions and therefore have the free will to choose whether to do right or wrong. Of course, this would not apply to children, to people with severe mental disorders, or perhaps to people with certain types of brain damage. However, if behaviour is fully determined by factors outside the person's control, then they do not have free will and cannot be responsible for their actions.

Many psychologists take a middle road in this debate. If our behaviour was entirely based on free will, no laws or predictions would be possible. The fact that psychologists have identified many laws (e.g. attribution errors or operant conditioning) suggests that free will in a pure form does not exist. However, in many situations people do choose between different alternatives and have a strong sense of free will. So we can see human behaviour as determined by general laws but with free will operating in specific situations. This is a version of *'soft determinism'*. The different approaches also differ in their degree of determinism. For example:

- The biological approach represents *'hard determinism'*. It sees our behaviour as mostly determined by our biology and genetic make-up.

- Social learning theory represents soft determinism. It assumes that social and environmental factors are important in determining behaviour. However, we also have cognitions (thoughts and feelings) that help us to choose between alternatives and allow for a degree of free will.

- The humanistic approach specifically assumes that humans have free will and can make choices that decide the course of their lives. It rejects determinism in all of its forms, and therapy based on the humanistic approach encourages people to

Nature and nurture

This has been one of the longest lasting and most important debates in psychology. Today we would refer to it as genetic or inherited influences versus non-genetic or environmental influences. The central question is the extent to which our behaviour is determined by the genes we inherit from our parents versus the influence of environmental factors such as home, school and friends. The extreme positions would be that behaviour is entirely determined by genes, or by our environment. The answer is most behaviours reflect a combination of the two.

Perhaps the most controversial area has been the study of intelligence, as measured by IQ. If intelligence is entirely determined by inherited genetic factors it would imply that educational programmes for deprived groups in society are largely a waste of time. More generally, the role of genes has been investigated in most areas of psychology. These include the development of perception, aggressive behaviour, eating disorders and many other psychopathologies, gender role development and addictive behaviours.

Nowadays it is accepted that genes and environment can interact in complex ways:

▧ Passive gene–environment interaction. This is where parental genes affect the way they treat their children. For instance, parents with music ability automatically encourage this in their children.

▧ Active gene–environment interaction. This is where the child's genetic make-up actively affects its environment. For instance a quiet child will prefer solitude and passive activities, which can affect their development and later behaviour. A musically gifted child may actively pursue friends who are also musical.

▧ Reactive gene–environment interaction. The child's genetic make-up, for instance their looks or temperament, produces particular reactions in parents and friends that affect development and behaviour. Parents or teachers may notice musical ability and encourage development.

Different approaches in psychology place different emphases on nature and nurture, for example:

▧ The biological approach tends to emphasise genetic influences rather than the environment.

▧ The behaviourist approach assumes all behaviour is caused by learning (environmental) and has no role for inherited factors.

▧ The psychodynamic approach assumes innate or inherited drives are modified by early experience, representing interaction of genes and environment.

Ethical issues

In your work for the AS you will have come across many ethical issues in relation to experiments. Milgram's work on obedience and other studies of social influence are legendary for the ethical issues they raise. Virtually all psychological studies involve ethical issues such as deception, privacy and psychological and physical harm. An area of particular concern is *socially sensitive research*. This is research with potentially wide implications. Examples are studies of gender differences or gay and lesbian relationships.

To deal with ethical issues in psychological research bodies such as the British Psychological Society have produced detailed guidelines on how psychologists should act. Any single study can be evaluated in terms of ethical issues and how successfully the researchers coped with these issues. An important aspect of these guidelines is the potential importance of the research. For instance, it is argued that Milgram's hugely unethical studies on obedience were justified because they showed under the right circumstances people inflict pain on others. Often ethical issues are a matter of judgement and there is no simple right or wrong answer.

Although ethical issues are usually discussed in relation to particular studies, there are also ethical aspects to whole research areas. Probably the best example has been the study of racial differences in IQ. It has been argued that psychologists who work in this area assume from the start that such differences exist and will favour white ethnic groups over black ethnic groups. Should such research be done? Evolutionary psychology often makes assumptions about the way our ancestors lived and uses these assumptions to justify stereotyped views of men and women; for instance, that women should be at home looking after children rather than developing careers in the workplace. Other controversial areas include research into non-traditional relationships such as gay and homosexual partnerships.

The use of non-human animals in psychological research

Psychology has a long tradition of using non-human animals in a variety of ways. The principles of behaviourism were largely based on Skinner's work with rats and pigeons. Until the introduction of modern scanning methods our knowledge of brain function depended heavily on studies with monkeys, cats and rats.

One reason that non-human animals were used was that procedures would have been unethical if inflicted on humans. Depriving rats of sleep until they die, or as with Harlow, separating baby monkeys from their mothers to look at the effects of separation, would not have been allowed with human participants.

Work with non-human animals is now regulated by an Act of Parliament and requires a licence from the Home Office for any study. The Act encourages researchers to minimise the suffering involved, to reduce the number of animals required, and if possible to use other experimental methods that do not involve animals. When assessing a proposal the Home Office also requires a detailed assessment of the scientific value of the research. Bateson (1986) suggested that research with non-human animals be evaluated on three dimensions:

▓ the degree of suffering involved

▓ the scientific quality of the research proposal, e.g. is the methodology sound and reliable?

▓ the potential benefit to society of the results.

Using these criteria we could say depriving rats of sleep until they die is of less value to society than Harlow's work, which did show that comfort and security were vital parts of infant attachment.

There are many other issues in research with non-human animals. For example, how far can we generalise findings to humans, i.e. how similar are the behaviours involved? In comparative psychology researchers may use observational techniques in the animal's natural habitat which would not appear to have many ethical issues. However, simply invading an animal's natural territory might itself be stressful.

Gender bias

Gender bias in psychological theories and studies is not the same as *gender differences*. There are gender differences in many aspects of behaviour, and the study of these differences has a long tradition in psychology. A typical experiment would compare a group of females and a group of males on a particular task, or perhaps it would study cognitive development in a group of girls and a group of boys to see if there were any differences. However, if a study used only male participants, but assumed the findings applied to both males *and* females this would show gender bias. There are two main forms of gender bias:

▓ Alpha bias assumes real differences between males and females. This approach can devalue females, for instance in Freud's theory of psychosexual development. Freud's view was that women in many respects were 'failed men', associated with the absence in women of a penis. On the other hand, an alpha bias can raise the profile of women. A good example is Gilligan's theory of morality, which proposes that the morality of women is different to that of men but not inferior.

▓ Beta bias assumes that there are no differences between men and women, or that any differences are trivial. This approach often assumes that findings from studies using only male participants can simply be applied to females as well. Although it is not so much the case now, the majority of early studies in psychology used only male participants. Such a study has what is called an androcentric ('male') bias, and because of this most psychological theories show a beta bias, i.e. the results are simply generalised to women.

Cultural bias

All psychological research has to be done somewhere. It is therefore *culturally specific*. However, this does not mean that the results can automatically be applied to other cultures. Although we are now more aware of cultural issues, much classic psychology, carried out in Europe and America, was assumed to apply to the rest of the world. The idea that research findings from one culture can simply be generalised to all cultures is called *ethnocentrism*. More specifically, the generalisation of results from Europe and America is sometimes called *eurocentrism*. Good examples of eurocentrism include early theories of relationship formation, such as social exchange theory, which are heavily based on Western capitalist ideas of personal possessions and worth.

The opposite view to ethnocentrism is *cultural relativism*. This is the idea that all cultures are different and equally worth studying. This has led to many studies comparing cultures in terms of, for instance, infant attachment, relationship formation and adolescent development. Two terms that often occur in relation to cultural bias are:

▓ Etic analysis: behaviour is universal and that cultural differences can be ignored. A good example is the application of Western-based psychiatric diagnosis to non-Western ethnic groups. Behaviour that looks abnormal in such groups may have different causes to similar behaviours in Western groups.

▓ Emic analysis: behaviour is culturally specific, i.e. an example of cultural relativism. Traditionally this approach uses cross-cultural research. Margaret Mead studied adolescent development in several tribes in New Guinea and compared the results with adolescent development in the West.

Emic analysis is preferable to etic as we become more aware of cultural influences on behaviour.

In each of the topics there are references to relevant issues and debates. In the examination you will be expected to refer to those relevant in your answers.

Biological rhythms and sleep

Introduction

The following three chapters cover biological rhythms, sleep states and disorders of sleep. These areas are closely related as sleep states themselves represent biological rhythms. Some disorders of sleep may also reflect problems in the control of biological rhythms.

Most people spend approximately 30 per cent of their lives asleep, i.e. more than 20 years. For centuries philosophers, artists, poets and scientists have speculated on the nature and functions of sleep. However, only since the 1950s has the proper scientific study of sleep been possible. Therefore the material in the following chapters represents research from the last 50 years.

Despite the relatively short length of time that it has been studied, a great deal has been discovered about sleep and its relationship to biological rhythms. The development of techniques to measure brain activity during sleep and waking (the electroencephalograph) was a vital step in understanding the nature of sleep and the fact that we have different stages of sleep during a single night. Although this was a fascinating discovery, it did make life more complicated, as instead of looking for a single function of sleep, we had to explain the functions of the different stages. Some of these ideas are reviewed in Chapter 2, Sleep states.

Along with the increasing interest in sleep and its functions there was a growing awareness that biological rhythms could have a significant influence on human behaviour. Biological rhythms are found in plants as well as animals (as discussed in Chapter 1, Biological rhythms) and they appear to be a fundamental part of our evolutionary heritage. People probably have hundreds of different biological rhythms, including the sleep–waking cycle and the release of hormones into the bloodstream. What has brought biological rhythms into focus is the way that our modern social and work routines can act against those rhythms such as the sleep–waking cycle. The consequences of this can be disastrous as we see later in Chapter 1, Biological rhythms.

Disruption of biological rhythms can cause sleep disorders, but there are many other disorders with a variety of different causes, as shown in Chapter 3, Disorders of sleep. Because of the growing interest in biological rhythms and sleep, we are now much more efficient at identifying disorders and the underlying problems. Problems with sleep are widespread and a major cause of unhappiness and depression.

The scientific study of biological rhythms and sleep is unusual in that it combines many different approaches and methods of investigation. The recording and measurement of brain activity in humans has been mentioned above. Evidence also comes from lesion and drug studies in non-human animals, and also from the study of animals' behaviour in their natural environment. So we have theories about brain function during sleep, for example, and also theories about why predators sleep more than prey animals. Research into biological rhythms has looked at hamsters and the role of brain structures, but also at how police officers are affected by shift work.

Specification	Topic content	Page

1 Biological rhythms

Introduction

Learning objectives:

- ▦ understand the different types of biological rhythm and their distribution throughout the living world

- ▦ understand the roles of endogenous pacemakers and exogenous zeitgebers in the control of biological rhythms

- ▦ be aware of relevant research studies and their findings, and be able to evaluate them.

▦ Key terms

Biological rhythms: regular patterns of physiological, behavioural or cognitive activity. They are usually divided into circadian (24 hours), ultradian (less than 24 hours) and infradian (more than 24 hours).

Menstrual cycle: an example of an infradian biological rhythm, with a regular cycle length of 28 days.

Hibernation: hibernation in animals is an example of an infradian biological rhythm. As it occurs at yearly intervals, it is also sometimes called a circannual rhythm.

Circadian rhythms: biological rhythms with a cycle length of 24 hours.

Infradian rhythms: biological rhythms with a cycle length of more than one day.

Ultradian rhythms: biological rhythms that have more than one cycle in 24 hours.

Biological rhythms are found throughout the living world. The term refers to regular variations in biological activity, and includes changes in the levels of brain chemicals, increases and decreases in body temperature over a single day, and the shift between sleeping and waking. Some plants open and close their flowers in tune with night and day, while beach-living algae (single-cell plants) burrow into the sand when the tide comes in, and re-emerge when it recedes. Some rhythms, such as the **menstrual cycle** in mammals and **hibernation** in squirrels and hedgehogs, are longer, and given the variety of rhythms it is necessary to classify them into different types:

- ▦ **Circadian rhythms** (sometimes referred to as 'diurnal'): this term refers to 24-hour rhythms, such as body temperature in humans (one peak in 24 hours), and the sleep–waking cycle.

- ▦ **Infradian rhythms**: these are rhythms that have a cycle length (the time between successive peak activity) of more than one day. They include the menstrual cycle (28 days) and hibernation (rhythms with a periodicity of a year are sometimes referred to as 'circannual').

- ▦ **Ultradian rhythms**: these have more than one cycle in 24 hours. An example would be the alternation of slow-wave sleep and REM sleep during the night.

A key question is how these biological rhythms are controlled. Sometimes it looks obvious: we go to sleep when it is dark and wake up when it is light; birds migrate and squirrels hibernate when food becomes scarce in each winter. These observations suggest that biological rhythms are controlled by environmental factors such as light, temperature and food availability. Such environmental factors are called exogenous (or external) **zeitgebers**, from the German word for 'timegivers'. However, many studies have shown that things are not that simple. For example, if beach-living algae are kept in the laboratory in constant conditions and without tides, they still burrow into the sand and emerge at times in tune with the tidal flows at their home beach. Squirrels kept in similar constant laboratory conditions still prepare for hibernation as winter approaches in the world outside, by putting on weight and decreasing body temperature.

These observations suggest that control of body rhythms is more complicated than first thought, and involves more than external zeitgebers. If rhythms are maintained in the absence of environmental stimuli or 'cues', then there must be some internal 'clock' that regulates biological rhythms in the absence of zeitgebers. These internal clocks are known as **endogenous pacemakers**. Understanding the relationships between external zeitgebers and endogenous pacemakers is a key aim of this topic, and it is discussed in detail on pages 6–9. Firstly we will look in a little more detail at the different types of biological rhythm.

Different types of biological rhythm

Circadian rhythms

Circadian (from the Latin for 'about a day') rhythms occur over 24 hours. The sleep–waking cycle involves one period of each in 24 hours, while our body temperature has one peak (in the afternoon) and one trough (in the early morning) in the same period. Many hormones, brain **neurotransmitters** and other physiological processes show a similar circadian variation in activity, and altogether there may be over 100 bodily processes linked to this 24-hour periodicity. Why should this be?

Nocturnal animals are active and alert at night, but they need to sleep and keep safe during the day. **Diurnal** animals reverse the pattern, being active during the daytime and sleeping at night. Either way it makes sense for the body's physiological processes to be tuned in to the sleep–waking cycle, so that energy is provided when needed. For example, the rising body temperature during the daytime in diurnal animals such as humans allows for increased metabolic activity and energy expenditure during the daytime. As night approaches, body temperature falls, allowing for decreased energy expenditure. The central circadian rhythm in humans is the sleep–waking cycle. This is referred to later in this chapter and it is dealt with in detail in Chapter 2, Sleep states.

Infradian rhythms

These biological rhythms have a periodicity of more than one day, and include the female menstrual cycle and hibernation. In the introduction we saw how an infradian rhythm such as hibernation would seem a sensible adjustment to severe winter weather and lack of food, but that squirrels kept in the laboratory also show the hibernation pattern. Therefore the control of hibernation must involve both external zietgebers, such as day length and temperature, and endogenous pacemakers that control the infradian rhythm even in the absence of external zeitgebers.

In recent years there has been increasing interest in a human psychological disorder known as **seasonal affective disorder (SAD)**. This is a form of depression that regularly affects vulnerable people in the winter months. In this sense it qualifies as an infradian biological rhythm. People with SAD become depressed in the winter, and tend to eat more and sleep more.

Research into treatments for SAD provides a clue as to its cause. For some, but not all, sufferers, brief exposure to bright light first thing

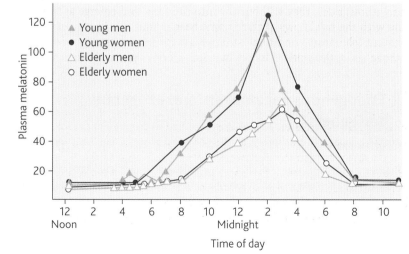

Fig. 1 *Levels of melatonin for young and elderly men and women over period of a day*

Take it further

What does the graph in Figure 1 tell you about melatonin levels in older and younger men and women? What trends or pattern can you see?

Key terms

Melatonin: a hormone secreted by the pineal gland that has an important role in many aspects of biological rhythms. It is involved in the control of our sleep–waking cycle; the presence of light reduces melatonin levels, while they increase during the hours of darkness.

Rapid eye movement (REM) sleep: one of the two distinctive types of sleep seen in mammals. It is characterised by a desynchronised EEG pattern, rapid eye movements and a paralysis of the skeletal muscles. REM sleep is associated with dreaming.

Suprachiasmatic nucleus (SCN): a group of neurons in the hypothalamus of the brain. These neurons have their own regular rhythms of activity. The SCN is our most important endogenous pacemaker and in turn controls the pineal gland and the release of melatonin.

Pineal gland: a small structure in the brain that secretes the hormone melatonin which in turn regulates many of our biological rhythms. The pineal gland is controlled by the SCN.

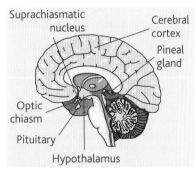

Fig. 3 *The suprachiasmatic nucleus (SCN) and the pineal gland*

AQA **Examiner's tip**

The study of the different types of biological rhythms can seem complicated. Start by making sure that you can describe clearly at least one example of each of the main types of rhythm.

in the morning can be effective against SAD. One effect of light is to suppress the activity of a brain chemical, **melatonin**, which has a central role in the sleep–waking cycle (see Figure 1). Darkness increases melatonin activity, while daylight reduces it, and these effects seem vital to normal functioning of the sleep–waking cycle. There is some evidence that melatonin pills can be effective in preventing jet lag. People with SAD may be less reactive to the effects of light and so their melatonin system is disrupted. The exposure to bright light in the morning may resynchronise the melatonin system and reduce SAD.

Ultradian rhythms

These are rhythms of less than a day's length. The most relevant example comes from the pattern of human sleep. During a night's sleep we move systematically through different phases of sleep – light slow-wave sleep to deep slow-wave sleep, then back up to light slow-wave sleep and into a phase of **rapid eye movement sleep (REM)**. One cycle takes 90 minutes on average. The control of this cycle involves a network of centres in the brain communicating through a variety of neurotransmitters. Some key elements, such as the **suprachiasmatic nucleus (SCN)** and the **pineal gland**, are discussed below.

There are other examples of ultradian rhythms. Some studies of alertness in humans show that it can vary with a periodicity of about 90 minutes. There is also evidence for a basic rest–activity cycle in human behaviour that also has a 90-minute periodicity (Friedman and Fisher, 1967).

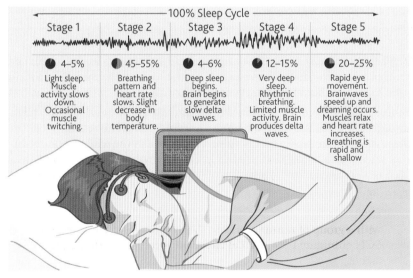

Fig. 2 *Stages of sleep*

Endogenous pacemakers and exogenous zeitgebers

Introduction

This brief review of the various types of biological rhythm demonstrates how widespread they are. A key issue is how biological rhythms are controlled. They are clearly intended to help us adapt to our environment, most obviously with rhythms such as the sleep–waking cycle and hibernation. But evidence also shows that they can operate in the absence of environmental cues. This brings us to the relationship between endogenous pacemakers and exogenous zeitgebers. To remind you:

- Endogenous pacemakers are internal or inbuilt **body clocks**. As regular rhythms of activity can be recorded in the developing human embryo it is probable that these pacemakers are innate, i.e. an inherited genetic mechanism.
- Exogenous zeitgebers are environmental stimuli or cues that play a vital role in regulating biological rhythms.

The most important zeitgeber is light, and a great deal of research has identified the main pathways involved in linking light to biological rhythms.

Light, endogenous pacemakers and sleep

Two key brain structures in the control of biological rhythms are the suprachiasmatic nucleus (SCN) and the pineal gland. The SCN is a small group of neurons in the hypothalamus of the brain. The electrical activity of these neurons has an inbuilt or endogenous circadian rhythm, and this pattern is maintained even when the SCN is isolated from the rest of the brain, showing that it is truly endogenous and probably genetic. In fact several genes involved in the control of the endogenous body clocks have been discovered, e.g. the PER3 gene. Their precise mechanisms have not yet been uncovered. A direct pathway links the SCN to the retina of the eye. The retina is where light impulses are received and converted into nerve impulses, and this pathway would allow light input to regulate activity of the SCN. Stephan and Zucker (1972) were amongst the first to show that damaging the SCN in rats disrupted a number of circadian rhythms, including 24-hour cycles of locomotor activity and the sleep–waking cycle.

Research study: Stephan and Zucker (1972)

In one of the earliest controlled and scientific studies on endogenous pacemakers, Stephan and Zucker investigated the effects of damage to the SCN on circadian rhythms.

Rats housed in the laboratory with 12 hours of light followed by 12 hours of dark show a circadian rhythm of drinking and locomotor activity. They drink more and are more active during the dark period.

Stephan and Zucker compared a group with damage to the SCN with a group of normal controls. They found that damage to the SCN eliminated the normal circadian patterns of drinking and activity.

They concluded that the SCN is one of the key pacemakers in the brain controlling circadian rhythms.

Methodological issues

Compared to the Siffre case study (see page 8) this was a more scientific and controlled study of endogenous pacemakers. Stephan and Zucker also damaged other parts of the hypothalamus to show that this did not affect circadian rhythms. However, the surgical procedure was very difficult, for instance only 11 out of 25 rats survived the damage to the SCN. There is a possibility, therefore, that the severity of the operation might have affected the rat's behaviour. However, the use of controlled lesions to other areas, and the fact that later studies confirmed the role of the SCN, suggest that this was not a major factor in this study. The study did use

Key terms

Body clocks: otherwise known as endogenous pacemakers, they regulate biological rhythms.

Link

Approaches, issues and debates

To explain the control of biological rhythms by just referring to endogenous pacemakers (body clocks) would be an example of biological reductionism. We gain a better understanding of biological rhythms if we move beyond the endogenous pacemakers and look at the interaction with exogenous zeitgebers such as light.

Link

The functions of the hypothalamus are outlined in the *AQA Psychology AS* student book on page 145.

Link

Approaches, issues and debates

The use of non-human animals in research (see page xii) is a controversial area. Studies such as Stephan and Zucker (1972) involve highly unethical procedures, but, along with similar studies, it has told us a great deal about endogenous pacemakers and biological rhythms. Society has to decide if sacrificing animals in scientific studies is justified by the value to society of the findings.

Key terms

Free running: a term used to describe biological rhythms in the absence of external zeitgebers. An example would be Siffre's cave study where sleep–waking cycles were investigated in the absence of natural light.

rats, which raises the issue of generalising from rats to humans. Although it is likely that human endogenous pacemakers will be organised in a similar way, this can only be confirmed by studies on humans.

Ethical issues

The use of non-human animals in research (see page xii) involves a balance between the value of the findings against the stress to the animal. The fact that so many rats died during this study is a major concern. It should not matter that these were rats rather than primates such as monkeys or chimpanzees. Given the extreme severity of the procedures, it is unlikely that such studies would be permitted today. Note that this study was carried out in 1972 – since then regulations covering animal experimentation have been tightened.

This research group found similar effects of SCN destruction in ground squirrels (Zucker, Boshes and Dark, 1983). They also demonstrated that the circannual rhythm of testosterone secretion in male hamsters was eliminated by SCN damage (Rusak and Zucker, 1975). So the SCN is one of the key endogenous pacemakers or biological clocks in the brain.

The next stage in the system is a pathway connecting the SCN to the pineal gland in the forebrain. The pineal is where the hormone melatonin is manufactured, and this pathway allows the SCN to control the manufacture and secretion of melatonin. This is a vital role as melatonin, after release from the pineal, has widespread effects on the rest of the brain and on the body's physiological systems. Amongst its effects is the control of sleep and waking behaviour. Injections of melatonin produce sleep in sparrows (Abraham, Gwinner and Van't Hof, 2000), while chickens wake up at dawn as melatonin levels fall (remember that light reduces melatonin activity in the brain) (Binkley, 1979).

We have already seen how biological rhythms can continue even when zeitgebers such as light are absent. This can be explained by the *endogenous* rhythmic activity of neurons in the SCN and pineal gland. The fact that the SCN can be directly affected by light falling on the retina of the eye means that the endogenous biological clock (i.e. the SCN and the pineal) can be perfectly synchronised with light and dark phases of the outside world. This pattern – in which the endogenous clock is capable of maintaining biological rhythms in the absence of zeitgebers, but which needs light input for perfect synchronisation – is supported by many research studies, one of which is discussed here.

Research study: Siffre (1975)

In this unusual study a French geologist, Michel Siffre, spent six months (179 days) in an underground cave in Texas. There was no natural light, and in the absence of this critical zeitgeber biological rhythms become what is called **free running**. The cave was artificially lit, and Siffre could use a telephone to ask for the lights to be turned off when he slept and turned on when he woke. He could eat and sleep when he wanted. During his stay in the cave a variety of physiological functions were recorded, including body temperature, heart rate, blood pressure, and of course his sleeping and waking pattern.

There were two key findings:

- Siffre's sleep–waking circadian rhythm extended from the normal 24 hours to between 25 and 32 hours, i.e. his 'days' became longer. When he emerged on the 179th day, in his terms it was only the 151st day.

- His body temperature circadian rhythm was more stable. It extended slightly to about 25 hours, but remained consistent. One outcome of this was that Siffre's sleep–waking cycle became desynchronised from his body temperature rhythm. Under normal conditions they are synchronised, so that we regularly go to sleep when body temperature is falling and awake when it is rising.

In the absence of environmental zeitgebers such as light, our endogenous pacemakers or body clocks can still regulate biological rhythms. However, this regulation is not perfect so the rhythms are not perfectly tuned into the 24-hour cycle.

Methodological issues

Unlike the Stephan and Zucker study described above, which was a controlled laboratory experiment, this is a single case study on one man. Therefore we can only generalise the findings with caution. However, other studies have confirmed the results; for instance Aschoff and Weber (Kleitman, 1965) found that the sleep–waking cycle of students kept in an underground bunker under similar conditions to Siffre also extended, to between 25 and 27 hours. Although the general picture is supported, remember that there will also be individual differences in how each participant reacts to the absence of natural light.

The results match overall conclusions regarding the roles of endogenous pacemakers and external zeitgebers. Body clocks such as the SCN have their own rhythmic activity, but they can be influenced by light reaching the retina of the eye. Therefore, under normal circumstances the inbuilt rhythm is perfectly synchronised with the outside world. Only under artificial conditions such as Siffre's cave can we see how they operate independently.

Ethical issues

Standard ethical procedures are difficult to apply in the case of these unusual studies. Siffre was a volunteer and was fully aware of the nature of the study. However, no one could predict the effects on him as no one had experienced such a long period of 'free running' biological rhythms before. In fact Siffre did report feelings of depression, suicidal thoughts and memory problems as little as 80 days into the study. After it was over he also reported long-lasting psychological consequences of the six months of isolation. There is no record of any counselling or psychological support offered over this period, which would be an essential part of any psychological study today. However, on a more optimistic note, in late 1999 Siffre took part in a similar study, spending two months in a cave in the French Alps!

Hint

How science works

Case studies such as Siffre can be criticised, as the findings are difficult to generalise to other people. However such studies are still extremely interesting, especially when they are supported by research using larger numbers of participants. In neuropsychology, for instance, we have learnt a great deal about the brain from studying individuals who have suffered damage to particular parts (e.g. prosopagnosia, see page 79).

There must be at least two independent endogenous pacemakers. Siffre's body temperature and sleep–waking cycle were regulated but became desynchronised, showing that they were under separate control. Later research suggests that there may be around 100 separate pacemakers regulating the activity of various physiological processes.

■ Take it further

Using your knowledge of psychology and especially evolutionary aspects, try to imagine why at some stage in human evolution it might have been advantageous for women living together to menstruate at the same time. Remember that women having synchronised menstrual cycles means that they are likely to be pregnant at the same time.

■ Key terms

Pheromones: these are biologically active chemicals in animals' sweat and urine that convey information to other animals of the same species. They might indicate sexual receptivity, or they can be used to mark out territory.

■ Infradian rhythms

We have already seen how annual rhythms such as hibernation persist even when squirrels are kept in constant conditions in the laboratory, showing that there is at least one biological clock regulating this infradian rhythm. In normal circumstances we assume that hibernation involves this internal clock and external zeitgebers such as day length, which becomes shorter in the winter. Sensitivity to day length would ensure that hibernation is perfectly tuned in to the outside world.

The menstrual or oestrous cycle is another infradian rhythm controlled by endogenous pacemakers but which can be sensitive to external zeitgebers. There are anecdotal (non-scientific) reports that the menstrual cycles of women living together for long periods eventually synchronise, i.e. they all follow the same monthly cycle. In 1980, Russell, Switz and Thompson provided a possible explanation. They found that if sweat from one woman (the donor) was rubbed on to the lips of a recipient woman, eventually the menstrual cycles of donor and recipient would synchronise. Their explanation was that **pheromones** (biologically significant chemicals) in the sweat were picked up by the recipient and these altered the menstrual cycle of the recipient, i.e. the pheromones acted as an external zeitgeber.

Key points

- Biological rhythms are regular variations in biological activity.
- There are various types of biological rhythm. Circadian rhythms have a 24-hour cycle; infradian rhythms have a cycle length of more than one day; ultradian rhythms have more than one cycle every 24 hours.
- Biological rhythms are controlled by endogenous (natural) pacemakers in the brain.
- Zeitgebers are external stimuli such as light that influence biological rhythms so that they are synchronised with the outside world.

■ Summary questions

1. Outline the three main types of biological rhythm.
2. Outline the role of melatonin in the sleep–waking cycle.
3. Light is one of our most important zeitgebers. Give an example of research into one other zeitgeber and outline the results of this research.
4. Outline and evaluate Siffre's cave study. What does it tell us about the roles of endogenous pacemakers and exogenous zeitgebers in the control of biological rhythms? Are these conclusions limited by the fact that it was a single case study?

Disrupting biological rhythms

- understand the consequences of disrupting biological rhythms

- use research findings on the effects of shift work and jet lag to assess the consequences of disrupting biological rhythms

- use research findings to understand methods of reducing the effects of shift work and jet lag.

Key terms

Shift work: working patterns which enable factories and organisations to work around the clock. It means that employees are often required to work at times when they should be sleeping. Shift work is therefore a major source of disruption to biological rhythms.

Jet lag: jet lag can occur in people travelling east to west or west to east. It is caused by the rapid change in zeitgebers, especially light, in relation to our biological rhythms such as the sleep–waking cycle.

Introduction

The interplay between endogenous pacemakers and external zeitgebers is designed to keep physiological processes and behaviours such as sleep–waking cycles and hibernation perfectly in tune with the outside world. Over the year, days gradually shorten and nights become longer, and activity and physiological processes adjust their cycles to these zeitgebers.

Of course, for humans there can be exceptions. Eskimos live in a world of endless day in the summer and endless night in the winter, yet they maintain fairly regular sleep–waking cycles throughout. This shows us that there are other zeitgebers that we can use to regulate biological rhythms, such as the patterning of work and social activities.

External zeitgebers such as day length change only slowly in the normal course of events, allowing our biological rhythms time to adjust to the changes. However, the increasing complexity of human society has produced situations in which zeitgebers change rapidly, and this can have dramatic effects on biological rhythms and the behaviours they affect. The best examples are shift work and jet lag.

Shift work

Some people can suffer so badly from the disruption of circadian rhythms caused by **shift work** and **jet lag** that these disorders are listed in the International Classification of Sleep Disorders. These problems did not exist until the last century, when Edison's invention of the electric light in the late 19th century freed us from dependence on natural light and candles. Henry Ford could only set up his 24-hour car assembly line in 1914 with the aid of electricity, while widespread jet travel has only been available since the 1950s.

The electric light has transformed modern society. We can now work and shop for 24 hours a day, and socialise until the early hours of the morning. Before electric light our activities were largely dictated by natural light and dark. Now we can sleep when we like, and the outcome is that our average sleep time nowadays, about 7.5 hours, is about 1.5 hours less than 100 years ago (Coren, 1996). However, the most dramatic effects are seen when we challenge our inbuilt body clocks by changing external zeitgebers more rapidly than they are used to.

Shift work was introduced with the assembly line and 24-hour working. The traditional pattern would be to divide the 24-hour day into three eight-hour periods, midnight to 8am, 8am to 4pm, and 4pm to midnight. Shifts would change at intervals of, say, one week, and the traditional rotation was backwards; one week on 4pm to midnight, one week on 8am to 4pm, and one week on midnight to 8am. It is estimated (Coren, 1996) that one in five workers in America are on shift work of one sort or another. This can of course include junior doctors, nurses and air traffic controllers.

The effects of this are predictable. Many shift workers are operating machinery or making decisions at times when their internal body clock is completely out of synchronisation with the external world, especially the light–dark cycle. Apart from effects on performance, this leads to frequent reports of fatigue, depression and illness.

- Our body clock prepares us for sleep when it is dark, and particularly between 2am and 4am. It is no coincidence that some of the most disastrous industrial accidents have occurred during this phase of shift work, including the Chernobyl nuclear explosion and the near melt-down at the Three Mile Island nuclear reactor.

- Decisions made that led to the loss of the Challenger space shuttle were made by technicians who had been working 10–12-hour shifts for the previous two weeks. It is likely that this would have affected their judgement.

- An additional factor is that workers on night shifts then have to try to sleep during the day. This can be interrupted by sunlight, by the noise of the rest of the world going about its business, and by the natural desire to take part in social and family activities. So night-shift workers may be sleep deprived as well as suffering desynchronisation of their circadian rhythms at work.

The increasing scientific interest in sleep and biological rhythms over the last 50 years has led to various suggestions for reducing the psychological and physical consequences of shift work. A leading researcher in this area, Charles Czeisler, has shown convincingly that applying our knowledge of body clocks and zeitgebers can be extremely effective.

At a Utah chemical plant that used the traditional backwards shift rotation, with seven days on each rotation, workers reported high levels of stress, sleeping difficulties and health problems, all of which affected productivity. Czeisler, Moore-Ede and Coleman (1982) introduced a *forwards* shift rotation (this is effectively the same as **phase delay**, discussed below in relation to jet lag; our body clock adjusts better to phased delay than to the opposite, **phase advance**), and increased the time on each shift to 21 days, allowing the body clock to adjust properly. After nine months workers reported feeling less stressed, with fewer sleeping difficulties and health problems, and increased productivity.

Gordon *et al.* (1986) found similar results in a study on Philadelphia police officers. Moving them from a backwards shift rotation to 18 days on a forward rotation led to a 30 per cent reduction in sleeping on the job and a 40 per cent reduction in accidents on the job. Officers reported better sleep and less stress.

There have been other approaches to coping with shift work:

- Permanent non-rotating shift work. Phillips *et al.* (1991) found similar positive results to Czeisler when she introduced permanent shifts into a Kentucky police force. This means that officers choose one of the three eight-hour shifts and stay on it permanently. This allows the body clock to synchronise with external zeitgebers (which normally takes 16–20 days). This approach is not popular as very few people would be happy with permanent night work.

- Planned napping during shifts. Although this has been shown to reduce tiredness and improve performance (Sack *et al.*, 2007) it is not popular with employers or, more surprisingly, with employees.

- Improved sleep during the day for night-shift workers. This involves keeping the bedroom as quiet and dark as possible, and avoiding bright lights even in the house. However, as mentioned above, this can be very disruptive of family life and can lead to its own pressures.

Key terms

Phase delay: this particularly applies to air travel and jet lag. If we fly west from London to New York and arrive at, say, 5pm local time, our body clock tells us that it is 10pm (London time). To adjust to local time we need to delay our sleep time. This is known as phase delay. Studies suggest that phase delay is easier to adjust to than phase advance.

Phase advance: when we fly from west to east, time differences mean that local time at our destination is later than that indicated by our body clock. This means that our biological rhythms have to advance to catch up with local time. Studies suggest that we find phase advance more difficult to adjust to than phase delay.

Rapid rotation. This is the principle that rotating shift work patterns every two or three days avoids even trying to adjust circadian rhythms and the disruption it causes. However, it also means that most of the time rhythms are out of synchronisation, and there is controversy over the success of rapid rotation in coping with shift work (Coren, 1996).

▥ Jet lag

Jet travel provides the best example of how biological rhythms can be rapidly disrupted, and it is certainly the one most frequently encountered. If you leave the UK at 10am and fly to New York, you arrive around six hours later. Your body clock tells you it is 4pm, but because of the different time zones, local time is actually 11am. You would feel physically ready to sleep when local time is about 5pm.

This dislocation between the body clock and local zeitgebers (besides light these can include social cues such as meal and work times) can lead to jet lag – an unpleasant feeling of extreme tiredness, depression and slowed mental and physical reactions. Using our knowledge of internal body clocks and external zeitgebers we can see why this happens:

▥ Our sleep–waking body clock is reset by the light of morning in order to keep to a 24-hour rhythm. Our body is alert during the day and preparing for sleep during the evening.

▥ Using the example above, we arrive in New York with our body clock five hours ahead of local time. Our body clock tells us to sleep when it is about 5pm local time, and to wake up when it is about 3am local time. To fit in with local time, i.e. when meetings are arranged or shops are open, we are trying to be alert and active when our body is trying to sleep.

▥ This leads to feelings of tiredness and confusion.

▥ Note also that other body rhythms, such as body temperature, may also be disrupted and become desynchronised from the sleep–waking cycle (as happened with Siffre in his cave, page 8). This adds to the general feeling of disorientation.

Jet lag can affect the alertness and performance of aircrew, and it is established that jet lag is worse when you travel west to east rather than east to west (Coren, 1996). Recht, Lew and Schwartz (1995) looked at US baseball teams. The United States is large enough to have four different time zones when you travel east to west or west to east, so that New York on the east coast is four hours ahead of San Francisco on the west coast. They studied results over a three-year period and showed that teams travelling east to west before a game won 44 per cent of their games, but those travelling west to east won 37 per cent, significantly fewer. Although it is possible that some teams were simply better than others, the length of the study means that this variable should have evened itself out.

The reason for this east–west west–east difference appears to be the demands it makes on the body clock. Travelling east to west the clock ends up ahead of local time and has to 'wait' for local time to catch up. Travelling west to east the body clock ends up behind local time and has to advance to catch up. It appears that the clock finds it easier to phase delay than to phase advance.

Various factors affect the severity of jet lag:

▥ Direction of travel, as discussed.

▥ Number of time zones crossed.

Biological rhythms

- Age. There is some evidence that jet lag decreases with age (Sack *et al.*, 2007).
- Individual differences. Some people are more resistant to the effects of jet lag than others, a characteristic known as 'phase tolerance'.

There are also a number of techniques that have been shown to reduce jet lag (Coren, 1996):

- Sleep well before the flight, so that you do not start off sleep-deprived.
- Adjust your flight behaviour in anticipation of the time at your destination. If you are going to arrive in the daytime, stay awake on the plane. If it is going to be dark when you arrive, try to sleep on the plane.
- Avoid caffeine and alcohol. These have been shown to make jet lag symptoms worse.
- When you arrive, immediately adjust to local zeitgebers. Stay up if it is daytime, sleep if it is night time.
- Go out into the morning daylight as soon as possible – sunlight is the most effective way of resynchronising your body clock to local time.
- There is some evidence that melatonin can speed up resynchronisation and reduce jet lag. Beaumont *et al.* (2004) found that melatonin given at bedtime three days before travel and for five days after arrival significantly reduced the symptoms of jet lag.

However, if your trip is for only one or two days there will not be enough time to fully synchronise your body clock. There is a school of thought that in these cases you should actually stick to your original sleep–waking patterns and not try to adjust. Of course this is usually difficult as it leaves you out of sync with the local social and business life.

Conclusions

The consequences of disrupting biological rhythms can be seen in people engaged in shift work or suffering jet lag. It can lead to fatigue, depression and physical illnesses. There is also evidence that disruption of biological rhythms and the sleep deprivation it leads to can reduce the efficiency of our immune system (Sack *et al.*, 2007). This probably explains the levels of illness in shift workers.

Shift work is vital to the functioning of Western industrialised societies, and we now take jet travel for granted. Other examples of disruption, such as in parents of babies, have been with us forever. However, our increasing knowledge of the roles of endogenous body clocks and exogenous zeitgebers does allow us to understand why these consequences occur, and to design effective ways of coping with them.

Key points

- Biological rhythms can be disrupted by shift work and jet travel. This means that our rhythms are preparing the body for sleep at a time when we want to be awake and alert.
- Disrupting biological rhythms can lead to fatigue and depression, and can also impair performance, leading to industrial accidents.
- Our knowledge of the interaction between pacemakers and zeitgebers leads to methods of reducing the impact of shift work and jet lag.
- Many of these methods involve restoring the normal link between pacemakers and zeitgebers as quickly as possible.

AQA Examiner's tip

The specification refers to the consequences of disrupting biological rhythms. If you are not careful, this can become a simple list of consequences. You would receive some credit, but it is far more impressive if you can quote one or two pieces of research evidence to support your statements. Studies showing the effectiveness of strategies to deal with disruption of biological rhythms are valuable as evaluation and commentary.

Summary questions

5 Using your knowledge of the sleep–waking cycle, outline the reasons why shift work and jet lag may affect mood and performance.

6 Czeisler *et al.* (1982) found that a forwards shift rotation and an increased time on each shift reduced the negative effects of shift work. Explain these findings.

7 Jet lag is often reduced by following the external zeitgebers at your place of arrival rather than your biological rhythms. Explain this finding using your knowledge of endogenous pacemakers and exogenous zeitgebers.

2 Sleep states

Nature of sleep

Learning objectives:

■ describe and evaluate the use of the electroencephalograph in sleep research

■ understand the different stages of sleep, in particular the characteristics of REM and NREM sleep

■ describe the patterning of REM and NREM through the night.

Introduction

Of all human behaviours, sleep is one of the best known but most mysterious. We all sleep, and adults will have spent one-third of their lives asleep – around 25 years in a normal lifetime. Sleep has been investigated intensively by scientists for over 50 years, but although we can describe many characteristics of sleep, we still have no idea what it is for. There are many hypotheses regarding the functions of sleep, but still no definite answer as to why we sleep.

We know that sleep is necessary. All complex animals, including humans and other mammals, sleep. Even reptiles and birds sleep. From this straightforward observation we can draw one important conclusion: sleep is necessary, i.e. it must have important functions for the animal's survival.

To emphasise this conclusion, we can look at aquatic mammals such as the dolphin. Mammals breathe air, so even though they live in water (either rivers or the sea) dolphins have to come up to the surface to breathe. This makes sleeping a real problem, as in this state of unconsciousness the dolphin cannot come up to the surface and so might drown. Dolphins have therefore evolved extraordinary methods to enable them to sleep. In some species only one side of the brain sleeps at a time, alternating sides so that each gets some sleep. Others have perfected 'microsleeps', so that instead of one long sleep session several hours long, they sleep frequently but for very short periods of a few seconds at a time. In this way they are never unconscious for long enough to put them in danger of drowning.

These adaptations show how essential it is for dolphins to sleep, and they reinforce the conclusion that sleep must have essential functions. The key problem is working out what these functions are. Before reviewing some approaches to this problem, we first need to consider the nature of sleep.

Key terms

Electroencephalograph (EEG): a recording of the electrical activity of the brain. Electrodes on the scalp pick up electrical activity from the millions of neurons in the brain. Different patterns of EEG activity can reflect different brain states, such as arousal and the stages of sleep.

Desynchronised EEG: a reading that has no regular pattern of electrical activity. This type of EEG reading is typically recorded when the brain is in an active and aroused state.

Types of sleep

We have already seen that the sleep–waking cycle is a circadian rhythm, with one episode of each in 24 hours. However, sleep itself is a complicated mixture of different types of sleep. The breakthrough in this area of sleep research came in the 1950s with the use of the **electroencephalograph (EEG)**. This is a technique, developed in the 1920s, that uses electrodes on the scalp to record the electrical activity of the brain. Berger (1929) demonstrated that the EEG picked up the electrical activity of billions of brain neurons and could be used to identify different states of the brain. Two major EEG patterns identified by Berger were:

■ **Desynchronised EEG**: see Figure 1 (overleaf). This is usually recorded when somebody is awake.

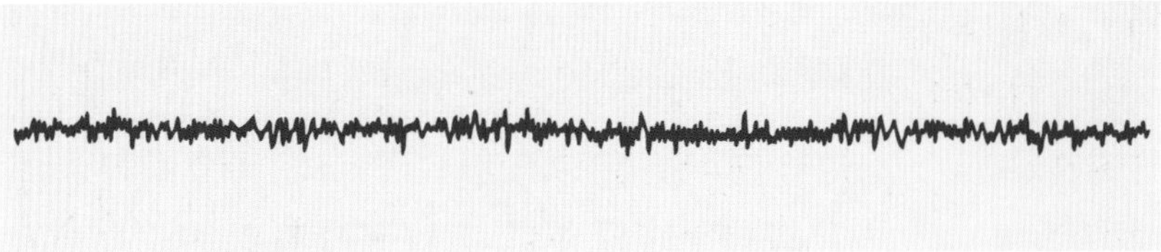

Fig. 1 *Desynchronised EEG*

■ **Synchronised EEG**: see Figure 2. Frequency is measured in hertz (Hz), the number of waves per second. A synchronised EEG indicates that millions of neurons are firing together in unison. This is usually recorded when somebody is asleep.

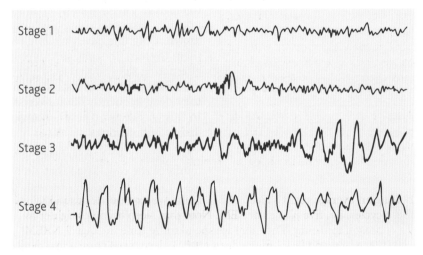

Fig. 2 *Synchronised EEG*

In the 1950s, Aserinsky and Kleitman (1953) and Dement and Kleitman (1957) were the first to use EEG recordings to show that sleep was a far more complicated brain state than previously thought. They demonstrated that various states of human sleep and arousal could be identified through their EEG patterns (see Figure 3).

Stage 1

Stage 2

Stage 3

Stage 4

Fig. 3 *EEG stages of sleep*

Non-REM sleep (NREM)

When we first fall asleep the EEG is dominated by larger and slower waves as we enter **NREM**. There are four stages to NREM (see Table 1).

Along with these EEG changes, a number of physiological changes are associated with falling asleep. As we move from drowsiness through the stages of NREM to deep stage 4, so respiration, heart rate and blood pressure fall. Blood flow to the brain slows, indicating that the brain is becoming less active.

Table 1 *Stages of NREM*

Stage of NREM	Characteristics
Stage 1	EEG characterised by theta waves (4–7 Hz)
Stage 2	EEG dominated by theta waves, but also with bursts of **sleep spindles**; these are phases of fast (12–16 Hz) EEG activity that last for a second or so
Stage 3	**Delta waves** (1–4 Hz) first appear and the number of spindles falls. Delta waves also have larger amplitudes than theta waves
Stage 4	The EEG is dominated by large, slow delta waves. This is the deepest stage of NREM, when people are most soundly asleep

Rapid eye movement (REM) sleep

The above description of falling into a deep sleep is not too surprising, as sleep was always thought to be a time of decreased activity and rest. However, Aserinsky and Kleitman (1953) and Dement and Kleitman (1957) then made a startling observation in their EEG recordings. After falling through the stages of NREM into deep stage 4, sleep would lighten and participants would move back up to NREM stage 2. At this point, 75 minutes or so into sleep, the EEG becomes fast and desynchronised, similar to the pattern for the awake, aroused person. However, the body muscles lose tone (i.e. they relax completely, leaving the body effectively paralysed apart from occasional twitches of the fingers and toes). There are also movements of the eyes, from which this phase of sleep gets its name.

Although heart rate and blood pressure increase and there may be penile erections in males and increased vaginal blood flow in females, the person is still difficult to awaken. This is surprising as the 'aroused' EEG pattern is associated with increased brain activity and energy consumption (which is close to the waking level). This contrast between an aroused brain and a sleeping state and largely unresponsive body led to REM also being termed **paradoxical sleep**.

After around 15 minutes in REM, we move back into stage 2 NREM and move down the stages into deep stage 4 NREM. Then the process repeats itself, taking about 90 minutes for a complete NREM/REM cycle. Note that this is an ultradian biological rhythm, with more than one cycle in 24 hours.

During an average night's sleep of 7–8 hours we experience around five of these cycles, i.e. five phases of REM. Note that sleep becomes lighter as we approach morning. Therefore we spend more time in stage 2 NREM and REM sleep and less time in deep NREM sleep, see Figure 4 (overleaf).

Dreaming

Along with their other pioneering discoveries, Aserinsky and Kleitman (1953) and Dement and Kleitman (1957) also discovered that REM sleep was associated with dreaming. By waking participants at various times they established that those woken during REM reported dreaming about 80 per cent of the time. In contrast, those woken during NREM reported dreaming only about 20 per cent of the time. Additionally, the dreams reported during REM were far more vivid and intense than those reported during NREM.

Since that time, REM has been seen as 'dreaming sleep'. One problem with this label is that REM and dreaming are very different creatures. REM is a physiological state identified by objective scientific

▮ **Key terms**

Sleep spindles: bursts of high-frequency electrical activity seen in the deeper stages of NREM.

Delta waves: seen in the EEG of a person in the deeper stages of NREM, these have a large amplitude and a frequency of about 1–4 Hz.

Paradoxical sleep: an old-fashioned term for REM sleep.

▮ **Take it further**

If you have a dog or cat, watch when they go to sleep. At some point they will start twitching their paws and if you look closely you will see eye movements. They are in a phase of REM.

Hint

How science works

Objectivity is seen as critical to the scientific method, and so it is impossible to study subjective phenomena such as dreams (not visible to an observer) scientifically.

Link

See Chapter 37, The application of scientific methodology in psychology, for a discussion of the key features of the scientific method.

Key terms

Ascending reticular formation (RF): a network of millions of neurons buried deep in the brain. It controls the brain's arousal state, and within it there are centres that are important for the regulation of sleep and waking.

Locus coeruleus: a group of neurons buried in the reticular formation that are important in the control of REM sleep. These neurons secrete the neurotransmitter noradrenaline.

Raphe nuclei: a group of neurons buried in the reticular formation that is important in the control of NREM. They secrete the neurotransmitter serotonin. The raphe nuclei work with the locus coeruleus to regulate the ultradian rhythm of NREM and REM sleep.

Noradrenaline: a brain neurotransmitter secreted by neurons at the synapse. Pathways using noradrenaline are important in states such as sleep and arousal and in feeding behaviour.

Serotonin: a brain neurotransmitter secreted by neurons at the synapse and thought to be important in emotional states. Pathways using serotonin are involved in behavioural states such as sleep and depression.

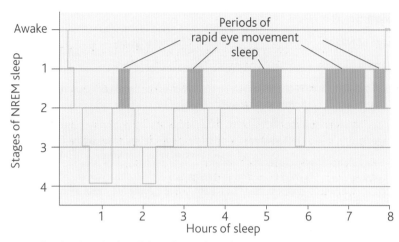

Fig. 4 *The ultradian rhythm of sleep during the night*

measurements of activity in the brain and body. Dreams are 'subjective'. We only know they exist through our own experience and the verbal reports of participants. There is no objective method of recording them. This means that scientific psychology has problems studying dreams and their functions. Therefore the focus for psychologists should be on the nature and functions of REM, rather than the content and symbolism of dreams.

Sleep and biological rhythms

Before moving on to the functions of sleep we need to consider the relationship between sleep and biological rhythms. In Chapter 1, Biological rhythms, we saw that the sleep–waking cycle is an excellent example of a circadian rhythm. This is controlled by endogenous pacemakers such as the SCN and the pineal gland, fine tuned by the influence of external zeitgebers, in particular light onset.

The ultradian rhythm represented by the cyclical shifts between NREM and REM during a night's sleep must be separately controlled. The pioneering work of Michel Jouvet (1969) established that critical structures for the control of REM and NREM lay in the **ascending reticular formation (RF)**, a network of millions of neurons buried deep in the brain. In a series of experiments using lesions and electrical stimulation Jouvet identified the **locus coeruleus** as being critical for REM sleep and the **raphe nuclei** as essential for NREM. In addition he found that REM seemed to depend upon the brain neurotransmitter **noradrenaline** and NREM depended on the neurotransmitter **serotonin**.

Later research has complicated the picture, with other structures in the RF and elsewhere involved in an intricate system that controls the patterning of REM and NREM during a night's sleep. It is beyond the scope of this book to go into detail on this subject, but the overall picture is clear. The ultradian rhythm of NREM and REM depends upon endogenous pacemakers buried deep within the brain.

Key points

- The sleep–waking cycle represents a circadian rhythm. Sleep itself is made up of two distinct types of sleep, REM and NREM.
- REM sleep is associated with an arousal pattern in the brain, eye movements, and a loss of muscle tone.
- NREM sleep is associated with a loss of brain activity, and the EEG of people in deep NREM sleep is dominated by large slow waves.
- REM sleep is associated with reports of dreaming, and in fact it is sometimes referred to as dreaming sleep.

Summary questions

1. Explain the difference between a synchronised and desynchronised EEG pattern.

2. Outline the key characteristics of REM sleep. How are the phases of REM organised during a night's sleep?

3. A night's sleep involves an ultradian rhythm. Describe this rhythm and outline the brain mechanisms that control it.

AQA Examiner's tip

Make sure you understand the implications of the different stages of sleep for theories of the functions of sleep. Do not learn the 'nature of sleep' independently from the 'functions of sleep'. For example, the characteristics of REM sleep need to be explained by any theory about the functions of REM.

Functions of sleep

Learning objectives:

Learning objectives:

- understand the evolutionary approach to sleep and how to evaluate relevant research evidence

- understand the restoration theory of the functions of sleep and how to evaluate relevant research evidence

- consider evidence for memory consolidation during sleep.

Introduction

Above we emphasised the fact that sleep is essential for all complex animals. The next simple question is: what function does sleep serve? Unfortunately, even after 50 years of intensive research we do not know the answer. However, we do have a number of hypotheses, some of which are reviewed below. Before describing these, there are some important facts that act as a background to any explanation:

- Across the animal kingdom there is a huge range in the patterning of sleep and waking. Adult humans sleep for between six and eight hours on average. Horses and elephants sleep for about three hours a night, and mice for between 14 and 20 hours every day.

- The two types of sleep, NREM and REM, are so different in terms of their EEG and general physiology that they are certain to have different functions.

- Newborn humans sleep for about 16 hours a day, and 50 per cent of this is REM sleep. As they grow this gradually reduces until they reach the adult pattern of 6–8 hours' sleep of which about 25 per cent is REM. This observation must be explained in any full account of the functions of sleep.

- Sleep has both *behavioural* and *physiological* characteristics. Animals are unresponsive and often inconspicuous when they sleep, while the two states of sleep are associated with EEG and other physiological changes. It may be that sleep therefore functions on different levels; both the behavioural side (for example being inconspicuous) and the physiological side may have advantages for the animal.

One approach that has concentrated on the behavioural side is the evolutionary perspective.

Evolutionary explanations

The basic principle behind evolutionary explanations of behaviour is that behaviours evolve and develop if they provide selective advantages for the animal involved. In relation to sleep we can see that even though it may not be obvious, sleep has evolved into an essential behaviour because it provides some selective advantages.

The evolutionary approach to sleep has focused on **ecological niches**. These refer to the lifestyles of animals, i.e. how and where they live, and involves many factors that have been shown to be relevant to sleep:

- Environment – for example, aquatic or terrestrial. We have already seen how the bizarre sleeping patterns of aquatic mammals such as dolphins are an adaptation to their environment. Another aspect of the animal's environment is that virtually all animals are either diurnal (day living) or nocturnal (night living). This means that they are adapted to be active only in part of every 24 hours, and for the remainder they will be inactive.

- Predator or prey – is the animal a carnivorous (meat eating) predator or an animal that is preyed upon? Prey animals are often herbivores (grass eaters) and are clearly more vulnerable than predators, especially when asleep.

Key terms

Ecological niche: this refers to an animal's living conditions. These can include habitat (e.g. whether it lives on the land or in the water), whether it is a predator or prey animal, and whether it is nocturnal or diurnal.

- Sleep site – does the animal sleep in a relatively safe deep burrow or in a more exposed location, for example on the African savannah?
- Size – we have already seen that large animals tend to sleep less than smaller animals. Is this to do with lifestyle, or do large animals have a different physiology to small animals?

Ecological factors

There were a number of early explanations of sleep that focused on ecological factors.

- Predator–prey status: Meddis (1975) proposed that sleep keeps vulnerable prey animals safe at times when normal activities are impossible, i.e. diurnal animals cannot forage for food at night, and therefore they simply stay out of harm's way by sleeping.
- Hibernation theory: Webb (1982) uses the analogy of hibernation to explain sleep. Animals such as bears and squirrels hibernate over winter to conserve energy at times when hunting and foraging are impossible. Similarly, sleep is a time of relative inactivity when animals will conserve energy resources. This is particularly important for small animals such as mice that tend to have a high **metabolic rate**. This is the rate at which animals burn up resources, so small animals sleep more in order to conserve energy.

Research evidence

Allison and Cicchetti (1976) studied sleep in 39 animal species and found that prey animals sleep for significantly less time than predators. This might imply that sleep is a dangerous time for prey animals and goes against Meddis's ideas. However, prey animals are often herbivores, and it has been shown that herbivores sleep for less time than carnivores (Lesku *et al.*, 2006), so it might be this fact that explains the predator–prey relationship.

A more commonsense argument against Meddis's proposal is that sleep leaves an animal unreactive and vulnerable. If safety was the only consideration then it would be more effective to stay awake and alert, but quiet, than to fall asleep.

There is clearer evidence in favour of the hibernation/energy conservation approach. Findings show that basal metabolic rate (BMR), essentially the rate at which the body burns up energy, is *positively* correlated with sleep time, i.e. the higher the BMR the more the animal sleeps (Berger and Phillips, 1995; Zepelin and Rechstaffen, 1974; Lima and Rattenborg, 2007). Small animals have higher BMR than larger animals, and so they sleep more.

So sleep would be more beneficial for small animals, although remember that only NREM represents energy conservation as the body's physiological processes slow down. In REM, energy consumption is only slightly less than in waking behaviour. These conclusions are largely supported by a recent analysis by Lesku *et al.* (2006).

Research study: Lesku *et al.* (2006)

In this study Lesku *et al.* analysed data on sleep patterns from 54 species and looked at a range of variables, including:

- body mass
- brain mass
- basal metabolic rate (BMR)

Key terms

Metabolic rate: the rate at which animals burn up resources. Animals with a high metabolic rate need to eat more, but they also conserve more energy when they are asleep.

Link

Approaches, issues and debates

The evolutionary explanation of sleep relies heavily on studies with non-human animals. Although these are not laboratory experiments they still have ethical issues. For instance, observation in the wild may disturb the animal's natural behaviour. Other observations will be based on animals in captivity (zoos). Apart from ethical issues, behaviour in captivity may not be the same as behaviour in the wild. Recent reports suggest that the giant sloth sleeps for far longer in the zoo than it does in its home environment. Can you think why this might be?

Hint

How science works

Many of the conclusions in this area rely on correlations between different measures, e.g. sleep time and body size, sleep time and metabolic rate. Remember that correlations simply mean an *association* between two variables, and we cannot conclude that one *causes* the other. For instance, small animals sleep more than large animals, but this may not be to do with body size, but simply that small animals tend to have safer sleeping sites than large animals.

- sleep exposure index – this is an assessment of the animal's sleep site and how safe it is
- trophic position – this index relates to whether the animal is a herbivore or carnivore.

Their key findings were that:

- Brain mass is *positively* correlated with the amount of REM sleep, but it has no association with NREM.
- The sleep exposure index is *negatively* correlated with the amount of REM. The more dangerous the sleep site, the less REM sleep.
- Trophic position was correlated with the amount of REM and with total sleep time. Herbivores generally had less REM and total sleep time than carnivores.
- Basal metabolic rate is *negatively* correlated with NREM and total sleep time. The authors acknowledge that this contradicts previous findings (e.g. Zepelin and Rechstaffen, 1974), and a possible explanation is that they calculate the BMR in a different way. Other authors support the positive relationship between BMR and sleep time, while Savage and West (2007) propose that the *brain's* metabolic rate is the key variable. In their study sleep time in 96 species was positively correlated with BMR but had a stronger positive relationship with brain metabolic rate.

Methodological issues

Results in this type of research are based on correlations between variables such as brain mass and sleep time. Strong correlations can indicate a powerful relationship between variables, but cannot say whether the relationship is 'cause and effect', i.e. whether brain mass in some way 'causes' an increase in REM sleep. To establish cause and effect we need to use controlled experiments, often in the laboratory.

On the other hand, this research has high ecological validity, as it was often based on observations of animals in their natural habitat.

Ethical issues

- As they were using data collected in a number of other studies over the years, there are no ethical issues with this type of review.

Link

For more information on the advantages and disadvantages of correlational designs, see Chapter 38, Designing psychological investigations.

Lesku *et al.*(2006) demonstrated that sleep time and the relative proportions of NREM and REM can be influenced by a range of factors that need to be considered for each separate species. This complexity accounts for the range of sleep patterns found in the animal world, although there are still problem species – for example, the sloth is a relatively large mammal yet it sleeps for 20 hours a day.

Most studies in this area are *correlational* designs, and cannot identify cause and effect. It can also be difficult to disentangle correlations between sets of variables. For example, herbivores sleep less than carnivores. Herbivores have to graze for many hours each day and so have less time to sleep. However, herbivores are also prey animals, and prey animals in general sleep less than carnivores. So we cannot say for certain which of these factors is more important in determining sleep time in animals that are both herbivores and prey.

The evolutionary ecological approach has identified many factors related to sleep time and patterning:

▓ Body mass or size is *negatively* correlated with sleep time; large animals sleep less than small animals.

▓ Brain mass is *positively* correlated with the amount of REM sleep.

▓ Basal metabolic rate, and in particular brain metabolic rate, is *positively* correlated with sleep time.

▓ Animals with more exposed sleep sites sleep less than animals with safer sleep sites. This is particularly the case with REM sleep.

▓ Herbivores sleep less than carnivores.

The challenge is to identify how these factors interact for any particular species.

Evaluation

The classic studies in this area consist of observations and measurements of sleep patterns in as many species as possible. Measurements cover ecological niche, physiological characteristics such as body size and metabolic rate, and EEG recordings of NREM and REM. Currently data exists for about 90 different animal species. Researchers then correlate the various measures to identify significant associations between different factors. However, correlations cannot confirm cause and effect relationships, and there is always the possibility that some other unidentified factor is influencing the observations.

Evolutionary approaches across psychology also assume that any current behaviour or characteristic must have an evolutionary advantage, and so we try to find the advantage in, for example, NREM or REM. However, some characteristics may simply be neutral for the animal, providing neither advantage nor major disadvantage. No one doubts that sleep overall has major and important roles, but perhaps some of its detailed characteristics are simply evolutionary hangovers.

Finally, one of the most positive features of the evolutionary approach with its focus on ecological factors is that it takes the whole animal and its lifestyle into account. It is not a *reductionist* approach, but it tries to explain sleep in terms of the whole animal and its environment.

Some of the factors identified through the evolutionary approach have clear links to physiology, for example the relationship between metabolic rate and sleep, and between brain mass and REM sleep. These links should be remembered as we move on to consider restoration theories of sleep.

▓ Restoration theories

Restoration theories are quite simple in outline but complicated in detail. Sleep has always been seen as a time of rest and recuperation, when the body restores itself after the day's activities. So the simple view of the restoration approach is that the physiological patterns associated with sleep are produced by the recovery processes of the body, especially the brain. Immediately several questions arise:

▓ What is used up during the day's activities that is restored during sleep?

▓ Do NREM and REM have different roles in restoration theories?

▓ Do the characteristics of NREM and REM fit with restoration theories?

▓ Does evidence from sleep deprivation studies support restoration theories?

▓ Link

Approaches, issues and debates

The evolutionary approach is often seen as reductionist, comparing modern human behaviour directly to that of our ancestors. With sleep functions, though, the approach has broadened out to include a variety of ecological and physiological variables that might influence sleep patterns. Used in this way, the evolutionary approach cannot be criticised as reductionist.

Biological rhythms

One of the earliest systematic restoration theories was presented by Oswald (1969 and 1980). He noticed that people recovering from severe trauma to the brain, such as drug overdoses, spent more time in REM sleep. It was also known that new skin cells (our skin cells are constantly being replaced) grow more quickly during sleep, and Oswald linked this to the increased release of the body's growth hormone during deep NREM. He then proposed that REM sleep was for restoration of the brain, while NREM was essential for restoration of the body.

The proposed role of REM in maintaining and restoring brain function did explain one of the key observations referred to earlier. Newborn babies spend a third of every day in REM sleep. This is a time of massive brain growth, with the development of new **synaptic connections** between **neurons** requiring neuronal growth and the production of neurotransmitters. We know that REM is an extremely active phase of sleep, with brain energy consumption similar to waking behaviour, so Oswald's theory would explain this activity and why it is so dominant in the newborn.

Research evidence

Before considering other restoration theories we should look at some of the evidence relevant to Oswald's model. He predicted that burning up more resources during the day should lead to longer sleep times. In addition he argued that sleep deprivation should have an effect on brain function and behaviour.

Physical exercise and sleep

The evidence here is contradictory. Shapiro *et al.* (1981) found that runners slept longer and spent more time in NREM after running a marathon, supporting Oswald. However others (e.g. Horne and Minard, 1985) have found that exhausting physical exercise leads to people going to sleep faster but not sleeping longer than normal.

Effects of sleep deprivation

Studies of sleep deprivation are critical to arguments about the functions of sleep. If NREM and REM have essential roles, then deprivation should lead to clear-cut effects. This area of research has produced a range of fascinating case studies.

Peter Tripp, an American DJ, raised money for charity by staying awake for 201 hours. After a few days he developed signs of mental disturbance, with hallucinations (seeing spiders) and paranoid delusions, thinking that his food was drugged. At the end of his marathon effort he slept for 24 hours and awoke feeling restored and back to normal.

In 1964 an American student, Randy Gardner smashed Tripp's record by staying awake for 264 hours (about 11 days!). He developed blurred vision, his speech became disorganised, and he became mildly paranoid (Dement, 1976). On his first recovery night he slept for 15 hours, and over the following nights recovered about a quarter of the sleep he had lost. What was interesting was the type of sleep he recovered – about two-thirds of deep NREM and about 50 per cent of REM were recovered (Dement, 1976).

Although these were uncontrolled single case studies, they do allow some conclusions to be drawn regarding the effects of total sleep deprivation (TSD):

■ People can endure long periods of TSD with no long-term effects.

Key terms

Synaptic connection: the microscopic gap between one neuron and the next. Information is conducted across the synapse by the release of neurotransmitters. The development of new synaptic connections between neurons is a crucial part of brain growth.

Neurons: the brain is made up of around 100 billion neurons. Neurons are specialised to transmit electrical activity and are connected to each other by synapses. The electrical activity codes information in the brain.

Fig. 5 *DJ Peter Tripp in sleep deprivation for charity*

Fig. 6 *Randy Gardner beat Peter Tripp's record in 1964 by staying awake for 264 hours*

- TSD can have effects on mental functioning, i.e. the brain, but these effects show significant individual differences.
- After TSD only a small proportion of sleep lost is recovered.
- Recovery is concentrated on the deep stages of NREM and REM.

Evaluation

Although fascinating in their own way, the cases of Tripp and Gardner have to be treated with caution. There was little control over them, for example laboratory studies would use EEG recordings to monitor the person's state; Tripp and Gardner may well have had periods of 'microsleep' to keep them going. They provide clues to the effects of TSD, but more systematic studies would be needed to confirm the results.

Studies in non-human animals have shown that prolonged sleep deprivation leads to death. In rats this occurs after about 19 days. However, to keep them awake very stressful procedures have to be used, for example having them fall into a water bath if they fall asleep. It is impossible to separate the stress of these procedures from the effects of the sleep deprivation itself.

Human fatal familial insomnia is a rare inherited condition in which people sleep normally until middle age and then simply stop sleeping. Death usually follows within two years, and is associated with damage to the thalamus in the brain. Again it is impossible to separate the effects of the sleep deprivation from the underlying brain damage.

The sleep laboratory

Tripp, Gardner and fatal familial insomnia are all interesting but largely **anecdotal** accounts of sleep deprivation. The systematic and scientific study of sleep, including sleep deprivation, had to wait until the widespread use of the sleep laboratory. This is set up so that participants can have their EEG and physiological measures recorded constantly, and can also be given tests of memory and attention, etc. to identify effects of deprivation. Conditions are highly controlled so that results are reliable and can be generalised. The simultaneous measurement of all these EEG, physiological and psychological variables is known as polysomnography.

Horne's restoration theory

Jim Horne has been a major British sleep researcher for many years. From an analysis of laboratory controlled studies of sleep deprivation he proposed a restoration theory similar in some ways to Oswald's, but very different in other ways. He based his conclusions on key observations:

- Sleep-deprived participants given cognitive tasks can maintain reasonable performance by putting more effort in. Eventually, though, deprivation produces effects on memory and attention, i.e. brain processes (see the research study below).
- Moderate sleep deprivation appears to have few if any effects on the body.
- When allowed to sleep, deprived participants make up far more of the REM and deep NREM sleep that they have lost than the lighter stages of NREM.

 Key terms

Anecdotal: uncontrolled observations or hearsay. It is often contrasted with the collection of evidence through controlled scientific experiments.

Hint

How science works

The development of the sleep laboratory and the use of polysomnography is an excellent example of how the study of sleep functions in humans has become more objective and scientific over the last 50 years.

■ **Research study: Horne and Pettitt (1985)**

These researchers were interested in whether incentives would help participants (Pps) overcome the effects of sleep deprivation. They had three groups of Pps. Group 1 were sleep deprived for 72 hours and were not given incentives. Group 2 were sleep deprived for 72 hours but were given financial incentives to complete the task. Group 3 were a control group who were not sleep deprived and were not given incentives.

Pps were repeatedly tested on an auditory vigilance task in which they listened to tones, and had to respond when they heard a tone that was slightly shorter than the rest.

The researchers found that the performance of group 2 was as good as the control group after one night of sleep deprivation, whereas group 1 performed significantly worse. Even after two nights of sleep deprivation group 2 still performed significantly better than group 1.

Horne and Pettitt concluded that the motivation provided by the financial reward could overcome the effects of sleep deprivation. They argue that sleep deprivation initially affects motivation more than our cognitive abilities. Eventually though, sleep deprivation does affect cognitive performance.

They also found that all Pps were completely recovered and performed normally after just eight hours' sleep. They therefore concluded that not all sleep was necessary for the return of normal cognitive functions. Horne later referred to the sleep that was recovered as 'core sleep'.

Methodological issues

The groups in this study were very small with only five Pps in each. This means that results might be difficult to generalise. The researchers also note that sleep-deprived Pps would have occasional microsleeps; there was no checking to see if these were comparable across all of the Pps. Finally there should have been a control group who were not sleep deprived but did have the incentive.

Ethical issues

Sleep deprivation is very stressful, but Horne and Pettitt did follow appropriate ethical procedures, obtaining full informed consent.

■ **Take it further**

Horne and Pettitt did not have a control group who were not sleep deprived but were given the financial incentive. Can you work out why this would have been an important group to compare with the other groups?

■ Key terms

Core sleep: this term was introduced by Horne to refer to REM sleep and the deepest stages of NREM. Horne found that recovery after sleep deprivation was concentrated on these components. He concluded that these were the most essential parts of sleep, so called them core sleep.

Optional sleep: this was a term introduced by Horne to describe the lighter stages of NREM. After sleep deprivation these stages were not recovered and so Horne refers to them as optional, i.e. not essential.

Horne therefore proposed that:

■ REM and deep NREM are essential for normal brain function, i.e. during these phases of sleep the brain is restoring itself. Horne refers to REM and deep NREM as **core sleep**.

■ Light NREM sleep appears to have no obvious function, and Horne refers to this as **optional sleep**. He suggests it may have a role in keeping the animal inconspicuous.

■ There remains the problem of restoration of the body. As we enter NREM there is a surge in the release of growth hormone. However, if this hormone is to help in repairing body tissues, it requires a supply of amino acids and proteins. By the time we go to sleep, perhaps six hours after the evening meal, the nutrients supplied by the meal are no longer available in the blood stream for the growth hormone to use. Therefore, although the reason for the surge in growth hormone remains unclear, it is unlikely to include tissue repair. Horne suggests that body restoration could take place in periods of 'relaxed wakefulness' during the day, when energy expenditure is very low and nutrients are likely to be available.

A final question for the brain restoration approach is exactly what is being restored? Basically we do not know. Likely candidates include various aspects of brain metabolism, growth of new synaptic connections, or synthesis of neurochemicals, including neurotransmitters.

This last hypothesis receives some support from the action of antidepressant drugs. We have already seen how people deprived of sleep recover REM in particular. If they are specifically deprived of REM (by being woken up in the sleep laboratory whenever they enter a phase of REM), REM recovery is even more dramatic, and referred to as **REM rebound**. This supports Horne's proposal that REM is vital for brain recovery.

However, people on antidepressant drug therapy often show a reduction in REM sleep, and no REM rebound when they come off the drugs. These drugs have a particular action in the brain. They increase levels of neurotransmitters, in particular noradrenaline and serotonin. Stern and Morgane (1974) suggest that the function of REM is linked to the synthesis of neurotransmitters used up in daytime activities. Antidepressant drugs increase these chemicals, so there is less need for REM sleep and no REM rebound.

The brain restoration view of REM also explains the high proportion of REM in newborn babies. This is a time when the brain is growing rapidly with millions of new synaptic connections being formed every day. If REM is essential for growth of new connections and/or the supply of neurotransmitters used in synaptic communication, then more REM would be needed during periods of brain growth.

Evaluation

The strongest evidence in favour of the restoration approach comes from studies of sleep deprivation. Even though work with non-human animals is largely invalidated by the stressful methods needed to keep the animals awake, human studies show that deprivation produces effects on memory and attention, and if prolonged, confusion, hallucinations and paranoia occur.

The evidence is strongest for restoration of brain processes. There is little convincing evidence for restoration of body tissue during sleep.

Evidence against restoration ideas is that energy expenditure during the vital REM phase of sleep is similar to waking levels. However, specific restoration of neurotransmitters or growth of new synapses would require energy expenditure. The increased amount of REM in the newborn supports this approach, that REM is for restoration of specific processes rather than for general brain repair.

Restoration theories in their pure form ignore the evolutionary/ecological approach. In this sense they are *reductionist*, focusing only on physiological processes of brain and body. Most of the evidence comes from studies with humans. If the theories are to be extended to non-human animals, then the ecological factors shown to affect sleep patterns will have to be included.

Key terms

REM rebound: this is seen after people are specifically deprived of REM sleep in a sleep laboratory. When allowed to sleep they show a dramatic recovery of REM and this is known as REM rebound. This is evidence supporting the importance of REM sleep.

Link

Approaches, issues and debates

As a science, psychology involves testing hypotheses. The restoration theory of sleep leads to specific hypotheses that can be tested, e.g. sleep deprivation will impair memory and learning, or energy expenditure during the day will increase sleep at night. Studies to test these hypotheses lead to findings and conclusions that help us decide which theory is more reliable.

AQA Examiner's tip

Examination questions on the functions of sleep will involve evaluation of evolutionary and restoration approaches. However, it will often be relevant and creditworthy to compare these approaches. Make sure you have a clear understanding of some points of contrast.

Biological rhythms

Memory consolidation

Since the scientific study of sleep began in the 1950s, there has been a popular view that sleep might be a time when memories acquired during the day were 'consolidated' into permanent memories. However, it was some time before clear evidence emerged that some forms of learning were dependent on sleep. When asleep you are both quiet, and passing through the sleep stages. The effects of sleep may not then be due to sleep stages specifically, but simply to being quiet and undisturbed. A common problem in early studies was a failure to control for the effects of simply being quiet and undisturbed. If you learn a task in the morning you might show less recall in the evening because of the intervening activities of the day. If you learn it in the evening and then sleep, you might recall better because you have avoided the interference, not because sleep itself is essential for consolidation of learning.

Development of the sleep laboratory allowed controlled studies to be carried out, and these demonstrated the beneficial effects of sleep. For example, Karni et al.(1994) used selective disruption of REM and NREM sleep and showed that improvement on a simple visual discrimination task (participants had to discriminate line patterns) depended on REM sleep but not on NREM sleep.

Walker et al.(2002) developed this approach and showed that motor learning (participants had to learn and repeat finger key-press sequences) improved if sleep followed training but not if training was followed by a similar period of wakefulness. Additionally there was a significant positive correlation between the amount of improvement (i.e. memory consolidation) and the amount of stage 2 NREM.

The most convincing evidence comes from studies using simple learning tasks, involving the simplest form of memory, **procedural memory**. The evidence for the dependence of more complex forms of learning (e.g. learning word lists) on sleep is inconsistent (Walker and Stickgold, 2004).

Key terms

Procedural memory: one of the simplest forms of memory and relates to the learning of simple motor skills such as using a keyboard or riding a bike.

Summary questions

4 Elephants sleep for about three hours in 24, and mice for about 15. What sort of factors would the evolutionary approach use to explain this difference?

5 Outline and evaluate findings from studies of sleep deprivation, especially their implications for restoration theories of sleep.

6 Discuss whether evolutionary explanations and restoration theories explain why we need both REM and NREM sleep.

Key points

■ Evolutionary explanations study factors such as the environment, predator/prey status, sleep site, and brain and body size. All of these have been related to sleep patterns.

■ Body size and metabolic rate are positively related to sleep time.

■ Herbivores, prey animals and animals with exposed sleep sites sleep less than other animals.

■ Restoration theories focus on physiological recovery of the brain and body.

■ Research evidence shows that sleep deprivation affects brain function more than the body. In particular REM and deep NREM sleep are associated with brain recovery.

■ There is increasing evidence that REM and NREM sleep are important for memory consolidation. So far, though, only simple forms of learning have been studied.

Lifespan changes in sleep

Learning objectives:

■ understand changes in sleep patterns over the lifespan

■ consider implications of changes in sleep patterns over the lifespan.

■ Introduction

The study of ways in which patterns of sleep may change across a person's life may help to explain the functions of sleep. We saw above that sleep in a newborn baby is very different to sleep in adults; babies will sleep for 16–20 hours a day, and of this 50 per cent will be REM sleep. In fact, in premature babies born at 30 weeks, the proportion of REM can be as high as 80 per cent. During its first year the baby's patterns of sleep and activity begin to settle down.

■ How sleep patterns change

We know that our endogenous biological rhythms are synchronised with signals from the outside world, especially the light/dark cycle. This synchronisation happens during the first year. At around one year of age, rest–activity patterns are stabilising, with 6–8 hours' sleep at night supplemented by daytime naps of 1–2 hours. The proportion of REM approaches the adult ratio of about 25 per cent. Between one and two years old, the adult pattern of sleep–waking is established though there may still be short naps in the daytime.

The changes in sleep patterns from birth to two years are dramatic and their significance is considered below. However, it is also interesting to see whether sleep patterns alter significantly across the rest of the lifespan. Many studies have been done, but a key problem is that there are large individual differences in sleep patterns. One technique to overcome this is to combine the results of many similar studies in a meta review. This approach identifies consistent trends across a large number of studies.

Ohayon *et al.* (2004) performed such a meta review using 65 studies of sleeping patterns that between them covered an age range of 5–102. They identified a number of significant trends:

■ Total sleep time decreased steadily from about 470 minutes at five years old to 370 minutes at age 70.

■ The percentage of stage 1 NREM increases from 5.8 per cent at age five to 6.8 per cent at age 70.

■ The percentage of stage 2 NREM shows a similar increase over the lifespan from 47 per cent at age five to 55 per cent at age 70.

■ The most dramatic finding was a decrease in the percentage of deep NREM (stages 3 and 4) from 24 per cent at age five to only about 9 per cent at age 70.

■ The percentage of REM sleep decreases slightly but steadily over the lifespan from about 25 per cent at age five to about 19 per cent at age 70. This slight decrease was confirmed in a recent study by Floyd *et al.* (2007), which found a decrease in REM of 0.6 per cent per decade.

Ohayon *et al.* also looked at gender differences. They found that males had higher mean scores for total sleep time, percentage of deep NREM and percentage of REM. Females showed a higher percentage of stage 2 NREM compared with males.

There are other changes across the lifespan. There is a decrease in sleep efficiency, which is the ratio of time asleep compared with time in bed. This is due to the fact that older people have more episodes of waking during sleep than children and young adults. Older people also report more sleep disorders. These are discussed in Chapter 3, Disorders of sleep.

Conclusions

Changes in sleep patterns over the lifespan ought to tell us something about the functions of sleep and its different components. The single most striking observation is the large amount of REM in the newborn baby and its decrease over the first year or so to adult levels. Of course, the baby's brain is doing lots of things during this period. It is developing physically, in terms of neuronal connections, and it is also processing an enormous amount of information. Basic motor systems are developing, along with cognitive processes such as perception, learning and memory.

In theory, REM in the newborn could be related to any of these functions. REM plays a role in restoration, approaches to the function of sleep, and perhaps in memory consolidation. At the moment we have no way of deciding what the exact function of REM is.

Changes in sleep patterns between the ages of five and 70 are variable. There is roughly a 16 per cent increase in stages 1 and 2 NREM, and a dramatic 60 per cent decrease in deep NREM. Deep NREM has been linked to restoration theories, with Horne proposing that it is part of 'core sleep' essential for efficient brain function. Other studies have shown that it seems to be vital for the consolidation of simple learning.

The steady reduction in deep NREM, significant as early as age 30, implies that the need for these functions declines with age. Older people with Alzheimer's disease (senile dementia) show a particularly dramatic loss of deep NREM. They also have major problems with learning and memory and other brain functions, supporting a link between deep NREM and normal cognitive processes.

Key points

- There are significant changes in sleep patterns over the lifespan.
- Babies have a high proportion of REM sleep which declines to adult levels over the first year.
- There is a significant decrease in deep NREM (slow-wave sleep) between the ages of five and 70.
- REM sleep shows only a slight decrease between the ages of five and 70.

Summary questions

7 Outline two key changes in sleep patterns over the lifespan.

8 Consider explanations for the high proportion of REM sleep in newborn babies.

Insomnia

Learning objectives:

- understand the classification of sleep disorders
- explain the differences between primary and secondary insomnia
- understand some of the explanations for insomnia and the role of personality.

Key terms

Insomnia: a condition where people have difficulties sleeping. This can involve the quality or length of sleep.

Apnoea: frequent episodes during sleep when breathing stops for a few seconds. This leads to daytime sleepiness and causes insomnia.

Narcolepsy: a genetic condition with symptoms of sleep paralysis, cataplexy, hypnagogic hallucinations and daytime sleepiness.

Sleepwalking: parasomnia that occurs during the lighter stages of NREM. It is most common in children.

Dyssomnias: these are conditions such as insomnia and narcolepsy that affect the quality and duration of sleep, leading to daytime tiredness.

Parasomnias: these are events occurring during sleep, such as sleepwalking and nightmares, that do not lead to daytime sleepiness.

Nightmares: these are terrifying dreams that occur in REM sleep and they are especially common in children.

Types of disorders

Sleep disorders are an increasingly important area of research. It is estimated, for instance, that **insomnia** (problems with the quality and length of sleep) affects up to one-third of the American population. For about 10 per cent it is a long-lasting (chronic) problem (Morin *et al.*, 1999). Sleep disorders affect an individual's quality of life by leading to daytime tiredness and possible problems with work and relationships.

Unfortunately the recent increased interest in sleep has led to the diagnosis and classification of many different sleep disorders. The most recent edition of the *International Classification of Sleep Disorders* (*ICSD-2*), published by the American Sleep Disorders Association, describes 70 specific disorders divided into eight categories. Here we will review only a sample of these disorders.

We have already considered some disorders, as sleep problems associated with shift work and jet lag both appear in the *ICSD-2*. A few of the more common disorders such as insomnia and sleep **apnoea**, and some of the more dramatic ones such as **narcolepsy** and **sleepwalking**, are considered here.

Before looking at specific conditions, we can divide sleep disorders into two general categories:

- **Dyssomnias** are problems with the amount, quality or timing of sleep. They include insomnia and narcolepsy, and often produce daytime tiredness that affects daily activities.
- **Parasomnias** are behavioural or physiological events that occur during sleep. Examples include sleep walking and **nightmares**. Parasomnias are rarely associated with daytime sleepiness.

Insomnia

The general definition of insomnia is that it involves problems in falling asleep, maintaining sleep and reductions in sleep quality so that sleep is non-restorative thus leading to daytime tiredness. This can then affect daytime work and social functioning. Of course we all have periods of insomnia, perhaps related to study or relationship problems, but these are usually shortlived. Therefore, to define a clinical syndrome a tighter definition is needed (Morin *et al.*, 1999).

Diagnostic criteria for insomnia

The diagnostic criteria for insomnia include one or more of the following:

- sleep onset latency (time taken to fall asleep) of more than 30 minutes
- sleep efficiency (time in bed actually spent asleep) of less than 85 per cent
- increased number of night-time awakenings

■ symptoms occurring three or more times a week.

In addition, the duration of insomnia is important:

- ■ Transient insomnia lasts less than one week. It is often associated with something in particular, for example jet lag or short-term life stresses such as examinations.
- ■ Short-term insomnia lasts for between one and four weeks.
- ■ Chronic or clinical insomnia lasts for more than one month and has a significant and distressing effect on daytime work and social functioning as a result of tiredness and irritability.

A key distinction is between primary and secondary insomnia:

- ■ **Primary insomnia** is a chronic insomnia occurring in the *absence* of any psychological or physical (medical) condition that might explain the disorder.
- ■ **Secondary insomnia** is a chronic insomnia that can be explained by a pre-existing psychological or physical (medical) condition. Besides psychological and medical conditions, other sleep-related phenomena such as sleepwalking and sleep apnoea can lead to insomnia.

Primary insomnia

Primary insomnia is a chronic insomnia, as defined above, with no obvious psychological or physical cause, and it is not associated with other sleep problems. It is often defined by exclusion, i.e. if an exhaustive life history and assessment of psychological and physical health reveals no obvious cause for insomnia, then it can be classified as primary insomnia.

The most severe form of primary insomnia is **idiopathic insomnia**. This begins in childhood and is effectively lifelong. In its severest form it does not vary with life circumstances or psychological well-being, i.e. it is not linked in any simple way with anxiety and arousal. People usually learn to live with idiopathic insomnia and function reasonably well. In some cases it is associated with high levels of depression. Fortunately it is an extremely rare condition.

There are no clear explanations for either idiopathic insomnia or primary insomnia in general. However, in earlier chapters we saw that sleep mechanisms are extremely complicated, involving control centres throughout the brain and an interplay between endogenous pacemakers (body clocks) and external zeitgebers ('time-givers'). Neurotransmitters such as melatonin, serotonin, noradrenaline and acetylcholine are also heavily involved. So it is reasonable to speculate that primary insomnia is caused by some basic malfunction in our sophisticated sleep control systems. This may be genetic, as there is some evidence that idiopathic insomnia runs in families (*ICSD*, 2005).

Given the strong evidence that the body clocks controlling our biological rhythms are 'inbuilt' (inherited), then a reasonable speculation is that a slight inherited bias or error in sleep control mechanisms prevents the normal pattern of sleep developing. Although idiopathic insomnia does not vary with arousal level, other forms of primary insomnia do seem more common in people with already high levels of anxiety. In these cases the additional anxiety-related arousal may disturb a sensitive sleep control system and lead to insomnia. Further evidence for this is the clear evidence that insomnia is often associated with *clinical* anxiety states such as generalised anxiety or obsessive-compulsive disorder. This is an example of a secondary insomnia.

■ **Key terms**

Primary insomnia: problems with the quality and duration of sleep leading to daytime sleepiness, with no obvious cause.

Secondary insomnia: problems with the quality and duration of sleep leading to daytime sleepiness, caused by a pre-existing condition such as narcolepsy or depression.

Idiopathic insomnia: lifelong serious insomnia beginning in childhood with no obvious cause.

■ **Hint**

How science works

Research into sleep disorders has led to interventions or treatments that help patients with insomnia or sleep apnoea, for example. Therefore uncovering the psychological or physiological factors that lead to sleep disorders may have immediate applications in the real world. (I)

Secondary insomnia

Many cases of chronic insomnia can be clearly associated with something psychological, physical (medical) or parasomnia (sleep-related events such as sleepwalking and sleep apnoea). This type of insomnia is therefore referred to as secondary insomnia. Some common causes include the following:

- Psychological disorders such as depression, anxiety states and schizophrenia are associated with insomnia. It has been estimated that around 40 per cent of patients seeking treatment for insomnia have an associated psychological disorder (Morin *et al.*, 1999).
- Medical conditions such as heart failure, Parkinson's disease and asthma can lead to insomnia. In addition, treatments for medical conditions can lead to insomnia, for example the use of steroid therapy for asthma.
- Drug use can lead to insomnia. Examples include stimulants such as amphetamines and alcohol, and the overuse of sleeping pills ('hypnotics') can lead to disrupted sleep patterns and increased insomnia.
- Parasomnias. Sleep apnoea, which is discussed below, is a disruption of breathing during sleep that leads to repeated wakenings through the night. Sleepwalking is another parasomnia that clearly disrupts normal sleep. It is important to note that for many people the insomnia linked to these conditions does not actually lead to daytime sleepiness or distress.
- **Fatal familial insomnia (FFI)**.

Explanations and treatments for insomnia

At one level, explanations for insomnia can be straightforward. Each of the factors listed above is a satisfactory explanation for insomnia. In some cases, such as sleep apnoea and FFI, we can even map out the underlying mechanisms in some detail. We also know that drugs such as amphetamine, alcohol and hypnotics affect brain neurotransmitters and probably lead to insomnia by disrupting the control of our complex sleep systems.

However, the detailed mechanisms behind some of the commonest forms of secondary insomnia – those associated with psychological disorders such as anxiety and depression – are more difficult to explain. Some clues come from effective treatment methods (Morin *et al.*, 1999). These are *not* on the specification but can give some insights into the causes of insomnia. This is similar to the way in which the success (or not) of treatments for psychological disorders has helped to identify the causes of schizophrenia and depression.

Drugs

If insomnia is secondary to depression or anxiety, then drugs to treat those conditions (antidepressants and anti-anxiety drugs such as the benzodiazepines) can lead to reduced insomnia. In fact, the most prescribed drug over the last 40 years for psychological disorders has been **nitrazepam** (trade name **Mogadon**), marketed as a sleeping pill. Unfortunately, while increasing sleep time, there is clear evidence that sleeping pills reduce sleep quality, disrupting the normal ultradian pattern of REM and NREM sleep. They can lead to morning sleepiness and increased insomnia when the drugs are stopped.

▥ Key terms

Fatal familial insomnia (FFI): a rare genetic condition in which the person sleeps normally until middle age, then develops severe insomnia that eventually leads to death. It is associated with the loss of brain neurons.

Nitrazepam: a sleeping pill ('hypnotic') and one of the most prescribed drugs over the last 40 years. It comes from the benzodiazepine class of drugs.

Mogadon: the trade name for nitrazepam.

AQA Examiner's tip

Occasionally in this book there will be material that is not on the Specification, such as treatments for insomnia. To do well in the examination you do not need to know this material. However, it will have been included to provide additional material that would be relevant to some questions. For example, effective treatments for insomnia tell us something about the possible underlying causes. You will not be asked a question directly on treatments for insomnia.

■ Link

For more information about treatments for psychological disorders, see Chapters 25–28.

Stimulus control therapy

This is based on the idea that insomnia is a conditioned (learned) response to various cues such as night-time and the environment of the bedroom. Because insomnia has become associated with night-time and the bedroom, a new association between sleep and these cues needs to be learnt. Procedures include (Morin *et al.*, 1999):

- only going to bed when sleepy
- only using the bedroom for bed and bed-related activities such as sleeping and sex
- waking and getting up at the same time every morning
- not taking naps in the daytime.

The effectiveness of this technique supports a role for conditioning and learned associations in the development of insomnia.

Cognitive behavioural therapy (CBT)

People who suffer from insomnia often report that they become extremely anxious at bedtime. They know they should go to sleep quickly and sleep for 7–8 hours. If they do not, then they will not be able to cope with daytime activities and their quality of life will suffer. The more they try to sleep, the worse it gets. CBT is aimed at correcting these faulty cognitions. Causes of insomnia are discussed and maybe elements of stimulus control therapy are introduced. Assumptions such as always needing 7–8 hours' sleep a night are challenged. In this way the anxiety caused by faulty cognitions is reduced.

The success of this method supports a role for cognitive processes and anxiety-related arousal in insomnia.

Over-arousal

A role for over-arousal is supported by the effectiveness of relaxation techniques. Progressive muscle relaxation and imagery techniques (visualising pleasant and relaxing situations) reduce physiological arousal and can be effective in reducing insomnia.

▌ **Hint**

How science works

In trying to explain human behaviour we often rely on more than controlled experiments. In psychopathology for instance, the effectiveness of antipsychotic drugs supported the dopamine model of schizophrenia. Similarly, the effectiveness of CBT for insomnia would support a role for faulty cognitive processes and anxiety in causing insomnia.

▌ **Key terms**

Longitudinal study: form of research that is often used in 'developmental areas' where a group of participants are studied for extended periods of time.

▌▌ Research study: Gregory *et al.* (2006)

There is evidence that insomnia is related to high levels of anxiety and depression. Gregory *et al.* (2006) were interested in the relationship between family conflict and the later development of insomnia. It is unusual in that it is a **longitudinal study**.

Based in New Zealand, a group of children have been followed from their birth in 1972 up to the present day. A wide range of variables have been studied regularly during this time.

One of these variables was the level of family conflict. This was assessed using questionnaires to measure levels of tension, hostility and distress in the family. It also included events such as separation and divorce.

Gregory *et al.* found that the degree of family conflict experienced by the child between the age of nine and 15 was significantly correlated with the frequency of insomnia at age 18. The researchers controlled for other factors such as socio-economic status, gender, health and depression.

They conclude that their study demonstrates a possible causal connection between family conflict and later sleep problems. They suggest that insecurity may lead to high levels of anxiety and a tendency to focus on family difficulties. This fits in with research showing that insomnia is often linked to high levels of anxiety.

Methodological issues

Although this was a large study with over a thousand children followed from birth, the actual incidence of insomnia at age 18 was only 15 per cent, the majority of the insomniacs being females. This is a relatively small group in which to study the effects of so many variables. The study was also correlational, meaning that we cannot determine cause and effect relationships. It may be that family conflict and later insomnia are both influenced by some factor that was not measured in the study, such as the personality characteristics of the people involved.

Finally, as the researchers admit, the relationship between family conflict and later insomnia, although significant, was modest. This suggests that other factors are involved in the development of insomnia.

Ethical issues

This longitudinal study began when the children were born, therefore informed consent would have been needed from the parents involved. Once the children were over 16, they would have been required to give their own informed consent. Information would have been collected through questionnaires and interviews, and some of these might have included intrusive personal questions. Participants would therefore have been given the right to withdraw at any time. The researchers obtained full ethical approval from the Otago ethics committee.

Causes of insomnia – conclusions

▥ Psychological factors. These can be extremely important. Conditioned (learned) associations and faulty cognitions (expectations) contribute to insomnia.

▥ Anxiety-related arousal. This is a central issue. Arousal is incompatible with sleep, and whether it is due to a clinical anxiety or depression, or simply due to worries about the sleep problems themselves, techniques to reduce arousal are likely to be effective. Presumably high levels of arousal interfere directly with the brain's complex sleep mechanisms.

▥ Problems with the brain mechanisms of sleep. Drugs can reduce insomnia, but they may also reduce the patterning and quality of sleep. Unfortunately the sleep system is very complex and we do not have drugs to target specific parts of the system. Until we know more about what has gone wrong with sleep mechanisms in cases of insomnia, we are unlikely to produce truly effective drug therapies.

▥ Personality factors and genetics

You will know from your own experience that there are many individual differences in sleeping habits. Although everyone needs some sleep, Napoleon reputedly needed only 4–5 hours per night, and Margaret Thatcher (one of our longest-serving Prime Ministers) functioned efficiently on a similar amount. On the other hand Albert Einstein slept around 10 hours a night (Wickens, 2004). The shortest sleeping time validated in a sleep laboratory is around one hour each night (Meddis, 1977).

■ Key terms

Neuroticism: a personality type characterised by high levels of anxiety and bodily arousal.

Chronotype: a personality type defined by when in the circadian rhythm of sleep and waking you are most alert.

Larks: people with a chronotype that makes them most awake and alert in the morning.

Owls: people with a chronotype that makes them most awake and alert in the evening.

Clock genes: a number of genes involved in the control of our endogenous pacemakers (body clocks).

■ Link

For more information about the use of muscle relaxation and CBT to reduce arousal and anxiety levels, see page 34.

■ Link

For more information about the biological circadian rhythm of sleep and waking, see page 5.

On average, people sleep for 7.5 hours, with 16 per cent sleeping more than 8.5 hours and 16 per cent sleeping less than 6.5 hours (Empson, 1993). Interestingly, both sleeping less and more than average are associated with slight but significant increases in mortality (death). We do not know the mechanisms behind these effects or the causal links involved (Van Dongen, Vitellaro and Dinges, 2005).

Although sleep duration appears to be a relatively stable characteristic, with a significant genetic component, there are no clear psychological or personality differences between long and short sleepers (Van Dongen *et al.*, 2005).

There are two areas in sleep research that do bear directly on the issue of personality in relation to sleep. The first is the role of arousal and anxiety.

Clinical anxiety

We have seen that clinical anxiety states are often a cause of secondary insomnia. Anxiety is associated with high levels of physiological arousal, and arousal clearly acts against any tendency to sleep. So people with anxious personalities are more likely to suffer from insomnia. This is supported by the effectiveness of therapies such as muscle relaxation and CBT which aim to reduce arousal and anxiety levels and thus combat insomnia. It is also supported by twin studies showing that high levels of sleep disturbance, mostly insomnia, were associated with high levels of neuroticism (Heath *et al.*, 1998). **Neuroticism** is a personality trait that is significantly correlated with anxiety. Vahtera *et al.* (2007) have also shown that vulnerability to sleep disorders following traumatic life events such as divorce is highly correlated with the personality trait of anxiety.

Clinical anxiety and depression are major causes of insomnia, and even in the general population a tendency towards anxiety in particular makes sleeping problems, especially insomnia, more likely.

Chronotype

A second area where personality and sleep patterns overlap is in **chronotype**. This is the technical term for the common observation that some people are aroused, alert and functioning well in the morning ('early birds', or '**larks**'), and some people function well in the evenings ('**owls**'). In between these morning types (larks) and evening types (owls) we have an intermediate type who functions pretty well throughout the day.

The difference between extreme morning types and evening types is genetic and is based in the biological circadian rhythm of sleep and waking. It turns out that the circadian rhythm in morning types is roughly two hours ahead of that in evening types (Kerkhof and Van Dongen, 1996). As our sleep–waking behaviour, arousal and alertness are all linked to phases of our circadian rhythms, larks and owls peak in alertness at different times.

These characteristic individual patterns are stable over time and seasons, and represent a distinctive personality trait. They are controlled by our endogenous body clocks (endogenous pacemakers), which in turn are controlled by so-called 'clock' genes on our chromosomes. So far several **clock genes** have been identified, but much work needs to be done to discover the detailed control systems.

Your particular chronotype is almost certainly genetically determined. Other aspects of sleep, such as duration, REM/NREM patterning, vulnerability to narcolepsy and nightmares, etc. show a modest heritability (genetic influence) although there is lots of room for environmental factors (Van Dongen *et al.*, 2005). However, if you are a lark it is counter-productive to pretend you are an owl as you are fighting against an inbuilt tendency and it is likely to lead to sleep disorders. If you are at one or other extreme, go with the flow and work when your biological rhythms tell you to!

A final word on gender. This has not been researched much in relation to sleep and sleep disorders. More women than men suffer from insomnia, making up about 60 per cent of patients in sleep clinics (Morin *et al.*, 1999), although women tend to have higher levels of neuroticism and anxiety, which make insomnia more likely. The ICSD has categories of premenstrual insomnia and hypersomnia (too much sleep), recognising that in some cases hormonal changes during the menstrual cycle may influence sleep patterns. However, findings are inconsistent and few studies specifically look for gender differences in sleep and sleep disorders.

Key points

- There are many sleep disorders, categorised into dyssomnias (problems with the amount, quality or timing of sleep) and parasomnias (events occurring during sleep).

- Insomnia is divided into primary insomnia, with no obvious cause, and insomnia secondary to psychological or medical conditions.

- Anxiety and arousal are key factors in secondary insomnia, and there is evidence for a role for learned associations and unrealistic cognitions.

- People can be characterised in terms of their chronotype (circadian phase preference), into morning 'larks', evening 'owls' and an intermediate type.

- The sleep–waking circadian rhythm in larks is roughly two hours ahead of that in owls. Evidence supports a genetic origin for these personality differences.

Link

Approaches, issues and debates

Gender bias: the fact that little research focuses on gender differences in sleep disorders is an example of the beta bias in psychology and science – the assumption that results from studies with males will automatically apply to females.

Summary questions

1. Outline key differences between dyssomnias and parasomnias.

2. Outline *three* factors that can lead to secondary insomnia.

3. Evaluate evidence linking personality factors to sleep patterns and sleep disorders.

Other sleep disorders

Learning objectives:

- describe symptoms of sleep disorders, including sleep apnoea, narcolepsy and sleepwalking

- understand explanations for sleep disorders such as sleep apnoea, narcolepsy and sleepwalking.

Key terms

Obstructive sleep apnoea (OSA): apnoea caused by obstruction of the upper airways, preventing efficient passage of air to the lungs.

Central sleep apnoea (CSA): apnoea caused by problems in the brain's control of breathing and respiration.

Cataplexy: sudden loss of muscle tone during waking, leading to collapse. This is a key symptom of narcolepsy.

Sleep apnoea

We have already discussed sleep apnoea as a cause of secondary insomnia. The term 'apnoea' (US spelling: apnea) relates to repeated episodes of breathing failure during sleep. These typically last for between 20 and 40 seconds, although they can go on for several minutes in rare cases. For clinical diagnosis there need to be at least five episodes a night. The person may or may not be fully conscious during an episode, but either way sleep is disturbed and the sufferer will complain of insomnia and daytime sleepiness. Other features include:

- snoring
- morning headaches
- dry mouth in the morning.

There are two types of sleep apnoea:

- **Obstructive sleep apnoea (OSA):** this is when the breathing passages from the mouth to the lungs (the upper airways) are obstructed and breathing is inefficient. There can be a narrowing of the airways, enlargement of tissue at the back of the mouth or enlargement of the tonsils deep in the throat. OSA is highly correlated with obesity (which contributes to narrowing of the airways), and the typical patient is a middle-aged overweight man or woman. OSA affects about 4 per cent of men and 2 per cent of women.

- **Central sleep apnoea (CSA):** the main symptom of several episodes of breathing failure during the night leading to insomnia and daytime sleepiness is the same as for OSA. However, it tends not to be associated with snoring but with a choking sensation, and there are no obvious problems with the upper airways. CSA is often linked with heart problems and cerebrovascular disease (problems with the blood supply to the brain), and probably represents malfunctions in the brain's control of respiration and cardiac (heart) function.

Treatment of OSA can be effective. Surgery can widen the upper airways if they are physically obstructed, while weight loss can be a key element (Grunstein *et al.*, 2007). Also popular is the use of a breathing mask during sleep that creates continuous positive airway pressure (CPAP). CPAP effectively drives air through the upper airways into the lungs.

CSA is more difficult to treat as the problem is probably in the brain mechanisms of respiration. Drugs to help the underlying condition of heart failure or cerebrovascular disease can indirectly help in CSA.

Narcolepsy

Narcolepsy is one of the more dramatic sleep disorders, affecting around one person in 2,000 (Black, Brooks and Nishino, 2004). It is characterised by four major symptoms:

- Extreme daytime sleepiness, with repeated short episodes of sleep throughout the day.

- **Cataplexy:** this is the sudden and unexpected loss of muscle tone while awake. It can lead to immediate collapse (but not loss of consciousness) lasting from a few seconds to a few minutes. Some sufferers may have several cataplexic attacks per day. Cataplexy can be brought on by emotional arousal of any sort, for instance laughter or sexual arousal.

■ **Hypnagogic hallucinations**: these are dreamlike experiences occurring during wakefulness, especially during the transitional period between sleeping and waking up.

■ Sleep paralysis: an inability to move, often occurring when falling asleep or waking up.

Only around 50 per cent of sufferers show all four symptoms, but most exhibit cataplexy and at least one of the other symptoms. In terms of our sleep mechanisms, the symptoms of narcolepsy seem to reflect the invasion of REM sleep phenomena into waking life. We think this because:

■ During REM sleep the bodily muscles lose tone. This would account for cataplexy and sleep paralysis if it occurred during waking behaviour.

■ Dreams occur mainly in REM sleep. Hypnagogic hallucinations would represent the intrusion of dreams into the waking state.

■ When people with narcolepsy fall asleep they move directly into REM sleep, rather than following the normal pattern of moving through the stages of slow-wave sleep first. So when they fall asleep in the daytime, they immediately show cataplexy as they are in REM sleep.

Narcolepsy is also unusual in that we do know some details of what has gone wrong with our sleep mechanisms. The clue was provided by dogs. It turns out that some dogs have a tendency towards cataplexy, especially when excited. They also fall straight into REM sleep. This tendency can be increased by selective breeding, and allows narcolepsy to be directly studied.

A gene defect is responsible for narcolepsy in dogs. The gene, on chromosome 12 (Lin *et al.*, 1999), is responsible for regulating brain receptors for a neurochemical called **orexin**. Without receptors orexin cannot function, and it was proposed that lack of orexin or its receptors was the cause of narcolepsy in humans. This was confirmed when Thannickal, Moore and Niehuis (2000) found that orexin-producing cells in the hypothalamus of the brain were drastically reduced in people with narcolepsy.

In narcolepsy, therefore, levels of orexin are greatly reduced (Sakurai, 2007). Injecting orexin into areas of the brain involved in sleep, such as the locus coeruleus and raphe nuclei, increases levels of REM (Wickens, 2005), suggesting that orexin is centrally involved in the control of REM sleep.

At present we cannot explain the loss of hypothalamic orexin-producing neurons. Narcolepsy usually develops in the teenage years, and while MZ twins have a higher concordance rate than DZ twins, it is only around 30 per cent, suggesting that the condition is not entirely inherited. Environmental factors are also important.

What is equally frustrating is that although we have a clear neurochemical candidate for the cause of narcolepsy, at the moment we have no effective treatment. Drugs that increase orexin levels should, in principle, help in narcolepsy, but such drugs are not yet available. Treatment usually involves stimulant drugs such as methylphenidate

Key terms

Hypnagogic hallucinations: these are REM dreams occurring during the switch from sleeping to waking.

Orexin: a brain chemical (neurotransmitter). Loss of orexin function is associated with narcolepsy.

Link

For more information about REM sleep, see page 17.

Fig. 1 *Dr William Dement holding a dog displaying the signs of cataplexy*

Link

For a reminder about the locus coeruleus and raphe nuclei, see page 18.

Link

The use of MZ and DZ twins in describing the effects of genetics and environment on behaviour is discussed in detail in Chapter 21, Evolution of intelligence.

Key terms

Ritalin: a stimulant drug used as a treatment for narcolepsy.

Modafinil: a stimulant drug used as a treatment for narcolepsy.

Night terrors: the person awakes terrified, confused and disoriented. They usually remember little of the experience. Night terrors are not nightmares, as they occur in NREM sleep.

Link

Approaches, issues and debates

Psychodynamic explanations for disorders such as sleepwalking and nightmares can look superficially convincing. However, these explanations, such as instinctual energies spilling over from REM to NREM sleep, do not lead to hypotheses that can be tested using objective scientific methods. Whether you believe them or not becomes a matter of personal opinion.

(trade name **Ritalin**; this drug is a popular therapy for attention deficit hyperactivity syndrome), amphetamine and newer drugs such as **modafinil**. Stimulants act against the daytime sleepiness that occurs in narcolepsy.

Sleepwalking

Sleepwalking is an example of a parasomnia, an event occurring during sleep that does not result in severe insomnia or daytime sleepiness. Around 30 per cent of 5–12-year-olds may have episodes of sleepwalking, but in only 1–5 per cent does it occur regularly. It tends to run in families, suggesting some genetic involvement, and although most children grow out of it, it can also occur in young adults.

Sleepwalking usually takes place in the deeper stages of NREM early in the night. It cannot happen in REM as the body muscles are relaxed.

During sleepwalking the individual usually carries out routine automatic tasks, but these can sometimes be quite complicated, such as making tea or selecting channels on the television. Usually in sleep the brain inhibits motor activity. For reasons we do not understand, in sleepwalking these over-learnt routine activities are activated. In fact, in one or two cases people have escaped murder charges by claiming they were sleepwalking at the time! For this to happen there has to be evidence of a strong family history of sleepwalking and the individual themselves must have clearly demonstrated the disorder before the incident.

Sleepwalkers often have no recollection of their actions in the morning, even if awoken during the episode (contrary to popular wisdom, this is quite harmless). For most people, usually children, sleepwalking is harmless and they eventually grow out of it. When it causes distress to the individual and their family, it is classified as a sleep disorder.

Sleepwalking can look purposeful, and this has led to some psychodynamic explanations. For example, there is a suggestion that it represents a desire to sleep where the person slept as a child, although this does not explain the wide range of automatic acts that the sleepwalker can display. Another interpretation is based on Freud's ideas that during our dreams we are working through unconscious anxieties. Moving from REM sleep into NREM prevents this process, and so unconscious instinctual energies spill over into NREM and are channelled into motor activities, i.e. sleepwalking. This interpretation has also been applied to night terrors (see below). As with most psychodynamic ideas, this explanation is impossible to test scientifically.

Nightmares and night terrors

A final word on two conditions that people often confuse but which are very different. Nightmares are unpleasant, often terrifying dreams. As such they occur in REM sleep and often have a story-like structure which can be recalled in every unpleasant and vivid detail. **Night terrors** relate to when the person awakes in a terrified state, screaming and crying. They can be confused and disoriented and hard to wake, and when awake they remember little of the experience that led to the terrors apart from perhaps a single image. This is because night terrors occur in NREM sleep; they are not dreams in the standard sense.

Nightmares and night terrors occur in adults but are far more common in children. They are essentially harmless and require nothing beyond reassurance. Most children grow out of them as they mature.

Fig. 2 *Night terrors*

Key points

- Sleep apnoea is characterised by episodes of breathing cessation during sleep.

- Obstructive sleep apnoea is due to problems with the upper airways; it is highly correlated with obesity.

- Central sleep apnoea involves the brain mechanisms regulating breathing and heart function.

- Narcolepsy has four major symptoms – cataplexy, sleep paralysis, hypnagogic hallucinations and extreme daytime sleepiness. The first three represent the intrusion of REM-sleep phenomena into waking behaviour.

- Sleepwalking, nightmares and night terrors are parasomnias. Sleepwalking and night terrors occur in SWS, while nightmares are unpleasant dreams and therefore occur during REM sleep.

Summary questions

4 Outline the key symptoms of sleep apnoea.

5 Discuss the relationship between symptoms of narcolepsy and REM sleep.

6 Evaluate explanations for either sleep apnoea or narcolepsy.

Biological rhythms end of topic

How science works: practical activity

- Do some research using textbooks and the web, and find the average sleep times for at least 10 animal species.
- Similarly, find or estimate the average body weight of each species.
- What is your hypothesis?
- Perform a Spearman's rho correlation test on the two sets of data.
- Does the calculated correlation coefficient support your hypothesis?
- What are your conclusions?

Further reading and weblinks

Carlson, N.R. (2007) *Physiology of Behavior*. Boston: Pearson.

This book provides comprehensive coverage of sleep physiology, functions and disorders. It also covers biological aspects of gender development, feeding behaviour and psychopathology.

Coren, S. (1996) *Sleep Thieves*. New York: Free Press.

This is an extremely readable account of all aspects of sleep, from the earliest scientific studies to the problems of shift work and jet lag.

www.sleepnet.com.

This website focuses on sleep disorders, with over 200 links to additional sites and information.

www.circadian.com.

A search of this website will reveal information on circadian rhythms (the emphasis is on the problems of shift work).

Perception

Introduction

What is perception?

'Perception' refers to the ways in which information received through our sense organs, i.e. eyes, nose, ears, tongue, skin (sensation), is transformed into meaningful experiences of objects, events, noises, tastes and touch. Sensation is a biological process that relates to the responses of our sensory receptors and sense organs to environmental stimuli. Perception is more of a cognitive process involving the recognition and interpretation of stimuli once they have registered on our senses.

Look around the room where you are sitting and register some of the objects and people in it. You will immediately recognise a door, a window and, perhaps, some desks and chairs. If there are fellow students with you, you will probably recognise them and know their names. The noise outside on the road will instantly tell you that traffic is passing by, and if a strong, flowery smell reaches your nose, you will know that the person next to you has overdone it with the perfume today.

This may all seem very simple to you – our perception of the world appears to be immediate and direct and we have no conscious awareness of the brain activity underlying this apparently straightforward ability. However, in spite of the ease with which we perceive our environment, we know that it involves complex brain processes. It has been estimated that more than half of the adult human brain deals in some way with the processing of visual information (Sereno *et al.*, 1995). The most sophisticated of modern computers cannot be programmed to match the perceptual competence of a small child. Another indication of the intricate mechanisms involved in perception comes from case studies of people who suffer perceptual impairment as a result of brain damage. Small lesions in the brain can give rise to very specific and sometimes bizarre perceptual difficulties. For example, some people can no longer recognise faces, including their own. This disorder, known as prosopagnosia, is discussed later in the topic.

Perception involves all of the senses, but psychologists have conducted more research into visual perception than any of the other perceptual systems and this is reflected in the AQA specification. Over the next few pages we shall consider two broad types of theory that attempt to explain perceptual organisation: direct and indirect. Psychologists have also been interested to discover how the visual system develops from infancy to adulthood. This kind of research forms part of a wider debate about the contribution of nature (innate factors) and nurture (environmental influences) to human development. We shall look at the nature–nurture debate within the context of visual perception in Chapter 5, Development of perception. Another important aspect of human perceptual processing is face recognition. This is a specialised ability which has attracted a great deal of research interest and (in Chapter 6, Face recognition and visual agnosias) we shall consider theories of face recognition and look at the reasons why this ability sometimes breaks down.

4 Theories of perceptual organisation

Introduction

Learning objectives:

■ understand the basic processes involved in vision

■ describe and evaluate some of the methods used to investigate perception.

▦ The visual system

In order to understand visual perception, it is useful to have a basic understanding of the way the visual system works.

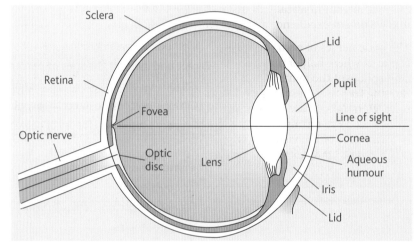

Fig. 1 *The structure of the eye*

Our sense organs receive electromagnetic energy from the environment and convert it into electrical activity in the brain. In the visual system, the energy is in the form of light. When light reaches the cells at the back of the eyeball, it starts off a chain of activity that leads, approximately 100 milliseconds later, to a conscious visual experience (see Figure 1).

The front of each eyeball is covered by a protective layer called the sclera (the white of your eye). An opening in the sclera, called the cornea, bends incoming light rays so that they fall directly on the retina at the back of the eyeball. There is a mechanism to control the amount of light that can enter the cornea at any one time. This is a ring of coloured (usually brown or blue) muscle called the iris. In the centre of the iris is the pupil, through which light passes. The iris can contract, making the pupil smaller, or dilate, making the pupil larger, depending on the prevailing light conditions.

You can see the pupil contraction for yourself: Pull the blinds or turn down the lights in your classroom. Ask a fellow student to sit close to you so that you can see their pupils. Under these dim conditions, you should notice that the pupils are quite large. Shine the beam of a torch into their eyes (take care that the beam is not too strong) and you will see how quickly the pupils constrict. If you turn the torch off, the pupils will dilate again. This is a reflex action and cannot be controlled voluntarily.

Immediately behind the pupil is the lens. This spherical body completes the task of the cornea by bringing light waves into focus on the retina. By changing its shape (a process called 'accommodation'), the lens can focus light rays from near and distant objects.

Link

A newborn infant cannot accommodate and has a fixed focal distance of approximately 19 cm. See page 63.

We lose elasticity in the lens as we grow older and it becomes increasingly difficult to focus on objects that are close to us. The lens can also become dense and cloudy as a result of disease or old age. This condition is known as a cataract and can cause blindness. At the back of the eye is the retina, a sort of screen consisting of layers of millions of light receptors (rods and cones) and nerve cells. In the middle of the retina is the fovea, a tiny spot but one that is densely packed with cones. This is the area that produces the clearest vision. The receptors convert the light into electrical activity which is then carried by the retinal cells via the optic nerve into the brain. There is a blind spot at the point where the optical nerve leaves the eyeball because there are no light receptors there.

We do not usually notice the blind spot in our everyday lives, but you can demonstrate it in the Take it further task. This demonstrates something important about our perceptual processing – we seem to 'fill in' missing information automatically to make sense of the visual environment so that we do not experience any holes in the visual field.

The optic nerves of each eye come together at the optic chiasm (see Figure 2) where half of the fibres from each eye cross over to the other hemisphere of the brain and half remain in the same hemisphere. Fibres carrying responses from the left visual fields of each eye terminate in the right lateral geniculate nucleus (LGN) and responses from the right visual field of each eye terminate in the left LGN. LGN cells then project to the receiving area of the visual cortex on each side of the brain, also known as V1, where complex visual processing takes place.

Take it further

On a sheet of paper, draw a diagram like the one shown below. The line should be six inches long and the X and the square should be about one inch in from either end. Hold the sheet out in front of you at arm's length. Now close your left eye and focus your right eye on the figure X. Make sure that you keep your right eye focused on the X and move the sheet slowly towards you. At the point where the image of the square falls on your blind spot, you will notice that the square seems to vanish completely. However, you do not experience a gap where the square should have been. Instead, you will have seen an unbroken black line.

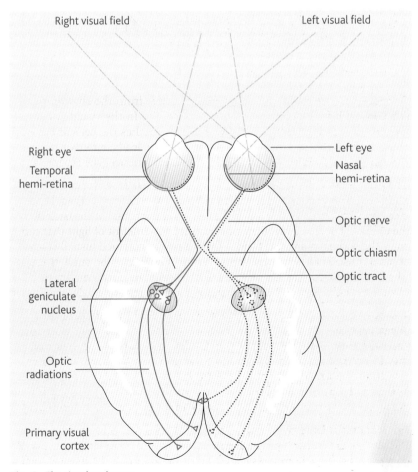

Fig. 2 *The visual pathways*

Perception

Perception

Table 1 *Different techniques used to investigate visual perception*

Method	Description	Commentary
Lesion experiments	Surgical removal or destruction of a specific part of an animal brain followed by observation of the consequences for perceptual awareness. Conclusions can then be drawn about localisation of function (i.e. neurons responsible for a particular function are located in a particular brain area)	Modern equipment ensures highly controlled experiments and accurate pinpointing of specific brain areas It is not always easy to draw accurate conclusions from observing animal behaviour after the surgery
Clinical studies	Investigation of the consequences for perceptual ability of accidental damage or disease in specific brain areas	The effects of brain damage in humans can be observed – lesion studies would not be ethical with human participants By definition, the researcher has no control over the location or extent of damage caused by accident or disease so any conclusions are limited
Single-unit recordings	A visual stimulus is presented to an animal while a fine electrode inserted in the brain registers activity from single sensory cells. This activity is recorded and analysed by a computer	This is a way of finding out how individual cells (as opposed to larger brain areas) contribute to perceptual processing In spite of the important discoveries about the functional properties of single cells, there is a need for caution in drawing conclusions about the functioning of a mass of neurons on the basis of responses in single cells
Brain imaging	These techniques were first developed in the 1970s for medical purposes. In computerised tomography (CT), the individual lies on a trolley that can be placed inside a long tube and a highly focused X-ray beam is passed through their body. X-rays can be passed through the head from many different angles so that a detailed picture can be built up of the different structures within the skull. The CT scan can reveal damaged areas and this can be helpful in people with perceptual impairments in order to isolate the areas responsible for the impairment. Magnetic resonance imaging (MRI) scanners pass radio waves through the head in various directions. These detect minute magnetic changes which inform us about brain function. The usual procedure is to ask individuals to perform different perceptual tasks during the scan in order to identify the parts of the brain that are active during those tasks	This is a non-invasive technique that allows investigation of living, human brains The techniques are expensive and technically complex requiring careful and expert interpretation
Psychophysical experiments	A typical experiment uses a series of carefully controlled visual stimuli, usually presented on a computer, and requires participants to make judgements about them, e.g. which is the brighter of two images. The difference between the two images is manipulated to find the point at which the participant can accurately discriminate between them	These are useful for testing predictions from theories of perception It is not always easy to draw inferences about the underlying neural structures
Artificial intelligence (AI)	This aims to produce a computer capable of carrying out various types of cognitive processing, including perception, in the same way as a human brain. It has been used particularly in investigating how we recognise objects and detect edges	AI research has been important in furthering our understanding of how the brain processes visual information Computers are not human and no machine has yet been programmed that can rival human perceptual processing

Methods of investigation

Various scientific techniques have been developed to investigate perception (see Table 1). Each technique has its own strengths and limitations and investigators often use a combination.

Key points

- Our sense organs receive electromagnetic energy from the environment and convert it into electrical activity in the nervous system. In vision, the electromagnetic energy is in the form of light.

- Light rays enter the eye through the cornea and are projected onto the retina. Photoreceptors convert light into neural information which is then transmitted to the brain via the optic nerve. The optic tracts travel through the brain to the visual cortex where higher-level processing of visual information takes place.

- Various methods have been devised to investigate visual perception, some involving non-human animals. However, recent advances in technology have made it possible to use non-invasive methods to investigate perception directly in human participants. Each method has its own strengths and limitations.

Summary questions

1. What is the difference between sensation and perception?

2. Why do you think we are usually unaware of our blind spot?

3. Various investigative methods are outlined in Table 1 above. Try to explain in a little more detail the strengths and limitations of using clinical studies to investigate perception.

Link

See also techniques used in infant research, page 61.

Hint

How science works

The development of different methods of investigation is important in the development of any science, including psychology. Various methods have different strengths and limitations, and it is important when you evaluate them to show that you understand both their strengths and weaknesses. (F)

Perception

Direct and indirect theories of perception

Learning objectives:

▓ understand the distinction between bottom-up and top-down processing

▓ describe and evaluate Gibson's direct theory of perception

▓ describe and evaluate Gregory's indirect theory of perception.

Link

The models of memory that you learned about at AS are based on the information-processing approach, see page 4 of the *AQA Psychology A AS* student book.

Bottom-up and top-down processing

As we move around in our everyday lives, we are presented with a diverse and continually changing array of sensory information, and the patterns of light reaching our retinas shift and change. In spite of this, we seem to manage to maintain a stable view of our visual environment. We are able to perceive the world around us not only with remarkable speed but also, usually, with a high level of accuracy. This suggests that perception is an organised process and that we use mechanisms to impose some order on our experience of the visual world. Various theories have been proposed to explain the processes involved in perception.

Traditional theories of visual perception fall into two broad categories:

▓ Direct theories – according to this type of theory, perception depends on bottom-up processing.

▓ Indirect theories – according to this type of theory, perception depends largely on top-down processing.

These terms come from the information-processing approach and have been applied to virtually every aspect of cognition, including perception.

Bottom-up processing theories

These are based on the assumption that we work upwards in our analysis of the visual world from basic sensory inputs at the bottom level towards the higher, more cognitive levels of the brain. We start with an analysis of sensory inputs, i.e. factors such as the patterns of light reflected from the objects around us. This incoming information is relayed to the retina where the process of transduction into electrical impulses begins. These impulses are then passed into the brain where they trigger further responses along the visual pathways until they arrive at the visual cortex for final processing. It is assumed that there is enough information contained in the sensory input to allow the individual to make sense of the visual world without recourse to stored knowledge or problem-solving skills. Bottom-up theories are also often called data-driven theories. This is because data, arriving at receptors in the form of sensory input, drives or determines the perceptual process.

Top-down processing theories

These are based on the assumption that we can only perceive our visual world accurately if we use stored knowledge and problem-solving skills to interpret raw sensory data from the environment. This higher-level information works downwards from the top in order to make sense of sensory inputs – in other words, we access higher cognitive levels right from the beginning of the perceptual process. This kind of processing is also called concept-driven processing because prior knowledge (i.e. mental concepts stored in memory) drives the perceptual process.

Gibson's bottom-up direct theory of perception

J.J. Gibson (1950) believed that perception is a direct process which does not rely on stored knowledge or past experience but is part of an inbuilt adaptive mechanism for survival. He viewed the organism and its world as inseparable and believed that organisms exist only because they have successfully adapted to local conditions and can obtain food and avoid predators. His theory of direct perception is sometimes described as an ecological approach because of his beliefs about evolutionary biology. His key idea was that the light pattern reaching the eyes is so rich in sensory information that recognition can take place without the need for any higher cognitive input. He called this rich sensory input 'the optic array'. Gibson was particularly interested in explaining how perception works in the real world and he was critical of theorists like Gregory (see page 53) who used artificial, laboratory-based studies to investigate perception. He preferred to work in applied research using his findings in practical applications. He was involved, for example, in developing training programmes for pilots during the Second World War. In particular, he was concerned with training pilots to accomplish the difficult and dangerous task of landing the plane safely. This led him to think about depth perception and to formulate his own ideas about how perception works.

Gibson's ideas are complex and he developed his theoretical framework over a long research career spanning more than 30 years. In this chapter, we will focus on some of the central elements of his theory: the optic array, the importance of movement, invariant information and the direct nature of perception.

The optic array

Gibson believed that the starting point for the perceptual process is the optic array or the structure of light in the environment. Light alone is insufficient for accurate perception. The light has to be structured by the objects, surfaces, edges and textures that reflect it. Lift your eyes away from your book and look at some of the objects around you. You will probably perceive the objects and their surfaces, edges and textures easily. In fact, you can only see them because of the thousands of light rays that are reflected from them and which then converge into the cornea of your eye. If you stand up, the structure of the optic array changes and provides your visual system with more information about the visual scene.

Movement

We are rarely static when we view the world around us and most of our perception occurs when we are moving through the environment either walking, running or driving, etc. Even if we are sitting down, our eyes move constantly and we turn our heads or alter our position in our seats. Similarly, the objects and people we are viewing are also often in motion relative to us. Gibson was not so much interested in the structure of light at any single time but in how the structure changes as the observer moves. He calls this the ambient optic array. Movement of the observer within the environment provides rich information about the relative positions of objects and surfaces.

Invariant information

Even though there are constant changes in the optical image that reaches the eye as we move around and change our viewpoints, there are some properties in the ambient array that are invariant. According to Gibson, this invariant stimulus information is automatically extracted by the perceptual system and we use it to gauge depth, distance and orientation of the objects around us. There are three main sources of invariant information:

- texture gradient
- optic flow pattern
- horizon ratio.

Perception

Texture gradient

Texture gradient is an important concept in Gibson's theory. In our visual environment, we are presented with surfaces which have different textures, e.g. a smooth road, a pebbly beach, a grass-covered field. Gradient refers to the fact that we view these textures from different angles and distances. The individual elements of the texture (e.g. the pebbles on the beach or the separate blades of grass) appear to be closer together as the distance from the viewer increases. You have probably experienced this for yourself. Think about standing at the edge of a roughly mown field; the grass at your feet will probably look quite rough and long whereas the grass at the end of the field looks smoother and well tended. In general, if the texture is coarse, we assume the object is close to us; as the texture becomes smoother, we assume it is further away.

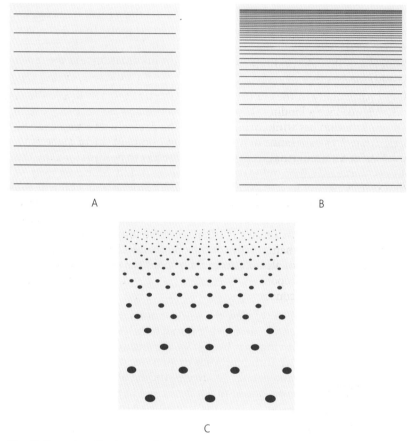

Fig. 3 *Examples of texture gradient*

Texture gradient can also help us to detect changes in orientation – sudden as opposed to gradual changes in the texture often indicate a change in the direction of the surface, e.g. horizontal floor to vertical wall (see Figure 4).

Optic flow patterns

Optic flow patterns (OFPs) are created as elements in the environment pass around a moving observer. Imagine you are looking out of the side window of a moving car or a train. You will see a gradient of flow, i.e. the speed of movement is more rapid in the foreground but slower in the background. This is similar to the depth cue of motion parallax,

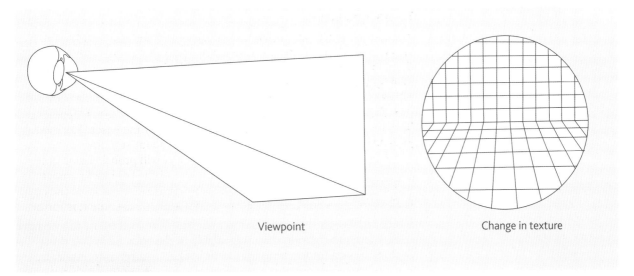

Viewpoint   Change in texture

Fig. 4 *A change in texture from floor to wall is sudden, not gradual*

but Gibson thought that the flow of the whole visual field was more important than the relative movement of isolated objects. He investigated OFPs particularly in the context of aircraft landing and taking off. When a pilot approaches a landing strip, the point towards which they are aiming remains motionless while the rest of the visual environment seems to move outwards as if fanning away from that point. These OFPs provide pilots with vital information about their direction, speed and altitude.

Horizon ratio

Horizon ratio is the extent of an object that is above the horizon, divided by the extent of the object that is below the horizon. The horizon ratio principle states that two objects of the same size standing on a flat surface will have the same horizon ratio. This is invariant with the observer's position so, although objects seem larger to an observer as they get closer, the proportion of the object that is above and below the horizon will remain constant.

Fig. 5 *Horizon ratio in context*

Direct perception

According to Gibson, we 'pick up' information from the invariants in the optic array and this leads directly to perception.

We have considered some of Gibson's key ideas, but there is one other central concept which is probably the most controversial. This concerns the way in which we attach meaning to what we see. Gibson believed that our visual perception does not occur in a vacuum because it takes place in a rich environmental context which includes our:

▓ physical situation (in our kitchen, in a garden, etc.)

▓ psychological state (happy, thoughtful, optimistic, etc.)

▓ physiological state (thirsty, hungry, tired, etc.).

In order to recognise objects and to understand what they are for, we have to use more information than is available in the optic array. We must combine it with information that feeds back to us from our physical surroundings and from our psychological state. According to Gibson, all objects in our environment offer us the opportunity to make use of them in some way. How we choose to use them depends on a combination of factors. For example, if we are thirsty, we are likely to see a glass as something to put a drink in; if we have just picked some roses and no vase is available, we might see it as a container for flowers. Similarly, the same object can offer different opportunities for different species, e.g. a flower offers a bee the opportunity to gather nectar, but it might offer a human the opportunity to pick it for a buttonhole. Gibson called these opportunities 'affordances'. He suggested that most objects afford (offer) us opportunities to make use of them, e.g. chairs afford 'sitting on', stones afford 'throwing', etc. We 'pick up' these meanings directly from the environment because we are closely attuned or adapted to it. Gibson called this pick-up process 'resonance' and used the analogy of listening to the radio to explain this. If we do not fine tune it, we simply hear a hissing noise. However, if we tune the radio finely to a particular part of the electromagnetic spectrum, it will resonate to the signal there and we will hear clear, meaningful speech and music. In a similar way, individuals resonate to certain elements in the environment that specify the affordances of the objects around them.

Commentary

▓ Gibson's theory has offered a powerful challenge to many of the mainstream ideas about perception and has stimulated considerable debate. In particular, he highlighted the importance of movement in understanding perceptual processes. He also stressed the need to study perception in the natural environment and showed how traditional laboratory methods sometimes underestimate the amount of information available in the stimulus input.

▓ Visual perception is known to be a very fast and generally accurate process and this fits with the idea of direct perception.

▓ Gibson was not concerned with explaining perception in physiological terms. Nevertheless, independent biological research has provided evidence of neurons in the visual cortex which could be responsible for some of the perceptions Gibson described. For example, Graziano Andersen and Snowden (1994) have identified neurons which could underpin the perception of optic flow patterns.

▓ One of the weakest aspects of Gibson's theory is the concept of affordances. Humans live within a particular cultural context in which knowledge about the use of objects is learned rather than

Link

Approaches, issues and debates

Gibson emphasises the direct nature of perception and does not consider the role of experience and stored knowledge. In this sense it is a more reductionist approach than Gregory's. If the evidence shows that perception is influenced by expectancies, for instance, then Gregory's constructivist approach provides a more detailed and comprehensive explanation of perception than Gibson's more limited approach.

'afforded'. Bruce and Green (1990) have suggested that affordances only provide an adequate explanation of the visually guided behaviour of lower animal forms, e.g. insects which do not need a conceptual representation of their environment.

People have been shown to be susceptible to visual illusions. If perception is the direct process that Gibson describes and if it depends on invariant and unambiguous properties of the visual array, this should not happen. Gibson responded by pointing out the artificial conditions in which experiments using illusions were carried out. However, this does not entirely answer the criticism because some illusions affect us in everyday life.

Gregory's top-down theory of perception

Gregory's indirect theory of perception is embedded in the much older, but still active, **constructivist approach**.

Constuctivists like Gregory believe that the stimulus input arriving on our sensory organs from the environment is frequently ambiguous or unclear in some way. In order to interpret or make sense of our visual world, we have to approach the process of perception as if it is a problem-solving task. When we are faced with unusual or incomplete visual stimuli, we have to draw inferences or make a best guess as to what we are viewing. Instead of perceiving directly as suggested by Gibson, we frequently have to use indirect, top-down processes. These processes are usually unconscious and we have no direct awareness of making inferences while viewing our environment. Although the top-down processing involved in perception is mainly unconscious and happens within milliseconds, the process is regarded as indirect. This is because the visual information has to be processed at a high cognitive level way beyond the basic sensory registration in order to be perceived accurately and meaningfully. For this reason, this type of theory is sometimes called 'intelligent perception'.

To give an example, imagine you are looking at the noticeboard in the student common room and read the following handwritten notice:

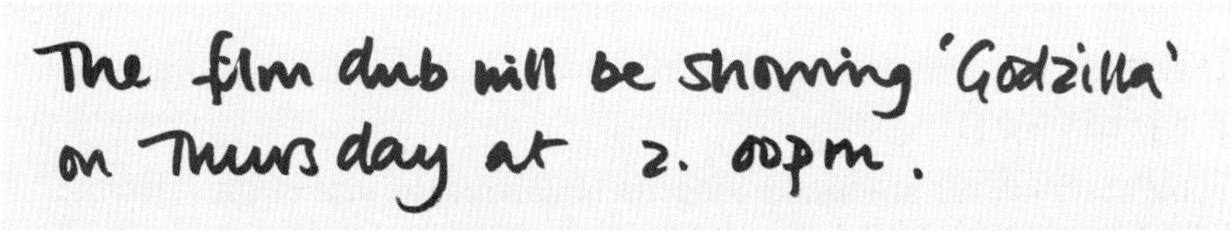

The film club will be showing 'Godzilla' on Thursday at 2.00pm.

Fig. 6

You should have had no problem reading this quickly and accurately. However, look at it again carefully. Exactly the same sensory input that you interpreted as 'cl' in club, is perceived milliseconds later as a 'd' in Thursday. Similarly, the 'z' in Godzilla is the same as the '2' in 2.00pm. The reason you had no difficulty in understanding this message is that you used context and stored knowledge to guide your perception, so you infer that, although 'dub' is an English word, it makes no sense in this context, and 'Thursclay' does not exist as an English word so you do not consider it as a possibility.

According to Eysenck and Keane (2000), there are three major assumptions that all modern constructivists like Gregory share:

Perception is an active, constructive process which goes beyond direct registration on the senses.

Link

See pages 54–57 for some examples of visual illusions.

Key terms

Constructivist approach: a theoretical approach developed more than 100 years ago by the German psychologist Helmholtz who believed that we combine a number of different factors in order to 'construct' our final perception. According to this view, perception is a process that relies on inference.

Perception

■ Perception is the end product of the interactive influences of the stimulus input combined with internal hypotheses, expectations and knowledge. Motivational and emotional factors can also contribute to this perceptual processing.

■ Since perception is influenced by internally generated hypotheses and expectations, which may not always be correct, it is prone to error and people can make perceptual mistakes.

Gregory agreed with Gibson about the importance of environmental cues such as texture gradient and motion parallax, but he rejected Gibson's contention that perception is a direct process with no need for higher cognitive input. Instead, Gregory believed that retinal images are inherently ambiguous (e.g. in terms of the size, shape and distance of objects). In addition, many properties of objects that are vital to guide our behavioural response to them cannot be signalled by the eyes, e.g. their hardness, weight, temperature, whether they are edible or not, etc. Because the visual input is so impoverished, Gregory believes that perception has to be an active process requiring a dynamic search for the best possible interpretation of the available data. He called this process hypothesis testing.

Gregory believed that we do not need much sensory data in order to draw appropriate inferences. He cites a study by Johannson (1975) as support for this idea. Johannson attached flashing lights to the major joints of an actor and then filmed him as he moved about a darkened room. When the actor was stationary, participants viewing the film could not make sense of the array of lights. However, as soon as the actor began to walk about, participants recognised that the movement was produced by a person walking.

There is considerable research support for the idea that our perceptions are influenced by prior expectations or stored knowledge. The related concept of perceptual set, first introduced by another constructivist, Allport (1955) refers to the idea that past experience produces a predisposition to perceive an object/situation in a particular way. It is thought that perceptual set makes perception more efficient because it reduces the choice between alternative interpretations of a scene and therefore speeds up the recognition process.

Diener (1990) demonstrated the effects of perceptual set by using pairs of words like those in Figure 7.

Look at the words and make judgements about the size of the letter P. The letter P in the second word is usually perceived to be a capital and to be bigger than the P in the left-hand word which is perceived as smaller and in lower case. In fact the letter Ps are physically identical. It is simply your set and expectations based on your knowledge about the relative proportions of upper- and lower-case letters that have distorted your perception.

One of the consequences of the constructivist idea of perception is that we sometimes formulate the wrong hypotheses and so make perceptual errors. One particular type of error that interested Gregory is the perception of visual illusions.

Look at the drawing in Figure 8.

This drawing could be seen simply as a set of interlocking two-dimensional shapes such as triangles, squares and trapezoids. However, most people interpret it as a representation of a three-dimensional cube. What is more interesting is the finding that, if you look at it for

■ Link

See page 50 for more about motion parallax.

AQA Examiner's tip

Note that experimental studies can be capable of more than one conclusion. Gregory cited the Johansson study as support for his constructivist theory. However, other researchers have claimed that it supports the Gibsonian view that biological motion provides invariant information.

Fig. 7 *Pairs of words used by Diener (1990)*

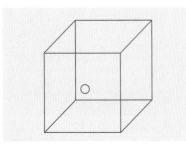

Fig. 8 *A Necker cube*

Perception

long enough, it will suddenly appear to change orientations. Once you have experienced this, the cube will then continue to 'jump' backwards and forwards between these two orientations. Gregory explained this in terms of his theory of hypothesis testing. No clue is provided in the drawing to tell us whether the cube is resting on a flat surface or jutting out towards us like a square cupboard fixed to a wall. In the absence of any surrounding context, either of these hypotheses is equally likely, so our brain flips between the two. If the picture had contained more information, e.g. the cube had been drawn sitting on a table top, the ambiguity would have been eliminated and only one hypothesis would have made sense.

The Necker cube is a type of illusion called an ambiguous figure where the same physical stimulus results in two different but equally likely perceptions. There are several well-known illusions that fall into another category called distortions. The two best known of these are shown in Figure 9.

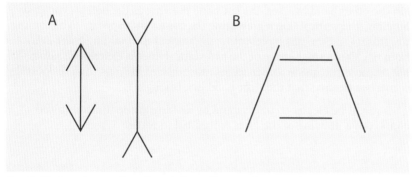

Fig. 9 *Illusions that are distortions:* **A** *the Müller-Lyer illusion;* **B** *the Ponzo illusion*

The Müller-Lyer is a powerful illusion where the line with the outward fins at each end is perceived as considerably longer than the line with the inward fins, even though the actual lines on the page are of equal length (check with a ruler if you do not believe it!). In the Ponzo illusion, most people 'see' the top horizontal line as longer than the bottom one, even though they are actually the same length.

Gregory has explained these illusions in terms of misapplied constancy scaling. To understand his explanation, you will need to understand what is meant by size constancy.

Size constancy

Our visual world is constantly changing as we walk around or move our head and eyes, and yet we perceive our environment as remarkably stable. If our perceptions were based purely on the retinal image (proximal image) objects would appear to grow in size and change shape and colour as we moved around. In most circumstances, however, our distal stimulus (our perceptual experience of what is 'out there') remains the same regardless of changes to the proximal stimulus. Size constancy refers to our ability to see objects as more or less the same size regardless of our own distance from them. If you walk towards a bookshelf to pick up a copy of your textbook, the image of the book that falls on your retina will increase in size the nearer you get. However, you do not believe that the book is getting bigger – you use the information from the expanding image on the retina to work out that you are now closer to the bookshelf than you were before. In other words, the retinal image provides you with depth and distance cues. This means that smaller objects are perceived as being further away. Size constancy is a way of maintaining a stable visual world and is usually helpful to us in making sense of the world. However, in certain circumstances, we misapply the rules and so we misinterpret the visual stimulus.

Gregory's explanation of the Müller-Lyer illusion

Gregory believes that, in Western culture at least, we learn from a very early age to interpret two-dimensional drawings as if they were three-dimensional objects. The perceived object will be determined by our cultural context. So, when we look at the Müller-Lyer drawing, our past expectations make us think it should represent something solid. We live in what Gregory calls a 'carpentered environment', i.e. where buildings are usually rectangular and contain outside edges and inside corners. So the object that seems to fit the bill most closely in this case is the corner of a room or building. We 'see' the right-hand version as the inside corner of a room (the vertical line represents the inside corner which appears to be going away from us and the fins represent the edges of the ceiling that seem to be coming towards us). On the other hand, we 'see' the left-hand drawing as the outside corner of a building (the vertical line representing the corner that appears to be coming towards us and the fins representing the sides of the building going away from us). Our retinal image of the two vertical lines is exactly the same, but, because the inside corner seems more distant from us than the outside corner, we assume that the right-hand line is longer.

This might be clearer to understand by looking at the illusion in the context of a drawing of the lines embedded in walls.

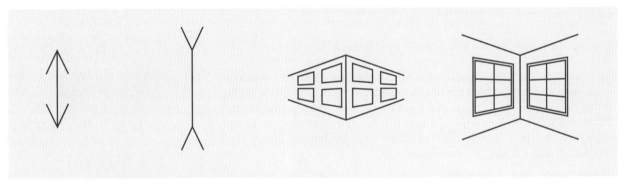

Fig. 10 *The Müller-Lyer illusion in context*

Gregory is not suggesting that we consciously make these comparisons to architectural edges when we look at the Müller-Lyer illusion – he believes that it is an automatic process that results from our well-learned experience of translating two-dimensional images into three-dimensional objects.

There is some support for his explanation from cross-cultural studies. Pedersen and Wheeler (1983) investigated the illusion with two groups of American Navajos. One group had lived all their lives in Western society and had grown up surrounded by a carpentered environment. The other group had not integrated into American cities and still lived in tribal communities in round houses. Navajos in the first group were much more susceptible to the Müller-Lyer illusion than those in the second group.

However, Gregory would find it hard to account for the findings of a study by De Lucia and Hochberg (1991). They constructed a three-dimensional version of the Müller-Lyer illusion and found that the illusion persists even when there are no depth cues. They stood wooden models shaped like fins on a flat surface (see Figure 11).

Perception

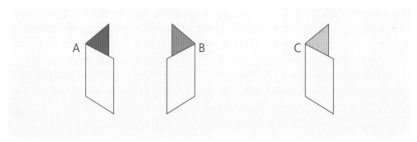

Fig. 11 *A 3-dimensional version of the Müller-Lyer illusion*

The distance between A and B appears shorter than between B and C, and yet the actual distance is the same. This shows that the Müller-Lyer illusion cannot depend on misapplied size constancy.

Day (1989) offers a very simple explanation of the Müller-Lyer illusion. He says that when we look at the lines, we have to consider two factors:

▒ the actual length of the vertical lines
▒ the overall length of the whole figure.

In this illusion, there is a conflict between these two factors and so we make a compromise estimate of length. The overall length of one figure is longer than the other version and so we estimate that the length of the vertical shaft itself must also be longer. This is in keeping with data from an earlier study where the fins were drawn in a different colour from the shafts (Coren and Girgus, 1972). In these conditions, viewers usually saw the two vertical shafts being of equal length which suggests that they had not taken the differently coloured fins into consideration.

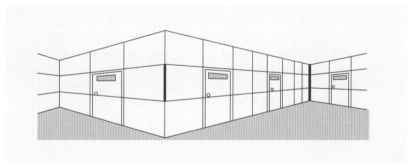

Fig. 12 *A 3-dimensional version of the Müller-Lyer illusion*

Commentary

▒ There is considerable research evidence to support the idea that we often make use of stored information and past experience to guide our perceptual processes.

▒ Gregory and other indirect theorists have over-emphasised perceptual errors in their research. In the real world, perception is remarkably accurate.

▒ This is linked to Gibson's main criticism of indirect theories, namely that their research is largely based on highly artificial stimuli presented briefly and often in fragmented or incomplete condition in laboratory settings. He felt that this cannot be generalised to perceptual processing in the real world.

▒ Indirect theories can account for visual illusions more satisfactorily than direct theories. However, Gregory's explanations of distortions are not universally accepted.

■ One problem with Gregory's explanation is that certain illusions are extremely persistent, i.e. we are still susceptible to them even when we know our perceptual system is being tricked. Gregory explains this by saying that we operate two systems: perceptual and conceptual, and one can override the other. However, this is not a very satisfactory answer because he does not explain how the two systems work.

■ We have noted several times in this chapter how accurate our perception is in general and how we manage to maintain a stable and constant visual world. If our perception relied totally on hypothesis testing and best guesses, we might expect to make far more perceptual mistakes than we do.

Key points

■ Perception is a complex activity and yet we manage to achieve it speedily, accurately and without conscious effort.

■ Theories to explain perception have fallen broadly into two categories: top-down (exemplified by Gregory) and bottom-up (exemplified by Gibson). It is almost certainly the case that neither approach can adequately explain perception on its own.

■ We almost certainly use a mixture of bottom-up and top-down processing. When viewing conditions are good and unambiguous, we can probably extract sufficient information directly from the visual environment to form accurate perceptions. However, in difficult conditions, when we are presented with degraded or incomplete visual information, we need to use our experience and stored knowledge to help us make perceptual sense.

■ Research in the field of visual perception has advanced considerably since Gibson and Gregory first proposed their theories. Although both continue to be influential, newer models, e.g. Marr (1982), have offered computational models of human perception, while others, e.g. Milner and Goodale (1995), have proposed a more complex two-system model in which there is a distinction between vision for perception and vision for action.

Summary questions

4 Constructivists explain size constancy in terms of top-down processing. How do you think Gibson might explain size constancy?

5 Look at Figure 9, showing the Ponzo illusion, and try to explain this in terms of misapplied size constancy.

6 Explain some of the strengths and limitations of using cross-cultural research to investigate Gregory's theory.

5 Development of perception

The nature–nurture debate

Perception

Learning objectives:

- understand the nature–nurture debate and, in particular, how it relates to explanations of perceptual development

- describe methods used to investigate the nature–nurture debate and understand their strengths and limitations.

Link

You learnt about the behavioural approach in the psychopathology section of *AQA Psychology A AS*, page 241. It is discussed in more detail in the Intelligence section of Unit 3 of this book, page 239.

Link

Approaches, issues and debates

The central debate in the development of perception is nature–nurture, or the influence of genetics versus the influence of environmental factors. This debate is also relevant to many other areas of psychology, and your understanding of the debate in relation to perception will help you to use it effectively when you come to other topics on the course.

Introduction

There has been a long-standing philosophical debate about the extent to which humans are shaped by their biological inheritance (nature) or by external, environmental factors (nurture) and this is known as the nature–nurture debate.

At one extreme of the debate, nativists believe that we are born with certain innate abilities and that, although some of these abilities can be incomplete or immature at birth, they develop through a process of maturation which is genetically programmed and does not rely on learning. In other words, we are shaped by our genetic inheritance and the constraints of our basic anatomy and physiology. For example, humans are 'programmed' to walk upright and, as long as they have no physical disability, they will do so without any training as soon as their muscular and skeletal systems are mature enough. On the other hand, humans are not pre-wired to fly and no amount of physical maturation or learning will enable them to do so. At the other extreme, empiricists believe that a child develops their abilities through experience with their environment. Environmental factors include personal experience and circumstances, but also influences from the social, cultural and political context in which the child grows up.

Behaviourists, such as Watson and Skinner, represented the extreme view of environmental determinism. According to them all behaviour is directly shaped and controlled through various types of learning and systems of rewards and punishments. Biologists, on the other hand, adopt the nature side of the debate, and believe that innate biological mechanisms and systems determine our psychological make-up.

Few psychologists now take either of these extreme positions and most would agree that our psychological abilities arise from an interaction between innate and environmental factors. Language ability is a good example to illustrate this interaction: there is now strong evidence that human language acquisition is an innate process. We are 'hard-wired' to speak a language and we possess an inbuilt mechanism that is programmed to recognise grammatical structure. However, the actual language that we speak, e.g. Chinese, English, French, etc., will depend on the language that we hear spoken around us as we develop. Similarly the range and richness of our vocabulary will largely depend on the models we are presented with. One interesting finding that clearly illustrates how innate and environmental factors affect one another comes from speech perception research in infants. Werker and Tees (1984) showed that infants up to the age of about six months can discriminate between a huge range of sounds found in world languages. However, this ability has disappeared by the time they are about nine months and they seem only to be able to discriminate sounds from the particular language spoken around them. In other words, an external influence, i.e. the language spoken around them, seems to have affected the plasticity of the brain and shaped it to adapt to specific environments. In the field of visual perception research, Riesen (1965) has provided another example of the interdependence of biology and environment. He reared chimpanzees in total darkness and, after a few months, tested their perceptual abilities. They were unable to recognise objects in their environment unless they accidentally knocked into them and they did not take avoidance behaviour when objects moved suddenly towards them. One conclusion was that the chimps lacked experience of the visual world and had not had an opportunity to learn the skills of object recognition and depth perception. However, it was found that, in the absence of light stimulation, nerve cells in the retina and visual cortex had started to atrophy. This suggests that biological and environmental factors interact to bring about accurate perception.

The nature–nurture debate in visual perception

We have already seen in Chapter 4, Theories of perceptual organisation, some of the complexity involved in perceptual processing. Psychologists are interested in finding out how much of this ability is innate and how much is a result of learning and experience.

Our biological visual system clearly imposes some constraints on our perceptual processes. For example, we can only focus clearly up to a certain distance because of the limited flexibility of the lens and we are only able to see a restricted range of the electromagnetic spectrum, e.g. we cannot see X-rays or infrared without special equipment. We also know that damage to the brain (e.g. prosopagnosia) can cause severe disruption to our perceptual processing. To this extent our perception is governed by innate mechanisms. However, we are constrained not only by our bodies, but also by the environment in which we grow up and this will vary for different individuals in a way that biological mechanisms do not.

The nature–nurture debate began as a theoretical, philosophical debate, but it is now a topic of interest for psychologists who have tried to find evidence relevant to the innate/acquired controversy in the area of visual perception. Various methods have been adopted to investigate this question and they all have strengths and limitations. Most of the evidence that supports the nativist view comes from human infant studies while other sources of evidence have tended to demonstrate the importance of environmental factors. Some of these sources of evidence are considered here.

Neonate studies

The most obvious way to investigate the nature–nurture debate in perception is to study the behaviour of newborn human infants. If perceptual abilities are innate, it should be possible to observe them in **neonates**, whereas if they are learned, these skills would be absent in the newborn. However, there are several problems with such research:

- It is difficult to hold infants' attention – they lose interest or even fall asleep during testing.
- There are ethical concerns about using babies in experiments.
- Just because an ability cannot be observed does not necessarily mean that it is not innate: it might be a question of maturation – the basic ability is innate but the visual system has not developed sufficiently to show it.

Hint

Gregory (see page 53) believes that environmental factors are paramount and that we can only perceive effectively because we use stored knowledge and past experience to make sense of our visual environment. However, Gibson suggests that affordances and invariants allow us to perceive the world effectively without additional, constructive processes. He does not deny that the perception of affordances and invariants has had to be learned, but the difference is that this learning has taken place over the course of millions of years of evolutionary history and not in the course of an individual perceiver's lifetime.

Link

For more information about the limited flexibility of the lens, see page 45.

Link

For more information about prosopagnosia, see page 79.

Key terms

Neonates: newborn or very young infants.

▥ Communication can be a problem – babies cannot understand instructions or tell us what they are experiencing – how do we know, for example, that a baby prefers to look at faces rather than other objects? Much of this research is based on inferences.

Table 1 *Some of the methods used in neonate research*

Technique	Explanation
Preferential looking (PL)	Two distinctive stimuli are projected on the walls or ceiling of a 'looking chamber' in which the baby is placed. If the baby looks at one for longer than the other, it is assumed that the baby can distinguish between the two and that one stimulus is preferred
Habituation	The researcher repeatedly presents the same stimulus and waits until the infant becomes so familiar with it (habituates to it) that they lose interest. A novel stimulus is then presented and, if the infant starts looking again, it can be assumed that they can tell there is a difference between the two
Sucking rate	The infant is given a dummy that is connected to a monitor that measures the sucking rate. Infants usually suck faster when their interest is aroused. When they become habituated to a stimulus, sucking rate declines. If it increases again, when a novel stimulus is presented, it is assumed that the baby can distinguish between the two stimuli
Conditioning	Every time the baby looks at a particular stimulus, they are rewarded by being shown a colourful toy or rattle. The infant quickly learns to look towards it. If the stimulus is then shown as one of an array of other stimuli and the infant still shows a preference for it, it is assumed they can distinguish it
Heart and breathing rate	A change in the infant's heart and/or breathing rate usually indicates that a novel stimulus has been recognised
Positron-emission tomography (PET) and functional magnetic resonance imaging (fMRI)	These are advanced techniques which allow researchers to see which part of the brain is active during any particular test

▮ **Hint**

How science works

It is important to understand the ethical and methodological limitations of these research methods. You will not achieve high AO2 and AO3 marks by simply saying that studies 'lacked ecological validity' or 'lacked generalisability'. You need to explain why. (F, J)

Researchers have developed some creative techniques to try to avoid some of these problems (see Table 1), but they cannot be completely resolved. That is why researchers have turned to other sources as well, but these have their own limitations:

▥ Non-human animal studies – these avoid some of the ethical problems of research with human neonates, but it can be difficult to apply findings from animals to humans.

▥ Clinical studies – these take the form of case studies of people who have suffered some kind of brain damage that affects their perceptual abilities. In the context of the nature–nurture debate, one of the most interesting sets of patients are those who have been blind since birth but who have surgery later in life that enables them to see. These people provide a sort of natural experiment because their visual deprivation occurs without any intervention from the investigator. These patients are normally adults and, unlike neonates, they can understand instructions and explain what they are experiencing.

Link

For a reminder about natural experiments, see *AQA Psychology A AS*, page 107.

Take it further

It is beyond the scope of this chapter to discuss animal, clinical and distortion studies in detail. However, these sources of evidence have yielded interesting findings in the nature–nurture debate which could be used effectively in an exam answer on the topic, so it is worth doing some extra reading.

However, by definition, these patients are not typical and might have developed heightened awareness in their other senses (e.g. touch, hearing, etc.) so they do not necessarily tell us much about normal perceptual functioning.

■ Human distortion studies – these involve adult volunteers who wear special equipment that distorts their visual world. If such individuals are quickly able to adapt to their new distorted world, it is assumed that learning plays a huge role in our perceptual abilities. If the individual is not able to adjust, it is assumed that perceptual capacity is innate and difficult to modify. The advantage of these studies is that they involve adults who can follow instructions, report what they are experiencing and move freely about their environment. However, such studies are very artificial.

■ Cross-cultural studies – these studies investigate perceptual abilities in people from very different cultural and environmental backgrounds, see page 68.

Key points

- The nature–nurture debate concerns the relative contributions of innate, biological and external, environmental factors to our behaviour.

- The debate arose in the discipline of philosophy but has since been addressed by psychologists who have considered it in several research contexts including that of visual perception.

- At one extreme end of the debate, nativists believe that we are either born with our perceptual abilities or that we develop them through a process of genetically programmed maturation.

- At the other end of the debate, empiricists believe that humans develop perceptual abilities through experience of their environment.

- Most contemporary psychologists believe that perceptual abilities depend on an interaction of biological and environmental factors.

- Various methods have been used by psychologists to investigate the nature–nurture debate in perception but they all have certain limitations.

Summary questions

1 Why do you think modern psychologists no longer adopt an extreme nativist or an extreme empiricist position?

2 Explain some of the strengths and limitations of using non-human animals to investigate the nature–nurture debate in visual perception.

The development of perceptual abilities

Learning objectives:

- understand what is meant by depth and distance perception

- describe and evaluate research into the development of depth perception in humans

- understand what is meant by visual constancies

- describe and evaluate research into the development of visual constancies in human infants

- understand the contribution of cross-cultural research to the nature–nurture debate

- describe and evaluate cross-cultural studies of visual perception.

Introduction

Until the 1960s most psychologists took the empiricist view that human infants possessed very little perceptual ability. However, as the methods shown in Table 1 (page 61) were developed, it became clear that babies are more perceptually aware than had been thought.

The development of depth and distance perception

Judging depth and distance is a skilled activity, but we do not think about it because we do it automatically. We manage to transform the somewhat blurred, two-dimensional, upside-down image on the retina into a meaningful experience of a three-dimensional world. Depth perception involves the understanding of absolute distance (i.e. the distance that the observer is away from the viewed object) and relative distance (i.e. the distance between two objects). This is used when, for example, you judge whether a small packet will fit in the postbox. On the whole, we are more accurate when judging relative rather than absolute distance.

Primary cues

Various cues are available to us when we make judgements about depth. Some of these cues are not dependent on learning or experience. These are called 'primary cues' and usually depend on the fact that we have two eyes working together (binocular). The cues are:

- Convergence – the muscles of the eye contract and pull the eyes inwards when we focus on an object that is close to us.

- Retinal disparity – because our eyes are roughly 6 cm apart, each eye receives slightly different information from the environment, resulting in slightly different images on the two retinas. However, as we move about in everyday life, we are usually not aware of this. Our brain seems to combine the two images in a process called stereopsis. The brain then makes use of this stereoptic information to form an impression of depth. The greater the disparity of an object in the two images, the closer it is perceived to be.

Common tasks such as threading a needle or inserting cards into cash machines are performed 30 per cent faster and more accurately using both eyes rather than just one (Sheedy *et al.*, 1986). However, it is clear that we can still perceive depth even if one eye is closed, so we must be able to use monocular cues (requiring the use of only one eye) as well. The only monocular, primary cue is:

- Accommodation – the lens can change shape depending on whether the viewed object is nearby or far away.

Secondary cues

Most of the other monocular cues seem to depend on learning and experience and are classed as secondary cues. One secondary monocular cue is texture gradient. Constructivists believe that this cue depends on prior learning, but Gibson (1950) believed that this provided direct perceptual information.

Perception

Link

For more information about Gibson's view that texture gradient provides direct perceptual information, see Chapter 4, Theories of perceptual organisation, page 48.

These are often also called pictorial cues because they are used by artists to convey depth in two-dimensional drawings and paintings. If neonates have an innate capacity for perceiving depth and distance, it seems likely that they are relying on primary rather than secondary cues.

Research study: Gibson and Walk (1960)

In order to investigate depth perception in human infants, Gibson and Walk carried out a classic experiment. They constructed a special piece of equipment called the visual cliff. This consisted of a flat sheet of glass placed above a table. A black-and-white check-patterned material was stuck on the underside of the glass which extended halfway across the table length (the shallow side). At this halfway point, the check material was placed about four feet below the glass (the deep side). This arrangement gave the impression of a deep drop halfway across the table even though the glass top continued to provide a solid surface. Gibson and Walk tested 36 babies aged between six months and 14 months by placing them individually on the shallow side of the apparatus and encouraging them to crawl the length of the table (i.e. across that apparent cliff edge) by having their mothers call to them from the other side.

They found that babies would happily crawl across the shallow surface but would not cross over the apparent cliff edge. If they accidentally toppled over, they showed a fear reaction. Gibson and Walk concluded from this that babies had innate awareness of depth. In particular, they believed that the babies were able to use the cue of **motion parallax** to detect depth.

Methodological issues

The researchers had to use babies who were able to crawl and so all of the babies in their study were at least six months old. Critics of the visual cliff study suggested that babies of that age could have learned to perceive depth in the first six months of life. In other words, it is impossible to conclude from this study whether depth perception is innate or learned.

Researchers often try to respond to criticism by modifying their studies in some way. Gibson and Walk decided to carry out the same experiment, but to use non-human animals. This is because the young of many other species can walk immediately after birth. Therefore, it was possible to use animals such as chicks, rats, kittens, etc. soon after they were born and before they could possibly have learned any behaviours. Animals placed on the shallow side would not move across to the 'deep' side, and animals placed by the researchers on the 'deep' side either froze or refused to stand up. Rats were the only animal that seemed unafraid to cross from the shallow to the deep side. Rats have quite poor vision compared to humans and rely on other senses to a greater extent. However, when the rats' whiskers were removed depriving them of an important sensory guide, rats, too, would not cross the cliff edge.

Animal studies have their own methodological issues. While it is often easier to use non-human animals from a practical and ethical point of view, it is difficult to generalise findings from one species to another. Humans are cognitively far more complex than lower-order animals and we must be cautious in concluding that perceptual development occurs in the same way in humans and non-human animals.

Key terms

Motion parallax: a depth cue that refers to the movement of an object's image across the retina. If there are two stationary objects at different distances from the observer and the observer moves sideways, the image of the nearer object moves faster across the retina than the one further away, e.g. on a moving train trees close to the railway line appear to move faster relative to trees further away.

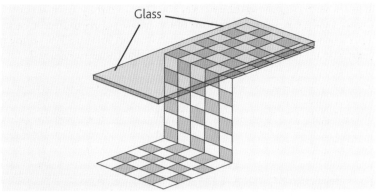

Fig. 1 *Gibson and Walk's visual cliff*

Ethical issues

In the original experiment, Gibson and Walk used young infants. It is, of course, impossible to obtain consent from young children so, in these cases, parents are asked for their permission. In this study, mothers were in the room with the infants at all times. The mother, in fact, played an important role in the study, as she provided the incentive for the child to crawl across the 'cliff'. However, the babies were subjected to mild distress as they were separated from their mother by what appeared to be a frightening obstacle. They were all picked up and comforted as soon as possible, but researchers must always weigh up very carefully the benefits of the research against any possible harmful effects however mild.

Experiments with non-human animals also raise ethical issues and there are now strict rules governing the use of animals in scientific research.

> **Hint**
>
> Researchers could not use neonates for this study. The design of the apparatus required babies to crawl across the surface and to respond to their mother's call. Neither of these abilities would have been present at birth.

By using the method of heart rate monitoring, Campos, Langer and Krowitz (1970) were able to use infants that were only two months old on the visual cliff. There was a significant decrease in heart rate when the baby was moved from one side of the apparatus to the other, in other words across the 'cliff'. This physiological change suggests that babies were able to detect depth differences between the two sides. An interesting later finding was that babies of nine months showed an increase rather than a decrease in heart rate. An increase indicates anxiety and suggests that babies of this age were not only aware of the depth change but also recognised the danger involved. The work of Campos *et al.* suggests that avoidance behaviour is learned and does not emerge until the age of about nine months. Using a different technique, Yonas (1981) demonstrated avoidance behaviour in infants as young as two months. He showed infants a video of an object appearing to loom towards them and found that these very young babies flinched and moved their heads away.

> **Hint**
>
> Depth awareness appears to be innate, but avoidance behaviour might only be acquired through a process of learning. This is another example of biology and environment interacting.

> **Hint**
>
> **How science works**
>
> When evaluating human infant research it is important to note the different techniques used by researchers and to realise that sample sizes are usually very small. We have already noted the importance of methodology in drawing appropriate conclusions from research. The fact that Compos *et al.* drew different conclusions from Yonas illustrates this point well.

Overlap and familiar size

As noted above, very young babies are more likely to use primary rather than secondary depth cues because they clearly depend on innate factors. However, infants do seem to be able to apply some of the secondary cues at an early age although they do not acquire them all at the same time. Bruno and Cutting (1988) found that infants as young as three months can use motion parallax before they learn to make use of some of the other cues. Another secondary cue is called 'overlap' – if one object

Perception

appears to overlap or partially cover the view of another, we assume that the first object is situated in front of the one it seems to overlap. Granrud and Yonas (1984) investigated this with human infants. They showed babies two-dimensional cardboard shapes like those in Figure 2.

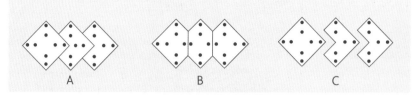

Fig. 2 *The cardboard shapes used in the Granrud and Yonas study*

Babies tend to grasp for objects which seem nearer to them than others. The shapes in (A) give the appearance of depth (even though they are actually drawn on a flat piece of card) because one shape overlaps another. The shapes in (B) and (C) do not contain depth cues. Granrud and Yonas found that seven-month-old babies reached for the left-hand shape in (A) but not in (B) or (C), suggesting that they were influenced by the depth cue. This was not the case for five-month-olds, suggesting that the ability to make use of the overlap depth cue emerges at around seven months.

Granrud *et al.* (1985) also showed that babies can use another monocular cue – familiar size. They gave seven-month-old infants two wooden objects to play with (see Figure 3) for 10 minutes.

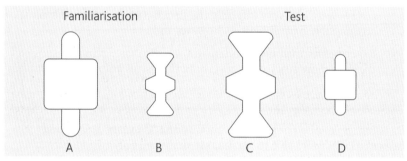

Fig. 3 *The wooden objects used by Granrud* et al. *(1985)*

Object (A) was considerably larger than object (B). After the 10-minute familiarisation period, two identically shaped wooden toys were presented simultaneously at the same distance from the baby, but this time their sizes were reversed. The hypothesis was that infants sensitive to the cue of familiar size would perceive object (C) to be closer if they recalled, from the familiarisation period, that this shape had been the smaller of the two. Seven-month-olds did indeed reach out for object (C), but five-month-olds did not. It seems that, as with the cue of overlap, the ability to use the cue of familiar size develops sometime between five and seven months.

Hint

This study shows how cognitive processes are interlinked. The results of the study by Granrud *et al.* show that babies can only use the cue of familiar size to perceive depth if they remember the size of objects.

Visual constancies

Visual constancies relate to the ways in which we maintain a stable visual environment even though the image on our retinas is constantly changing. You do not think the shape of a clock on the wall is changing just because you are looking at it from an unusual angle, or that the colour of your shoes has gone from dark to light brown as you move about. As you walk towards someone, the size of their outline on your retina will gradually increase. You do not think for a moment that they are actually increasing in size, but you realise that the change in retina size means that the distance between you is decreasing. In other words, you understand that the size of the person or object remains constant. We manage to maintain a remarkably stable visual world by keeping size, shape, brightness and colour constant. Psychologists have been interested in finding out whether this ability is innate or learned.

▥ Research study: Bower (1966)

The classic experiment on size constancy in infants was carried out by Bower (1966). He conditioned (see Table 1 on page 61) nine infants aged between six and nine weeks to turn their heads in response to a 30 cm cube placed 1 m away. Each time the baby turned its head towards the cube, it was rewarded by a peek-a-boo game from an adult who popped up in front, smiled and tickled the baby and then bobbed down again. Once he was sure that the baby recognised the 30 cm cube and associated it with a reward, Bower introduced three different cubes:

▥ Cube 1: a 30 cm cube positioned 3 m away; the same size cube but further away, thus producing a retinal image one-third the size of the original.

▥ Cube 2: a 90 cm cube positioned 3 m away; a larger cube further away, producing exactly the same retinal image as the original.

▥ Cube 3: a 90 cm cube positioned 1 m away; a larger cube at the same distance as the original, producing a retinal image three times greater than the original.

You will need to think carefully about this to understand what Bower was trying to do. The baby had been trained to respond to a 30 cm cube at 1 m distance. This would produce exactly the same retinal image as cube 2, i.e. a bigger cube but further away. However, only cube 1 was the same actual size as the original. If babies have size constancy, then they should look towards cube 1 more than towards either of the other two. Bower found that most head turns did indeed occur in response to cube 1 (actual results: cube 1 had 58 head turns, cube 2 had 22 head turns, and cube 3 had 54 head turns). Retinal size was clearly not the crucial factor as babies looked least at the stimulus which had the same retinal image as the original. He concluded from his study that babies have innate size constancy.

Methodological issues

It is very difficult to draw conclusions about perception from studies with young babies. They cannot speak or understand instructions and they become bored or fatigued quite easily. For this reason, researchers have had to think up ingenious ways of investigating their perceptual abilities (see Table 1 on page 61). However, researchers can only make assumptions when they use these techniques.

Given the uncertainty about drawing conclusions from such studies, it is important for other researchers to be able to replicate findings. Replication would add weight to Bower's original conclusions. Slater, Mattock and Brown (1990) reported that, under certain conditions, size constancy could be demonstrated in infants as young as two days old. However, not all psychologists agree with Bower's conclusions and they have found it difficult to replicate his findings.

Ethical issues

Bower used very young infants in this study and put them in unfamiliar surroundings. However, it is unlikely that they suffered any real distress and, in fact, they were 'rewarded' with a peek-a-boo game. It is very important to obtain the consent of parents when using young children in research.

Bower conducted a further study to try to find out which cues babies were using to gauge the distance of the cubes (see depth perception on page 63).

He modified his original experimental techniques to include some depth/distance cues:

- texture gradients and motion parallax
- texture gradient alone
- retinal disparity and texture gradient.

Bower found that babies were not able to judge the actual size or the distance of cubes in the second condition. This suggests that texture gradient is not available as a cue for young babies. They responded most accurately in the first condition. Since texture gradient did not seem to help them, Bower concluded that they were using motion parallax. They responded reasonably well in the third condition, suggesting that retinal disparity might also be used to a limited extent.

Bower also believed that shape constancy was innate in human infants. He conditioned two-month-old babies to respond to a rectangle and then found that the babies continued to show this conditioned response to rectangles that had been tilted so that the retinal image was now that of a trapezoid. Slater and Morrison (1985) found similar results using the habituation technique.

Cross-cultural studies

A number of studies have been conducted with different cultural groups to investigate the nature–nurture debate. If certain perceptual abilities can be demonstrated in one cultural group but not another, it could be assumed that the ability is dependent on learning rather than on innate biological mechanisms.

We have already seen that there is some interaction between our sensory systems and environmental stimuli. It might be the case that aspects of our environment and culture alter the internal expectations and inferences that we bring to a new perceptual situation. If you are reading this book, you have probably grown up in a crowded, built-up environment. Imagine how different your visual world would be if you lived in the wide-open spaces of the desert or the snowbound Arctic. Cultural factors might also play a part. For example, people from industrialised societies are exposed to many visual stimuli, e.g. photos and television pictures which are not available to some communities living in less technological societies.

The Müller-Lyer illusion

Much of the evidence for cross-cultural differences in perception comes from research using visual illusions. The most widely used illusion is the Müller-Lyer.

Hint

You could use this study to support the conclusions of Gibson and Walk (page 64) about the importance of motion parallax.

Take it further

Kaye and Bower (1994) demonstrated that babies can recognise the visual shapes of objects that they have only experienced through touch or feel. The study involved two different-shaped dummies in the mouths of 12-day-old human infants. You may find it interesting to read about that study.

Link

For an example of the Müller-Lyer illusion, see page 55.

Segall, Campbell and Herskovits (1963) showed the Müller-Lyer illusion to various cultural groups including people from different parts of Africa, the Philippines and North America. They found that people from built-up Western societies were significantly more susceptible to the Müller-Lyer illusion than people from less urbanised groups. They explained this finding in terms of the **carpentered world hypothesis**. Segall et al. believed that this tendency to interpret trapezoid shapes as rectangles and acute angles as right angles is so well reinforced in people that it becomes an automatic and unconscious process from an early age. Also, from a young age Westerners are used to interpreting two-dimensional drawings as three-dimensional objects. So, when presented with the Müller-Lyer drawing they interpret it as the inside corner or outside edge of a room. They then use misapplied size constancy to perceive the apparent closer line to be shorter than the line that was apparently further away. On the other hand, people brought up in non-carpentered environments would not have learned to interpret lines and acute angles in that way and so would not be fooled by the Müller-Lyer illusion.

However, not all researchers agree with Segall et al.'s conclusions. Gregor and McPherson (1965) found no differences in susceptibility to the Müller-Lyer illusion between groups of urbanised and traditional aboriginal Australians, although both groups were less prone to the Müller-Lyer illusion than Europeans. Jahoda (1966) also failed to demonstrate the effect when she compared two Ghanaian tribes who lived in different environments. She believed that the differences that Segall et al. had demonstrated could be accounted for by cultural factors other than the carpentered world. In particular, she felt that the differences might reflect the lack of familiarity with drawings and photos among non-Western groups.

Two or three dimensions?

We are so used to looking at paintings, drawings, cartoons, photos and moving film/video images that we do not think about it as an interpretative task. Pictures are not accurate representations of our visual world, for example they are flat, often in black and white and yet we usually have no trouble in understanding what they depict. Deregowski (1980) has reported on a number of cross-cultural studies in which pictures were used as stimulus material. Many of these studies are old and were not carried out according to rigorous scientific principles, but they do offer some interesting insights. One example came from a missionary in Malawi who showed local people black-and-white drawings of an ox and a dog. They were puzzled at first, but when the missionary pointed out individual features, e.g. the nose and ears of the dog, they were then able to recognise the whole figure as an animal. This suggests that object recognition can occur quite quickly if attention is appropriately directed.

However, it seems to be more difficult for people from non-Western cultures to understand the implied spatial relationships in two-dimensional pictures. In the West, we automatically seem to assume that a two-dimensional picture represents a three-dimensional figure. For example, Hudson (1960) showed Zambian and British schoolchildren a line drawing of a geometric figure. He then gave them some sticks and modelling clay and asked them to build a model of the figure in the picture. He found that the British children made three-dimensional models, while the Zambian children made two-dimensional models.

Link

For more about size and shape constancy see page 66.

Key terms

Carpentered world hypothesis: the idea that Westerners live in a visual world dominated by lines, angles and rectangular buildings. Westerners continue to 'see' these buildings as rectangular even when viewed from an angle that produces a trapezoid shape on the retina.

Link

For more support for the carpentered world hypothesis, see the Pedersen and Wheeler study (1983) on page 56.

Take it further

There is even a suggestion there could be a biological reason for cultural differences in the susceptibility to the Müller-Lyer illusion. We know that susceptibility to the Müller-Lyer illusion declines with age. One reason for this appears to be the increasing difficulty older people have in detecting contours. Pollack and Silvar (1967) found that contour detection deteriorates as retinal pigmentation becomes denser with age. Pollack suggested that retinal pigmentation, which might be denser in dark-skinned people, could be responsible for the reduced susceptibility found in the non-European samples in Segall et al.'s study. Students need to be aware that there can be different interpretations of the same data.

Perception

The effect of artistic conventions

Western artists make use of various depth cues to give the impression of depth and distance. These so-called pictorial cues include linear perspective, texture gradient, overlap, height in the visual plane, and familiar size.

Table 2 *Different monocular pictorial cues*

Cue	Description
Overlap (superimposition)	An object which appears to overlap or cut off the view of another and is perceived as being closer to the viewer
Relative size	In an array of similar objects, one that projects a smaller image onto the retina is assumed to be further away
Familiar size	Objects that are known to be large, e.g. an elephant, a lorry, are assumed to be far away even if they project a small image onto the retina
Height in the visual field (elevation)	Objects placed higher up seem to be further away
Texture gradient	Texture or grain appears to become smoother as distance increases
Linear perspective	Parallel lines (e.g. a road or rail track) appear to converge as they recede into the distance
Aerial perspective	Objects with clear, distinct images are assumed to be closer than objects which are blurred (e.g. distant hills, buildings)
Shadowing	Shading is used to indicate dents or bumps in a surface

However, other cues which we use in our everyday life such as retinal disparity, accommodation and convergence (see page 63) cannot be used with two-dimensional drawings and, because pictures are static, motion parallax is also not available. Hudson (1960) showed two-dimensional pictures to various African cultures and asked them to identify the objects in the pictures and then to explain the relationship between the various figures (see Figure 4).

He asked them questions such as 'Which is closer to the man?' and 'What is the man pointing his spear at?' People were usually able to identify the objects in the pictures but found it much more difficult to understand the implied depth. For example, they assumed the man was pointing his spear at the elephant rather than at the antelope. This

Fig. 4 *An example of the pictures used by Hudson*

suggests that they do not perceive depth in the same way that Westerners do, and that this must be a learned ability. However, it is important to note that Hudson's pictures did not make use of primary depth cues (see page 63) or of motion parallax and texture gradient. Hagen and Jones (1978) found that the understanding of depth improved when more depth cues (aerial perspective and texture gradient) were included in the pictures. So, it is possible that some cues such as texture gradient are more salient to people from non-Western cultures than others. It is also clear that people from these cultures can quickly learn to interpret pictorial cues when they have been exposed to a formal, Western-style education (Pick, 1987).

It seems then that the difficulty non-Western groups have in perceiving pictures accurately is due to lack of familiarity with the pictorial conventions of Western art. Hagen and Jones (1978) found that non-Western groups who found it difficult to understand black-and-white photos or line drawings could readily interpret coloured photos. In other words, the closer the picture is to real life, the more easily understandable it is.

Myopia

A rather different line of cross-cultural research concerns the development of myopia (short-sightedness). This is a good illustration of the interaction of biological and environmental influences. Myopia occurs when the eyeball is too long causing the retinal image to become blurred. This clearly affects accurate perception, although it can usually be alleviated by wearing glasses. There is strong evidence that myopia runs in families (Gwiazda *et al.*, 1993). In other words, some people are predisposed genetically to develop myopia. However, cross-cultural studies have shown that environment can also be a powerful factor. Myopia is more common in cultural groups that experience more formal education and engage in close work. Myopia became much more common in Inuit children after the introduction of Western education (Mutti, Zadnik and Adams, 1996) and it is more prevalent in male orthodox Jewish teenagers who study for up to 16 hours per day than Jewish females who study 8–9 hours per day (Zylbermann, Iandau and Berson, 1993).

Link

Approaches, issues and debates

The cultural bias in much psychology has already been mentioned. The value of cross-cultural research is shown in studies such as Hudson (1960). Cultural factors can influence perceptual abilities and this provides evidence for the role of nurture, or environmental factors, in the development of perception.

Summary

The nature–nurture debate in relation to perceptual development has not been fully resolved. Human infant, animal and cross-cultural studies have all provided useful information about the relative contributions of innate and environmental factors. However, all of these types of research have particular ethical and practical difficulties which can make the findings hard to interpret. What does seem clear is that we have to combine innate and learned factors in order to perceive the world around us accurately and to attach meaning to what we see. We appear to be born with certain 'hard-wired' abilities which require interaction with our environment to develop appropriately. Studies of people from other cultures suggest that the particular environment in which we grow up can have a powerful influence on how we interpret visual input.

Key points

■ Depth and distance perception are important for understanding the relationship between objects in our visual world.

■ We make use of a variety of cues to help us understand depth/distance.

■ Some of these cues (primary) rely on biological mechanisms, while others (secondary) appear to depend on some experience with the world.

■ Various ingenious techniques have been devised to investigate the development of depth perception in human infants. Studies based on the visual cliff seem to indicate that depth perception is innate, although there are some problems of interpretation with this research.

■ Visual constancies allow us to maintain a stable visual world. Babies have been shown to possess size and shape constancy from a very early age.

■ Cross-cultural studies have provided some interesting insights into visual perception. However, they are often poorly controlled, have limited samples and suffer from experimenter bias, so we must interpret the findings with caution.

■ Many cross-cultural studies use pictures as the stimulus material so may simply reflect lack of familiarity with Western art rather than limitations of perception in the real world.

■ Many of the studies are quite old now and, although cross-cultural psychology is a growing area, research into differences in visual perception is no longer a key interest.

Summary questions

3 Explain why depth perception is an important perceptual ability for human infants.

4 What are some of the problems involved in investigating depth perception in infants?

5 Explain some of the limitations of cross-cultural research into visual perception.

6

Face recognition and visual agnosias

Introduction

Learning objectives:

- understand the importance of face recognition research and some of its applications

- understand the difference between feature analysis and holistic theories of face recognition

- understand the debate about whether face recognition is a highly specialised mechanism.

Hint

How science works

One way of evaluating face recognition research is to consider some of its practical applications. For example, it has been used in E-fits (electronic facial identification techniques) to enhance witness identification of suspects. It has been used in Australia to prevent passport fraud and in the USA to prevent people from obtaining fake identification cards and driving licences. (I)

Take it further

More uses for facial recognition are currently in development, for example at ATMs and as computer log-ins. How do you think face recognition research can help in applications such as these?

Hint

Can you think of any other reason why recognition might have declined so dramatically amongst the college lecturers over a period of eight years?

Face recognition

Pattern recognition is the process by which we transform the raw data provided by our sense receptors into a meaningful whole picture. Face recognition is a particular kind of pattern recognition that has attracted a great deal of research interest.

Recognising faces is a very important aspect of human social functioning. We know from developmental research that babies show an early preference for looking at pictures of faces rather than other visual stimuli, and adults also seem to process human faces rather differently from other visual stimuli. Most faces are broadly similar in that they have the same features – a mouth, eyes, a nose, a chin, eyebrows and a hairline – within the same configural arrangement. In spite of this, we are remarkably good at recognising familiar faces and distinguishing between different faces. Even if a face is unfamiliar to us, we readily make certain judgements about it, for example the person's gender and approximate age and whether they look happy, angry, afraid, etc. Gender, for example, seems to be a feature which is readily discernible even when the normal cues of clothing and hairstyle are missing. Bruce *et al.* (1993) took photos of the faces of a large number of men and women. In order to eliminate obvious clues about their gender, the women had no make-up on and the men were close shaven, and both sexes wore close-fitting swimming caps to conceal their hair. Observers were asked to judge whether the photos were of males or females. In spite of the lack of obvious gender cues, participants were 96 per cent accurate in their judgements.

Familiar faces

We are generally much better at recognising faces with which we are familiar. Not surprisingly, one reason why we are better at recognising familiar faces is that we are frequently exposed to them. Bahrick (1984) gave lecturers sets of photos and asked them to distinguish between their own students and others that they had never taught. Immediately after the end of term, recognition was very good, but accuracy dropped significantly after a year and, when tested after eight years the lecturers performed at no better than chance levels. This suggests that exposure to faces needs to be regularly maintained otherwise recognition for familiar faces will decline.

One reason why we are good at recognising familiar faces is that we have had the opportunity to view them from a number of different angles so we can build up a more complete mental picture of them. Ellis and Shepherd (1992) have demonstrated that recognition is more accurate for faces that have been seen from more than one angle. Bahrick (1984) found that participants were able to recognise photos of other students from their classes much more easily than photos of people they had only seen before in two-dimensional picture form.

The processing of faces

It has been suggested that face recognition is a highly specialised function and that the processing of faces differs from that of other objects. Technologies such as functional magnetic resonance imaging (fMRI) have demonstrated neural activity uniquely related to viewing faces. These studies suggest that the right hemisphere of the brain may be more specialised for processing faces than other objects.

Kanwisher, McDermott and Chun (1997) used fMRI to record the brain activity of individuals who were shown a series of faces and common objects. Their research showed that the fusiform gyrus (see Figure 1) became significantly more active when the subjects were presented with faces than when they were looking at other objects. Results from these studies suggest that this region of the brain is specialised for processing faces.

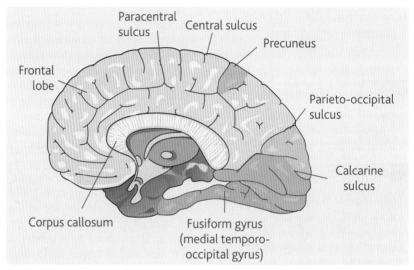

Fig. 1 *Fusiform gyrus*

However, not all researchers agree with this conclusion. Although we often assume that faces are unique, statistically they are quite similar, so high-level cognitive processing is needed to differentiate them. This would mean that faces are nothing more than a particularly difficult class of perceptual object which we have learned to distinguish through experience. Gauthier *et al.* (2000) used fMRI to record the brain activity of people who were shown pictures of birds and cars and were asked to identify the type of bird/car. They found that the fusiform area is also active during this task and concluded that this area of the brain is not exclusively dedicated to face recognition. They suggested that humans have much more experience in distinguishing between human faces than, for example, distinguishing between different birds. However, people who have expertise in that particular area, e.g. keen birdwatchers, would use this part of the brain to identify different categories of birds. This interpretation implies that the brain does not have a specialised mechanism for recognising faces, but that the fusiform area is specialised for the recognition of any object category for which we possess expertise. The idea of expertise is supported by the well-replicated research finding that we find it more difficult to recognise faces of people from other races – this is probably largely due to our lack of experience/expertise with this task. This is still a controversial area and research has produced conflicting evidence.

Think about Gauthier *et al.*'s conclusions. They assumed that the fusiform area is specialised for expert processing. If this is the

■ Hint

How science works

Researchers draw conclusions or inferences from their own investigations, but these can be challenged by other researchers who carry out their own studies rather differently and then come to another conclusion.

Gauthier *et al.*'s (2000) work is an example of how psychologists use the methods of science. Their model is based on previous findings and leads to a particular hypothesis or prediction. This hypothesis can be tested experimentally, and the results used to support or disconfirm their model.

case, people who are expert in car identification should find it very difficult to carry out a face recognition task and a car recognition task simultaneously. This is because the tasks would be competing for the same, specialised part of the brain. On the other hand, people who have no expertise in car identification should be able to do the two tasks simultaneously because only the face recognition task would require fusiform activity while the car identification task would use a different part of the brain. Gauthier *et al.* (2000) tested this prediction and found that this is exactly what happened.

Key points

- Face recognition is a specialised form of pattern recognition.

- Face recognition is an important area of research because it has a number of practical applications.

- We are generally better at dealing with familiar faces rather than unfamiliar faces.

- There is some debate as to whether face recognition is a highly specialised mechanism or whether it is simply one type of complex processing.

Summary questions

1 How might face recognition systems be used at ATMs and as computer log-ins and why?

2 Do you think that the results of Bahrick's 1984 study (page 73) would have been the same if students (not lecturers) had been the participants and were required to recognise photos of their former lecturers after eight years? Give reasons for your answer.

3 Explain why Gauthier *et al.* believe that the fusiform gyrus is not solely dedicated to face recognition.

Perception

Theories of face recognition

Learning objectives:

- understand the difference between feature analysis and holistic processing

- describe the components of the Bruce and Young model of face recognition

- evaluate the Bruce and Young model of face recognition.

Link

This is a method used in the information-processing approach. See Chapter 1, Models of memory, in the *AQA Psychology A AS* student book pages 17–18.

Feature analysis and holistic processing

Imagine you are in a busy shopping mall: you are looking for your friend and suddenly you spot her among the crowd. How did you manage to single her out and recognise her? This is the kind of question cognitive psychologists are interested in trying to answer. One way in which they approach this is to formulate computer models to mimic face recognition.

A computer would need to:

- store information about the faces to be remembered in a memory bank
- compare each face it encountered with the information stored in memory to seek a perfect match
- recognise the face if there is a good match
- reject the face as unfamiliar if there is no match.

However, there are different ways in which this matching process could occur. One possibility is that the memory bank could contain a set of features of the face to be remembered, for example your friend has:

- a thin face
- brown eyes
- a mole on her left cheek
- long hair
- full lips, usually coloured with bright red lipstick.

Each feature observed in the face could be compared against the stored list of features. If the features match, the face is recognised as that of your friend. However, if the observed face has blue eyes rather than brown, it would be rejected as unfamiliar. According to this kind of feature analysis theory, we look at individual parts of the face (features), i.e. hair, mouth, eyes, nose, and then build up towards recognition of the whole face. In other words, face recognition is a bottom-up process.

We certainly use features to help us in the face recognition process. Shepherd, Davies and Ellis (1981) carried out a study to investigate this idea. They briefly showed participants pictures of unfamiliar faces and subsequently asked them to describe the faces they had seen. It was found that the features most frequently recalled were (in order) hair, eyes, nose, mouth, eyebrows, chin and forehead. Participants did not tend to describe the faces in terms of their overall shape, the spacing of features or the expression on the face. However, it could be that, when asked simply to describe faces rather than identify them, outlining the features might be the easiest way. It does not necessarily tell us about the normal process of face recognition.

There are other problems with a simple feature-based theory. Yin (1969) demonstrated a phenomenon now known as the 'inversion effect'. His participants were able to recognise pictures of objects turned upside-down about as often as they could recognise them the right way up. However, they found it much more difficult to recognise *faces* that had been turned upside-down than they did to recognise faces the right way up. Yin suggested that inversion of an image impairs holistic processing but does not interfere with feature processing. Since Yin's participants showed a compromised ability to recognise inverted faces but not other inverted objects, he argued that faces must be processed in a holistic way, while other objects are processed feature by feature. Similarly, Bruce and Valentine (1986) used faces of well-known celebrities but scrambled their features. In other words, the features remained the same but their layout on the face was distorted. People found the scrambled faces much harder to identify than the normally configured faces. This again suggests that we find it easier to process faces holistically, i.e. to process the face as a whole (spacing, overall shape, etc.), including stored information related to it, for example emotion. This is said to be a top-down theory.

Bruce and Young's theory of face recognition

This model, first proposed in 1986, has been the most influential model of face recognition. Bruce and Young (1986) argued that face perception is mainly a holistic process that might involve several independent sub-processes working in unison. They identified eight separate components of the face recognition process. Some of these components are linked sequentially and others in parallel (see Figure 2 overleaf).

1 Structural encoding: constructing various representations and descriptions of faces.

2 Expression analysis: drawing conclusions about an individual's emotional state from an analysis of their facial features.

3 Facial speech analysis: looking at facial movements, particularly lip movements, to help understand speech.

4 Directed visual processing: specific facial information is processed selectively, e.g. seeing whether the individual has a beard.

5 Face recognition units: stored structural descriptions of familiar faces.

Hint

The words 'model' and 'theory' can be used interchangeably by psychologists to describe certain accepted ways of looking at things. Models tend to be able to be represented with box diagrams, and theories may be more descriptive or abstract, but there are no hard and fast rules.

6 Person identity nodes (PINs): stored information about known individuals, e.g. their occupations, interests, etc.

7 Name generation: names are stored separately from other information.

8 Cognitive system: this holds additional information which might help the recognition process. For example, if you see someone in your local pub who looks like Victoria Beckham, the cognitive system would assess the likelihood of seeing her in that setting and prevent misidentification.

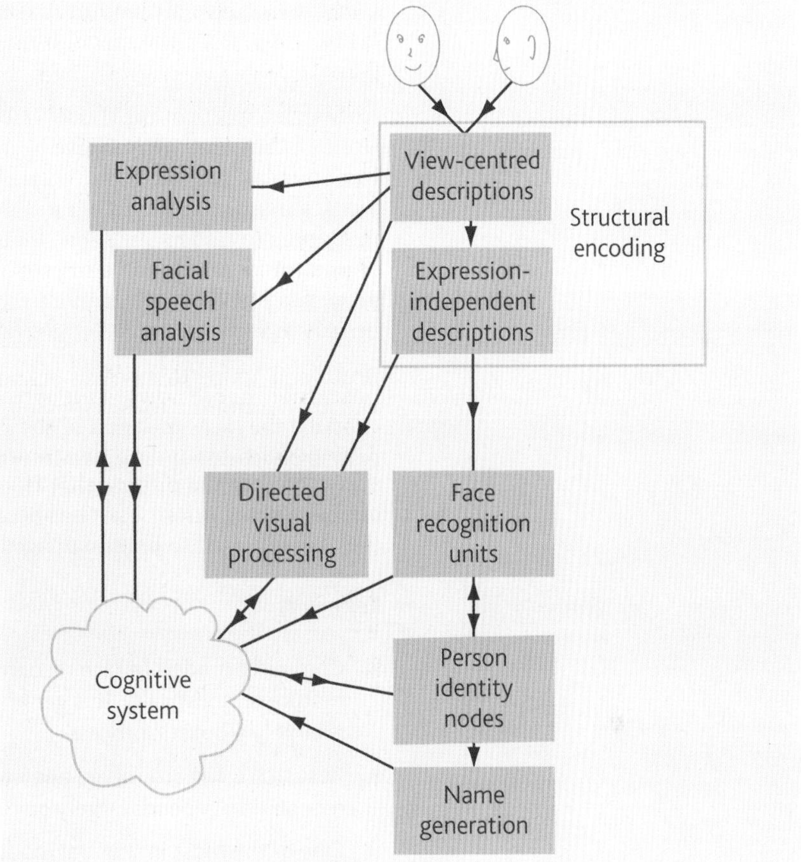

A 'view-centred description' is derived from the perceptual input. Simple physical aspects of the face are used to assess age, gender, etc. Most analysis at this stage is on a feature-by-feature basis. This initial information is used to create a structural model of the face, which can then be compared to other faces in memory and across views. This explains why the same person seen from a novel angle can still be recognised. There is some evidence from research with monkeys (Perrett and Oram, 1993) that different templates of the same faces (i.e. full-faced, profile, rear view, etc.) are stored in the brain.

Fig. 2 *Bruce and Young's face recognition model*

Note that this model predicts that familiar and unfamiliar faces are processed in slightly different ways. Recognition of familiar faces depends mainly on structural encoding, face recognition units, PINs and name generation. Once the structural encoding stage has been completed, unfamiliar faces are processed in terms of expression analysis, facial speech analysis and directed visual processing.

▤ Link

Approaches, issues and debates

Non-human studies can be useful where similar human research is ethically or methodologically impossible. However, generalisation to humans is not always straightforward.

▤ Evaluation of the model

This model has been very influential and can predict and explain many research findings, for example it is consistent with many of the findings from brain-damaged patients (see pages 79–80).

The idea that there is a series of independent stages in the face recognition process has been supported by research. Young *et al.* (1993) asked 22 people to keep diaries of their everyday errors in person recognition. A total of 1,008 errors were recorded and almost 20 per cent of these referred to instances when someone knew a lot of information about the person but could not think of their name. In contrast, no diarist reported being able to name a face whilst knowing nothing else about that person. This supports the idea that naming is a separate process. Similarly, people often reported a feeling of familiarity but an inability to think of any personal details about the person. This suggests that the face recognition unit has been activated but not the PIN. There is also support for the model from case studies of people with brain damage.

Although aspects of the model have been well supported by research, some of the components have been less well explained than others. In particular, the role of the cognitive system is unclear. This model focuses mainly on the recognition of familiar faces and is of limited value in helping to understand how, for example, eyewitness identification of unfamiliar faces can be improved. It also does not account for the processes involved in learning to recognise new faces and storing these images in memory.

Bruce and Young themselves acknowledge the weaknesses in the model and are continuing to develop and refine it.

The model is neutral on the question of whether face recognition is a special perceptual process that is qualitatively different from other types of object recognition. This has become a central issue for researchers and they have looked to brain-damaged patients to find an answer.

Key points

- Computer models of face recognition can operate either feature by feature or holistically. It is generally agreed that human face recognition is largely a holistic process.
- Research using scrambled and inverted faces suggests that human face recognition depends largely on holistic processing.
- One of the most influential models of face recognition was proposed by Bruce and Young. This model contains a number of independent modules working in parallel.
- The model has been influential but only offers a limited explanation of face recognition.

Summary questions

4 Describe the inversion effect and explain why it helps us to understand how faces are processed.

5 Explain why the Bruce and Young model is a top-down theory.

Visual agnosias

Learning objectives:

- define what is meant by visual agnosias, in particular prosopagnosia

- understand how the study of people with prosopagnosia contributes to face recognition research.

Key terms

Prosopagnosia: also known as face blindness, this is an inability to recognise faces and it cannot be explained by sensory impairment. People with this disorder can recognise a face as a face, but they are not able to link the face with anything they once knew about the person such as their name, age, occupation or relationship. (Agnosia is a clinical condition characterised by disordered visual perception of shapes and/or objects.)

Take it further

Two broad types of prosopagnosia have been identified. Find out what they are. How do you think this distinction supports the Bruce and Young model?

Hint

You may have wondered why case study patients are usually referred to by initials rather than by their full name. This is an ethical consideration to maintain patient confidentiality.

Prosopagnosia

Bodamer first coined the term **prosopagnosia** in 1947 when he described three cases, including a 24-year-old man who suffered a bullet wound to the head and lost his ability to recognise his friends and family and even his own face. Since then a number of case studies have been reported and they have offered valuable information about face recognition in normal humans. Individuals with prosopagnosia differ in their abilities to interpret faces, and it has been the investigation of these differences which has suggested that stage theories (such as Bruce and Young's model) might be correct.

Below are some of the questions addressed in the study of prosopagnosia.

Is face recognition a specialised process?

If face recognition is a specialised mechanism, we would expect to find that people with prosopagnosia can individuate non-face objects even though they are unable to distinguish faces. The case study evidence here is contradictory.

DeRenzi *et al.* (1991) reported on VA who could identify his own handwriting and could distinguish between coins from different currencies and yet was profoundly prosopagnosic. Another prosopagnosic patient, RM, (described by Sergent and Signoret, 1992) could accurately distinguish between his large collection of model cars better than control participants. However, this simply shows that inanimate objects are processed independently.

What happens to non-human animal recognition in people with prosopagnosia?

This question has been tested and several case studies have been reported where prosopagnosic individuals have retained their ability to differentiate between non-human animals. Mr W, a farmer suffering from prosopagnosia (Bruyer *et al.*, 1983) was still able to recognise different cows within his herd. On the other hand, MX, another farmer, (Assal, Favre and Anders, 1984) unusually regained his ability to recognise human faces six months after being diagnosed with prosopagnosia, but he was no longer able to recognise his cows. WJ (described by McNeil and Warrington, 1993) took up farming after his diagnosis, and, interestingly, was able to learn to distinguish between his sheep even though he remained profoundly prosopagnosic. Such findings support the idea that face recognition is at least anatomically distinct from other types of object processing including non-human animals. However, some researchers have been unable to replicate these findings.

Are the processes of face recognition independent?

According to the Bruce and Young model, expression analysis occurs in parallel with, but independently of, face recognition. This view is supported by clinical evidence. For example, Kurucz, Feldmar and Werner (1979) found prosopagnosic patients who could correctly identify some familiar faces but were unable to recognise their facial expression, while Bruyer *et al.* (1983) found the reverse pattern in other patients.

Perception

It seems that the mechanisms for facial speech analysis and face recognition are also independent. You may not be aware of it, but most people lip-read when they are listening to someone face to face in order to help speech perception. This reliance on lip-reading has been demonstrated in the McGurk illusion.

McGurk and MacDonald (1976) showed participants a video of someone enunciating single-syllable sounds while the audio track played a different sound. Participants presented with one sound on the audiotape, e.g. 'ba', while simultaneously watching someone make mouth movements consistent with 'ga', actually reported hearing a fusion of the two sounds 'da'. This is a perceptual illusion.

Some prosopagnosics have been shown to be susceptible to this illusion, demonstrating that they can carry out speech analysis even though they cannot recognise faces. Campbell, Landis and Regard (1986) have described two case studies: D had profound prosopagnosia and could not recognise familiar faces, identify facial expressions or judge the sex of an individual from their face. However, she was susceptible to the McGurk illusion, suggesting that speech analysis is a separate process. Similarly, patient T was not susceptible to the McGurk illusion and could not lip-read but was able to identify facial expression accurately.

Case study research has been carried out by many different researchers using different patients and testing methods. Young *et al.* (1993) conducted a very strictly controlled study in which they tried to eliminate all of this variability. Under these rigorous conditions, they still found strong evidence for the independence of the abilities to identify facial expression and to recognise identity.

Link

See pages 54–7 for more information about perceptual illusions.

Hint

How science works

Case studies are very useful for providing information about face perception. They allow us to investigate the effects of highly specific brain damage in humans without unethical manipulation. However, there are problems with case study research in terms of generalising findings to the normal population.

Key points

- Prosopagnosia is a relatively rare disorder in which individuals lose the ability to recognise familiar faces.

- A number of case studies have been reported which provide clues about the face recognition process in normal humans.

- Prosopagnosia research lends support to the Bruce and Young model.

Summary questions

6 How does research with prosopagnosic patients help to resolve the question of whether face recognition is a specialised process?

7 Why do you think it might make sense to have a dissociation between the functions of expression analysis and person identification?

8 Explain why research carried out on individual patients needs to be regarded with caution.

Perception end of topic

Fig. 3 *Bugelski and Alampay's 'rat-man' figure*

Link

See Chapter 38, Designing psychological investigations, page 515, for details on research methods.

Link

You can refresh your memory about statistical tests for nominal data and find the formula by looking at Chapter 39, Data analysis and reporting on investigations, page 533.

How science works: practical activity

You can investigate the effect of expectation on perception by running a small experimental study. You will need to obtain an ambiguous picture which can be interpreted in two different ways. A good example of this is the rat-man figure used by Bugelski and Alampay in a classic experiment (Bugelski and Alampay, 1961), see Figure 3.

Use an independent group design because it is important to keep your participants naive.

Find (or draw) two other simple, line-drawing pictures of things related to each of the interpretations of the ambiguous figure (for example, if you are using the rat-man figure find one picture of a cat and one picture of an old lady).

Show one group the picture of the cat for a few seconds, then show them the ambiguous figure and ask them to write down immediately what they see. Show the other group the picture of the old lady for a few seconds, then show them the ambiguous figure and ask them to write down immediately what they see.

Record their answers. This will give you nominal data that you can put in a table. You can then analyse the results by using a Chi-squared test. Make sure that you have sufficient numbers of participants to make a Chi-squared analysis possible.

Decide whether you also need a control group (i.e. a group of participants who only see the ambiguous figure and are not shown anything else). Why do you think a control group might be useful here?

You will need to write a brief, clear set of standardised instructions.

You will need to debrief your participants after the study.

Further reading and weblinks

Bruce, V. and Young, A. (2000) *In the Eye of the Beholder: The Science of Face Perception*. Oxford: Oxford University Press.

This is a comprehensive book on the subject of face recognition by two of the leading researchers in this area. It is accessible but quite a challenging read for A Level students.

Eysenck, M.W. and Keane, M.T. (2000) *Cognitive Psychology: A Student's Handbook* (4th edn). Hove: Psychology Press.

Perception is a complex topic and many of the textbooks that are available are pitched at a high level which is beyond the scope of the A Level specification. If you want to read more about perception, it is sometimes more straightforward to look at the perception chapter in a general cognitive psychology textbook. The Eysenck and Keane book provides a more detailed coverage of all of the issues covered in this topic.

Gregory, R.L. (1997) *Eye and Brain: The Psychology of Seeing* (5th edn) (revised). Oxford: Oxford University Press.

This book is written by Gregory himself and contains a detailed but accessible account of his ideas on visual perception.

Rookes, P. and Willson, J. (2000) *Perception: Theory, Development and Organisation*. London: Routledge.

This is a readable book aimed at A Level students who want to develop their knowledge of topics on the specification.

Sacks, O. (1986) *The Man Who Mistook His Wife for a Hat*. London: Picador.

This is an entertaining and highly readable collection of true case studies, one of which, Mr P., could not recognise his wife from her face although he could identify her from her voice.

www.bbc.co.uk/science/humanbody

You can find some good interactive activities on the BBC website. These change from time to time, but there are often activities related to sensation and perception.

www.scientificpsychic.com/graphics

This site has a large selection of visual illusions.

www.faceblind.org/facetests/fgcfmt/fgcfmt_intro.php

This is a site where you can take the Cambridge face recognition task – it will take about 20 minutes.

Relationships

Introduction

In this topic we will consider the social psychology of interpersonal relationships. Relationships – the connections formed with others – are one of the most important aspects of most people's lives. From birth we are surrounded by others: the first relationships we have are generally with the adults and children who make up our family. As we enter nursery and school, the social circle widens to include peers, friends and, later, partners. Here, we will consider how relationships are formed, why we choose to 'hook up' with some people rather than others, how relationships become close and how likely it is that a couple who meet at college will still be together 20 years later.

Psychologists have traditionally been interested in a fairly small range of human relationships. Social psychologists have been concerned with romantic relationships whereas developmental psychologists have been interested in the relationships (or 'attachments') formed between young children and their caregivers, usually mothers and fathers. Only recently have researchers started to look at the connections between these two different areas of relationships in their study of possible continuities between relationship experiences. This is considered in Chapter 9, Effects of early experience and culture on adult relationships.

In Western cultures, for example in the UK, USA and Australia, romantic relationships are generally formed when people meet face to face or via social networking and internet sites. In early adulthood, many people experiment with a variety of romantic relationships, dating a range of people and trying out different relationships. Moghaddam (1993) argues that there are three assumptions about relationships that are largely taken for granted by those living in Western cultures:

- Relationships are voluntary. This means that people are generally free to choose their own partners, although family often say whether or not they like the partner or approve of the choice.
- Relationships are temporary. Although breaking up may be painful (and expensive), relationships can be ended by either partner. A couple who are married can file for divorce.
- Relationships are individualistic. This means that they are arrangements between two individuals rather than between two families.

These assumptions are not shared in other parts of the world or, indeed, by some cultural and religious groups living in the UK. Many relationships are partly or even wholly arranged, and parents and family have a much greater say in the choice of partner. They may also be permanent, so that couples are faced with staying together however difficult their relationship becomes. Chapter 9, Effects of early experience and culture on adult relationships, examines some of the cultural differences that relate to how relationships are formed and organised.

The study of interpersonal relationships has presented challenges for social psychologists as many research methods available in the psychologists' 'tool kit' have failed to capture the complexity and the shifting nature of human relationships (Miell and Dallos, 1996). Throughout this topic we will be looking at the methodological challenges posed for psychologists studying interpersonal relationships.

Relationships

7

Romantic relationships theory

Theories

Learning objectives:

- describe how relationships start and the processes involved in attraction

- understand the importance of rewards and needs in the formation of relationships

- discuss economic explanations of how people regulate their relationships and why they sometimes split up

- explain the models of how relationships break down

- understand difficulties and challenges of research in this area.

Key terms

Interpersonal attraction: this relates to being interested in another person and wanting to get to know them better.

Link

Approaches, issues and debates

The study of relation formation identifies many factors that could be involved. However, it can imply that we have no free will over our relationships; that they are determined by these various factors out of our control. As we have a strong sense of free will when it comes to relationships, this is a criticism of such a deterministic approach.

Getting relationships started

How are relationships formed? This chapter starts by considering how and why people are attracted to each other. We will then go on to consider two explanations of how some dating relationships become long term – the filter model and need/reward theory.

Boy meets girl, girl meets girl, boy meets boy. What factors will influence whether or not these individuals are attracted to each other and begin a relationship? Until the late 1970s, the study of relationships focused almost exclusively on the processes involved in **interpersonal attraction**. The topic area was appealing to social psychologists as it was relatively easy to study using the research methods available at the time – experiments set in the laboratory and the field. From this early research, a number of important factors in attraction were identified including proximity (physical closeness which provided the opportunity to meet), physical appearance and similarity of attitudes and social background.

Contact

Contact between two people is essential in order for attraction to take place. Until fairly recently, most people met face to face – at school, at work or at play. Relationships were generally formed between people who lived near each other. In 1932, Bossard found that more than half of 5,000 couples who applied to get married in Philadelphia lived within a few minutes' walk of each other. In 1950, Festinger *et al.* compared the friendships formed by students in halls of residence and found that people were far more likely to be friends with those who lived on the same floor or corridor than those from the floor above or below. Living near someone or working at the same place allows regular and relatively easy contact so two people can begin to get to know each other. Today, physical proximity is less important as a prerequisite for attraction, as improvements in communication technologies such as text messaging and internet use mean that it is possible to get to know someone with little face-to-face contact. However, regular contact – whether this is face to face or via a social networking site – remains important because it allows two people to become familiar with each other.

Physical appearance

Once two people have become aware of the existence of each other, physical appearance plays some role in attraction. What makes someone physically attractive? This is usually a combination of *architectural* factors (facial features, body shape and size) and *dynamic* factors (how someone dresses and talks, their facial expressions). In the next section of this chapter we shall consider the physical features which make men and women attractive and why these preferences may have evolved. However, what seems to be important in early attraction is that two people are of a similar level of attractiveness. Murstein (1972) was one of the first to note this effect which he termed the **match hypothesis**. Murstein argued that whilst we might desire the most physically attractive partner in theory, in reality we know that we are unlikely to get or keep them so we look for someone of a similar level of attractiveness as ourselves. This makes us less likely to suffer rejection. Murstein studied 99 couples who were dating and compared them with randomly paired couples. He found that the real couples were consistently rated as more alike in levels of attractiveness. Silverman (1971) supported these findings by rating dating couples in bars. The 'matching' concept can also be applied to friends. McKillip and Riedel (1993) found that pairs of friends were also fairly closely matched in levels of physical attractiveness.

Similarity of attitudes and social background

Once two people have started talking to each other, interests, hobbies and attitudes become important. The importance of similar attitudes in attraction was researched in detail in the 1970s and Byrne proposed the **law of attraction**. Whilst some feel that Byrne overestimated the importance of shared attitudes, there is no doubt that they play a role in attraction. Communication is easier when two people share attitudes, and shared interests are also important as spending time together is easy and rewarding. Conversely, differences in attitudes can lead us to dislike people (Singh and Ho, 2000).

A similar social background in terms of education and socio-economic class is also important. Kendel (1978) found that teenage pairs of close friends were similar in many respects including ethnic background, religion and the economic background of their parents. Hill, Rubin and Peplau (1976) also found similarity of race, class and religion in dating couples and in pairs of friends.

■ The formation of relationships

Once two people have met and started the process of getting to know each other, how likely is it that they will go on to develop a **close relationship**? Lots of relationships fail to get off the ground or simply fizzle out. There are many reasons why two people may not pursue a relationship with each other even when there is a strong attraction: they may be involved with someone else, wary from a previous split or decide that the relationship is not viable due to practical factors such as living too far apart. Alternatively, the relationship may appear to work for a period of time but may terminate at a later date as it fails to meet the partners' needs. Two explanations of relationship formation are the filter model and the reward/need theory.

Filter model

The filter model (Kerckhoff and Davis, 1962) argues that relationships develop through three 'filters', so that different factors are important at different times. Kerckhoff and Davis referred to the '**field of availables**' as the possible people that we could have a relationship with. They argued that we 'filter out' potential partners for different reasons at different times, so that the field of availables is gradually narrowed down to a relatively small '**field of desirables**' – those who we would consider as potential partners.

■ The first of the filters involves *social/demographic variables*. This filter exerts its influence often without us even being aware of it. Most people tend to mix with others who are pretty similar to them in several ways – they live in the same area and go to college or work

Fig. 1 *A perfectly matched couple?*

■ **Take it further**

To carry out your own correlation study into the match hypothesis, collect photos of couples from magazines, papers or websites. Keep a record of who was paired with whom, then separate the photos into two batches – one with male photos and one with female photos. Ask a sample of people to rate each photo using a scale which you will need to devise. You can assess whether couples are matched for attractiveness by calculating the average score given to the male and female member of each couple and plotting these on a scattergram.

■ Key terms

Match hypothesis: the tendency to form a relationship with someone who is of a similar level of attractiveness to oneself.

Law of attraction: the idea that how much we like someone is directly related to how similar our attitudes are.

Close relationship: a connection between two people which involves interdependence in many areas of their lives.

Field of availables: the name given to the large group of people we could potentially have a relationship with.

Field of desirables: those we would see as potential partners.

Relationships

together. A much larger group of people who live in other places and come from different backgrounds are rarely encountered. This means that there is a fairly small selection of people, who are often similar in educational and economic background and social class, that make up the 'field' from which potential partners are chosen. Individual characteristics play a small role at this stage.

▥ Once two people have started going out together, the next important filter is *similarity of attitudes and values*. If the couple share ideas and beliefs, communication should be easier and the relationship may progress. However, if they appear to be very different, to think differently and share few views about the world, it is likely that the relationship will not progress much further as communication may be difficult. At this stage people with different attitudes, values and interests are filtered out.

▥ Once a couple have become established in a relationship which is fairly long term, the third filter comes into play. This is *complementarity of emotional needs* between the two people – how well the two people fit together as a couple and meet each other's needs.

Kerckoff and Davis (1962) tested their model using a longitudinal study of student couples who had been together for more or less than 18 months. They were asked to complete several questionnaires over a seven-month period in which they reported on attitude similarity and personality traits with their partner. It was found that attitude similarity was the most important factor up to about 18 months into a relationship. After this time, psychological compatibility and the ability to meet each other's needs became important, supporting the claims made by the filter model.

▥ The filter model is a useful way to think about the factors which are influential in relationship development and when they might come into play. A factor which may be important at one time in a relationship, such as similar attitudes, may assume less relevance later on in the same relationship.

▥ The filter model emphasises the importance of demographic factors and similarity of attitudes as 'filters' in relationship development. Evidence shows that both of these continue to be important in relationship survival. Sprecher (1998) found that couples who were matched in physical attractiveness, social background and interests were more likely to develop a long-term relationship. A longitudinal study of couples over 21 years found that those who were similar in educational level and age at the start of their relationship were more likely to stay together. They also became more similar in attitudes as time went on (Gruber-Baldini, Schaie and Willis, 1995).

▥ The division of relationships into stages fails to capture their fluid and dynamic nature. In real life, relationships flow seamlessly. Some may develop faster and others slower than the filter model suggests.

Reward/need theories

In order for a relationship to progress from early attraction, the two people involved need to be sufficiently motivated to want to continue getting to know each other. Reward/need theory argues that a long-term relationship is more likely to be formed if it meets the needs of the partners and provides rewards. People enter relationships with a range of needs including biologically based social needs, such as sex, and emotional needs, such as giving and receiving emotional support and feeling a sense of belonging. The relative strength of these needs varies

> ▥ **Hint**
>
> You can remember the three filters in this model using the mnemonic DAN for demographic, attitudes and needs.

Fig. 2 *Star-crossed lovers Romeo and Juliet*

Relationships

between individuals. What is important is that the relationship meets some of the needs of the two people involved.

As well as meeting needs, relationships provide many different types of reward. Some of these are fairly straightforward such as having fun together and sharing activities. It seems obvious that a relationship is more likely to get off the ground if the two people enjoy time spent together and find each other's company rewarding. Rusbult and van Lange (1996) argue that rewards are important in determining if and how a relationship between two people will develop. People who do not know each other well often exchange rewards initially on a 'tit for tat' basis (I will cook for you tomorrow if you cook for me on Thursday). The exchange of rewards in this way was identified by Clark and Mills (1979) who used the term '**exchange relationships**' to describe couples operating on this basis. As the relationship progresses, rewards may begin to be exchanged in a less reciprocal way which Clark and Mills termed '**communal relationships**'. Here, rewards are given as a result of concern for the well-being of the partner and a desire to please them, rather than with the thought of receiving payback. The move from giving rewards on an exchange to a communal basis may be an important aspect in forming a close relationship.

Different rewards become possible as people get to know each other better. Intimacy develops through self-disclosure as people gradually reveal more personal information about themselves to their partner. **Self-disclosure** enables casual relationships to become much closer and it is also rewarding as it implies trust in the other. It is often reciprocal – when one partner discloses it is often matched by disclosure in the other. Research has shown that self-disclosure is regulated by norms relating to when information should be revealed, what can be told, and what should be avoided (Duck and Miell, 1986).

- Both the filter model and reward/need theory suggest that long-term relationships are most likely to be formed where partners meet each other's needs, although they have different views about when needs become important.

- Evidence shows that the meeting of needs is an important factor in the long-term survival of relationships. Smith and Mackie (2002) argue that long-term, happy relationships meet many of the needs of the two people involved, whereas unhappy relationships entail unmet needs.

- Reward/need theory acknowledges that both rewards and needs are personal to individuals. This view is supported by the Social Affiliation Model (O'Connor and Rosenblood, 1996) which argues that each individual has an optimal level of social contact. Their research found that students differed dramatically in their **need for affiliation**, with some desiring large amounts of social contact and others being happier with their own company/space.

■ Should I stay or should I go?

Economic theories are a group of explanations which look at how couples regulate their relationships. These theories share the view that people keep an eye on what they are putting in and getting out of a relationship and they may choose to move on if a better 'deal' is offered by someone else. Economic theories help to explain how couples keep their relationship going and the decision to stay or go if the relationship gets into difficulties.

■ Key terms

Exchange relationships: these involve the exchange of rewards largely on a 'tit for tat 'basis.

Communal relationships: these take place when partners offer rewards without expecting rewards in return.

Self-disclosure: the sharing of increasingly personal and intimate information which shows trust and enables two people to get beyond superficial contact.

Need for affiliation: this relates to how strongly an individual is motivated to form connections with other people.

Economic theories: an influential group of theories which argue that people run relationships in a similar way to running bank accounts, keeping an eye on what is being put in and taken out by the partners.

AQA Examiner's tip

You will need to be able to explain how relationships form. Make sure that you can describe the important factors in attraction and explain how they relate to the two main theories of rewards and filters.

Social exchange theory

Homans (1971) borrowed concepts from economics and from Skinner's theory of operant conditioning to develop social exchange theory. He acknowledged that relationships involve rewards, but he also noted that they involve costs. Costs come in different forms: relationships involve costs of money, time and the incalculable emotional costs produced by loss, betrayal and jealousy. Homans argued that we run our relationships by keeping an eye on the exchange of rewards and costs. Whether or not we are satisfied depends on the ratio between costs and rewards which Homans referred to as the '**outcome**'. If the rewards in the relationship outweigh the costs, the relationship was said to be in a state of 'profit'. If the costs outweigh the rewards, the result is a state of 'loss' which leads to dissatisfaction with the relationship. Social exchange theory argues that people are basically selfish, aiming to minimise their costs in the relationship and to maximise the rewards they receive.

Interdependence theory

Thibaut and Kelley (1959) developed social exchange theory further. They viewed relationships as similar to business transactions in which people keep an eye on the 'balance sheet' of their relationship, comparing it with previous relationships and alternatives that may be on offer, just like you might compare the interest rate offered by different bank accounts! They identified two types of comparison:

- The comparison level (CL) – this involves comparing the current relationship with a general expectation of how rewarding relationships are, created from your previous experiences. If the current relationship seems more rewarding than those you have experienced previously, you are likely to be satisfied.

- Comparison level for alternatives (CL Alt) – this involves comparing the current relationship with other possible relationships on offer. If the current relationship compares favourably (or there are no alternatives available) you are likely to be satisfied.

Social exchange theory predicts that an individual may decide to leave a relationship if the ratio of costs and rewards ceases to be positive and the relationship runs in a state of loss. This could happen if the costs in the relationship outweigh the rewards, if the CL suggests that the relationship is less rewarding than expectations or if the CL Alt offers a viable and attractive alternative.

Evaluation

- Social exchange theory assumes that people spend a considerable amount of time and effort monitoring their relationships. This assumption has been challenged. Argyle (1987) argued that people only really begin to count the costs and monitor relationships *after* they have become dissatisfied with them. Duck (1994) agrees that, in general, people do not keep an eye on other alternatives which are on offer and only start to consider alternatives when they become dissatisfied with their current relationship.

- Studies have shown that both rewards and costs involved generally increase as a relationship develops (Argyle, 1996). Relationship closeness involves rewards *plus* costs, not rewards *minus* costs.

- Social exchange theory views people as self-centred and likely to leave relationships in a state of loss where costs outweigh rewards.

Key terms

Outcome: the overall balance between rewards and costs in a relationship.

AQA **Examiner's tip**

In your exam write out CL and CL Alt in full the first time you use it to show you know they mean comparison level (CL) and comparison level for alternatives (CL Alt).

However, it is apparent that people continue to stay in relationships which are extremely unrewarding, for example those suffering domestic abuse or violence. One reason given for this is often the amount that has been put into the relationship in the past – **investments**.

Investment model

Rusbult and van Lange's investment model (1996) argues that in order to understand decisions to stay or leave relationships, we must take into account investments. The investment model argues that the best predictor of whether or not a couple will stay together is commitment, which is made up of a number of factors including:

▓ satisfaction with the relationship – a feeling that the relationship provides rewards that are unique

▓ a belief that the relationship offers better rewards compared with any alternatives on offer (CL Alt)

▓ substantial investments in the relationship – a network of mutual friends, shared property and emotional investments made in the past. These factors act as barriers to dissolution.

The difference between this approach and social exchange theory is the emphasis on investments rather than a focus on current rewards and costs. These may be very important in helping to understand why people stay in relationships which are unrewarding and appear to offer little but costs!

Impett, Beals and Peplau (2002) tested the model using a prospective study of a large sample of married couples over an 18-month period. They found that commitment to the marriage by both partners predicted relationship stability, supporting Rusbult and van Lange's model.

Rhahgan and Axsom (2006) studied a group of women living in a refuge and found that each of Rusbult and van Lange's three factors (satisfaction, CL Alt and investments) contributed to women's commitment to stay with their partner, supporting the investment model.

Jerstad (2005) studied men and women and found that investments, notably the amount of time and effort put into the relationship, were the most important predictor of whether or not someone would stay with a violent partner. Those who had experienced the most violence were often the most committed – almost as if their previous experiences were 'investments' which would be rendered worthless if they left.

Equity theory

Equity theory (Walster, 1978) agrees that people weigh up rewards and costs within relationships but argues that people have an expectation that relationships should be fair. According to equity theory, couples keep an eye on what both they and their partner are putting in and getting out. If this is roughly equal they are likely to feel reasonably satisfied with the relationship. However, if this is unequal, with one partner putting in a great deal more effort than the other or getting much more out, the relationship will be experienced as 'inequitable' and this will lead the relationship into problems. This feeling of inequity will lead the 'loser' in the relationship to feel dissatisfied and the 'winner' to feel guilty. If the relationship is of relatively short duration one partner may simply end it. However, if the couple have been together for a long time and both have invested in the relationship in terms of time and money, they may well

▓ **Key terms**

Investments: things which have been put into the relationship, such as time, which will be lost if it breaks down.

Equity: the idea that relationships should be run in a fair way. Equity can be measured using the Hatfield Global Measure, which uses a scale from +3 (I am getting a much better deal than my partner) to –3 (I am getting a much worse deal than my partner).

■ **Hint**

How science works

There are several models that try to explain the maintenance of relationships. The scientific approach tries to test these models using controlled experiments to find the best explanation. It is a problem for psychology that relationships are very complicated, with many variables involved. It is a challenge for the psychologist to design valid and reliable studies in this area.

▓ **Link**

Approaches, issues and debates

Equity theory argues that relationships are more likely to break down when they are inequitable. This can be seen as reflecting the views of individualistic, Western cultures. Cultural bias takes place when culturally specific concepts such as 'equity' are assumed to be culturally universal.

Relationships

be motivated to repair the relationship by restoring equity. This could be done by:

- ■ reducing inputs – putting less effort into the relationship
- ■ increasing outputs/rewards – encouraging the other person to put more effort into the relationship.

■ Research study: van Yperen and Buunk (1990)

Van Yperen and Buunk (1990) carried out a longitudinal study using 259 couples recruited by way of an advert in a local paper. Eighty-six per cent were married and the remainder were cohabiting. They obtained a score for equity in the relationship using Hatfield's Global Measurement of Satisfaction (Hatfield *et al.*, 1990) and found that about 65 per cent of men and women felt that their relationship was equitable, about 25 per cent of men felt over-benefited, and about the same number of women felt under-benefited.

One year later the couples were asked about satisfaction in their relationship. Those who felt their relationship was equitable at stage 1 were the most satisfied, the over-benefited were next and the under-benefited were least satisfied, supporting the equity theory.

Methodological issues

This study uses a longitudinal design with a follow-up period of one year. This enables researchers to provide a more detailed analysis rather than a snapshot of relationships.

Ethical issues

The area of relationships is extremely personal and requires the fully informed consent of those who take part. The researcher needs to be sensitive.

■ Hint

How science works

Concerns relating to validity have led researchers such as Van Yperen and Buunk to use longitudinal research. Longitudinal studies would hold participant variable constant and depict the sequence and continuity rather than show snapshots of relationships (F).

De Maris (2007) assessed the importance of equity in relation to marital dissatisfaction and later breakdown using a sample of 1,500 American couples. He found that a woman's sense of being under-benefited was most important in predicting later disruption.

Other research has shown the importance of equity in gay and lesbian relationships. Dwyer (2000) argues that lesbians put a considerable value on equity within a relationship.

Together the findings of these studies imply that equity is indeed important in relationships, but probably more so for women than men (van Yperen and Buunk, 1990).

Miell and Croghan (1996) argue that the equity principle is more important in Western, individualistic cultures and less important in collectivist cultures. Other critics argue that truly intimate relationships do not involve counting inputs and outputs.

■ How do relationships end?

Economic explanations consider *why* people might choose to leave relationships. An alternative approach was taken by Duck's four-stage model dissolution (1988) demonstrating *how* relationships end – the process of splitting up. Duck argues that the decision to move from one

AQA Examiner's tip

Ensure that you can define the important terms used in these theories, such as CL, CL Alt, equity and investments. Try to explain the differences between social exchange, investment and equity theories in relationship breakdown using these terms. You might find it useful to map out these different explanations using mind map techniques.

phase into the next is made when the individual reaches a threshold or decision point:

1 The intra-psychic phase – the start of the break-up process is the unhappiness or dissatisfaction of at least one of the members of the couple. The focus at this point is usually on the partner's behaviour and how they are failing in the relationship. The unhappy party may talk to their friends about the relationship. When they reach the threshold of being unable to stand it they voice their concerns to the partner and the dyadic phase begins. *Threshold – I cannot stand it any more*.

2 The dyadic phase – the unhappiness is now out in the open air. The couple may engage in 'our relationship' discussions and talk through possible changes to resolve the difficulties. They may choose to call in intervention teams such as couple counselling – if this is partially successful the relationship may continue. Otherwise the issues may fail to be resolved and the next threshold is eventually reached. *Threshold – I would be justified in leaving*.

3 The social phase – the relationship problems are now aired publicly as the couple start to tell their friends and family about the difficulties and the possibility of a split. Friends may offer support or take sides. The break up is now becoming pretty inevitable. *Threshold – I mean it*.

4 The grave-dressing phase – the last phase takes place after the couple have officially split up. Both parties try to get their side of the story/explanation of the break-up across to people that they want to think well of them. Each partner creates their own version of what went wrong and who/what was to blame. These versions are usually face-saving to demonstrate that they are not a totally bad person who is rubbish at relationships and not to be trusted!

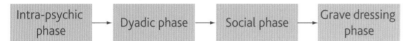

Fig. 3 *Duck's four-stage model of dissolution*

▮ Thinking about methods

In the 1970s and 1980s most research into relationships operated within the scientific tradition using experimental methods, for example Byrne's research into attitudes. Critics have argued that these methods focused on 'isolated slices of relationships', that they explored behaviours which are part of relationships (for example, attraction) but failed to consider the complexity. Steve Duck has been an influential critic of relationship research and has argued that relationships are better studied as processes rather than states. They exist in time and are fluid; they progress, improve, develop or deteriorate. Even though they involve periods of relative stability, they rarely stand still, and we should develop methods of studying them as processes rather than taking 'snapshots' of them at different points. This has led to a move towards longitudinal research such as that carried out by van Yperen and Buunk (1990) to investigate equity in relationships. However, we must also note that the process of looking at something under a microscope may alter it – asking people to reflect on equity in their relationships may produce effects that would not occur without the research.

Key points

■ Factors including proximity, similarity and physical appearance are important in initial attraction.

■ Relationship formation has been explained by the filter model and reward theories.

■ Economic explanations help to understand how couples regulate and maintain their relationships.

■ Relationships may break down due to lack of rewards or inequity.

■ Some people continue to stay in unrewarding relationships due to investments and commitment.

■ The process of splitting up has been described in a four-phase model.

Summary questions

1 Outline the filter and reward theories of relationship formation.

2 Explain what is meant by investments. How are they important in understanding relationships?

3 Compare the explanations for relationship breakdown given by exchange and equity theory. Which do you consider to be most convincing and why?

Sexual selection and human reproductive behaviour

Learning objectives:

- understand why certain physical features are attractive to men and women

- describe what men and women seek in potential partners

- explain differences in the reproductive behaviour of men and women

- understand the explanations for behaviours given by parental investment theory and sexual strategies theory.

Fig. 1 *Female beauty*

Link

You can read more about the evolutionary explanations of these on pages 95–6. Think about the potential reproductive advantages of these physical preferences.

Introduction

This chapter considers how evolution may have shaped the sexual preferences, behaviours and relationships of men and women today. The evolutionary perspective on relationships argues that human reproductive behaviours have their origins in the evolutionary past and exist because they conveyed survival or reproductive advantages to our distant ancestors. This perspective draws from the ideas of Charles Darwin on *natural selection* and *sexual selection*. We shall start by examining some of the differences in what men and women find attractive and the qualities they seek in partners. We will then go on to consider differences in human reproductive behaviours. Finally we will discuss two evolutionary explanations of human reproductive behaviour: Trivers' (1972) parental investment theory and Buss and Schmitt's (1993) sexual strategies theory.

The evolutionary basis of physical attraction

Cunningham (1986) investigated what types of female faces are found attractive by males. He systematically varied the size of female facial features including eyes, nose and mouth and found that men were most attracted to features usually associated with young children – large eyes, small noses and chins. Some features associated with maturity such as prominent cheekbones and narrow cheeks were also found attractive as were dilated pupils and wide smiles. Waynforth (2005) found that masculine facial features including a square jaw, ridged eyebrows, small eyes and a symmetrical face were preferred by women especially those seeking a short-term partner. Using computer-manipulated images, Bruce and Young (1998) have found that there is a preference for symmetrical faces in both men and women.

Langlois *et al.* (2000) carried out a meta-analysis of 919 studies into physical attractiveness and found that there was considerable agreement within cultures as to who was attractive and who was not. There was also some agreement between cultures. Langlois *et al.* also found that a preference for attractive faces is shown in very early childhood and has emerged strongly by the time children are around 26 months old.

Body shape has also been investigated. Singh (1993) found that across cultures there is a preference for a female waist–hip ratio (WHR) of 0.7, which produces a typical hour-glass shape. This preference exists despite cultural differences for curvier or slimmer figures. In males, the ideal WHR is around 0.85 to 0.9 which signifies a tapering figure from wide shoulders down to narrowing hips (Gross, 2001). Longer-than-average legs are attractive to both men and women. Pawlowski (2008) asked a sample of 218 males and females to rank the attractiveness of seven pictures of men and seven of women which were digitally altered for leg length. He found that in both sexes 5 per cent longer legs than average were seen as the most attractive.

Partner selection

When it comes to long-term preferences for mates, we can examine partner preferences by looking at the qualities sought in personal adverts and on dating websites as well as those gathered from questionnaire-based research. Dunbar and Waynforth (1995) carried out a study using 900 personal adverts taken from North American newspapers. They found that a younger partner was important to just under half of the men (42 per cent) compared to only a quarter of the women. Physical attractiveness was sought by 44 per cent of men compared with 22 per cent of women.

As this study was carried out in the USA, it is important to ask if the preferences appear to be culture specific or if they are the same across cultures. A substantial cross-cultural study was carried out by David Buss (1989) in which he looked at partner preferences in men and women in 33 countries taken from five continents. Data was collected from a total of 4,601 men and 5,446 women aged between 16 and 28 years. Buss found that the following preferences appeared strongly across cultures:

- Men valued physical attractiveness more than women did.
- Men valued women who were younger than themselves.
- Women valued financial capacity of potential partners and qualities associated with financial success (ambition and industriousness) more than men.

Others have assessed partner preferences of homosexual people. Bailey and Zucker (1995) looked at the preferences of both gay and straight men and found them to be very similar. Both showed a large amount of interest in the physical attractiveness of their partner and in uncommitted sex. Both types of men were relatively uninterested in the financial status of potential partners.

Kenrick *et al.* (1995) set out to compare the age preferences of heterosexuals and homosexuals and to see how far they resembled each other. Using 783 singles adverts taken from a range of New York magazines, they found strikingly similar preferences in gay and straight men. Both were happy with the idea of a partner who was up to five years older or younger when they were in their twenties. However, as both groups aged, their preferences moved gradually towards younger partners, and this continued across adulthood.

Sprecher (1998) identified a range of *personal qualities* found important in partners. These were the 'desirable' personality of the partner (warmth and kindness), reciprocal liking (that the other person liked them) with similar attitudes and interests. Interestingly, these qualities were pretty much the same as those valued in friends!

Differences in reproductive behaviours

As well as differences in partner preferences we can also consider human reproductive behaviours. Whilst there are clearly many similarities between men and women's behaviour, there are also some fairly clear differences which have been documented by research studies:

1 The tendency to engage in casual sex. A much documented difference in behaviour between males and females is the tendency to engage in casual sex (Buss and Schmitt, 1993). On balance, men tend to be much more likely to have short-term relationships or one-night stands than women. This was demonstrated beautifully in Clark and

Hatfield's studies (1989 and 1990) where a sample of male and female students approached total strangers of the opposite sex on campus and propositioned them with one of three requests which were:

▥ to go out with them that night
▥ to go back to their house with them
▥ to have sex with them.

Clark and Hatfield found that whilst 50 per cent of both men and women agreed to go out that night, unsurprisingly none of the women propositioned by men agreed to sex with a stranger. However, 75 per cent of the men approached agreed to sex – although only 69 per cent of them agreed to go back to the person's house! (Presumably the other 6 per cent were going for an alfresco approach.) Even when Clark modified the experiment in 1990 and assured participants about the trustworthiness of the stranger, the results were still the same – women did not generally agree to casual sex. The general unwillingness to engage in uncommitted sex is also found in lesbians (Buss and Schmitt, 1993).

2   Men tend to seek and desire a greater number of sexual partners than women. Buss and Schmitt (1993) asked how many sexual partners people would ideally like over the next two years, the next decade and during their lifetime. On average, men would like 8 partners over the next two years compared to women's 1 partner. Over a lifetime, the averages were, respectively, 18 (men) and between 4 and 5 (women).

3   Differences in sexual jealousy. Whilst both men and women feel jealousy at betrayal by a partner, evidence shows us that what makes them jealous may be different. Buss (1993) asked male and female students to imagine their current boy/girlfriend either having sex with someone else or in love with them. Whilst engaging in these rather dubious fantasies, they were wired up to measure stress responses. The researchers found that men became most distressed at the image of their partner being sexually unfaithful, whereas women became most distressed at the idea of their partner in love with someone else. Schützwohl (2004) replicated this study asking students to make a choice between sexual and emotional infidelity in their partner. He measured their decision times to respond and found that those who selected the adaptive response took less time than those who selected the less adaptive option.

4   Sexual fantasies and dreams. Ellis and Symons (1990) found that men are more likely to have sexual dreams than women especially those involving multiple or anonymous partners and strangers.

Many of the studies carried out in this area have ethical implications. For example, Clarke and Hatfield's studies on university campuses involved deception and a lack of informed consent. The studies carried out by Buss and Schmitt (1993) and Schüzwohl (2004) into sexual jealousy involved some degree of stress and emotional distress by their very nature, even though participants consented to take part. There are also issues with demand characteristics. In Buss and Schmitt's 1993 study, it is likely that participants were influenced to produce socially desirable responses, and it may be easier or more socially acceptable for men to report sexual dreams and fantasies than women.

How can these differences be explained?

How might these preferences and behaviours have arisen? Evolutionary theory sees them as originating through the processes of **natural selection** and **sexual selection**. According to the principle of natural

AQA **Examiner's tip**

Make sure you can describe some of the main differences between men and women in reproduction behaviour. You will also need to back these up with reference to research studies.

▥ Key terms

Natural selection: variation within any species leads to some individuals being better equipped to survive and breed than others. Those who are reproductively successful and who leave more offspring will have their characteristics passed on in the gene pool.

Sexual selection: the process by which characteristics are selected because they are attractive to the other sex. The genes which code for these are passed on to offspring.

selection, members of any species vary in physical ways as well as behaviours – for example, height, body shape and hair colour. If a variation of some kind produces a reproductive advantage which enables its owner to leave more offspring, then these characteristics will be passed into the gene pool. Over a period of time most members of the species will come to possess the feature or the behaviour.

Sexual selection operates on similar principles to natural selection. Darwin was initially puzzled by bodily features such as the male peacock's spectacular tail, which appeared to offer no survival value and indeed made the peacock much more vulnerable to predators as it hampered the bird's ability to fly. However, the peacock's long and glorious tail was found to be valued by peahens that actively preferred mates with beautiful tails. In order to explain this, Darwin proposed the concept of sexual selection, suggesting that some bodily features and behaviours exist because they are valued by the other sex and are deemed attractive, thus leading to increased opportunities for mating.

We can distinguish between two types of sexual selection. Intra-sexual selection takes place when members of one sex (often males) compete for access to the other sex (females). An example of this is the way in which male stags fight over females. Inter-sexual selection takes place when members of one sex (often females) choose from the available pool of male mates on the basis of features which they find desirable. For example, a female stickleback will choose a male to fertilise her eggs on the basis of how beautiful the nest that he builds is and how vigorously he performs a zigzag dance.

Parental investment theory

One influential explanation of mate selection and human reproductive behaviour is Robert Trivers' **parental investment** theory (1972). This approach argues that differences between males and females have their origins in the different amount of parental investment made by males and females.

The human male's investment in offspring is relatively small. He has large amounts of sperm and remains fertile throughout his life. He is also capable of many matings and the only limit on the number of offspring he can produce is in the number of available female partners. Each takes little in terms of time and energy. The best way to maximise his reproductive success is to have many matings with multiple fertile partners.

In contrast, the human female's investment in each offspring is substantial. The gamete she supplies (the ova) is around one hundred times larger than the sperm, and she has a limited supply of these (generally producing one ovum per month). Her reproductive life is shorter at around 30 years, limiting the total number of offspring she can produce. Following conception, her pre-natal investment continues to be large. She carries the growing foetus for around 40 weeks feeding it from her own supplies of nourishment, which uses thousands of calories. Then she must give birth and continue to invest in the baby. In the distant past, this would have involved breastfeeding for at least two years after birth. Therefore her investment in comparison to the male's is substantial and her best chance of reproductive success it to ensure the survival of her few precious offspring.

■ Key terms

Parental investment: the amount of time, energy and effort put in to aid the reproduction and survival of a child (offspring).

■ Link

Approaches, issues and debates

The evolutionary approach has been criticised for reducing complex human experiences and emotions to the level of genes selected for survival advantages. The attractiveness of features such as youth and economic resources may be explained at higher levels by referring to social learning theory and cultural expectations.

Evaluation of parental investment theory

▪ Parental investment theory helps us to understand *mate preferences*. As a woman invests heavily in each child, she should seek a man with good genes to father her children, a man who shows commitment to remaining in the relationship and helping her raise offspring. If he also has material resources, her offspring will be more likely to survive. This helps to explain Buss's cross-cultural finding that women valued material resources and industriousness in potential partners. In contrast, males who make less parental investment will be more reproductively successful if they have multiple matings with young, fertile females. This helps us to understand why youth is universally important to men.

▪ Trivers' theory also explains why men are more likely to engage in *short-term sexual relationships* and women are more reluctant. As they require little investment of time and effort and have few costs, they can be seen as positive to men as they increase reproductive success. In contrast, females are less likely to be attracted to one-night stands as the men do not display a commitment to help to raise the offspring which may result.

▪ Trivers' theory helps us to understand the observed *differences in sexual jealousy*. Men become distressed at sexual betrayal as it means that they may end up investing in babies which are not theirs. In contrast, women are more distressed at emotional betrayal as this may lead their partner to move his support and investments to another woman, which may threaten the survival of the woman's offspring.

▪ Where Trivers' theory is weaker is in the relative rigidity of the behaviours it suggests. Parental investment theory ignores the obvious evidence that not all mating is about long-term relationships and that women, as well as men, clearly engage in short-term relationships, one-night stands and affairs.

▪ Trivers' theory also tells us little about homosexual relationships which are non-reproductive. For example, it struggles to explain the reluctance of lesbians to engage in short-term, uncommitted sex when the risk of reproduction is not a threat. It also struggles to explain the preference for younger partners that is shown by older gay men. Tooby and Cosmides' (1992) modular mind explanation argues that the same principles can be used to understand relationships and that age preferences shown are inbuilt in men regardless of sexuality.

▪ **Take it further**

Find out about Tooby and Cosmides' (1992) 'modular mind' evolutionary explanation, which argues that age preferences for younger mates are inbuilt in men regardless of sexuality.

Sexual strategies theory

Sexual strategies theory was developed as an extension of Trivers' theory by Buss and Schmitt (1993). It accepts the basic premise of parental investment theory, that differences in parental investment between males and females lead to differences in mating behaviours. However, sexual strategies theory argues that mating is essentially 'strategic' and that humans have a complicated range of mating strategies – both short and long term – which are selected depending on the situation. What this means is that the range of possible reproductive behaviours is large and strategies are flexible. Rather than all women seeking commitment all of the time and all men seeking youth and sexual availability, sexual strategies theory argues that different strategies will come into play depending on the situation. Sexual strategies theory differentiates between the strategies that men and women might use when pursuing a short-term mate (e.g. a one-night stand or date) and a long-term partner:

- Strategies for short-term relationships: according to sexual strategies theory, a short-term partner needs to be able to be identified as sexually available. For men, the most important qualities will be fertility (tied again to youth) and willingness to engage in activity without commitment. For women, a short-term fling can provide benefits, for example as 'mate insurance' in case her proper mate disappears. It should involve a generous male as a miserly one is unlikely to provide resources later to possible offspring. He should also be physically attractive and provide good genes.

- Strategies for long-term relationships: when selecting a long-term partner, both sexes need to assess potential candidates for qualities related to resources and commitment. For men it is of crucial importance that the woman they select will have good parenting skills otherwise offspring from the relationship may not survive. Even more important is faithfulness as they need to ensure that any offspring they invest in are biologically theirs. For women, it is important to identify a potential partner who will supply resources to offspring and will offer commitment and protection.

Sexual strategies theory argues that whilst we are 'hard-wired' to find certain characteristics desirable because they are advantageous in evolutionary terms, 'socially based' characteristics such as an outgoing personality or shared interests are also desirable. People are seen as strategists, using their hand of playing cards to secure reproductive success.

Research study: Norman and Kenrick (2006)

According to Trivers' parental investment theory, women are less likely to engage in one-night stands as they may choose a man without good genes or one who is not committed to raising potential offspring. However, one-night stands offer clear reproductive benefit to males with little effort. In contrast, sexual strategies theory argues that short-term relationships can provide reproductive advantages for both men (reproduction) and women (mate insurance).

Norman and Kenrick (2006) set out to see if there were differences between men and women in the criteria for embarking on one-night stands. In a series of experiments, Norman and Kenrick asked participants to 'design' a short-term partner using a 'mate budget'. They were forced to choose between different characteristics such as kindness, physical attractiveness, vitality, generosity and humour and then asked if they would sleep with the partner they had designed. Norman and Kenrick found that both men and women were most interested in the physical attractiveness of potential one-night stand partners.

They argue that although there may be a difference in willingness to enter short-term relationships, those who *do* look for remarkably similar attributes in their potential partner. Norman and Kenrick argue that the males' preference for physical attractiveness is essentially the same in short-term relationships as in long-term relationships – physical attractiveness signals youth, which provides a powerful visual signal that a female is likely to be fertile. In contrast, the females' preference for physical attractiveness can be explained by sexual strategies theory as physical attractiveness provides good genes, which signals resistance to disease.

Methodological issues

This is an unusual and innovative study. However, the use of self-report measures may be influenced by social desirability effects. It is unclear as to how far rational judgements made in experiments of this nature reflect what actually happens in one-night stands.

Ethical issues

Given the sensitive nature of this research, participants would need to be briefed carefully in order to give fully informed consent. Studies of this nature may be deemed offensive to members of some religious groups

Evaluation of sexual strategies theory

▓ Unlike parental investment theory this approach takes into account the obvious fact that women do engage in short-term relationships and in extra-relational sex (affairs).

▓ Like Trivers' parental investment theory, sexual strategies theory can offer an explanation for many of the observed differences in reproductive behaviours. It helps to explain the qualities that men and women seek in both long- and short-term encounters and acknowledges that both of these may aid reproductive success, although in very different ways.

▓ Evidence supports the claim that socially based desirable characteristics can be used to attract partners. Dawson and McIntosh (2006) used 151 internet personal adverts and analysed them for references to attractiveness, income and personality characteristics. They found that males and females who possessed the evolutionary advantageous qualities such as material resources and/or physical attractiveness tended to decrease their emphasis on socially based characteristics. In contrast, those who were weaker on the evolutionary benefits tended to emphasise their socially based advantages. Sexual strategies theory therefore helps us to understand how men and women use both of the evolutionary advantageous qualities to attract partners and how those who are weaker in these qualities compensate by offering socially based characteristics.

▓ Reproductive behaviours – for example, female choosiness – are also said to have their origins in genes and to exist today because of the reproductive advantages they conveyed in the evolutionary past. Bell (2002) argues that 'evolutionary grounded arguments only concentrate on the idea that successful behaviours ensure the survival of the animal, reproduction and furtherance of the animals' genes'. He argues that the same behaviour can be explained at a moralistic level (it is wrong to engage in casual sex) or an emotional level. For example, female choosiness can be explained by cultural rather than evolutionary factors. In Western society, social norms tend to see men as hunters pursuing women as prey. Female choosiness can be explained by gender role socialisation and the cultural double standard which sees casual sex as acceptable (and even desirable) for boys but not for girls.

Hint

When you are revising this material, go back to the differences in men's and women's reproductive behaviours and apply parental investment theory to each of these. How well can it explain each difference? How does sexual strategies theory explain them?

Link

Approaches, issues and debates

Evolutionary explanations of relationships can be seen in the light of the debate of **reductionism**. In this case, the explanation of partner choices is given at the level of genes. Men and women are said to be genetically predisposed to find certain features attractive. So men are attracted to younger women, which implies fertility; and women are attracted to older men, which often goes with economic resources.

Bell's commentary illustrates how in psychology there are often different levels of explanation. The less reductionist socio-cultural explanation qualifies the evolutionary explanation and together they more aptly reflect the complexity of human social behaviour.

Key terms

Reductionism: the term given to explanations of human behaviours at a low level of analysis.

Relationships

Take it further

Many of the studies discussed here could be considered 'socially sensitive' as they have implications for the groups represented. Discuss how the findings of some of the studies on reproductive behaviours might be reported in the tabloid press. Do you think research into human sexual behaviour should be carried out?

Key points

- Men and women differ in what they find physically attractive and in the qualities they seek from long-term partners.

- There are broad differences in sexual behaviours between men and women, including the tendency to engage in one-night stands, patterns of sexual jealousy and the desire for greater numbers of partners and sexual variety.

- These differences have been explained by Trivers' parental investment theory (1972) and Buss and Schmitt's sexual strategies theory (1993).

- Parental investment theory argues that women invest more than men in offspring, which drives their general choosiness and makes them seek commitment. Men are seen as generally promiscuous in this model.

- Sexual strategies theory argues that men and women use different strategies and look for different qualities when seeking short- and long-term partners. Reproductive behaviour is seen as complex and flexible.

- Trivers' theory has some problems explaining short-term and homosexual relationships.

Summary questions

1. Outline the qualities sought in long-term mates.

2. With reference to research evidence, describe two sex differences in human reproductive behaviour.

3. Outline the explanation given by Trivers' parental investment theory for differences in reproductive behaviour.

4. Compare the explanations of one-night stands given by parental investment theory and sexual strategies theory. Which do you think is more convincing and why?

9

Effects of early experience and culture on adult relationships

The influence of childhood and adolescent experiences

Learning objectives:

- understand how early attachments may influence adult relationships

- understand the differences between horizontal and vertical relationships

- explain how attachments may influence relationships with peers and how relationships with friends and peers may impact on later relationships.

Key terms

Continuity hypothesis: the claim that early relationship experiences continue in later adult relationships.

Attachment style: a characteristic way of behaving in relationships, for example a tendency to be trusting or jealous.

Horizontal relationships: those between individuals of similar status or power.

Link

You may wish to go over Ainsworth *et al.*'s ideas about secure and insecure attachments and the Strange Situation methodology from the *AQA Psychology A AS* student book, pages 58–60.

Introduction

The approaches we have considered so far have largely overlooked explanations of how and why relationship experiences differ between and, indeed, within individuals. You have probably noticed from looking around your friends that some people seem to be happy within a long-term relationship, others are more likely to 'play the field' and some lurch from one relationship disaster to another! Are some people inherently good at relationships and, if so, where do these skills come from? Developmental social psychologists have set out to see if early attachments between children and their caregivers and children's friendships with peers have an influence on later relationship experiences in childhood and adulthood.

The continuity hypothesis

Attachment theorists such as Bowlby argued that the early relationships with our primary caregivers provide the basis for later adult relationships – an idea termed the '**continuity hypothesis**'. According to attachment theory, the young child develops an internal working model (IWM) from their first relationship with their primary carer. This consists of a view of themselves as loveable or otherwise, a model of other people as basically trustworthy or not to be relied on, and a model of the relationship between the two. Young children also develop characteristic **attachment styles** in their early relationships which influence later relationships by providing the child with beliefs about themselves, other people and relationships in general.

Ainsworth, Bell and Staydon (1971) divided attachment styles into three types using the 'Strange Situation' methodology – secure (Type B), insecure avoidant (Type A) and insecure ambivalent (Type C). Research has taken place to establish whether these attachment types influence the relationships a child develops with those of the same age – friends and peers – and whether they persist in adolescent and adult relationships as the hypothesis predicts. Here we will examine both of these threads of research to assess the extent of the continuity.

Relationships with peers

Most children do not grow up in a vacuum but within a rich, social environment surrounded by siblings, peers and friends. Relationships with peers are characterised as **horizontal relationships** as they take place between two people of roughly equal knowledge and power such as siblings or friends and are characterised by equality. Peer relationships provide young people with the opportunity to develop and practise 'social competence' – relationship skills and abilities.

Attachment theories suggest that the child's attachment classification may influence their popularity with peers so that the child who has a secure attachment style should be more confident in interactions with friends. Considerable evidence has supported this view. Waters, Wippman and Sroufe (1979), Jacobson and Willie (1986) and Lieberman (1977) have all found that children classified as 'secure' go on to be more socially skilled in their friendships than both types of insecure children. Lyons-Ruth, Alpern and Repacholi (1993) carried out a longitudinal study which suggested that infant attachment type at 18 months was the best predictor of problematic relationships with peers in five-year-olds. Type D – disorganised attachments – seemed to struggle most to make friends with their peers. Hartup *et al.* (1993) argues that children with a secure attachment type are more popular at nursery and engage more in social interactions with other children. In contrast, insecurely attached children tend to be more reliant on teachers for interaction and emotional support (Sroufe and Fleeson, 1986). These studies support the claim that secure attachments with parents enable children to be good at later friendships.

However, an alternative explanation of the link between attachment type and childhood popularity/peer relationships is offered by **social learning theory**. This approach also predicts a continuity between the child's relationship with their parents and their ability to make friends, as it suggests that children will learn relationship skills from their parents via modelling – observation and imitation. Parke (1988) argues that families indirectly influence their child's later relationships as they guide and modify the child's social behaviour to help them develop social skills. Russell and Finnie (1990) observed Australian pre-school children with their mothers in a situation where the child was introduced to unfamiliar peers. They found that the children who were classed as 'popular' had mothers who suggested strategies to help the child interact with other children and to 'ease' them into the group. In contrast, children classified as 'neglected' had mothers who tended to encourage their child to play with toys and materials but did not offer ways of helping them with interaction. This study therefore suggests that rather than attachment type, popular children may simply be those whose caregivers model and teach important social skills.

Continuities to adult relationships

As young people develop into adolescents, time spent with parents and family decreases and time spent with peers increases. At this age, friendships become increasingly intimate with higher levels of self-disclosure of inner feelings and secrets. Bee (1995) argues that teenagers use their peer group to make the transition from the protected place within the family to the wider adult world. Dunphy (1963) carried out a series of observational studies of a high school in Sydney, Australia and identified two important types of social group:

■ the clique – a same-sex group of 4–6 young people usually aged around 12–14

■ the crowd – a larger group made up of several cliques, some male and some female.

This collection of cliques and crowds allows the adolescent to try out their fledgling relationship skills. Again, there is evidence to suggest that attachment style can influence adolescent sexual relationships. Moore (1997) carried out a study using 100 adolescents aged 14–15. She measured their attachment style using the adult attachment interview and asked a close friend of each teenager to rate their behaviour for social acceptability. Moore found that secure teens were less likely to engage in risky sexual activities (i.e. unsafe sex) than their insecure counterparts. However, those rated as secure were more likely to have had sex than those

Key terms

Social learning theory: the idea that behaviours are learned through observation of role models and imitation of their actions.

AQA **Examiner's tip**

There are two different explanations for how and why attachments might influence children's relationships. Make sure that you understand and can explain the difference between them.

rated as insecure. Moore concluded that secure attachments can help to 'set up' adolescents to handle the transition to adult sexual relationships.

In another study, Feeney and Noller (1992) examined the link between attachments and relationship breakdown. They studied 193 students and found that the three attachment styles differed: those with avoidant attachments were (unsurprisingly) more likely to split up. However, they also found evidence for changes in attachment type when relationships changed from casual to committed, showing that attachment type is not completely fixed.

Continuities to adulthood

Another thread of research has considered the possibility of continuities between childhood and adult relationships. Hazan and Shaver's (1987) Love Quiz is one of the most famous of these studies which you may already have met at AS Level.

Link

You can read more about the adult attachment interview in the evaluation in Table 1 on page 104.

Research study: Hazan and Shaver (1987)

Hazan and Shaver set out to test the question 'Is love in adulthood directly related to the attachment type as a child?' Their research involved a Love Quiz in their local North American paper, the *Rocky Mountain News*, which asked people to write in to the paper regarding two things:

1 Which of three descriptions best fitted their feelings/experiences about romantic relationships?

   a I am somewhat uncomfortable being close to others; I find it difficult to trust them completely; difficult to allow myself to depend on them. I am nervous when anyone gets too close, and often others want me to be more intimate than I feel comfortable being.

   b I find it relatively easy to get close to others and am comfortable depending on them and having them depend on me. I don't worry about being abandoned or about someone getting too close to me.

   c I find that others are reluctant to get as close as I would like. I often worry that my partner doesn't really love me or won't want to stay with me. I want to get very close to my partner and this sometimes scares people away.

2 A simple adjective checklist which described the relationship they experienced with their parents.

Hazan and Shaver tested two samples. The first included 215 men and 415 women (aged between 14 and 82) randomly selected from the many responses to the newspaper advert. The second group consisted of 108 students with a mean age of 18 years.

Hazan and Shaver found a strong relationship between childhood attachment type and adulthood attachment type. Secure Type Bs had relationships that had lasted, on average, twice as long as those classed as insecure. The main findings of this study are shown alongside Ainsworth *et al.*'s in Table 1 overleaf. We can see here that adult and infant attachments are distributed in a very similar way.

Methodological issues

Hazan and Shaver used self-reporting measures of childhood and adult attachments and categorised individuals' responses into

Table 1 *Characteristics of childhood and adult attachment types found by Ainsworth* et al. *(1971) and Hazan and Shaver (1987)*

Attachment type	Ainsworth *et al.*'s Strange Situation	Hazan and Shaver's Love Quiz
Insecure avoidant – Type A	15% of the sample did not orient their behaviour towards their mother. They showed some distress at her departure but did not seek comfort from her when she returned. They also rejected the stranger's attempts to comfort them. The relationship style of these babies involved keeping a distance and avoiding closeness.	25% of sample 1 (newspaper responses) and 23% of sample 2 (students). These adults were doubtful about the existence of true love. They feared closeness and were less accepting and forgiving of their partners.
Secure – Type B	70% of the sample fell into this category. These babies used their mother as a safe base and were happy to explore the room when she was present. They showed distress by crying when she left, and welcomed her back on her return, settling back down to play fairly quickly. They were wary of the stranger and treated them very differently to their mother.	56% of adults fell into this category. This group expressed a belief in lasting love. They tended to be happy and trusting in relationships and were generally high in self-esteem. They were happy to trust others and not afraid of closeness or getting involved.
Anxious ambivalent – Type C	15% of the sample were very upset at separation but were not easily comforted when the mother returned. They appeared to be angry and rejected the mother's attempts to comfort them. These babies seemed to expect the relationship to be difficult and they alternated between seeking closeness and wanting distance.	19% of sample 1 (newspaper responses) and 20% of sample 2 (students). This group experienced emotional extremes of jealousy and passion. They reported a desire to 'merge' with their partner.

different attachment styles. This approach is useful as it generates large amounts of data from which generalisations can be made. However, it is subject to demand characteristics and participants may give socially desirable answers when describing relationships. Retrospective accounts rely on memory, which may be incomplete.

For this reason, psychologists have sought methods to use with adults which get around these difficulties and which equate more or less to Ainsworth *et al.*'s Strange Situation, such as the adult attachment interview devised by Main, Kaplan and Cassidy (1985).

Ethical issues

Hazan and Shaver's study (1987) considers the sensitive area of attachments and relationships. As the first sample were self-selected readers of a newspaper, it is unlikely that they were fully debriefed after the study.

The limits to continuity

Hazan and Shaver's study supports the claim that childhood attachments influence later adult relationships, and others' studies have confirmed this to be generally true. However, evidence has also shown that early relationships do not always predict later ones and pointed to the important influence of other factors on adult security including life events. Zimmerman *et al.* (2000) studied a group of children growing up in Germany and found that child attachment type did not predict adult attachment type. Life events such as the divorce of parents or parental illness/death had much more influence on later security. In agreement, Hamilton (1994) found that children could move from being classed as secure to insecure when major life events took place in their lives.

Others have pointed to the possibilities of change in the opposite direction. Rutter, Quinton and Hill (1999) identified a group of people who had experienced problematic relationships with their parents but had gone on to achieve secure, stable and happy adult relationships which they termed 'earned security'. These pieces of research indicate that early attachments are not the only factors which influence security in adult relationships.

Others such as Sternberg and Beall (1991) point to a range of methodological problems inherent in attachment research. These include the problems of demand characteristics: participants often give the answers they perceive to be 'correct' and they are asked to recall often fuzzy memories of relationships with parents. One method which has been devised to get around these problems of self-report is the adult attachment interview devised by Main, Caplan and Cassidy (1985). This looks at how the individual talks about their past rather than what is said. It consists of a standardised interview in which a set of questions explores how adults describe the relationships they had with their parents in order to measure their current feelings about relationships. The focus of the analysis is not on the content of the interview but on the way the individual talks about their past relationships. The interview is coded by trained observers who look for a number of factors including the internal consistency (whether the individual makes contradictory statements) and coherence (if the points fit together). The adult attachment interview is an extremely useful tool as it is relatively free from demand characteristics: an adult can claim to be secure but may actually be classified as insecure from their narrative.

Other researchers such as Feeney and Noller (1992) have pointed out that relationship styles in adulthood can vary, so the same individual could be secure in a relationship with one partner but insecure in a later relationship, challenging the idea that attachment styles are consistent across different relationships.

Finally, Hartup *et al.* (1993) argues that researchers know surprisingly little about the extent of cross-age linkages between attachments and later relationship experiences. This is because it is difficult to assess cause and effect. It is possible that the child's temperament may influence their early attachment style and later friendships.

Wood, Littleton and Oates (2002) argue that we need to distinguish between *relatedness* (the way we relate to others which stems from our attachment style) and *relationships* which result from the interplay between two people's attachment styles. So, for example, whilst an insecure person may be generally lacking in trust in adult relationships, they may act very differently when they are with a secure, trusting and trustworthy partner rather than with an insecure partner.

Key points

- Early attachments with carers can have an impact on childhood friendships and later adult relationships.

- Secure attachments with parents help children to interact with peers. Parents also teach social/interaction skills explicitly to their children.

- Horizontal relationships with peers are an important part of development and provide a place to develop social skills and competence.

- Those adults who recalled secure childhood attachments in the Love Quiz believed in love and had relationships which lasted longer.

 Hint

How science works

Studying relationships poses a range of methodological challenges for researchers. Tools such as the Adult Attachment Interview (Main, Kaplan and Cassidy, 1985) have been devised to avoid the problems of relying on verbal accounts and self-report.

 Link

Approaches, issues and debates

Attachment theory helps to explain continuities between early attachments and later friendships and relationships. This explanation can be seen as deterministic as it assumes that early relationship experiences cause later experiences. Other factors such as life events can influence later relationships, making the link probabilistic rather than deterministic, making this an example of 'soft determinism'.

AQA **Examiner's tip**

You can see that there is an important debate at stake here relating to the extent of the impact of attachments. Make sure that you can present evidence for both sides of the argument. It is fine, of course, to come down on one side or another as long as you can back up your argument!

 Link

You can refresh your memory about the free will–determinism debate by looking at page xi of the Introductory chapter on approaches, issues and debates.

Relationships

- Adults who recalled insecure childhood attachments were more prone to jealousy and fears of being abandoned.

- Whilst there is some continuity between early childhood attachments and later relationships, other factors such as 'life events' can affect later security.

- After difficult childhoods, some adults achieve 'earned security' through positive marital relationships.

- It is difficult to assess the extent of cross-age linkages in relationship experiences.

- The link between childhood attachments, peer relationships and adult relationships should be seen as probabilistic rather than deterministic.

Summary questions

1 Explain what is meant by the 'continuity hypothesis' and give one piece of evidence which supports this hypothesis.

2 Discuss methodological difficulties with assessing adult attachment styles.

3 What functions are served by horizontal relationships?

4 Compare ethological and social learning explanations of children's social competence. Which do you find the most convincing?

The nature of relationships in different cultures

Learning objectives:

■ understand the meaning of the term 'culture'

■ describe how marriages are arranged

■ explain the findings of research into arranged marriages in both collectivist and individualistic cultures

■ describe economic marriage practices including the dowry and bride price.

Fig. 1 *An arranged Japanese marriage*

■ Key terms

Culture: the beliefs and customs of a social group which distinguish it from other groups.

Collectivist cultures: cultures where the welfare of the group is seen as more important than the welfare of the individual.

Well wishers: interested parties such as parents, relatives or friends who help to identify potential partners.

■ Introduction

The term '**culture**' is used in many different ways in everyday language. In social psychology culture is defined as 'a set of cognitions and practices that identify a specific social group and distinguish it from others' (Hogg and Vaughn, 2005). Gross (1999) argues that culture has two main aspects. The objective aspects of culture include aspects which can be seen, such as buildings, pictures, music or food, whereas subjective aspects include the beliefs, values and social norms which regulate behaviour in groups.

Most of the research we have considered so far has been carried out in northern Europe or the USA, which are considered to be Western or individualistic cultures. Here, partners are freely chosen and relationships are temporary and can be ended if the couple become unhappy. Relationships are effectively arrangements or alliances between two people. In contrast, relationships in **collectivist cultures** have been characterised as:

■ obligatory (i.e. they are chosen by others, as in arranged marriages)

■ permanent (unable to be terminated) and

■ collectivist (seen as alliances between families or social groups rather than an arrangement between two individuals). (Moghaddam, Taylor and Wright, 1993)

We shall examine how these principles work by considering research into arranged marriages before moving on to look at economic arrangements such as the dowry system.

■ The psychology of arranged marriages

Arranged marriages are one of the most common forms of marriage arrangement across the world in collectivist cultures. As recently as 1993, one in four marriages in Japan was arranged (Iwao, 1993). In 1994, UNESCO initiated a large-scale research study into changes in family patterns in Asia as part of their 'International Year of the Family' (Batabyal, 2001).

Batabyal (2001) has carried out a series of reviews into the processes involved in arranged marriages. He suggests that they are based on the idea that young people are unlikely to make the right choice when choosing a lifetime partner for themselves as they are likely to choose on the basis of attraction, which is unlikely to produce a lasting, stable relationship. For this reason, decisions regarding marriage are best made by parents or **well wishers**. Although they may be organised differently in different places, the first stage of the process is the identification by well wishers of a range of possible candidates who are chosen on the basis of family and economics. These are presented to the person wishing to marry who is known as the 'agent'. Batabyal notes that in modern arranged marriages, the 'agent' has a great deal of choice when deciding and has an explicit opportunity to refuse the potential partner if they do not like the look of them. Should they do this, well wishers will seek other candidates of a higher quality to present to the agent.

Arranged marriages in collectivist cultures

In India, either arranged or love marriages are possible for those seeking partners. Umadevi, Venkataramaiah and Srinivasulu (1992) compared preferences for arranged or love marriages in female, Indian students from professional and non-professional backgrounds. They found that both groups of women were happy with the idea of arranged marriages when they involved the consent of the two young people involved. They were also comfortable with the idea of love marriages if the parents approved of the choice. This shows the importance placed on the family's approval of the marriage partners in modern India.

Other studies have set out to compare how 'successful' arranged and love marriages are by considering how happy the couples are and how satisfied they feel with their relationships. These studies have yielded somewhat contradictory findings. Gupta and Singh (1982) set out to compare love and liking in 'arranged' and 'love' marriages. They studied 100 professional, degree-educated couples living in Jaipur, India, 50 of whom had arranged marriages and 50 of whom had 'chosen' or ' love' marriages . They were asked to use liking and love scales after one, five and 10 years of marriage to indicate how much they currently liked and loved their partner. Gupta and Singh found that in love marriages, both love and liking were high at the start but both decreased during the course of the marriage. In contrast, whilst both were much lower at the start of an arranged marriage, love and liking for the partner grew, and at 10 years exceeded that in love marriages. Similar findings were obtained by Yelsma and Athappilly (1988). However, Xioahe and Whyte (1990) carried out a study in the People's Republic of China – a rapidly modernising country – which indicated that women in love marriages were much more satisfied than those in arranged marriages.

These rather contradictory findings suggest that research cannot be generalised across different countries but should be considered in relation to the specific social and economic changes that are taking place. There is variation within as well as between cultures.

Arranged marriages in individualistic cultures

Other researchers have examined marital preferences in second- and third-generation immigrants. When people migrate, they are rapidly exposed to the views of other cultural groups which often produces changes in thinking and behaviour especially amongst younger migrants. The process of internalising the views of another culture is known as **acculturation** (Hogg and Vaughan, 2005) and it is reasonable to suspect that where there are differences in values between the home culture and the dominant culture there may well be acculturative stress. Zaidi and Shuraydi (2002) carried out a study of attitudes towards arranged marriages in a group of second-generation, Pakistani, Muslim women who were brought up in Canada. They interviewed 20 single women aged between 16 and 30 regarding their views about the types of marriage available and found that most favoured Westernised marriage practices involving greater amounts of partner choice. Despite this, many perceived their fathers to be resistant to change. This study demonstrates the importance of considering arranged marriages in Western cultures and shows the need for regular research to 'map' cultural changes.

Zaidi and Shuraydi's study demonstrates the relationship choices facing second- and third-generation migrants. Berry (1986) has identified these as:

■ Integration – keep the values of the home culture, but relate to the dominant culture.

Link

Approaches, issues and debates

Cultural bias may occur when measuring tools devised in one culture are applied to relationships in other cultures. Gupta and Singh (1982) used Rubin's Liking and Loving scales, devised in the US.

Link

Approaches, issues and debates

Culture bias occurs when **etic** constructs are assumed to be **emic**. For example lack of equity is rarely the cause of relationship dissatisfaction in collectivist cultures, though a Western researcher might assume this to be a source of dissatisfaction.

Key terms

Etics: culturally specific constructs.

Emics: constructs which are universal across cultures.

Acculturation: internalising the views of another culture.

Link

Approaches, issues and debates

There is a tendency to assume that the way things are done in one's own culture is normal. It can be difficult for a researcher to avoid his or her own cultural bias so research may be better carried out by those working within and belonging to a particular culture as they would understand it better.

- Assimilation – give up the home culture and take on the views of the dominant culture.
- Separation – keep the home culture and do not integrate with the dominant culture.
- Marginalisation – give up the home culture but fail to take on the dominant culture.

▦ Relationships as economic alliances

In many parts of the world, relationships take place within a context of negotiation and economic transaction. One of the most common long-standing practices is the **dowry**. The practice of giving dowries was common in the UK until the end of the 19th century and continues in many parts of the world today. Srinivasan and Lee (2004) carried out a study of attitudes to the dowry system in Bihar, a northern province of India and found that the practice of dowry giving was becoming more rather than less widespread despite the modernisation taking place in social attitudes in India. In addition the size of the dowry was increasing. Of the 4,603 women studied, almost two-thirds disapproved of the dowry system.

Key points

- Most research into relationships has been carried out in Western, individualistic cultures.
- Arranged marriages are common across many cultures.
- Partners are presented by well wishers, and the marrying 'agent' is often able to reject would-be suitors.
- Some research shows that arranged marriages are stronger in liking and loving than 'chosen' marriages, but other studies disagree.
- It is important to distinguish between arranged marriages which have taken place in collectivist cultures and those of second- and third-generation migrants.
- Economic arrangements such as the dowry are still common today.

▦ Summary questions

5 How are arranged marriages generally organised?

6 Discuss the view that arranged marriages can be as happy and stable as love marriages.

7 Evaluate the claim that research into relationships has suffered from cultural bias.

▦ Key terms

Dowry: a sum of money and/or gifts given by the bride's family to the groom at the start of the marriage.

▦ Take it further

In order to investigate cultural bias for yourself, you could look at the portrayal of arranged marriages in Western newspapers where they are often depicted as 'forced' marriages.

▦ Link

You may wish to look back at the Introductory chapter on approaches, issues and debates to remind yourself about cultural biases in psychology.

Relationships

Relationships end of topic

How science works: practical activities

We have seen that similarity seems to be an important factor in the formation of relationships and friendships. Kandel (1978) found that teenage pairs of close friends were similar in many respects including ethnic background, religion and economic background of parents. Hill, Rubin and Peplau (1976) also found similarities of race, class and religion in dating couples and in pairs of friends. You can investigate this for yourself. First you will need to decide if you intend to look at similarity in pairs of friends or dating couples. You should set a minimum time that they have been friends/known each other, such as six months. You will need a sample of at least 10 pairs of friends or 10 couples in order to produce sufficient data to carry out statistical analyses.

When you have decided if you are studying friends or couples you will need to consider exactly how you intend to measure similarity. You could focus on attitude, personality or demographic similarity (social background) as all of these have been found to be important. If you decide to focus on attitude, you will probably be able to find ways of measuring attitudes using internet sources. Personality measurements such as Eysenck's EPI should also be readily available. If you decide to measure demographic similarity you will need to devise a method to 'measure' social background. Your measurements should allow you to produce a score for both members of each pair. You can plot these on a scattergram to see if there is any apparent similarity and then go on to correlate these using a Spearman's Rank Order test of correlation.

When you have devised your measuring scale, you will need to think through the ethics of this carefully. How do you intend to ask for informed consent from your participants and how will you debrief them afterwards? You will need to keep the results anonymous and confidential.

You can investigate partner preferences by carrying out an analysis of personal adverts in a similar way to that used by Dunbar and Waynforth (1995). You could choose to focus on comparing heterosexual male and female adverts in terms of qualities sought and advertised, or you could compare adverts by gay men and women seeking partners.

When you have decided on the focus of your research, you will need to decide where you intend to collect adverts from. This could include newspapers (free or otherwise), magazines or internet dating sites. You will also have to consider how many adverts you intend to study and think about the different ways of choosing them to ensure a fair and unbiased sampling.

Link

You may like to refresh your memory about graphs and statistical testing in Chapter 39, Data analysis and reporting on investigations, page 532.

Link

You may wish to look again at sampling methods on page 524.

Although this material is in the public arena and people clearly intend for their adverts to be read, you will still need to consider the ethical issues involved in the study. Clearly you cannot contact anonymous advertisers to ask for consent and you cannot debrief them.

When you have made these decisions, you will need to decide exactly how you intend to score the qualities advertised. A pilot study will be helpful at this stage to enable you to see the kinds of qualities referred to. In order to ensure that you have inter-rater reliability, you could devise a recording/scoring scheme with a classmate or partner then score the adverts separately using your system. Hopefully you should find that the results agree.

Further reading and weblinks

Hogg, M.A. and Vaughan, G.M. (2005) *Social Psychology* (4th edn). Harlow: Pearson Education.

This has good coverage of the social psychology of interpersonal relationships.

You can find out more about the measurements used in Hazan and Shaver's Love Quiz study by going to http://psychology.about.com/od/loveandattraction/a/likingloving.htm. This site also has some great information on Rubin's liking and loving scale along with lots of other measurements for assessing relationships.

Films: If you are interested in how relationships are organised in different cultures you may like to watch the film *Bride and Prejudice* (2004) directed by Gurinder Chadha.

Introduction

Key terms

Aggression: deliberately unfriendly behaviour that is often intended to cause harm, usually observed through verbal or physical acts.

Acts of **aggression** manifest themselves in many ways. Think about the current problems in Afghanistan, the continuing troubles of the West Bank and Gaza strip, the atrocities of 9/11 or, closer to home, the horror of 7/7. Acts of terrorism are just one of the many guises aggression can take.

Aggression is a behaviour that often surrounds us as we are growing up. We observe it on the news: another murder, another country goes to war, another situation where a neighbour's frustrations are vented physically. Yet it is not a geographically specific behaviour, it is a universal phenomenon within which there are cultural variations. For example, in some tribal communities, e.g. the Yanomamo Tribe of the Upper Amazon Rainforest, the showing of aggression is an expected behaviour and battle scars are admired as they show that the individual has used aggression effectively to defeat another.

Aggression is not easily defined. The image conjured up in most people's minds would be a fight or disagreement between individuals that results in physical or verbal altercation. To achieve a greater understanding of the topic of aggression and the motives that lie behind this recurrent human behaviour, social psychologists have tried to work out what causes it. This topic initially examines Albert Bandura's social learning theory. This is followed by other social psychological explanations; deindividuation, cue arousal and relative deprivation explanations. Finally, explanations of institutional aggression are examined.

Like many other areas of psychology, human behaviour can be viewed from many perspectives. By simply restricting an analysis of aggressive behaviour to social psychological explanations other causes would be ignored. To explore this further it is necessary to look at the likely biological and physiological factors that lie behind aggressive behaviour. For some people, aggressive behaviour might be more likely at a particular time of the month – suggesting hormonal changes. Other authorities would argue that aggression can be attributed to genes. Some psychologists stress that damage to the structure of the brain could result in changes in behaviour. We often have to try to understand the behaviour that we show today as being the product of the generations before us. The examination of aggression looks at the contribution made to understanding this human behaviour from the evolutionary perspective. The group display of aggression seen at sporting events and in lynch mobs provides an example of what we understand about group behaviour and aggression.

This topic finishes with an evaluation of the theories, and a reminder that a good explanation of aggression would draw on several of the theories mentioned.

Copyright © AQA, 2009. Please refer to the current version of the specification on AQA's website at www.aqa.org.uk/qual/gce.php

10

Social psychological approaches to explaining aggression

Social psychological theories

Learning objectives:

- understand social psychological theories of aggression
- explain the cause of aggression according to the social learning theory
- evaluate social learning theory.

Key terms

Imitation: copying, showing the same behaviour as another.

Social cognitive perspective: an explanation that suggests that behaviour has a social origin and includes cognitive processes such as perception, recollection and interpretation.

Reciprocal determinism: one process or entity relies on another.

Introduction

During your study of psychology you will have noticed that aspects of human behaviour can be explained in more than one way. Often these varying explanations conflict. Aggression as a topic is no different. The explanations of different approaches that are provided by psychologists are what give psychology its unique perspective on understanding human behaviour. The following points list the social psychological explanations of aggression that follow in this chapter:

- the power of imitation
- the loss of personal identity
- situational factors, or
- the perceived inequalities between what a person has and what they think they should rightfully have.

Social learning theory

Social learning theory originated from the work of Gabriel Tarde (1912). He argued that the key characteristics of **imitation** were:

- the behaviour of role models
- the copying of the behaviour of those of a higher status
- the degree of contact with role model
- the degree of understanding of the behaviour.

For Tarde, these were ways in which our social behaviour and responses could be shaped by the actions of others.

Bandura's social learning theory

Bandura (1963) combines the logic of both social psychology and cognitive psychology in his **social cognitive perspective** of human behaviour. Bandura thought that behaviour may be motivated not only by inherent psychological factors, but also by more socio-environmental factors. He argued that the individual and the social environment were linked, something he called **reciprocal determinism**.

Bandura thought that social learning theory had, at its heart, four basic processes:

- Attention – how much do you concentrate on the model showing the behaviour?
- Retention – storing the behaviour you witnessed.
- Reproduction – copying the behaviour you witnessed.
- Motivation – having good reason for showing the witnessed behaviour again, e.g. a real or imaginary incentive.

The central part of these processes was the presence of a role model from whom behaviour could be copied. This model would be a person who seems similar to the child (e.g. in age or sex) or who is in a position of power (e.g. a pop idol, teachers or parents). While the role model is important, the child still needs to have a level of self-confidence that lets them imitate the behaviour. Bandura referred to this as **self-efficacy**.

Supporting his theory: Bandura's Bobo doll studies

Bandura's explanation of social learning theory was based on research that has become well known, his Bobo doll studies. Both the original study and variations of the study helped Bandura to develop the view that human behaviour is often shaped by the sociocultural processes of social learning.

Research study: Bandura, Ross and Ross (1961)

In the original study a total of 72 child participants were used. Each child went through the process individually but they were grouped in conditions as described. There were an equal number of boys and girls throughout. Half of the participants in the experimental groups were exposed to an aggressive model and the other half a non-aggressive model. Within the aggressive experimental group half would view a same-sex role model interacting aggressively with the Bobo doll, while the remainder would watch an opposite-sex role model doing the same. The same balance was used in the non-aggressive condition. The control group of 24 children went through the same process but did not see an adult role model interact with the Bobo doll. Before making observations in the experimental set up, Bandura *et al.* got the teacher and experimenter (both of whom would have had plenty of contact with the children) to rate them on level of aggressiveness. This provided Bandura *et al.* with a good benchmark for comparisons in behaviour as a result of the experimental stimulus.

Initially the child entered a playroom with an adult role model and an experimenter. The child played in one corner, while the adult role model went to another corner of the room. The adult had a construction set, a mallet and a Bobo doll that was 5 feet tall. The experimenter left, and after a few minutes of playing with the construction set the aggressive role model started to hit the Bobo doll. The role model used both physical and verbal violence. Physical actions included hitting the Bobo doll repeatedly with the mallet. Verbal comments like 'take that Bobo' or 'sockeroo' were also heard by the child. In the non-aggressive condition the role model simply ignored the Bobo doll and continued to play with the construction set.

Ten minutes later the experimenter returned. The role model was asked to leave. The child was then asked to follow the experimenter to another playroom, which contained some lovely toys. Frustration was created in the child by only giving them a few minutes in this room before they were told that these nice toys were for other children. The child was then taken to another room with other toys. In this last room there were some aggressive toys (e.g. the Bobo doll, a mallet and a dart gun) and some non-aggressive toys (e.g. paper and crayons, toy lorries and cars, dolls and a tea set) to see which the children would play with, and if they would repeat the verbal statements of aggression of the role model. Sitting behind a two-way mirror, Bandura and his colleagues were able to observe the children's behaviour.

Key terms

Self-efficacy: knowing your own abilities and being confident with them.

AQA Examiner's tip

If the exam question asks you to outline a social psychological explanation of aggression and you choose social learning theory, that is fine. But remember that you need to outline the theory and not just Bandura's Bobo doll study. Candidates often provide too little information about the theory that underpins Bandura's thinking – the Bobo doll study was simply there to support his reasoning.

Hint

How science works

Bandura uses experimental evidence to back up his theory. Scientific explanations are those that are based on experimental evidence. The validity of the theory is assessed by the amount and quality of research evidence that supports it. While Bandura uses his own evidence, other researchers have similarly identified imitation to be a causal factor in aggression. **(G)**

Fig. 1 *A child 'playing' with the Bobo doll*

Aggression

Hint

The issue with Bandura's study is the level of consent he had from the parents of the children who participated. Under the current British Psychological Society Code of Ethics and Conduct, parents/legal guardians must be fully informed and give written consent for children's participation in research.

Link

Bandura used structured observation methods. For more information about observational methods, see the section on Psychological research and scientific method, page 516.

AQA Examiner's tip

To evaluate a theory or a study well, you must go beyond the simple statement that 'a problem with this study is that it has low ecological validity'. If you make a point in your essay, imagine the examiner asking you 'Why?' and provide an explanation that makes clear the consequences or implications of the problem you have identified.

Key terms

Vicarious reinforcement: witnessing another person showing a behaviour and being rewarded for it.

Take it further

Develop an article for a psychology magazine in which you critically analyse the research methodology of Bandura. To what extent do the Bobo doll studies provide support for his theory? What are the theoretical implications for Bandura's methodological pitfalls.

The children who witnessed the aggressive role model's behaviour were far more likely to show aggressive behaviour themselves, and the gender of the role model had a significant influence on whether the behaviour was imitated. Boys showed more aggressive behaviour when the role model was a male. For girls, while the same trend in results was seen, it was less significant. This might be partly explained by the generalisation that boys on the whole are more aggressive than girls.

Methodological issues

Using laboratory-based research (in Bandura's case across a small number of rooms that were the same for each child) there was environmental continuity between each child. However, due to its artificial nature, it lacked realism when compared to everyday life. Also, the experiment was only performed in one cultural setting so other potential cultural influences were ignored. The children's behaviour may have been the product of demand characteristics of the experiment and the desire on the part of the child to 'please the experimenter' as children often wish to please adults. To this extent Bandura might well have overplayed the importance of the *intended* role model as the influencing force. Bobo was a toy originally made for punching, and knowledge of this could have further influenced the children's behaviour. On a positive note, there was a well-defined method of coding the behavioural responses of the children to give a measurable outcome.

Ethical issues

Confidentiality surrounding the names of those concerned in the study was maintained, yet selected films of the behaviour are widely available on the internet and this suggests a compromise of confidentiality. Indeed, the children taking part in the study were unaware that their behaviour was being filmed. This makes an even stronger case for the ethical criticism of the lack of informed consent. It is unlikely that Bandura would have had the *fully* informed consent of the parents/guardians of the children taking part.

In variations to his original study, Bandura showed that rewarding the behaviour of the model encouraged the imitation of it. This process is known as **vicarious reinforcement**. In further experiments, the significance of punishment on changing aggressive behaviour was not as noticeable.

Evaluation of Bandura's social learning theory

Positive points

■ Bandura's theory helps us to explain why children might copy. The theory has face validity (i.e. it is true at face value) through its explanation of how the behaviour of role models such as television personalities and pop stars can be imitated. For example, Jamie Bulger (a very young child) murdered by two boys aged 10 and 11 was a case that the media focused on inherently, not least because before the murder the two boys had been allowed to watch *Child's Play 3*. This was an issue that newspaper articles highlighted dramatically.

■ Social learning theory has been applied to other antisocial areas. For example, Burgess and Akers (1966) used social learning theory to explain deviancy.

▓ Bandura's research focused society's attention on the power of the media, not just in areas of aggression but in other related areas, e.g. health (anorexia and bulimia).

Negative points

▓ Bandura's theory falls foul of the criticism of **imposed etic**. Bandura is a Western researcher working in a first-world country. He assumes that processes of learning are the same for all people in all countries and cultures (i.e. universal).

▓ By suggesting that the child would passively absorb the observed behaviour and imitate it without a logical thought for the implication of it, Bandura's view, like most of behaviourism, is 'behaviourally **deterministic**'.

▓ Runciman (1966) raises a valid issue that challenges Bandura's explanation. It is possible that aggressive behaviour might be shown due to one's relative deprivation – the perceived difference between what you have and what you think you should have.

▓ Dollard *et al.* (1939) suggested that aggressive behaviour is not due to imitation alone. According to them, aggression is the result of frustration building up (psychoanalysis) and the presence of environmental cues (behaviourism) that signal aggressiveness.

▓ Although Bandura was aware of potential biological factors influencing aggressive behaviour, he never gave them the academic attention that they deserved. For example, some authorities would argue that aggressive behaviour could be linked to genetic, bio-chemical or neuro-anatomical causes.

▓ Deindividuation

What does deindividuation mean? One definition is:

the loss of one's sense of individuality

Reber and Reber, 2001

Put simply, deindividuation refers to the process of **decreased self-assessment** and **awareness** in situations where identification of an individual is difficult if not impossible. For example, a child with a Power Ranger's mask on is deindividuated. An individual football supporter amidst a much larger crowd of supporters is deindividuated, as is a person in a crowded music arena. So, any situation where individual identification is restricted ensures that changes in the normal standards of behaviour occur.

Singer, Brush and Lublin (1965) show very clearly that when inhibitions are lowered in a group situation the topic of conversation can change quite dramatically. For example, they showed that in a 'discussion of pornography' members liked the group more and made increased contributions on the topic when they felt that their individuality had been reduced.

So it would seem so far that:

Group situation → Inhibitions reduce → Change in normal standards of behaviour

Zimbardo suggested that further contextual factors such as **sensory overload**, altered states of consciousness, level of arousal and reduction of responsibility could equally increase the likelihood of antisocial behaviour. In each case inhibitions surrounding normal behaviour are reduced.

▓ Key terms

Imposed etic: when a researcher imposes their idea and assumes that their view is appropriate irrespective of cultural differences.

Deterministic: a debate in psychology suggesting that our behaviour is controlled either by one factor solely (hard determinism) or by general laws, but allowing free will to operate in some situations.

Decreased self-assessment: in relation to deindividuation, this means the reduction in evaluation of your own behaviour in a given situation.

Awareness: in relation to deindividuation, this refers to the limited attention we give ourselves in certain situations.

Sensory overload: the senses are bombarded by too much information and they become overloaded and unable to deal with it all. As a result, inhibitions are lowered.

▓ Link

Approaches, issues and debates

Issues and debates in psychology have been used in this evaluation of Bandura's theory. For more information about determinism and cultural bias see the introductory chapter, page xi and page xiii.

Aggression

AQA Examiner's tip

Always read the title of the essay question carefully. Often the essay will not require such an in-depth analysis of the changing focus of deindividuation research as is found here. Indeed, often a comment showing your awareness of this will suffice.

Link

For more information about Milgram's studies of obedience see your *AQA Psychology A AS* student book, pages 184–225.

Link

For more information on naturalistic observations, see your *AQA Psychology A AS* student book, page 112.

Zimbardo (1969) showed dramatically the effect of reduced inhibitions. He used female undergraduates in a 'study of learning'. A stooge is used to play the role of a student. The female participants played the teacher. The 'student' had to complete a set of tasks (very similar to those given by Milgram in his studies of obedience) and electric shocks were delivered to the 'stooge student' if they completed the tasks wrongly.

Half of the female participants were wearing large laboratory coats and hoods to cover their faces. They were talked to in groups of four, they were never referred to by name and were the deindividuated group. The other group of participants wore their normal clothes, they were given large name tags and introduced to each other formally. All participants could see the 'student'. They were also told that she was either 'honest' or 'conceited and critical'. Irrespective of the description of the student learner, the deindividuated participants delivered twice as many shocks as the individuated ones. Those participants that had large name tags tended to give different amounts of shocks depending on the description given.

Diener (1976) conducted a naturalistic observation of 1,300 trick-or-treating children in the US. Diener noted that when the children were in large groups and wearing costumes that meant their identity could not be revealed, they were more likely to perform antisocial actions such as stealing money or sweets. The group 'reduces the possibility of personal identification', which means that behaviour may deviate from normal moral standards.

In a similar vein, Silke (2003) analysed 500 violent attacks occurring in Northern Ireland. Of those 500 a total of 206 were carried out by people who wore some form of disguise so that their individual identity was not known. Silke further noted that the severity of the violent incidents sustained was linked to whether the perpetrator was masked or not. It seems from evidence such as this that aggressive acts can be explained by the deindividuation theory.

Evaluation of the deindividuation theory

One of the fundamental problems of this theory is the fact that it cannot provide an explanation for the simple fact that not all crowds or groups perform aggressive actions. This was seen in the work of Gergen *et al.* (1973), in which lowered levels of individuation did not result in aggressive actions. In Gergen *et al.*'s study, 12 subjects (six men and six women) were taken to a dark room. There was no light at all in this room. Another group of 12 subjects were taken to a lit room. This was the control group. The groups were given no specific requests or instructions from the experimenter, so they could use the time as they wished. During the hour that the participants were in their rooms it was interesting to see what they actually did. Gergen *et al.* made the following general observations about the 'dark room group'. In the first 15 minutes their behaviour was generally polite and social (small talk, exploration), but by 60 minutes the normal barriers to intimate contact had been overcome, and the pitch black nature of the situation meant that inhibitions were lowered. Indeed, most participants 'got physical'. At least half cuddled, and about 80 per cent of the group felt sexually aroused.

In the modern age, computer-mediated communication (i.e. by way of email, text, etc.) is common. The one general trait of this communication is that you are deindividuated. You do not need to show someone what you look like, there is no need for embarrassment, and topics of conversation may be more perverse or varied. Bloodstein (2003) noted that those individuals who had speech problems such as stuttering showed fewer of these problems when wearing a mask. It might be that not being able to be identified increased their self-efficacy and decreased opportunities for **evaluation apprehension**. Mullen (1986) has also shown that in violent situations where people are being attacked, individuals who went to provide help to the victim often would do so if they could mask their true identity, for example by wearing a hat and dark sunglasses.

In his correlational study, Watson (1973) noted that from a total of 24 cultures studied, those warriors that disguised their individual identity through the use of face paint/garments tended to use more aggression, as evidenced through the increased likelihood of torture, death or mutilation of captives.

To simply suggest that the cause of aggression was due to the lowering of inhibitions is somewhat narrow. Furthermore, in a meta-analysis of deindividuation research conducted by Postmes and Spears (1998), much of the previous research examining deindividuation held the view that the *group influenced the psychology (the thinking and action) of the individual*. Postmes and Spears' analysis of over 60 studies investigating deindividuation did not discover a consistent finding of deindividuation acting as a psychological influence on the individual's state and behaviour.

Their meta-analysis reveals that there are no consistent research findings to support the argument that reduced inhibitions and antisocial behaviour are more likely to be seen in large groups or crowded situations where anonymity can be maintained with ease. Interestingly they suggest that behaviour change of individuals in group situations has more to do with *group norms* than anything else.

Cue arousal

While it is clear that frustration could lead to anger, it is not always the case that frustration will lead to the showing of aggressive behaviour. There needs to be a cue or stimulus to spark the aggressive behaviour. Building on Dollard's (1939) frustration/aggression hypothesis, Berkowitz and LePage (1967) argued that if cues (such as a knife or a gun) are present in the situation, they will influence the individual's behaviour, turning anger to aggression.

Research study: Berkowitz and LePage (1967)

Two US psychologists conducted an experiment using 100 undergraduate psychology students from the University of Wisconsin. They thought that just seeing a firearm (or any aggressive cue) could trigger aggression in a person who was already angry since the cue would already have been associated with violence. Each of the participants was paired with what they thought was a genuine participant but this was actually a stooge. The participants were told they were taking part in 'a study of the physiological reactions to stress during problem-solving tasks'. In the first condition, the subject was placed in one room and the stooge was placed in an adjoining room. Mild electric shocks were given by the stooge via a shock key, and the subject was told that the number of shocks given was indicative of their performance on the problem-solving task. The poorer the performance the more shocks were given.

Those subjects that received the most shocks were in the angry group. The group that were not angry only received one shock from their partner. In the second part of the experiment, the subject and stooge changed rooms. The real subject now had to judge their

Key terms

Evaluation apprehension: fear of being assessed by others, which often limits a person's confidence and affects their social behaviour.

Link

Approaches, issues and debates

Saying that aggression is caused by the losing of one's inhibitions (as well as identity) suggests that it is the presence of the group that determines the aggressive behaviour. This argument is a determinist one in the free will and determinism debate.

Link

For more information on normative social influence see your *AQA Psychology A AS* student book page 198.

partner's performance on the task. In some cases a 12-gauge shotgun and a .38 calibre revolver were left in plain view of the table. In other cases a badminton racket and shuttlecocks were present. Berkowitz measured the number of shocks to the partner as a measure of anger.

Berkowitz and LePage found that the angry group of subjects gave more shocks and held the shock key down for longer when the shotgun and revolver were present, compared to the other participants in the control condition where the badminton racket and shuttlecocks were present.

Methodological issues

▦ This research study was conducted in the artificial environment of the laboratory. The task was not an everyday one, and the presence of firearms was unusual. Therefore it is possible that the subjects fulfilled the experimenters' expectations because that was what they thought they had to do. So the behaviour was not normal behaviour, it was simply the result of demand characteristics.

▦ Kellerman (2001) notes that 'the strongest proof of the validity of any study is the independent replication by others'. The greatest problem with the study is that in subsequent replications no consistent trends have been established.

▦ **Consequentiality** – it is possible that the results of the study were affected by the knowledge that it was 'only an experiment'. Kleck and McElrath (1991) looked at 21 'weapons effect' studies and stated that the effect only worked on those individuals who had no prior experience of guns. Furthermore, the more closely the experimental situation reflected real life, the less likely there was to be an effect. Kleck and McElrath argued that it should not be too surprising since the consequences of the actions were neither serious nor permanent. When the result of the action is lethal, this is quite a different matter.

Ethical issues

▦ The psychology students had no idea that their 'partners' were stooges. Furthermore, the level and number of shocks given initially by the stooge to the real participant was in fact determined by the experimenter, not the stooge as the participants believed. In both cases it is clear that the participants have been deceived, which is an ethical issue.

▦ The electric shocks used, while only mild, were real. The researcher has a duty of care to protect participants, which clearly was not the case here.

▦ Suitable debriefing following the experiment (explaining the nature of the study, the reason for deception, the way the results will be used and analysed and providing an arena for the subject to ask questions) was not given.

Key terms

Consequentiality: the effect of knowing the purpose or potential outcome of the task that needs to be done. Psychologists argue that if the subject is made aware of the consequences of the task, they will take it more seriously.

Evaluation of cue arousal theory

At a theoretical level, while these studies are providing a more logical explanation than the original frustration–aggression hypothesis, the theory ignores important individual differences that exist between people. Furthermore, other studies have not supported the findings of Berkowitz and LePage. For example, Buss, Booker and Buss (1972) replicated the

Aggression

original Berkowitz and LePage study and found no convincing evidence that a cue such as the production of a gun would actually increase arousal and therefore cause participants to be more aggressive. Ellis, Weinir and Miller (1971) did an experiment that was similar to the original Berkowitz and LePage study, but their results were the opposite. This was further reinforced by the studies of Cahoon and Edmonds (1984, 1985) and Anderson and Anderson (1996). Only a few experiments have found even slightly convincing evidence of a weapon acting as a cue arousal trigger, and it is more likely that aggressive behaviour is caused by other factors. It is a weakness of the cue arousal theory that important cognitive and biological causes of behaviour are not mentioned in the explanation. **Multidimensional** explanations could be more accurate.

Relative deprivation

This theory originated from the work of Hovland and Sears (1940) who noted that during the 1930s recession in the US there was an increase in anti-black violence and lynchings. Stouffer (1950) advanced the first formal attempt at creating a relative deprivation theory.

There are many examples of riots that came about as the result of inequalities between groups of people, e.g. the Los Angeles riots in 1992 (in the USA), the Brixton riots in 1981 and the Handsworth riots in 1981 and 1985 (in the UK). The apparent hostility towards Islam is an issue which some psychologists feel could 'spark race riots unless urgent action is taken' (Doward and Hinsliff, 2004). Whichever example you choose to use in the exam, the basic underlying common denominator is the difference in opportunity between two groups. One group can see what the other

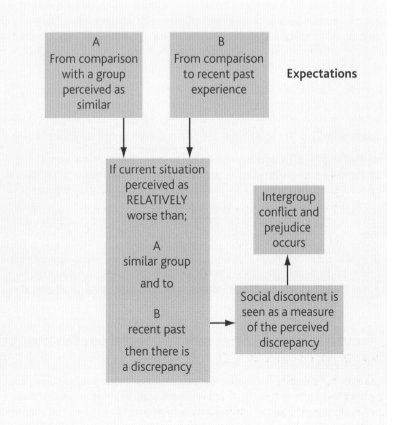

Fig. 2 *The processes involved in relative deprivation*

Link

Approaches, issues and debates

The cue arousal explanation provides an interesting combination of two approaches the behaviourist approach and the psychodynamic approach. The building up of frustration is symbolic of Freudian notions of psychic energy and the observing of an aggressive stimulus in a situation reminds us of the basic principles of classical conditioning in behaviourism.

Key terms

Multidimensional: a perspective or explanation that encompasses more than one view.

Hint

How science works

The practical application and implications of research are central to the effectiveness of science. (I) Relative deprivation as a theory relates practically to the many instances of civil unrest around the world. The degree of practical application and explanation should be a measure of the success of the view scientifically.

Aggression

Key terms

Fraternalistic relative deprivation: the inequality and injustice experienced and felt as part of a 'collective' group (e.g. specific ethnic minorities) in comparison with other collective groups.

Egoistic relative deprivation: the inequality and injustice experienced when you compare yourself to other individuals.

AQA Examiner's tip

Reference to real-life examples of issues that you are discussing is good. This shows confidence in dealing with and understanding the concepts being discussed. Make sure your example is appropriate.

Take it further

Compare and contrast the different social psychological explanations of aggression.

- How are they different?
- What is central to their explanation?
- What deficits do they all have in common that other (non-social psychological) explanations have been able to account for?

groups have, and they believe that they should have access to those things, e.g. wages, housing or job opportunities/security, etc. This difference between what they think they should have and what they actually have is the basis for relative deprivation and therefore the basis for the aggression.

Runcimann (1966) would have called such relative deprivation **fraternalistic relative deprivation**, since this involves a group-to-group comparison. He separates this from **egoistic relative deprivation**, which involves a comparison between individuals. A conscious comparison generates feelings of difference which can be seen as the basis for further antisocial behaviour.

One of the dominant explanations of militancy today states that militant action is a result of the relative deprivation of one group over another, and that reducing difference between groups would therefore reduce aggressive behaviour. Although bordering on sociology rather than psychology, the encouragement of social mobility (the transition of individuals up and down a class system) would in Wright and Klee's (1999) mind provide a means by which the effects of relative deprivation could be reduced. They argued that the more opportunities there are for social mobility, the less likelihood there is that aggression and discriminatory behaviour will be shown.

Evaluation of relative deprivation theory

There are plenty of examples of rioting behaviour that seems to have been sparked by one group's perceived relative deprivation over another. The race riots of 1919 in Chicago, the Notting Hill riots of 1958, or the more recent Bradford and Oldham riots in 2001 all contained elements of relative difference in opportunity for one group over another. A further source of support comes from the militant striking behaviour of groups of workers. In 2008 the police service held a ballot for its members relating to strike action because of 'perceived inequalities over pay'. Likewise, for the first time in its history, members of the coastguard agency went on strike over similar issues. These 'perceived inequalities' are at the heart of relative deprivation theory.

A potential problem with this theory is that it says very little about how we decide what group to compare ourselves with. There are clearly cognitive processes at work here in terms of self-perception and comparison, yet the relative deprivation theory seems to ignore these.

Relative deprivation has been applied to other areas of antisocial behaviour, for example Kanin (1985) in examining date rapists. Kanin suggests that the individual's heightened need for sexual contacts and acts is not matched by their ability to achieve these. This mismatch between their individual need and their ability (unlike others) to satisfy their need leads to the aggressive act of rape.

However, there are plenty of examples of situations where there is a clear difference between groups and yet this does not cause aggression, which shows it should not be assumed that perceived differences always result in direct aggressive action.

Evaluation of social psychological explanations

The main issue with most of the approaches explained above is internal and external validity. Considering external validity, most of the research in this field has been done in a laboratory and so it is possible that there was a participant reaction to the experimental procedure (demand characteristics). As Orne (1962) noted, participants are often helpful to the experimenter – sometimes too helpful. Participants behaving in the way they thought they were supposed to is a likely confounding variable in the Bandura *et al.* (1961) Bobo doll studies. In most laboratory-based work, the nature of the task and often the environment is artificial, leading to questions about how much the experiment represents everyday life or ecological validity.

Nevertheless, from a social psychological viewpoint we can look at the explanations for aggressive behaviour and see that they do provide relatively convincing explanations for this behaviour. Like any theory in psychology, social psychological theories typically explain things in a simple way. To say that aggression is just caused by imitation, or as a result of built-up frustration and the presence of appropriate cues, seems short-sighted. There is little consideration of how environmental factors might contribute to aggressive behaviour such as overcrowding. Farah (2000) studied refugee camps on the West Bank. It was noted that if the camps were overcrowded, there was an increase in violence within them. Temperature and noise also contributed.

Finally, the social psychological explanations fail to take account of important biological processes that might also influence the showing of aggressive behaviour. This point is considered in more detail in Chapter 11, Biological explanations of aggression.

Key points

- Social learning theory in its present form is based upon the reworking of earlier researchers' work such as Tarde (1912) and Rotter (1954). While Bandura brought the composite view of social cognitivism to the study of aggression, the earlier work provided a firm foundation for later research.

- Social learning theory is a well-established explanation, and has raised awareness of the power of the media to influence younger children through observing and imitating the behaviour of their role models. This is especially true, with increased attention being paid to the leniency of sentences given to celebrities who are guilty of antisocial behaviour.

- Deindividuation is the loss of one's identity.

- The nature of thinking in deindividuation theory has changed over the years. Some researchers suggest that the group affects the individual's psychology (thinking and action). Other researchers suggest that the individual simply follows group norms. The meta-analysis of Postmes and Spears (1998) charts these changes in theoretical direction. Their research also cautions the reader not to assume that deindividuation alone causes aggressive behaviour. They note that there are avenues of research within the normative cues associated with the social context that equally provide potential causes for the aggressive behaviour being shown.

- Cue arousal theory (Berkowitz and LePage, 1967) builds on the earlier work of the frustration/aggression hypothesis (Dollard, 1939). Cue arousal suggests that while there are close associations between frustration and anger, it is not always the case that frustration will lead to the showing of aggressive behaviour. There needs to be a cue or stimulus to spark the aggressive behaviour.

- Relative deprivation theory originated with the work of Hovland and Sears (1940), although it was Stouffer (1950) who advanced the first formal attempt to create a relative deprivation theory. Runcimann (1966) further studied relative deprivation, isolating different types: fraternalistic relative deprivation and egoistic relative deprivation.

Link

For more information about internal, external and ecological validity and confounding variables see the section on Psychological research and scientific method, page 520.

Summary questions

1 As you are walking home from college you see your friends and decide to go over to them and say hello. One friend then decides, in a sudden angry frenzy, to kick a litter bin to the floor. Your other friends cheer him on. How might social learning theory explain this behaviour? Use another theoretical approach to criticise the social learning theory explanation of this.

2 Can deindividuation alone explain aggressive behaviour? Give reasons for your answer.

3 What does relative deprivation suggest? Can you give any examples of aggressive behaviour that could be explained by this theory?

Aggression

Explanations of institutional aggression

▒ Key terms

Situational forces: a general term referring to those factors present in social situations that can collectively encourage the showing of certain (aggressive/ antisocial) behaviours that would otherwise not be seen.

Individualistic (dispositional) forces: those characteristics of the individual (i.e. their personality) that contribute to the showing of behaviours usually regarded as antisocial or aggressive.

Self-selected sampling: where subjects volunteer themselves for a study after seeing an advert.

▒ Link

For more information on sampling techniques see the section on Psychological research and scientific method, page 524.

Fig. 3 *The prisoners and the prison guards had different uniforms*

▒ Introduction

This form of aggression involves the behaviour of those people serving in institutions (such as the police, security services and military) as well as criminal and terrorist groups (i.e. those who are bound together by a common purpose to be aggressive). Explanations of institutional aggression usually consider two different forces:

▒ **situational forces**
▒ **individualistic (dispositional) forces**

▒ Situational forces

As you might remember from your AS studies in social psychology, a famous researcher called Philip Zimbardo conducted a study that has come to be known as the Stanford Prison Study. Using **self-selected sampling** (this technique is notoriously unrepresentative as participants are either willing to help or need the money on offer!) Zimbardo recruited 24 male participants. Each participant was subjected to physical and psychological testing to ensure that they would be 'suitable for the study'. It is important to note here that all of the participants were deemed 'normal'. No participant was assessed as being any more or less aggressive than the others, therefore the testing allowed an even basis for comparison. Participants were randomly allocated to the role of prisoner or prison guard. Those that were prisoners were formally arrested at their homes and taken 'down to the station' for finger printing and to be searched. They were then blindfolded and moved to the prison (a basement in the psychology building at Stanford University, that had been converted into a semi-realistic prison). Zimbardo's instruction to the guards was that they should maintain control within the prison, but they were not allowed to use physical violence.

While at first the behaviour of both groups was relatively limited and non-intrusive, by the end of the first day the prisoners had taken off their numbers in protest. The prison guards became ever more controlling and issued more and more punishments. The longer the study went on, the more degrading and perverse the punishments and requests of the prisoners became. Consider the following conversation between a guard (Hellmann) and two of the prisoners, numbers 7258 and 2093.

> 'While you have got your hand in the air, 7258, why don't you play Frankenstein. 2093, you can be the bride of Frankenstein, you stand right here.'
> 'You go over there' says sarge. Sarge asks if he could act it out.
> 'Of course you should act it out. You be the bride of Frankenstein, 7258 you be Frankenstein. I want you to walk over here like Frankenstein and say "I love 2093"'
> As 7258 starts to walk towards his bride, Burdan (a guard) stops him in his tracks.
> 'That ain't no Frankenstein walk. We did not ask you to walk like you.'
> Hellmann grabs 7258 by the arm very aggressively, pulls him back, and makes him walk the proper Frankenstein walk.
> 7258: 'I love you 2093.'

'Get up close! Get up close!' shouts Burdan.
7258 is now inches away from 2093.
Hellman pushes them together, his hands on each of their backs, until
their bodies are touching.

Zimbardo, 2007 (page 119)

Link

For more information about
Zimbardo's Stanford Prison Study,
see your *AQA Psychology A AS*
student book, page 192 or visit the
website at www.prisonexp.org.

Hellmann turned out to be the most degrading of all the guards. So was it
in his upbringing? Hellmann came from a middle-class, academic family.
He was a musician and described himself as a scientist at heart. He said he
was a person who lived a natural life, loved music, food and other people;
a person that clearly held great love for his fellow human beings. Both
Hellmann and Burdan were assessed physiologically for abnormalities and
psychologically for their stability to take part in this study and they, like the
prisoners, showed no preference to either be guards or prisoners. So it could
be argued that the situation in which they found themselves had corrupted
their normal way of thinking as they subjected the prisoners to a relentless
series of 'little experiments' (as described by Hellmann).

An example of institutional aggression occurred in the Abu Ghraib prison
atrocities, in which Iraqi prisoners of war were subjected to dehumanising
and degrading treatment. Zimbardo, as the expert witness defending one
of the prison guards, argued that the behaviour of the prison guard was
the product of the situational forces of being a guard in that particular
prison environment, and not due to dispositional characteristics of the
person concerned. Zimbardo's thoughts about Abu Ghraib automatically
focused on the circumstances in the prison cell block that could have
tipped the balance and led even good soldiers to do bad things.

Human behaviour has more than one simple influence, and so the
behaviours witnessed at Abu Ghraib were the result of interplay between
several key factors:

- *Status and power*: those involved were the 'bottom of the barrel'. They
  were army reservists on a night shift. With little of their own power,
  these soldiers were trying to demonstrate some control over anything
  that was inferior to them (i.e. the prisoners). Unlike most military
  personnel, these soldiers even had to take orders from civilians.
  Furthermore, there was often no superior officer checking what they
  were doing.
- *Revenge and retaliation*: revenge for hurting and killing fellow US
  soldiers. Humiliation was used as a way of 'teaching the prisoners a
  lesson'.
- *Deindividuation and helplessness* of the situation: Zimbardo (2007)
  makes reference to the Mardi Gras effect: 'living for the moment
  behind a mask that conceals one's identity and gives vent to
  libidinous, violent and selfish impulses'. In short, you show behaviour
  instantaneously in response to the situation without any planned
  conspiracy or negative reasoning.

Such situational factors combined can be seen as an influence on
behaviour – shaping an otherwise good individual so that they act in an
evil way.

Individualistic (dispositional) causes

It has been suggested that the horrifying behaviours of the soldiers at Abu
Ghraib were, as General Myers (chairman of the Joint Chiefs of Staff)
explained, by 'a few bad apples'; the abuses were not systemic, they were

Aggression

simply the work a few 'rogue soldiers'. This is a very different view, with a very different cause, and it is a common reaction. Here the institutional aggression witnessed is seen to come from the individual themselves, not as a result of the systems and institutions. In police shootings, where there are fatalities and the police are at fault, a certain line of argument seems to emerge. Whenever rank-and-file police officers perform badly, police chiefs attribute the bad behaviour to the few 'bad cops' and claim that it is not representative of the police as a whole. This suggests that there are aspects of a person's disposition that make them more likely or capable of performing aggressive or derogatory actions.

One problem with this view is that we do not completely understand ourselves as human beings. The view assumes that we are rational individuals who uphold our moral responsibilities in every social situation. But do we? When some of their group 'go wrong', most institutions of social control like the military or the police will depersonalise them from the institution. In other words they compare their *individual* behaviour to the otherwise morally superior behaviour of the rest of the institution. But this attitude and position, commonly exhibited by institutions to avoid the wrath of the public as a result of their action, is simply a defence. It hides the reality of human action being largely determined by situational factors. For example, I drive a car along a road, I see a person lying helpless in the road and the situation imposes on me a duty to act in a certain way. In the same way, the situation of Abu Ghraib imposes behaviours on the prison officers. By appreciating the power of situational forces:

> [this] should encourage us to share a profound sense of humility when we are trying to understand the unimaginable, senseless acts of evil: violence, vandalism, suicidal terrorism, torture or rape. Instead of immediately embracing the moral high ground that distances us good folks from the bad ones and gives short shrift to analysis of causal factors in that situation the situational approach gives those 'others' the benefit of attributional charity.

Zimbardo, 2007 (page 320)

Evaluating explanations of institutional aggression

Researching this field of aggression is difficult. To the lay person, an examination of the research available reveals that there are only limited studies that are well documented. Even then researchers have to tease out, often from biographical detail, the essence of individualistic or situational causes that lie behind behaviour.

The evaluation of explanations of institutional aggression might further be exercised through their application in practical situations. Below are some applications of this research.

Security forces

Using Bernard's angry aggression theory to examine the causes of institutionalised aggression in the police, it could be argued that factors such as the chronic stress of police work, along with the inability to respond to the actual sources of that stress, increase the aggressive nature of responses that police make. Bernard's view of there being a police subculture is not new and can be traced back to the earlier work of Westley (1970). Like Westley, Bernard advances the idea that aggression is seen as 'just', 'acceptable' and in some situations 'expected', in part

Hint

How science works

A researcher in this area is dealing with information that is socially sensitive. Thought has to be given as to how the material gained by the research will be collected, used and, most importantly, published. (L)

Furthermore, given the nature of the incidences of institutional aggression, it would be very hard for a researcher to control all variables in these often natural situations. Where there is limited control of variables, cause and effect relationships cannot be established. (F)

because the working environment of most police officers is mainly structured by what Bernard calls codes of deviance, secrecy, silence and cynicism. So it is the working environment of the police officers that in a sense leads them to show aggressive behaviours. Robert Agnew's research (1992) supports this assertion. In this research the general strain theory suggests that negative experiences and stress generate negative **affective states** that may, in the absence of effective coping strategies, lead to violent behaviour.

Strain emerges from negative relationships with others. The strain occurs when individuals feel they are not being treated in a manner that they think is appropriate. If this happens, a subsequent disbelief in the role of others will occur. According to Agnew, it is clearly possible that anger and frustration can result from these negative relationships.

Terrorism

In the analysis of terrorist action, Black (2004) says 'pure terrorism is unilateral self help by organised civilians who covertly inflict mass violence on other civilians'. The idea suggests that the motive behind such action is to improve a situation and this is achieved by imposing negative behaviour such as violence on a mass scale, and applying the principle of collective liability (i.e. targeting random civilians rather than the military). Black believes that the root cause of current terrorism is a culture clash.

Deflem (2004) extends this view by suggesting that the division between situational and dispositional causes may not be as clear as we think. For example, he talks about the 'predatory characteristics' of terrorism that help us to see the terrorist action, but these should be seen within a wider understanding of 'anti-modernist impulses', e.g. an opposition to free markets, liberal democracy and associated Western norms. Deflem says that 'contemporary terrorism represents contrasting institutional balance of power dominated by family, ethnicity and religion'. Barber (1996) had previously made this point with his catchy term 'Jihad versus McWorld'! Barak (2004), looking at suicide terrorists, suggests more of a dispositional nature to this aggressive motive. Barak's writings show how a key motivational component of violent behaviour is issues of shame, esteem and repressed/suppressed anger.

On a lesser scale, this could be compared to the situation of disaffected young males who participate in street violence in a gang or gun culture in the UK or the USA. Often these individuals experience both economic and political marginalisation. However, the main thread of Barak's argument is somewhat lost when we examine the background of many of the 9/11 terrorists, the 7/7 bombers or those that tried to bomb the London Underground system later in 2007. Many of these Islamic terrorists were university educated and came from very supportive and often materially affluent families. We must also be careful when examining the research into terrorist action as there are some methodological flaws.

An analysis of the historical actions of terrorist groups, where the choice to act and the frequency with which they act, does give psychologists an insight into the workings of the group. To some extent, a profile can be developed. However:

- Terrorist action is often unique.
- There is a real lack of empirical data for each terrorist event, so the drawing of conclusions is limited and very difficult to substantiate.

Key terms

Affective states: feelings and emotions.

AQA Examiner's tip

When using the topic of terrorism as an example to which theories of institutional aggression could be applied, make sure that the examiner is aware of your knowledge of the friction between those that believe the cause of terrorist acts are external societal factors and others who would see the cases as being more individual and dispositional. You need to convey in your answer your awareness of dispositional versus situational explanations.

Aggression

Link

Approaches, issues and debates
Aggression, depending on the approach taken, can be seen as having myriad different causes. A comparison between this chapter and the next shows the two sides of a very familiar debate in psychology between nature (the genetic basis) and nurture (the socio-environmental basis) of human behaviour.

There is not really a 'typical terrorist' since terrorist groups are now more fluid and increasingly globally mobile.

Aggressive behaviour seems more dynamic than simply having social or institutional motives. Closer examination of the individual aggressor suggests that much of the observable behaviour that we see has a deeper biological and physiological cause. This is considered in Chapter 11, Biological explanations of aggression.

Key points

- Cue arousal was originally based on the work of Dollard and the links between frustration and aggression. The suggestion is that the presence of aggressive cues in the locality will be enough to act as a cognitive trigger to aggressive action.

- Relative deprivation refers to the inequalities that exist between either one group of people and other groups of people or one individual and other individuals. It is the relative deprivation of 'one' compared to 'another' that is seen as the cause of the aggressive behaviour.

Summary questions

4 Using the quotation from Zimbardo's Stanford Prison experiment (pages 124–5), create a summary statement about the situationalist view.

5 Use a recent news report of either a terrorist action or an incident of police/security force brutality and provide a possible explanation for the behaviour using this situational point of view.

6 Assuming that aggression in the confines of an institution is dispositional, what might you think the characteristics of the individual are? What kind of personality might he/she have?

7 Read the quote from Zimbardo (2007) on page 126. What is he arguing?

8 Consider aggressive over-reaction in the police. To what extent can the views of Bernard and Agnew be supported by your knowledge of up-to-date examples of police aggression? Support your answer with recent occurrences of this behaviour. Could institutional aggression simply be put down to such factors?

9 Is terrorism the irrational action of an individual or a result of the situation in which the person finds themselves? Explain your argument.

11

Biological explanations of aggression

The role of genetic factors

Aggression

Learning objectives:

- understand how biological and physiological processes affect aggressive behaviour

- understand how biological explanations of behaviour are split into genetic, biochemical and neuro-anatomical explanations

- describe the various biological and physiological processes that lie behind aggressive behaviour

- evaluate the effectiveness of the various biological explanations of the cause of aggression.

Link

Approaches, issues and debates

The question of whether aggression is caused by genetic factors links to the wider debate of nature versus nurture. Psychologists with a biological and physiological background tend to see aggression as being singularly influenced by these underlying internal systems. Of course, in reality both environmental influences and internal biological ones are equally as important. They are in many ways two sides of the same coin.

Key terms

47 XYY karyotype: a male with 47 chromosomes. A normal individual will have 46. The extra chromosome is found in the sex chromosomes. For the male with this genetic disorder, they have XYY.

Introduction

Biological explanations of any human behaviour start with the assumption that what causes the behaviour is some internal (rather than external) factor. Often the cause can be reduced to a single biological process, although there is some disagreement as to what that process might actually be. There is a series of paths that bio-psychologists have tended to follow. These can be summarised as:

- genetic influences
- biochemical influences: hormones; the neurotransmitter serotonin
- brain structure influences.

The point that links the different paths is the idea that aggression is simply the by-product of complex internal physiological processes. Social psychological theories do not consider these causes at all.

Is aggression caused by genetics?

Sandberg (1961) first identified what is scientifically known as the **47 XYY karyotype**. Whilst most individuals have 46 chromosomes (23 from each parent), it is possible for a male to have an extra Y sex chromosome, making them XYY. The research of Court-Brown between 1965 and 1967 found that of the sample of 314 patients, those with XYY would be 'best hospitalised due to an increased likelihood of aggressive behaviour'. The request for hospitalisation was based upon common knowledge of traits associated with each of the sexes. Many psychological and medical textbooks of the time adopted this view of XYY males without considering the research critically. Media depictions of XYY males have contributed to the widely held belief that the XYY male is more aggressive.

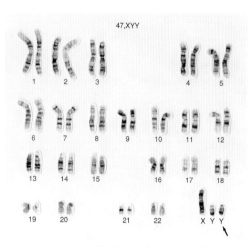

Fig. 1 *A human karyotype from an individual with an extra Y chromosome*

AQA Examiner's tip

When developing your evaluation skills remember that you can evaluate each of the biological explanations on their own, given that their explanations are so fundamentally different. This is in addition to providing evaluative assessment through comparison to other theories more generally.

▍ Hint

How science works

Researchers need to be aware of how society uses science to inform decision making. (L) Court-Brown's claims of what should be done to 47 XXY karyotype individuals ensured that many other academics took at it as read that XXY individuals were dangerously aggressive, when in reality it was a completely different story.

▍ Link

The use of animal research is questionable at the best of times. There are clear arguments both for and against. The use of animals in research is heavily regulated, and only Home Office approved and licensed premises have the ability and permission to conduct such research. The question that must be answered eventually is: does the end finding justify the use of the animal in the research in the first place?

▍ Key terms

Genotype: the genetic make-up of a person.

Thematic apperception testing: a projective psychological test in which the emphasis is on trying to make unconscious thought processes, emotions, etc., conscious.

The link between XYY males and increased aggressiveness was an early assumption that Court-Brown made prior to the examination of the patients. This was a point that was later retracted, although it was too late because many other scientists had incorporated this incorrect view into their thinking. While the XYY genotype may have some effects on the physical make-up of the male (e.g. increased height), XYY males are not likely to show the increased levels of aggression that researchers in the 1960s suggested.

How aggression is passed from generation to generation has been looked at through animal studies. Nelson (2006) noted that selective breeding experiments can lead to more aggressive behaviour in animals. Earlier, Cairns (1983) showed this in his study of mice. He created highly aggressive males and females that would show their aggressiveness in middle age rather than when they were young or old. This research on selective breeding techniques shows how important genetic processes are to understanding human behaviour. Obviously these are observations of animals, and the issues about generalising from animals to humans are relevant here. Science is limited in this respect by the ethics of using humans in genetic research. Whilst the study of animals cannot give us a true understanding of aggression in humans, studying a wider range of animals allows researchers to create more informed models.

In 1984 Theilgaard researched the personality traits of XYY men compared to XY men and men with XXY (thought to be more feminine). Part of the research compared the aggressiveness of the XYY to XY men. Theilgaard's background research showed that about 1 in 1,000 males are XYY, and that 'no single characteristic except height … has been associated with the XYY condition'. Since research in this area is conflicting, it is not possible to conclude that XYY alone causes increased aggression. Research that examines the behaviour of XYY males seems to show no consistent link between **genotype** and aggressive nature. The basic measure of looking at XYY and XY males who are inmates in prisons and comparing this to the general population does not provide a consistent objective measure of the validity of this view. Using **thematic apperception testing**, Theilgaard showed that XYY men tend to give more aggressive and less anti-aggressive interpretations of the images used in the thematic apperception test (e.g. images similar to Rorschach ink blots) compared to XY males. She therefore concluded that the issue is complex: XYY males might seem to be more aggressive, but these tendencies did not mean that they would readily perform acts that were violent and resulted in prison or institutionalisation.

▍ Hint

Research ethics limit the content of research to some degree, particularly research that directly involves human participants. By studying as many different animals as possible, while models might not be 100 per cent accurate for humans, they are at least formed on wide-ranging research.

▍ Link

Approaches, issues and debates

Any view that simply focuses on genetics as the cause for aggression is reductionistic because it has no scope to appreciate other influences on this behaviour, for example biochemical and aspects of brain structure.

Evaluation of genetic factors in aggressive behaviour

Table 1 *Genetic factors in aggressive behaviour*

Claim	Evidence for	Evidence against
Genetics can be seen as the only influence on aggressive behaviour	As the research of the XYY karyotype suggests (Sandberg, 1961; Nelson, 2006; Cairns, 1983), using both animal research and research observations in humans with this condition, a greater number of aggressive behaviours tend to be reported	Theilgaard (1984) appears to be right when she says that the issue as a whole is complex, since there are potentially many influences on behaviour, e.g. biochemistry (hormones and neurotransmitters) and neurophysiology (brain structure and the effects of brain damage)
Through genetic transmission, aggression can be passed from one generation to another	Animal studies have examined this (e.g. Nelson, 2006), and selective breeding experiments showed how this was possible	It is very difficult to separate the influence of genetics (nature) from environmental upbringing (nurture). An aggressive environment can also lead to those aggressive traits being shown
Social/environmental factors are played down as influences of aggression	Some evidence, and the media coverage of the issue, seem to strengthen the view that genetics are bound up with the behaviour of the XYY individuals	See Chapter 10 (Social psychological approaches to explaining aggression), examining explanations such as social learning theory, deindividuation, cue arousal and relative deprivation, which show that there are clearly social/environmental influences that simply cannot be ignored

Key points

- Sandberg (1961) first identified the 47 XYY karyotype. Court-Brown's research between 1965 and 1967 suggested that such individuals needed to be hospitalised (a statement that was not substantiated with evidence).

- The media have encouraged the belief in the XYY phenomenon with programmes such as *Doom Watch* and films such as *Alien 3* and *XYY Man*. This limits the potential for explaining aggression by other means due to its deterministic focus.

- Animal studies using selective breeding techniques support a genetic base. While generalisation from animal studies is limited, this research nevertheless shows the importance of understanding genetic processes and foundations of behaviour.

- Theilgaard (1984) examined the personality traits of a sample of XYY men and compared these to a sample of XY men. She focused on levels of aggressiveness between the two groups.

- Theilgaard's research concluded that in all occurrences of XYY (about 1 in every 1,000) the only factor that seems to be linked is their height. Levels of aggressiveness fluctuated so no definitive conclusion could be drawn.

Take it further

Using the internet, investigate the XYY phenomenon. Think about the following question:

- To what extent can genetics alone explain the causes of aggressive behaviour?

Summary questions

1. How many chromosomes does the XYY male have?

2. How common is this genetic disorder?

3. Critically analyse the contribution of genetics to our understanding of aggressive behaviour.

Aggression

The role of neural and hormonal mechanisms in aggression

Learning objectives:

■ understand the effect of hormones on aggressive behaviour

■ understand how hormones and selected neurotransmitters can influence aggressive behaviour

■ evaluate the contribution of research into neural and hormonal influences on aggressive behaviour.

AQA Examiner's tip

Reference to specific relevant court cases such as these shows how the psychology you are discussing has real-life consequences. Such examples inform your commentary.

Key terms

Androgens: male sex hormones, the most important one being testosterone.

Leydig cells: a system of cells in the testes that make testosterone.

Circadian rhythm: biological rhythms with a cycle length of 24 hours.

Link

Approaches, issues and debates

Much scientific research takes place in Western, industrialised societies, which are often where the facilities for research can be found and the financial incentives to study it. This can mean it is culturally specific and generalisation to other cultures is more difficult and subject to cultural biases.

Hormonal influences on aggressive behaviour

This topic considers biochemical influences on aggressive behaviour. Hormones seem to affect many aspects of our life. In the UK since the 1980s there has been a series of high-profile cases where hormonal fluctuations surrounding pre-menstrual tension have been used as grounds for claims of temporary insanity. In *R* v *Smith* (1979) 3 All ER 605, 611 (CA) (and in a range of other related cases since), a murder charge was successfully reduced to manslaughter when PMT was taken as a contributory factor behind the killing that occurred.

The lawyers acting for the females in these cases argued that their clients were acting as 'automatons' of their body. Here, the aggressive act is said to be caused by uncontrollable hormonal changes associated with the monthly cycle. Nelson (1995) reviewed research into how hormones influence aggressive behaviour. Generally there does seem to be a positive correlation between the level of **androgens** circulating in the body and aggressive behaviour in female and male prisoners. Methodologically such assertions weaken, since levels of androgens were not measured at the precise point when the aggressive act was being performed. Therefore, we cannot be 100 per cent sure that this was the only variable affecting behaviour.

Testosterone is an androgen and it is produced by the **Leydig cells** in the male testes and in the adrenal cortex. The release of this hormone is rhythmic following a natural **circadian rhythm**. Evidence could be used to argue that androgens have an effect on aggression. For example, during puberty aggression increases when androgen levels are higher (especially in males as androgens have masculinising effects). Animal research further supports these conclusions. Wagner, Beuving and Hutchinson (1979) show that if a male mouse is castrated, overall levels of aggression tend to reduce. If the castrated mouse receives testosterone aggression levels increase. Results are plotted on the graph in Figure 2.

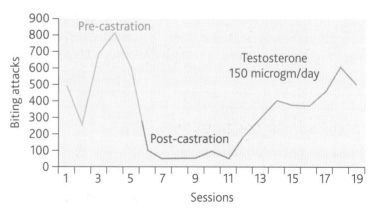

Fig. 2 *Graph showing the changing levels of aggression shown in male mice pre- and post-castration*

Wagner *et al.*'s research is correlational. But, as for all correlations, you cannot establish cause and effect. It cannot be stated that hormones cause aggressive behaviour. In males, androgens encourage aggressive behaviour to be shown, but likewise they could encourage social dominance, impulsiveness and competition. It is probably not surprising that Pillay (2006) noted that testosterone has long been associated with varying athletic qualities, including 'aggressive behaviour and spatial abilities'. In his study of 94 athletes testosterone levels differed according to which sport was played (soccer, wrestling, basketball, softball and swimming). Using samples of saliva, the level of testosterone was measured. The results indicated that those males and females in aggressive sports had the highest level of testosterone. Kimura (1999) adds to this finding, noting that female spatial ability also tends to improve with high levels of testosterone. So the outcome of high testosterone levels is not always negative and aggressive. In her review of the role of testosterone in aggression, Simpson (2001) argues that 'testosterone is only one of a myriad of factors that influence aggression and the effects of environmental stimuli have at times been found to correlate more strongly'.

This ignores the potential for individual difference. Harisson *et al.* (2000) noted that after giving testosterone to 56 men (aged 20–50), when given a frustration-inducing computer game, aggressive responses were significantly increased. But this effect was not the same for the entire sample. If anything, the changes were largely psychological and few had any noticeable physical effect on behaviour.

However, what is clear is that testosterone does have a role to play in this complex formula of human aggressive behaviour. In their 2007 research, Huston *et al.* show how men with high levels of testosterone often perform well in competitive tasks but poorly on cooperative tasks. The **basal model of testosterone** would suggest that testosterone causes a change in a person's dominance. The more testosterone that a person has, the more competitive and dominant they become. It follows that a man with a high level of testosterone will take part in antisocial behaviour (such as fighting or showing other signs of aggression), and on the whole will be more dominating. Support for this assertion comes from Mazur and Booth (1998) who, after reviewing a number of studies in this field, concluded that men with higher levels of testosterone 'are more likely to divorce, or remain single; be arrested for offences other than traffic violations; to buy and sell stolen property; to incur bad debts; and to use weapons in fights'. The **reciprocal model of testosterone** effect suggests that testosterone levels vary with the person's dominance. The level of the testosterone is the effect of, and not the cause of, the dominance. This can be seen more clearly in Mazur and Booth (1998) where 2,100 air force veterans were studied. Over a 10-year period, the veterans were given four medical examinations. Interestingly their testosterone levels varied – they reduced when married and increased upon divorce. This finding is consistent with Mazur and Booth's original view.

Serotonin and aggression

Serotonin is a neurotransmitter. Over the last 50 years there have been numerous investigations into the effect of serotonin on aggression and these have involved a variety of animals. Research in this area suggests that the serotonin influences aggressive and violent behaviour. Davidson, Putnam and Larson (2000) suggested that serotonin may provide an *inhibitory function* so that when comparing violent criminals to

---

AQA Examiner's tip

You might not recall the exact results of the study, but if you remember the broad trend in results it will be enough to support your case that hormone replacement on castrated mice increases levels of aggression.

Hint

How science works

Mazur and Booth's review of literature in their research is highly selective. The research that they cite is research that often has not been reviewed by peers. This is a weakness methodologically since peer review is an essential means of establishing the validity of research. (K)

Key terms

Basal model of testosterone: the model that suggests that an individual's level of testosterone influences their level of dominance. The more testosterone, the more competitive and hence more dominant they become. Dominance here is the effect of testosterone.

Reciprocal model of testosterone: this is the reverse of the basal model of testosterone, and suggests that testosterone levels are influenced by changes in the level of dominance that an individual has.

Link

Approaches, issues and debates

If it is the case that the reduction of serotonin increases the incidence showing aggressive behaviour as Davidson, Putnam and Larson (2000) seem to suggest, then this views human behaviour in a very deterministic fashion after all – the showing of aggressive behaviour seems not to be the result of free will.

Aggression

Key terms

Serotonin 1B receptor: also known as HTR1B, this is a neurotransmitter that acts on the central nervous system inducing behavioural changes.

CSF: cerebrospinal fluid – a colourless solution that bathes and protects the brain and spinal cord.

Tryptophan: an amino acid found in food that is essential to the production of the neurotransmitter serotonin in the brain.

Serotonergic: containing or releasing serotonin.

Hint

How science works

The study of this negative relationship between serotonin and aggression is based upon correlation research. Such research does not allow for cause and effect relationships to be unequivocally established. (E)

AQA Examiner's tip

Descriptive comments on neurotransmitters are complex at the best of times, so keep your comments brief and to the point. Where possible reinforce what you say with a practical example such as those found below.

non-violent ones, the levels of serotonin found in violent criminals were markedly lower. Research on mice where the **serotonin 1B receptor** was not functioning found an increase in aggressive behaviour, a point that was further reinforced by research involving Vervet monkeys. Reducing the serotonin levels of the monkeys resulted in an increase in aggressive behaviour, whereas increasing serotonin levels resulted in a decrease in aggressive occurrences.

Serotonin (also known as 5-hydroxytryptamine – 5HT), has effects all over the body. It would seem that 'low serotonin levels in the brain can result in impulsive behaviour, aggression, overeating, depression, alcohol abuse and violent suicide' (Lenard, 2008).

Studies of domestic pets, which have been bred for reduced aggression, show that they seem to have higher levels of serotonin. Researchers in Russia looked at silver foxes; these animals have been tamed by humans for more than 30 years. They found that they all had higher levels of serotonin and 5-HIAA (5-hydroxyindoleacetic acid) than would normally be expected. They also had a higher level of tryptophan hydroxylase (an essential enzyme used in the production of serotonin) and a lower level of monoamine oxidase (an enzyme that is essential for removing serotonin from the synapse). In the USA, NIAAA (the National Institute of Alcohol Abuse and Alcoholism) investigators took blood and **CSF** samples from 49 free-ranging monkeys living on an island. They found that:

> those monkeys with the lowest serotonin levels stand the greatest chance of getting injured and/or dying young ... monkeys with greater serotonin levels spent more time grooming other group members and stayed in close proximity to others ... in other words they were more affectionate.

Lenard, 2008

Reducing serotonin increases aggressive tendencies. This is consistent with the work of Linnoila and Virkkunen (1992) who reported that low levels of serotonin are linked to 'impulsivity and explosive acts of violence'. As Cleare and Bond (1997) poetically put it, 'serotonin depletion tends to ruffle people's feathers'. In clinical trials, **tryptophan** on its own or combined with Desyrel 5HTP (a **serotonergic** drug) has historically been given to juvenile delinquents (Morand *et al.*, 1983) and unpredictable institutionalised patients (Greenwald, Marin and Silverman, 1986) to reduce their aggressive tendencies.

Caution should still be used before simply attributing the cause of aggression to serotonin levels. Summers *et al.* (2005) observed in their research that globally acting serotonergic drugs do modify aggressive behaviour, but this cannot be singularly identified as the only cause of activity in regions of the brain that could ultimately have serotonergic effects on aggression.

Hint

In any research, when using human subjects the issue of the ethical treatment of humans becomes apparent. Scientists have a duty to ensure that their research looks after (rather than uses) participants as a means by which to further understand and make better our human existence. The following of humanistic, moral and religious beliefs ensures that psychology can continue to use members of the public in their investigations. The question is whether all research is so ethically sound.

Evaluation of neural and hormonal factors in aggressive behaviour

Table 2 *Neural and hormonal factors in aggressive behaviour*

Claim	Evidence for	Evidence against
Hormones control aggressive behaviour	There is no doubt that levels of testosterone and their influence on aggression have been well documented in animal studies (Wagner *et al.*, 1979) and in humans (Nelson, 1995). Research shows that testosterone – an androgen – tends to be linked to higher levels of aggression at the points in life when testosterone is plentiful, e.g. puberty. High testosterone levels can be desirable for athletes (Pillay, 2006) given the link to high levels of competition and the athletes' need for more muscular bodies	Remember what Simpson said: 'testosterone is only one of a myriad of factors that influence aggression and the effects of environmental stimuli have at times been found to correlate more strongly' (Simpson, 2001). Other environmental factors such as temperature, noise and overcrowding have an influential role in the showing of aggressive behaviour
Neurotransmitters influence aggressive and violent behaviour	Davidson *et al.* (2000) would argue that the role of serotonin is to inhibit aggressive tendencies. Certainly research on animals supports this conclusion – since when rats have low levels of serotonin an increase in aggressive behaviour is seen. Tame domestic pets have much higher levels of serotonin. Serotonin has an influence, but it is not the only influence on behaviour	Neurotransmitters on their own, out of the context of the wider physiology of the brain, ignore the influence that brain structure has on demonstrating aggressive behaviour. The case of Phineas Gage is a good example of an individual who after suffering brain injury showed heightened levels of aggression (see page 136)

Brain structure and aggression

It is a mistake to just assume that aggressive behaviour is simply the result of abnormal levels of brain neurotransmitters or fluctuating levels of bodily hormones, since underlying these systems are the fundamental structures of the brain. These are a finely tuned set of systems that work together. Research in this area is varied, but it seems to agree that systems such as the hypothalamus and amygdala are associated with aggressive responses. Although dated, in the 1940s Bard and Mountcastle (1948) looked at 'rage' in cats caused by a detachment of the higher and lower brain through lesioning. From this they concluded that it is the hypothalamus that initiates the aggressive behaviour, and the cerebral cortex that reduces this behaviour. In the 1960s, Flynn (2006) found that stimulating the lateral hypothalamus in cats made them more likely to show 'predatorial aggression', but when the medial hypothalamus was stimulated 'vicious attack behaviour' was more likely.

As well as the effect of the hypothalamus on aggressive response behaviours shown by humans, research has suggested that the amygdala might also be part of this system. This was initially investigated as far back as the 1930s, when the careful lesioning of the amygdala of aggressive animals was shown to have a taming effect. In humans, if an **amygdalectomy** is carried out it reduces violent behaviour, although this comes at a high price as emotion is also lost.

Social regulation and social interaction are functions that involve the frontal cortex, and aggressive behaviours are part of our social interaction repertoire. Research has shown that the frontal cortex is closely connected to the functioning of the amygdala and hypothalamus, and therefore it is in a good position to influence the other brain areas that stimulate aggressive responses. Individuals with frontal lobe damage often show impulsive behaviour, irritability, shortness of temper and they are easily provoked. One of the best examples of such brain injury is that

Hint

Animal research indicates that specific locations of the brain can be stimulated, resulting in the showing of aggressive behaviour. The difficulty for the researching psychologist is that they need to be absolutely sure that the same is true of humans. After all, the human brain is far more complex than that of many animals.

AQA Examiner's tip

Animal studies provide one source of evidence for the influence of brain structure on aggressive behaviour. But these are only animal studies. A human reference is needed. Phineas Gage is a well-documented human example which provides evidence of how aggressive behaviour was influenced by brain injury.

Key terms

Amygdalectomy: surgical removal of part of the brain called the amygdala. The amygdala is a structure of the limbic system in the anterior temporal lobe that is responsible for processing emotions.

Aggression

■ **Take it further**

Use the internet to investigate the case of Phineas Gage.

■ Describe what actually happened to him.

■ Critically analyse the extent to which Gage's case provides evidence for the argument that brain structure influences aggressive behaviour. Make sure you explain your answer.

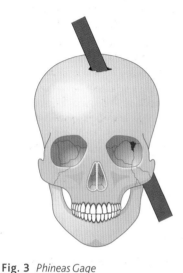

Fig. 3 *Phineas Gage*

of a railway worker called Phineas Gage. Gage was studied in detail by his physician Harlow who published research on him in 1868.

Gage was the foreman of a work gang responsible for excavating rock in preparation for the construction of a new railway just outside Cavendish, Vermont, USA. On 13 September 1848, there was an accident. A tamping iron, which was 1.1 m long and just over 3 cm in diameter, entered the left side of Gage's face, passed through his jaw, up and behind his left eye and exited through the top of his head. Amazingly, after leaving hospital Gage managed to survive some 11 years following the accident, but there were noticeable changes in his persona – he was unable to stay in a job for very long and he became aggressive.

Animal research conducted by Zagrodzka *et al.* (1998) using cats showed that damage to the central nucleus of the amygdala was a significant contributory factor to 'predator-like' attacks. Interestingly in laboratory-based research (Potegal, Ferris and Delville, 1994) involving rats, the corticomedial amygdala was identified as a potential centre for mediating and regulating aggressive reaction. Potegal (1991) showed that hamsters have more active neurons in and around the medial nucleus of the amygdala during acts of aggression. No other increases in neural activity were recorded in any other areas. Such research does inevitably relate to work performed on animals. Yet Potegal *et al.* (1994) argue that generalisation between animals and humans should be more viable – human and animal differences are *qualitative* (i.e. the basics are the same, but the details are different). The underlying neural circuitry related to emotional expression seems more similar, allowing for more avenues of generalisation. This assertion is supported by the work of Blair, Colledge and Mitchell (2001). Blair *et al.* studied aggression in humans that had been institutionalised due to psychopathic tendencies. He proposed that psychopathy involves damage to the amygdala, and this is further supported by various findings in non-human animals.

■ Evaluating the brain structure argument

Table 3 *The brain structure argument*

Claim	Evidence for	Evidence against
Brain injury or damage causes people to become aggressive	Phineas Gage is an example of how an otherwise quiet, hard-working and shrewd character can be turned into a very negative and aggressive individual as the result of a brain injury	It is easy to assume that brain injury can cause a change in behaviour. Gage's case is very convincing. But this is a case study of just one individual. So generalisability is limited. Furthermore, we are relying on the accuracy of the medical notes made by Harlow (Gage's physician)
The amygdala has an influential effect on mediating aggressive responses	Studies involving cats, rats and hamsters show that neural processes surrounding amygdala functioning can explain aggressive changes in behaviour. Research by Blair *et al.* (2001) shows that in cases where humans have been hospitalised for psychopathic tendencies, this is often caused by damage to the amygdala	A lot of research into the influence of the amygdala on aggressive behaviour stems from animal research – so there are problems of generalisation. This is disputed by Potegal *et al.* (1994)

To assume that aggressive behaviour has just one cause – either genetic or hormonal or brain-structural – is too simple, since such a narrow focus ignores the myriad of other factors that contribute to aggressive behaviour.

There are theoretical differences between explanations of aggression. But even then, a narrow focus just on biological factors ignores the fact that culture might influence the aggressive behaviours shown as a result of socialisation, as in the Arapesh tribe (Mead, 1935) or the Simbu tribal people (Brown, 1986). Anderson and Dill (2000) and Freedman (2002) argue that aggression might be learned through observing the various forms of media available to people. Biological views also ignore situational factors. For example, Bushman (1993, 1997) and MacDonald, Zanna and Fong (1996) show how alcohol disrupts information processing – so an accidental comment or behaviour is interpreted as meaningful, therefore contributing ultimately towards aggressive behaviour. Other situational factors such as temperature, crowding or even noise can explain aggressive behaviour (Carlsmith and Anderson, 1979; Kenrick and MacFarlane, 1986). Finally, the biological approach ignores the argument that the showing of aggressive behaviour might simply be the result of frustration, which ultimately becomes an aggressive action through the identification of aggressive cues in the environment.

Key points

- Hormones seem to influence many parts of our lives. Cases in court have shown that a woman's pre-menstrual tension can be used to reduce a charge of murder to manslaughter.

- Animal research shows that raised levels of testosterone lead to aggressive behaviour.

- Serotonin has also been identified has having an influence on the showing of aggressive behaviours. It is argued that serotonin has an inhibitory function. That is, it stops such behaviours. So if serotonin levels are low, its inhibitory effect is reduced and this results in more aggressive behaviours being witnessed.

- Increased levels of testosterone have been associated with increased levels of aggression. Levels of testosterone seem to fluctuate over time. Levels have been seen to increase during puberty (and more aggressive behaviours are shown), to decrease upon marriage and to increase upon divorce.

- Physical damage to the brain can alter the processing of information. Cases such as that of Phineas Gage show that when damage does occur, the resulting changes in behaviour are dramatic.

Summary questions

4 Which hormones in particular have been studied in psychological research of aggressive behaviour? Why?

5 What is serotonin and what appears to be its function?

6 Brain structure explains aggressive behaviour. Discuss.

■ Take it further

You are asked to prepare to present a seminar on the biological explanations of aggression. Your audience will be non-psychologists, but you have to ensure that they understand what influence each biological factor has on aggressive behaviour. You therefore need to either (a) produce a PowerPoint slide show, or (b) create an A3 summary mind map.

For both the slide show and the mind map you need to do the following:

- Describe what biological influences there are on aggressive behaviour. How do they influence levels of aggression? (Be specific.)

- Critically evaluate these different influences on aggressive behaviour. (Consider the explanation but also the methodology of the studies used to support them.)

■ Link

Approaches, issues and debates

Animal research reveals some neurological and biochemical influences upon aggression. The question is, does the end result of animal research justify the means? Researchers need to consider the ethical issues. Bateson (1986) emphasised the need to maintain a delicate balance between the advancing of psychological understanding while also trying to ensure that any suffering experienced is limited.

Aggression

Evolutionary explanations of human aggression

Learning objectives:

- understand how evolutionary psychology explains aggression
- explain how jealousy and infidelity can influence aggressive behaviour
- understand how to evaluate evolutionary explanations of behaviour.

Link

Approaches, issues and debates

The evolutionary approach embodies the view that the behaviours and cognitive processes that enable an individual to survive will ultimately be passed on to the next generation as part of an inherent survival strategy. This belief firmly implicates this evolutionary psychology within the nature side of the nature–nurture debate.

Key terms

Ethologist: someone who studies animal behaviour.

What is evolutionary psychology?

Evolutionary psychology is not an area within psychology as such; it is a way of viewing or thinking about topics within it. Evolutionary psychology traditionally combines Anthropology, cognitive science, neuroscience and evolutionary biology are all combined in the approach taken by evolutionary psychology to areas of human behaviour such as aggression. Evolutionary psychologists believe that innate brain function and knowledge both help the individual to adapt to their environment.

The evolutionary psychologist takes the view that by understanding the human brain and the way it has evolved we will be able to explain behaviours such as aggression. Evolutionary psychologists try to identify how aggression developed in the first place. They would say knowing the evolutionary roots of aggression helps us to understand it today.

Evolutionary psychologists use a variety of forms of evidence to substantiate their claims. Both human and animal research have been used.

Aggressive behaviour by animals

Craig (1921) provided the first major attempt at understanding aggression from the ethological point of view since Darwin's work in the late 1800s. Craig made it clear that, in animals, 'even when the animal does fight, he aims not to destroy the enemy, but only to get rid of his presence and interference' (Van Der Dennen, 2005). Animals do not necessarily try and kill other animals in their fights; their aim is to get the attacker to back down or submit, and they will only use physical force if necessary.

Lorenz (1966) was an **ethologist** who wrote a famous book, *On Aggression*. In it he stressed that humans are animals and therefore show similar behaviour patterns to animals. For Lorenz there were four main drivers behind the behaviour of any animal (human or not). These were: fear, reproduction, hunger and aggression. At the core of Lorenz's argument was the idea that aggression itself could *only* occur within (and not between) a species.

For Lorenz, the functions of aggression were:

- It would help to ensure that only the fittest and strongest were selected (females select males as mates who appear to offer the greatest chance of survival for them and their offspring).
- It would ensure survival of the young (parents show aggression in protecting their offspring against predators).
- It would help to distribute a species in a balanced way as animals would have their own territories.

Lorenz noted that there are several types of social organisation and relationships, for example, family and social life, tribes and rat packs, anonymous crowds and love and friendship. In each, the type of aggression that may be shown is very different. For example, the aggression surrounding family and social life differs dramatically from that related to rat packs and tribes. Lorenz formulated the idea that animals show **ritualised aggression**. Like Craig (1921), he noted that often little harm was observed as a result of ritualised aggression. For example, when stags show ritualistic rutting behaviour, they seem to be very aggressive, but rarely is any real damage done.

Morris (1990) states that animal disputes show a remarkable amount of restraint. Gross (1998) refers to jackdaw behaviour to illustrate this. Even when two jackdaws are about to attack each other, if one displays an **appeasement tactic**, for example showing the nape of its neck to the aggressor, the other jackdaw will not attack.

Lorenz's work has been criticised by other ethologists and academics from different disciplines. Some researchers have argued that Lorenz's research is simply outdated. Barnet (1973) states that Lorenz's work 'does not in fact represent the methods or opinions current in **ethology**'. Other scientists have suggested that Lorenz perhaps oversimplified his explanations by suggesting there are parallels between non-human animals and humans. For example, Lehrman (1953) questions whether it is correct for a researcher to make comparisons between species and assume that what might be true for animals might be the same for humans. He suggests that even though two behaviours seem similar, we cannot necessarily assume that the underlying mechanisms are similar.

Aggressive behaviour by humans

Fromm (1973) also questions Lorenz's view. He states that human aggression comprises two forms – **benign aggression** and **malignant aggression**. Examples of malignant aggression include organised violence such as gang warfare, the ethnic cleansing in Serbia or the attempted eradication of Jews from Germany during the Second World War. An example of benign aggression in humans is that of a parent defending their child from harm by attacking the threat.

Nelson (1974) states that Lorenz should have considered three basic factors that can affect aggression:

▥ The process of learning: Bandura shows how people may learn aggressive behaviour through the observation of others. We know that aggressive impulses can be shaped through learning strategies (as is shown in anger management programmes, for example).

▥ Structural causes: according to Nelson, structural causes relate to the nature of social life. If you think about it, a society without norms or rules is one where aggression is likely to be widespread.

▥ Psychological causes of aggression: psychological explanations highlight the failings of the biological approach. In the animal kingdom, often the aggressive action is directed towards an 'actual enemy', for example a threat or challenge, but in humans often this is not the case since aggression can be motivated by many different personal factors (e.g. mood or feelings) and situational factors (e.g. heat or over-crowding).

In some cases of human aggression the victims of the violence and aggression are not even thought of as fellow humans (Fromm, 1964; Erikson, 1956). This might be the case particularly in situations of unprovoked random attacks. Rapoport (1965) explains this further by suggesting that 'man by virtue of his ability to manipulate symbols, attaches the label ìenemyî to entire categories of things: other animals,

Fig. 1 *Stags rutting*

▥ Key terms

Ritualised aggression: the showing of aggression as a basis for the assertion of power and maintenance of status.

Appeasement tactic: a behaviour that, if shown, stops the aggression by the competitor, and avoids imminent injury. The animal that uses this tactic admits defeat and shows submissive behaviour.

Ethology: the study of animal behaviour.

Benign aggression: this is similar to animal aggression, it involves an impulsive act if threatened.

Malignant aggression: an evil act, not instinctive.

■ Hint

How science works

Lehrman (1953) questioning an issue is a characteristic of science (**B**). Scientists are expected to evaluate methodology, evidence and data, and resolve conflicting evidence (**F**). The criticisms are well-founded here since he is questioning the robustness of the evolutionary psychologists' generalisations from animals to humans.

Aggression

other people, even inanimate objects and ideas … accordingly aggression ceases to be lead by the situation.'

There are significant differences between animals and humans, which makes generalisation almost impossible. The aggression shown in humans might well be adaptive and useful, i.e. a product of evolution, but it is not usually ritualistic, although it can be. In fact, it could be argued that the use of weapons by humans means that aggression is destructive and not ritualistic. This is a view that is broadly shared by Tinbergen (1968), who suggests that while humans, like 'animals' might fight each other, humans are the only species in which aggression is not part of an elaborate system of ritual (e.g. for mating) but is rooted in a deep desire to harm another.

■ Evolutionary explanations of human aggression

The acts of terrorists such as those on 9/11 or war in general can also be explained through the application of Tinbergen's ideas and evolutionary theory. Advances in weapons technology mean that aggressors no longer need to be physically close to those they are attacking. Terrorists use their actions to cause fear, and in war the use of weapons technology distances the aggressor from the recipient of the aggression. As Tinbergen notes, the crews of planes that are eager to drop bombs on a 'target' would often not be so eager to stab or burn children (or adults) with their own hands. Because attackers are no longer physically close to their targets, it is likely to be the case that appeasement or distress signals that would have stopped acts of aggression no longer apply.

According to Krueger *et al.* (2002), the evolutionary approach concerns itself with how the skills and the methods of dealing with the environment have evolved into behaviours used in today's society. Many of these evolutionary changes were seen in the **Pleistocene era**. Evolutionary psychologists have argued that since then, human evolution has generally been static (e.g. Brody *et al.*, 2004). The evolutionary psychologists believe that a series of psychological mechanisms affect behaviour and these do not vary much between individuals (they are *universal*). They think that the behaviour witnessed is very closely linked to the **reproductive success** of the individual.

Therefore, the evolutionary psychologist would be most likely to suggest that aggression is the result of sexual competition. Females invest heavily in terms of parental issues (e.g. time, energy, food, etc.). The males compete for females so that they can pass on their genes. Evolutionary psychologists show that aggressive behaviour in males is a means by which they can ensure their reproductive success. For example, Kenrick, Trost and Sheets (1996) state that men have to compete with other men in order to gain access to women. The dominant image for a man nowadays is 'a provider of valuable resources'. What this means practically is that men need to be more assertive and aggressive.

Waller (2002) has applied aspects of the evolutionary perspective to explain mass killings and genocide. He noted that humans have evolved living in groups and so they have needed to define the boundaries of behaviour of the group, formulating an in group ('us') and an out group ('them'). This way of thinking about 'us' and 'them' is of course likely to result in aggression. Waller suggests that such examples of behaviour could be caused by our ancestral past, in which **xenophobia**, the need for people to feel socially dominant and the holding of ethnocentric perspectives, together, lead to acts of aggression and violence.

AQA Examiner's tip

Remember that the examiner wants to see that you understand the theory you are writing about. The news is full of examples of acts of aggression that are committed daily. Try applying your knowledge of theories to current news stories.

■ Key terms

Pleistocene era: a period of time between 1.8 million and 11.5 million years ago.

Reproductive success: refers to the process of successfully passing on your genes to the next generation. This is measured by the number of surviving offspring left behind by an individual.

Xenophobia: a general dislike or fear of people from other countries or cultures.

Link

See Chapter 8, Human reproductive behaviour, for more on sexual selection.

Such evolutionary explanations of aggression are plausible. Anitei (2007) focuses on *Australopithecus* (the first grouping of common ape ancestors of the human), who lived about 4 million years ago and had remarkably small stumpy legs, which meant they could hold a strong squat position, useful in male-male combat. They held this adaptive characteristic for over 2 million years.

Buss (1999) reminds us that it would be foolish to assume that aggressive behaviour was just male versus male. While male-to-male violence could explain some instances of aggression, it cannot explain all. The use and form of aggression by women has redeveloped. In women, physical aggression is limited, in part as a result of physiological differences and strength, but verbal aggression is more common. Buss comments how female-to-female verbal aggression is often aimed at reducing the 'attractiveness' of competitors in the eyes of males, a strategy which would have evolutionary advantage for the name-caller.

The influence of infidelity on aggressive behaviour

Infidelity means the process of being unfaithful to your partner, which ultimately includes having sexual relationships with someone other than your partner. Undoubtedly the infidelity of one partner has an impact not only on the relationship as a whole but also on the quality of interpersonal communications between partners and others. Evolutionary psychologists argue that the act of infidelity triggers an emotional state within the individual as it is a perceived threat to the relationship and the current status quo. Buss, Larsen, Western and Semmelroth (1992) argued that this would naturally lead to the showing of behaviours that would reduce and eliminate the threat. Often such action is violent or aggressive.

Sexual infidelity for both males and females ultimately triggers sexual jealousy. But evolutionary psychology suggests that these cues or triggers are different for males and females. Brunk *et al.* (1996) suggest that from the male's point of view, infidelity by a female brings with it not only uncertainty of paternity, but also a profound sense of sexual jealousy. However, for the female that becomes pregnant after an act of infidelity, the associated sexual jealousy is influenced not by parental uncertainty but by the lack of time or economic resources that are given to her and her offspring by her mate. Indeed, Brunk *et al.* (1996) assert that it is the lack of emotional support that makes most women aggressive, whereas for men anger and subsequent aggression is based upon suspicion of the wife's infidelity.

What does become clear is that infidelity and subsequent jealousy both contribute to aggressive action.

The influence of jealousy

Nowadays it is not unusual on a night out at a pub, club or social event to witness violence or acts of aggression that have been influenced by jealousy. Harvey, Sprecher and Wenzel (2004) summarise research in this area. The research is varied and focuses on different causal factors behind the jealousy. According to Cascardi and Vivian (1995), when participants of studies are asked to explain the cause of the aggression in the relationship, jealousy is the most commonly attributed cause. Other work has suggested that this is a reliable finding. For example, researchers Canary, Spitzberg and Semic (1998) argue that couples with relationship conflicts commonly reported that the anger and aggression was contributed to by jealousy. However, it may also be the case that

Hint

How science works

Scientists, through their research into incidents of aggression such as 9/11 or war in general, are aware that their research has very real applications and implications (L). Indeed, ideally most researchers would assert that their principal aim is to encourage 'human betterment' through a better understanding of the social behaviours that we show, for example aggression.

Link

Approaches, issues and debates

By looking at infidelity and jealousy from the perspective of both males and females, evolutionary psychologists take steps to avoid gender bias in their research into explanations of aggression.

Aggression

AQA Examiner's tip

Society is riddled with social problems, not least the aggressiveness that is often witnessed after a night out partying. Try applying your knowledge of explanations to this sort of event to illustrate your point.

■ Link

Approaches, issues and debates

Evolutionary psychologists state jealousy can be explained adaptively through mate retention, suggesting that this behaviour is aimed at species survival. Any trait with survival value is a trait that is passed on in further generations. A further example of the 'nature' side of the nature–nurture debate.

some violent males lack effective ways of mediating and responding to situations of jealousy, compared to non-violent males (Holtzworth-Monroe and Anglin (1991). In conclusion, Harvey *et al*. show us that the underlying possible influences of jealousy are complex and often multidimensional.

Haden and Hojjat (2006) comment on the differences in sexual jealousy of young women and men. They focus on aggressive responsiveness in situations of partner rivalry. In two separate studies they found that men were more likely than women to consider aggressive action against the rival, whereas women tended to be more emotionally and behaviourally reactive. In the USA, Morenz and Lane (1996) observed that 'murder-suicides' (where an individual is murdered, then the perpetrator kills his or herself), accounted for 1,000–1,500 deaths a year. They argued that the causal factor here could be rejection or other events beforehand. Evolutionary theory explains jealousy as the desire to keep one's mate. Males have a tendency to show mate tending and guarding activities including the showing of aggressive activities to avoid sexual infidelity (this is also supported by Buss and Shackelford, 1997), whereas females display such behaviours less frequently.

Key points

- After the work of Darwin, Craig (1921) was the next to attempt to apply the principles of ethology to explain aggressive behaviour.

- Lorenz (1966) advanced the notion of ritualised aggression to encompass animal behaviour that was aggressive (e.g. stags rutting). Other ethologists have furthered this analysis by stating that animals know when to stop being aggressive; after all, few ever kill their enemy. Gross (1998) refers to jackdaws as an example of this.

- Lorenz's early work suffered much criticism, often from within the ranks of his own ethological colleagues. The biggest problem for Lorenz was assuming that you could generalise findings from animals to humans. This view is fraught with many difficulties.

- Nelson (1974) provides a well-structured criticism of Lorenz. Nelson argues that Lorenz's work misses three fundamental issues that could equally affect human behaviour: (a) processes of learning, (b) structural causes, (c) psychological factors. Lorenz ignored all of these influences.

- Jealousy has a basis of explanation with the adaptive argument. Harvey *et al*. (2004) show support for the assertion that jealousy is a motivator for violence, and suggest that the causes of jealousy are complex.

Summary questions

1. In what way might aggression be 'adaptive'?
2. To what extent can jealousy provide a motive for aggressive action?
3. How would terrorist action be explained through the evolutionary perspective?

Group display of aggression in humans

Learning objectives:

- understand the nature of group display in humans

- understand psychologists' attempts to explain group display in humans

- be able to apply the notions of group display to specific examples of crowd behaviour.

Take it further

Investigate Freud. Think of a football match. How might Freud explain the behaviour and the mood of the crowd? Think critically and list any problems with adopting his point of view.

Link

See Chapter 10, Social psychological approaches to explaining aggression, page 117 for more on deindividuation and the effect of reduced inhibitions.

AQA Examiner's tip

Reference to Freud's older theories of group display provide a good benchmark in your essays for comparison, showing the benefits of the more contemporary theories over the classic ones.

Key terms

Contagion: the atmosphere and views of the group become infectious and spread rapidly amongst group members.

Circular reaction: the emotions and behaviour of the individuals in a crowd are copied from one to another and intensified in the process.

Classic theories

Melnick (1986) comments on British tabloid headlines about crowd disorder following football games. Articles have titles like 'Smash those Thugs', 'Murder in the Soccer Train!', 'Mindless Fighting Hooligans'. Both psychologists and sociologists are interested in how crowds operate. They have produced models and explanations. The two disciplines differ in how they explain crowd disorder; for example, sociologists focus more on the role of the media as an 'amplifier' of the antisocial behaviour, whereas psychologists are more concerned about the factors that exist within a group that lead to the demonstration of antisocial behaviour.

Freud

Sigmund Freud argued that the mindset of an individual in a crowd differed from that of an individual on their own. He noted that there would be a merging of minds within the group based on sharing the same opinion; the enthusiasm for being in the group would mean that normal inhibitions surrounding behaviour were reduced.

Influence from the group

A different point of view was held by Le Bon (1896). His 'pathological' viewpoint suggested that crowd behaviour was more the result of individuals' personalities. Le Bon argues that the atmosphere of the group causes **contagion** and 'group members fall under the influence of a collective mind' (Le Bon, 1896). Group members are suggestible, taking on the views of the group and imitating actions of others within the group. They are like a sponge soaking up the views of the group and imitating the actions shown within it. The group provides a situation in which contagion can occur – group behaviour is taken up quickly, usually because of the atmosphere surrounding the group. This leads ultimately to the creation of what Le Bon called a 'group mind'. In the 20th century, Blumer (1939) argued that in a **circular reaction** individuals reproduce the behaviours and emotions of those around them, which subsequently intensifies or amplifies the original emotion and behaviour. Blumer felt that this could explain the processes involved in social unrest.

Convergence theory and emergent norm theory

This theory suggested that the motive behind group behaviour is convergence upon a specific location by like-minded individuals with similar points of view (for example, a football crowd). Subsequently, Turner and Killian (1957) developed the idea of convergence theory and proposed a theory known as emergent norm theory. They argued that crowd behaviour as such is 'normless'. So where an individual has no norms to follow, as the situation is unique, they look to see what other people are doing and base their behaviour on that. If one person's behaviour is distinctive and stands out within an otherwise normless group, this person will get the attention of the crowd. The distinctive behaviour is gradually taken on as the norm for that group, which ultimately governs the behaviour of the group as a whole. Essentially this view dictates that crowds are not a passive group of people – in fact, they

Aggression

are a logically thinking mass of individuals. This view does help to explain why crowd behaviour can at times be unpredictable; it is because it is ultimately governed by the norms identified and accepted by the group.

Value-added theory

In 1963 Neil Smelser created the value-added theory to better understand and predict collective behaviour. He suggested that certain prerequisites (situations or conditions) were needed in order for a group or a social movement to develop. The stages he suggested were:

▓ Stage 1: structural conduciveness. The actual social situation and conditions must allow for collective action.

▓ Stage 2: structural strain. Some parts of the social system do not function effectively.

▓ Stage 3: growth and spread of a generalised belief. This shared view assigns causes and determines a response or action.

▓ Stage 4: precipitating factors. Collective belief is strengthened, the search for alternatives gathers pace.

▓ Stage 5: mobilising the collective for action. Leaders and workers emerge. Hierarchy of order is established.

▓ Stage 6: reaction of agencies of social control. Agencies of social control attempt to interfere with the operation of the collective.

Smelser argues that social life and the processes we follow within it affect how individuals behave. If society is not well regulated (i.e. suitably policed with good sanctions) that might change an individual's view on appropriate behaviour. So the individual assesses his or her own needs. If society offers certain incentives and rewards that the individual is interested in, selfishness may prevail and they might not think too carefully about how they achieve the goal. Self-interest and preservation become more important than respect of others.

Although essentially a sociological theory, the impact of value-added theory on psychological understanding of the behaviour of groups is important since it shows how human behaviour is often the net result of careful regulation at a societal level. Any imbalance leads to individual changes to behaviour. Other theorists, such as Sztompka (2004), lend support to this view, believing that group behaviour does not just happen. It is the result of a logical and systematic evolution through progressive stages of development. Smelser and his value-added theory exhibit this point well.

▓ Evaluation of theories of crowd behaviour

To simply assume that there is one cause for group behaviour is problematic. As this topic has identified, there are a number of different interpretations and explanations for group behaviour which each suggest a slightly different underlying motive or cause. Levy (1989) summed this up nicely by stating that every theory of crowd behaviour tends to take a slightly different perspective.

Freud provided a very early contribution to the analysis of group behaviour. Not everyone agreed with his suggestion of the merging of minds within the group and the sharing of a similar view that generates enthusiasm for group membership, but it has provided other researchers with a foundation upon which to study group behaviour. But much of Freud's work is dogged by the same criticism of methodological flaws surrounding the theories that he generated. For example, in the main it would seem that Freud did not follow the principles of science in using the **hypothetico-deductive method**.

Aggression

Le Bon (1896) provided an interesting explanation of group behaviour. However, Freud criticised Le Bon's idea that the 'group' had a soul of its own. Instead, Freud emphasised how the group behaviour was the result of identification with a leader. Le Bon's theory is also criticised by some researchers who claim that in fact many crowds do not take on a 'life of their own' which is different and separate from the thought and behaviours of the individuals who comprise the group. Instead, as Smelser suggests, specific conditions and situations may be found to be responsible for the behaviour.

Convergence theory focuses more on how individuals are rational and how, as like-minded people come together, the formation of the crowd and then its behaviour can be seen as rational and logical. This is in contrast to contagion theories such as that of Le Bon, which are more concerned with irrational forces.

Turner and Killian's emergent norm theory provided a way of explaining most crowd behaviour. But the theory has been criticised for not explaining exactly how norms might emerge. Also, not all crowd behaviour scenarios can be explained by the theory. For example, Berk (1974) suggests that behaviour that looks irrational (a crowd running out of a building, say) may in fact be rational (the building is on fire). Emergent norm theory tried to provide a different explanation to earlier models, and to this extent there was great praise for the explanation. However, the theory does not take into account non-verbal processes which occur in crowds, so for this reason can be seen as incomplete.

Smelser's value-added theory received a mixed reception academically. While it is a logical theory, and the stages seem intuitively to make sense, some researchers have commented that it does not take into account the complexities of crowd behaviour. Other researchers such as Evans (1969) and Marx (1972) commented on the positive nature of the theory since some other models like contagion theory view crowd behaviour as irrational and negative. However, this model also suffers from another flaw – it is hard to test. Berk (1974) summarises this when he says that:

> Crowd events occur with great speed, are difficult to anticipate, often happen several at a time, sometimes cover a broad geographic area, have processes leaving few traces, are not conducive to interviewing members during the process, frequently produce unreliable unremembered accounts and create a risk of injury to the observer.

Berk, 1974

Sports crowds

In applying the theoretical models to sports crowds, Hockling (1982) argues that each of the different theories can explain elements of crowd behaviour. He observed a basketball game. Convergent theory explained similar behaviours by committed members of a crowd. Booing responses to referee decisions can be explained by contagion theory, whereas the standing up of all spectators when the national anthem is played could be explained by emergent norms. Although there is some agreement between authorities about which explanation is most plausible, there is not a unanimous view. Guttman (1986) notes that there is no single theory appropriate to explain the behaviour and violence of sports crowds. An explanation which comprises ideas from all theories seems most logical.

Aggression

Fig. 2 *Rioting sports crowd*

■ **Key terms**

Stigmatisation: the act of making something or someone stand out as different from others. Giving a negative label to a person or thing.

Symbolic interactionist: a major sociological view that suggests that people behave in a way that is influenced by their interaction with and interpretation of others.

Lynch mobs

According to the Tuskegee Institute, between 1882 and 1951 there were 3,437 lynchings of black people (Gibson, 1979). Deane and Beck (1996) suggest that lynchings were justified (by lynchers) to keep white control and to ensure that the status differences between blacks and whites remained. Other writers see the function of lynchings was more a way of keeping 'them [blacks] in their place' (Cox, 1945) and ensuring that there was no challenge to the dominant position that white Americans held. The Ku Klux Klan were notoriously well known for their prejudiced views and their methods of killing; lynching was only one means of exerting their supremacy over their usually lower-status (mainly, although not solely) black victims. Lynchings may also have served a political purpose as well (Blalock, 1967). The majority political group of the time could have seen a minority group as one that could challenge the majority position. Lynching was a means of control through fear.

Zimbardo (2007) argues that dehumanisation is crucial to understanding 'man's inhumanity to man'. The inhuman form of aggression that involved the torture and violent murder of blacks was not seen as a crime against humanity. The lynching of black people by mobs of white people in many of the cities across the USA was the result of black people's **stigmatisation** as 'niggers', so they were not seen as individuals (Ginzberg, 1988). Asked how a group of otherwise normal individuals could perform such appalling actions, Zimbardo refers to the work of the famous **symbolic interactionist** Erving Goffman. Goffman talks about those in society that are socially discredited. He states that:

> under such conditions it becomes possible for normal, morally upright, and even idealistic people to perform acts of destructive cruelty [e.g. lynchings]. Not responding to the human qualities of the other persons automatically facilitates inhumane actions.

Goffman, 1959

■ **Link**

For more contemporary examples of aggression in the Abu Ghraib prison, see page 125.

The same underlying process of dehumanisation might well explain the Rape of Nanking in 1937, the My Lai massacre in the Vietnam war, or more recently the treatment of prisoners at the Abu Ghraib prison in Iraq.

No aggression here: crowd celebrations

Although large groups of people often create the very situational variables needed for aggression and violence. This is not always the case. Cassidy *et al.* (2007) investigated the Mela – a month-long Hindu festival that takes place in India every few years. It is the largest gathering of people on earth – in 2007 over 50 million people attended it over the month. Hence it provides psychologists with an interesting crowd situation that is not characterised by aggression. The research discovered that during the Mela the crowds behaved well and increased generosity, support and orderly behaviour was noted. The Mela shows how crowd behaviour and collective living can promote good, non-aggressive behaviour where a strong sense of common identity and close proximity is beneficial instead of being the causal factors for subsequent harm. Therefore, crowds need not always lead to the occurrence of aggressive behaviour.

Fig. 3 *Hundreds of thousands of people attend the annual Mela celebrations*

Key points

- Group display in humans has been studied by a variety of psychologists both classic and contemporary. Freud and Le Bon, although arguing from different points of view, very much laid the foundation for the gradually evolving nature of the study of group behaviour.

- Group displays of behaviour can be shaped by a number of factors. Some psychologists such as Le Bon believe that crowd behaviour is explained through the individual taking on the 'psychology of the crowd'.

- Other explanations of crowd behaviour have tended to centre on issues such as situational factors (convergence in one location) or the understanding that crowds are normless situations (where group members look to others to see how to act when norms of behaviour are not readily available).

- In both sports crowds and lynch mobs the psychology of the groups seem to ensure that the action is carried out with great emotion and loyalty to a cause.

Link

Approaches, issues and debates

As part of Cassidy *et al*'s research of the Mela celebrations observations of behaviour were made. These would have to be conducted in accordance with the British Psychological Society's ethical guidelines. These suggest that for observational research observations can take place without the informed consent of others if the observations are conducted in a location where people would otherwise expect to be observed by others, for example public places.

Aggression

Summary questions

4 In what way have large groups of people been characterised by the media as bad? Give some recent examples from your analysis of the news.

5 What is the main difference between the early work of Freud and Le Bon compared to the later attempts at understanding group behaviour such as that provided by Turner and Killian and Smelser.

6 How does psychology attempt to explain crowd behaviour?

Aggression end of topic

▥ How science works: practical activity

You can investigate the topic of aggression by using a questionnaire. This would examine aggression by investigating the views of both younger and older age groups. First, you might want to establish the ethical and methodological advantages of using the interview/questionnaire technique instead of laboratory experimentation.

This activity aims to assess to what extent people believe that the media affects aggression through imitation.

▥ The questionnaire that you develop needs to access both qualitative and quantitative data, which means that you need to make use of both open and closed questions.

▥ For your questions to be standardised between the different age groups, you might decide to make use of statements which have a 1–5 Likert scale attached. For example:

Television programmes contain moderate levels of violence and aggression.

1	2	3	4	5
Strongly agree	Agree	Neither agree nor disagree	Disagree	Strongly disagree

In order to develop open-ended questions, think about the issues you most want to examine and get more detail on. For example, why might your respondents think the television as a form of media is a means of encouraging aggressive action? Do the older and younger generations have different views on this?

You will need to think carefully about how you analyse your data. The questionnaire/interview that you create will lend itself to both quantitative and qualitative analysis. You could look at tabulating the quantitative data of each participant and working out measures of central tendency and dispersion for the data given. You could also analyse the qualitative data gathered from the interviews. **Transcribe** the interviews and code the responses thematically. Do common themes emerge?

Finally, think about the ethical issues that this study raises. You might want to create a table like the one below which identifies the ethical issue, why it is a problem and how it can be overcome.

Ethical guideline	Why it is an issue in your study	How it can be overcome
Protection of participants (mental distress)	The answering of the questions involves the divulgence of personal views which might reveal some prejudices. Some participants might be a little distressed about how this information will be used	If participants feel distressed they are to be reminded that they are free to withdraw from the investigation at any time

▥ Link

For more information about the structure of interviews/questionnaires and the styles of questions that can be used see the section on Psychological research and scientific method, page 517.

▥ Key terms

Transcribe: write up exactly what was said.

Aggression

Further reading and weblinks

Anitei, S. Early humans had short legs to fight over females: fighting with weapons later allowed the development of longer legs. Softpedia News12 March 2007, http://news.softpedia.com/news/Early-Humans-Had-Short-Leggs-For-Fighting-Over-Females-49109.shtml.

An interesting read that provides further information about the evolving nature of the human body adapting to its social physical climate.

Zimbardo, P. (2007) *The Lucifer Effect: How Good People Turn Evil*. London: Rider Books.

This book examines the reasons behind evil behaviour and offers explanations for cases such as Abu Ghraib.

www.aber.ac.uk/media/Modules/TF33120/tv-violence_and_kids.html

There are lots of websites that you can visit to learn more about the Bandura study. A look at this site will be worthwhile.

www.bbc.co.uk/dna/h2g2/A1093439

Theories of aggression are succinctly summarised on the BBC website.

www.flyfishingdevon.co.uk/salmon/year2/aggression/aggression.html#male_aggression_testosterone

Biological influences upon aggression are well summarised on this website.

www.medicine.mcgill.ca/mjm/v06n01/v06p032/v06p032.pdf

Find further information about biological influences upon aggression on this website.

www.life-enhancement.com/article_template.asp?ID=208

This National Institute of Alcohol Abuse and Alcoholism investigation provides interesting insight into wider socio-economic and lifestyle choices and how they influence aggression.

http://people.exeter.ac.uk/tpostmes/deindividuation.html

This website charts the deindividuation theory of aggression, which has a very varied history of development.

Eating behaviour

Introduction

Our contemporary attitudes to food have changed dramatically since earlier times in evolution when the major concern was simply finding enough to eat and survive. Even over a shorter period, such as the last 100 years, there have been dramatic changes in food availability and choice in Western and other advanced societies. This has led to parallel changes in attitudes to food at individual and cultural levels, and to the emergence of a range of eating-related problems.

The basis of eating behaviour is our need to take in adequate nutrition in order for our body's physiological systems to work effectively. Chapter 13 (Biological explanations of eating behaviour) reviews the biology of eating behaviour and its evolutionary history. Food is a basic requirement and we have evolved sophisticated biological machinery to make sure we eat enough of the right things. However, there is an enormous choice of foodstuffs, and our preferences are also affected by culture, mood and health concerns. These are reviewed in Chapter 13, Biological explanations of eating behaviour.

A major concern in our modern society, particularly for women, is body image dissatisfaction and dieting. It is clear that dieting is often unsuccessful, and Chapter 14 (Eating behaviour) also considers why this should be. A related concern is the increasing frequency of eating disorders such as anorexia nervosa, bulimia nervosa and obesity. Along with eating behaviour in general, these have biological (including genetic), psychological, social and cultural aspects. These are reviewed in Chapter 15, Eating disorders.

Eating behaviour is unusual in that it involves all levels of explanation. We cannot understand eating behaviour without having some awareness of the underlying biological systems. However, familiarity, early experience and learning, family and peer pressures, media influences and cultural attitudes can all influence our diet. This means that eating behaviour is an excellent area in which to demonstrate your understanding of different approaches in psychology. There are also many issues and debates relevant to research into eating behaviour and its disorders. Again, you will be able to show your awareness of these, and how they can inform our understanding of this fascinating area.

Eating behaviour

Biological explanations of eating behaviour

The role of neural mechanisms involved in controlling eating and satiation

Learning objectives:

▊ understand the role of neural mechanisms involved in controlling eating and satiation

▊ evaluate research into the mechanisms of feeding and satiation

▊ outline and evaluate research into evolutionary explanations of food preference.

▊ Key terms

Homeostasis: how the body maintains a constant internal environment; the best example is body temperature, which is regulated around a set-point of 98.6 °F.

▊ Take it further

Think about your own eating patterns. Are they regular or do you wait for hunger pangs? If you snack between meals, what do you eat? What characteristics of the snack food do you find most appealing? Do you feel that your diet is more determined by family, friends or your own preferences? When we look at our own eating patterns, it often turns out that there are many influences other than just the biological drive.

Although to stay healthy people need a diet containing carbohydrates, fats and protein as well as small amounts of vitamins and mineral salts, the focus of eating behaviour research has normally been on body weight. This is largely decided by the fats and carbohydrates that people eat and so research has focused on these dietary components.

Today there is enormous interest in the psychological factors that can affect a person's eating habits, but some of the clearest research findings have come from research into the brain (neural) mechanisms controlling eating behaviour. Before looking at some of this research, we need to consider some general points about feeding behaviour in humans.

Humans, along with all mammals, are homeostatic animals. The term **homeostasis** is technically defined as 'the maintenance of a constant internal environment'. In simple terms this means that we try to keep our body's physiology consistent within narrow limits. The best example is body temperature, which is regulated at 98.6 °F. If it falls we generate heat through activity or wearing warmer clothes, and if it rises we lose heat through perspiration or wearing less. Our body is designed to operate at 98.6 °F and it is therefore critical that we maintain that body temperature. It is sometimes referred to as our body temperature set-point.

Our diet is essential to homeostasis as it provides the nutrients that allow physiological processes to be regulated within narrow limits. One of the most obvious signs of homeostasis is that outside of the growth phases of childhood and in conditions such as pregnancy humans regulate their body weight within reasonably narrow limits (of course there is concern at the moment over increasing levels of obesity in children and adults and this is discussed in Chapter 15, Eating disorders).

To maintain a consistent body weight people therefore have to regulate their eating behaviour and food intake. To study this we can first discuss overall patterns of eating behaviour. For example, do we simply wait until we feel hungry before eating? How is the frequency and size of meals regulated so that long-term body weight stays fairly constant? We can find some clues in everyday behaviour:

▊ We do not usually wait until we feel hungry before we eat. Meals, at least in prosperous countries, follow a regular pattern so that hunger is anticipated and we rarely experience uncomfortable levels of hunger.

▊ We usually feel full or 'satiated' at the end of a meal, which is long before the nutrients have been fully absorbed into the body. What signals tell the brain that enough food has been eaten in a given meal?

▊ If the brain mechanisms controlling eating behaviour are sensitive to body weight, what signals alert them to changes in body weight?

Research into eating behaviour provides some answers to these questions. The earliest studies focused on the role of the digestive tract.

▉ The digestive tract

The aim of digestion is to break food down into essential components such as sugar and amino acids. The process begins in the mouth where food mixes with saliva. Saliva contains **enzymes**, chemicals that are vital in breaking down complex carbohydrates into sugars and converting proteins into **amino acids**. After swallowing, food passes through the **oesophagus** into the stomach where the process of digestion continues. From the stomach food passes to the **duodenum**, the first part of the small intestine. The duodenum and small intestine contain a cocktail of enzymes that complete the process of digestion. The products of digestion, such as glucose and amino acids, are absorbed into the bloodstream through the walls of the small intestine. The waste products of digestion pass into the large intestine and are eventually excreted.

▉ Insulin and glucagon

Insulin and **glucagon** are two hormones released from the **pancreas gland** and they play a vital role in eating behaviour and body weight regulation. Insulin controls blood glucose levels by allowing glucose in the blood stream to enter the cells of the body. Glucose is the main energy source for cells and it is vital to their function. Insulin also converts glucose to glycogen. **Glycogen** is stored in the liver and in muscles and, along with fatty tissue, it makes up the main energy reserve for the body. Finally, insulin is also crucial in allowing fats in the bloodstream to be stored in fat (or 'adipose') cells. **Adipose cells** make up the fatty tissue of the body and are another key energy reserve. They are also important in determining body weight.

In the condition known as **diabetes**, insulin levels are low. This can be due to damage to the cells of the pancreas gland that secrete insulin (type I diabetes) which usually occurs early in life. Type II diabetes occurs usually later in life when the pancreas gradually fails to secrete enough insulin. This is often associated with obesity and is far more common than type I diabetes.

In the absence of insulin, levels of blood glucose rise (**hyperglycaemia**) and this can have potentially disastrous consequences including confusion, delirium, loss of consciousness and, in the long term, heart attacks and blindness. Diabetes requires regular treatment with insulin, although this has to be carefully monitored. Too much insulin means that more glucose is stored within cells and therefore blood levels of glucose fall dramatically. This too can have serious consequences.

We return to the role of insulin and glucose metabolism when we review brain mechanisms of eating behaviour (page 157).

▉ Neural mechanisms and eating behaviour

We are aware of the taste of food in the mouth and the presence of food in the stomach. The role of taste in eating behaviour is considered later in this chapter. The role of the stomach was investigated in some of the earliest and most bizarre studies in biopsychology. For instance, Cannon persuaded his colleague Washburn to swallow a deflated balloon (Cannon and Washburn, 1912). He then inflated the balloon in Washburn's stomach and used it to measure stomach contractions in relation to Washburn's feelings of hunger. It turned out that Washburn's hunger pangs were correlated with stomach contractions. This would suggest that the presence or absence of food in the stomach is an important signal to the brain mechanisms of

▉ Key terms

Enzymes: chemicals that are vital in enabling nutrients in our diet, such as carbohydrates and proteins, to be broken down so that they can be absorbed into the body.

Amino acids: during digestion food is broken down into basic units. Proteins are broken down into amino acids so that they can be absorbed into the body and then used as building blocks for the proteins that the body needs.

Oesophagus: part of the digestive system connecting the mouth to the stomach.

Duodenum: food leaving the stomach enters the duodenum, the first part of the small intestine.

Insulin: hormone secreted by the pancreas gland. It enables glucose and fats in the bloodstream to be stored within cells. It is therefore vital to the control of blood glucose levels.

Glucagon: a hormone released from the pancreas gland that is important in glucose metabolism. It facilitates the release of glucose from the liver so that it can be used by the body.

Pancreas gland: endocrine (hormone-secreting) gland situated near the liver. It secretes insulin and glucagon, which are hormones vital in the control of glucose and fat metabolism.

Glycogen: complex carbohydrate found in muscles and the liver and an important energy reserve for the body. Food intake raises blood glucose levels, and insulin converts some of this blood glucose into glycogen.

Adipose cells: the fat storage cells of the body. After digestion insulin enables fat in the bloodstream to be stored in adipose cells.

Diabetes: caused by low blood insulin which leads to high levels of blood glucose. Type I occurs at a young age and is caused by early damage to the pancreas gland. The more common Type II occurs later in life when the pancreas gradually fails to secrete enough insulin. It is associated with obesity. Diabetes can have severe health consequences.

Hyperglycaemia: high levels of blood glucose caused by low levels of insulin found in diabetes. There can be severe health consequences such as delirium and coma.

Eating behaviour

■ Key terms

Hypothalamus: a structure in the forebrain which controls the pituitary gland and the autonomic nervous system. It also contains centres for control of feeding behaviour.

Ventromedial nucleus: see ventromedial hypothalamus (VMH).

Ventromedial hypothalamus (VMH): part of the hypothalamus that functions as a satiety centre to inhibit feeding.

VMH rat: rat with a lesion (damage) to the ventromedial hypothalamus, causing overeating and obesity.

Satiety centre: a centre in the brain that inhibits feeding in response to signals from the body. The ventromedial hypothalamus is a key satiety centre.

Lateral hypothalamus (LH): part of the hypothalamus that functions as a feeding centre, stimulating feeding in response to signals from the body.

Aphagia: failure to eat when hungry. Can be caused by damage to the lateral hypothalamus.

Feeding centre: a centre in the brain that triggers feeding in response to signals from the body. The lateral hypothalamus is a key feeding centre.

feeding. However, it was soon pointed out that people who had lost all or part of their stomach through cancer were still able to regulate their food intake. This did not mean that the stomach was unimportant, but that there were other mechanisms involved in food intake regulation.

In 1942, Hetherington and Ranson published one of the most famous studies on the control of eating behaviour. They demonstrated that lesions of an area in the **hypothalamus** of the brain caused rats to overeat and become dramatically obese. The area of the hypothalamus involved is called the **ventromedial nucleus**, and the obese rat with a lesion to the **ventromedial hypothalamus (VMH)** rapidly became known as the **VMH rat**. It appeared that the lesion destroyed a centre vital for the control of feeding behaviour, as its destruction led to an increase in feeding and body weight. Hetherington and Ranson assumed it was a '**satiety centre**', i.e. it was normally activated when the animal was full or satiated at the end of the meal and its function was to inhibit or stop feeding.

In 1951, Anand and Brobeck found that a lesion in another area of the hypothalamus, the **lateral hypothalamus (LH)**, led to a loss of feeding behaviour in rats, also known as **aphagia**. They suggested that this area was a feeding or eating centre whose normal function was to stimulate feeding in hungry rats.

Later studies confirmed these findings. Electrical stimulation of the VMH inhibited feeding, while stimulation of the LH produced feeding, so confirming their normal functions. The apparent discovery of a satiety centre and a **feeding centre** led to a fairly straightforward model of the neural control of feeding behaviour (see Figure 1). When blood glucose levels fall this is sensed by the hypothalamus, hunger is experienced and the lateral hypothalamus is activated, leading to feeding behaviour. Food intake leads to an increase in blood glucose. This is picked up by the hypothalamus and the VMH is activated and stops feeding.

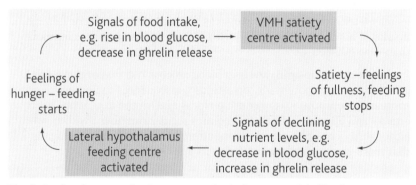

Fig. 1 *Feeding, hunger and satiety centres – the dual centre model of feeding*

Although much of this pioneering work is now over 50 years old, contemporary research has confirmed the central role of hypothalamic centres in feeding behaviour. However, we have also become aware of the complexity of the pathways involved. For instance, a key question is what signals are involved in telling the hypothalamic centres when to start and when to stop feeding. Using the background material covered above, we can outline some of these processes.

Signals for starting a meal

■ In Western countries we usually eat to a set schedule, and the digestive system starts preparing itself by releasing saliva and enzymes just before a meal time (Pinel, 2007). This represents a *learned* response, anticipating the presence of food.

▇ The taste and smell of food also act to prepare the digestive system. The role of taste and smell are considered in the next section on evolutionary influences, but you know from your own experience that the sight, smell or taste of a desirable food, often chocolate, can lead to eating even when we are not genuinely hungry.

▇ It has been known for many years that an empty stomach sends signals to the brain to start eating. Although these signals may include direct neural pathways from the stomach to the brain, an important role is played by a hormone, **ghrelin**. This hormone is secreted from the stomach, and the amount released is directly proportional to the *emptiness* of the stomach, i.e. as the time from the last meal increases and we feel hungrier, so ghrelin secretion is increased. Injections of ghrelin increase food intake and body weight in animals and humans (Cummings, 2006), and it may be significant that **gastric bands** (see page 176) used to treat obesity, reduce ghrelin secretion from the stomach. There is evidence that ghrelin acts directly on the brain mechanisms of feeding behaviour, including the hypothalamus (Cummings, 2006).

Research study: Cummings *et al.* (2004)

In this study Cummings *et al.* investigated changes in blood ghrelin levels over time between meals. Six participants (pps) were allowed to eat lunch, then ghrelin levels were monitored from blood samples taken every five minutes (from a tube or catheter inserted into a vein) until the pps requested their evening meal. Pps assessed their degree of hunger every 30 minutes.

Findings were that ghrelin levels fell immediately after eating lunch, reaching their lowest level at about 70 minutes. Then they slowly began to rise, peaking as pps requested their evening meals. Importantly, in five out of the six pps ghrelin levels were closely correlated with the degree of hunger reported by the pps. The authors concluded that ghrelin levels directly reflect stomach emptiness and are closely related to subjective feelings of hunger. This supports a role for ghrelin as a key appetite signal in humans.

Methodological issues

▇ Pps were isolated from time and context cues so that any changes in ghrelin levels would be due to hunger rather than reflecting an automatic response to signals that meal time was approaching (feeding mechanisms often *anticipate* food intake – see Chapter 15, Eating disorders).

▇ There were only six participants (because of the complicated technical and physiological procedures involved). All were male. Therefore, there could be problems of generalising results to the wider population in general and to females in particular.

▇ Data was correlational, so we cannot say that ghrelin *causes* feelings of hunger.

▇ The results support previous work on the role of ghrelin in stimulating appetite.

Ethical issues

The study involved inserting a catheter into the pps' vein so that blood samples could be collected. The researchers obtained approval for this from their local Ethical Committee. Pps were volunteers who gave informed consent and who were fully debriefed afterwards.

▇ **Key terms**

Ghrelin: a hormone released from the empty stomach that signals the hypothalamus to stimulate feeding.

Gastric band: a band placed around the stomach to reduce its capacity. This means that feelings of satiety ('fullness') occur when smaller meals are consumed. It is used as a treatment for severe obesity.

Eating behaviour

Signals stopping the intake of food – meal size

Feeding is not under strict biological control. We know that people eat more of tastier food (so do rats), and they eat more in the company of other people (de Castro, 2004). We also know that regulation of food intake must involve short-term *and* long-term factors. Short-term factors regulate the size of a particular meal; however, a meal ends before food has been absorbed and converted into the fat stores that determine our body weight. So our long-term regulation of body weight must involve different factors to those that control meal size:

▓ From the early work of Cannon and Washburn it is known that the presence of food in the stomach can signal satiety (a feeling of fullness) to the brain (Carlson, 2007). These signals probably pass directly from the stomach via neural pathways to the brain mechanisms that control feeding behaviour.

▓ As food is digested and passes from the stomach to the duodenum, a short section of the intestinal tract that leads to the small intestine, it stimulates the release of another key hormone. This is **cholecystokinin (CCK)**, and it appears to have the opposite effect to ghrelin. Studies have shown that injections of CCK in animals and humans *reduce* meal size (Smith, Gibbs and Kulkosky, 1982), while animals with a genetic mutation eliminating the CCK system become obese. So there is good evidence that CCK signals satiety to the brain and contributes to the control of meal size.

▓ We have seen that ghrelin probably acts to promote eating as the stomach becomes emptier. It may also be that the *fall* in blood ghrelin levels during a meal acts as another satiety signal.

▓ An early hypothesis on the control of meal size was the **glucostat theory**. This proposed that blood glucose levels were a key signal to the brain, falling when we were hungry and rising as we eat. Blood glucose levels do respond rapidly to food intake, but it was quickly shown that there were problems with the theory. Glucose levels do not vary much under normal circumstances and not enough to be an effective signal of hunger and satiety. Additionally, people with diabetes often have long-term high levels of blood glucose, but most have normal appetites.

Signals controlling food intake – body weight

Signals controlling meal size are involved in what we call short-term regulation of food intake. We saw above that animals, including humans, regulate their body weight in the long term. There are exceptions, and conditions such as obesity and anorexia nervosa are considered in Chapter 15, Eating disorders. Long-term regulation of body weight must involve a different set of factors, as we stop eating a meal well before it can have an effect on body weight.

Body weight is determined by muscle mass and, more importantly, by body fat. Fat is stored in specialised cells called **adipocytes**, and fatty tissue is made up of these adipocytes. During early development, especially in the first year of life, the number of adipocytes can be affected by diet. However, after this period, the number is set, and the only way our fat stores can vary is through how much is stored in each cell. Our food intake over a period of time is regulated so as to maintain a fairly constant body weight. To do this the mechanisms controlling feeding in the hypothalamus and related structures must receive a signal indicating the body's fat reserves, as this is the major determinant of body weight.

▓ **Key terms**

Cholecystokinin (CCK): a hormone released from the duodenum in response to the presence of food. It acts as a satiety signal to the hypothalamus to stop feeding behaviour.

Glucostat theory: the theory that blood glucose levels are the main signal to the hypothalamus controlling feeding behaviour. Blood glucose is thought to be one of many signals used by the brain.

Adipocytes: see adipose cells (on page 153).

The clue to the identity of this signal came from studies of a strain of mice that are genetically obese, i.e. their obesity is inherited. These mice, called simply 'ob' mice, are missing a gene that produces a hormone called **leptin**. It turns out that this hormone is released from the adipocytes (fat cells) into the bloodstream, and travels to the hypothalamus where it acts as a **satiety signal**. As more fat is stored in adipocytes so more leptin is released and the hypothalamus is stimulated to *reduce* food intake. The **ob mice** do not produce leptin and so they eat continuously and become obese. We also know that injections of leptin into the ob mice stop them eating as much and their weight eventually returns to normal (Carlson, 2007).

If life was simple then leptin would seem to be a potential treatment for human obesity, as we would expect the overweight human to have *low* levels of leptin in their bloodstream. Unfortunately, this is not the case. There are some rare individuals who are overweight because of a genetic leptin deficiency, but the majority have normal or even higher-than-normal levels of leptin. The problem in these cases seems to be that the brain mechanisms controlling feeding behaviour are insensitive to the effects of leptin.

Back to the hypothalamus

Earlier in this chapter we discussed the classic work on hypothalamic centres for feeding and satiety. Researchers have now unravelled even more of the complex systems controlling feeding behaviour and body weight. Many neurotransmitters are involved, some of which inhibit feeding and others which stimulate feeding behaviour. Hormones such as leptin act on neurons in the hypothalamus that are part of the satiety, or fullness, centre. In contrast, ghrelin acts on neurons that are part of the feeding centre.

▓ Conclusions

In this review of the biological basis of eating behaviour, we have seen that it involves a complex set of factors. These include the sight, smell and taste of food, the presence of food in the stomach and intestines, and the release of hormones from the stomach and intestines. After absorption, insulin and glucagon are important in processing fats and carbohydrates, and we have seen the importance of adipose tissue in the regulation of body weight. Finally, you should have gained some sense of the complexity of the brain mechanisms controlling feeding, with several neurotransmitters interacting to stimulate or to inhibit feeding. Chapter 14 (Eating behaviour) and Chapter 15 (Eating disorders) consider the social and psychological aspects of feeding behaviour, but when considering issues such as dieting, obesity and anorexia, it is important to remember that feeding behaviour fulfils a basic biological need.

▓ Evaluation

There is no doubt that we are biological organisms and our eating behaviour relies on complex biological systems. Therefore, an understanding of these systems plays a key role in explaining the regulation of human eating behaviour. It is relevant to normal regulation, but also to disorders such as anorexia nervosa and obesity (see Chapter 15, Eating disorders).

The biological approach is reductionist, focusing only on the biological systems regulating food intake and body weight. It ignores

▓ Key terms

Leptin: a hormone released from fatty (adipose) tissue. It acts as an indicator of body weight to hypothalamic mechanisms controlling long-term food intake.

Satiety signal: any neural or hormonal process that tells the hypothalamus to inhibit feeding, usually in response to the presence of food in the stomach and duodenum.

Ob mice: genetically obese mice. They lack a gene that controls the production of the satiety signal leptin from adipose tissue. With no leptin, they overeat and become obese.

AQA Examiner's tip

The biology of eating behaviour is very complicated. You will be expected to have a basic knowledge of the need for control of food intake and body weight, and some of the key processes involved. Focus on the principles, in particular that the key centres in the hypothalamus need signals to tell them when to start and when to stop feeding. You should be able to outline at least two of these signals.

Eating behaviour

Link

Approaches, issues and debates

Explaining feeding behaviour purely in terms of biological mechanisms is a *reductionist* approach. Although we need to understand the biological mechanisms in order to provide a full picture, we also know that feeding is affected by many other non-biological variables such as mood, experience, and culture. The biological approach cannot provide a complete explanation. Your awareness of alternative approaches and explanations will be a key element in evaluating any explanation of feeding behaviour.

the psychological, social and cultural factors that influence our eating behaviour. A full description of eating behaviour requires research into all of these areas as well as biology.

Although the number of studies on humans is increasing, the area still relies heavily on research with non-human animals. This is particularly the case with the role of neurotransmitters in the hypothalamus and the functions of ghrelin and CCK release from the stomach and duodenum. This raises the problem of generalising from animals to humans. It is likely that there will be subtle differences in the control of feeding between humans and other animals.

Key points

- Feeding behaviour provides the various nutrients that the body needs to function effectively. The focus of research is on the control of carbohydrate and fat metabolism in relation to body weight.

- The hypothalamus in the brain contains feeding and satiety centres that are central to the control of feeding behaviour.

- Insulin, a hormone released from the pancreas gland, allows blood glucose to enter cells to provide the energy they need to function. It also converts some glucose to glycogen that is stored in the liver and muscles where it functions as an energy reserve. Finally, insulin promotes the storage of fats in adipocytes, which make up our fatty tissue and are our main energy reserve. Glucagon, another hormone released from the pancreas gland, generally has the opposite effect to insulin.

- Ghrelin, released from the empty stomach, signals the hypothalamus to stimulate feeding behaviour.

- CCK, released from the duodenum, is a satiety signal that tells the hypothalamus to stop feeding behaviour.

- Leptin is a hormone released by the fat cells (adipocytes) that signals the hypothalamus to stop feeding behaviour when our fat reserves are high. It is important in the long-term regulation of body weight.

Summary questions

1. Is hunger the only signal we use to decide when to eat?

2. Outline the role of insulin in the metabolism of glucose. What happens if insulin levels are low, as in diabetes?

3. Outline the dual-centre model of feeding behaviour and give two pieces of research evidence that support it.

4. Name one satiety signal that the hypothalamus uses to stop feeding behaviour, and one signal that it uses to stimulate feeding behaviour. Give one piece of research evidence for each.

Evolutionary explanations of food preference

Learning objectives:

- describe evolutionary explanations of food preference

- evaluate research into evolutionary explanations of food preference.

Humans are biological organisms and need a range of different nu~~~ to survive. These include carbohydrates, fats, proteins, amino acids vitamins and trace elements such as zinc and magnesium. Our feed system is designed to identify the things we need and to reject things we either do not need or that might be dangerous such as toxins (pois~ Throughout evolution, the components of our diet have come in a var of forms, such as fruit, nuts, berries, leaves and vegetables, and meat. During evolution we have evolved a digestive system suited to breaking down these foodstuffs into the nutrients we need, so that they can be absorbed into the bloodstream and metabolised (processed) by the body.

In the previous section we reviewed the mechanisms of feeding behaviour. Each of these components, such as the digestive system and the brain mechanisms regulating food intake, have an evolutionary aspect. However, this section focuses on the evolution of the human diet and how we identify the foods that we need.

Taste and smell

These are the key senses in identifying the foods we need and those that might be dangerous. Our sense of smell (**olfaction**) is sensitive to around 10,000 fragrances. The sense of smell is used by animals not just to identify foods, but as a means of social communication (for example, the role of **pheromones** in courtship and mating), navigation, identifying predators, etc. (Young and Trask, 2002). However, in relation to food preferences, the sense of taste (**gustation**) is critical.

Taste depends upon taste receptors located on the tongue. When we eat, food is dissolved in saliva, broken down into its basic building blocks (molecules), which then combine with the taste receptors. This combination triggers activity in the gustatory nerve that carries taste information into the brain. Taste receptors work hard; it is estimated that they are replaced every 10 days or so.

Taste receptors are specialised to identify five key taste qualities, each of which can be linked to a particular aspect of diet:

- Sweet: this would be used to identify foods rich in carbohydrates. These would provide the calories that we burn up in energy expenditure.
- Sour: a sour taste is associated with food that has gone off (for instance milk) and may therefore contain harmful bacteria.
- Salt: this is critical to the normal functioning of cells in the body, and it would therefore be important to identify foods providing this nutrient.
- Bitter: a bitter taste is associated with plant chemicals that might be poisonous to humans.
- **Umami**: this has been discovered relatively recently and represents a meaty or savoury quality. This would indicate a good source of protein.

Of course we do not always find pure sources of these tastes. Most foods and certainly most meals are a complicated mixture of several tastes, and it is the *pattern* of stimulation across thousands of taste receptors that gives us our sensation of flavour.

Key terms

Olfaction: the sense of smell.

Pheromones: chemicals secreted in sweat and other body fluids that play an important role in social communication, particularly in courtship and sexual and reproductive behaviour.

Gustation: our sense of taste.

Umami: one of the five key taste qualities that we can identify in food; it has a meat or savoury quality.

Eating behaviour

Key terms

Omnivores: animals, such as humans, that eat fruit, nuts, leaves and meat – a wide-ranging diet.

Hint

How science works

We cannot use conventional scientific methodology to test evolutionary hypotheses in the laboratory. We use *converging* evidence from the fossil record, observations of living hunter-gatherer societies, or studies on our closest primate relatives, to give some examples. The extent to which these different types of evidence support the same theory of our diet and its evolution makes that theory more reliable. (C)

Take it further

Development of the hunter-gatherer society placed different demands on males and females. Many evolutionary psychologists think that these different demands led to gender differences in behaviour that are still with us today. These might involve parental investment, technical abilities or differences in cognitive abilities such as map reading and verbal communication. Thinking of the males and females you know, can you see these sorts of differences? Do you think it is reasonable to explain them in terms of evolution or do you feel they are more due to socialisation during early childhood and learning of gender roles?

Evolutionary origins of the human diet

We can also look at the evolutionary origins of the human diet. It is useful to compare it with our nearest relatives, i.e. the great apes (chimpanzees and gorillas) and monkeys. The human evolutionary line split from the great apes about 6 million years ago. As all modern apes and monkeys live largely on fruit, nuts and plants, it is likely that our earliest ancestors had a similar diet. Chimpanzees may occasionally eat meat in the form of grubs, insects and smaller monkeys if they get the chance. However, the human line rapidly became full **omnivores**, i.e. animals that regularly eat meat as well as fruit, nuts and plants. It is significant that even in modern hunter-gatherer societies meat still makes up a large fraction of the diet, 20–90 per cent depending upon the season. In contrast, chimpanzees will have a maximum of 4 per cent meat in their diet (Buss, 2008).

Even though today vegetarianism has become a choice for many people based on health, ethical and moral grounds, we are still animals that are specialised to eat meat. This is particularly evident in the digestive system:

- We have a relatively long duodenum and small intestine specialised for the digestion and absorption of protein.
- Chimpanzees, gorillas and monkeys have a relatively long large intestine, specialised for the digestion of plant materials.

The advantage of a diet containing meat is that meat is a rich source of protein. It is a far more efficient means of obtaining protein than foraging for plants and leaves. Large occasional kills would mean that early humans would spend less time feeding themselves and the group. Hunting would also require the development of very specialised skills:

- Tool making and tool use; carcasses of dead animals need to be cut up and the meat scraped off.
- Weapon making and use.
- Hunting requires skills of navigation and social cooperation. Social cooperation itself puts pressure on the evolution of language and other high-level social skills (e.g. deception, altruism).

These skills would provide the selection pressure for a larger brain, i.e. individuals with brains capable of these complex actions would have been more likely to survive and breed. The evolution of a hunter-gatherer society would have other implications:

- Division of labour: the physical demands of hunting would be more suited to males, while females would be more occupied with child care and gathering berries, leaves, etc. close to the camp.
- Skilled hunters would acquire great prestige. In modern hunter-gatherer societies the successful hunter shares his kill with other members of the group outside his own family. This gives him esteem and power in the group, as well as sexual favours and greater opportunities to spread his genes (this is a form of the legendary 'sex for meat' hypothesis). In fact, in some modern tribes women can divorce husbands who are not successful at providing food (Buss, 2008).

So we can see that the evolution of our diet has had widespread consequences for human society, although we are now less concerned about divisions of labour due to the widespread availability in Western society of every type of food. Also, women today are less likely to be impressed by a man doing the supermarket shopping than they would have been if he brought home a gazelle in hunter-gatherer times! However, there are clearer examples of our evolutionary heritage in relation to food preferences.

Omnivores have a wide-ranging diet and can therefore exploit many different food sources. However, this also leaves them open to a variety of plant toxins and infections from food that has gone off. Meat is a major source of food poisoning even today. During evolution various methods have evolved to cope with this problem:

- Cooking, introduced at least half a million years ago, is one solution for killing bacteria in meat (Wrangham *et al.*, 1999). This would provide a species advantage for our ancestors over other species. Cooking also makes food easier to chew, and it is noticeable that our chewing teeth, the molars, have decreased in size during evolution (Lucas *et al.*, 2006).

- Spices have always been a part of the human diet. Surprisingly, spices such as onion and garlic are extremely effective at killing bacteria and would have helped the survival of our ancestors. We would not have a genetic tendency for using spices, but **cultural transmission** would quickly spread the word that use of spices would help prevent food poisoning. Today, more spices are used in hot countries (where food goes off more quickly) and in meat (Sherman and Hash, 2001), which is far more dangerous if spoiled.

- Our bitter and sour taste receptors are designed to help us identify foods that have gone off. These tastes lead to a facial expression of 'disgust' that is similar across human infants and other young primates such as chimpanzees and monkeys (Steiner *et al.*, 2001). The feeling of disgust motivates us to avoid these foods in future.

- **Food neophobia**: this is another evolutionary aspect of food preferences. 'Neophobia' means 'fear of the new'. Applied to food it means that animals have a powerful tendency to avoid foods they have not come across before. Although this can lead to a dull diet, it does mean that you always eat food that you know is safe and avoid new foods that may be harmful. An aspect of this neophobia is that we tend to show greater liking for foods as they become more familiar (Frost, 2006). Encouragingly, we do show a preference for variety in foods that we know are safe; children will eat more Smarties if they are multicoloured than if they are all the same colour!

- **Taste aversion learning**: if we eat a food that makes us sick, it would be an evolutionary advantage to avoid that food in future. This can be shown in humans, but has been most dramatically demonstrated in non-human animals. Garcia, Rusiniak and Brett (1977) made wolves sick with lamb's meat contaminated with a mild poison and wrapped in sheepskin. When allowed to approach live sheep, the wolves would approach, sniff, and then leave the sheep alone. They had learnt to associate the poison with sheep. Rats also show powerful taste aversion learning. If poisoned at the same time as they are fed with both a familiar and an unfamiliar food, they will in future avoid the unfamiliar food, as their previous experience tells them that the familiar food is safe. Taste aversion learning is highly specific and extremely intense. Just one experience will affect the animal's behaviour for months as it contributes to keeping the animal alive.

Babies and young children can show a range of taste preferences. In some cases this is very narrow, such as surviving largely on peanut-butter sandwiches. Some of their dislikes are understandable; some vegetables,

Key terms

Cultural transmission: the spread of skills, technologies and ideas through communication and modelling rather than genes.

Food neophobia: common in the animal kingdom, this is an avoidance of unfamiliar foods. It is part of the system for avoiding dangerous foods.

Taste aversion learning: a powerful form of learning in which an animal learns to avoid a particular food after one bad experience with it.

Eating behaviour

■ Key terms

Embryo protection hypothesis: the proposal that morning sickness in the early stages of pregnancy evolved to help the mother avoid foods that might be dangerous to the developing baby.

■ Link

Approaches, issues and debates

Biological explanations of eating behaviour, especially the evolutionary approach, imply that much of our diet is determined by nature rather then nurture (genetics rather than the environment). This ignores the cultural and social changes in food availability and choice over the years of human evolution. Although eating behaviour has a biological and therefore 'nature' element, it is also heavily influenced by environmental 'nurture' factors.

such as broccoli and Brussels sprouts, contain chemicals that can be toxic to the very young (Nesse and Williams, 1994). In adults diets settle down and stay fairly constant. One exception is women in the early stages of pregnancy. It is a cliché that early pregnancy is associated with dietary changes, and in particular the avoidance of certain foods, so much so that disgust and vomiting can be the reaction. This 'morning sickness' is found in at least 75 per cent of women and has a convincing evolutionary explanation –the **embryo protection hypothesis** (Profet, 1992).

Surveys show consistently that the foods most avoided by pregnant women are coffee, tea, meat, alcohol, eggs and vegetables (Buss, 2008). Morning sickness is most severe in the early weeks of pregnancy, when the baby's major body organs are developing and the baby is most vulnerable. Usually it then eases off and disappears as the baby becomes fully formed. Alcohol and coffee and tea (which contain caffeine) can damage the baby's major organs. Meat and eggs are common sources of toxins such as bacteria, while some vegetables contain toxic chemicals harmful to the developing foetus.

The sickness reaction therefore helps the mother to avoid foods that may be harmful, while vomiting prevents any toxins entering the mother's bloodstream and affecting her baby. Of course standards of hygiene are now fairly rigorous and morning sickness is therefore something of an evolutionary hangover. It is an impressive example of how evolution selected out changes in feeding preferences that would help survival of the species.

■ Evaluation

- ▥ Our biological systems for controlling food intake have a long evolutionary history, and there are many similarities between humans and other animals. It is therefore sensible to investigate this evolutionary background.

- ▥ Fossil evidence on changes to our digestive system (e.g. our teeth, the structure of the digestive system, etc.) support hypotheses on the evolution of meat eating and the shift to a hunter-gatherer society. However, there is a limited amount of fossil evidence, and evolutionary explanations are often speculative.

- ▥ The shift to meat eating helps to explain the selective pressure on brain evolution in order to cope with new technical and social skills.

- ▥ An evolutionary approach can explain many features of our digestive systems, e.g. our range of taste qualities.

- ▥ The evolutionary approach can also explain some unusual aspects of food preferences, such as morning sickness.

- ▥ As part of the biological approach, evolutionary explanations are reductionist. They do not take into account cultural transmission of behaviours related to food and feeding, and they do not place enough emphasis on social and cultural changes in, for example, the widespread availability of food. In Western societies we no longer behave as hunter-gatherers, and the evolutionary approach is therefore extremely limited.

Key points

- Modern humans are omnivores and we use a wide range of foods to supply the nutrients that we need. Our digestive system, in particular our sense of taste, has evolved to identify safe foods and avoid harmful foods.

- The introduction of meat as an important part of the human diet led to the evolution of the hunter-gatherer society. This, in turn, gave a selective advantage to the evolution of skills such as weapon making and tool use, and social cooperation.

- Our food preferences are affected by food neophobia, the inherited avoidance of unfamiliar foods.

- Taste aversion learning is a powerful form of learning based on a single bad experience with food. It helps animals to avoid foods that are dangerous.

- Morning sickness involves avoidance of certain types of food in the early stages of pregnancy. The embryo protection hypothesis states that it probably evolved to protect the developing baby from foods that might harm it.

Summary questions

5 Name three taste qualities and explain their significance for our food preferences.

6 Explain two consequences that followed the evolution of an omnivorous (meat-eating) diet.

7 Learning through operant conditioning usually takes many learning experiences. Why is taste aversion learning so rapid?

8 Outline the embryo protection hypothesis. Why can it be considered an 'evolutionary hangover'?

Factors influencing attitudes to food and eating behaviour

Learning objectives:

- understand the role of learning and familiarisation in the development of food preferences

- describe the role of parents and peers in the development of food preferences

- understand and evaluate the relationship between food and emotional states such as depression

- understand the role of cultural factors in food preferences.

Link

Approaches, issues and debates

With eating behaviour there is no simple right or wrong answer to the question of what influences our attitudes to food and our eating behaviour. A lot of human behaviour is complicated and sometimes a sensible conclusion is to say that many different factors at different levels – biological individual, social, cultural – are involved. This is sometimes called an 'eclectic' approach.

Introduction

The biology of eating behaviour is extremely complicated. It has evolved to make sure that we take in the right nutrients in order for our body to function efficiently. The most important aspect is energy regulation. The billions of cells that make up the body are constantly active and in order to function they need energy in the form of calories from carbohydrates such as glucose and from fat. When we take in more calories than we need the excess is either converted into fat stores or converted into heat – this is called thermogenesis. Finally, of course, we expend energy when performing physical activity.

If we take in more calories than we use then we put on weight. If we burn up more calories than we take in, we lose weight. Weight regulation therefore sounds simple: eat less, exercise more. However, the existence of the diet industry and the fact that dieting is a major preoccupation for millions of women and an increasing number of men shows that life is not that simple. In the second part of this chapter we look at reasons why losing weight by dieting is difficult.

The last chapter emphasised the biological aspects of eating behaviour. There is no doubt that the main aim of eating is to maintain the body's physiological systems. An important concept is homeostasis, i.e. all body systems try to maintain a constant level of functioning, and an adequate diet is crucial to this. Below we shall see how the homeostatic regulation of body weight, for instance, can act as a barrier to dieting and weight loss.

We know that what we eat is not only aimed at maintaining homeostasis, it is also affected by cognitive processes such as learning and experience. Emotional state, cultural attitudes, health concerns, etc. also influence eating behaviour. The first part of this chapter reviews some of these influences, and shows that in humans some of our biological drives have become modified by emotional and cognitive factors.

There are some obvious factors that influence what we eat. In the last chapter we reviewed the biological functions that our diet is designed to fulfil. Our diet must contain carbohydrates, fats, protein, amino acids, vitamins and trace elements if we are to survive and stay healthy. Animals in the wild have established patterns of feeding, usually from a limited choice – Koala bears survive mainly on eucalyptus leaves. Of course, some people today survive in harsh or impoverished environments on what we call a subsistence diet – simply finding enough food to stay alive. Choice is not available in such conditions.

However, in affluent societies, especially in the West, food choice is very wide. Carbohydrates, fats and proteins come in a bewildering number of food types, and it is obvious that people develop their own preferences and range of diets. Many factors influence our diet – psychological, social, cultural – showing that despite feeding behaviour having basic biological functions, it can be modified by many other influences.

Before considering some of these influences, we need to outline what a good diet might consist of, at least in Western societies:

- Fruit and vegetables: in the UK the advice is to have at least five portions per day, although only a minority manage this. There is no clear evidence that five portions is necessarily better than four or six but, in principle, fruit and vegetables are an important part of a balanced diet.
- Moderate amounts of meat and fish.
- Bread or cereals (called complex carbohydrates).
- Moderate amounts of milk and other dairy products.
- Small amounts of fatty food and sugar (a simple carbohydrate).

A balanced diet will provide the trace elements, vitamins and amino acids that we also need. Across Western countries most people, while not achieving the ideal, have a reasonable diet. Some groups, in particular students and the elderly, tend to have less-healthy diets with low levels of nutrients, vitamins and energy. There is also increasing concern that children's diets contain too much fat along with low levels of fruit and vegetables. However, these problems are insignificant when compared with the developing worlds of South Asia, Africa and Latin America. Many children in these regions suffer severe malnutrition, with around 180 million at risk. Malnutrition is the major cause of death for these children.

This chapter is concerned primarily with eating behaviour in Western societies, but we should not forget that in many countries the issue is the lack of availability of food, not variations in diet and consumption.

▥ Development of food preferences

Familiarity and preference – the role of learning

1   As we saw in the last chapter, babies are born with taste receptors for sweet, sour, salt, bitter, and umami taste qualities. So they can identify and distinguish between different foods from an early age. They like sweet tastes, and in fact sweet foods are effective in reducing distress in babies (Benton, 2002). This leads us to ask whether we have innate (genetic) food preferences.

2   We saw in the last chapter that food neophobia (page 161) is widespread in the animal kingdom as a basic survival mechanism (new foods may be poisonous). Neophobia is also found in babies and children, although it decreases with age. However, experience and familiarity increase food preferences. Birch and Marlin (1982) found that exposure of two-year-olds to a new food over six weeks increased preference for that food; a minimum of 8–10 exposures was necessary for the initial dislike (neophobia) to change to a preference. The children have *learnt* that the food is safe.

3   Birch (1999) proposes that we are born not with innate (genetic) food preferences, but with an innate ability to associate food tastes and smells with the consequences of eating that food. In this way we learn from experience the foods that are good for us and the foods that are not.

Parental attitudes and food preferences

Parents, usually the mother, provide food for the child. Therefore, it is obvious that the mother's attitude to food will affect the child's preferences. If the mother is concerned over health aspects of food she

▤ Link

Approaches, issues and debates

The study of feeding behaviour and its disorders has focused largely on Western and other industrialised societies. It has ignored third world countries whose main aim is to avoid starvation rather than cope with obesity. This is an example of research that is culturally biased.

▥ **Take it further**

Think about your own diet in terms of the key elements – fruit, vegetables, meat, dairy products, etc. How close do you come to a balanced diet?

▤ Link

Approaches, issues and debates

Birch's (1999) proposal that we inherit an ability to associate food tastes and smells with the consequences of eating that food is an excellent example of an approach that is neither nature nor nurture, but an interaction between them. We learn (nurture or experience) what is good for us, but that learning depends upon brain circuits that are innate (nature).

Eating behaviour

will work harder to make sure her child has a balanced diet. If the mother is less aware or less concerned over health issues such as obesity, she will take less care over the child's diet. As expected, there is a significant correlation between the diets of mothers and children (Ogden, 2007). Parents, especially the mother, provide key role models for the child.

Once the child reaches school, peers become important. Studies have shown that modelling using admired peers can increase consumption of fruit and vegetables (Lowe, Dowey and Horne, 1998). Throughout childhood children are also exposed to widespread food advertising on television, using peer models, animations, etc., to make the food seem more attractive. This can be effective in developing preferences, but unfortunately advertised foods tend to be high in fat and carbohydrates, probably contributing to problems such as childhood obesity.

A common technique, used by many parents and based on operant conditioning, rewards consumption of a disliked food with a desired food – 'You can have some ice cream if you eat your vegetables'. Unfortunately studies have shown that while this technique may work in the short term, in the long term it increases the desirability of the reward food and decreases liking for the non-preferred food (Ogden, 2007; Birch, 1999). Similarly, punishing poor eating habits by denying access to a desired food simply increases the preference for the desired food.

Link

Approaches, issues and debates

This is an example of the principles of social learning theory (see Chapter 10, Social psychological approaches to explaining aggression, page 114), learning through observing models being rewarded.

AQA Examiner's tip

It is easy in this topic to discuss eating behaviour in a commonsense way but it is necessary in the examination to support what you say with research evidence.

Research study: Nicklaus et al. (2004)

Based in France, this study used data collected between 1982 and 1999 on the food preferences of children aged 2–3 at nurseries. Children were allowed free choice of a variety of foods, and these preferences were recorded. In 2002 the children and their families were contacted and invited to take part in a follow-up study.

Those who agreed to take part were given questionnaires on their current food preferences, and for the younger participants (pps) parents were also interviewed. There were between 68 and 99 pps in each of four age categories (4–7, 8–12, 13–16 and 17–22 years old). The main findings were:

- Overall correlations between food preferences at age 2–3 and preferences at 4–7 were significant. Correlations at later ages were non-significant.
- Preferences for cheese and, to a lesser extent, vegetables, remained fairly stable between ages 2–3 and early adulthood (17–22 years old).
- There was some increase in preference for vegetables with increasing age.
- There were decreases in preference for meat products in females as they got older, but this remained fairly stable in males.

The researchers concluded that preferences in adolescence and early adulthood become influenced by exposure, for example, to vegetables. There may also be ethical concerns over killing and eating animals and health concerns (less meat and more vegetables) especially in females. This supports a role for psychological, social and cultural factors in influencing food preferences in adolescence and early adulthood. However, individual preferences at later ages were related to preferences at age 2–3, especially for cheese, and for around 50 per cent of foods in other categories, showing the importance of early experience.

Methodological issues

Food preferences at 2–3 years old were recorded from actual choices, but the follow-up study had to use questionnaires and interviews. These may not provide a completely accurate picture of food preferences, as pps may feel a need to present a 'healthier' view in their answers. Foods were also categorised into groups, so some data on individual foods might be lost. However, the results support previous research on the role of familiarity and social/cultural variables on food preferences.

Ethical issues

There would be few ethical issues with this type of study. The data at 2–3 years old was collected by observation, and at later ages by invitation followed by questionnaires and interview. There was no need for deception, and pps could give fully informed consent.

Fig. 1 *Experience and familiarity increase food preferences*

Food preferences in the adult

As we have seen, children's food preferences are a complicated mix of innate taste receptors, familiarity and experience with food, and the influence of parents, peers and the media. However, even as adults our preferences can change.

Attitudes to health

In the Western world there is increasing concern over diet and health. Obesity is increasing, along with its associated risks of heart disease and diabetes. There is growing awareness of the need for diets that are less fatty and include more fruit and vegetables, and this has led to many adults altering their attitudes to food and changing their diets and those of their children (Ogden, 2007). A downside of this relates to dieting itself. Mothers dissatisfied with their body size or shape can pass this concern on to their daughters, affecting the girl's attitude to food and feeding. This is considered in more detail in Chapter 15, Eating disorders.

Social factors

Parents aware of the health consequences of poor diets may try to change the family's eating habits. However, this depends upon knowledge of healthy diets, the motivation to change, and the time and perhaps the financial resources to put the changes into effect. Those higher up the socio-economic scale are more likely to be aware of healthy diets and try to follow them. The TV chef Jamie Oliver began a campaign in 2007 to improve the diets of schoolchildren and their parents, but the slow progress of the campaign shows how hard it is to shift established attitudes to food. In an age when both parents may be working, the availability of cheap fast food that is quick to prepare and easy to eat in front of the TV is a major problem in changing attitudes to food.

Food and emotion

We have looked at food preferences in relation to biological regulation, early experience, social learning from parents, peers and media, health concerns and socio-economic factors. But food has many other functions besides the dietary ones. These may be religious, with special meals on certain festivals, or ceremonial banquets at weddings. Providing meals can be an expression of love and caring, and the vast number of recipe

■ Hint

How science works

Recently there have been a number of government and media campaigns to improve the diets of people in the UK. These campaigns are based on scientific findings on what foods are good for us and what foods are bad for us, and also on what we know about the causes of problems such as obesity. In this way science can directly influence decision-making in society. (L)

■ Take it further

Going back to your diet, what do you think were the key influences in deciding your preferences? Have they changed over the last few years, and if so, why? Do you have health-related concerns? At this stage, do you think your friends or your parents have any influence over your diet?

Eating behaviour

books and TV cookery programmes shows the widespread interest in food and preparing meals. However, a key area concerns the emotional aspects of food and feeding behaviour.

Hunger is associated with increased arousal, vigilance and irritability, while after a meal we feel calmn and sleepy and have generally pleasurable feelings. More strikingly, studies have shown that people who are stressed or depressed increase the carbohydrate (especially sugar) and fat content of their meals (Gibson, 2006). This change is associated with better mood and more energy (Macht, Gerer and Ellgring, 2003). We also know that most people find sweet tastes (as in carbohydrates like sugar) pleasurable.

This effect is so widespread (we saw on page 165 that sweet tastes calm down babies) that two mechanisms have been proposed to account for it.

■ *The serotonin hypothesis*: carbohydrates such as chocolate contain the amino acid **tryptophan**. This is used by the brain in the manufacture of the neurotransmitter **serotonin**. Low levels of serotonin are associated with depression (see Chapter 27, Depression), and it has been proposed that people with stress or depression take in more carbohydrates because it leads to increased levels of serotonin in the brain. This reduces their depression (Gibson, 2006).

Unfortunately this increase in serotonin levels only occurs when we take in pure carbohydrates, which is extremely rare. The presence of even a small amount of protein, as in chocolate, prevents the tryptophan entering the brain, and so serotonin levels will not change (Benton, 2002). The serotonin hypothesis is unlikely to explain the antidepressant effects of high carbohydrate diets.

■ *The opiate hypothesis*: we have already met some brain neurotransmitters such as serotonin. In the brain we also have **opiate** (or opioid) neurotransmitters. Two examples are **enkephalin** and **beta-endorphin**. They are released from neurons and act at synapses with opiate receptors. As their name suggests, opiates (also referred to as **endorphins**) are chemically very similar to the opiate drug heroin, and heroin acts on these brain opiate pathways. Heroin is a highly addictive drug which can also produce pleasurable feelings and euphoria. Therefore, it seems likely that the brain's opiate pathways are part of our **reward system**, a network of pathways that control our feelings of pleasure and reward.

Our reward system is activated by natural rewards such as food and drink. If the rewarding properties of food depend upon the opiate/endorphin system, then we would expect some interaction between opiates and feeding behaviour, and this is what we find (Grigson, 2002; Gibson, 2006):

■ Opiate drugs increase food intake and increase the perceived tastiness of food.

■ Blocking the endorphin system with the drug naloxone reduces food intake, especially sweet foods, and suppresses thoughts about food. This shows that the system is involved in feeding regulation.

■ Sweet foods increase the release of endorphins in the brain.

So we feel better after eating sweet carbohydrates as these foods in particular activate our natural reward pathways. This effect would be more obvious in people with depression or those highly stressed, but even in normal circumstances sweet foods can improve mood.

Because food is so vital we are very efficient at learning associations between taste and consequences (e.g. taste aversion learning, see Chapter 13, Biological explanations of eating behaviour, page 161). This applies

■ Key terms

Tryptophan: an amino acid found in food that is essential to the production of the neurotransmitter serotonin in the brain

Serotonin: a brain neurotransmitter secreted by neurons at the synapse and thought to be important in emotional states. Pathways using serotonin are involved in behavioural states such as sleep and depression.

Opiate: drugs such as heroin and morphine. Also naturally occurring neurotransmitters in the brain, involved in feelings of pleasure and also in pain reduction.

Enkephalin: an opiate neurotransmitter in the brain. The release of enkephalin is associated with feelings of pleasure and euphoria.

Beta-endorphin: an opiate neurotransmitter in the brain, similar in action to enkephalin.

Endorphins: opiate neurotransmitters such as enkephalin and beta-endorphin.

Reward system: a system of pathways in the brain that control feelings of reward and pleasure. The system is activated by natural rewards and by drugs such as heroin.

to positive effects as well – we *learn* to associate the mood-improving effects of carbohydrates, especially sugars, with the sweet taste. So when we taste the food, we have expectations about the consequences, and this applies to physiological systems as well:

▓ Glucose reliably improves performance on cognitive tasks. However, if people are given a glucose drink but are told it is a placebo (an inactive solution with no glucose), then the effect disappears. Our *expectations* override the actual intake of glucose.

▓ The sweet taste of a glucose solution immediately produces a release of insulin from the pancreas gland, anticipating a rise in blood glucose levels. This happens even with drinks sweetened with saccharine, a compound that is not processed by the body. However, we have learnt that sweet tastes usually mean glucose, so our body prepares itself. Anticipation and expectation on the basis of learning and experience are vital parts of our feeding behaviour (Gibson, 2006).

▓ Culture and food

We have already mentioned the major effect that culture has on food – in some parts of the world, food is scarce and there are high levels of malnutrition and starvation. A second major effect of culture is the availability of different types of food. Eskimos live largely on seal meat because that is what is available.

Although the globalisation of the food market means that even in remote communities food choice is increasing, at least in the sense that fast food is now available worldwide, differences are still found. Wardle *et al.* (1997) surveyed the diets of 16,000 young adults across 21 European countries. In general the number eating a basic and healthy diet was low, with females doing better than males. There were also differences between countries:

▓ People in Sweden, Norway, Denmark and Holland eat the most fibre, and those in Portugal, Spain and Italy eat the least fibre.

▓ People in Italy, Portugal and Spain eat the most fruit, and those in England and Scotland eat the least.

▓ People in Poland and Portugal have the highest salt intake, and those in Sweden and Finland have the lowest intake.

A great deal of interest has focused on the so-called 'Mediterranean diet' found in countries bordering the Mediterranean Sea. People in these countries seem to have lower levels of heart disease and obesity than in other European countries. Key differences in the diet are:

▓ Use of olive oil as a source of fat. The fat in olive oil is unsaturated, and it is thought to be healthier than the saturated animal fats widely used, for instance, in the UK.

▓ High levels of fruit and vegetables are consumed.

▓ Moderate levels of cheese and other dairy products are eaten.

▓ Moderate levels of fish and poultry are consumed.

▓ Low levels of red meat are eaten.

▓ There is a low to moderate intake of wine.

In general lower levels of processed foods are consumed and more natural products are used. However, cultural differences are being reduced with the spread of highly processed fast foods with high saturated fat content. Exposure of ethnic groups to new diets can have dramatic effects. Studies on the Pica Indians of New Mexico show that those who stay in their communities have low levels of obesity. However, those who move to

■ Link

Approaches, issues and debates

Diet can show clear cultural variations, as Leshem's work demonstrates. However, we cannot conclude that these are environmental or 'nurture' effects rather than inherited tendencies ('nature'). Where groups such as the Bedouin have lived in the same environment for many generations, it may be that their diet today is a mixture of innate (genetic) factors and culturally transmitted preferences (nurture).

AQA Examiner's tip

A wide range of factors influence our attitudes to food and our eating behaviour, and it is impossible to say which ones are most important. You need to be aware of the different factors and the relevant evidence. Most importantly you need to be aware that eating behaviour depends upon early experience and learning, media, family and cultural influences, but also our biological requirements for a balanced diet.

■ Summary questions

1 Explain the role of novelty and familiarity in the development of food preferences in children.

2 Outline and evaluate the role of brain mechanisms in explaining the effects of food on emotional states.

3 Evaluate the role of cultural influences on diet and food preferences.

areas heavily influenced by American culture and diet develop high levels of obesity.

On the other hand, a series of studies by Leshem (2009) shows the persistence of cultural effects on diet. He compared Bedouin Arab women living in desert encampments with Bedouin women who had lived for at least one generation in an urban setting. He compared both with a group of Jewish women also living in an urban environment:

■ The diet of urban Bedouins was hardly different from that of desert Bedouins, with both groups differing significantly from the Jewish women.

■ Bedouin groups had a much higher intake of energy, especially carbohydrates, and protein.

■ The Bedouin groups also had significantly higher levels of salt intake.

Higher salt intake is probably related to the high fluid and salt loss associated with living in the desert. It is impressive that this adaptation survives the move to an urban community with easy access to a range of foods.

In another study, Leshem compared the diets of ethnic communities living close to each other in Israel with equal access to shops and food. In the Muslim community intake of carbohydrates was twice that of the Christian group, and they also took in higher levels of protein, fats and salt. Interestingly, the mean body mass index was virtually identical.

These findings show that cultural influences on diet are profound and persist even where there is equal access to the same foods. These differences may originate in adaptations to previous environments, as with salt intake in the Bedouin people. In some groups there are strict religious guidelines on what may or may not be eaten, and these will survive whatever the surrounding environment.

Early humans were omnivores, eating leaves, fruit, seeds and meat wherever they could find or catch it. Our current eating patterns are far more complicated. Outside the developing world there is access to a wide range of natural and processed foods. Food production and preparation have become industries in their own right, and our innate feeding systems have found it hard to cope. Chapter 15, Eating disorders, looks at the causes of the obesity epidemic, but below we review why, in an age of plenty, so many people, especially women, try to diet and why it is so difficult.

Key points

■ Feeding preferences in babies and young children reflect a balance between neophobia and learning through familiarity. Repeated exposure increases food preference.

■ Parents, especially the mother, influence food preferences in children by providing the child's diet and acting as role models. The mother's attitudes towards food are crucial. Later, peers become an important model in the social learning of food preferences.

■ The parents' awareness of health risks associated with diet can influence the child's attitude to food. This is affected by knowledge, motivation and socio-economic status.

■ Sweet-tasting foods improve mood, especially in depressed and stressed people. Evidence suggests that they activate opiate/endorphin reward pathways in the brain.

■ Culture can have significant effects on diet as a result of the availability of food, specific environments and religious beliefs.

Explanations for the success or failure of dieting

Learning objectives:

▥ understand the aims of dieting

▥ describe and evaluate cognitive models of dieting behaviour

▥ understand the biology of body weight regulation in the context of dieting

▥ describe and evaluate different methods of weight loss.

▥ Link

Approaches, issues and debates

Historically, dieting and eating disorders have been studied in Western industrialised societies, showing a Eurocentric bias. In addition, research into dieting has mainly studied women and ignored men who have a preoccupation with body image; this is a gender bias. However, there is now an increased awareness of cultural and gender differences in feeding behaviour, dieting and eating disorders, and this is reflected in the range of modern research studies.

▥ Introduction

It has been estimated that at any one time 40 per cent of the female population is trying to lose weight, usually by dieting. A multi-million pound dieting industry has grown up over the last 20 years, advertising various diets and strategies guaranteed to help you lose weight. This industry is aimed at females, girls and women.

▥ Why do so many females want to lose weight?

If you are obese (see Chapter 15, Eating disorders), whether you are male or female, losing weight has enormous benefits for health and self-esteem. However, many women diet when only mildly overweight if at all. It is assumed that people who diet are dissatisfied with their bodies. This means that their actual body size and shape does not match their ideal size and shape. In some cases, especially in relation to eating disorders, the person has a faulty perception of their actual body, seeing it as larger than it is. However, in many cases women have an accurate perception, and are simply dissatisfied with it. Why should this be? Ogden (2007) suggests several possible factors:

▥ Media influence: this is explored in more detail in Chapter 15, Eating disorders (page 179), but it is clear that media images of women have become slimmer over the last 50 years. Exposure to slimmer models has been shown to increase body dissatisfaction, and it is assumed that many women will try to match what they see as an idealised size and shape.

▥ Family: although the research evidence is inconsistent, a number of studies have found a relationship between mother and daughter's body dissatisfaction and weight concerns. It may be that the mother acts as a model for body dissatisfaction, or it may be a more complicated product of the relationship.

▥ Ethnicity: again evidence is mixed, with some studies finding more body dissatisfaction in white women, and some in black and Asian women. Interestingly, research suggests that the frequency of eating disorders cross-culturally is proportional to their exposure to Western media (see page 179). This may relate to increased body dissatisfaction in ethnic minorities in Western societies.

▥ Social class: there is evidence that eating disorders such as anorexia nervosa are found more frequently in higher-class social groups, suggesting more sensitivity to body dissatisfaction. More recent research now finds that eating disorders and concerns over body size and shape are becoming more equally spread across social groups.

▥ Peer groups and social learning: although not mentioned by Ogden, peer groups are a key source of models and reinforcement. Dieting may become a norm for the group, and the girl is rewarded by praise from her friends for sticking to a diet and perhaps losing weight.

So a number of factors may be involved in developing body dissatisfaction and the desire to lose weight through dieting.

██ Key terms

Preload/taste test: an experimental technique used in the study of the control of eating behaviour. After a preload meal, participants are asked to 'taste' foods. In fact the amount they eat on the taste test is measured. Dieters tend to eat more rather than less on the taste test after preload, supporting Herman and Polivy's boundary model of dieting.

Restrained eaters: a term used for people attempting to diet.

██ Does dieting work?

The short answer is 'no'. Some women can lose weight simply through dieting and they maintain that weight loss. However, most women cannot (Mann *et al.*, 2007), and even more bizarrely they often end up eating more. This is so common it has been extensively researched, often using a methodology known as the **preload/taste test**. Participants are given a food preload which is either high in calories (e.g. a chocolate bar) or low in calories (e.g. a plain unsweetened biscuit). They are then given a taste test, for instance deciding which of a variety of foods is sweetest, saltiest, most preferred. What they do not know is that it is the *amount* of food they eat in a given time that is measured.

A number of studies have been done comparing dieters (usually referred to as '**restrained eaters**') with non-dieters ('unrestrained eaters'). After a calorie-rich preload, restrained eaters should feel full and eat less at the taste test, and this is what some early studies found. However, many other studies (e.g. Herman and Mack, 1975) have found the opposite; they found that restrained eaters eat *more* after a high-calorie preload than after a low-calorie preload, whereas non-restrained eaters consume less.

██ Research study: Herman and Mack (1975)

This was one of the earliest studies using the preload/test method. The participants (pps) were 45 female students. They were told that it was a study on taste experiences.

Method

This was an independent design, with 15 participants in each of three conditions. The first group received no preload. The second group were given one milkshake as a preload. The third group were given two milkshakes as a preload. Groups 2 and 3 were asked to rate the taste qualities of the milkshakes. All participants were then given three tubs of ice cream of different flavours and given 10 minutes to rate their taste qualities. They were told they could eat as much of the ice cream as they wanted.

Finally all pps were given a questionnaire to assess their degree of dietary restraint (dieting).

Results

For each group (no preload, one milkshake preload, two milkshake preload) pps were divided into either high restraint (dieters) or low restraint (non-dieters) sub-groups. Herman and Mack found that low-restraint pps ate less of the ice cream in the two milkshake preload condition than in the one or zero preload conditions. This is what you would predict, as they would be 'fuller' after two milkshakes compared to one or zero preloads.

However, high-restraint pps ate significantly *more* ice cream in the one and two preload conditions than in the zero preload condition. In addition, Herman and Mack found a significant positive correlation across all pps between score on the eating restraint questionnaire and amount eaten after two preloads, i.e. the higher the restraint score (the more the pps were attempting to diet) the more they ate after two milkshake preloads.

Conclusions

Herman and Mack conclude that the results support a boundary model of dietary restraint. Restrained eaters have a 'cognitive' dieting boundary for food intake. Once this is overcome (by the milkshake preloads) the 'what the hell' effect takes over and eating is disinhibited. So they eat *more* in the preload condition than in the zero preload condition; the opposite pattern to low restraint pps.

Methodological issues

The restraint questionnaire was given *after* the feeding tests, so the division of each group into high- and low-restraint pps was what we call **post hoc**, i.e. after the study had been designed and carried out. Ideally this should be done before the study, but Herman and Mack felt that giving the questionnaire before the feeding tests would have alerted the pps to the general purpose of the experiment. This might have biased the results. It did mean that the distribution of high- and low-restrained pps differed across the groups. For example, there were nine high-restraint and only six low-restraint pps in the second group. This uneven pattern reduces the reliability of the findings.

The correlation between restraint scores and food intake after two preloads is only suggestive. Correlations cannot show cause and effect, and some other variable may have produced the association, e.g. high restraint may be linked to depressed mood, and it is this that leads to increased eating.

A final point is that no account was taken of individual differences. Group sizes were quite small (especially after the division into high- and low-restraint pps). Some pps may have liked ice cream more or less than others. Although three different varieties were provided to try to deal with this, it is still possible that dislike of ice cream might have biased the findings.

Ethical issues

Pps received course credit for taking part, which implies some degree of coercion, i.e. they were not pure volunteers. However, the study did not involve unethical procedures, with pps able to eat as much or as little as they liked. There was an element of deception, essential if the experiment was to be valid, but pps were given a full debrief afterwards.

> ### Key terms
>
> **Post hoc:** a term used in research methods to describe manipulations or statistical tests carried out after the study has been completed rather than being planned beforehand.
>
> **Boundary model:** introduced by Herman and Polivy, this model explains why restrained eaters sometimes eat more after preloads than with no preload. Restrained eaters have a cognitive and a physiological boundary controlling eating. The preload takes them past the cognitive boundary, and they then eat until they reach their physiological boundary (see Figure 2 on page 174).

This overeating after a high-calorie preload in restrained eaters is a form of behavioural disinhibition. Several theories have been put forward to explain it, the most comprehensive of which is Herman and Polivy's (1984) **boundary model**.

You will recall from the last chapter that the body's fat stores seem to act as a 'body weight set-point'. Under normal circumstances mechanisms controlling food intake do not allow our weight to fluctuate very much from this set-point. This is an important aspect of homeostasis. If our weight reduces, feeding is stimulated, if it increases, feeding is inhibited. In restrained eating, or dieting, the person is also setting a cognitive limit on food intake. So restrained eaters have two potential boundaries for food intake – one is physiological and set by the body weight set-point, the other is cognitive and set by the person concerned. It will be less than the physiological boundary (see Figure 2 on the next page). In other words:

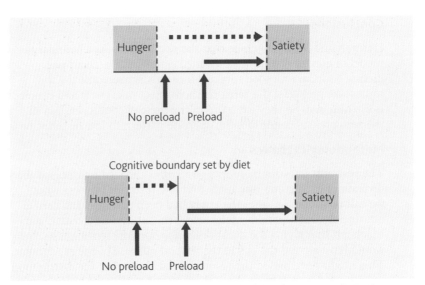

Fig. 2 *Food intake boundaries in unrestrained eaters (above) and dieters (below)*

- The unrestrained eater will eat until they reach satiety ('fullness'), the physiological boundary determined by their body weight set-point.
- The restrained eater will eat until they reach their cognitive boundary, determined by the diet they have set themselves.
- With a low-calorie preload, the restrained eater is still within the diet boundary, and on the taste test eats enough to reach this boundary, i.e. not very much.
- With a high-calorie preload, the restrained eater is pushed *beyond* the diet boundary before they even start the taste test. This disinhibits their feeding behaviour and they simply eat until they reach the physiological satiety boundary, i.e. more than in the low preload condition.

This disinhibition of behaviour after you violate a self-imposed limit is also called the 'what the hell effect'. It has also been seen in people trying to give up smoking or alcohol (Ogden, 2007). You are determined not to smoke, but once you violate this by having a cigarette there is a sense of 'what the hell' and you carry on smoking. The dieter who eats more than their self-imposed limit feels the same, a sense of 'why bother?'.

Evaluation

- The boundary model is a good example of combining physiological and psychological factors to explain feeding behaviour.
- However, much of the experimental work is carried out under controlled conditions in the laboratory. This gives it high levels of reliability but low levels of ecological validity. Dieting in the real world may involve more complicated issues than are studied in the laboratory.
- It does not specify the cognitive and emotional (affective) processes that lead to the 'what the hell' effect.

Other characteristics of restrained eaters have been identified which contribute to their problems maintaining a diet:

- Restrained eaters (in common with women diagnosed with anorexia or bulimia nervosa) tend to become preoccupied with food and thoughts of food. They may then try to deny that food is important and suppress their thoughts about it. However, studies have shown that when instructed *not* to think about something, we actually think about it more. It has been demonstrated using thoughts about sex, mood and white bears (Ogden, 2007). Restrained eaters may therefore overeat as a *rebound* effect from trying to suppress thoughts about food.

- Restrained eating is associated with lowered and depressed mood. As we saw in the last section, food can be used to raise mood. In addition, depression is linked to low self-esteem. So the restrained eater has increased motivation to eat. However, if they violate their dietary limit, they tend to attribute it to their own useless nature and their inability to stick to the diet. So they continue to overeat, following the 'what the hell' effect.

- Dieting to reduce weight below the body weight set-point is also difficult because the body will try to restore the set-point in any way it can. Besides increased feelings of hunger, the body will also reduce its basal metabolic rate (BMR) as weight is lost. The BMR is the rate at which cells burn up energy. A lower BMR *reduces* energy expenditure, making weight loss difficult even on a diet. Fewer calories are being taken in, but fewer are being used up. Slow weight loss on a diet reduces the motivation to stick to it.

Laboratory studies have shown that restrained eaters often overeat even after high-calorie preloads. Reviews of controlled studies of dieting in the real world similarly conclude that reducing calorie input through dieting is not an effective method of losing weight (Mann *et al.*, 2007). In the long term, between one- and two-thirds of dieters end up actually regaining more weight than they lost on the diet. Finally, repeated attempts at dieting (called 'yo-yo dieting') can in the long term increase the chances of heart disease.

So research into dieting looks rather depressing. However, there is hope. Research suggests that successful weight loss is possible when combined with lifestyle changes (Powell, Calvin and Calvin, 2007). These involve low-calorie (especially low-fat) diets with lifestyle changes such as:

- physical exercise
- group and individual support
- self-monitoring: the person is encouraged to keep a diary and records to monitor their progress. This encourages their sense of being in control.

It is also important to set realistic goals. Although on average weight loss was only 7 lb on the programmes reviewed by Powell *et al.*, it was sustained over at least two years, and this level of weight loss has significant health benefits for the overweight.

Weight loss – pharmacological and surgical techniques

It is so hard to lose weight by dieting that many people use drugs or surgery instead. Given the widespread desire to lose weight, especially amongst women, this is an extremely lucrative market for drug companies and there are several compounds on the market:

- **Orlistat**: this drug prevents the absorption of fat from the intestine so that it is excreted rather than processed into fatty tissue. It can produce substantial weight loss (Powell *et al.*, 2007), but it is associated with unpleasant side effects such as intestinal discomfort and oily faeces.

Hint

How science works

The study of the psychology and physiology of dieters and non-dieters has helped us understand why dieting is often difficult and unsuccessful. However it has also helped develop psychological and medical interventions that can help people lose weight successfully. (I)

AQA Examiner's tip

The failure of attempts to diet often reflects a conflict between psychological (cognitive and emotional) factors and biological homeostatic mechanisms. To do well in the assessment you need to be aware of this. You will not need in-depth knowledge of the biological mechanisms, but you will need to understand the idea of body weight set-point.

Eating behaviour

Key terms

Orlistat: a drug used in the treatment of obesity. Orlistat prevents the absorption of fat from the food we eat.

Key terms

Sibutramine: a drug used in the treatment of obesity. It acts on brain serotonin pathways involved in the regulation of food intake.

Link

See Chapter 15, Eating disorders, for more information about body mass index.

Sibutramine: this acts on serotonin pathways in the brain that are involved in brain regulation of food intake. Again it can lead to significant weight loss, but side effects include increased blood pressure.

Drugs are never recommended for long-term use, and as they are not tackling the psychological aspects of dieting, weight gain is likely when the drugs are stopped. Along with side effects their use would only be recommended when obesity becomes a serious threat to health. The weight-loss drug Rimonabant was withdrawn in Europe over fears that it leads to psychological disorders such as anxiety and depression.

Surgery is recommended only for the serious or morbidly obese (those with a body mass index above 35 or 40). The two basic types are:

■ Gastric band: this is a band that is placed around the stomach and reduces its effective size. Therefore, less food needs to be consumed before the person feels full.

■ Gastric bypass: a tube is inserted between the top of the stomach, where food goes in, and the duodenum. This significantly reduces the effective size of the stomach and only small meals can be eaten.

These techniques mean that stomach factors in feeding (such as ghrelin release, see Chapter 13, Biological explanations of eating behaviour, page 155) are avoided and appetite is reduced. These surgical procedures can be very effective. However, apart from the dangers of stomach surgery, they are associated with side effects such as abscesses, pneumonia and other lung infections, and have a significant mortality rate of 2–4 per cent. They would only be used where obesity has itself become a life-threatening condition.

Key points

■ People diet when dissatisfied with their bodies. Many factors, such as media influence, family, ethnicity, social class and peer groups may contribute to body dissatisfaction.

■ Dieting often fails. Research studies demonstrate overeating in restrained eaters. The boundary model explains this using two satiety boundaries; one is the cognitive boundary set by the dieter, the other is the biological body weight set-point.

■ Successful weight loss is possible if dietary changes are combined with lifestyle changes such as physical exercise, social support and self-monitoring.

■ Pharmacological and surgical techniques can lead to effective weight loss, but they are associated with a range of side effects.

Summary questions

4 Outline factors that may contribute to body dissatisfaction and so lead to dieting.

5 Outline and evaluate the boundary model of overeating in restrained eaters.

6 'Dieting is difficult because the body is constantly trying to restore homeostasis and the body weight set-point.' Discuss the interaction between psychological and biological factors in dieting.

15 Eating disorders

Diagnosis and classification

Introduction

Over the last 20 years there has been increasing interest in eating behaviour in general and eating disorders in particular. By now most people are aware of conditions such as **anorexia nervosa (AN)** and **bulimia nervosa (BN)**. This is partly due to their dramatic symptoms, such as a failure to eat, or perhaps a pattern of binge eating and then purging. However, it is also due to the apparent increase in these disorders over recent years, and the fact that AN is a life-threatening condition.

In fact conditions sounding very much like AN and BN can be found in literature over the centuries. Equally, certain professions have long been associated with issues concerning body weight; these include ballet and athletics. We have seen in previous chapters that a range of factors can influence our attitudes to food and our eating behaviour, including biological mechanisms and cultural factors. A key question is whether eating disorders can be explained using these factors, or whether additional influences are operating.

Categories and symptoms

The *Diagnostic and Statistical Manual for Mental Disorders* (*DSM-IV*) identifies three categories of eating disorder. These are anorexia nervosa, bulimia nervosa and eating disorders not otherwise specified (**EDNOS**). AN can be further divided into AN restricting type and AN binge eating/purging type.

The four major symptoms of anorexia nervosa are:

- body weight 85 per cent or less of normal weight for age and height
- distorted perception of body weight/shape, and/or denial that the weight loss is severe
- intense fear of becoming fat
- loss of three consecutive menstrual cycles in women (amenorrhoea).

The AN restricting type involves a refusal to eat, while the AN binge eating/purging type involves episodes of binge eating followed by purging. This means removing food from the body by way of vomiting, laxatives or enemas. Both of these sub-types of AN are associated with significant weight loss and the other symptoms of AN. Note that the AN binge eating/purging type is distinguished from bulimia nervosa as there is significant weight loss.

The main symptoms of bulimia nervosa are:

- repeated episodes of binge eating (though this is hard to define, it usually means eating more in a two-hour period than most people would), followed by purging, exercising or fasting
- the individual feels a loss of control during their binge-eating episodes

Fig. 1 *Sufferers of anorexia and bulimia often have a distorted perception of their body weight or shape*

Key terms

Obesity: weight above normal for age and height. Usually defined as a body mass index of 30 or greater.

AQA Examiner's tip

The Specification refers to psychological and biological explanations of one eating disorder, for example anorexia nervosa, bulimia nervosa or obesity. Therefore, you may concentrate on one out of the three. However, increasing your breadth of knowledge about eating disorders will give you more scope to demonstrate your understanding and for evaluation and commentary.

- the cycle of bingeing and purging occurs at least twice a week for at least three months
- the individual's self-esteem is extremely dependent on their body weight and shape.

The EDNOS category of eating disorders is made up of six eating disturbances that do not match the diagnosis of AN or BN. Examples might be anorexia (refusal to eat) but with body weight above 85 per cent of normal or without amenorrhoea, or cycles of bingeing and purging occurring less than twice a week. Because of these less precise criteria, the frequency of EDNOS is two or three times greater than that of diagnosed anorexia and bulimia nervosa, and this is a major problem for researchers (Striegel-Moore and Bulik, 2007). Another problem is that some of the criteria for AN and BN themselves are very vague. For example, how much would a normal person eat in two hours?

Obesity was in early versions of the *DSM* as an eating disorder but it was removed in the 1980s. However, given the rapid increase in cases over the last 20 years it is now the largest category of problems associated with feeding behaviour. Explanations for this increase are a matter of major social concern.

Anorexia nervosa (AN) and bulimia nervosa (BN)

Although described as two different syndromes in the *DSM-IV*, people with AN or BN have much in common, in particular a dissatisfaction with body weight and/or shape. Anorexia nervosa often develops over time into bulimia nervosa, although the reverse is rare (Polivy and Herman, 2002). Both conditions affect young women far more than any other group (around 90 per cent of cases are female) and they are extremely resistant to treatment. Some 30–40 per cent will show no improvement after five years, while AN in particular is associated with a mortality rate of about 8 per cent, often through suicide (Polivy and Herman, 2002). Although these are dramatic conditions, they are rare (AN affects around 0.3 per cent of males and 0.9 per cent of females, BN around 0.5 per cent of males and 1.5 per cent of females). This is a problem for researchers as participants for studies can be hard to find.

Both AN and BN have in common a preoccupation with body weight and shape, which can be associated with distorted perceptions of their actual body weight/shape and body dissatisfaction. This leads to disrupted eating patterns – starvation or binge-purge cycles. Explaining the core symptom of body dissatisfaction might therefore cover both disorders, and there is general agreement on a broad framework for such a psychological approach.

Psychological causes

Eating disorders (EDs) can be identified in literature going back to the 12th century (Keel and Klump, 2003), although the first formal description of anorexia nervosa was in the 19th century (Gull, 1874) and bulimia nervosa as late as the 1970s (Striegel-Moore and Bulik, 2007). So AN in particular has been around a long time. However, there is clear evidence that both AN and BN increased significantly between the 1970s and the 1990s (Keel and Klump, 2003), and many studies have tried to explain this increase in what are particularly female disorders.

Eating disorders have been identified in all of the cultures studied, but it has been noted that the frequency is affected by reactions to images of Western lifestyles portrayed via media such as television. For instance, Hoek *et al.* (1998) found that the black inhabitants of the Caribbean island of Curaçao had a much lower rate of anorexia nervosa than the white population. They concluded that this was because the white population aspired to more Western lifestyles, especially in relation to idealised images of women, while the black population still valued larger female body sizes.

In a major review of cross-cultural studies of eating disorders, Keel and Klump (2003) drew several important conclusions:

- Anorexia nervosa is not a **culture-bound** disorder. It is found in all of the cultures studied, even in those not exposed to Western influences. However, the frequency is *proportional* to the degree of influence. The more Westernised the society, the more AN is found.
- Bulimia nervosa is more culturally specific. It is found in Western industrialised societies, but not in societies *not* exposed to Western influences.

So what are the influences that affect the frequency of anorexia nervosa across all cultures and why is bulimia nervosa found in Western societies only?

Media images of the idealised woman have become taller and slimmer over the last 50 years, as demonstrated by the winners of Miss World contests and the images of women in newspapers, magazines, films and on television. There is general agreement that this is an important factor in the development of eating disorders (Striegel-Moore and Bulik, 2007). The argument is that:

- Girls internalise culturally defined standards of female beauty, including slimness.
- In some girls, this creates a tension between the real self and the ideal self.
- This leads to dissatisfaction with their own body weight and shape, which in turn leads to dieting and an obsession with food.
- In some vulnerable girls, this can lead to a fully fledged eating disorder.
- The process may be helped by imitation of role models (social learning) and direct reinforcement by praise from family and friends for losing weight (operant conditioning).

There is much evidence to support the role of the media in developing body dissatisfaction in females. For example, Groesz, Levne and Murnen (2002) did a **meta-review** of 25 studies and concluded that body dissatisfaction significantly increased after exposure to media images of thin women. The increase in dissatisfaction was greatest in those with most dissatisfaction before exposure. There is also Becker *et al.*'s (2002) famous study in Fiji. They found that eating disorders were absent in Fiji before the introduction of television and exposure to Western influences. After five years there were significant numbers of women with anorexia nervosa and bulimia nervosa. Given that everyone is exposed to these images, why do only a few develop an eating disorder? It seems obvious that there must be some factors making these people more vulnerable. One area that has been looked at is the psychological characteristics of people with eating disorders and their families.

Women who develop eating disorders tend to have low self-esteem, to be perfectionists (eating disorders often occur together with obsessive-compulsive tendencies) and to have high social anxiety. In addition, those with bulimia nervosa tend to have high levels of impulsivity

Key terms

Culture-bound: specific to one particular social or ethnic group.

Meta-review: statistical approach that combines data from several studies all investigating the same hypothesis. A meta-review gives a more reliable overall picture of, for example, the relationship between media and body dissatisfaction.

Link

Chapter 17, Social contexts of gender roles, outlines processes involved in the development of the self and gender identity. These processes act as a background to the model of EDs above.

Link

Approaches, issues and debates

Although there are an increasing number of cross-cultural studies into eating disorders, it is fair to say that the focus is still on Western industrialised societies, indicating a cultural bias in research.

Eating behaviour

Key terms

Enmeshment: term used to describe families where parents are emotionally over-involved with children. The child then finds it difficult to develop an independent self-concept.

Take it further

Some of the characteristics of people with eating disorders are aspects of personality, such as low self-esteem and perfectionism. Using your psychological knowledge, how might we develop these types of personality? What approaches might be used to explain their development?

(Striegel-Moore and Bulik, 2007). Studies of their families show that parents tend to be high achievers and controlling. The concept of '**enmeshment**' has also been used. This refers to the over-involvement of parents with the child, so it is difficult for the child to feel autonomous (independent).

Research study: Bardone-Cone *et al.* (2008)

These researchers were interested in the interaction between various personality characteristics and the symptoms of bulimia nervosa. Two hundred and four adult women were recruited through advertising and eating-disorder clinics. All satisfied the *DSM-IV* diagnostic criteria for bulimia nervosa. They then completed questionnaires assessing:

- perfectionism – having high standards, and interpreting mistakes as failures
- self-efficacy – a sense of confidence in one's own abilities and being able to control events in one's life
- eating-disorder symptoms – this assessed body dissatisfaction and the frequency of bulimic symptoms.

Using complex statistics the researchers analysed relationships between the personality variables and bulimic symptoms. They found that concern about body weight and body dissatisfaction were positively related to bulimic symptoms, but *only* when combined with *high* levels of perfectionism and low levels of self-efficacy. They conclude that body dissatisfaction is a predictor of bulimia nervosa, but only when combined with high levels of perfectionism, and low levels of self-efficacy. The perfectionist is very self-critical and sees body dissatisfaction as a 'mistake' that they can control. So, in the presence of low levels of self-efficacy, they indulge in bingeing and purging/vomiting.

Methodological issues

- The participants were well-educated Caucasian women. This would limit the extent to which the findings can be generalised for example to other ethnic groups and cultures.
- The participants had already been diagnosed with bulimia nervosa. We do not know whether some or all of the personality characteristics were *secondary* to the condition or contributed to its onset.
- The results support previous work on the involvement of body dissatisfaction, perfectionism and self-efficacy in the cause of bulimia nervosa (Bardone *et al.*, 2000).

Ethical issues

The study was formally approved by the relevant ethical committee. Participants provided written consent and were fully debriefed.

Psychodynamic interpretations of eating disorders

In one of the earliest models of anorexia nervosa, Bruch (1973) proposed that AN was an attempt by the individual to exert some sort of control. They felt used and exploited and were struggling for autonomy – to feel independent from their parents. Eating behaviour was one area that they could control (i.e. increase their self-efficacy) and feel autonomous.

- Crisp (1980) developed similar ideas, based on the fact that self-starvation and the loss of body weight in AN led to postponement of menstruation in pre-pubertal girls and loss of menstruation (amenorrhoea) in post-pubertal girls. He proposed that this was an attempt by the girl to remain in a pre-pubertal state and postpone the onset of adulthood, something that Crisp thought they were unable to cope with.

- Minuchin, Rosman and Baker (1978) took a family systems approach. They suggested that a child develops anorexia nervosa as a means of diverting attention away from other family problems. It is a misguided attempt to keep the family together, for example in cases where the parents are having relationship problems.

There is no doubt that most cases of eating disorders involve complex interactions between children and parents. However, it can be difficult to identify family problems that come *before* the eating disorder and those that are *caused by* the eating disorder. Although psychodynamic interpretations seem to fit descriptions of some cases, they are difficult to test using rigorous scientific methods. Evidence comes mainly from case studies, and these always have issues of reliability as they cannot be replicated. However, various forms of psychotherapy and family therapy have been used in the treatment of eating disorders and they can be effective (Wilson, Grilo and Vitousek, 2007).

Biological explanations

As with all psychological disorders, there has been rapid progress over the last 20 years in the identification of the biological bases of eating disorders. This has been accelerated by the widespread use of brain scanning and other advanced techniques. However, it is important to remember that eating disorders are psychological and any biological approach has to explain the behaviour and characteristics associated with eating disorders.

The biological approach can include evolutionary ideas as well as genetics, and the structure and neurochemistry of the brain. All of these areas have been linked with eating disorders.

Evolutionary approaches

The adapted to flee famine hypothesis (AFFH)

Guisinger (2003) suggested that anorexia nervosa is a reflection of behaviours that were adaptive in the **environment of evolutionary adaptation (EEA)**, maybe one million or more years ago. When our ancestors were hunter-gatherers they needed to move on regularly as food supplies in the local area were exhausted. Guisinger notes that key characteristics of people with anorexia nervosa are restlessness and high levels of activity. She contrasts this with the usual response to starvation and weight loss, which would be inactivity and depression.

She therefore hypothesises that high levels of activity and a denial of hunger would help the individual to migrate in response to famine in their local area.

As with all evolutionary explanations of human behaviour we have no direct evidence for this model. It does not explain why anorexia nervosa is found predominantly in women when it would have seemed sensible for it to have affected both men and women in the EEA. It is also impossible to test scientifically but has to rely on a great deal of

Link

Approaches, issues and debates
There are different approaches to explaining eating disorders. An effective way of demonstrating your understanding is to balance the approaches against each other, e.g. in terms of explaining symptoms, or whether they can be experimentally tested.

Key terms

Environment of evolutionary adaptation (EEA): many examples of modern human behaviour are thought to have originally evolved many thousands of years ago, when the environment was very different. Behaviours that were able to adjust or adapt then may not be adaptive in today's environment. To understand them now we have to consider their origins in that EEA.

speculation. However, it does explain some characteristics of AN, such as the denial of hunger and the increased level of activity.

Genetics of eating disorders

It is by now generally agreed that there is a significant genetic component to eating disorders. Although it has been known for some time that eating disorders can appear regularly across generations in the same family, this could be because families share not only genetic factors but also similar environments. A better approach is to compare monozygotic (MZ) twins, with identical genetic make-ups, with dizygotic (DZ) twins, who, like brothers or sisters, are not genetically the same. However, DZ twins (like MZ twins) are brought up together, sharing similar environments, so they act as a control for environmental factors. If MZ twins are more alike for a particular characteristic (such as anorexia nervosa) than DZ twins, then the difference between MZ and DZ twins is likely to be due to genetic factors rather than the environment.

This was first demonstrated for anorexia nervosa and bulimia nervosa in the early MZ/DZ twin studies of Holland *et al.* (1984) and Kendler *et al.* (1991). Concordance rates for MZ twins were significantly higher than those for DZ twins in both AN and BN. By now many twin studies have been done, and recent reviews (Klump *et al.*, 2001; Bulik *et al.*, 2006) conclude from these studies that the genetic contribution to both anorexia nervosa and bulimia nervosa is between 50 per cent and 80 per cent.

Therefore, we can conclude that genetics play a significant role in eating disorders. However, there are some issues in this area:

■ Anorexia nervosa and bulimia nervosa are rare conditions. Therefore, some genetic studies are based on very few numbers of participants and so lack reliability.

■ Virtually all studies have been done in Western (European and American) populations. We do not know if the same results would be found in, for example, African and Asian countries.

■ Simply identifying a genetic contribution is only the first step. We have no idea what it might be that is inherited. For example, it is difficult to imagine a gene for body image dissatisfaction. In addition, nobody suggests that genes will be the complete answer, as no study has found an MZ concordance rate of 100 per cent. This leaves room for environmental (non-genetic) influences of between 20 per cent and 50 per cent. A key question for today's researchers is how any genetic tendencies interact with environmental factors.

■ Link

Approaches, issues and debates

MZ/DZ twin studies provide evidence for genetic factors in behaviours such as eating disorders. However, if the concordance rate for MZ twins is less than 100 per cent, they also provide evidence for non-genetic environmental influences on behaviour. With eating disorders it seems clear that they reflect neither nature nor nurture, but an interaction between the two.

■ Research study: Holland *et al.* (1984)

■ Aims: to investigate the genetic contribution to anorexia nervosa using MZ and DZ twin pairs where one of each pair has been diagnosed with anorexia nervosa.

■ Justification: MZ twins are genetically identical. If a characteristic is entirely determined by genetics, then both twins must have it. DZ twins are genetically only as similar as brothers and sisters. However, they do share the same environment, so they act as a control for the fact that MZ twins also share the same environment. In theory, the only difference between MZ and DZ twins is the fact that MZ twins have the same genes.

- Participants: 16 MZ female twin pairs and 14 DZ female twin pairs. One of each pair had been diagnosed with AN. Whether they were MZ or DZ twins was decided for most pairs by blood-group analysis. For the remainder a 'physical similarity' questionnaire was used.

- Findings: Holland *et al.* found that if one MZ twin had AN, then the probability of the other twin having AN was 55 per cent. This is known as the concordance rate. The concordance rate for the DZ twins was 7 per cent.

- Conclusions: the concordance rate (CR) for MZ twins was significantly greater than the CR for DZ twins. As the only difference between MZ and DZ twins is the greater genetic similarity of MZ twins, the findings point to a significant genetic involvement in anorexia nervosa.

Methodological issues

- Anorexia nervosa is a rare condition and many studies are therefore based on small numbers of participants. This study is no exception. In addition, allocation to MZ or DZ twins was done on the basis of physical similarity for a few of the twin pairs. This is not a completely reliable method for distinguishing MZ and DZ twins.

- MZ/DZ twin studies assume that environmental influences are the same for both types of twin, and the only difference is in their genetics. However, MZ twins are probably treated more similarly than DZ twins whilst growing up (for instance, they look the same and are often dressed the same), and this extra closeness might contribute to the higher concordance rate.

- The concordance rate for MZ twins was 55 per cent. If anorexia nervosa was entirely genetic it would have been 100 per cent, so non-genetic (environmental) factors are almost as important as genetic influences.

- However, as we have seen, studies over the last 20 years have supported a significant genetic component in anorexia nervosa. The accumulation of research data is more convincing than any single study.

Ethical issues

Studies using participants with psychological disorders such as anorexia nervosa must be carefully vetted for fully informed consent and the right to withdraw at any time. Pps should also have access to professional help and counselling if required.

Serotonin and eating disorders

Serotonin is a brain neurotransmitter that is involved in many behavioural functions, including depression and obsessive-compulsive disorder. Early studies (Kaye *et al.*, 2005) found a reduction in levels of the important serotonin metabolite 5-HIAA in people with eating disorders. This would suggest that brain serotonin pathways were underactive. However, most of these early studies were on people with ongoing AN and BN, and it is always possible that the illness itself had produced the changes in serotonin activity. In AN especially, the loss of body weight itself produces many hormonal and brain changes as the body tries to cope. It was not possible to conclude that serotonin abnormalities *caused* the eating disorder.

Eating behaviour

However, the introduction of brain-scanning techniques has transformed the area. In PET scans, a drug that combines with serotonin receptors is injected. It travels to the brain and binds to serotonin receptors. A brain scan is taken and the drug shows up as brightly lit areas. These can be measured, and this gives us an estimate of the number of serotonin receptors in different parts of the brain. This is a far more direct method than measuring serotonin.

Using PET scans it has been shown that there are fewer serotonin receptors in the brains of people with eating disorders (Frank *et al.*, 2002; Kaye *et al.*, 2005). More importantly, they also show that these changes are found in people who have *recovered* from eating disorders, i.e. they are not due to loss of body weight or other physiological changes associated with AN and BN (Kaye *et al.*, 2005).

- A reduction in receptors suggests a dysfunction of the serotonin system in eating disorders. The brain serotonin system has been implicated in personality traits associated with eating disorders, such as obsessionality, perfectionism, anxiety and depression. It is also part of the neurotransmitter system of the hypothalamus that controls feeding behaviour. Therefore, it is likely to be involved in the causes of eating disorders.

- However, this still does not show conclusively that changes in the serotonin system *cause* eating disorders. The loss of weight in anorexia nervosa, for example, produces alterations in the body's physiological systems. These alterations may be so profound that they persist even after the person has recovered. But they are still *secondary* to the illness and not the cause.

- The only convincing way to show that dysfunction of the serotonin system causes eating disorders would be to show that the changes were there *before* onset of the eating disorder. But because eating disorders are so rare it would be impossible to test enough people and then follow them through to see which of them developed an eating disorder.

An integrated approach to eating disorders

Research evidence shows that psychological and biological factors are involved in eating disorders, but studies usually focus on one or the other. However, it is obvious that they must interact. The simplest model would be that a genetic vulnerability interacts with environmental factors, such as media influence or family dynamics, to produce eating disorders. Connan *et al.* (2003) have suggested a more detailed model of anorexia nervosa based on the characteristics of the disorder:

- Anorexia nervosa typically affects girls around the time of adolescence and early adulthood. However, there are a number of early signs. Mothers of girls who go on to develop AN have more difficult pregnancies. Babies are more likely to be premature and of low birth weight. Mothers have high levels of anxiety during the pregnancy and are more likely to be anxious and over-protective with the new baby. This leads to the higher levels of anxiety and *insecure attachment* between child and parent.

- Animal studies show that stress before birth ('maternal stress') and poor mothering afterwards can upset the hypothalamic-pituitary-adrenal (HPA) stress response in the developing child.

- This means that the child has an over-reactive stress system and copes poorly with stressful situations. In addition, high levels of stress hormones affect neurotransmitters such as serotonin in the brain.

Link

Find more detail on the HPA in the *AQA Psychology A AS* book, pages 143–6.

Eating behaviour

At puberty there is a surge of oestrogen in females. Oestrogen has been shown to have a direct effect on brain serotonin and to affect a number of brain systems, including those related to the control of mood, appetite and the HPA system. In vulnerable girls, this further imbalances systems that have already been disturbed by early experience.

Puberty and adolescence are times of significant psychological stress. The girl enters adulthood and has to cope with rapid bodily changes, changes in family and social relationships, and the development of full gender and self-concept.

In AN, the stress response is hyper-reactive, leading to a failure to cope successfully with adolescence. Attempts to cope lead to the behavioural symptoms of AN, influenced by the imbalanced brain systems referred to above.

The genetic influence might operate in various ways. Complications of pregnancy and the development of the HPA have a genetic component, as do the hormonal changes associated with puberty. So genetic factors could act to make the sequence of events outlined above more likely.

There is a certain amount of evidence for this model (Connan *et al.*, 2003), especially the early developmental problems associated with anorexia nervosa. We have also seen evidence for disturbances of brain function in the disorder, and levels of the stress hormone cortisol are raised in AN. However, much of the model is speculative, with little reliable research evidence. Yet it is an important attempt to show how the biological and psychological approaches might be combined. There is no doubt that the eventual understanding of EDs will require this type of combination.

Key points

- Anorexia nervosa and bulimia nervosa represent abnormalities of feeding behaviour. They are associated with a concern over body weight and the effect this has on self-esteem.

- There is strong evidence that changing media representations of women play a part in causing eating disorders. However, only a small number of women develop eating disorders, so other factors must be involved.

- Evidence suggests that symptoms of bulimia nervosa emerge when body dissatisfaction is combined with high levels of perfectionism and low levels of self-efficacy.

- Evolutionary hypotheses suggest that anorexia nervosa might be an adaptation to coping with famine in the EEA, as it is associated with increased activity and a denial of hunger.

- Twin studies show a clear genetic component in eating disorders, although concordances in MZ twins are never 100 per cent and we do not know what the genetic mechanisms might be.

- There is strong evidence for a disturbance of serotonin systems in the brain in eating disorders. This would explain some of the personality characteristics associated with EDs, but clear evidence for cause and effect is lacking.

▮ **Hint**

How science works

This is an excellent area in which to demonstrate your understanding that different approaches in psychology may all contribute to our explanations of eating disorders.

AQA Examiner's tip

You are required to know psychological and biological explanations for *one* eating disorder, either anorexia nervosa, bulimia nervosa, or obesity. Some explanations, such as body dissatisfaction and media influences, apply to both anorexia and bulimia nervosa, or you may use a more specific explanation, e.g. the adapted-to-flee-famine hypothesis of anorexia. Just be clear in your answer *which* disorder you are discussing.

▮ **Summary questions**

1. Discuss three problems with the *DSM-IV* classification of eating disorders.

2. Using research evidence, discuss the role of the media in the development of eating disorders.

3. Eating disorders are associated with changes in brain function, e.g. effects on the serotonin system. Discuss the difficulties of showing that these changes *cause* the disorder rather than being caused by the disorder.

Eating behaviour

Obesity

- understand methods of defining obesity

- describe and evaluate psychological, social and lifestyle changes that may contribute to obesity

- describe and evaluate biological explanations of obesity.

Introduction

As outlined above, obesity is not classified as an eating disorder in the *DSM-IV*. However, it is a major social issue and attempts to understand and treat obesity are a key concern of psychologists. More than one-third of the American population were classified as obese in 2004 compared with 15 per cent in 1980. In the UK it has been estimated that up to a quarter of adolescents are obese, with the number increasing steadily. Rates of obesity have increased in all countries except Japan (Anderson and Butcher, 2006).

Obesity is usually defined in terms of the body mass index (BMI). This is calculated by dividing your weight in kilograms by the square of your height in metres:

- BMI of less than 18.5 = underweight
- BMI of over 25 = overweight
- BMI of over 30 = obese
- BMI of over 40 = morbidly obese.

There are problems with this system. In particular, it takes no account of the ratio between fat and muscle; many body-builders and weightlifters would come out as obese on the BMI. It is also inappropriate to use with the developing child, where BMI should be compared with the norms for their age and sex. Alternative approaches include waist size and measuring the actual thickness of fatty tissue using callipers.

Anorexia nervosa and bulimia nervosa are severe but relatively rare conditions. Obesity, on the other hand, is now common, and it is related to poor health in general and a significantly increased risk of heart disease and diabetes. It is second only to smoking as a cause of death in the USA. There are some immediate points that can be made:

- The rapid increase in obesity over the last 20 years cannot be genetic, as genetic mechanisms cannot change that quickly.

- So we must look for non-genetic factors, in particular changes in patterns of feeding behaviour and in general lifestyle that might contribute to weight gain.

Psychological, social and lifestyle explanations

We saw in Chapter 13, Biological explanations of eating behaviour, that there is a simple relationship between food intake and weight gain. If you take in more calories than you burn up in energy expenditure, then you gain weight. Use up more than you take in, and you lose weight. There are three main routes to energy expenditure (Anderson and Butcher, 2006):

- **Basal metabolic rate (BMR).** All cells in the body are continually active, so even when we are at rest we are consuming energy. This is our BMR, which accounts for about 60 per cent of energy expenditure.

- Dietary thermogenesis. This is the energy we expend in digesting food, and it accounts for about 10 per cent of our energy expenditure.

- Physical activity and exercise. This accounts for about 30 per cent of energy expenditure.

Hint

How science works

Obesity is an increasing social and health issue especially in Western industrialised societies. If scientific research can identify the causes and therefore potential treatments for obesity, it would be making a profound contribution to the well-being of these societies. (I, L)

Key terms

Basal metabolic rate (BMR): all cells of the body are continually active and consuming energy, even when the body is at rest. The rate at which this occurs is the BMR.

Weight depends upon energy taken in versus energy expenditure. As we shall see below, there are physiological and genetic factors involved, but there are also a number of important non-genetic factors that can be linked to the increase in obesity, especially in children:

▓ There has been a huge increase in the availability and consumption of fast food and soft drinks over the last 20 years. Fast food generally has higher energy content (calories), often in the form of fat rather than carbohydrates, and lower nutritional content, while soft drinks also have a high energy content in the form of sugar. Portions have also increased in size (Anderson and Butcher, 2006).

▓ The increase in the number of working parents means that there is less time for meal preparation and more reliance on fast food. There is also less time for organising activities with children.

▓ The increase in television and computer games matches the increase in childhood obesity over the last 20 years. Early research suggested that each extra hour's viewing per day increases levels of obesity by 2 per cent (Dietz and Gortmaker, 1985). Besides the lack of exercise, TV viewing is associated with more fast snacks and exposure to food advertising.

▓ The food industry invests substantial sums of money into researching aspects of food that make it more attractive, such as taste and colour. It has been very effective in using research into feeding behaviour to persuade us to eat foods that have high energy content and little nutritional value.

▓ The 'built environment'. Rightly or wrongly city life is seen as increasingly dangerous, either as a result of crime or traffic. Children play less, and children and adults walk less and travel more by car. Physical activity has decreased.

These trends combine to provide a recipe for weight increase and obesity. Physical exercise (energy expenditure) has decreased over the last 20 years while food intake (energy input) has increased.

Evaluation

The social and psychological changes in feeding behaviour and lifestyle outlined above provide a convincing account of the increase in childhood and adult obesity. The most convincing aspect is that it fits with what we know about energy regulation in relation to feeding and body weight. However, the evidence is largely *correlational*, meaning that we cannot draw conclusions about cause and effect. In this area it is impossible to do controlled studies on the relationship between, for example, TV viewing and obesity; it would be unethical to manipulate viewing hours to observe the effects on obesity.

It also means that we do not know which of the factors is more important – is the change in diet more significant than the reduction in physical activity? We do have a convincing picture, but there are many details to be unravelled.

Finally, although obesity is widespread in affluent societies, most research is carried out in Europe and the USA. There is some evidence for cultural variations. For example, there is more obesity in children of low income Afro-Caribbean groups (Anderson and Butcher, 2006), which could relate to lifestyle differences or to genetic and physiological factors. However, cultural factors have not been widely explored.

▓ **Take it further**

Consider your own diet and lifestyle in terms of your energy input and energy expenditure. Does your diet contain lots of fast, fatty foods and sugary drinks? Do you walk to school or college? Do you play sport or take other exercise? Have any of these factors changed over the last five years? If your energy input and output seem unbalanced, can you identify simple ways in which you could restore balance?

▓ Link

Approaches, issues and debates

Although research into obesity can be criticised as culturally biased, as most of it takes place in Western industrialised societies, obesity is linked to factors found more often in such societies. These include the availability of high fat low-cost foods and more indoor activities for children such as computer games. So, compared with research into feeding behaviour in general, which varies across cultures but is still mainly studied in the West, the criticism that research into obesity is culturally specific is less severe as obesity itself is culturally specific.

Eating behaviour

▓ Biological explanations

You will recall from Chapter 13 (Biological explanations of eating behaviour) that the control of feeding behaviour is extremely complicated, with many hormones and brain neurotransmitters involved. If these systems are not regulated properly, the outcome could be over-eating (and obesity) or under-eating. Further, if the physiological causes of obesity were identified, then there is the potential for medical treatments, such as drugs, to be developed. As with the other eating disorders, there are evolutionary, genetic and physiological aspects to obesity.

Evolution and obesity

The main contribution to body-weight variation is made by our fat reserves. Humans have a higher proportion of fat in their bodies than other animals, with men averaging about 13 per cent and women about 25 per cent. Most animals in the wild have about 4–8 per cent (Wells, 2006). In particular we have far more fat than our closest primate relatives, gorillas and chimpanzees. Along with other characteristics, this key difference suggests an evolutionary explanation for obesity, suggested by Wells (2006):

▓ In our evolutionary ancestors, the higher proportion of fat would have served as a medium-term energy reserve in times of food shortages.

▓ This would have allowed them to survive seasonal changes in food availability.

▓ The move from hunter-gathering lifestyle to agriculture would have left early humans vulnerable to famine; large fat reserves would have increased their chances of survival.

▓ The higher proportion of fat in females is essential for normal functioning of the reproductive system (remember how menstruation stops as body weight falls in anorexia nervosa). It also provides energy for mother and child during pregnancy and early childhood. In particular the developing human brain consumes large amounts of energy.

▓ Our feeding behaviour and energy regulation evolved in times when the supply of food was unpredictable. Our systems for finding and eating food are complex and sophisticated, sensitive to smell, taste and dietary value. In contrast, our systems for controlling satiety are less sensitive, as eating more than we needed at that particular time would have built up fat reserves for times of hardship. It is notable that our satiety system, for instance the release of ghrelin from the stomach (see Chapter 13, Biological explanations of eating behaviour, page 155), is less sensitive to fats than to carbohydrates.

▓ We now live in a time of plenty, at least in Western and other affluent societies. Our evolutionary tendency to store more food than we need (this has been referred to as the 'thrifty gene') can therefore operate most of the time, leading to increased fat deposits, increased weight and obesity.

Evaluation

As with all evolutionary hypotheses, many of Wells' ideas are speculative. We do not know at what stage increased fat deposits in our ancestors emerged, or exactly how they related to lifestyle. Wells' hypothesis is supported by the adaptive value of having a system that stores extra energy reserves during times of plenty, for use when times are hard. It has also been shown (Poston and Foreyt, 1999) that groups usually living

▓ Link

Approaches, issues and debates

Evolutionary explanations of obesity can be seen as reductionist as they explain obesity through the relatively simple behaviour of our ancestors in the EEA (environment of evolutionary adaptedness). Such an approach minimises the influence of cultural and social factors in attitudes to food and feeding, and, as we have seen, these can be highly influential. A complete explanation of obesity requires research at all levels – biological, evolutionary, psychological, social, and cultural.

Eating behaviour

in harsher conditions, such as the Pima Indians of Mexico, develop high levels of obesity when exposed to the Western pattern of easily available energy-rich diets. Their 'thrifty' inherited system cannot cope with the change in environment.

Whether such an explanation can apply to the rapid increase in obesity levels over the last 20 years is doubtful. It is more likely that this evolutionary tendency *interacts* with the non-genetic factors discussed above.

Genetics and obesity

There is a popular view that a tendency to obesity is inherited. Studies do show a strong relationship between parent and child BMI (Anderson and Butcher, 2006), but of course the parents also provide the environment for the child, so it may be their attitudes to food and feeding behaviour that the child learns.

More convincingly, twin studies do show a higher concordance of about 50 per cent for BMI and BMR in MZ twins compared with DZ twins, showing a genetic influence. In fact it was thought for a long time that the obese person inherits a low BMR from their parents; thus they burn up calories at a lower rate and more energy is stored as glycogen (see Chapter 13, Biological explanations of eating behaviour, page 153) and fat, increasing body weight. However, studies show that obesity is not associated with a lower BMR, and this is usually in the normal range.

The discovery of leptin and the ob mouse (see Chapter 13, Biological explanations of eating behaviour, page 157) seemed a promising development. Leptin is a satiety signal, a hormone released from fat cells that travels to the hypothalamus and inhibits feeding. If someone inherits a deficiency in the leptin system then they may, like the ob mouse, develop obesity. Unfortunately it turned out that leptin levels were normal or even higher than normal in the obese person. This led to the interesting conclusion that in obesity the feeding system has become *insensitive* to the satiety effect of leptin. This may be genetically determined, but we do not know the mechanisms involved.

Genetic abnormalities have also been found in obesity, but they account only for a small minority (less than 10 per cent) of cases. In general there is no evidence for a *simple* genetic explanation for obesity. The rapid increase in obesity is a convincing argument against genetic factors. However, it may be that some obese people inherit a vulnerability to become overweight when there is an imbalance between energy input and energy output, i.e. they may store carbohydrates and fats more efficiently and so increase weight more rapidly.

Physiological factors

We have already mentioned some of the physiological characteristics relevant to obesity:

▪ Obese people do not on the whole eat more than the non-obese (Mobbs *et al.*, 2005) although they may eat a higher proportion of fat in their diet.

▪ So far, obesity has not been conclusively linked to problems with satiety signals such as leptin.

▪ Obesity is not associated with a lower BMR.

▪ However, we do know that weight loss reduces BMR as the body tries to compensate for the weight loss by reducing energy expenditure.

■ **Link**

Approaches, issues and debates

Obese individuals are sometimes accused of lacking 'willpower', and that they are overweight simply because they are greedy and cannot control themselves. This is an argument based on free will, the idea that we have control over our behaviour. However, research has shown that obesity can be due to genetic factors or to imbalances in brain mechanisms. This is a deterministic argument, which says that in some cases the person cannot help being obese because it is caused by factors outside of their control.

Eating behaviour

■ In people of normal weight, the reverse happens. BMR increases with feeding and weight gain, but significantly this does not happen in the obese (Mobbs *et al.*, 2005). This could be a key factor in weight gain in obesity. An increase in BMR would burn up more energy and help to prevent weight gain.

■ Bringing it all together

Apart from the rare cases where we can identify a genetic abnormality that produces obesity, it is unlikely that any of the factors discussed above will prove to be decisive. Any model of obesity must include all of them:

■ We have inherited feeding and energy regulation systems from the EEA which may now be maladaptive in times when energy-rich foods are plentiful.

■ As food has become easily available, so environmental and lifestyle changes have reduced physical activity, so the energy in/energy out balance has shifted.

■ A genetic vulnerability to obesity, perhaps based in subtle changes in the brain systems controlling feeding behaviour, promotes fat storage and reduces the BMR response to weight gain seen in people of normal weight.

Key points

■ Obesity is an increasing problem in Western societies. It is associated with an increased risk of major health problems such as heart disease and diabetes.

■ The rapid increase of obesity over the last 20 years must be related to non-genetic factors such as psychological, social and lifestyle changes.

■ Significant factors are the increased availability of high-energy food and decreased levels of physical activity.

■ Evolutionary approaches see obesity as an adaptive response to cope with periods of food shortage, but which is now maladaptive as food is plentiful.

■ Physiological changes associated with obesity have been hard to identify as there are no clear changes in BMR or the feeding system. A failure to respond to food intake and weight gain with an increase in BMR may be a key factor.

■ Summary questions

4 Obesity reflects an imbalance between our energy intake in the form of food and the energy we expend as BMR, dietary thermogenesis and physical activity. Explain four factors that might explain how this imbalance has increased over the last 20 years.

5 Outline and evaluate an evolutionary explanation for obesity.

Eating behaviour

Eating behaviour end of topic

How science works: practical activity

Using the internet, collect media articles on aspects of diet and health. These often involve the effectiveness of particular diets in weight loss, or the role of nutrition in causing or preventing conditions such as obesity, cancer, heart disease or senile dementia. Then rate the articles along various dimensions, such as:

- How scientific is the work? Is the article based on published, peer-reviewed research findings, or on supposition and hearsay? Why do we trust the former more than the latter?
- Were they experimental studies? A lot of the work in this area uses correlations. What are the problems with correlational studies?
- If the findings are in areas covered in these chapters, how do they relate to the material you have read? Do you find them surprising or do they fit with what you now know?

Further reading and weblinks

Ogden, J. (2003) *The Psychology of Eating: From Healthy to Disordered Behaviour.* Oxford: Blackwell.

The focus of this text is on eating behaviour, both normal and disordered, in particular psychological and social factors.

Ogden, J. (2007) *Health Psychology* (4th edn). Maidenhead, Berks.: Open University Press.

This volume has particularly good information on psychological and social approaches to eating behaviour, including models of dieting and causes of obesity. Again it covers other A2 topics including models of health behaviour and addiction.

Wickens, A. (2005) *Foundations of Biopsychology* (2nd edn). Harlow, Essex: Pearson Educational.

This book has excellent coverage of the biological bases of eating behaviour, including brain mechanisms, eating disorders and obesity. It also covers the biological aspects of other A2 topics, such as sleep, schizophrenia, depression and sexual development.

http://disordered-eating.co.uk

There are many websites dedicated to eating disorders. One which takes a balanced view in terms of psychological, social and biological causes is called Disordered Eating. The websites have a wealth of information, but be careful to look for material that has scientific validity rather than consisting of anecdotal material.

Gender

Introduction

'Men are from Mars and women are from Venus' – so wrote John Gray in 1992. This phenomenally successful book puts forward an argument which is taken by many to be 'fact', that men and women are biologically different. Pick up a newspaper or magazine and you will see the prevailing view that sex differences between men and women are natural. Men are rational whereas women are emotional; men are assertive and women are passive; men are aggressive, women are gentle. The list of claims goes on and on!

How true are all of these? In this section of the course we are going to look at the psychology of **sex** and **gender**. In order to do this, we need to examine the meaning of these terms. Although they are often used interchangeably in everyday life, the terms have different meanings.

There is little doubt that gender differences exist, but where do they come from? In this topic, we will examine the explanations given by biological and evolutionary psychologists and by social learning theorists about the relationship between sex and gender. As we will see, biological and evolutionary psychologists have taken the view that gender differences arise from biological sex, that men and women are 'hard wired' to act differently. In contrast, psychologists working within the behavioural approach have argued that gender differences arise from socialisation processes. Children are shaped and rewarded for gender-appropriate behaviours. They are immersed in a gendered environment in which role models are very different for boys and girls. In this environment, they rapidly learn what it is to be masculine or feminine. Biological and social explanations take different sides in the nature–nurture debate and many psychologists favour theoretical explanations which combine the interactions between nature and nurture, such as the biosocial model. As you will see, the psychology of sex and gender has been fraught with argument, counterclaim and political battle! Most recently, cognitive theories emphasising the importance of the child's understanding of gender have come to the fore.

While people may choose different ways in which to interpret gender, most people experience a clear relationship between biological sex and gender identity. Most women are biologically female and 'feel' feminine. But what happens when there is conflict between an individual's biological sex and their sense of gender identity? Trans-gendered people often report that they feel 'trapped in the wrong body'. What can these experiences tell us about sex and gender?

Key terms

Sex: the biological fact of being a male or female. In about 98 per cent of babies, biological sex is clearly established by the genitals and hormones.

Gender: the concepts of masculine and feminine. These are socially constructed ideas about the behaviours and qualities which are appropriate for men and women, such as being interdependent or emotional. The statement 'boys don't cry' demonstrates a commonly held idea about masculinity.

Link

Approaches, issues and debates

There are various explanations of gender development, but most involve an interaction between nature and nurture. Purely biological explanations are now seen as highly reductionist, ignoring psychological, social and cultural influences on gender development. The biosocial approach is an attempt to combine biological and social factors and provide a more complete view of gender development.

Specification	Topic content	Page

Introduction and some key terms

Fig. 1 *Masculine or feminine?*

Key terms

Androgyny: the co-existence of masculine and feminine qualities within the same person. For example, a man who is both adventurous and gentle or a woman who is brave and nurturing could be called 'androgynous'.

Introduction

This part of the chapter introduces you to some important terms and concepts in the psychology of sex and gender. As noted in the introduction, the terms 'sex' and 'gender' have different meanings. The word 'sex' refers to the biological fact of being male or female, whereas gender refers to the ideas of being masculine or feminine.

Whilst it is a fairly simple procedure to decide the sex of a baby at birth (at least it is in most cases), decisions about masculinity and femininity are much more subjective – one person may see something as masculine behaviour, but another may disagree. For example, one person may view David Beckham as a very masculine man whereas another may argue that he is in touch with his feminine side!

For a long time, psychologists made the logical assumption that masculinity and femininity were opposite points on a single dimension, so that each individual could be measured and placed somewhere in between the two extremes. Using this approach, an extremely masculine man such as Bruce Willis would be placed at one end whereas a 'girly' girl like Paris Hilton would be placed at the other. This assumption was challenged by Sandra Bem (1974) who developed the idea of '**androgyny**'. Bem drew on Jung's idea that each personality is comprised of a blend of two complementary characteristics, the anima (feminine) and the animus (masculine), and she argued that people possess both masculine and feminine characteristics. In order to investigate this, Bem developed an influential scale, the Bem Sex Role Inventory (BSRI). This scale identifies four different gender 'types', suggesting gender to be complex.

Research study: Bem (1974)

Bem asked 50 male and 50 female students to rate a list of 200 personality trait words (such as reliable, honest, gentle and assertive) in relation to how desirable they were for men and women. This was to generate gender stereotypes. From the original list of 200 items, Bem selected 20 words which were consistently rated as desirable for women (including affectionate, gentle, understanding and sensitive) and 20 which were rated as desirable for men (including assertive, dominant, independent and ambitious). Twenty neutral items which were seen as being neither masculine nor feminine were also selected.

These 60 items constituted Bem's Sex Role Inventory (BSRI). Bem then asked students to rate themselves on each of the 60 traits using a scale of 1 (almost never true of me) to 7 (almost always true of me). This produced a score out of 20 for each of the sub-scales – masculinity, femininity and neutrality – and enabled Bem to divide people into one of four gender types:

- Individuals with high scores on masculinity and low scores on femininity are generally masculine.
- Individuals with high scores on femininity and low scores on masculinity are generally feminine. The above two are referred to as 'sex-typed' individuals.
- Individuals with high scores on both masculinity and femininity are 'androgynous'.
- Those with a low score on both masculinity and femininity are categorised as 'undifferentiated'.

Bem's research confirmed her idea that people combine aspects of masculinity and femininity within their personalities. In later research Bem argued that sex-typed individuals tended to be restricted in their gender role behaviours and had poorer psychological health, whereas androgynous individuals had better psychological adjustment.

Methodological issues

Bem's SRI scale has been carefully developed using the 20 items which are most consistently seen as male and female. However, the use of students as raters may have produced bias in the scale as students may have more egalitarian views about gender than the general population.

Ethical issues

There are few ethical issues in the development of the scale. However, the use of the scale requires the informed consent of participants who may also need to be carefully debriefed. This is difficult for researchers to control especially when published scales appear on the internet for self-completion.

Fig. 2 *Blurring the boundaries between masculine and feminine*

Key terms

'Sex-typed' individuals: men who conform to a masculine stereotype and women who conform to a feminine stereotype.

Gender identity: the classification that the child/adult gives himself/ herself as male or female. In most cases, the child is either male and feels like a boy, or female and feels like a girl.

Gender dysphoria: being uncomfortable with your assigned gender and having a strong desire to become a member of the other sex. A man may feel he is a woman trapped in a man's body.

Another important concept refers to **gender identity**. This is your classification of yourself as male or female. As we shall see in Chapter 18, Psychological explanations of gender development, young children develop gender identity at around two years of age. For most people, gender identity and biological sex correspond; most women are biologically female and 'feel' feminine and most men are biologically male and 'feel' masculine. However, individuals who experience **gender dysphoria** experience conflict between their sex and gender identity and have a strong desire to become a member of the other sex. In everyday language this group of people are often referred to as 'transsexuals'. We will look at explanations of gender dysphoria to see what light it casts on our understanding of sex and gender.

The relationship between sex and gender

Here and in Chapter 17, we will look at the explanations offered by a number of different psychological perspectives for the development of gendered behaviour. As you will see, these perspectives differ quite radically in terms of the relationship they see between biological aspects of sex and gendered behaviour. The biological perspective sees a relatively straightforward relationship between the two. According to this approach, biological sex produces gendered behaviour in an unproblematic way. Men and women act in 'masculine' and 'feminine' ways because their hormones make them do so. In this perspective there is no real distinction between the terms 'sex' and 'gender'. Biological sex creates gendered behaviour. This view is shared by the evolutionary perspective, which takes the view that differences in gendered behaviour between men and women have been selected because they produced survival or reproductive advantages in the evolutionary past. Therefore this perspective sees the differences as coded in genes.

Chapter 17, Social contexts of gender roles, considers the alternative explanation offered for the development of gendered behaviour by the behavioural perspective. According to this approach, gendered behaviour is learned from the environment through mechanisms including observation, modelling and rewards and punishments. So, as a result of direct instructions boys learn not to cry; rewards teach them to be tough ('well done ... that hurt but you were a brave boy and did not cry'), and punishments, for example teasing, discourage behaviour such as crying. According to this view, if a boy grew up surrounded by female role models and was rewarded for feminine behaviour, he would behave in a feminine way. A similar view is taken by the biosocial theory which argues that biological sex provides a 'signpost' leading to differential treatment of males and females. According to these approaches, gender is much more flexible and does not arise directly from biology but from the meanings attached to biological differences within a particular culture.

This short section has perhaps made you aware that this debate is not simply a matter of academic difference. If gendered behaviours arise entirely from biological sex, then men and women cannot change how they act as they are largely programmed or determined by biology. Feminist psychologists have long objected to this view that 'biology is destiny' and have taken the view that gendered behaviour is much more flexible and changeable for both men and women. We will examine this important critique later in the chapter.

Biological differences between males and females

Biological psychologists search for the physical differences between males and females which may underlie gendered behaviour. In this part of the chapter, we are going to look at how sex differences develop by tracing the steps of a journey which starts with genes and goes on to consider hormones and brain structures. When we have identified these biological differences, and seen that there has been some debate as to the nature and extent of them, we will go on to consider what they tell us and what they may fail to help us understand about gendered behaviour.

What makes a baby a boy or a girl?

From genes to hormones to brain differences

The sex of a baby is determined at the moment of conception. An embryo has 23 pairs of chromosomes, each made up of one from the ovum and one from the sperm. The twenty-third pair of chromosomes determines the sex of the embryo. If the embryo inherits an X chromosome from both parents, it will become a girl. If it inherits an X chromosome from the mother and a Y chromosome from the father, it will develop as a male.

Between four and eight weeks after conception, the gene on the twenty-third chromosome instructs the gonads to release **hormones**. In the male embryo, the testes are instructed to release testosterone which acts on an area of the brain known as the **hypothalamus**. Without testosterone, the brain would develop in the female form (Green, 1995). In the female embryo, hormone release from the ovaries is very slight.

Link

Approaches, issues and debates

A purely biological view of gender and gender development is highly *deterministic*. It implies that we are programmed by biological factors, with no room for flexibility in development. Although biological influences are important, we know that gender is a complicated characteristic that is affected by many non-biological factors.

Key terms

Hormones: chemicals released from glands which act on target tissues and organs. Androgens are male hormones and oestrogens are female hormones.

Hypothalamus: a structure in the forebrain which controls the pituitary gland and the autonomic nervous system. It also contains centres for control of feeding behaviour.

Gender

Clear differences can be seen in the brains of adult men and women notably in the function and anatomy of the hypothalamus (Green, 1995), although these differences are not generally found in children under six years old. In 1985, Swaab and Fliers found evidence of an area of the brain which they called 'the sexually dimorphic nucleus' INAH 1 located in the hypothalamus. Analysing 13 men and 18 women aged between 10 and 93 years old, they found that the volume of the sexually dimorphic nucleus was 2.5 times larger in men with 2.2 times the number of cells – although the density of cells decreased with age. Whilst later studies contradicted this claim, two more areas INAH 2 and 3 were identified. LeVay (1991) found size differences only in INAH 3. The generally accepted view is that these differences in the hypothalamus arise from the pre-natal action of sex hormones, particularly testosterone. Green (1995) makes the point that testosterone may affect other brain structures such as those which influence aggressive behaviour, although there is no direct evidence for this.

Another sex difference is in the degree of lateralisation in male and female brains. The left hemisphere controls speech and language and the right controls spatial skills with information being passed between hemispheres through the **corpus callosum** (although this is different in left-handers). Shaywitz and Shaywitz (1995) used magnetic resonance imaging scans to examine the brain whilst men and women carried out language tasks, and they found that whilst women used both hemispheres, only the left was used by men.

There are examples of genetic conditions which differ from the usual XY pattern. One in 500 men have a condition known as Klinefelter's Syndrome where they have a chromosome pattern of XXY rather than XY. These men are unusually tall with enlarged breasts and are likely to be infertile. 'Super males' have an XYY pattern. They are taller than normal and some have suggested that they are more likely to be highly aggressive and commit violent crimes. Inter-sex babies are born with the characterisations of both sexes, for example one ovary and one testis. This condition is very rare with about 60 cases in the past 100 years in the US and Europe. Given these anomalies, the use of genetic testing to establish biological sex was abandoned at the 2000 Sydney Olympics where several female athletes were found to have a Y chromosome pattern but were female according to other indicators (Hollway *et al.*, 2002).

From biological differences to gendered behaviour

Male and female babies are exposed to both **androgens** and **oestrogens** and it is the relative balance of hormones overall that is important. Under- or over-exposure to hormones during the **critical period** of development may influence later gender-related behaviour. For example, boys who are exposed to too little testosterone may become less masculine whereas girls exposed to larger amounts than usual (through the mother's environment) may be born with genitalia resembling a male.

How can we tell what effect hormones may have on gender-related behaviour patterns? Here we are going to examine three sources of evidence in order to assess possible links between biological and behavioural differences: animal research, case studies of atypical individuals and correlational studies of normal populations.

Animal research

Using animal research, the experimenter is able to systematically manipulate an independent variable, for example the amount of a

Key terms

Corpus callosum: the interconnecting set of fibres that enable the two hemispheres of the brain to 'talk' to each other.

Androgens: male sex hormones, the most important one being testosterone.

Oestrogens: female hormones.

Critical period: a specific period of time in which something has to happen.

Link

For a reminder about correlational studies and case studies, look at the *AQA Psychology A AS* student book, pages 116–17 and page 121.

Gender

particular hormone, and observe the effects on behaviour. Young (1966) studied rats, a species in which males and females show very different sexual behaviours. Males mount females from behind and females adopt the 'lordosis' position – back arched and head low. Young gave doses of male hormones to female rats and vice versa during a critical period of their early development and found that they showed reversed behaviours, the males adopting the lordosis position and the females attempting to mount from behind. The exposure to testosterone was thought to have enlarged the sexually dimorphic nucleus.

Case study research

An alternative approach is to look for naturally occurring examples of high exposure to androgens using case studies. Research in this area is ethically sensitive. Money and Erhardt (1972) studied a group of girls who had been exposed 'in utero' to high levels of male hormones through the administration of an anti-miscarriage drug. These girls were compared with their non-exposed sisters, and mothers were asked to comment on the toys and games they played and the clothes they liked to wear. Mothers reported differences between the two groups, with exposed individuals playing more boyish games, having higher IQ scores and career aspirations. However, Hollway *et al.* (2002) note that many of the questions asked made assumptions and were leading (for example, 'Which of your daughters is the most tomboyish?') and that a follow-up study in 1974 found only one difference – the exposed girls were more physically active.

Hines (1994) examined the amount of 'rough and tumble' play shown by girls and boys aged 3–8 years old who had congenital adrenal hyperplasia (CAH), a condition in which embryos are exposed to high levels of male hormones. She compared them with an unaffected control group and found minor differences between CAH and control girls in that the CAH girls tended to prefer playing with boys. This study implied that over-exposure to male hormones had little real effect on behaviour. In 2004, Hines *et al.* compared a group of 25 women and men who had CAH with their unaffected male and female relatives. Both groups were asked to think back and recall their childhood gender role behaviour. They found that women with CAH tended to recall more 'boy-related' play behaviours and less interest in heterosexual relationships, whereas men with CAH did not differ from their unaffected male relatives.

Correlating hormone levels and gender behaviours in normal populations

More recently, researchers have looked for possible relationships between hormone levels and gender differences using 'physiological markers' which go with hormone exposure. These include the amount of testosterone in saliva and the ratio between the lengths of the second (index) and fourth (ring) finger.

Deady *et al.* (2006) looked at the relationship between gender role orientation and testosterone levels in 'child-free' young women, specifically looking at their views as to whether or not they intended to have children. They asked the participants to complete Bem's SRI as well as answering a range of questions including how 'broody' they felt and their ideal age for having a first child. They found that women with high salivary levels of testosterone tended to have lower scores relating to the desire to have children, suggesting that lower maternal drives may be related to higher levels of male hormones.

Others have turned to **2D:4DR** as a source of evidence. It has been suggested that high exposure to pre-natal androgens and low exposure to

Gender

Key terms

2D:4DR: the ratio between the lengths of the second (index) and fourth (ring) finger.

pre-natal oestrogens or a combination of both may be linked to **sexual dimorphism**. Typically, women tend to have a higher 2D:4DR than men, with their index finger being longer than their ring finger whereas men typically show the reverse pattern with a longer ring than index finger especially in the left hand. This difference is evident in foetuses in the first three months of pregnancy and 2D:4DR remains stable across childhood to adulthood.

Studies into 2D:4DR and gender differences in behaviours have yielded mixed results. Troche *et al.* (2007) correlated 2D:4DR with scores on Bem's SRI in four different European countries which have differing views of gender roles – Germany, Sweden, Spain and Italy – using a total of 176 female and 171 male university students. They found no evidence of a relationship between SRI and 2D:4DR, implying that gender role behaviour may not be related to exposure to male or female hormones in utero.

However, Rommsayer and Troche (2007) carried out a study using 423 male and 312 female university students. They asked each of their participants to complete a Bem SRI to measure their gender role orientation, then measured 2D:4DR on both hands. They found significant results only in males. Those who showed a more feminine sex role on Bem's SRI had a 2D:4DR pattern which indicated lower exposure to androgens and higher exposure to oestrogens in utero. Whilst it is difficult to draw conclusions from data of this nature, the implication of this is that masculinity *may* be related to the level of pre-natal male and female hormones that the foetus is exposed to.

Key terms

Sexual dimorphism: differences in bodily structure between males and females of a species. A common example of dimorphism is that males are often bigger than females.

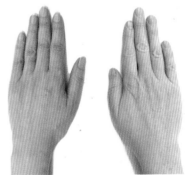

Fig. 3 *Typical index and ring finger lengths for males and females*

Commentary

The evidence from these biological studies has produced some support for the idea that some behavioural differences may have their origins in biology. Case study research has suggested that girls exposed to high levels of male hormones tend to play more physically and prefer playing with boys compared to their unaffected sisters. Deady's study found that women with high testosterone levels tended to have lower scores relating to their desire to have children.

The link between hormone levels and behaviours seen in 2D:4DR studies may be stronger in relation to masculinity than femininity. Rommsayer's study implies that lower levels of male sex hormones may correlate with androgyny as measured by Bem's SRI.

However, the differences seen in these studies are relatively small and there is a need for caution when interpreting their results. Whilst they can show possible relationships between hormone levels and gender-related behaviour, we cannot conclude that hormone levels *cause* 'masculinity' or 'femininity'.

Animal studies have also supported the claim that hormones are linked to gendered behaviour. However, we need to be cautious when generalising from animal studies.

Davies and Wilkinson (2006) argue with the assumptions of neuroscientists that brain differences between men and women are caused by pre-natal hormonal masculinisation of the male brain. They claim that this tells only part of the story and that other mechanisms are involved in differentiating the brains of men and women. They argue that genes located on the sex chromosomes can also influence 'sexually dimorphic neurobiology' directly, and they are developing this idea.

AQA Examiner's tip

You have seen here a range of sources of evidence used by biological psychologists in the search for sex and gender. Make sure that you can explain the strengths and weaknesses of these different research methods and also understand their findings.

This research may provide some insight into why men and women might be vulnerable to different mental disorders, for example depression in women and alcoholism in men.

If sex differences arise from biology then they might be expected to become evident before social experiences start to have an influence on the young child. Durkin (1995) argues that there is no evidence to point to early sex differences in behaviour or temperament between baby boys and girls and cites studies carried out by Prior *et al.* (1987) and Sanson (1985) which have supported the 'no difference' view. By around the age of one, boys begin to show higher levels of activity but, of course, this may reflect parental treatment.

Key points

- Sex refers to the biological fact of being male or female, whereas gender refers to the concepts of masculine and feminine.

- Bem's SRI identifies four gender types including sex-typed, androgynous and undifferentiated individuals.

- Biological psychologists search for physical differences between men and women which may underpin gender differences.

- Embryos become male through the action of sex hormones at around six weeks gestation. These influence the structure of the hypothalamus.

- Differences between men and women in the sexually dimorphic nucleus have been found in some studies, but others have failed to replicate these findings.

- Studies with rats indicate that some behavioural differences are found when female rats are exposed to large amounts of male hormones in utero.

- Case study research has found some behavioural differences between girls who have been exposed to high levels of male hormones in utero and their sisters who have not.

- Studies of 2D:4DR in normal populations imply that there may be a stronger link between hormones and masculinity than between hormones and femininity.

Summary questions

1. Explain what is meant by the terms 'sex', 'gender' and 'androgyny'.

2. Explain the relationship between sex and gender according to the biological perspective.

3. Outline two types of evidence which have been used to assess the links between sex hormones and gendered behaviour.

4. What are the difficulties in drawing conclusions from these types of evidence?

Evolutionary explanations of gender roles

Learning objectives:

- describe the parental investments made by males and females

- explain how behavioural differences may have been linked to reproductive success

- understand the criticisms that have been made of the evolutionary account of gender differences.

Key terms

Reproductive success: refers to the process of successfully passing on your genes to the next generation. This is measured by the number of surviving offspring left behind by an individual.

Parental investment: the amount of time, energy and effort put in to aid the reproduction and survival of a child (offspring).

Link

You may have come across parental investment theory in Chapter 8, Human reproductive behaviour. You can look back at this on page 96.

Link

Approaches, issues and debates

The evolutionary approach has been criticised for reducing complex human experiences and emotions to the level of genes selected for survival advantages. Behavioural predispositions such as female choosiness can be explained at higher levels by referring to cultural expectations.

Introduction

In this sub-topic we are going to consider how and why different behaviours may have evolved for men and women. As you will see, the evolutionary perspective has generated some of the fiercest debate and opposition from feminist psychologists. Evolutionary psychologists take the view that gendered behaviours have their roots in the past and took shape via the mechanisms of natural and sexual selection. According to the evolutionary approach, gender differences are neither deliberate nor conscious; they exist today because they enhanced or helped men and women perform particular types of roles in the past. The evolutionary and biological perspectives therefore agree that biological sex produces gendered behaviour. Trivers' parental investment theory argues that the origin of behavioural differences between men and women lies in different ways of achieving **reproductive success**.

Parental investment theory

Trivers (1972) argued that behavioural differences between men and women evolved due to different reproductive strategies which led to reproductive success in the past. Trivers noted that for males, each offspring involves relatively little **parental investment** and a man's involvement in producing a child could theoretically be limited to a few minutes of copulatory activity. In fact, a male's best chance of reproductive success would be to produce as many offspring as possible through mating with as many willing, fertile females as he can find!

In contrast, reproduction for the human female involves considerable investment. A female ovulates about 400 times in her lifetime and her supply of eggs is limited to one or at best two a month. Following conception, she will carry the growing baby for nine months supplying the nutrients it needs. After this she has to give birth – in the evolutionary past and still for many women across the world, this is a hazardous business. Then she will need to care for the baby and in the past that meant breastfeeding it until it was at least two years old. Given this substantial input, the best strategy for reproductive success for a human female is to ensure the survival of her few precious offspring. Survival is more likely if there are two parents around to provide protection and food. For this reason, the best strategy for a female is to carefully select a male with 'good genes' who will help her to raise offspring. Reproductive success will be further guaranteed if the male is powerful and resourceful.

Parental investment and behavioural differences

Parental investment theory can help us to understand some of the differences in behaviours between men and women. Differences in 'sexual style' may be linked to differential reproductive success. Uncommitted sex or promiscuity is seen as an optimal strategy for males as this would enable them to leave larger numbers of offspring. In contrast, choosiness would be more beneficial for females as a carefully selected mate would be important in ensuring survival of their few precious offspring. This may explain the differences seen between men and women in their readiness to engage in casual sexual encounters which was found in Clark and Hatfield's studies (1989 and 1990).

Gender

■ Link

You may wish to look in more detail at the studies carried out by Clarke and Hatfield (1989 and 1990) on page 95 in Chapter 8, Human reproductive behaviour.

■ Hint

How science works

Although the evolutionary approach to gender roles is controversial, some people do accept it and then suggest that male and female roles, even in today's society, should be based on this approach, i.e. that females should stay at home and nurture children, while men should go out and compete in the workplace. This would be an example of how scientific findings, even controversial ones, can influence social policy and decision-making. (I, L)

■ Link

Approaches, issues and debates

The biological and evolutionary approaches emphasise the role of nature and genes in gender development but have little to say about the role of experience or nurture.

Parental investment theory may also help to explain the tendency to form relationships or 'pair bonds'. Wilson (1978) argued that our ancestors moved to living in 'pair bonds' because the arrangement provided further benefits in reproductive success. Females gained protection from the presence of a permanent, live-in male as this helped to guarantee provision of resources such as food and shelter and aided the survival of themselves and their offspring. Males benefited as they were able to guard their mates from other interested males and ensure sexual fidelity. This was advantageous as it meant that males could gain a measure of parental certainty in a situation where offspring are 'mummy's babies, daddy's maybe's'.

Parental investment theory can explain differences in aggression between men and women. As the female's best approach to mate choice in the past was to be choosy, this produced a situation in which males would need to compete for females in order to be reproductively successful. This meant that physical and behavioural characteristics which led males to be successful in competitions/fights would be passed into the gene pool. So, larger males with size, strength and dominance would be more likely to win mates over smaller or less-dominant males. This can help to explain why human males are usually about 1.15 times bigger than females (Hollway *et al.*, 2002). In species such as chimpanzees – where there is greater pressure for male competition – males tend to be about 1.3 times bigger than females.

■ Commentary

Evolutionary explanations help us to understand why physical differences such as body dimorphism exist between men and women. They also help us to see how sex differences in behaviours such as promiscuity or choosiness may have their origins in our hunter-gatherer past. However, researchers such as Sternglanz and Nash (1988) have argued with the sociobiological claim that a 'love 'em and leave 'em' attitude leads to greater reproductive success for males. They suggest that males who have sex in a one-night stand or short relationship are unlikely to leave the female pregnant given the odds of conception. If pregnancy occurs, they argue that the baby would have less chance of survival without two parents to fend for it and feed it, implying that this promiscuity does not lead to reproductive success for males!

Others have disputed the evolutionary interpretation of studies such as Clark and Hatfield's which show an unwillingness in women to engage in casual sex, arguing that gender differences in behaviour may not simply reflect biology and evolution. Instead, they suggest that cultural views account for these differences and particularly the view in Western societies that 'nice girls don't', but that masculinity is related to a readiness to have sex at any time, a view perpetuated by magazines such as *FHM* and *Loaded*. Cassidy (2007) argues that evolutionary psychology tells us nothing about non-heterosexual relationships or those which are non-reproductive.

Just because differences exist, it does not imply that they are desirable! Buss (2000) argues that our evolutionary legacy may well lead to all manner of unhappiness in modern relationships between women and men and that 'the problem for contemporary humans is that this ancestral heritage of sexual style and predispositions can impose considerable costs in feelings of rejection, jealousy and unhappiness'.

Thornhill and Palmer (2000) have taken evolutionary explanations further to explain – and some would argue, justify – sexual violence. 'The natural history of rape' is a highly controversial sociobiological account in which Thornhill and Palmer argued that the act of rape can be understood using the mechanisms of evolution by natural selection. Their claim was that rape – defined as copulation with an unwilling female – was a feasible strategy to aid reproductive success and could therefore be seen as an adaptation. Alternatively, it could be viewed as a by-product of gender differences in which men's optimal reproductive style is promiscuity and women's is choosiness. Thornhill and Palmer argued that rape could therefore be seen as an evolved tactic which would be used by men who were unable to compete for status and resources successfully and who would therefore be unable to attract mates.

As I am sure you can imagine, these claims have met with resistance, refutation and outrage! Critics have argued that 'The natural history of rape' justifies unacceptable male violence as 'natural'. Others have argued that rape is motivated by a desire for power and dominance rather than sex, especially as it often involves older and younger victims of non-fertile ages.

Both the biological and evolutionary perspectives see gender differences in behaviours as having their roots in genes which have been selected for their survival value. This places them firmly in the 'nature' camp of the nature and nurture debate. Some researchers such as LeVay (1993) take a hard-line view on the subject. In *The Sexual Brain*, LeVay argues that sex differences in human behaviours are rooted in biological mechanisms which will eventually be revealed using traditional, laboratory-based scientific methods. Other evolutionary psychologists have taken a less hard-line view and have argued that genes *predispose* men and women to act in certain ways rather than *programming* them, allowing for some environmental influence.

The extreme view put forward here has been criticised as being deterministic as it implies that men and women have little choice or control over their behaviours: women are natural 'nurturers' and men are naturally aggressive and promiscuous. Some have taken these suggestions even further to argue that equal opportunities policies in the workplace are doomed to fail as men are 'naturally' more competitive, risk taking and likely to progress up the career ladder (Cronin and Curry, 2000). Not surprisingly, these views have come under fire from feminist psychologists due to their political implications and the permanence they imply. Here we can see that the debate is not simply academic but has far-reaching implications which may impact on lives and opportunities. In Chapter 17, Social contexts of gender roles, we will consider the alternative view of gender put forward by psychologists working in the behavioural perspective.

Link

Approaches, issues and debates

Extreme biological views such as those put forward in The Sexual Brain (LeVay, 1993) are heavily deterministic. They also have social and political implications as they imply an inability to change behaviour. For this reason such research can be regarded as socially sensitive.

Key points

- Physical and behavioural differences between men and women may have their roots in reproductive success.

- Differences in parental investments between men and women may have led to differences in sexual style and aggression.

- Pair bonding and mate guarding may have evolved to ensure parental certainty.

- Male competition for mates may have led to differences in size and aggression.

- Evolutionary arguments have been criticised for ignoring the role of culture and socialisation in behaviour.

- Biological and evolutionary accounts of gender have been criticised for being deterministic.

Summary questions

5 Explain what is meant by reproductive success.

6 How does parental investment theory explain differences in sexual style and aggression between men and women?

7 Discuss some criticisms which have been made of evolutionary explanations of gender differences.

Gender

17 Social contexts of gender roles

Social influences on gender roles

Learning objectives:

- understand how reinforcement from parents and peers may influence gendered behaviours

- explain how observational learning from role models is important in development of gender

- be able to describe how experiences at school might reinforce gendered behaviours.

Key terms

Operant conditioning: this refers to Skinner's idea that the likelihood of any behaviour being repeated depends on its consequences.

Positive reinforcement: this occurs when a behaviour is followed by something pleasant (which increases the likelihood that the behaviour will be repeated).

Meta-analysis: the combination and review of the data from many studies which have used similar methodology to investigate the same subject.

Link

You can read more about positive and negative reinforcement by looking at page 242.

The behavioural perspective

In this chapter we are going to examine how gender role behaviours may be shaped by the environment that a child is brought up in. This draws on the behavioural perspective which takes the view that gendered behaviours are learned through the mechanisms of operant conditioning and social learning. If this is so, it would be reasonable to expect gender role behaviours to differ across cultures depending on the types of behaviours and qualities which are reinforced in those cultures. As we will see, the behavioural perspective perceives a much less direct relationship between biological sex and gender: if gender role behaviour is simply taught and shaped, theoretically it should be possible to encourage girls and boys to develop masculine or feminine behaviours. We will start this section by considering the importance of reinforcements from parents and peers, then we will move on to consider the role of observational learning by examining Bandura's social cognitive learning theory (1977).

The role of reinforcement by parents and peers

Parents may teach their children about gender-related behaviour through **operant conditioning** – the distribution of rewards and punishments. Behaviours which produce positive consequences such as compliments or attention are more likely to be repeated than those which produce unpleasant consequences such as teasing. For example, parents may provide **positive reinforcement** and compliment their daughter when she is wearing a 'pretty' dress but not when she is wearing jeans. They may cheer their son for a tough tackle in football but not if he comes off the pitch crying! Reinforcements may be offered for gender-appropriate choice of toys. So boys could receive negative comments when happily engaged in ironing, and the same could happen to girls when they are climbing trees, which may dissuade the behaviour in the future. Of course, parents may choose to reward their children differently depending on their own beliefs about gender.

How important is parental reinforcement in the production of gender role behaviours? Maccoby and Jacklin (1974) set out to test if parents in the 1970s treated boys and girls differently. They found that parents reinforced sex-typed behaviours including games and toy choice, as social learning theory predicts. In other areas there was a remarkable degree of uniformity in the treatment of the two sexes. An updated review of this area was carried out by Lytton and Romney in 1991.

Research study: Lytton and Romney (1991)

Lytton and Romney carried out a **meta-analysis** of studies that had looked at the parental treatment of boys and girls. They were concerned that previous research studies had focused on mothers and overlooked the role of fathers, and only considered young children under the age of around six. Lytton and Romney also wished to assess if the more egalitarian climate of the 1990s would produce less parental reinforcement than in 1974.

Lytton and Romney selected a range of studies which had considered the parental treatment of boys and girls with a total of 27,836 participants. Some 158 were carried out in North America and the remaining 17 in other Western countries. They examined eight areas of socialisation and their main findings were as follows:

- There was little evidence for differential treatment in terms of the amount of interaction, communication and warmth between sons and daughters.
- The only difference in the North American studies was in encouragement of sex-typed activities in play and household chores. For example, girls were more likely to be encouraged to help with housework and boys with outdoor tasks.
- In Western countries other than the USA, there were differences in the encouragement of sex-typed activities as above and also in physical punishment. Boys were more likely to be physically punished (i.e. smacked) than girls.
- Fathers tended to treat their sons and daughters more differently than mothers.
- Differential treatment decreased over age, so was most noticeable with younger children and less noticeable with older children.

This meta-analysis supports the claim that boys and girls receive different reinforcement for activities considered to be sex-appropriate.

Methodological issues

This is a substantial meta-analysis with a very large sample size. However, most of these studies have been carried out in Westernised countries, making the findings specific to those Westernised countries.

Ethical issues

As this is a meta-analysis, no data was collected, meaning there are no direct ethical issues here. An important ethical issue in the original studies would be parental consent.

Similarly, Siegal (1987) found that fathers were more likely than mothers to respond negatively, especially when their sons carried out 'feminine' play activities. Fagot, Leinbach and O'Boyle (1992) found that toddlers aged two to three who had mastered the labels 'girl' and 'boy' had mothers who were more likely to 'police' cross-sex play, further supporting the claim that parental reinforcement is important in the ideas that a child develops about gender.

Peers and reinforcement

Peers also play an important role in reinforcement and regulate what they perceive to be 'cross-sex' play. Langlois and Downs (1980) noted that when boys played with girls' toys, they were likely to be ridiculed and teased by their male peers. Archer and Lloyd (1982) found that children as young as three criticised peers who engaged in cross-sex play

Link

You can read more about the development of gender schemas in Chapter 18, Psychological explanations of gender development.

Gender

■ **Hint**

To make sure you understand the different types of reinforcement, analyse the research studies above using the terms 'positive and negative reinforcement' and 'punishment'.

■ Key terms

Social cognitive learning theory (SCLT): this takes the view that behaviours are learned through observation of role models and imitation of their behaviours. The child plays an active part in deciding which models to copy.

Vicarious experience: learning through observation of another person's actions rather than through direct experience.

Egalitarian family: parents share parenting and economic work.

Traditional family: one parent takes responsibility for childcare and housework and the other for economic work.

and were less likely to play with them. It is therefore no surprise that sex differences in children's behaviours appear first of all in social settings (Maccoby, 1992) – the girl who is quite happy playing with the cars in the sandpit at home is less likely to do that at playgroup and instead joins the girls in the Wendy House.

Peers are such systematic reinforcers of sex-typed play that Harris (1998) and Durkin (1995) have argued that they play a more important role in gender role reinforcement than parents. Durkin (1995) suggests that 'the critical variable may not be vertical reinforcement (i.e. parents) so much as horizontal social engagement (i.e. peers)'.

■ The role of observational learning

Social cognitive learning theory (SCLT) was proposed by Bandura and Walters (1963) as social learning theory, but later modified to acknowledge the role of higher-order cognitive processes. SCLT argues that children learn gendered behaviours in similar ways to other behaviours such as aggression. Bandura acknowledged the importance of reinforcements in learning behaviours but also argued that learning takes place through observation of role models and imitation of their behaviours. Children are exposed to a variety of role models: parents, older siblings, friends, television characters, sporting figures and celebrities. These models demonstrate different ways in which masculinity and femininity are interpreted and enacted within today's society. For a child to imitate the behaviour of a role model, they must pay attention to the behaviour and store a representation of it in their memory. In order to repeat the behaviour, the child should be capable and motivated to reproduce the behaviour.

What would motivate a child to copy the behaviour of one role model rather than another? According to social cognitive learning theory, behaviours are most likely to be copied if they are seen to bring rewards to the role model. This is referred to as learning through **vicarious experience**. SCLT also acknowledges that children do not passively imitate role models but are highly selective, choosing dominant and powerful individuals as models (Bussey and Bandura, 1984).

Parents as models

Parents may serve as role models and show children the gender role behaviours expected of them. Dads may take their sons fishing and mums their daughters shopping. If this is so, then parents who show strong gender role segregation (where men carry out male tasks such as repairing cars and women do the housework) should, technically, have children who adopt these roles.

Fagot *et al.* (1992) measured the effects of parenting style by comparing 27 **egalitarian families** where the father and mother shared the parenting relatively equally with 42 **traditional families** where child rearing was carried out by Mum while Dad was at work. They interviewed the parents when their children were aged about 18 months old and they observed them playing with the toddler at the age of 28 and 48 months. When the children reached the age of four, they were given a variety of gender-labelling tasks to examine their own gender schemas. Children in 'traditional' families tended to use gender labels earlier and showed more gender role stereotyping at age four than those in the egalitarian families, supporting the view that parents are important role models.

Television and magazines

From a very young age, most children in Western cultures are avid watchers of television, and by the time they reach 18 many have spent more time in front of the television than at school! Durkin (1995) has argued that television provides a 'plentiful source of sex-role models' and that gender stereotypes are alive and kicking on TV. A variety of studies (e.g. Morgan, 1982) have found that the more television a child watches, the stronger the sex-role stereotypes they hold. However, whilst it is clear that there is an association between television watching and sex-role stereotypes, we cannot assume that one causes the other. Duck (1990) has argued that children are far from passive in their consumption of television and that they select their role models carefully, choosing those who are powerful and attractive.

Viv Groskop, the parent of an 18-month-old daughter and a four-year-old son, reflects on the ideas of masculinity and femininity put forward in TV programmes aimed at very young children.

> It all started with Lola, the googly-eyed heroine of the CBeebies series Charlie and Lola. First created by the children's writer Lauren Child, Lola is a very sweet little girl. Intelligent, funny and rather rebellious, she winds up her brother, has an incredible vocabulary and truly possesses a mind of her own. She is therefore the closest the CBeebies channel comes to having any kind of feminist icon. All good stuff, except for one fatal flaw – she just had to be given a love of pink milk.
>
> … Since having a daughter … I have started to watch it [children's television] through the eyes of a little girl and suddenly I don't like what I see.
>
> … I already don't like her interest in Upsy Daisy from In the Night Garden whose main interaction with the world consists of repeatedly performing an elaborate curtsey and giggling uncontrollably with her hand over her mouth like a Japanese geisha.
>
> … [CBeebies] is packed full of macho heroes: Fireman Sam, Underground Ernie, Lazy Town's Sportacus, Bob the Builder, Tommy Zoom, Finley the Fire Engine, Lunar Jim. A few of these have female side kicks but none ever goes much further than being the token woman. Their femininity is often weirdly denoted usually by obligatory pigtails or bunches, even on grown women … .
>
> As a rule, female characters conform to a 1950s stereotype of women: submissive and decorative. Lunar Jim's lady astronaut friend Ripple is weedy … Over the course of many episodes I have witnessed Firewoman Penny in Fireman Sam save the day only once.
>
> Worst of all when female characters pop up on CBeebies, they always have an affinity for pink.

The Guardian, *2 November 2007. For the full article*
see www.guardian.co.uk/world/2007/nov/02/gender.uk

Magazines also give different 'gender messages' to boys and girls. Boys' magazines focus on sport, popular television programmes and computer games whereas girls' magazines focus on fashion, body products and the lives of celebrities. Peirce (1993) carried out a content analysis of magazines aimed at young teenage girls between 1987 and 1991 including *Seventeen* and *Teen*. In over half of the stories, girls were

Hint

How science works

The extract from the *Guardian* expresses a commonly-held view that media representations of masculinity and femininity are heavily stereotyped. However even widely accepted views may be wrong. It is one aim of the scientific approach to confirm such views using carefully-designed studies published in peer-reviewed journals, such as the Peirce (1993) content analysis referred to below. (K)

Gender

Link

For a reminder about content analysis, see the *AQA Psychology A AS* book, page 131.

Take it further

Collect some data yourself to examine the constructions of masculinity and femininity shown in magazines aimed at pre-teen boys and girls. Select two or three best-selling magazines aimed at roughly the same age for each sex. Carry out a content analysis of the articles, images and adverts in them. What do they suggest about what it is to be a successful boy or girl in today's society?

Link

Approaches, issues and debates

Note that most of the research described is heavily biased towards Western industrialised societies. It is likely that gender stereotypes will vary from culture to culture, and the next section reviews some of this work. The cross-cultural perspective is vital in developing an understanding of gender roles.

Take it further

The study by Renzetti and Curran was carried out in 1989. Girls have started to outperform boys in many areas of the school curriculum, and you could investigate whether their findings hold true today. Sample the comments made on male and female students' work and class them as related to either intellectual quality or presentation. This data could be subject to a chi-squared test to look for significant differences.

portrayed as unable to solve their own problems and dependent on others to sort out issues in their lives. Almost half of the problems shown in the magazines related to relationships with boys, reinforcing the view that femininity is about relationships rather than career achievement.

Hust (2006) has examined boys' use of media in constructing ideas about masculinity. In a qualitative study, 26 boys, both black and white aged between 13 and 14, were interviewed about 'what it means to be a boy', and the posters they chose in their bedrooms were analysed. The boys identified a range of components in their ideas about masculinity. To be young and male involved being sporting, sexually proficient, stoic (like the film character Rocky Balboa) and risk taking (think of the television programme *Jackass*). Hust argues that the media provides a very limited set of ideas about masculinity for boys, which provides them with an unhealthy range of role models and options regarding masculinity.

The impact of schools

Time spent at school may also influence gender role behaviours. Children in the UK start school at four years old and continue until at least 16. Most of this time is spent in a mixed-sex environment although a small proportion of children are still in single-sex schools at secondary level. In the last few years we have seen something of a moral panic as girls have started to outperform boys at all stages of the National Curriculum, achieving better grades in GCSEs and A-levels. Connell (1995) notes that boys are slower to read, more likely to drop out of education, be excluded, disciplined and taught in Special Needs programmes. Hollway *et al.* (2002) argue that children learn and maintain gender identities within the classroom, and Connell argues that schools 'enforce gender regimes'. How might the school environment reinforce gendered behaviours?

- One possibility is in the role models shown to children. In primary schools, the majority of teachers are female, so it is easy for girls to identify with learning and the source of authority. Young boys may fail to identify with a female teacher, and consequently they label learning and academic achievement as for girls.

- At secondary level, the division of labour between male and female teachers may reinforce gender stereotypes. Women tend to teach humanities and men teach maths and sciences. Colley (1994) has noted that children rapidly divide the curriculum into boys' and girls' subjects. So, subjects are far from being neutral and gender free. Subjects such as physics, history and IT are 'for boys' and sociology, geography and psychology are 'for girls'. This may relate to the sex of the teachers involved in the subjects.

- Finally, reinforcement may perpetuate gender stereotypes in the classroom. Renzetti and Curran (1989) found that boys were more likely to receive praise for the intellectual quality of their work whereas girls were often praised for the neatness of their work.

Commentary

The behavioural approach emphasises the contribution of the environment (i.e. nurture) to gender role development. The theories and studies we have considered in this part of the chapter have shown how the environment provides gendered role models at school, on television and in magazines, and these images surround children with ideas of masculinity and femininity. Play is 'policed' and reinforced by parents and peers, and schools may provide a gendered curriculum for children.

The behavioural approach also implies that **culture** may have an influence on gender role development. Different cultures may encourage and reinforce different gender patterns of behaviour for girls and boys. In the next section of this chapter we will assess how far this appears to be true by examining studies of gender in different cultures.

Key points

- Differential reinforcement is offered for sex-typed behaviours especially from fathers to sons.

- Peers are powerful regulators of gender-appropriate play.

- Social learning theory argues that gender is learned through observation and imitation of role models.

- Television and magazines provide traditional and limited role models of masculinity and femininity.

- There are correlations between the strength of sex-role stereotypes and the amount of television watched.

- Schools may influence gendered behaviours via the hidden curriculum, role models and reinforcements.

Summary questions

1. Explain how reinforcement by parents and peers may regulate gendered behaviours.

2. Describe the main principles of social cognitive learning theory.

3. How are gendered behaviours maintained and regulated in the classroom?

Key terms

Culture: the beliefs and customs of a social group which distinguish it from other groups.

AQA Examiner's tip

An effective way to evaluate either approach in the exam is to consider evidence for the other side of the argument.

Link

Approaches, issues and debates
You can see here that the biological and behavioural approaches have very different views on the origins of gender roles.

Cross-cultural studies of gender roles

Learning objectives:

- explain ways of classifying different cultures

- describe studies which show gender role development in collectivist cultures

- understand difficulties in assessing the role of culture in gender role development.

Key terms

Traditional: a culture where there are clear differences in men's and women's roles and power.

Egalitarian: a culture where gender roles are more flexible and equal.

Masculine culture: values stereotypically 'male' qualities such as independence or achievement.

Feminine culture: values stereotypically female qualities such as cooperation.

Anthropologist: person who studies different cultures and societies.

Link

You can read more about Hofstede's classification of cultures by looking at Chapter 9, Effects of early experience and culture on adult relationships, page 107.

Fig. 1 *Gender roles in other cultures*

Distinguishing different kinds of cultures

We have already noted the dominance of Western research and theory in psychology and the importance of considering research studies carried out in other cultures. Most of the research that we have considered so far has taken place in economically developed countries such as the US, Australia and northern Europe. These studies have shown how parents and peers encourage the development of masculine behaviour in boys and femininity in girls. We have also seen that there is some flexibility and choice over the way in which gender is enacted. So, it is relatively acceptable in the UK for men to stay at home and raise children, for women to pursue careers, or either sex to adopt a relatively androgynous way of life. A very simple way of classifying cultures is to divide them into **traditional** or **egalitarian**. Cultures with some choice and flexibility over gender roles have been characterised as egalitarian as men and women have greater gender equality. In traditional cultures, men and women have different gender roles to each other which are clearly defined. It is more difficult for individuals to make choices outside these very prescriptive roles.

A more complex system of classifying cultures has been proposed by Hofstede (1989) using four dimensions. We will consider two of them here – masculine/feminine and individualistic/collectivist. According to Hofstede, **masculine cultures** have a high regard for stereotypically 'male' qualities such as achievement and competition. Examples of this type of culture would be the UK, US and Japan. In contrast, **feminine cultures** value stereotypically female qualities such as interpersonal harmony and cooperation. Examples of feminine cultures would include Pakistan and India. In individualistic cultures, identity is defined through personal choices and achievements, whereas in collectivist cultures, membership of family, work and community groups is most important.

Gender roles in other cultures

Early studies carried out by **anthropologists** such as Margaret Mead in the 1930s identified a range of apparent cultural differences in the ways in which gender was enacted. Mead's study of three tribes in New Guinea found that interpretations of gender roles were very different to those in Western societies. In the Arapesh tribe, both men and women appeared to show behaviours which fitted the Western stereotype of femininity, and in Mundugumor society both sexes behaved in a fairly macho way. Mead was most interested in the third tribe, the Tchambuli, where the gendered behaviour was apparently the opposite of that expected in Western society. Women and girls were 'possessive, definite, robust and practical' whereas men engaged in flirtatious behaviour and 'coquettish play acting' (Mead, 1935). However, as Mead extended her studies to include indigenous peoples in Samoa, she changed her original viewpoint and suggested that there were indeed cultural similarities in the ways in which gender was organised. Although her ideas and methods were criticised by later anthropologists, Mead's work pointed to the importance of cultural factors in the development of gender and challenged the widely held view that gender differences resulted purely from biological sex.

Whiting and Edwards (1975) suggested that gender roles were organised in similar ways across a range of traditional cultures. They looked at 11 non-Western societies and found that girls were encouraged to spend more time with their mothers and were more likely to be given domestic and childcare roles within the household in all of them. In contrast, boys were more likely to be assigned tasks outside the house including feeding and herding animals. This meant that girls spent more time with younger infants and adults, whereas boys spent most of their time with peers. Across cultures, younger girls were found to be more responsible and nurturing than boys, who 'caught up' with responsibility in early adolescence. Whiting and Edwards concluded that the behavioural differences seen in boys and girls come about because of the tasks they are given. Girls are taught how to be responsible at a young age as they are exposed to female role models and develop skills of caring for younger siblings – effectively children become the company they keep! (Bee, 1995.)

Individualistic versus collectivist cultures

Other researchers have chosen to compare gender roles in collectivist and individualistic cultures. Chang, Guo and Hau (2002) compared 145 American and 173 Chinese students living in their respective countries. They were given a 10-item Egalitarian Gender Roles Attitudes Scale which measured their attitudes to gender equality at home and in the workplace. Chang *et al.* found that there were cultural differences between the two groups. Male and female American students emphasised the importance of equal gender roles at work whereas the Chinese sample emphasised the importance of equality at home and in the family (i.e. sharing housework and childcare). This may reflect the fact that gender equality at work is taken for granted in China, a communist country. Leung and Moore (2003) compared Australians of English and Chinese origin using Bem's SRI and found cultural differences in line with Hofstede's dimensions. Both male and female English Australians showed masculine traits which are valued in individualistic cultures, and male and female Chinese Australians showed feminine traits valued in a collectivist culture.

These research studies imply that cultural values and expectations have a strong influence on the development of gender roles and expectations. Leung and Moore's study shows us that cultural differences may well 'override' gender differences. There may be more similarities between males and females within a culture than between males and males of different cultures!

Differences within cultures

As we noted above, attempts to classify cultures tend to oversimplify the differences which exist within cultures. Although North America and Italy are both classed as individualistic cultures, studies suggest that there are differences in the ways in which masculinity is interpreted. Tager and Good (2005) compared ideas about masculinity in a sample of North American, southern Italian and northern Italian males and found less conformity to traditional ideas about masculinity in Italians. Further, northern Italian men held less-traditional ideas than their southern counterparts! This demonstrates clearly that we should not generalise when considering cultural differences, as gender role development depends on many factors.

 Link

Approaches, issues and debates

Studies such as Whiting and Edwards (1975) can be used to support the nature side of the nature–nurture argument in relation to gender role development. In general, cultural influences consistently emphasise the importance of the environment in the development of gender roles, and can be seen as a counter-argument to the biological approach.

Link

You can refresh your memory about Bem's SRI by looking back at Chapter 16, Biological influences on gender, page 194.

Gender

211

Commentary

The studies we have considered have shown us how different qualities may be encouraged in males and females in different cultures. This points to the importance of environmental factors in the development of gender roles. We have seen that there may be greater similarities between males and females from a collectivist culture than between males from an individualistic and a collectivist culture, suggesting that cultural influences may generally override biological factors. In the next chapter, we will see how biosocial theory argues that both factors operate together so that gender roles are produced as a result of the interpretation of biological differences within a specific culture.

Key points

- Cultures can be distinguished using different dimensions or systems.
- Hofstede's model differentiates masculine/feminine cultures and individualistic/collectivist cultures.
- Cross-cultural studies indicate that collectivist cultures encourage the development of feminine traits for both men and women.
- Individualistic cultures encourage the development of masculine traits in both men and women.
- Gender roles vary within as well as between cultures.

Summary questions

4 Explain what is meant by the term 'culture' and outline two ways in which cultures have been classified.

5 Discuss the claim that there are differences in gender roles between different cultures.

The biosocial approach to gender development

Learning objectives:

- explain what is meant by biosocial theory
- be able to describe how concepts of gender are constructed
- understand the critique of gender research offered by social constructionists.

Key terms

Biosocial theory: this argues that it is the interaction between biological factors and social factors which leads to the development of the child's gender identity and gendered behaviour.

Social constructionist theory: this argues that concepts of gender are not natural but are 'made' or constructed within a particular time and place through language.

Fig. 3 *The start of gendering …*

Introduction

We have seen that both biological and environmental factors play an important role in the development of gender roles. The biosocial theory argues that we need to consider how these factors work together to produce gender roles. **Biosocial theory** argues that the interpretation of biological sex within a specific social and cultural context influences the treatment given to the child, and it is this which leads to the development of gender role behaviour and gender identity.

The start of gendering – labelling of sex

The sex of a baby is often one of the first things asked by the new parents and announced by the midwife who delivers the baby. As we have seen, most infants are clearly labelled as male or female immediately after birth. The sex of the baby is often seen as more important than temperament, and labelling of the baby as a girl or boy has all sorts of influences on how the baby is treated, starting with the selection of baby cards and presents.

Differential treatment

You may have noted from the above exercise that boys and girls are portrayed in very different ways in baby cards. Once the child's sex has been labelled, biosocial theory argues that the sex label serves as a 'signpost' by which the baby's needs and behaviours are interpreted. So, people may treat the baby differently on the basis of their biological sex depending on their own particular views about gender differences. A classic study which demonstrated this clearly was the Baby X, Baby Y study by Smith and Lloyd (1978) who dressed babies in unisex 'snow suits' and gave them boys' or girls' names. They found that when the same baby was dressed and named as a boy, they would be played with very differently to when dressed and named as a girl.

The constructed nature of gender

Social constructionist theory argues that the ways in which people see and understand the world are not 'natural' but are constructed or made. In Western societies, the idea of gender is constructed by dividing people into two categories on the basis of their biological sex – male or female – and assuming that male equals masculine and female equals feminine. When John Grey published *Men are from Mars, Women are from Venus* in 1993, most people understood what the title implied: that men and women have different views, behaviours and instincts. The two gender categories are

Take it further

Look at the cards available for newborn babies. Almost all cards use the term 'boy' or 'girl' and few refer to welcoming a new baby. The implicit message is that sex is important. Carry out a content analysis of the images in the cards and the colours used. You might also like to look at the verses inside the cards and the language used. Are the two genders portrayed in different ways?

constructed as different species so the term the 'opposite sex' is used, further perpetuating the view that men and women are fundamentally different. Try replacing 'opposite' with 'other' and see how strange it sounds!

Social constructionists argue that constructions of gender differ across time and culture. So the idea of what a 'real man' is like would be very different in the 1940s to now. Edley and Wetherell (1995) argue that there are many different ways of 'doing' masculinity and femininity, so the ideas of 'new man', 'metro sexual' and 'ladette' are recent ways of reshaping gender ideas. This means that we should think in terms of multiple masculinities and femininities (i.e. many different ways of enacting gender).

This view has been supported by research carried out by Connell (1995) and Mac an Ghaill (1996) who have identified a range of different 'masculinities' adapted by men today. Mac an Ghaill distinguished four sub-cultures of masculinity in British schools including:

- the 'academic achievers' who pursued and valued success in academic subjects
- the 'macho lads' who rejected formal schooling
- the 'new entrepreneurs' who located themselves within technical, IT subjects and
- the 'real Englishmen' who rejected traditional school values and prioritised difference, independence and autonomy.

A book written by Antonia Young (1996) has drawn attention to a very different way of interpreting gender in Albania. In *Women who become men: Albanian sworn virgins*, Young (1996) describes how women take on men's roles when there is no male member of a family to take on the masculine duties. Avowed virgins take a pledge never to marry, they dress as male, cut their hair short and take on the male responsibilities. They are given all of the rights and privileges normally reserved for men (*The Guardian*, 7 May 1996).

Commentary

The biosocial theory argues that behavioural differences arise from the interactions between biology and socialisation rather than purely biological or environmental causes. This theory sees gender-related behaviour as flexible rather than fixed, making it much less deterministic. This assumption offers opportunities to create and develop aspects of the self which may be otherwise constrained by traditional ideas of masculinity and femininity.

Key points

- The biosocial explanation argues that gender differences in behaviour cannot be explained solely through biology.
- Gendered behaviour is produced from an interaction between biology and environment.
- The labelling of a baby as a boy or girl leads to differential treatment which produces the child's sense of gender identity.
- Western societies view gender as having two categories (masculine and feminine) and see men and women as different species.
- Social constructionists argue that ideas about gender are constructed (made) rather than natural and are distributed through language.
- Constructions of gender differ across time and culture.

Link

Approaches, issues and debates

The biosocial theory combines both biological (nature) and social (nurture) influences on gender development. Combining the approaches provides a far more realistic and valid model than either one alone.

Summary questions

6 Outline the biosocial explanation of the development of gender.

7 Discuss the claim that femininity and masculinity are socially constructed concepts.

Gender

Psychological explanations of gender development

Cognitive theories

Learning objectives:

- describe cognitive explanations of how children develop an understanding of gender (including Kohlberg) and gender schema theory

- assess the evidence on which cognitive theories are based.

Key terms

Schemas: sets of ideas about an object or activity which come from past experience and may be taken in from the wider culture. A gender schema refers to the set of ideas about what activities, toys and behaviours are appropriate for a particular sex – boy or girl.

Gender roles: the sets of behaviours that are seen as appropriate for males and females.

Hint

Make sure that you understand the different methods used to assess children's understanding of gender. These will provide you with a useful 'evaluation tool' when discussing theories.

How do children develop an understanding of gender?

In this chapter we are going to look at how children develop an understanding of gender. They have to grasp a number of ideas. Perhaps the most simple of these is the ability to class themselves and other people correctly as male or female. As you will recall from Chapter 16, Biological influences on gender, this is referred to as gender identity. They also need to grasp the concept that gender identity is permanent and does not change despite changes in appearance. Most young children develop ideas, known as **schemas**, as to what behaviours, games and clothes are appropriate for males and females. Finally, they are likely to adopt some of these as **gender role** behaviours.

In order to investigate children's understanding of gender identity and gender roles, developmental psychologists have used a range of methods including:

- *Observation*: observing children allows us to see aspects of gender role behaviours including who they play with, the toys they choose and the games they play.

- *Scenarios or vignettes*: vignettes are short stories which ask children to make a judgement about some aspect of gender. Damon (1977) used vignettes about children who engaged in cross-gender play, for example, 'George likes to play with dolls'. Damon asked children aged 4–9 a series of questions like, 'Is it OK for George to play with dolls?' Others have used a similar technique by describing tasks or showing pictures of activities such as cooking and asking children to choose a doll to carry out the activity.

- *Preferential looking techniques*: with young children who have not yet begun to talk, more inventive methods are needed. Preferential looking involves presenting two pictures simultaneously to a young child, for example a man changing a tyre and a woman baking a cake, and measuring how much time they spend looking at each one. You will read more about this method in the studies by Slaby and Frey (1975) and Campbell *et al.* (2000).

Cognitive explanations of gender development

Here, we are going to examine two cognitive explanations of gender development. These theories share the view that the child's thinking and understanding of their gender identity as boys or girls is what leads to the adoption of gender role behaviours. Kohlberg's cognitive developmental theory (1966) argued that the child develops an understanding of gender in three stages and it is only *after* the child has fully understood that gender is constant, at around age five, that they show gender role behaviour. Martin and Halverson's gender schema theory (1981) agrees with the cognitive nature of gender development, but argues that children develop schemas about gender and gender role behaviours earlier than Kohlberg suggested.

Cognitive developmental theory

According to Kohlberg (1966), the child's understanding of their own gender identity forms the basis of their enactment of gender role behaviours. Kohlberg argued that the child's understanding of gender develops gradually through three stages which are loosely linked to age across early childhood. In each of these stages, the child grasps increasingly more complex concepts about the nature of gender.

1 *Gender identity*: the first and most simple concept the child has to grasp relates to their own sex – that of a girl or boy. Between the age of about two and three-and-a-half, the young child starts to use the label 'boy' or 'girl' to refer to themselves and then to other people. However, the child of this age has a very limited understanding of what it means to be a girl or a boy and does not understand that gender is stable, generally for life!

2 *Gender stability*: when the child reaches the age of about three-and-a-half they begin to realise that their own sex will not change. Whilst the two-year-old would seriously claim that he is a boy but is going to be a mummy when he grows up, the four-year-old knows that he will grow up to be male and become a daddy if he becomes a parent. However, the child of four or five years old is still misled by superficial changes to appearance, and may believe that sudden changes in appearance (such as head shaving) may lead a woman to become a man.

3 *Gender constancy*: between four-and-a-half and seven years of age, the child works out that gender is constant – that is, that people stay the same gender despite superficial changes in their appearance. Whilst the three-year-old might feel that Britney Spears with a shaved head has turned into a man, the six-year-old would not fall into that trap. To some extent, this stage can be seen as the child's ability to 'conserve' in Piaget's terms – the ability to know that despite superficial transformations of appearance, the underlying 'thing' remains the same.

Kohlberg argued that once a child understands that their gender is constant, they become highly motivated to behave in a way that is expected of them as a boy or girl. Therefore, this theory predicts that children should pay attention to same-sex role models and show systematic gender role behaviours only after they have a full understanding of their gender and a strong sense that it is for life. The implication of this theory is that gender role behaviours should appear at around or after the age of five.

- Evidence has shown that Kohlberg's stages occur in the order and at the ages he suggested. McConaghy (1979) found that children aged three-and-a-half to four tended to use hair length and clothes to decide upon the sex of a doll, rather than its genitals.

- Slaby and Frey (1975) studied children aged between two and five who were divided into high- and low-gender constancy groups. They were shown a silent film in which two adult models – one male and one female – carried out a simple stereotyped gender role activity such as baking a cake or changing a wheel. The film was constructed using a spilt-screen model so the child could watch both films and their eye movements and direction of gaze were recorded to assess which film they looked at most. Slaby and Frey found that the child who had

Link

You can read more about Piaget's ideas on conservation by looking at page 273.

Gender

reached high levels of gender constancy spent more time watching the same-sex model than those who had low levels of gender constancy, supporting Kohlberg's claim that children pay attention to same-sex models after the stage of constancy has been reached.

In a more realistic study, Ruble (1981) considered the relationship between gender constancy and the child's responsiveness to television adverts for 'girl' and 'boy' toys. Children who had reached gender constancy were sensitive to the implicit message of the advert that certain toys were 'right or wrong' for boys or girls. Their behaviour was also influenced in that their willingness to play with the toy advertised depended on how 'gender' suitable they felt the toy was.

Whilst Kohlberg's theory provided the basis for thinking about children's understanding of gender, theorists such as Bem (1981) and Martin and Halverson (1981) have argued that children begin to pay attention to gender-related behaviours much earlier than Kohlberg has suggested. These theories have claimed that children start to construct schemas about gender by the age of around two and that it is these schemas which drive gender role behaviour.

Gender schema theory

Gender schema theory (Martin and Halverson, 1981) was based on an idea originally developed by Bem (1981), who was mentioned in Chapter 16, Biological influences on gender. Martin and Halverson agreed with Kohlberg that the child's thinking is at the basis of their development of gender role behaviours. However, they argued that the process starts much earlier than Kohlberg had suggested. According to gender schema theory, children gain their gender identity between the age of two and three when they work out that they are a boy or a girl. At this stage, their gender schema is extremely simple, consisting of two groups – boys and girls. Their own group is viewed as the 'in group' and the opposite sex is viewed as the 'out group'. Schema theory argues that they then actively seek out information about the appropriate behaviours and actions of their own group. Boys pay close attention to boy-related toys, games and activities and focus on finding out about these; they pay minimal attention to anything which they perceive as 'girly' such as dolls. Girls, in contrast, focus on finding out actively about girly things and avoid finding out about anything which they perceive as belonging to boys. Therefore children look to the environment to develop and build their gender schemas, which become progressively more complex. So toys, from being neutral, become categorised as boys' or girls' toys; games, sports, school lessons, even musical instruments are categorised as 'right' for girls or boys. Campbell *et al.*'s studies (2000, 2004) below demonstrate how young children's gender schemas develop rapidly in early childhood to encompass toys and activities.

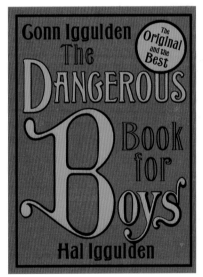

Fig. 1 *Schemas for boys?*

Research study: Campbell *et al.* (2000, 2004)

Campbell *et al.* used the visual preference technique using a sample of babies aged three months, nine months and 18 months. They found that three–month-old babies showed a very minor preference for watching babies who were the same sex as themselves and this was more noticeable in males. By nine months, boys distinctly preferred to look at and watch 'boy toys', and this continued through to 18 months. Both girls and boys showed a preference for watching male activities, although this was much stronger in boys.

This study provides support for the idea that babies develop schemas about gender long before they start to speak, and that these schemas drive their attention. Quite young children are 'tuned in' to pay attention to the group they belong to, and this ability seems to be much stronger in boys than girls.

A second study in 2004 used a longitudinal design. Some 56 children were studied at 27 months and 39 months. The study took place in the children's homes. They were seated on their parent's lap, shown a photo album of pictures and asked to point to:

- the boy or girl (the gender-labelling task)
- the girls' or boys' toy (football or brush and comb set)
- the boys' or girls' game/activity (skipping or football).

After this, the child was given 10 toys used in the study and filmed for 30 minutes as they played with them. Parents were prevented from influencing the play.

Campbell found that at two years old, just over half of the children (53 per cent) completed the gender-labelling task, and by three years old 94 per cent could correctly label their sex, as Kohlberg's stage theory predicts. Stereotyping of toys and activities was seen in 20 per cent at two years old, but about half of the sample (51 per cent) were labelling toys as suitable for boys or girls by three years old. Labelling of gender-related activities was only visible in about one in six toddlers by the end of the study. Campbell's study indicates that between the age of two and three, children's gender schemas show rapid development.

Methodological issues

This study uses a range of methods to assess children's gender schemas, providing rich and detailed data. The use of a longitudinal design allows the researcher to see how gender understanding grows.

Ethical issues

As this study took place in the children's homes, there was little stress for the children who participated. Research with young children should aim to minimise disruption or stress.

Similarly, Poulin-Dubois *et al.* (2002) studied a group of 63 Canadian toddlers aged two to three years. They were asked to choose a doll to carry out a series of tasks which were classed as male (shaving), female (vacuuming) and neutral (sleeping). Girls aged 24 months chose the gender-appropriate doll for the tasks whilst boys did not, implying that girls as young as two had identified gender stereotypes. Boys were around 31 months old before they demonstrated similar stereotypes. This study agrees with Campbell's findings and shows that young children between two and three years old select and pay attention to models on the basis of their sex.

Where do gender schemas come from?

These studies have shown us that children develop simple gender schemas which rapidly become more complex and take in games, activities, school subjects and sports. However, cognitive theories have not considered how schemas might develop. Tenenbaum and Leaper (2002) argue that parents' gender schemas are more influential in shaping

AQA Examiner's tip

Schema theory and Kohlberg's cognitive development theory share some similarities but also make some different predictions about the age at which children will start to show gender role behaviour. Make sure you can identify these differences and relate them to research evidence.

children's views about gender than the ways parents behave in terms of reinforcement or modelling. For this reason, they carried out a meta-analysis looking for possible links between parents' and children's views about gender. This has shown a link between parents' and children's gender schemas.

Research study: Tenenbaum and Leaper (2002)

Tenenbaum *et al.* carried out a meta-analysis of 43 studies involving 10,193 participants. The studies had looked for a relationship between the gender schemas held by parents and their offspring. This is clearly a complicated area with many possible variables – how old the child is and whether they are a boy or a girl and the different beliefs about gender held by their mother and father. In a complicated statistical analysis, Tenenbaum and colleagues looked for possible relationships between the gender schemas of:

- mothers and their daughters
- mothers and their sons
- fathers and their daughters
- fathers and their sons.

The overall correlation between the parents' gender schema and that of their child (of any age or sex) was +0.16. Although this is a small correlation it is statistically significant, indicating that gender schemas of parents and their children *are* alike and more so than would be expected by chance.

Methodological issues

This is a substantial meta-analysis with a large sample size. However, the vast majority of studies took place in Western industrialised countries such as North America, Israel and Europe, with only one study taking place in the Pacific Rim (Japan and Korea).

Ethical issues

As this is a meta-analysis, no data was collected so there are no direct ethical issues. In the original studies considered here, the principle of parental consent would have been important. Gender is also an issue which many people have strong feelings about, and researchers would need to be aware of, and show respect for, different viewpoints.

Tenenbaum's findings imply that children absorb gender schemas from their parents in a subtle way. What they see around them every day in the home – how labour is divided, who cleans the toilet and who earns what, etc. – may be taken for granted and absorbed as the norm.

Evaluation of gender schema theory

Both of the cognitive theories covered here see the child as active, seeking out information about gender and trying to make sense of the gendered world they live in. In both of these theories, the direction of development goes from cognitive concept (i.e. the schema of boy/girl) to information processing (looking at the world through the lens of gender) and then to gender preferences (I am a boy – boys play with cars – I like playing with cars). The difference between Kohlberg's theory and schema theory is the age at which this process takes place.

Hint

How science works

Cognitive theories were developed to explain gender development. They have led to many studies and findings, but their failure to account how schemas themselves develop is a major limitation. A more successful approach would account both for the role of schemas and for their development. (A)

Link

To refresh your memory about the interpretation of correlation coefficients see page 515 and page 533.

Gender

Research studies by Campbell *et al.* (2000) and Poulin-Dubios *et al.* (2002) have shown that children pay attention to same-sex role models much earlier than Kohlberg thought. In fact, young children appear to be tuned in to gender even before they start to speak.

One strength of the gender schema theory is that it helps us to understand why children's beliefs and attitudes about sex roles are so resilient and even rigid! Parents are often baffled by their young children's rigid interpretation of gender (as if the gender police were out there). This is explained by the fact that children only pay attention to those things which are consistent with and confirm their schemas. Therefore, if they see someone engaging in behaviour which contradicts a schema (such as the female mechanic who services my car so well) they will fail to notice it. Studies have shown that when young children watch films which depict people contradicting gender role behaviours, they simply tune them out.

Gender schema theory emphasises how schemas develop but not where they originate. This emphasis on the cognitive aspects of the child tends to overlook the impact of parents and surrounding culture such as friends, school and media that we considered in Chapter 17, Social contexts of gender roles. Tenenbaum's meta-analysis has shown the importance of parents' beliefs on the gender schemas developed by children.

Key points

- Children's understanding of gender develops in three stages loosely linked to age.
- These stages are gender identity, gender stability and gender constancy.
- Kohlberg argued that children become motivated to pay attention to and learn about gender when they have reached the stage of constancy.
- Gender schema processing theory argues that once the child has labelled themselves as a boy or girl, they become motivated to learn about their in group and ignore the out group.
- Campbell's study shows how young babies pay more attention to same-sex models from around nine months old, supporting gender schema theory.
- Meta-analyses have shown that children's gender schemas correlate with the schemas held by their parents.

■ **Take it further**

Think about how you could investigate possible links between the gender schemas held by A-level students and their parents. Devise some measurement of gender schemas using a questionnaire. Correlate the scores for a sample of students with the scores of one (or even both) of their parents using Spearman's rho.

■ **Link**

You can read about Spearman's rho in Chapter 39, Data analysis and reporting on investigations page 535.

Summary questions

1 Outline Kohlberg's three stages of gender understanding.

2 Explain one criticism of the cognitive development theory.

3 Explain what is meant by the term 'gender schema'.

4 How do children develop gender schemas?

5 What are the main differences between cognitive development theory and gender schema theory? Which do you find more convincing and why?

Psychological androgyny and gender dysphoria

Link

You can look back at the definitions of androgyny and gender dysphoria in Chapter 16, Biological influences on gender, pages 194 and 195.

Key terms

Androgyny hypothesis: this claims that individuals who score highly on *both* masculinity and femininity are psychologically healthier than sex-typed individuals.

Introduction

As we have seen above, most boys develop a male gender identity and most girls develop a feminine gender identity. However, this is not the case for all children. We noted in Chapter 16, Biological influences on gender, that androgyny refers to the coexistence of both masculine and feminine characteristics in an individual. A much more extreme – and often distressing – situation is the state of gender dysphoria in which the individual feels trapped in the wrong-sex body. Here we will find out what psychologists have learned about the development of an androgynous gender identity and gender dysphoria.

Explaining androgyny

Why might some people develop an androgynous rather than a sex-typed gender identity? Stainton Rogers and Stainton Rogers (2001) reviewed a number of different theoretical explanations which have attempted to explain the development of androgyny. These explanations share the view that androgyny is a conscious and deliberate choice made by some individuals who choose to reject traditional and constraining ideas of masculinity and femininity. As you read these explanations you will notice that they were developed during a similar period of time – the 1970s and 1980s. It is no coincidence that this era saw dramatic developments in gender equality between men and women and in the advancement of gay rights. This provided an environment in which androgyny as a gender 'choice' flourished.

The first models of androgyny, referred to as 'conjoint models' were presented by Bem (1974) and Spence *et al.* (1975). These approaches argued that a balancing of masculine and feminine characteristics was desirable and healthy within a personality. This approach led to the **androgyny hypothesis** (Bem, 1975), which claimed that androgynous individuals were psychologically healthier than sex-typed individuals such as masculine men and feminine women. However, conjoint models produced a description of the benefits of androgyny rather than the causes.

Olds (1981) argued that androgyny is a developmental stage reached only by some people. According to developmental theories, some individuals are able to develop and move beyond acceptance of traditional sex roles. This is similar to the view presented by Bem's later schema theory which argues that androgyny takes place when an individual comes to see the world without gender stereotypes.

Finally, behavioural models (Orlofsky, 1977) argue that androgyny is a form of behaviour or action and is demonstrated by what people do rather than what they think. This approach views androgyny as a way of life in which the individual gains competence in a wide range of skills associated with both masculine and feminine qualities such as leadership and nurturance. By this approach, androgyny is seen as a lifestyle choice.

Bem's work made an important contribution in the 1970s and 1980s and challenged the prevailing view that sex-typed individuals were well adjusted.

Gender

Initial studies carried out by Bem and Lenney (1976, cited in Lefkowitz and Zeldow, 2006) supported Bem's claim of androgyny equalling psychological health. However, later studies in the 1980s contradicted the androgyny hypothesis, suggesting that individuals who had most masculinity items (e.g. masculine men and masculine women) were better adjusted overall (Zeldow *et al.*, 1985).

Feminist psychologists such as Hollway (2002) have criticised Bem's ideas about androgyny and argued that they imply that individuals need to change their ways of thinking and seeing the world. Instead, she argues that social changes in the amount of power afforded to men and women need to take place. She also objects to Bem's acceptance of male characteristics, such as competitiveness and dominance, as desirable for women.

Old's developmental model sees androgyny as an advanced stage of gender role development but fails to explain how and why this takes place in some people and not others. This criticism can also be applied to lifestyle models.

Research into gender dysphoria

As we saw in Chapter 16, Biological influences on gender, individuals who experience gender dysphoria experience conflict between biological (assigned) sex and gender identity and are often referred to as 'transsexuals' in everyday language. Their experience is of being trapped in the wrong body. Gender dysphoria is the 'core symptom' of gender identity disorder (GID). This diagnostic category occurred in the *Diagnostic and Statistical Manual of Mental Disorders* (*DSM*) for the first time in 1980. GID is a relatively rare condition with an estimated incidence of one in 11,000 people. In order for GID to be diagnosed, a number of criteria have to be met:

- The person must experience ongoing identification with the opposite sex (i.e. 'feel' like a man/woman).
- They must feel a strong sense of discomfort with their own biological sex.
- The experience must affect their ability to function in everyday life.
- No biological condition (such as androgen insensitivity syndrome) should occur at the same time.

In order to investigate GID, studies take place comparing 'target samples' (those with dysphoria) with non-affected individuals. Two main research methods have been identified by Drummond *et al.* (2008):

- Retrospective case studies involve looking back at people who have been diagnosed with GID and piecing together the past. These methods are subject to memory bias and selective recall.
- Prospective studies involve taking a group and following them across childhood and early adulthood to map change and development. This often involves children who show moderate to strong cross-gender behaviour and who are referred to clinics by worried parents.

Research evidence suggests that gender dysphoria diminishes over adolescence and early adulthood so that most children who show cross-sex identification do not go on to request sex changes. Green (1997) studied a group of 44 boys referred in childhood to a clinic for strong feminine behaviours and compared them to a group of 30 control boys matched for age. A follow-up at the age of 18 found that only one of the original 44 remained gender dysphoric and had opted for reassignment surgery. Similar findings were produced by Zucker (2005) with boys.

Link

Approaches, issues and debates

Early work on gender and gender identity assumed that the only options were male and female. The study of androgyny has removed this bias approach and established that people may have an androgynous gender identity, and many of us will have both male and female sex-typed characteristics. Work on androgyny and gender dysphoria has confirmed that gender identity can be far more complicated than originally thought.

Gender

Research study: Drummond *et al.* (2008)

Drummond *et al.* studied a sample of 30 girls referred to a gender identity clinic between the age of two and three. At age seven a variety of measurements were used including observation of free play, a playmate preference questionnaire and measurement of sex-typed behaviours. At the follow-up at 18, the young women were asked about their current gender identity, their desire to be a man or to live and be treated as a man, and about their sexual orientation and fantasies.

Drummond *et al.* found that 88 per cent of the girls who had shown strong GID at age seven showed no signs in early adulthood. Only 12 per cent of the original sample had continued to show gender dysphoria, supporting the findings of Green (1997) and Zucker (2005) that GID decreases from childhood to adulthood.

Drummond *et al.* concluded that cross-gender identification in childhood may be a risk factor for later GID, but the lack of clear continuity between childhood and adulthood implies that other factors may be more important.

Methodological issues

This is an example of a prospective study with follow-up at age eight and 18. This avoids some of the difficulties associated with retrospective studies as noted above.

Ethical issues

As with all case study research, this is an exceedingly sensitive area. Researchers must balance the need to provide treatment with research interests into causes.

Key points

- Androgyny refers to the blending of masculine and feminine characteristics within an individual.
- The androgyny hypothesis claimed that androgynous people were psychologically healthier. This has received mixed support from research.
- Conjoint models have been criticised by feminist psychologists for their acceptance of masculine qualities as desirable.
- Developmental and behavioural models fail to explain why some people progress beyond traditional sex roles and adopt androgynous lifestyles.
- Gender dysphoria is the main symptom of GID.
- Studies show that early childhood cross-sex behaviour may lead to clinical GID in about one in five people.

Summary questions

6 Describe the main characteristics of androgyny and gender dysphoria.

7 Outline two explanations of the development of androgyny.

8 Evaluate some of the criticisms of research into androgyny and gender dysphoria.

Gender end of topic

How science works: practical activity

In this topic we have seen that psychologists have turned to correlational studies in order to assess possible relationships between hormone levels and gender role behaviours. We have also seen that there is some debate within the psychological community as to what exactly this shows. You can investigate it for yourself by carrying out a 2D:4DR study.

In order to do this, you will need to devise some way of measuring accurately the ratio of the second and fourth fingers in a sample of adults. You will need to read through Chapter 16, Biological influences on gender, to decide whether to use both hands or just left or right. (You will recall that there is some debate about this!) You will also need to measure gender role behaviour using Bem's SRI (see the weblink in the Further reading section below for a copy of this). This will produce scores for both masculinity and femininity. You will be able to correlate the scores for both of these measurements with the 2D:4DR score to assess a possible relationship.

When you have devised your measuring scales you will need to think carefully about the ethical issues involved in this study. How should you ask for consent and how much information should you give your participants? You will also need to decide which measurement to carry out first – the SRI or the finger measuring. You should think about how you intend to debrief participants at the end of the study if they ask the inevitable questions. You will need to stress that this a growing area of research and there are no clear answers yet.

Finally you may like to read more about other interesting (and obscure) finger studies taken from an article by Marc Abrahams in the *Guardian* (6 November 2007; see the weblink below). One of these studies has found a difference between social science and humanities teachers who participated in the 2D:4DR!

Further reading and weblinks

Bee, H. (1995) *The Developing Child*. New York: HarperCollins.

This has excellent coverage of theories of gender development.

Stainton Rogers, W. and Stainton Rogers, R. (2001) *The Psychology of Sex and Gender*. Maidenhead: Open University Press.

This gives an excellent overview of critical thinking about sex and gender.

The internet has a large number of resources relating to Bem's Sex Role Inventory. You can find a self-completion copy of the SRI with the score sheet by going to www.neiu.edu/~tschuepf/bsri.html.

You can read more about the symptoms of GID by going to www.psychnet-uk.com/dsm_iv/gender_identity_disorder.htm.

See http://education.guardian.co.uk/egweekly/story/0,,2205519,00.html for Marc Abrahams' 'Talk to the Hand' article (published in the *Guardian* on 6 November 2007).

Intelligence

Key terms

Intelligence: the ability to solve problems and adapt to the environment.

Introduction

In this topic, we will consider the issue of intelligence. **Intelligence** is a word that you are likely to have used and met many times in different situations, but – like many other words in psychology – it is used in a much more specific way than in everyday life. As you will see in the three chapters that follow, there has been considerable debate as to what is meant by intelligence and what intelligent behaviour is in both humans and non-human animals. A simple, working definition of intelligence which applies to both human and non-human animals is the ability to solve problems and adapt to the environment.

The first chapter in this section looks at theories about the nature of intelligence. As you read the chapter, you will see that there is some debate between researchers. Some argue that intelligence can be seen as a general ability which affects how an individual functions in many different areas, and others argue that there are different kinds of intelligence or 'multiple intelligences'. This is an important debate with implications for schooling and education, and you will see that this has generated competing explanations. We will move on to consider how intelligence can be measured using intelligence tests.

The second chapter looks at intelligence in non-human animals. You may have had experience with your own or other people's domestic pets which has shown them to be capable of many sophisticated forms of learning. A range of ways in which animals have been shown to learn and adapt to their environment are examined, including classical and operant conditioning and social learning. Some more unusual abilities in animals are also considered. These may demonstrate higher levels of intelligence, including the ability to recognise themselves, to communicate and to deliberately deceive other animals for personal gain.

It is often claimed that modern humans are more successful than other non-human animals because they are more intelligent! The third chapter of this section examines how and why human intelligence may have evolved. It traces the path taken by humans from the environment of evolutionary adaptation thousands of years ago to see how the human brain has developed. As you will see, this process is a little like a detective hunt in which evolutionary psychologists search for clues and work from often challenging and incomplete evidence. This process involves building hypotheses about the skills and behaviour seen today and the pressures of the past environment which may have led to these skills evolving via natural selection.

Specification	Topic content	Page
Theories of intelligence		
• Theories of intelligence, including psychometric and information processing	**Intelligence**	
	• What do we mean by intelligence?	228
• Gardner's theory of multiple intelligences	• Theories of the nature of intelligence	229
	• Measuring intelligence: the psychometric approach	235
Animal learning and intelligence		
• The nature of simple learning (classical and operant conditioning) and its role in the behaviour of non-human animals	**The nature of simple learning**	
	• Classical conditioning	239
	• Operant conditioning	241
	The role of operant and classical conditioning	
	• Limitations of behaviourist explanations of learning	245
• Evidence for intelligence in non-human animals, for example self-recognition, social learning, machiavellian intelligence	**Intelligence in non-human animals**	
	• Social learning	247
	• Theory of mind	249
	• Machiavellian intelligence	250
	• Self-recognition	250
Evolution of intelligence		
• Evolutionary factors in the development of human intelligence, for example ecological demands, social complexity, brain size	**Evolutionary factors in the development of human intelligence**	
	• Introduction	252
	• How evolution works	252
	• The human brain	253
	• Evolution and machiavellian intelligence	255
	• Evaluation of evolutionary factors in the development of human intelligence	256
• The role of genetic and environmental factors associated with intelligence test performance, including the influence of culture	**Genetics, environment and intelligence test performance**	
	• Measuring the genetic influence	258
	• Evaluation	262
	• Environmental and cultural effects on IQ	263
	• Conclusions	265

Intelligence

Learning objectives:

- explain what is meant by the term 'intelligence'

- understand the differences between hierarchical and multi-factorial models of intelligence

- describe the evidence on which theories are based

- understand difficulties in drawing conclusions from evidence

- describe methods of testing intelligence and the advantages and disadvantages of different tests.

Key terms

Individual differences: the study of how people vary in intelligence and personality.

Psychometrics: methods of measuring psychological qualities such as intelligence and personality.

Information processing approach: this views the human mind as analogous to a computer and identifies the cognitive skills involved in mental activities.

What do we mean by intelligence?

The study of intelligence is part of the psychological area of **individual differences** – this concept loosely refers to the ways in which people vary. A quick glance around your psychology class will remind you how varied people are! Two ways in which people vary are personality and intelligence, and these areas of individual differences have been the subject of much study. The measurement of individual differences is referred to as **psychometrics**. We will start by examining the debate as to whether or not there are different kinds of intelligence before moving on to consider how intelligence can be measured.

Research study: Sternberg *et al.* (1981)

Sternberg *et al.* set out to establish what experts and laypeople in the US think intelligence is. They asked a variety of experts drawn from different psychological fields to rate a series of different kinds of mental abilities and activities in terms of how characteristic they were of intelligence. They found a large degree of agreement as to which mental abilities made up intelligence. Sternberg then asked a group of non-psychologists to repeat the same activity and found strong agreement with the expert panel as to the factors that made up intelligence. These factors included:

- verbal intelligence – the ability to use words and language

- problem-solving abilities – the ability to meet novel situations and come up with solutions

- social competence – the ability to get on with, handle and understand other people.

In later studies, Sternberg and other researchers found that ideas about intelligence varied in other cultures. In Taiwan, strong emphasis was placed on interpersonal competence (Yang and Sternberg, 1997), i.e. the ability to understand and work with other people. In Kenya, initiative and the ability to handle real-life problems were valued (Grigorenko, 2001). These studies imply that ideas about intelligence relate to cultural context and the demands of a particular social group. We shall return to this point when we consider Sternberg's **information processing approach** to intelligence.

Methodological issues

Sternberg *et al.*'s study involved a comparison between experts and laypeople. This provided a wide sample in order for generalisations to be made. The use of cross-cultural samples in these studies strengthened the method even more.

In these studies, Sternberg *et al.* selected a range of different mental abilities. These were likely to reflect their own views (and biases) about the nature of intelligence.

Ethical issues

The topic of intelligence is a socially sensitive one as performance in tests can have serious implications for education and work. Participants in the study would need to give their fully informed consent to take part and would require sensitive debriefing about their performance on the tests.

Theories of the nature of intelligence

One main area of debate between psychologists has been of the very nature of intelligence. Early theorists such as Francis Galton argued that intelligence consisted of a single, underlying intellectual ability, whereas others such as Gardner have argued persuasively that there are different kinds of intelligence or **multiple intelligences**. Theories of intelligence can loosely be divided into the following categories:

- **Uni-factorial models**: these take the view that intelligence is a single quality which enables an individual to perform well in a range of intellectual activities and skills. These theories often link intelligence with genetic factors and assume that it develops independently of social context.

- **Hierarchical models**: these argue that intellectual abilities exist within a hierarchy. General intelligence is at the top and different intellectual skills can be seen at lower levels of the hierarchy. Examples of these types of models include Horn and Cattell (1966) and Carroll (1993).

- **Multi-factorial models**: these take the view that intelligence is composed of a range of abilities and they highlight the role of environmental factors and learning in the development of intelligence. An example of this type of theory is Gardner's theory of multiple intelligence.

Uni-factorial and hierarchical models

Francis Galton, a cousin of Charles Darwin, was one of the first to study intelligence, although in a way that we would consider rather unscientific today! Galton believed intelligence was a single factor or quality which individuals had in differing amounts and he set out to discover if people were 'generally' clever across a range of different mental activities.

In 1884, Galton set up a stall in the South Kensington Museum in London where ordinary people could have their mental abilities tested. More than 9,000 men and women took part in Galton's studies paying a princely 3 pence to be tested. (This is clear evidence of Galton's own intelligence as it was usual for psychologists to pay people to take part in studies rather than the other way round!) Galton gave his participants a range of tests including tests on reaction times and perceptual tasks, for example discriminating between different sounds. However, he found that there were no overall patterns to each individual's performance on different tasks, forcing him to abandon his method and his view of intelligence. Galton's search for general intelligence was taken up by Spearman (1904, 1927) who argued that intelligence consisted of a single factor which he called 'g' (for 'general' intelligence). This term is still widely used today.

This approach has been developed into the idea that intelligence can be seen as a hierarchy of intellectual skills. Hierarchical models agree that there are distinct mental abilities, but claim that they stem from general intelligence at the top of the hierarchy. Here we consider two of these models.

Hierarchical models

Horn and Cattell (1966) conceptualised intelligence as consisting of a hierarchy with two levels. General intelligence at the first (top) level was divided into five '2nd order factors' which are shown in Figure 1.

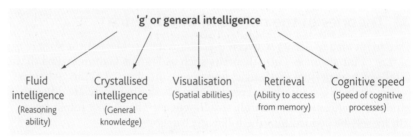

Fig. 1 *Two-level hierarchical model for 'g'*

Carroll's 1993 model agreed with Horn and Cattell that general intelligence is at the top of the hierarchy but conceptualised three levels in that hierarchy. At the second level, Cattell argued that there are three different types of intelligence, **crystallised intelligence**, **fluid intelligence** and visual perception. Each of these three types is further divided into two sub-types at the third level of the hierarchy as shown in Figure 2.

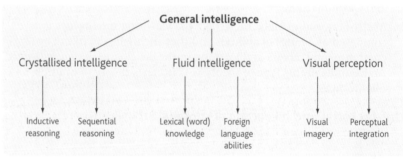

Fig. 2 *Three-level hierarchical model for 'g'*

Multi-factorial models

Other psychologists have argued that there are different kinds of intelligence rather than a single, mental ability. Thurstone (1938) obtained results which challenged Spearman's claim of a general, single intelligence. Thurstone argued that there were different kinds of intelligence which existed relatively independently from each other. So, for example, an individual could theoretically have a high score in one type of intelligence, such as verbal ability, but have a low score in another such as spatial ability. Thurstone used a sample of students who were asked to carry out a large number of different tasks. From these, he reduced intelligence down to a set of factors which he called primary mental abilities.

Guilford (1956, 1959) agreed with Thurstone that intelligence was comprised of many factors. However, his model conceptualised intelligence as consisting of three axes (pretty much like a cube) each with a different aspect of intelligence, allowing for a staggering 180 different aspects of intelligence.

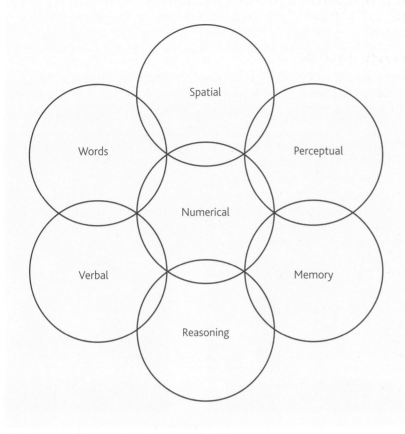

Fig. 3 *Seven of Thurstone's primary mental abilities*

Gardner's theory of multiple intelligences (1983, 1999, 2006)

Howard Gardner has argued that there is no single form of intelligence but a number of different kinds. He defines intelligence as the 'bio psychological potential to process information' (2006). In 1999 he proposed that there were eight distinct kinds of intelligence which he called 'domains'. According to Gardner, each domain operated as a relatively separate system or 'encapsulated module' in the brain. These eight domains of intelligence are shown in Table 1. Gardner has also suggested that there may be a ninth type of intelligence which he terms 'existential', but he is not yet convinced of its separate existence.

Fig. 4 *Matt Bellamy from the band Muse: an example of musical intelligence*

Table 1 *Gardner's eight intelligence domains*

Domain	Definition
Linguistic	Ability to understand language and communicate using spoken and written words
Logical/mathematical	Ability to perform mathematical operations with speed and accuracy
Spatial	Ability to understand physical relationships between objects, for example to make mental rotations of shapes or understand maps
Musical	Ability to appreciate or produce music, for example to discriminate pitch and rhythm
Bodily/kinaesthetic	Ability to use the body to solve problems, to construct objects or to make displays (for example sculpture, dance, surgery)
Intrapersonal	Ability to be in touch with, monitor and understand one's own feelings
Interpersonal	Ability to notice and understand the feelings and moods of other people
Natural	Ability to recognise, categorise and label man-made and natural objects

■ Link

You can refresh your memory about the method and calculation of correlations by looking at page 535 of Chapter 39, Data analysis and reporting on investigations.

The first of Gardner's three domains are familiar components in standard intelligence tests (as we shall see later in this chapter), whereas the last five have not traditionally been measured. Gardner argues that in order to understand how people's minds work we need to understand how the different intelligences interact. In a major revision of his theory in 2006, Gardner argued that we can identify two 'over arching intelligence profiles' or intelligence types:

■ **Searchlight intelligence**: this involves regular shifting between different domains of intelligence of roughly equal strength. It is often shown by politicians and business people who may have strong logical intelligence, good linguistic intelligence and the ability to read other people (interpersonal intelligence).

■ **Laser-like intelligence**: this involves dominance by just one or two of the domains and is characteristic of artists and scientists who show very high levels of intelligence in one area but not in others. For example, Albert Einstein was said to lack interpersonal intelligence.

Fig. 5 *Tony Blair has searchlight intelligence; Albert Einstein had laser-like intelligence*

The search for general versus multiple intelligence

Attempts to test Gardner's theory in schools have also produced some support. For example, Feldman *et al.* (1988) created an 'intelligence fair assessment' called 'Spectrum' aimed at pre-school children aged between three and four years old. This involved testing each domain in its most natural state – for example, testing kinaesthetic intelligence through observing children in sport and movement classes and testing interpersonal intelligence through watching children interact in the playground. Feldman's study found distinct intelligence profiles in young children, supporting Gardner's claim of multiple intelligence (MI).

A more formal method of looking for multiple intelligences is to use the technique of **factor analysis**. This is a statistical technique used in the debate between those who argue for 'g' and those in favour of multiple intelligences. Using this technique, correlations are calculated between scores on different IQ tests and sub-tests. If intelligence arises from a single underlying factor ('g') then theoretically participants who score highly on one test (let us call it A) should also score highly on other tests (let us call them B and C). If, however, Thurstone and Gardner are correct and there are different kinds of intelligence, correlations will be high when two tests measure similar factors (for example, spatial and mathematical/logical) but they will be low or close to zero if tests measure different factors (such as bodily/kinaesthetic and musical intelligence).

Colman (1990) has argued that the results from studies using factor analysis are ambiguous and difficult to interpret. This means it is often difficult to see if they provide clear support for either general, hierarchical or multiple intelligence. The Visser, Ashton and Vernon (2006) study is presented in some detail here so that you can see what the evidence is like.

▓ Research study: Visser, Ashton and Vernon (2006)

Visser, Ashton and Vernon tested Gardner's MI theory using a sample of 200 adults. Of these, 171 were university students and the remaining 29 were partners, friends or family of the students.

Each adult carried out two tests on each of Gardner's eight intelligence domains and the scores overall were correlated using factor analysis. Visser *et al.*'s findings were as follows :

▓ There were high correlations between pairs of scores on linguistic, logical/mathematical, spatial, naturalistic and interpersonal domains. Individuals who scored highly on any one of these would have a high score on the others.

▓ There were low correlations between pairs of scores on the above 'traditional' domains and the others, notably musical and spatial intelligence. So an individual could have a high musical ability score but a low score on the linguistic or mathematical domain.

▓ The lack of correlation was most noticeable for kinaesthetic intelligence which did not correlate well with any of the other domains.

As Colman (1990) has suggested, the findings of this study are difficult to disentangle in order to provide clear, unequivocal support for either theory. The high correlations between scores on the traditional 'cognitive' domains imply that these abilities may well be underpinned by a single intelligence factor (or 'g'). However, the low correlations with other domains imply that there may well be other kinds of intelligence, offering limited support for Gardner's MI theory. Visser *et al.* conclude that this study offers some support for hierarchical models of intelligence.

Methodological issues

Participants in this study took part in a battery of intelligence tests. Order effects (notably fatigue) would need to be prevented using careful counterbalancing.

The use of a predominantly student sample raises issues of how far it is sensible to generalise these results to other populations. University students are likely to score highly in traditional domains for university entrance such as linguistic and mathematical intelligence.

Ethical issues

As with all studies in intelligence, this research raises important ethical issues. Participants would need clear briefing as to the nature of the exercise in order to give their fully informed consent to participate. Freedom to withdraw would also be important.

AQA Examiner's tip

Although factor analysis is quite a complicated technique, it is worth thinking about it as it will help you to understand the evidence and rationale behind some of the studies in this area.

Sternberg's triarchic theory: an information processing approach (1985, 1997)

Sternberg's theory grew out of developments in cognitive psychology in the 1970s and 1980s and it draws on the information processing approach. Sternberg (1985) argued that we need to consider the cognitive or mental processes which are involved in intellectual activities and the speed and accuracy of these processes. He believes that differences in performance between individuals on intelligence tests can be explained

Key terms

Triarchic theory: a theory made up of three sub-theories.

by the cognitive processes they use, how effective they are and the speed and accuracy of their operation. His theory is sometimes referred to as triarchic as it is made up of three 'sub-theories'.

Sternberg's model (his **triarchic theory**) relates to mental processes as components and identifies five main components involved in intelligence. These are shown in Table 2.

Table 2 *Sternberg's triarchic theory*

Components	Function
Meta components	These make the decisions about which mental processes need to be used in a task. These are the higher order thinking/control processes
Performance components	These execute the plans and carry out the task
Acquisition components	These are used to acquire new information and knowledge
Retention components	These are used to retrieve information stored in memory
Transfer components	These are used to apply information from one task to another

We can illustrate how these components work by looking at an example.

Mick goes out with £20 and buys two rounds of drinks in his local. Sam drinks vodka at £3.00, Katy drinks halves of cider at £1.50 and Mick has a pint which costs £3.00. Tom usually drinks pints too, but he does not have a drink as he is driving. Can Mick go home on the bus (£1.50) and buy a kebab at £5.00?

The meta components first decide upon strategies, in this case, setting up equations (adding the cost of a round, multiplying by two and subtracting from 20) and discarding irrelevant information (Tom drinks pints). The performance components are used to solve the equation. Retention components keep the costs of each round in memory, and transfer components are used if similar problems have been met before.

Sternberg has recently developed these views to include the notion of successful intelligence. Drawing on his earlier views that ideas of intelligence vary in different cultures, he defines successful intelligence as the ability to achieve success in one's own society or culture. According to Sternberg, successful intelligence depends on capitalising on your strengths and compensating for your weaknesses, and on balancing the use of analytical, creative and practical abilities. He argues that we need to rethink ideas about intelligence and 'to move beyond conventional theories' (2006).

Evaluation: implications for education

One way in which we can assess these competing approaches is to consider how they have been used/applied in education. The assumption that intelligence resulted from a general factor led to the idea in the 1950s and 1960s that intelligence could be assessed (for example using the 11+ test) and children could be given different forms of education based on their performance. This idea has largely fallen out of favour and Gardner's theory has found support from educationalists and teachers (Searle, 2003) who have welcomed the idea of different kinds of intelligence in education. Supporters argue that MI theory has provided an opportunity to move away from 'one size fits all' intelligence testing

Hint

How science works

Theories of intelligence are an excellent area for demonstrating the application of scientific findings. The idea that different children may have different abilities that need to be developed in more individual ways in the education system has already influenced educational policy in the UK.

Take it further

You can find out more about the government's 'gifted and talented' programme in education by going to www.ygt.dcsf.gov.uk. Guidelines on what constitutes gifted and talented are given by the QCA and can be seen at www.qca.org.uk/qca_1960.aspx.

to a much more individualised educational programme which makes the most of children's strengths. It also acknowledges that children have different skills and abilities. 'Gifted and talented' programmes within schools acknowledge that children may be gifted academically or talented in different areas such as music and sport.

Sternberg's information processing approach moves intelligence away from the 'it or them' (single versus multiple) debate to consider the activities used in processing information. This has important practical applications to education as it identifies the cognitive skills used in intellectual activities. The failure to solve problems can be the result of a variety of things such as the failure to select appropriate strategies. The information processing approach is currently proving extremely useful in helping learners to develop thinking skills in schools in Personal Learning and Thinking Skills (PLTS) programmes. It is also usefully applied to problem solving in everyday situations.

Measuring intelligence: the psychometric approach

As we noted above, the term 'psychometrics' relates to methods for measuring intelligence. The modern psychometric view of intelligence takes the view that intelligence:

- can be measured
- is relatively consistent across time within individuals
- varies between individuals who can be compared using test scores.

Searle (2003) has argued that 'at the heart of psychometrics lies the identification of differences between the intelligence of individuals'. Two common types of psychometric tests used today are the Wechsler scales and Raven's Progressive Matrices. These tests rest on different assumptions about the nature of intelligence and what should be measured, and they are used in different settings.

The statistical approach to intelligence

The first useful test of intelligence was devised by Binet and Simon in France in 1905. They were asked by the French government to devise a way of assessing which children would benefit from remedial education. Binet devised a set of 54 tasks, starting with simple activities such as following a lighted match with your eyes and becoming progressively more demanding such as counting backwards from 20. Binet and Simon gave the tasks to children of different ages and found – unsurprisingly – that older children could do more of the harder tasks. From this, they established **test norms** for children of each age.

Binet developed the concept of mental age, which referred to how many tasks the child could correctly answer. If, for example, an eight-year-old could only answer tasks for a five-year-old, their mental age was classed as five. A 10-year-old who could answer tasks set for a 12-year-old would have mental age of 12. This led to the development of the concept of **intelligence quotient (IQ)** which was calculated by dividing mental age by the chronological age and multiplying by 100. A child with a mental age of 10 and a chronological age of eight would have an IQ of $10/8 \times 100 = 125$, and a child with a mental and chronological age of eight would have an IQ of 100.

$$IQ = \frac{MA}{CA} \times 100$$

Hint

As you read the next section, think back to the theories/models of intelligence that we have considered so far. What assumptions are made by each test about the nature of intelligence?

Fig. 6 *One of Binet's 54 items – what would be the time if the hands were reversed?*

Key terms

Test norms: the average performance in a test of children of a specific age.

Intelligence quotient: a score calculated by comparing mental and chronological age and multiplying by 100. Average IQ is 100.

Binet's system worked well when considering the intelligence of children but had limitations when applied to adults. This is because intelligence does not increase in the same way across adulthood as it does during childhood, so an adult of 40 is likely to produce a similar score to a 20-year-old. When this is worked through logically, it leads to an IQ score of 50 (20/40 × 100). For this reason, Wechsler (1939) introduced a purely statistical definition of intelligence.

Wechsler's statistical approach involved giving IQ tests to large samples of people and examining the distribution of their scores. He found that IQ test scores typically fell into a **normal distribution** (Figure 7). Most people's scores were close to the average of 100, with 68 per cent scoring between minus 1 and plus 1 standard deviations (SDs) from the mean. Ninety per cent of people would have scores between minus and plus 2 SDs. Extremely high or low IQs outside 2 SDs occurred in 5 per cent of the population.

> ## Key terms
>
> **Normal distribution:** the pattern found when many people's scores on a continuous variable such as height or IQ are measured and the frequency is plotted.

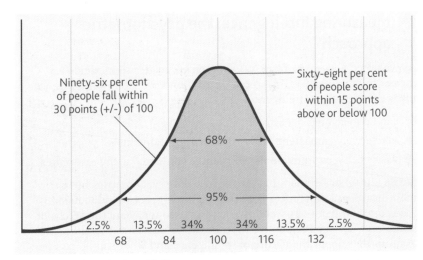

Fig. 7 *Normal distribution with IQ scores*

The Wechsler scales and Raven's progressive matrices

Two commonly used tests are the Wechsler scales and Raven's Progressive Matrices (PM). Three graded Wechsler scales are aimed at adults, children and pre-schoolers. The scales produce scores for verbal IQ, performance IQ and a full-scale IQ measurement. The WISC-R consists of 11 sub-scales, measuring a range of abilities such as digit span (how many separate numbers can be recalled) and block design. Whilst some of the Wechsler sub-scales measure fluid intelligence or problem solving, others measure crystallised intelligence and stored knowledge. Colman (1990) has argued that many of the items rely on verbal comprehension and seem to measure knowledge and memory rather than pure thinking ability.

In contrast, Raven's PM, originally produced in 1938 and revised and republished in 2008, measure fluid intelligence – non-verbal abilities and abstract reasoning. This means that they rely much less on learned knowledge. Like the Wechsler scales, there are different tests for different abilities:

■ the Coloured Progressive Matrices (CPM) are used for children under eight

■ the Standard Progressive Matrices (SPM) are used for children of eight and above and adults.

Each test item consists of a set of patterns and the task involves identifying, from a choice of options, the next item in the series. The items start easily and become progressively more difficult, requiring greater cognitive abilities to solve the tasks. These tests are widely used in research and occupational settings and have the advantage that they can be applied to a wide range of mental abilities irrespective of age, sex, culture or level of education (Searle, 2003). This makes them particularly attractive to global companies who need to select candidates from different cultures.

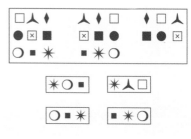

Fig. 8 *Items from Raven's Progressive Matrices*

Evaluation of the psychometric approach

As you can see, there are few direct links between theories of intelligence and intelligence tests. Whilst tests make implicit assumptions about intelligence in deciding what to include, they are generally devised by psychometricians whose interest is in testing and measurement. In fact, experts in the field have called for the need for collaboration and consistency between theorists of intelligence and test makers.

However, psychometric tests are extensively used today in educational and occupational settings and have been particularly widely used by military organisations. Evidence has shown that there is strong correlation between job performance and scores on ability tests (Schmidt and Hunter, 1998) and they are the best predictor of how well people will perform at work (Hunter and Hunter, 1984). Consequently, they are a popular tool for selectors and it is likely that you will at some point be required to take one of these tests as part of job selection procedures.

The claim that IQ scores form a normal distribution has also been challenged. Searle (2003) agues that whilst there are some generally unintelligent people at the bottom end of the normal distribution, there are fewer generally intelligent people at the top end, implying a lack of symmetrical scores.

An important factor overlooked by IQ tests and the psychometric approach is the role of motivation in intelligence test performance. Motivational models have recently emerged from the application of intelligence testing in occupational psychology and these consider how individuals apply the skills that they have. They are important in helping us to understand the gap often found between intelligence and performance (Searle, 2003).

An interesting critique of the psychometric approach has been made by James Flynn and termed 'the Flynn effect'. Flynn (1994) has drawn attention to a steady increase in average scores on tests of fluid intelligence of between 15 and 25 points over the last generation. Tests of crystallised intelligence have also shown increases but of less magnitude. Flynn argues that intelligence itself cannot have increased over that period and the improvements shown demonstrate that tests are not a valid measure of intelligence.

■ Hint

How science works

The widespread use of psychometric tests in education, in the workplace and in the military is one of the best examples of the application of psychological research. It is also one of the most important, as key decisions and appointments are made on the basis of such tests. (I, L)

■ Take it further

You can read more about the Flynn effect and look at one of James Flynn's lectures by going to www.psychometrics.sps.cam.ac.uk and search for 'beyond the Flynn effect'.

Key points

- ■ Intelligence can be seen as intellectual ability.

- ■ There is some debate as to whether intelligence is a single factor or comes in different, multiple forms.

- ■ Hierarchical models see different levels of intelligence organised under a single, general factor.

- ■ Factor analysis is a statistical method used to examine correlations between scores on different tests.

- ■ Studies using factor analysis show strong correlations between tests which measure traditional cognitive domains, but weak relationships between other domains of intelligence.

- ■ Multiple intelligence theories have found favour with educationalists.

- ■ Sternberg's information processing theory identifies the cognitive components involved in intelligence.

- ■ This approach is useful in helping learners to become more efficient.

- ■ The psychometric approach takes the view that intelligence is relatively consistent, can be measured and that scores are normally distributed.

- ■ Psychometric tests measure very different aspects of intelligence.

- ■ Theories about the nature of intelligence are produced separately to intelligence tests. The two approaches ask different questions about intelligence.

Summary questions

1 Outline the different domains of intelligence according to Gardner's MI theory.

2 What are the assumptions behind psychometric tests?

3 Explain two criticisms which have been made of the psychometric approach to intelligence.

4 Outline the method of factor analysis. What are the difficulties in drawing conclusions from factor analyses of intelligence?

5 Discuss the implications for education of theories about the nature of intelligence.

Animal learning and intelligence

The nature of simple learning

Learning objectives:

- describe the key features of classical conditioning

- describe the key features of operant conditioning

- understand the role of classical and operant conditioning in simple learning.

Key terms

Reflex: involuntary response to a stimulus.

Unconditioned stimulus (UCS): a stimulus that triggers an automatic (unconditioned) response.

Unconditioned response (UCR): a response to a stimulus that is automatic and involuntary (reflex).

Hint

How science works

Pavlov's observation that the dogs were producing saliva to novel stimuli and his subsequent studies to investigate why this happened are a good illustration of the scientific method (see the scientific process on page 508). He identified a problem, developed hypotheses about the problem and devised studies to test the hypotheses.

Learning has been described as taking place 'when some experience results in a relatively permanent change in the reaction to a situation' (Pearce, 2008). Simple forms of learning involve associative learning (i.e. learning to associate one thing with another). For example, as people learn to drive they learn to associate red lights with stopping the car. The stimulus of a red light becomes associated with the response of stopping. This is called stimulus-response (S-R) learning and these types of explanations of learning are associated with the behaviourists. Skinner (1938) pointed out that some S-R learning resulted in respondent behaviour (which is triggered automatically by certain stimuli), and other learning resulted in operant behaviour (which is linked to a stimulus but is voluntary). There are two behaviourist explanations of learning: classical conditioning, which deals with respondent behaviour, and operant conditioning, which deals with operant behaviour.

Classical conditioning

Classical conditioning was first described by Pavlov (1927). Pavlov was a physiologist who was interested in the salivatory **reflex**. This is an innate reflex that occurs when food is placed on the tongue. All animals have such innate reflexes. They are characterised by being involuntary and automatic responses to stimuli which are not altered by experience (i.e. they are not learned). However, during his studies of salivation in dogs Pavlov found that the reflex *was* affected by experience. He had an accurate method of recording saliva production and found the dogs were producing saliva before they had food in their mouths, for example to the sounds of the food being prepared or the sight of the food bowls. What he had found was that a stimulus that previously had not caused a response (such as clinking of bowls) now did. Somehow the dogs had learned (or been conditioned) to respond to the sound.

This finding formed the basis of Pavlov's studies into classical conditioning. In a series of studies he showed how reflex responses could be conditioned to a new stimulus. In one study he conditioned dogs to salivate to the sound of a bell. At the start of the study dogs produced saliva when food was put in their mouths. This is a reflex and is automatic and involuntary. Since this reflex requires no training or conditioning he called the food that caused it the **unconditioned stimulus (UCS)**. The response to this stimulus is the **unconditioned response (UCR)**. He then tested the dogs' response to a neutral stimulus, the bell. The bell was a neutral stimulus because it did not trigger the salivatory reflex. He then paired the UCS with the neutral stimulus by ringing the bell as the dogs were given food. The dogs responded by salivating because they had food in their mouths. He paired the two stimuli together a number of times. This is known as conditioning. After conditioning, the previously neutral stimulus of the bell caused the dogs to salivate. This is not a natural response but one that had been

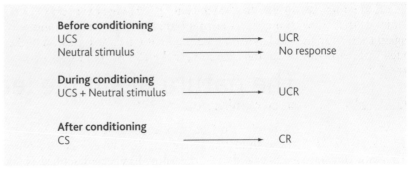

Before conditioning
UCS ——————————→ UCR
Neutral stimulus ——————————→ No response

During conditioning
UCS + Neutral stimulus ——————————→ UCR

After conditioning
CS ——————————→ CR

Fig. 1 *The process involved in producing a conditioned response*

conditioned. Pavlov therefore called the bell a **conditioned stimulus (CS)** and the salivation in response to it the **conditioned response (CR)**. The general process of classical conditioning is shown below.

Studies have shown that most things that animals can detect (sights, sounds, smells, tastes, etc.) can be linked to stimulus that produces a reflex (unconditioned response) to become a conditioned stimulus.

Timing of CS

The exact timing of the pairing of the CS and the UCS is important in the development of any CR. For example, if the CS is presented just before the UCS (forward conditioning) then conditioning tends to work. However, if the CS is presented after the UCS (backward conditioning) it tends to be much less effective in conditioning. The effect of the various timings is shown in Table 1.

Table 1 *The effect of the timing of CS and UCS pairing*

Type of pairing	Description of pairing	Effect of pairing
Forward	CS precedes UCS and overlaps with it	Tends to result in the strongest conditioning
Trace	CS precedes UCS and stops before UCS begins	Tends to result in conditioning, but the effects are weaker the longer the delay is between the two
Simultaneous	CS and UCS start and stop at the same time	Tends to result in weak or no conditioning
Backward	CS is presented after the UCS	It is difficult to produce conditioning with this timing

Extinction and spontaneous recovery

The unconditioned responses associated with reflexes do not fade or disappear over time. In contrast Pavlov found that conditioned responses do fade quickly. If the CS is presented without pairing to the UCS the CR becomes less and less strong until it stops completely. An example would be if the bell is rung repeatedly without any food then the dogs stop salivating to the sound of the bell. Pavlov called this process **extinction**. However, the CR does not disappear completely and often comes back without further conditioning. If there is a break in the testing of a dog and then the bell is rung again, there can be a response. This is called **spontaneous recovery**. Spontaneous recovery does not always happen, but it depends on when and how the CS is presented following extinction.

There are other lasting effects of conditioning following extinction. Animals that show extinction after conditioning are easier to condition again than animals that have never been conditioned. This has led to the idea that extinction is not the forgetting of the CR but an inhibition of the CR.

Generalisation and discrimination

Pavlov discovered that the CR could be produced by stimuli that are similar to the CS that the animal had been conditioned to. For example, if a particular bell tone is paired with food, the bell tone becomes a CS. However, other bells that are similar, but not identical to, the original also produce a response. Pavlov called this **stimulus generalisation**. Stimuli that are most like the CS produce greater responses than stimuli that are less like the CS. Animals can also learn to discriminate between different stimuli. This occurs during conditioning if one stimulus is paired with the UCS but others like it are not. For example, dogs are given food (UCS) while one particular bell is rung, but when other similar bells are rung they are not given food. The dogs then show **stimulus discrimination**: they show the CR to one bell only.

Operant conditioning

The role of operant conditioning in animal learning was described by Skinner (1938). Although he realised that classical conditioning played a role in learning, Skinner was more interested in operant behaviour and the effect the environment had on the likelihood that a voluntary behaviour would occur in the future.

Skinner's work on operant conditioning was a development of earlier work by Thorndike (1911). Thorndike was interested in how animals solved problems. In one study he built a puzzle box for cats. The cats were put inside the box and had to learn to operate a latch to get to some food outside the box. He found that on average cats took a long time to release the catch at first, but that after being put in the box a number of times ('trials') they became faster and faster. This has been called trial and error learning (the more trials, the less errors). This led to Thorndike's law of positive effect which states that any behaviour that is followed by a pleasurable outcome is more likely to be repeated.

Building on this idea Skinner studied behaviour in a controlled and scientific way using apparatus now known as Skinner boxes. These were a very plain environment that allowed him to eliminate extraneous variables. Typically they included only a device to measure a behaviour (such as a lever rats could push or a disc pigeons could peck at) and a means of delivering some food. When rats were put into a Skinner box the behaviour they were taught was to push a lever. At first the rats tried to escape and eventually in their exploration of the box they pushed the lever by accident. This was rewarded by giving some food (a food pellet). After rats had done this by accident a number of times they began to push the lever more and more often. The food reward encouraged the lever-pushing behaviour. Skinner called anything that made a behaviour more likely to happen again a reinforcer. Giving food after pushing the lever acted as a **reinforcement** of the behaviour.

The Skinner box not only acted as a controlled environment but also recorded the activity of the rat automatically. This allowed Skinner to show how subtle changes in the way reinforcement was given had profound effects on behaviour (see the schedules of reinforcement below).

Skinner found that operant conditioning depended on the relationships between ABC. Where ABC are:

■ Antecedents – the stimulus conditions before the behaviour (the box and lever)

■ Behaviours – what the animal does (pushes the lever)

■ Consequences – what happens after the behaviour (they are given food or reinforcement).

Skinner demonstrated that the voluntary, operant behaviour he studied is modified and maintained by the consequences of the behaviour.

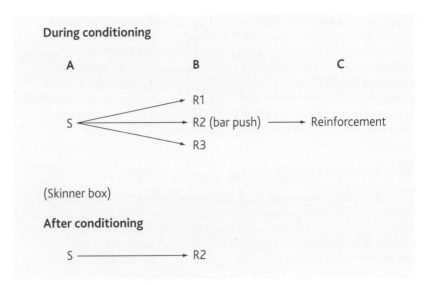

Fig. 2 *The ABC of operant conditioning*

Link

Approaches, issues and debates

Skinner's emphasis on the role of the environment in shaping behaviour has been described as environmental reductionism. He believed that psychologists should only study what happens to an animal (the stimulus), the animal's response and the consequence of the response. He did not accept that anything else affected behaviour.

Take it further

What type of schedule of reinforcement operates in gambling? Refer to the response and extinction rates in Table 2. Does this help to explain why gambling becomes a problem for some people?

Key terms

Positive reinforcement: this occurs when a behaviour is followed by a favourable stimulus (which increases the likelihood that the behaviour will be repeated).

Negative reinforcement: this occurs when a behaviour is followed by the removal of an aversive stimulus (which increases the likelihood that the behaviour will be repeated).

In classical conditioning the CR gradually shows extinction when the CS is no longer paired with the UCS. A similar process occurs in operant conditioning when reinforcement is removed. If a rat has been conditioned to push a lever by giving a food reinforcer, it will eventually stop pushing the lever when food is no longer given. This behaviour can start again without any further reinforcement and, in common with classical conditioning, this is called spontaneous recovery.

Schedules of reinforcement

Skinner found that a key feature in determining the way animals respond and how long a behaviour lasts is the way in which reinforcement is given. Initially animals were trained by giving a reinforcement each time the animal made the appropriate response. This is called continuous reinforcement. However, Skinner found that when reinforcement was given less frequently it altered the animal's response and extinction rates. Five ways of giving reinforcement and their influence on response and extinction rates are shown in Table 2.

Positive and negative reinforcement

In all of the examples of operant conditioning above reinforcement has been described as a pleasurable consequence of a behaviour (i.e. receiving food after pushing a lever reinforces the lever pushing). However, this only describes one form of reinforcement called **positive reinforcement**. Reinforcement can also be negative. **Negative reinforcement** is the removal of or avoidance of an aversive stimulus following an action by

Table 2 *The effect of schedules of reinforcement on response and extinction rates*

Schedule of reinforcement	Description	Effect on response rate and pattern	Effect on extinction rate
Continuous reinforcement	Reinforcement follows every single appropriate response	Response rate is low but regular	Extinction is very rapid
Fixed ratio (FR)	A reinforcement is given after a fixed number of responses (e.g. one reinforcement is given after 10 responses)	Response rate is very high. There tends to be a lull after a reinforcement followed by rapid responding	Extinction is fast
Variable ratio (VR)	A reinforcement is given after a number of responses, but that number varies each time around an average value (e.g. one reinforcement is given after eight responses and another after 12)	Response rate is very high and steady	Extinction is slow. VR tends to be the most resistant to extinction
Fixed interval (FI)	A reinforcement is given after a fixed period provided the response is made at least once during the period (e.g. reinforcement is given every 40 seconds)	Response rate is low. There tends to be pause after each reinforcement with an increase in responding towards the end of an interval	Extinction is fast
Variable interval (VI)	A reinforcement is given after periods that vary around an average time provided the response is made at least once during any period (e.g. reinforcement is given after 30 seconds in one period and 50 in another)	Response rate is moderate. The pattern is more steady than FI, but there is some increase in responding as time since the last reinforcement increases	Extinction is slow

the animal. For example, if an animal is conditioned to turn off a mild electric shock by pushing a lever, the removal of the electric shock acts as a negative reinforcement. Both positive and negative reinforcement strengthen behaviour and make it more likely to occur in the future. On the other hand, **punishment** weakens behaviour and makes it less likely to happen. Punishment is the presentation of an unpleasant stimulus after a behaviour. For example, if after pushing a lever the rat receives an electric shock, it makes lever pushing less likely to happen. The electric shock acts as a punishment.

Secondary reinforcement

The reinforcements described so far have all been primary. **Primary reinforcers** are innate and satisfy a biological need; they include food, water, sex and avoidance of pain. A primary reinforcer is a naturally occurring reinforcer. A **secondary reinforcer** on the other hand does not naturally act as a reinforcer. A secondary reinforcer is initially a

■ Key terms

Punishment: this occurs when a behaviour is followed by an aversive stimulus (which decreases the likelihood that the behaviour will be repeated).

Primary reinforcer: (also know as unconditioned reinforcer) this is a stimulus that reinforces behaviour naturally (e.g. food, water, etc.).

Secondary reinforcer: (also know as conditioned reinforcer) this is a stimulus that becomes reinforcing because of an association with a primary reinforcer (e.g. money).

AQA **Examiner's tip**

It is easy to confuse negative reinforcement and punishment because they both involve aversive stimuli. Remember that negative reinforcement involves the *removal* of or *avoidance* of an aversive stimulus and *strengthens* behaviour. Punishment involves the *presentation* of an aversive stimulus and *weakens* behaviour.

neutral stimulus. However, when it is paired with a primary reinforcer it begins to act as a reinforcer itself. For example, music does not act as a reinforcer for rats. However, if music is played each time rats receive food as reinforcement after pushing a bar, eventually rats will push the bar if music is played but no food is given. In the absence of food the behaviour should become extinct. It does not because the music acts as a secondary reinforcer.

Behaviour shaping

The simple behaviour of pushing a lever used in the examples so far seems to have little relevance to some of the complex behaviours that animals can learn. If learning a behaviour depends on the consequences of that behaviour, how do animals learn complex behaviour? For example, Skinner taught pigeons to hold small bats in their beaks to play ping pong. The chances of this happening by accident so that he could then reinforce it are extremely low. So how did he do it? The answer is by behaviour shaping or reinforcing successive approximations to the required behaviour. This is giving reinforcement for behaviour that gradually becomes more and more like the complex behaviour desired. In the case of the pigeons, they were first reinforced for pecking near the bat, then on the bat, then for grasping the bat and so on. If you have seen animals perform complex sequences of behaviour in films, they will have been trained using operant conditioning and behaviour shaping.

Summary questions

1 A puff of air into the eye causes the blink reflex. Describe the procedure for conditioning participants to blink to the sound of a buzzer. How would you make the conditioned response extinct?

2 In one study monkeys were taught to perform an action to get tokens. The tokens were then exchanged for fruit. When no fruit was available the monkeys continued to perform the behaviour to receive the tokens. What different types of reinforcement do the fruit and the tokens represent?

3 Outline the differences between ratio and interval schedules of reinforcement.

4 The schedules of behaviour were discussed using lever pushing in rats, but it can equally be applied to human behaviour. What type of schedules apply to each of the following? How do they influence human performance?
   a Weekly pay.
   b Turning on the TV.
   c Irregular self-employed payments.
   d Winning on a slot machine.

Key points

- Classical conditioning occurs when a stimulus (UCS) that causes a reflex (UCR) is paired with another stimulus that normally has no effect. After pairing, the second stimulus (CS) causes the same response (CR).

- Classical conditioning shows extinction, spontaneous recovery, generalisation and discrimination.

- In operant conditioning behaviour is determined by its consequences. Any behaviour that is reinforced tends to be repeated.

- Schedules of reinforcement alter both the response rate and extinction rate.

- Reinforcement can be positive (presentation of pleasant stimulus) or negative (removal of unpleasant stimulus).

- Reinforcement can be primary (innate, biological) or secondary (conditioned).

The role of operant and classical conditioning

- understand the role of conditioning in the behaviour of non-human animals

- explain the limitations of behaviourist explanations of learning.

The ability to learn is biologically important. Animals need to adapt to their environment and change behaviour to meet the challenge of new circumstances. Studies of classical conditioning have shown how animals can learn to react to new stimuli. So, for example, animals may learn to associate fear with a new stimulus if it is paired with a predator. Classical conditioning can also be useful in hunting and foraging. All animals need food, but some sources are potentially harmful. Learning which is beneficial and which is harmful helps animals survive. Garcia and Koelling (1966) demonstrated that classical conditioning could be used to cause animals to avoid food that made them ill. In studies of taste aversion they showed that just one pairing of a novel food with an emetic (a substance that causes vomiting) was enough to make rats avoid the food in the future. This happened even when the vomiting occurred some time after eating. Garcia, Rusiniak and Brett (1977) showed that this also happens with wild animals. They made coyotes ill by feeding them mutton wrapped in sheep hide that was laced with an emetic. When given the opportunity to attack sheep later, the coyotes turned away.

It is also important for animals to learn from past experience. Animals need to learn new behaviour in the search for food sources and shelter and to avoid threats. Operant conditioning explains how animals learn new behaviour because of the consequence of the behaviour. It also provides an explanation of how reinforcement and punishment in the past shape and guide behaviour. The study of schedules of reinforcement shows how subtle differences in the way reinforcement is given can change the ways animals respond and how long behaviours last. Furthermore, it can explain how animals can learn complex sequences of behaviour.

Limitations of behaviourist explanations of learning

Classical conditioning is able to explain how animals, including humans, can learn to react to new stimuli. However, it does have some limitations. Firstly, it is not clear that studies of classical conditioning can be generalised. Seligman (1970) notes that animals have evolved to survive in different environments and situations. Some animals might learn some things more easily than others. He called this concept 'preparedness'. Animals may be prepared to learn some associations but not others. Humans, for example, seem 'prepared' to learn to fear spiders and snakes but not kittens. Taste aversion studies also challenge traditional views of classical conditioning as they show it can work after just one pairing of the CS and UCS and is resistant to extinction. This does not fit the traditional description of acquisition and extinction.

Another problem is that classical conditioning is limited in explaining learning in animals. Classical conditioning only links a new stimulus to an existing response. Conditioning dogs to salivate to a bell instead of food does not teach a new response. However, animals learn many novel responses that help them to adapt to their environment. In contrast operant conditioning does explain how animals learn new and potentially complex behaviour. It provides a detailed account of how behaviour can be shaped by its consequences.

Link

Approaches, issues and debates

Behaviourists believe that all behaviour is learned. They argue that behaviour is due to nurture not nature. However the concept of 'preparedness' suggests that evolution (or nature) also plays a part in learning.

Nevertheless, operant conditioning and classical conditioning cannot explain all learning in animals. These behaviourist explanations of learning concentrate on the links between stimuli and responses and ignore the effect of any intervening factors such as thinking (or cognition). However, evidence suggests that these intervening, cognitive factors are important in animal learning. In one series of studies, Kohler (1925) showed that chimpanzees did not use trial and error to solve problems but, rather, studied the situation and then showed the appropriate response. Kohler called this insight learning. The chimpanzees seemed to solve the problem by using a mental representation of it. There is also evidence of latent learning in animals. For example, Tolman and Honzik (1930) allowed one group of rats to wander in a maze with no reinforcement, but reinforced another group when they reached the end. As predicted by operant conditioning, the rats in the reinforced group soon learnt to run to the end of the maze but the rats in the first group did not. However, when this group were given reinforcement (11 days into the study) they learnt to reach the end much quicker than the group that had been reinforced from the beginning. They showed latent learning of the maze and this is not explained by operant conditioning. Operant conditioning also fails to explain learning by imitation or observation (see below).

Key points

- Classical and operant conditioning provide two powerful explanations of learning in non-human animals.

- Classical conditioning provides an explanation of how animals learn to respond to new stimuli, and operant conditioning provides an explanation of how animals learn novel behaviour to adapt to their environment.

- The concept of preparedness raises a question of whether the results of classical conditioning from one species can be generalised to another.

- Taste aversion studies suggest that the gradual acquisition and extinction of conditioned responses described by Pavlov are not universal.

- Although operant conditioning is good at explaining trial and error-type learning, it fails to explain learning that involves cognition such as insight, latent learning or learning by imitation.

Summary questions

5 Describe how classical conditioning may influence foraging behaviour.

6 Describe how operant conditioning could explain how birds learn to use a new food source in a garden. What type of reinforcement do they receive?

7 Outline two limitations of classical conditioning and two limitations of operant conditioning.

8 Explain how a person might develop a taste aversion following a stomach bug.

Intelligence in non-human animals

Learning objectives:

- understand the concept of intelligence in non-human animals

- understand the role of social learning in animals

- evaluate evidence for theory of mind in animals

- understand the role of machiavellian intelligence in social animals

- analyse whether animals are capable of self-recognition.

Key terms

Theory of mind: the ability to attribute mental states to oneself and others.

Machiavellian intelligence: this type of intelligence is related to living in groups. It refers to the ability to manipulate other animals, to form advantageous alliances with other animals and sometimes to use deception to achieve your own ends.

The concept of non-human intelligence is difficult to define (or operationalise). Pearce (2008) discusses three characteristics that may be used to define and assess animal intelligence: adaptability, learning and information processing. He points out that few would disagree that adapting behaviour to circumstances is a sign of intelligence, but that it is difficult to identify the mechanisms that enable an animal to adapt (i.e. is the adaptation a result of learning or biology?). Therefore, the capacity to learn to adapt and the ability to process information are better characteristics to use. So far we have considered the role of simple learning in enabling animals to adapt. These explanations concentrate on the learning and adaptability of individuals. However, there are many other types of evidence of intelligence in non-human animals including social learning, **theory of mind**, **machiavellian intelligence** and self-recognition. These types of evidence for intelligence tend to require explanations of learning that are based on information processing (cognition).

Social learning

Many animals live in groups and are influenced by others. Even solitary animals need to interact with mates or may spend time with a parent. It is possible that some learning is not the result of individual experience but of social experience. Pearce (2008) has identified many ways that social learning could benefit animals. Animals can learn from copying rather than learning from the potentially dangerous process of trial and error. They could copy diet and thus avoid poor or poisonous food, copying others' reactions may help them to avoid predators, and problems may be solved by copying the solutions of others. There is evidence for each of these.

Diet and foraging

Some animals have a very varied diet that requires the animal to learn to discriminate between good and dangerous food sources. Rats are one such species that will eat nearly anything that is not poisonous. There is evidence that rats tend to go where others are feeding and thus are guided to safe food sources. There is evidence that rats can acquire from other rats a preference for a particular food even if they do not see the others eat it. In one study rats were paired up and one of the pair (the demonstrator) was placed in isolation and then fed a distinctive flavoured food (either cocoa or cinnamon). The demonstrator rat was then reunited with the observer for 30 minutes without any food. Next the observer was removed and given the choice of either cocoa- or cinnamon-flavoured food. The observer rats preferred the same flavour as their demonstrator had eaten (Galef, 1988). This preference can last up to 12 hours with just a single contact with the demonstrator. Other studies have shown that animals can acquire a preference for up to four flavours simultaneously (Galef, Lee and Whiskin, 2005).

Rats are usually reluctant to eat new flavours. The evidence therefore suggests it is the interaction with other rats that have eaten the food that changes the preference for the food. The mechanism of how this happens is unclear but Pearce (2008) suggests that the observers may detect odours on the demonstrator's breath or particles of the novel food on the demonstrator's whiskers.

Fear of predators

Wild monkeys have a strong reaction to snakes and this includes fleeing, alarm calls and facial expressions that seem to indicate fear. Monkeys that are raised in captivity or laboratories do not show these reactions (Pearce, 2008). This seems to indicate that the reaction is learned not innate. Mineka and Cook (1988) have shown that if a laboratory-reared monkey observes the reaction of a wild monkey to a snake, the laboratory-reared monkey (observer) shows the same fear response. This reaction seems to become acquired by the observer monkey and is subsequently shown in the absence of the wild monkey. The response can last up to a year after the initial observation of the wild monkey. Mineka and Cook (1988) suggest this is caused by a variant of classical conditioning. In this, the fear shown by the wild monkey is the unconditioned stimulus that triggers fear in the observer monkey. The snake becomes the conditioned stimulus that triggers the same conditioned response. Pearce (2008) calls this observational conditioning and notes that this can play an important role in learning to avoid predators.

Imitation

Some problems that animals face are so difficult that they may not be solved in a lifetime of trial and error by individuals. However, if the problem is solved by one individual it would be very advantageous to the group or even the species if the solution could be passed on. One potential mechanism for learning from another animal is imitation, where animals learn specific behaviours by observing others perform them.

It is difficult to find clear evidence of imitation from naturalistic studies. One often quoted source of evidence is the rapid spread of tearing the foil on milk-bottle tops by blue tits and great tits in Britain (Hinde and Fisher, 1951). This behaviour was first observed in one location in 1921, but by the late 1940s it was observed throughout Britain. One explanation of this rapid spread of a behaviour was that the birds learned by imitation. However, laboratory studies have questioned this explanation. Sherry and Galef (1984) have shown that if a bird is exposed to an already opened bottle it will drink the milk and is more likely to open the foil itself in the future. In other words, it learns by reinforcement not imitation.

Another famous example of apparent imitation was seen in one troop of Japanese macaque monkeys on an island (Kawai, 1965). To observe the monkeys easily a researcher left sweet potatoes on the beach. On one occasion a young female took a sweet potato to the sea and washed the mud off it. She repeated this behaviour on subsequent occasions presumably because the potatoes were better without mud. Fairly soon most of the younger monkeys also washed their potatoes. This behaviour has now become common in this troop of monkeys but it is not seen elsewhere. One explanation of this is that the monkeys learned by imitation. However, there is an alternative explanation. Nagell, Olguin and Tomasello (1993) suggest that the practice may be spread through stimulus enhancement. This occurs when an observer animal is more likely to direct their behaviour towards an object if they have seen another animal directing activity towards the object. In this case the object is the sweet potato. If the observer then follows the demonstrator (experienced) monkey to the sea because of social reasons, it may learn by accident that washed potatoes taste better. This may seem like a contrived explanation, but it has the advantage of explaining the spread of behaviour using established processes.

■ **Link**

Approaches, issues and debates

Many of the concepts discussed in this section (e.g. theory of mind, machiavellian intelligence and self-recognition) require an understanding of the processes that occur between a stimulus and a response. They require the study of thought. These processes are studied by cognitive psychologists.

Another behaviour that seems to be restricted to a few groups is nut cracking in wild chimpanzees. Marshall-Pescini and Whiten (2008) suggest this is a socially transmitted tradition and have investigated the behaviour with a group of sanctuary-living chimpanzees. They found it could be acquired in a few days and they discovered evidence of social learning.

Theory of mind

We often explain our behaviour by referring to a mental state (e.g. I drank because I was thirsty). We also make inferences about the mental states of others due to their behaviour (e.g. he drank a lot of water therefore he must be thirsty). This ability to attribute mental states is called theory of mind (ToM). The possibility that animals may possess ToM was first raised by Premack and Woodruff (1978). They showed a chimpanzee named Sarah a number of videos of humans attempting to solve problems. The video stopped before the solution was shown. Sarah was given the choice of two photographs – one showed an action that would result in a successful solution, the other would not. She consistently chose the one that would result in a successful solution. Does this suggest chimpanzees have a ToM? Pearce (2008) suggests there are two types of evidence to investigate this: deception and knowledge attribution.

Deception

If an animal has a ToM then it will understand that the behaviour of other animals will be influenced by the knowledge they have. This raises the possibility that animals might be capable of manipulating information to deceive others. Woodruff and Premack (1979) tested this possibility with chimpanzees. In their study, individual chimpanzees observed a person hide food under one of two containers before leaving the room. The chimpanzee was unable to reach the containers. In the next stage one of two trainers entered: either a 'cooperative' or a 'competitive' trainer. These were dressed differently and behaved differently. If the chimpanzee pointed to the correct container, the *cooperative* trainer gave it the food but the *competitive* trainer kept the food. However, if the chimpanzee pointed to the wrong container with the cooperative trainer, it did not receive food, but with the competitive trainer it received the food.

Woodruff and Premack found that some chimpanzees were able to get food in both conditions and this can be taken as evidence for ToM. Some chimpanzees seemed to mislead the competitive trainer. However, Pearce (2008) points out that the study required many trials before there was evidence of deception. It is possible that the results can be explained by a much simpler mechanism – they were caused by operant conditioning and discrimination. The animals learnt the appropriate response to each trainer (or stimulus) because of different consequences to their behaviour.

Knowledge attribution

If I see you put a sweet in a box I know you have the knowledge about its whereabouts because I have a ToM. Can animals attribute knowledge to others? This possibility was investigated by Povinelli, Nelson and Boyson (1990) using chimpanzees that had to choose a correct cup in order to get food. Individual chimpanzees were put in a room with two trainers. One of the trainers left the room. The trainer who remained placed food under one of four cups. The chimpanzee could see that food was being hidden but could not see which cup it was under. Only the trainer (the 'knower') who remained knew which cup contained the food. The other trainer

Hint

How science works

In science the law of parsimony suggests when we have two competing explanations we should accept the simplest or the one that makes the fewest assumptions. One explanation for the apparent deception in chimpanzees is that they have a theory of mind. This assumes that they are capable of thinking about the mental state of the trainers. The other explanation is based on operant conditioning and makes no assumptions. **(A)**

Intelligence

(the 'guesser') then returned. Both then pointed to a cup; the knower pointed to the correct cup and the guesser pointed to one of the incorrect ones. If the chimpanzees can attribute knowledge they should have chosen the cup that the knower pointed to. All chimpanzees did learn to do so.

This could be taken as evidence of ToM, but there is also a simpler explanation. It took hundreds of trials before the chimpanzees consistently chose the knower's cup. Over these trials the chimpanzee was consistently rewarded (reinforced) by choosing the knower's cup but it was never reinforced by choosing the guesser's cup. Thus the study could represent nothing more than learning to discriminate using operant conditioning.

Machiavellian intelligence

Animals that live in complex social groups need to learn to deal with others and to solve the problems that social relationships can bring (who to groom, who to share food with, who to be wary of, etc.). In other words, these animals need to develop a social intelligence. The machiavellian intelligence hypothesis put forward by Byrne and Whiten (1988) suggests that the intelligence seen in primates is not an adaptation to environmental factors but to the needs of complex social interaction. Machiavellian intelligence is a particular form of social intelligence where animals learn not only to manipulate their environment, but to deliberately manipulate others in a social group. This could involve exploiting or deceiving social companions for individual gain.

Byrne and Whiten (1987, 1988) describe a number of instances of baboons behaving in an apparently dishonest way to gain advantage. For example, a juvenile baboon watched as an adult dug up a large root and then, after looking around, screamed loudly. The juvenile's mother, who was dominant in the troop, then ran over and chased the other adult away. The juvenile then picked up the root and ate it. The juvenile's scream appears designed to mislead the mother and provoke an attack. However, this and other examples described by Byrne and Whiten raise the question of interpretation of intent of animals. Are they deliberately trying to deceive or are there simpler explanations? For example, an alternative explanation of the juvenile baboon's behaviour is that it is a conditioned response that occurred because of past experience. If the juvenile had approached an adult who was eating and had been threatened, a normal response would be to scream. The scream could trigger an attack by the mother and the juvenile would be left with the food; it would be reinforced for screaming.

Self-recognition

Another source of evidence of intelligence looks not at interactions with others but at interactions between the animal and itself in a mirror. Adult humans have an understanding that their image in a mirror is a reflection of themselves. They have self-recognition because they possess self-awareness or the concept that they are an entity separate from others. The question of whether other animals have self-recognition and self-awareness has provoked much debate.

Observational studies of great apes provide some evidence of self-recognition. Chimpanzees initially treat mirror images as other chimpanzees but soon show behaviour that indicates self-recognition. Pearce (2008) suggests that familiarity with mirrors 'brings out the worst' in chimpanzees, such as using mirrors to pick their teeth, extract mucus from their nose or closely inspect their anal-genital area! Whether these behaviours are good or bad they suggest that the chimpanzees are using the

Hint

How science works

Byrne and Whiten's evidence for machiavellian intelligence in baboons is based on observational research. It illustrates one of the problems of such research, interpretation of the findings. They have a record of what the baboons did but no control over variables, such as past experience, that might have influenced this behaviour. In the absence of any experimental data, any interpretation of the behaviour remains speculative. (F)

mirror image as a source of evidence about their bodies. This suggests self-recognition. Koko (the gorilla famous for her ability to use sign language) regularly uses a mirror for grooming (see www.koko.org for pictures).

However, the observational evidence is regarded by some as anecdotal. It could be merely coincidental that the behaviours were observed while the animal was in front of a mirror; they might have shown the same behaviour if the mirror was absent (Pearce, 2008). More convincing evidence comes from experimental studies. For example, in one study Povinelli *et al.* (1997) applied a dye to one eyebrow and the top of the opposite ear of chimpanzees that were familiar with mirrors. They then recorded how often the animals touched these areas in a baseline 30-minute period with no mirror. They then allowed the chimpanzees to look in mirrors and again recorded how often they touched the areas. During the baseline there was very little touching of the dyed areas, but when looking in mirrors the chimpanzees touched these areas regularly but did not touch unmarked regions any more than baseline levels. This seems to provide better evidence for self-recognition.

As with the observational evidence, the experimental evidence for self-recognition seems confined to the great apes. Other animals including Old World and New World monkeys, cats, dogs and parrots treat their mirror image as another animal. One exception may be elephants that can use mirrors to see areas of their body that have been marked, and they touch these areas with their trunk (Plotnik, de Waal and Reiss, 2006). Other animals, including parrots, seem to be able to use information from mirrors but show no self-recognition. One explanation for this is that animals can learn, through trial and error, to move using the mirror to achieve a goal.

The evidence for self-recognition in non-human primates is not universally accepted. For example, Heyes (1998) argues that the evidence from mirror studies does not warrant ascribing the concept of self-recognition or self-awareness to apes. The alternative explanation is based on the idea of body concept. Heyes argues that a body concept would allow an animal to discriminate between stimuli from its body and stimuli from outside. If an animal learned to correlate mirror information with stimuli from its body, it could react appropriately to the mirror image. This does not require an awareness of self.

Key points

- Social learning involves learning from other animals of the same species rather than from individual experience.

- There are a number of types of evidence of social learning, including learning diet selection and fear of predators. However, evidence for the role of imitation in animal learning is less clear.

- Studies of theory of mind in non-human animals are not conclusive. Sources of evidence, the ability to deceive and knowledge attribution are all open to alternative explanations.

- Most primates live in complex social groups and this requires the development of social intelligence. One form of social intelligence, machiavellian intelligence, involves manipulation of others in the social group.

- There is both observational and experimental evidence that the great apes are capable of self-recognition. However, there is disagreement about whether the use of a mirror to monitor the body needs a concept of self.

Summary questions

9 Outline some of the benefits that social learning could have for animals.

10 Describe an explanation of 'deception' in observational studies of baboons that does not use machiavellian intelligence.

11 Why is the experimental evidence of self-recognition more convincing than the observational evidence?

12 Explain how stimulus enhancement could account for apparent cases of imitation.

21 Evolution of intelligence

Evolutionary factors in the development of human intelligence

Learning objectives:

- describe the relative size and complexity of the human brain

- describe and evaluate the role of ecological demands in the development of human intelligence

- describe and evaluate the role of social complexity in the development of human intelligence

- understand the relationship between brain size and intelligence.

Key terms

Primates: a class of advanced mammals that includes monkeys, gorillas, chimpanzees and humans.

Genetic mutations: changes to genetic material that occur during fertilisation of the egg by the sperm. Mutations are often harmful and the embryo may not live. Occasionally, a mutation gives the offspring a slight advantage, and so it enters the gene pool.

Introduction

It is commonly accepted that the main reason for the success of modern humans is that we are more intelligent than other animals. As we saw in the previous chapter, non-human animals can show a variety of simple and complex learning. In some cases, they have skills beyond anything humans can do. For instance, some birds navigate their way accurately across thousands of miles of ocean and desert without the aid of GPS. So we have to be careful when we define intelligence. Human characteristics that seem to have developed beyond anything seen in the animal kingdom particularly relate to:

- planning and anticipating future events
- self-awareness and the ability to reflect on our own behaviour
- highly developed social communication.

All of these are heavily dependent on language and many psychologists feel that it is language that really distinguishes us from the rest of the animal kingdom.

The evolutionary approach in psychology assumes that the behaviour and characteristics of modern humans have evolved over millions of years from the behaviour and characteristics of our ancestors. In the first part of this chapter we look at ways in which the human brain differs anatomically from our nearest relatives, **primates** such as chimpanzees and gorillas. These differences can help to explain differences in intelligence. Then we consider various factors in the lifestyles of early humans that may have led to the evolution of these differences.

How evolution works

It is important to realise that evolution does not know where it is going. It is a common mistake to assume that we have large brains because, for instance, we have language. In fact, we have language because we have large brains. When we look at the evolution of intelligence we are looking for *selection pressures* that led to increased brain size and the development of high-level cognitive skills.

All animals inhabit a particular environment. As they breed, small changes can occur spontaneously in the genetic make-up of their offspring. These changes are known as **genetic mutations**. Sometimes these mutations are harmful and the offspring do not survive. Sometimes, however, the mutation gives that particular offspring a slight advantage. For example, we assume that the long neck of the giraffe began as a mutation that slightly lengthened the neck. It gave that animal a slight advantage in reaching leaves on trees, making it more likely that it would survive and breed, so passing this advantage on to its offspring. Over many generations additional mutations would have further lengthened the giraffe's neck. Therefore, the *selection pressure* leading to the long neck of the giraffe was the availability of nutritious leaves high up on trees.

In the same way mutations in the human genetic code would have given some individuals small advantages that led to increased chances of survival and breeding. We do not know exactly what these mutations were. We have evolved from ancestors that were almost certainly **arboreal** (tree living), that walked on all fours, had primitive skills that enabled them to use tools, and communicated through species-specific calls rather than language. All of these things have changed during the course of human evolution. It is unlikely that one dramatic mutation would have led to sophisticated use of tools in one generation, or that complex language would have emerged in one big leap from species-specific calls. The accumulation of many small genetic changes over many generations would have led to the high-level abilities of modern humans.

It is crucial to remember that each small change gave a small advantage to the animal concerned. This advantage would relate to the animal's environment and lifestyle. Therefore, when we look for factors influencing the evolution of the human brain and intelligence, the first consideration is always the environment and lifestyle of our ancestors. This is the **environment of evolutionary adaptation (EEA)**.

The human brain

The human ancestral line separated from our nearest relatives, the chimpanzees and gorillas, about 6 million years ago. Unfortunately, the fossil record, particularly for the period from 6 million to 2 million years ago, is very limited. The total number of skulls and parts of skeletons found would not fill the boot of a small family car. When skulls are found we can estimate the size of the brain, and from other parts of the skeleton we can work out whether, for instance, they were **bipedal**, and the shape and size of the teeth may indicate what their diet was. From 2 million years ago there is more evidence of tool making, and from campsites there are clues about diet and lifestyle.

Our earliest ancestors in the human line, the **australopithecines** (this means 'southern ape'), had brains not much larger than chimpanzees (about 400 cm³) but were probably bipedal. Chimpanzees can occasionally walk on two legs, but they are adapted for tree living and walking on all four limbs, so the evolution of bipedalism was a key step in human evolution.

Around 2 million years ago the first major expansion of the human brain occurred in *Homo erectus*, with a brain capacity of around 750 cm³. *Homo erectus* also made relatively sophisticated tools such as axes and bone scrapers, and used fire for cooking. Our close relatives, the Neanderthals, emerged around 400,000 years ago, dying out only about 40,000 years ago. They had a brain capacity as large or even larger than modern humans (1,100–1,500 cm³). Modern humans, *Homo sapiens*, evolved between 150,000 and 200,000 years ago, and have an average brain capacity of 1,350 cm³.

Absolute brain size is not a good index of intelligence. The brain controls the body's physiological systems and musculature, and larger bodies need larger brains for these basic functions. Elephants and whales have brains 4–5 times larger than ours. A better index is the ratio of brain to body; the higher the ratio, the more brain there is that is not dedicated to basic functions but perhaps handles higher-level cognitive abilities and intelligence. Using the brain:body ratio, humans come near the top of

Key terms

Arboreal: living mainly in trees, e.g. animals such as monkeys.

Environment of evolutionary adaptation (EEA): many examples of modern human behaviour are thought to have originally evolved many thousands of years ago, when the environment was very different. Behaviours that were able to adjust or adapt then may not be adaptive in today's environment. To understand them now we have to consider their origins in that EEA.

Bipedal: walking mainly on two legs rather than four.

Australopithecines: these were probably the first representatives in the human evolutionary line after it split off from the chimpanzees and gorillas.

Homo erectus: this human ancestor lived from around 2 million years ago and represents the first major increase in human brain size over the australopithecines and the chimpanzees.

Fig. 1 *Evolution of man*

the animal kingdom (in us the brain makes up about 2 per cent of body weight), but some small mammals do even better – the shrew comes in at about 3 per cent.

The encephalisation quotient (EQ)

A better method compares human brain size with other animals in the same class. In our case these are the mammals. Plotting brain size against body size, we can identify the 'average' ratio for mammals, but we can also identify animals that have a ratio that is greater than expected for their body size. This is calculated as the **encephalisation quotient (EQ)**. An EQ of 1.0 represents the standard value for the average mammal. An EQ of more than 1.0 represents a brain size greater than expected. Humans have an EQ of 7.0, the highest value found even compared with other intelligent mammals such as chimpanzees (2.5) and dolphins (4.5).

We can do the same exercise comparing the human brain with our closest living relatives, the non-human primates (monkeys, chimpanzees, gibbons, gorillas). It turns out that we have a brain that is three times larger than we would expect in a primate of our body size (Jerison, 1973; Passingham, 1982).

The expansion has not been equal across all brain structures. The human cerebellum, a structure involved in motor coordination, is smaller than expected, as is the olfactory area (concerned with the sense of smell). The greatest expansion has been in the frontal lobes, continuing a trend seen in all primates. The frontal lobes are involved in the highest cognitive functions – especially decision making and planning – and it is accepted that this development of the frontal lobes is the basis of our distinctive human intelligence.

There are a number of hypotheses about the factors that stimulated the evolution of the human brain, all of which have to consider the EEA of our ancestors – the *ecological* niche they had to survive in. We should also note that a large brain has disadvantages as well as advantages. It absorbs about 20 per cent of the energy produced by the food we eat. When babies are born, their brain is only about a quarter of its final size, so human infants have a very extended period of dependency. This has implications for the costs of parenting. So whatever advantages the increase in brain size has given us, they must be substantial to outweigh these disadvantages (Pinker, 1997). What might these advantages have been? There are several likely possibilities:

- Bipedalism: our earliest ancestors moved down from the trees onto the ground. Bipedalism allows predators to be spotted more easily. Crucially it frees up the hands for foraging (collecting leaves, fruit, insects, etc.) and for tool use.

- Diet: our ancestors moved from being **folivores** (living on leaves and plants), to **frugivores** (fruit eaters), to meat eaters. Each step involved greater cognitive demands. Leaves and plants are all around and easy to find. Fruits are scarcer. They need to be located (spatial skills), identified as ripe or not (so colour vision becomes important), and frugivores also need to be aware of the seasons so they can migrate to where fruit is available. Meat involves hunting and scavenging, so animals with skills in weapon and tool making, good spatial skills and group cooperation have the advantage.

- Meat is a concentrated source of energy and nutrients. The brain accounts for 2 per cent of our body weight but consumes 20 per cent of our energy intake. The move to a meat-based diet therefore allowed

Key terms

Encephalisation quotient (EQ): a measure of an animal's brain size that compares it with the brain size of its closest relatives. An EQ of greater than 1 indicates a brain larger than expected relative to that group of animals.

Folivores: animals that eat mainly leaves and plants.

Frugivores: animals that eat mainly fruit.

the physiological development of larger brains. Folivores in particular could not sustain the energy demands of a larger brain, while it is notable that other advanced primates such as chimpanzees also eat meat when they can find or catch it.

- Foraging range: there is evidence that the area within which animals gather food (their foraging range) is correlated with brain size (Walker et al., 2006). A wider range would be advantageous as it provides more chances of finding food. However, it also puts greater pressure on cognitive skills such as spatial navigation and spatial memory.

- Social complexity and group living: brain size in primates and other animals such as bats and aquatic mammals is significantly correlated with the size of the social group (Dunbar, 1992; Reader and Laland, 2002), leading to a popular hypothesis that the demands of group living led to selection for larger brains. Larger brains would allow for the complex social communication that makes an individual more effective in the group. Before considering this hypothesis in more detail, we should note that group-living primates, such as chimpanzees and gorillas, while having larger brains than monkeys, for instance, have not shown the very rapid increase in brain size seen in humans. Other factors must be involved.

- Migration: humans outstrip all other animals in their ability to migrate and colonise new environments. From their evolutionary origins in Africa humans have spread across the world, beginning with the first 'out of Africa' movement of *Homo erectus* around 100,000 years ago. Migration would be selected for during evolution as it opens up access to new resources. However, it places huge demands on cognitive skills – navigation, tool use (including boats/rafts), group cooperation and perhaps a distinctively human desire to explore the unknown.

Evolution and machiavellian intelligence

Brain size in animals is related to size of the normal social group. This has led researchers (e.g. Dunbar, 1992) to propose that group living and social complexity were key drivers of brain expansion. This idea has been developed in terms of the machiavellian intelligence hypothesis first put forward by Byrne and Whiten (1988), and which was discussed in Chapter 20, Animal learning and intelligence.

Living in groups has advantages and disadvantages. It provides protection from predators and access to food through cooperative foraging and hunting, and sexual partners are available. However, it has a downside, in particular competition from other group members for resources such as food and sexual partners. Animals that can successfully manipulate their alliances within the group are likely to be more successful in reproducing and passing on their genes. Several skills are required for this:

- Remembering the ranking of individuals in the group. Alliances with powerful members of the group are more advantageous (Seyfarth and Cheney, 2002).

- 'Strategic' alliances, i.e. ones that you hope to benefit from in the future, require you to remember the balance between favours you have done for others and favours they have done for you.

- You need an awareness of past and future, unlike more primitive animals that essentially live in the present. Realising the consequences of actions is a sign of planning and foresight.

- Manipulation: animals that are more successful at manipulating alliances for their own benefit will be more successful. Achieving

Link

Evolutionary aspects of feeding behaviour and hunting were discussed in Chapter 14, Eating behaviour.

Take it further

Evolutionary psychologists cannot do scientific experiments to test their hypotheses. Consider whether the methods they do use (fossil evidence, comparison with living non-human animals, study of Kalahari Bushmen, etc.) are valid and reliable.

■ Take it further

If you look back to Chapter 19, Theories of intelligence, you will see that nowadays some theories of intelligence suggest that we have several different kinds. Taking Gardner's theory as an example, see if you can speculate on which evolutionary factors, such as those mentioned in the text relating to group living, might relate to each specific intelligence.

AQA Examiner's tip

The specification refers to ecological demands (this includes the EEA and lifestyle factors such as bipedalism, diet and foraging range), social complexity (i.e. group size and group dynamics) and brain size. In your revision, be clear on what factors you might describe under each heading.

success often involves deception and deliberate manipulation of others, and this has been clearly demonstrated in chimpanzees (see page 249). Given boxes containing either food or a snake, they will lead a companion to the box with the snake; when the companion flees in terror, they can eat in peace (Pinker, 1997)!

■ Understanding others: you can manipulate other animals more effectively if you can 'read' their intentions. In humans we see this as developing a theory of mind (see page 299), and being able to understand the world from another's point of view. Evidence for theory of mind in non-human primates is limited, but it has been clearly demonstrated in some chimpanzees and gorillas.

■ Language: verbal communication is a far more effective method of communication than species-specific calls and mutual grooming. Therefore, it would have allowed for a far more complex machiavellian intelligence.

Skills in these areas would increase the chances of an animal surviving successfully and having offspring to carry their genes. Therefore, they would be selected for during evolution. Remember that the frontal lobes have expanded more than any other brain area during evolution, and these are the areas concerned with exactly the high-level cognitive abilities required for successful group living. Chimpanzees have larger brains than monkeys, and this may be due to their more complex group dynamics. However, even given their capacity to deceive and manipulate other chimpanzees, they are novices in manipulation compared to humans. Our abilities to understand others and plan for the future are far more sophisticated (i.e. 'not only do I know what you are thinking, I know what you think I am thinking') and stems from our increased brain size.

■ Evaluation of evolutionary factors in the development of human intelligence

The human brain and intelligence have evolved together over the 6 million years since our ancestral line split from the great apes (chimpanzees and gorillas) line. During that time we have moved from being arboreal to bipedal, from folivores and frugivores to meat-eating omnivores, we have colonised the world and developed complex social groupings. We can draw some general conclusions:

■ At different times our ancestors occupied different ecological niches; our EEA changed over time. Different niches involve different selection pressures, which would advantage those animals with appropriate skills such as tool use or spatial navigation. They would be more likely to have offspring, and those skills would spread through the human population over generations. However, at different times different skills would be appropriate. Therefore, there is no one answer to the question of which ecological factors propelled human brain expansion and the development of human intelligence.

■ Hunting meat, for instance, requires skills in making and using weapons, tracking and killing, social cooperation and distribution of the kill amongst the group. Saying that hunting was a key factor does not tell us which aspect of hunting was most important.

■ Using observations of a range of non-human primates from around a thousand published articles, Reader and Laland (2002) related the frequency of social learning (see page 255), innovation (showing flexibility in solving problems) and tool use to brain size. They showed that all three measures were significantly correlated with the size of frontal regions of the brain. They also found that the frequency of social learning was itself significantly correlated with frequency of innovation. This shows that it may be a mistake to consider the various factors in brain evolution as separate from each other; social learning is likely to involve group living, which may also be a driver for innovations in problem solving – as this would lead to increased status and rank in the group.

Key points

- The development of human intelligence must be due to the selection through evolution of characteristics that were adaptive in the EEA.

- The best measure of brain evolution is the encephalisation quotient. According to this, modern humans have a brain that is three times larger than that expected for a primate of our body size.

- Various factors have been suggested as contributing to the development of the human brain and human intelligence. These include bipedalism, diet, foraging range, group living and migration.

- An important factor is thought to be machiavellian intelligence. This would give advantages when living in groups. It involves the development of alliances for future gain and the manipulation and deception of others, and it would also depend on communication skills and language.

Summary questions

1. Briefly describe the encephalisation quotient and how it is measured. Why is it a better measure of brain evolution than simple brain size?

2. Outline some of the factors that may have contributed to the increase in human brain size and discuss whether different factors may have had an effect on this at different times.

3. Discuss how machiavellian intelligence may have been a key factor in expansion of the brain. Refer to the cognitive demands it makes on the individual.

4. The human ancestral line separated from other primates about 6 million years ago. Consider reasons why other group-living primates such as chimpanzees and gorillas do not show the same increase in brain size seen in humans over that period.

AQA Examiner's tip

Evolutionary explanations always have an element of speculation. Therefore, answers to questions may not be clear cut. The examiner will be looking for a clear line of argument based on what evidence there is, and an understanding that many factors may interact in the development of human intelligence.

Intelligence

Genetics, environment and intelligence test performance

Learning objectives:

- outline the nature–nurture debate as it relates to intelligence test performance (IQ)

- understand the use of family, adoption and MZ/DZ twin studies in identifying the relative contributions of genetics and the environment to intelligence

- describe and evaluate twin studies on the role of genetics in IQ scores

- describe and evaluate the role of cultural (environmental) factors in the development of intelligence.

Link

Approaches, issues and debates

The nature–nurture debate has been a central controversy in psychology for many years, and the interaction between genetics and environment in intelligence test performance a key area of study. This is partly because of the implications; if IQ is mainly determined by genetics (nature) rather than environment (nurture), then social changes to improve IQ are unlikely to succeed.

Human intelligence in its broadest sense has developed through evolutionary processes over millions of years and in that sense it is genetic. However, even though we have the capacity to use tools and language, we do not develop tool use or language if we do not have the right surroundings, i.e. the environment is also critical. In addition, there will always be individual differences in characteristics. Not everyone is a great hunter; some people are fluent with language and others struggle.

Humans also vary in their level of intelligence, and one of the longest debates in psychology is the extent to which these variations in intelligence are genetically determined and the extent to which they reflect environmental influences such as family environment, poverty, schooling, etc. This nature–nurture debate is important as it has implications for social policy. If intelligence is mostly genetic, why bother with enrichment programmes (i.e. better environments) to help deprived children? It is also controversial. If particular ethnic groups do badly in intelligence tests and intelligence is genetic, does this mean that these groups are innately (genetically) less intelligent?

Intelligence is a broad concept with several theories on the number and types of intelligence that people may possess (these are reviewed in Chapter 19, Theories of intelligence). However, the nature–nurture debate in relation to intelligence has focused on the intelligence quotient (IQ).

The development of the original Binet and Simon IQ scale was described in Chapter 19, Theories of intelligence (page 235). The value of the IQ is that it is a standardised measure that can be easily compared across ages and groups. Although more complex tests today use sub-scales to assess verbal and non-verbal IQ separately, overall IQ scores are still widely used in intelligence research.

Measuring the genetic influence

Sir Francis Galton began the study of nature–nurture in relation to intelligence in the 19th century. He was, incidentally, the cousin of Charles Darwin. By observing that 'success' and high intelligence seemed to run in families, Galton decided that intelligence was inherited from parents and largely genetic. However, he also began the first scientific studies of intelligence, and was the first to propose methods of studying the genetics of intelligence. These methods form the basis of what we do today.

The simplest approach to the nature–nurture problem is to assume that IQ is determined by a combination of genetic and environmental (non-genetic) influences. So if we can estimate the genetic contribution, we can calculate the degree of environmental influence. There are three main methods of estimating this genetic element (Plomin, 2004):

- Family studies: similar to Galton's methods, this approach looks at the distribution of IQ scores within a family. For instance, there is some evidence that birth order (whether you are first born, second born, etc.) and family size (number of children) are environmental factors that can influence IQ. On the other hand, there are also significant correlations in IQ between children and parents and between brothers and sisters, all of whom share a proportion of the same genes. However, they also share the same environment to a large extent, so we cannot disentangle the relative contributions of nature and nurture.

- Adoption studies: when children are adopted they are removed from the family environment. By seeing how similar their IQ is to their biological parents as compared with their adoptive (non-biological) parents we can get some insights into the genetics of IQ. However, adoption studies are much more powerful when combined with twin studies, as we shall see below.

- Twin studies: these have provided most of the reliable data in relation to nature–nurture and IQ. To understand this approach, we have to look at the genetics of twins.

MZ and DZ twins

Twins are babies that develop together and are born at the same time. This can happen in two ways:

- A single egg (or zygote) is fertilised, combining genetic material from mother and father. It then immediately divides into two separate eggs that develop into two babies. Because they come from the same original egg they are referred to as monozygotic ('one egg') twins. Again, because they originated in the same egg, they have exactly the same genetic make-up. They are also known as identical twins.

- Two maternal eggs are fertilised at the same time by two sperm. They develop in the womb as two babies and are born at the same time. However, as they develop from two separate eggs ('dizygotic' or 'two eggs') they are known as **dizygotic (DZ) twins**. They are not genetically identical, but share on average about 50 per cent of their genes. This is the same situation as for brothers and sisters not born at the same time. Dizygotic twins are also known as non-identical or fraternal twins.

Monozygotic (MZ) twins are genetically identical. Therefore, they will share any characteristic that is entirely determined by genetics (nature). This includes facial features and hair and eye colour, and explains why they are identical to look at. If a characteristic such as IQ is entirely determined by genetics, then two MZ twins should have the *same* IQ score. We can test this by correlating the IQ scores of sets of MZ twins.

However, as well as the same genes, MZ twins also share the same environment. They develop together in the womb, are born at the same time, and are usually brought up in similar ways, even down to wearing the same clothes. So if their IQs are similar, it could be due to the similar environments rather than genetics.

DZ twins also share similar environments (but see page 262). They develop together, are born together and brought up together. However, they are not identical to look at and they may be different genders. But the environment they grow up in is certainly more similar than that of siblings (brothers and sisters) of different ages. DZ twins share only about 50 per cent of their genes, and it is argued that this is the key difference between MZ and DZ twins. Both sets of twins share similar environments, but MZ twins are genetically identical. Therefore, if there is a higher correlation between the IQ scores of MZ twins compared with DZ twins, then the argument is that it must be due to their greater genetic similarity. This would support a key role for genetics in determining IQ.

Link

Correlation coefficients are discussed in Chapter 38, Designing psychological investigations.

Link

MZ/DZ twin studies have been used extensively in the study of psychopathology. See, for example, the work on genetic influences in schizophrenia, discussed in Chapter 26, Schizophrenia.

Key terms

Dizygotic (DZ) twins: twins who develop from two separate fertilised eggs and have no more in common genetically than any other siblings – on average, having about 50 per cent of the same genes. Also known as fraternal twins.

Monozygotic (MZ) twins: twins born from the same fertilised egg. Also known as identical twins, they have exactly the same genetic make-up.

Another opportunity for investigating the genetics of IQ comes on the rare occasions when twins are separated at birth and raised by different families ('reared apart' as opposed to 'reared together'). If IQ is determined more by genetics, then being reared apart should make little difference to the correlation between the IQ scores of MZ twins. However, if environmental factors are more important, then the IQs of MZ twins reared apart in different families should be less similar than MZ twins reared together in the same family.

Research evidence

A famous British psychologist, Sir Cyril Burt, was amongst the first researchers to investigate the genetics of IQ using MZ/DZ twin studies. However, his work in the 1950s has been controversial (see the research study) and his results, that showed a significant genetic contribution to IQ, have always been criticised. However, later studies have largely supported his conclusions.

Research study: Burt, Kamin and Jensen (1943, 1955, 1966, 1973 and 1974)

The eminent British psychologist Sir Cyril Burt first published IQ data on MZ twins reared apart in 1943, using 15 pairs of twins. In 1955 he published results on 21 pairs (the original 15 plus six additional pairs). Finally, in 1966 he presented data on a total of 53 MZ twin pairs. Burt died in 1971.

In the 1970s the role of genetics in intelligence was controversial and the debate was heated. Jensen (1973) and Kamin (1974) were on opposite sides of the argument, but both raised doubts about Burt's work. They pointed out that the correlations between MZ twins reared apart barely changed over the years – 0.770 in 1943, 0.771 in 1955 and 0.771 in 1966. Such consistency across different studies is most unusual.

Doubts were also raised over the sheer number of MZ twins reared apart that Burt managed to find – no one else over the same period had found anything like that number. Finally Burt acknowledged the help of two assistants in preparing his reports, but no trace of the assistants could be found. In the mid-1970s Burt's scientific reputation was destroyed, as there is no worse crime for a scientist than making up data. It also swung the argument *against* those who felt intelligence was largely inherited, as one of their main supporters had been shown to be a fraud.

However, the situation was to change again:

- Fletcher (1991) found convincing evidence that the two assistants did exist.
- Later studies, reviewed below, find correlations between MZ twins reared apart that are similar to Burt's values.

The idea that intelligence is genetic was not popular, as it argued that education and enrichment programmes were pointless. More controversially, it suggested that some groups might be *genetically* less intelligent. Therefore, some authors argue (e.g. Rushton, 1994) that critics of Burt's work were motivated by political views, and not by the scientific status of the work.

Hint

How science works

Scientific findings can only be trusted if we believe in the objectivity of the researcher and the reliability of the research methods. This is why we have systems of peer review before findings are published. The Burt controversy is an example of how personal beliefs and social and cultural factors can influence what should be a scientific debate. (K)

Methodological issues

The case against Burt is not proven. However, the whole episode raises serious issues:

▨ Science relies on experimentation, and although papers are peer reviewed (see Chapter 37, The application of scientific methodology in psychology, page 512) before publishing, the whole enterprise relies upon the integrity of the individual researcher.

▨ Research is influenced by the culture and society in which it takes place. Socially sensitive areas such as nature–nurture and intelligence have important social and political implications, and these can affect the research that is done and how it is interpreted.

▨ Science sees itself as objective. However, it takes place in a particular social and cultural context. The problems that it studies and the way results are used will be affected by that context.

Ethical issues

None applicable.

In one of these studies, Shields (1962) found that the correlation between the IQ of twins reared apart was 0.77, very close to the 0.76 of twins reared together. This would indicate that the environment has little influence. The correlation between DZ twins was 0.51, significantly less than for the genetically identical MZ twins.

Given that studies in this area are all very similar, using IQ tests and MZ and DZ twins, meta-analysis is a very valuable technique to use. This statistically combines the findings from a number of studies to provide a more accurate estimate of the influence of genetics on IQ. Ridley (1999) did such an analysis of all the family, twin and adoption studies up to that point. He built on a previous meta-analysis of 111 studies published by Bouchard and McGue (1981). Table 1 shows some relevant findings from Ridley's meta-analysis. The figures refer to the correlation (or concordance rate) between the IQ scores of various groups.

> **■ Hint**
>
> **How science works**
>
> MZ/DZ twin studies are based on correlations between IQ scores. Correlations do not imply causality, so we cannot conclude, for instance, that genetics 'cause' IQ. This is why research studies of environmental effects on IQ (page 263) are so important; many of them are experimental studies that can in principle show cause and effect relationships. **(F)**

Table 1 *Ridley's meta-analysis of IQ in twins*

Relationship	Correlation between IQ scores
MZ (identical) twins reared together	0.86
MZ (identical) twins reared apart	0.76
DZ (fraternal) twins reared together	0.55
Siblings (brothers and sisters) reared together	0.47
Siblings (brothers and sisters) reared apart	0.24

We can conclude the following from this meta-analysis:

▨ The correlations between MZ twins reared together and MZ twins reared apart are very close (0.86 and 0.76), suggesting that the different environments have little effect on IQ.

▨ The correlation between MZ twins reared together is significantly higher than the correlation between DZ twins reared together. This supports a strong genetic component in IQ scores.

Intelligence

Hint

How science works

As we have seen, the question of whether IQ reflects nature or nurture has been controversial. It is an example of *socially sensitive* research, as findings have implications for particular groups in society. This is a key issue in this area of research. (I, L)

■ Key terms

Heritability: the degree to which a characteristic or behaviour is determined by the genes inherited from parents.

- The correlation between DZ twins reared together is slightly higher than that of siblings reared together. As the genetic relatedness is the same for both groups, this is probably due to the greater similarity of the environment for DZ twins, as they are born at the same time and brought up together.

- The correlation between siblings reared together is larger than the correlation between siblings reared apart. As they have the same genetic relatedness, this must be due to environmental effects.

- These findings give strong support for a genetic component in intelligence as measured by IQ scores. They can be used to estimate the **heritability** of intelligence. Heritability is the extent to which a characteristic in a population is determined by the genes inherited from the parents. For intelligence this has been estimated as between 40 per cent and 80 per cent, with 50 per cent being a generally accepted estimate (Chipeur, Rovine and Plomin, 1990).

■ Evaluation

Twin studies have provided much valuable information on the genetics of IQ. However, there are several cautionary points:

- In some of the early studies the identification of MZ twins was not based on analysis of genetic material. It is possible that in some studies MZ twins were incorrectly identified.

- Adoption studies assume that the environments of the two twins are different. However, attempts are usually made to place adoptive children, especially twins, in similar environments (Maltby, Day and Macaskill, 2007). This would contribute to the similar correlations between MZ twins reared together and MZ twins reared apart.

- The correlation between the IQ scores of identical twins is never 1.0, as it would be if intelligence was determined *entirely* by genetics. This is evidence for a role for environmental factors.

- The comparison of MZ and DZ twins is based on the assumption that the environment of MZ twins is as similar as that for DZ twins. This is unlikely. MZ twins look identical and are often treated in exactly the same way by parents. Their environment is likely to be *more* similar than that of DZ twins. This would contribute to the greater correlation between the IQ scores of MZ twins.

- It is assumed that the environment of MZ twins is identical. However, as twins develop in the womb there may be slight differences in nutrients circulated by the mother to each baby. After birth there may be interactions of the sort reviewed on page 261. Characteristics of the child and the parent influence the interaction of genes and environment. Each child develops its own microenvironment, so that even MZ twins live in slightly different worlds. In modern calculations of genetic contributions to characteristics such as IQ, environmental effects are divided into *shared* (effects that the two twins have in common) and *non-shared* (effects specific to each twin).

- Finally, the old-fashioned model that saw genetic and environmental influences on IQ as *additive* is now seen as too simple. The additive model says that if genetic influences account for 50 per cent of intelligence, then a separate set of environmental effects account for the other 50 per cent. This ignores the sorts of interactions mentioned above. The role of genetics in IQ is likely to involve complex interactions with a range of environmental factors.

AQA Examiner's tip

The use of MZ/DZ twin studies in estimating the contributions of genetics and environment to intelligence can seem complicated. Examiners will be looking for a clear understanding of this methodology and why it helps us to identify the separate effects of nature and nurture.

Environmental and cultural effects on IQ

We have reviewed evidence for genetic influences on measured intelligence, and in this section we look at evidence for environmental and cultural factors.

Prenatal factors

This refers to influences affecting the baby before birth. The two main factors investigated have been maternal smoking and drinking. Mortensen *et al.* (2005), for instance, found that children of mothers who smoked more than 20 cigarettes a day during pregnancy did badly on IQ tests at ages 18 or 19. Incidentally they controlled for a range of other variables that could influence IQ, such as education and socio-economic status. Alcohol intake during pregnancy is also associated with later problems in IQ and general cognitive abilities (Maltby *et al.*, 2007). Heavy consumption can lead to **foetal alcohol syndrome (FAS)**; in this, the baby has low birth weight and often suffers mild brain damage and reduced IQ (Neisser *et al.*, 1996).

Nutrition

Adequate nutrition is obviously vital for normal growth of the body. This includes the brain, and there is good evidence that nutrition can affect IQ. Oddy *et al.* (2004) found that babies that were breast-fed for more than six months had better verbal intelligence at age eight than babies breast-fed for less than six months. In a landmark study, Benton and Roberts (1988) revealed that children given eight months of a dietary supplement containing several vitamins and mineral salts showed increases in non-verbal IQ scores (from 111 to 120). Children given placebos (a non-active treatment) showed improvements of four IQ points or less.

Later studies have not found such dramatic effects of supplements. Schoenthaler *et al.* (2000) did find increases in non-verbal IQ with dietary supplements, but only in children that had poor diets to start with. It appears that in children with an adequate diet, supplements have little or no effect, but they can improve non-verbal IQ in malnourished children.

The Flynn effect

Flynn (1984, 1987, 1994) was the first psychologist to identify an increase in IQ scores between the 1930s and the 1980s in all cultures studied. In America, for instance, between 1932 and 1978 the average IQ score for white Americans rose by 14 IQ points. In France between 1949 and 1974 they rose by 25 points, and in the UK they rose by 7 IQ points between 1940 and 1979. Twenty countries showed the **Flynn effect**, and the question was, why? There are several possibilities (Neisser, 1998):

- People have actually become more intelligent. This is unlikely as the increases in IQ scores have happened too quickly to be explained through genetic mechanisms. Any explanation has to be *environmental*.

- Education: there has been a steady trend for children to attend school and college for longer than previous generations. Length of education correlates with IQ scores. However, the Flynn effect is seen more with non-verbal IQ, whereas schooling is likely to affect both verbal and non-verbal scores.

Link

Genes and the environment can interact in different ways, particularly in relation to the child's interactions with its environment. Some of these ways are outlined in the Introductory chapter on approaches, issues and debates, page x.

Key terms

Foetal alcohol syndrome (FAS): seen in babies born to mothers who have consumed large amounts of alcohol during their pregnancy. The baby has low birth weight, often has mild brain damage and later may have reduced IQ scores.

Flynn effect: first identified by James Flynn, this refers to a steady rise in intelligence test scores between the 1930s and the 1980s. It has been found in all countries studied, and has no simple explanation. There is some evidence that the Flynn effect is now levelling out.

Intelligence

Nutrition and socio-economic status (SES): we have seen that nutrition can affect IQ in some groups, and intelligence is also correlated with SES. Mackintosh (1998), for instance, found a difference of 10 IQ points between professional and unskilled occupations after controlling for other relevant factors. Between 1930 and 1990 nutritional standards and SES have steadily increased in industrial societies such as the UK, the USA, Europe and Asia, and this has probably contributed to the Flynn effect.

Familiarity with tests: we live in an age of increased testing at all ages. Practice with tests will improve performance as teaching becomes geared to specific test requirements. However, this should apply to verbal as well as non-verbal IQ, and the Flynn effect is seen more with non-verbal tests.

Cognitive stimulation: Neisser draws attention to the enormous increase in visual media over the last 50 years. Children are exposed to an increasingly vast range of television, DVD and home computer-based visual information. Visual techniques are also far more common in schools and colleges. This input could stimulate non-verbal (visual) cognitive skills and lead to better scores in non-verbal IQ tests.

It is likely that no one factor alone is responsible for the Flynn effect, and you can also see that these effects are not independent. Schooling involves increased use of visual media, while SES is correlated with better nutrition and stimulating environments. Another element interacting with these is the increased publicity given to education and success. More parents will follow government initiatives in trying to help their children in the early years by providing a stimulating environment and helping them to learn to read and write.

Enrichment programmes

Although disputed by psychologists who believe intelligence is largely determined by genetics (e.g. Jensen, 1969), we have seen that environmental factors can be significant. Many people believe that environmental enrichment and stimulation can help improve intelligence, school performance and success in life. One of the first and most extensive enrichment schemes is the Head Start programme. This began in the USA in the 1960s. The aim was to provide additional educational help to deprived children in numeracy and literacy skills. A high proportion of these children have problems with speech and language, and most come from poor households.

Several studies have reviewed the effects of Head Start, but conclusions are controversial: children showed an initial gain in IQ scores, but this disappeared after 2–3 years (Locurta, 1991). However, long-term follow-ups show that Head Start children are less likely in later years to need special education services, and more likely to graduate from High School.

The positive effects of enrichment programmes are more clearly demonstrated in the Perry Pre-school project (Schweinhart, Barnes and Weikart, 1993). This gave 3–4-year-old African American children additional educational support over a two-year period leading up to formal schooling. A control group had no intervention. Results showed that the intervention group had increased IQ scores at age five (IQ of 95 versus 83 in the control group). A higher proportion of the intervention group graduated from High School, and they had higher levels of earnings and lower levels of involvement in crime than the control group.

Take it further

There is some evidence that the Flynn effect is levelling out. Using your knowledge of the factors outlined above, speculate why this might be. If we have seen the end of the Flynn effect, would it support one or more of the factors above as being the most important?

Cultural factors

'Intelligence' is sometimes talked about as though it is applicable to all people everywhere. However, the concept of intelligence only makes sense in a particular cultural context. 'Intelligence' means something different to us than to the Kalahari Bushmen. They would find it hard to succeed at GCSEs, while we would find it difficult to track a gazelle. Intelligent behaviour can only be understood in its cultural setting.

Attempts have been made to devise culture-free and culture-fair tests. *Culture-free* tests would measure some characteristic basic to intelligence and found in all societies. *Culture-fair* tests would be made up of questions and problems that did not favour one society or culture over another. In practice it is virtually impossible to devise culture-free or culture-fair tests. Non-verbal tests such as the pattern matching involved in Raven's matrices are a step in the right direction, as language-based questions are biased in favour of better-educated societies and ethnic groups.

However, a more profound problem is the attitude to intelligence testing itself. In the West we are used to being tested at all ages, in comparison to societies where schooling and testing may be non-existent. Our concept of intelligence is related to testing and measurement, whereas that of others may be related to everyday life. The Kpelle people of west Africa, when asked to sort a jumble of objects into groups (clothing, utensils, tools, foods), sorted according to a functional relationship, e.g. a knife with an orange (Glick, 1975). When asked how a fool would do the sorting, they immediately produced four piles of clothes, utensils, tools and foods! Who is to say which is the more intelligent approach?

What is certain is that cultural factors cannot be ignored in research on intelligence. All of the work quoted in this chapter is culturally specific, and we need to be careful before generalising findings to other cultures and societies.

Link

Approaches, issues and debates

The whole genetics/environment debate in relation to IQ can be heavily criticised as culturally-specific, with virtually all research taking place in Western and other advanced industrialised societies. When we look at other cultures we can immediately see that our concept of IQ, based on testing, is far too narrow to be applied to other societies.

■ Conclusions

There is clear evidence for a role for both genetic and environmental factors in the development of measured intelligence. Perhaps the simplest view is that we are born with an inherited potential, but environmental factors – nutrition, home environment, education, etc. – are critical in deciding how close we come to achieving that potential.

Key points

- The nature–nurture debate in relation to intelligence has a long history in psychology. It is a socially sensitive area, as findings have implications for educational and social policies.

- The comparison of monozygotic and dizygotic twins is a popular technique for separating out genetic and environmental contributions to intelligence test performance.

- Although twin studies can be criticised, findings do show a significant genetic contribution to intelligence of the order of 50 per cent. This also means that environmental factors are equally important.

- Research also shows that cultural/environmental factors can have a significant effect on IQ scores. These factors include maternal smoking and drinking during pregnancy, poor nutrition and socio-economic status.

Intelligence

- The Flynn effect relates to the steady increase in IQ over the last 60 years or so in all countries studied. There is no simple explanation for this, but people have proposed that education, familiarity with testing, increased cognitive stimulation and nutrition may all be involved.

- If environmental factors make a significant contribution to intelligence, then enrichment programmes should help children from deprived backgrounds. Although the evidence is not entirely consistent, such programmes have been shown to have beneficial effects.

- Intelligence is a culturally specific concept. It can only be understood within a particular society or culture, and findings should not be generalised from one culture to another.

Summary questions

5 What is the Binet and Simon IQ test? Briefly consider its contribution to research into intelligence.

6 Explain why it is important to use dizygotic twins as a control group in twin studies of genetics and intelligence.

7 Outline and evaluate findings from studies of MZ and DZ twins on the genetic contribution to IQ scores.

8 Early models of genetic and environmental influences on IQ scores assumed they were additive and did not interact. Explain why such an additive model is an oversimplification of gene–environment interactions in relation to intelligence.

Intelligence end of topic

How science works: practical activity

On the internet you can find many sites that allow you to take tests of various types. For example, on www.iVillage.co.uk choose one quiz for emotional intelligence (these assess how well you understand your own emotions and those of others) and one of the Mensa brain teasers. Do the two tests yourself.

Ask 10 people at random in your class to complete the two tests (after explaining what is involved and getting informed consent. Emphasise anonymity, confidentiality and the right to withdraw at any time). Assign each participant a number.

Tabulate the scores.

Carry out a Spearman's rho test of correlation between the two sets of scores. Then consider:

- What do the concepts of reliability and validity mean when applied to this type of web-based test?
- Do you think this is a reliable measure of aspects of intelligence?
- If the correlation is significant and positive, what would you conclude about the nature of intelligence as measured by these two tests? What theory of intelligence would it support?
- If there is no significant correlation, what would you conclude? What theory of intelligence would this support?

Further reading and weblinks

Lynch, G. and Granger, R. (2009) *Big Brain; the Origins and Future of Human Intelligence*. Basingstoke: Palgrave Macmillan.

This covers many ideas on the origins of the human brain and human intelligence. It is written in an accessible and entertaining style with many stimulating speculations.

Maltby, J., Day, L. and Macaskill, A. (2007) *Introduction to Personality, Individual Differences and Intelligence*. Harlow: Pearson Educational.

This is a comprehensive and clearly written textbook that covers all aspects of theories of intelligence, including the nature–nurture debate. It also contains excellent background material on different psychological approaches to personality, including psychoanalytic, cognitive and biological approaches.

Pearce, J.M. (2008) *Animal Learning and Cognition* (3rd edn). Hove: Psychology Press.

This book reviews all aspects of animal learning and intelligence, from classical and operant conditioning, problem solving and communication, to theory of mind.

If you Google 'intelligence' and 'brain evolution' many sites are listed. As a start, look at the following websites:

www.massey.ac.nz/~alock/hbook/brain.htm

This website includes many examples and links to most aspects of human evolution and the development of the human brain.

http://psychology.about.com/od/cognitivepsychology/p/intelligence.htm

There are some good summaries of concepts and theories of intelligence, and many links to related issues.

Cognition and development

Introduction

In this section of the course, we are going to look at how young children develop the ability to think and reason about a range of topics. Although you were obviously – once – a small child yourself, you have probably given little thought to how, or indeed what, young children think or believe. It is only when we are confronted with the different understanding of a small child that we come to appreciate that their beliefs about the world may be very different to our own. So, for example, when a two-year-old smacks the 'naughty chair' they have just fallen off, or rubs teddy's knee better when he falls out of the pushchair, we come to realise that young children assume that inanimate objects have human-like qualities and feelings in the same way that they themselves do. When a small child points out that the clouds are very still and asks if they are parked, we appreciate that their beliefs about the natural world are very different to our own!

We will consider research carried out by a range of influential psychologists who have been interested in children's thinking or **cognition**. Some of these, for example the Swiss developmental psychologist Jean Piaget and the American Lawrence Kohlberg, have produced elaborate theories to account for many aspects of children's thinking in different areas of cognition. Others, such as Simon Baron-Cohen have developed our understanding of a specific area such as social cognition.

Chapter 22, Development of thinking, looks at the process of cognitive development, and how our understanding of this has developed through the work of Piaget, Vygotsky and Bruner. The development of cognitive processes has been considered in two different ways: as a set of genetically preprogrammed stages that we work through as we mature; or as something that is influenced by culture and language.

Chapter 23, Development of moral understanding, considers the issues of moral development, or how children think about right and wrong. Most theorists have considered this process to take place in stages, with thinking gradually becoming more complex and sophisticated. The influence of gender on moral decision making (Gilligan) is explored, and the development of pro-social reasoning (Eisenberg) is also considered.

The development of social cognition is the focus of Chapter 24, Development of social cognition. Social cognition refers to the ways in which children think about other people and social situations. This section starts by considering how children develop a sense of 'self' and come to understand that they are an individual with a name and identity. The initial broad focus narrows to look at the work on perspective taking and how children develop the ability to understand the views of other people. Finally, we consider an area of emerging research interest, the role of biological factors in social cognition and the importance of 'mirror neurons' in these processes.

Key terms

Cognition: the term used to describe a range of mental activities associated with thinking. Common cognitive processes include reasoning, problem solving, paying attention and remembering.

Specification	Topic content	Page

Theories of cognitive development

Learning objectives:

- understand what is meant by cognitive development

- describe different explanations of cognitive development given by Piaget, Vygotsky and Bruner

- describe the evidence on which theories are based

- explain how theories have been applied to teaching and learning.

Key terms

Cognitive development: the development of thinking skills such as reasoning and problem solving.

Stages: periods of time loosely linked to age. Stages must be gone through in order and cannot be skipped.

Schemas: sets of ideas about an object or activity which come from past experience and may be taken in from the wider culture. A gender schema refers to the set of ideas about what activities, toys and behaviours are appropriate for a particular sex – boy or girl.

Operations: combinations of schemas.

Link

You met the idea of schemas in your *AQA Psychology A AS* student book. You might like to look back at pages 28–9 of that book.

What is cognitive development?

The term '**cognitive development**' refers broadly to the development of thinking skills. Goswami (1998) argues that there are two questions which need to be answered regarding cognitive development. The first relatively simple question is *what* develops (how children think and reason at particular ages) and the more complex question relates to *why* development takes place.

In this section of the chapter we are going to look at explanations of cognitive development given by three psychologists. The most famous of these is undoubtedly Jean Piaget, a Swiss biologist whose stage theory had a dramatic influence on teaching and education from the 1960s onwards. Lev Vygotsky, a Russian, had rather less impact at the time of writing due to suppression of his ideas under the Stalinist regime, although his theory has recently found favour with both developmental psychologists and educationalists. Jerome Bruner started his working life with an interest in the processes which underlie adult cognition. As we shall see, the backgrounds of each of these researchers influenced what they chose to study and the ideas they developed. Because Piaget's theory has been the basis for later explanations of cognitive development, we start by considering his ideas in detail.

Piaget's theory: genetic epistemology or the growth of knowledge

Jean Piaget (1896–1980) was a Swiss-born psychologist whose theory of cognitive development has had a huge influence on our understanding of how children develop the ability to think and reason. Piaget started his research life as a biologist and moved his interest to child development when he worked with Binet who was looking at intelligence testing. Piaget was fascinated by the wrong answers children gave to questions and became convinced that they revealed important differences between the thinking of adults and children. He carried out many of his own observations and studies using his three children, Laurent, Lucienne and Jacqueline. We shall start by examining the building blocks of Piaget's theory before going on to examine his claim that thinking skills develop in **stages** which are loosely linked to age.

The building blocks of Piaget's theory

Piaget believed that children (and indeed adults) constructed their understanding of the world through active engagement, trying out actions and seeing what effects they had. He argued that knowledge is stored in the form of **schemas** – mental ideas about actions, objects and situations. In very young babies, schemas consist of simple actions such as grasping objects. Combinations of schemas are known as **operations**: shaking a rattle would be the combination of two schemas, grasping and shaking.

Piaget likened the developing child to a scientist and believed that cognitive abilities developed through two important cognitive processes, **assimilation** and **accommodation**.

- Assimilation involves using an existing schema to deal with a new object or situation. For example, a toddler aged around 15 months has developed a simple action schema of 'posting' a circular shape into a shape sorter. Different-coloured circular shapes given to the toddler are promptly sorted using this schema and assimilated.

- Accommodation takes place when an existing schema will not work when faced with a new object or situation and has to be changed. If the toddler is given a different shape such as a square which will not fit into the circular hole, the posting schema needs to be altered so the child tries the shape in different holes. They will also need to adjust the 'posting' schema to incorporate rotating the shape slightly to make it fit a square-shaped hole.

We can also apply these concepts to adult learning. Consider the example of driving a car. You have been taking lessons in your instructor's Nissan Micra, but just before your test the instructor changes their car to a Corsa. Both cars are similar and you are able to apply your driving schemas and to 'assimilate' the new car without too much difficulty. However, a year after you have passed your test, you have returned from university for the summer vacation and are insured for your parents' new car which is automatic. Your existing driving schemas – which include using a clutch and changing gear – will not work and you must accommodate the schemas to fit the new situation.

Piaget believed that the cognitive development of young children did not take place at a steady rate but, rather, in leaps and bounds. Periods of stability were characterised by **equilibrium**: a mental state in which existing schemas could deal with most new information through assimilation. At other times, the child may meet many new objects and experiences which cannot be assimilated and this state is called **disequilibrium**.

Piaget's stages of cognitive development

Piaget believed that cognitive development takes place in stages which are loosely linked to age. Within each stage, children were seen to think in similar ways, with major changes or 'cognitive restructuring' taking place when a child moved from one stage into the next. Central to his theory was the idea that stages could not be missed out – moving on to a new stage relies on the skills and knowledge of the previous stage. Piaget identified four stages of cognitive development, summarised in Table 1.

> ### Key terms
>
> **Assimilation:** using an existing schema to deal with a new object or situation.
>
> **Accommodation:** modifying or changing an existing schema to deal with a new object or situation.
>
> **Equilibrium:** a state when existing skills or schemas can be used to deal with new situations.
>
> **Disequilibrium:** a state when existing schemas do not fit a new situation and so must be altered or adapted.

Cognition

Table 1 *Key ages and stages for Piaget's cognitive development theory*

Stage	Age	Characteristics
The sensorimotor period	0–2 years	Comprised of six sub-stages. The newborn baby develops from using automatic reflexes to the toddler who can carry out deliberate actions
The pre-operational period	2–7 years	The emergence of language allows the toddler to use words as symbols for objects. Thinking is limited and characterised by animism, egocentricism and a lack of reversibility
Concrete operations	7–11 years	This stage is characterised by the child's growing ability to decentre. The child develops the ability to perform mental operations and to reason about real (physical) objects and relations between them
Formal operations	11 onwards	The ability to think and reason about abstract ideas and problems is developed

■ Key terms

Object permanence: the ability to recognise that something or someone exists when it is out of sight.

Animism: the idea that objects have feelings. Roughly up to the age of four, children believe that inanimate objects have feelings.

Egocentric: not understanding that another person's viewpoint is different to your own.

■ Take it further

The development of object permanence can be related to the development of attachments which you studied in your *AQA Psychology A AS* student book. Look back at the stages of attachment formation. How can this be linked to the development of object permanence?

The sensorimotor period (birth to 2 years)

Piaget identified six sub-stages in this period, with thinking becoming gradually more skilled and complex. He noted that very young babies under the age of about six weeks deal with the world by using simple reflexes such as sucking anything put into their mouth and grasping anything placed in their hand. At around six weeks, these reflexes are no longer automatically triggered but become simple action patterns called 'primary circular reactions' initiated deliberately by the baby, for example grasping a toy. These are followed by more complex secondary and tertiary reactions and the stage comes to an end at around two years when language develops.

An important milestone in this stage was the development of **object permanence**, which Piaget believed developed at around nine months to one year. Piaget observed his own children in a simple experiment involving a toy and a cloth. The child was shown the toy which was then covered. Piaget was interested to find out when the child would begin to search for the toy. He found that children below the age of around nine months appeared to have no interest in the hidden object and literally acted as if it were 'out of sight and out of mind'. It was only after they were about nine months old that infants would remove the cloth and begin to search for the hidden toy.

Piaget's claims about the development of object permanence were challenged by Bower and Wishart (1972) who altered Piaget's procedure. Bower and Wishart placed a teddy bear in front of four-month-old babies; the babies would raise their hands to reach for the toy. When the lights were turned off so the room was dark, they observed that babies would still outstretch their arms to the bear. These findings suggest that Piaget may have under-estimated the age at which object permanence is established, a criticism we consider in some depth below.

The pre-operational period (two to seven years)

Around the age of two years, Piaget noted that the child's thinking became more complex. This complexity came about due to the development of language which enabled a toddler to use words (for example 'teddy') as symbols to stand for real objects, and this allowed them to refer to objects and situations which were not present – the basis of symbolic thought. It allowed the child to communicate and engage in pretend play.

Piaget drew attention to several characteristics of thinking in this stage. One of these was **animism** – the assumption made by small children that inanimate objects such as toys have human feelings and intentions. The following examples from Piaget (1973) demonstrate animism: 'It hurts where the wall hit me'; 'Naughty wind, smack wind'; and, holding a toy car up to the window, 'Motor see the snow'.

Piaget focused most of his description of this stage on limitations in the child's thinking, identifying a number of mental tasks which children seemed unable to do. These included the inability to decentre, conserve, understand seriation and to carry out class inclusion tasks.

Limitation 1: Egocentricity

Piaget believed that children in the pre-operational period were unable to see things from other points of view and were fundamentally **egocentric**. This was demonstrated in the famous study by Piaget and Inhelder (1967).

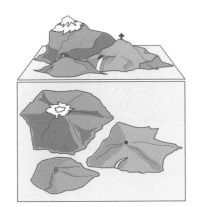

Fig. 1 *Piaget's three mountains*

Research study: Piaget and Inhelder (1967)

Piaget and Inhelder used a 'papier mâché' model of three mountains placed on a table (Figure 1). The mountains were different colours and topped by different features: a cross, a house and snow. Children aged between three and eight were encouraged to explore the model and walk around it to see it from all sides. A small boy doll was then placed at different points on the table and the children were asked to carry out several tasks to test their ability to 'see' from the doll's viewpoint.

- The child was given three cardboard shapes of the mountains and asked to arrange them to show what the doll could 'see'.
- The child was given 10 pictures and asked to select which one the boy doll could see.
- The child was asked to choose any picture and then say where the doll needed to stand in order to see that view.

In all of these conditions children under the age of about seven years were unable to show the doll's viewpoint. Instead, they tended to choose/create a scene that showed their own view, supporting Piaget's claim that young children are indeed egocentric.

Methodological issues

- You may have noted here that while this study is often referred to as an 'experiment' it does not technically fit the criteria for an experiment in terms of manipulation of an IV. Piaget himself referred to his methods as 'clinical observation' and designed studies which would enable him to explore children's thoughts and beliefs.
- Many researchers including Donaldson (1978) have suggested that children failed Piaget's task because it did not make sense to them. The critique given by Donaldson and others are examined in detail below.

Ethical issues

- Today there are strict ethical principles when working with children, including parental consent. However, at the time that Piaget was carrying out his experiments these principles were not in place and it is unlikely that informed consent was obtained from parents.

Link

Later on in this section the development of theory of mind (ToM) is considered. In normally developing children, the ability to work out that other people think, feel or believe something different to them develops around the age of two-and-a-half to three years, but this ability is delayed in children with autism. You can read more about this on pages 302–3.

Limitation 2: Conservation

A second limitation in the pre-operational child's thinking was the inability to **conserve** or to understand that when the shape or appearance of an object changes, the overall quantity remains the same if nothing is added or taken away. Piaget's studies involved giving children two equal amounts of a substance, for example beakers of juice, and asking if they were the same. He then transformed the appearance of one of these by pouring it into a large, tall glass (without spilling any!) (see Figure 2). Piaget tested conservation of number using two rows of counters arranged in parallel lines. When one row was spread out so it became longer, Piaget would ask the children if they were still the same. In both of these tasks, pre-operational children would be fooled and claim that the tall beaker had 'more' juice and the longer line had more counters. Piaget's method of asking the question 'are they still the same' is something we will return to below.

Key terms

Conserve: know that quantity remains the same despite changes in appearance.

Key terms

Compensation: referring to one aspect cancelling another out.

Reversibility: mentally reversing an action to see what a situation was like before.

Seriation: the ability to put objects into a series or order.

Class inclusion tasks: the ability to see one category existing within another, for example the categories of man and woman exist within the broader category of 'people'.

Link

Young children show a similar inability to conserve in relation to gender. For example, they may claim that a woman who has her hair cut has become a man as they are misled by external superficial changes. You can read more about this by looking at Chapter 18, Psychological explanations of gender development, page 216.

Piaget argued that pre-operational children fail conservation tasks like the two above because they focus or centre on one aspect of the change (e.g. height) but ignore the other (width). In contrast, children who have reached the stage of concrete operations will be able to focus on both aspects of the situation at once and explain that the level of juice may be higher but the glass is thinner, so one cancels the other out (**compensation**). They may also refer to **reversibility** ('we could pour it back').

Piaget found that the conservation of different substances occurred at different ages, with children succeeding on conservation of number before they could understand conservation of mass using plasticine. He referred to this process as 'horizontal decalage'.

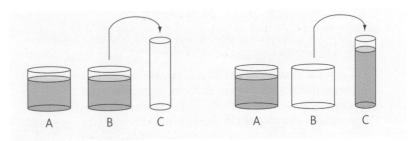

Fig. 2 *Conservation of volume*

Limitation 3: Seriation

A third limitation in the pre-operational child's thinking related to **seriation**, the ability to understand that objects can be organised into a logical series or order. For example, people can be ordered in terms of height from smallest to largest. This ability is important in relation to the development of mathematical skills. Piaget investigated this by showing young children Stick A which was longer than Stick B, then showing them Stick B which was longer than Stick C. When asked about the relationships between A and C which had not been seen together, pre-operational children were unable to infer, as you and I can, that Stick A was longer than C.

Limitation 4: Class inclusion tasks

A final limitation related to **class inclusion tasks**, the ability to work out how categories of objects relate to one another. For example, you are aware that vehicles, a super-ordinate category, contain lots of different examples such as lorries, cars, bicycles (subordinates or members of that category). Piaget used picture cards of animals such as five horses and three pigs. He asked children to count the number of horses, then the number of pigs and finally all of the animals together. He then asked the children: 'Are there more animals or more horses?' Piaget found young children were unable to answer correctly, leading him to conclude that this level of logic was not available to the child younger than six years old. Even at the age of seven, this skill was basic.

The concrete operational period (7 to 11 years)

Whilst the pre-operational stage was defined by inabilities to reason, the period of concrete operational reached at about seven years was marked by the growing ability to carry out these tasks. Concrete operational children were able to focus on more than one aspect at once (decentre), mentally reverse actions and to understand that things may cancel each other out (compensation), leading them to the ability to conserve volume, substance and weight. Class inclusion skills developed, as did the ability to put objects into series or order. This stage was named concrete operations because Piaget noticed that children at this stage could perform mental operations as long as they involved reference to real (concrete) objects or situations. So, for example, a concrete operational child would be able to order people in terms of height if they could see them. However, they would not be able deal with the same task in the absence of real objects using abstract reasoning or logic.

The formal operational period (11 years old onwards)

This was the final stage of development in which the child was said to develop logical reasoning and abstract thought. One of the key features of this stage was said to be deductive reasoning – the ability to generate various hypotheses (predictions) and test them systematically to find the solution. Piaget believed that by 11 or 12, adolescents could now problem solve logically rather than by trial and error. In contrast to concrete operational children, formal thinkers could consider hypothetical situations and concepts without needing actual objects in front of them. Piaget investigated this using the pendulum task in which children were given sets of weights and different lengths of string along with a bar to attach weights and string to. With this equipment they could make many different simple pendulums. The task set by Piaget was to find out what affected the speed at which the pendulum swung. Children in the concrete operational stage, aged under 11 or 12, would typically take a trial and error approach to the test randomly varying the factors without a systematic approach. In contrast, children who had reached the age of 11 or 12 solved the problem systematically by varying one factor at a time whilst keeping others constant. Such factors included the weight of the object attached to the string, the length of string and how hard the object was pushed. This study demonstrates clearly the differences in approach between concrete operational and formal operational thinkers.

Evaluation of Piaget's theory

Criticism of Piaget's methods

One common criticism of Piaget relates to the methods he used to assess children's reasoning, such as the three mountains task. Margaret Donaldson wrote an influential book in 1978 called *Children's Minds* in which she argued that pre-school children were capable of more sophisticated reasoning than Piaget had suggested. However, Donaldson pointed out that their understanding is 'embedded' in everyday familiar situations and they make use of context to work out exactly what is meant: children lack the ability to think outside situations in an abstract way.

A good example of this can be seen in relation to egocentricism. Donaldson argued that young children can understand another person's viewpoint if they are asked in a way which draws on their knowledge of an everyday situation which makes sense to them, such as a game of hide and seek. In Hughes' (1975) study, children aged between three-and-a-half and five were shown a 3D model of two intersecting walls (see Figure 3), and a toy policeman was placed at the end of one wall so that he could 'see' into two sections of the model. The children were asked to hide a doll where the policeman could not see it. Hughes found that 90 per cent of children aged between three-and-a-half and five correctly placed the boy doll in a place where the policeman could not see, suggesting strongly that children can take someone else's perspective if they understand the task. Even when a second policeman was introduced, children could complete the task.

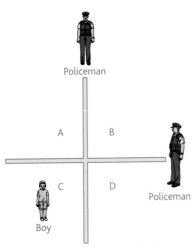

Fig. 3 *Hughes' 'hide and seek' policeman study*

■ **Key terms**

Human sense: tasks where children understand the motives and intentions of the characters.

■ **Take it further**

Find out about other studies which have been devised to test Piaget's claims using child-friendly methods such as McGarrigle and Donaldson's (1974) Naughty Teddy study. How exactly does it differ from Piaget's?

Donaldson argued that the problem with some of Piaget's tasks was that to small children they lacked '**human sense**': the motives and intentions of the characters should be made clear to them by drawing on familiar situations. We can see another good example of this in relation to the conservation tasks described above. When an adult asks the same question twice in the conservation experiments it is fairly reasonable for a child to assume that they got the answer wrong the first time! A 'human sense' version of this was devised by Paul Light. Pasta shells were placed in a beaker and transferred into a larger container in the standard Piagetian version of the task. In this condition 95 per cent of six-year-olds failed to conserve. However, when Light told the children that the glass beaker was chipped and had a sharp, dangerous edge before the transformation, 70 per cent of children passed the conservation task and answered that the quantity had not really changed. This demonstrates neatly the importance of children using context to make sense of situations.

However, others have counter-argued that whilst children show some abilities earlier than Piaget thought, these later experiments are not testing exactly the same reasoning abilities as Piaget was. For example, in Hughes' task it is much easier to decide where the boy cannot be seen than to work out exactly what the view is like from a particular place.

More recently researchers such as Siegler (1995) have begun to devise methods combining quantitative and qualitative data to develop a fuller understanding of the processes which take place when children move from one stage to another. One of these studies is included below. You might like to think about how this differs from Piaget's original method.

■ **Research study: Siegler (1995)**

Siegler devised a 'microgenetic method' to study conservation of number in five-year-old pre-operational children, combining experimentation and observation to 'see' the processes which take place when children learn to conserve. Siegler selected a group of children who had all failed the standard Piagetian number task in which a row of buttons was spread out to make a longer line. He then divided them into three groups, each of which received four 'training' sessions (the IV):

- The feedback group were told each time if they had got the answer right or wrong.
- The explanation group were asked to explain to the experimenter the reasons why they gave the answer, then they were told if they were right or wrong.
- The discussion group were told the correct answer by the experimenter then asked: 'Why do you think I know that?' This question asked them to focus on thinking about the experimenter's reasons for their belief.

After the four trials, all three groups were then retested on Piaget's conservation task. Siegler found significant differences in their abilities: more in the discussion group were able to conserve as they had realised that length did not predict number. Their development of understanding was found to be gradual rather than sudden.

Methodological issues

This study uses a combination of experimental methods – the control of an IV to expose children to different kinds of training – and qualitative methods, observing and recording their responses. This makes the data rich in approach but it also enables the research to draw conclusions about cause and effect.

Ethical issues

Parental consent is an important principle of research when using young children as participants.

Do the stages exist?

We have seen that researchers in the 1970s and 1980s drew attention to the abilities of children to carry out tasks earlier than Piaget thought when faced with more 'child-friendly' methods. Despite these findings, the claim that children understand and can reason at the level of action (doing) before the level of representation (abstract thinking) is accepted by most current theorists (Goswami, 1998). The major opposition to the idea of ages and stages has come to Piaget's claims about the development of formal operations in early adolescence. Keating (1979) reported that 40–60 per cent of college students fail at formal operational tasks, and Dasen (1994) has suggested that only about one-third of adults ever reach the formal operations, suggesting that this stage is not universal.

Piaget believed that progression from one stage to another was the result of maturation, implying that children cannot progress until they are ready. Studies such as Siegler's have pointed to the importance of practice, discussion and teaching in 'speeding up' or facilitating cognitive development. It is evident that Piaget underestimated the importance of social influences, language and context on cognitive development, points emphasised by Vygotsky's theory which is considered below.

Goswami (1998) has argued that Piaget's theory provided precise answers to the important questions of 'what' develops and 'why'. Although his theory is often seen as domain general (implying that cognitive abilities develop together at the same speed), he acknowledged that there would be variations with and between stages.

Modern developments in cognitive neuroscience mean that the study of children's cognition is now very similar to that of adult cognition, focusing on processes such as memory development (Goswami, 1998).

■ Piaget and education: discovery learning

Although Piaget did not apply his theory to education, later researchers took the principles of his theory and applied them to teaching and learning. An influential government review of primary education led by Bridget Plowden in 1966 was based strongly on Piaget's theory. As Margaret Donaldson (1978) commented in *Children's Minds*, this was not surprising as 'during the 1960s this work by Piaget and his colleagues was at the peak of its influence. It was very widely known and very widely accepted'. Almost every subsequent document on teaching and learning in primary schools has contained echoes of Plowden.

Piaget's theory had stated that thinking developed in stages loosely linked to age. The implication of this is that children will learn in different ways at different ages and will be particularly ready to learn certain things at

■ Link

Approaches, issues and debates

Theorists such as Piaget and Bruner emphasise the stage-like nature of children's development, seeing this as loosely linked to age. Stage theories of this nature have emphasised the importance of maturation and biological factors (nature) in the development of thinking but have tended to overlook the importance of social and cultural factors (nurture) which influence the nature and speed of development.

Key terms

Readiness: the idea that children are ready to learn certain things in specific ways at different times.

Discovery learning: the idea that children learn best through doing and actively exploring.

Link

Approaches, issues and debates

You can see that Vygotsky emphasises the importance of nurture including culture, language and environmental factors to cognitive development and thinking. However he has less to say about the possible role of innate factors (nature) in thinking.

Take it further

You can see the full Plowden report by going to Derek Gillard's website (www.dg.dial.pipex.com) and looking for the Plowden report (1967) in the documents section.

A short and interesting discussion of the report can be found at www.infed.org and search for 'the Plowden report'.

certain times – the **readiness** approach. This influenced how subjects were taught: the 'concrete' nature of thinking from age 7–11 implied that learning about science would be best developed by providing concrete, project-based work. Piaget's ideas also influenced the curriculum in terms of what was taught (i.e. subjects) at different stages. Abstract subjects, such as physics or chemistry, should not be introduced before the start of formal operations at secondary school.

Piaget had emphasised that learning was an active process in which children construct their own knowledge through exploring the environment and trying out schemas. This led to the idea that classrooms in infant and junior schools should provide the child with a rich environment to discover, filled with objects to explore. The water tray and sandpit, as well as providing messy fun, enable the child to experiment with transformation of substances leading to the development of conservation skills. Piaget's emphasis on the active nature of learning led to the term **discovery learning** being applied to his approach. This idea has been criticised by Sylva (1987) who argued that discovery learning is not always the best way forward.

You can see from the above paragraph that Piaget's theory said a good deal more about learning than teaching. His view of the child was of a solitary scientist, working out ideas and principles through action. This meant that his theory was essentially learner centred rather than teacher centred. The Plowden report (HMSO, 1967) emphasised the need to see children as individuals, requiring different attention. Teachers in the Piagetian classroom were viewed as facilitators, providing appropriate materials and resources to facilitate each child's learning. The role of the teacher was to identify the stage that the child was in and to sense when they were ready to deal with more demanding concepts from the next stage.

Vygotsky's theory of cognitive development

Lev Vygotsky (1896–1934) was a Russian whose ideas and writing were not widely published outside Russia until the 1960s. Because he died young, many of Vygotsky's concepts were relatively underdeveloped and have been reworked by later theorists. However, since his writing was rediscovered in the late 20th century, his ideas have found favour with many developmental psychologists and educationalists (Light and Oates, 1990). They have also dominated eastern European and Russian child psychology (Durkin, 1995). In contrast to Piaget, Vygotsky did not suggest that children develop the ability to think in specific, age-linked stages. Instead, he emphasised the importance of social interaction, language and cultural context to cognitive development.

The importance of social interaction, context and culture

Vygotsky believed that the ability to think and reason was 'the outcome of a fundamentally social process' (Light and Oates, 1990: 122) in which cognitive skills developed as the child interacted with other people. This did not just take place in formal interactions between teachers and pupils at school, it also took place in everyday, familiar contexts to the child – in the home, with family, siblings and friends. The key to cognitive development was interaction. Interaction enabled children to see adults and older children using problem-solving skills and cognitive tools and to internalise these mental skills to use themselves. The analogy that Vygotsky used was of the child as an apprentice, developing thinking skills and mental tools of the trade. It was this vital interaction which enabled children to develop mental skills and to learn to think. Tzuriel and Shamir (2007: 144) summarise Vygotsky's position, saying that cognitive development comes from the 'interplay between spontaneous, natural development and the social interaction of children with adults and peers'.

Vygotsky also emphasised that the cognitive skills developed by the child are heavily influenced by context and culture. A good example of this is shown in a study of Brazilian street children by Nunes (1992). Despite having almost no formal schooling, children who have jobs as street vendors have very well-developed mathematical skills which they have 'internalised' through working alongside adults and older children from an early age. This demonstrates the vital connection between context, culture and learning seen by Vygotsky (Mastergeorge, 2001: 75)

The importance of language

How exactly are mental skills internalised? Vygotsky believed that children were born with elementary mental functions such as attention and memory which developed into **higher mental functions** or complex thinking skills. The transition from simple to complex thinking was made possible by language. Vygotsky observed that young children often talk to themselves in monologues, commenting on their actions as they are playing. They may also talk to themselves when carrying out difficult tasks. Piaget had called these monologues 'egocentric speech' seeing them as further evidence of the child's egocentricity. However, Vygotsky argued that language itself became internalised at around age seven and this process enabled the child to think and perform complex reasoning tasks. Young children use monologues (talking to themselves) as they have not yet developed internalised speech.

Vygotsky believed that speech and language had two distinct functions and were used differently by younger and older children/adults. The most obvious use of language is **social speech**, using words to communicate with other people. This type of language is used by young children and adults. However, Vygotsky argued that at around 7–8 years speech becomes internalised as an inner voice which he called **intellectual speech**. This type of inner speech is used to regulate, plan and think and is the basis of higher mental functions. Vygotsky developed this argument to suggest that many mental abilities appeared on two 'planes', first of all socially with other people, then intellectually. This allowed a child to move from being able to do things only with the help of others to being capable of doing them alone.

The zone of proximal development and scaffolding

We have noted that Vygotsky believed that thinking skills developed through interaction. He was particularly interested in children's cognitive abilities when they were able to interact with an older or more knowledgeable other person. An important concept in Vygotsky's theory was the **zone of proximal development (ZPD)**. This was defined as the distance between the child's current developmental level, measured by the tasks they were able to achieve on their own, and their ability when helped by another person – peer or adult – who was more knowledgeable or experienced than themselves. For example, a two-year-old may be able to complete a four-piece jigsaw on their own (current developmental level) but unable to complete a ten-piece jigsaw despite many attempts. When helped by their older sibling who finds the four corners, the child is able to achieve the harder task.

> **Key terms**
>
> **Higher mental functions:** the ability to reason, problem solve and calculate.
>
> **Social speech:** used to communicate with others.
>
> **Intellectual speech:** used by older children and adults to think and problem solve.
>
> **Zone of proximal development (ZPD):** the gap between the tasks that the child can do on their own and those they can do with help.

■ Key terms

Scaffolding: help or support given to the child. The nature of the scaffolding can vary and depends on the child's current level of understanding and ability.

Whilst Vygotsky commented on the importance of the ZPD, he did not identify or explain the means by which this support could be delivered. An important development of his theory was the concept of **scaffolding** proposed by Wood, Bruner and Ross (1976). Scaffolding refers to support or help given to the child by a more knowledgeable other – an adult or peer – whilst working in the ZPD. Just as physical scaffolding supports a new building, mental scaffolding supports the child on a new task. Both can be removed at a later stage when the building/child can stand alone.

Evaluation of Vygotsky's theory

Many studies have demonstrated how adults and older children naturally 'scaffold' younger learners and provide support to help and extend their abilities on tasks outside their current level of performance. Wood and Middleton (1975) studied mothers helping young children to build wooden jigsaws and identified how scaffolding naturally takes place in interactions.

■ Research study: Wood and Middleton (1975)

Twelve mothers were asked to teach their own four-year-old children how to put together a wooden jigsaw puzzle/tower so that they could do it on their own. The mother–child teaching sessions were recorded on video and the tapes were then analysed. The types of support offered by the mothers were coded and categorised by the researchers into different kinds of help. Wood and Middleton identified five types of scaffolding/intervention which differed in the degree of help offered. These included:

- general suggestions ('Now you make something')
- specific verbal instructions ('Get four blue blocks')
- indicating materials ('You need to start with that one')
- preparing for assembly ('Turn it this way round')
- physical demonstrations ('The wooden peg fits in the small hole').

Wood and Middleton found that the most successful 'mothers as teachers' were those who adjusted the help they offered subtly, depending on the child's actions. These mothers would offer more direct help moving 'up' a level when children were struggling but would back off and move 'down' a level when their child appeared to be managing on their own. Wood and Middleton noted that help was carefully tuned and contingent or dependent on the child's actions.

Methodological issues

This study uses observational methods to provide rich, detailed data about the methods naturally used by mothers when playing with their young children. The use of video recording allows the play session to be watched many times by researchers. Although the sample is small, researchers working within this type of framework are less concerned with representative samples and generalising.

Data derived from observations of this nature is qualitative. In order to transform this into quantitative data (numbers), researchers need to code their observations into different categories. This process is a subjective one and is open to interpretation.

Ethical issues

This study took place with mothers present in the children's own homes. The experience was unlikely to be stressful for the children.

■ Link

You can find more about the analysis of qualitative data, and its validity and reliability, in Chapter 39, Data analysis and reporting on investigations, starting on page 544.

In another study, Moss (1992) examined mothers' scaffolding of pre-school children on tasks such as building a tower of blocks. Moss found that mothers naturally used three strategies when playing with their young children. These involved:

- staying one step ahead of the child, for example gathering a pile of large, square suitable blocks
- inhibiting or gently discouraging 'immature' strategies, such as putting bricks in their mouth
- reinforcing or consolidating useful new strategies, such as giving praise when the child lines up the bricks correctly.

Scaffolding does not just take place with young children. Pratt *et al.* (1992) studied parents helping older children with maths homework using long division. They found that some variation in children's performances was related to how successfully parents helped and scaffolded them during homework periods.

Durkin (1995) has pointed out that many studies of scaffolding have used rather contrived environments in which parents know they are being observed. However, studies carried out in natural environments have also demonstrated the existence and importance of scaffolding. For example, Greenfield and Lave (1982) looked at young Mexican girls learning the skill of weaving from older women. They found that the girls started by watching then worked alongside adults who gave them simple tasks to do and provided help and support to achieve them. This shows how scaffolding processes take place in everyday settings and different cultures.

We can see here that Vygotsky emphasised very different aspects of cognitive development to Piaget. Both theories may be seen as products of their own time and culture, demonstrating again the situated nature of knowledge. Vygotsky lived in a communist society that emphasised collective action over the role of the individual, and these ideas are reflected in his theory which emphasised the importance of interaction. Piaget, on the other hand, highlighted the individual nature of the child in cognitive development. Vygotsky emphasised the importance of culture and context in cognitive development and his theory can account for the cultural differences seen in cognitive development that we have noted. In contrast, Piaget's theories say little about cultural differences, implying that children go through the same developmental stages regardless of culture.

Another important difference between the two theories relates to their focus. Vygotsky's theory focuses on the processes underlying cognitive development rather than the outcomes. As Vygotsky's work has become better known, empirical support for his theories has started to grow. Since the 1970s his work has been applied in education. Later theorists, such as Jerome Bruner, have based much of their work on Vygotsky's theories.

Fig. 4 *Scaffolding in the real world*

Vygotsky and education: the importance of teaching

We have already noted that Vygotsky did not develop his ideas due to his early death. Since the rediscovery of his work in the late 1970s, researchers and developmental psychologists have begun to apply his ideas to teaching and learning. Two of the most obvious concepts are ZPD and scaffolding, considered above.

Unlike Piaget, Vygotysky strongly emphasised the importance of learning and instruction as he believed that cognitive development took place through joint activity and interaction. The teacher's role is to work sensitively within the ZPD, extending the child's skills and scaffolding them to achieve tasks they would be unable to deal with alone. We have examined a range of studies above, which have shown scaffolding in a number of different situations. Language and talk are seen as extremely important in the classroom.

Vygotsky did not restrict learning to a formal environment and instruction but argued that it took place in informal settings. All that was required for learning was a 'more knowledgeable other'. This could be a sibling, older child or peer of the same age who knows more about a topic. One aspect of Vygotsky's theory generating considerable research is the idea of **peer mentoring** which is sometimes known as 'peer assisted learning'. In peer mentoring, an older more knowledgeable child works with a younger child to develop the younger child's abilities on tasks. Evidence such as the study by Tzuriel and Shamir (2007) shows that this can benefit both children, not just the less experienced.

Key terms

Peer mentoring: cognitive benefits gained from children working together, especially when paired with a child of a different level.

Research study: Tzuriel and Shamir (2007)

In this study of peer-assisted learning in Israel, Tzuriel and Shamir looked at the impact of peer mediation on the ability of young children to master seriation tasks. A sample of 89 year 1 children was tested to ensure they were unable to carry out seriation. Each year 1 child was then paired with a year 3 'mediator':

- The experimental group of mediators took part in a programme which taught them how to use a mediation teaching style.
- The control group of mediators were give an equivalent teaching session on social interaction with their 'pupil'.

Following this each pair took part in a teaching session on seriation using a multimedia computer program, and the year 1 children were retested. Tzuriel and Shamir found that the year 1 children whose mediators had received peer mediation with young children (PMYC) training had gained more improvement than the control group. Interestingly, the most gains were made in pairs where there was a mismatch between the cognitive abilities of the mediator and pupil, in that one was of lower and the other was of higher cognitive ability.

Methodological issues

This study employs a control group who also take part in a training programme. This is designed to control for possible Hawthorn-type effects.

Ethical issues

In any study involving young children, full parental consent and school consent are required. Both researchers and schools need to ensure that parents are kept informed and feel able to withdraw their children if they decide to. Sensitive debriefing about children's progress and abilities is also essential in studies of this nature.

▦ Bruner's theory of cognitive development

Our third theory of cognitive development was produced by Jerome Bruner, an American. Bruner's research interests included language, adult cognition and problem solving during the late 1950s and 1960s when the **information processing approach** was rapidly gaining favour. Like Vygotsky, Bruner was more interested in the processes underlying cognitive development than the structure of cognition which Piaget had focused on. Bruner was strongly influenced by Vygotsky's ideas and wrote the introduction to a translation of Vygotsky's 1936 book *Language and Thought* when it was published in America in 1962. Bruner moved to carry out research at Oxford University in the 1970s where he investigated communication between mothers and babies before turning his interest to cognitive development in general. The concept of scaffolding which we introduced above was partly devised by Bruner working with David Wood.

Modes of thinking

As Bruner studied adult cognition, he became convinced that adults do not use a single method of thinking or reasoning to solve problems. This was in direct contradiction to Piaget's claim that adult thinking reaches formal operations where logical/abstract thought is utilised to solve problems. Instead, Bruner argued that adults select different strategies depending on the nature of the mental problem/task to be solved.

Bruner described three different ways of thinking which he called **modes of representation**. The first of these was the enactive mode. This involves representing a mental task in terms of actions. The second, iconic mode, involves representing a mental task in a visual form such as images or pictures. The third, symbolic mode, involves representing the task using language in the form of words. Bruner believed that each of these modes of representation was available for adults and children to use. When faced with a new task, adults and children were likely to go through each of the modes, from enactive to symbolic, in order to master the skill. A difficult task might lead a skilled adult thinker to revert to an easier method of representation.

Bruner accepted Piaget's claim that development of thinking took place in stages and he adapted Piaget's stages of pre-operations, concrete operations and formal operations. However, he rejected the idea that these were directly linked to age. Instead, he argued that all three modes of thought were available to older thinkers, although an individual might rely more on one than another.

Table 2 *Bruner's three modes of representation*

Mode of representation	Description
Enactive	Knowledge is represented through actions. For example, the child may count out 10, 100 and 1,000 pieces of pasta to understand sizes of numbers
Iconic	Knowledge is represented through pictures or images. For example, the child can visualise the size of each pasta heap and can therefore picture the difference between 100 and 1,000
Symbolic	Knowledge is represented through words. The child can understand the concepts of size and number using labels such as 'one hundred' and 'a thousand' without actions or pictures

▦ Key terms

Information processing approach: this views the human mind as analogous to a computer and identifies the cognitive skills involved in mental activities.

Modes of representation: different ways that tasks and knowledge can be represented internally.

Cognition

Evidence for Bruner's theory

Although Bruner's theory has not drawn extensive testing in the same way as Piaget's, his ideas have drawn support and are currently generating considerable interest in their application to education. An important study carried out by Bruner and Kenney (1965) demonstrated the modes of representation as well as supporting Bruner's claim that young children can learn tasks requiring logic and abstract thought if the mode of instruction and representation is appropriate.

■ Research study: Bruner and Kenney (1965)

Bruner and Kenney demonstrated the use of three different modes of representation in an interesting study using eight-year-old children. Firstly the children were given wooden blocks of different sizes, some rectangles and some squares.

In the first stage of the study, they were encouraged to play with the blocks and experiment with making different-sized squares. This was the enactive mode as it involved using actions to gain an intuitive understanding of the ways in which the blocks could be put together to make different shapes.

The children were then helped to construct diagrams and pictures of different-sized squares using the iconic mode.

Finally the symbolic mode was introduced. Children were instructed to give different shapes name labels (such as x, y or z). They were then taught to solve simple equations such as $x + y = z$.

Bruner and Kenney found that young children could solve the equations and work within the symbolic mode. They could also generalise their learning experience to new situations and problems, suggesting that young children can learn and understand complex, abstract ideas if they are taught them appropriately.

Methodological issues

This research study uses a range of different techniques based on observation and analysis of talk to assess children's growing understanding. Such methods provide insight into the processes involved in cognitive growth in a similar way to Siegler's study.

Ethical issues

It is important in research of this nature to ensure that young children do not become overwhelmed by cognitive tasks. The integration of research of this nature into the school classroom and everyday routine ensures that the environment is familiar and no more stressful for children than ordinary school.

■ Take it further

You can read an interview with Bruner by going to www.guardian.co.uk/education/2007/mar/27/academicexperts.highereducationprofile.

AQA Examiner's tip

One way of evaluating a theory is by making comparisons with other theories in terms of their assumptions and explanations.

You may have noticed that Bruner's theory shares many commonalities with Vygotsky and even some with Piaget. Wood (1988) has argued that Bruner's theory stands between those of Piaget and Vygotsky. Like Vygotsky, Bruner placed a strong emphasis on social experience and culture as the bases for cognitive development. Both Bruner's and Vygotsky's theories emphasise the importance of language. Language is viewed by Bruner as the most important 'cultural tool' available to help us think. Both theorists agree that language and cognition are so closely linked that they may be seen as two sides of the same coin (Wood,

1988). As we shall see below, Bruner's work has had considerable impact on educational policy, including curriculum design and ideas about accelerated learning.

▨ Bruner and education: the spiral curriculum

Bruner was the only one of our three theorists who specifically applied his own ideas to education. Still writing and practising now (although 91 years old at the time of writing!) Bruner has contributed to our understanding of how children learn and how they may best be taught. His ideas were set out originally in *The Process of Education* (1960) and *Toward a Theory of Instruction* (1966) and have been revised most recently in *The Culture of Education* (1996).

Bruner agreed with Piaget that children learn through enquiry and investigation. However, he rejected Piaget's idea of readiness and argued that any subject could be taught to a child of any age as long as the method of instruction was appropriate. Bruner argued that when first introducing a subject, the teacher should emphasise the basics of the subject and make sure that these are understood. The curriculum should return to these basics again and again each time at a higher level, building on these basic skills with more complicated material. For example, ideas of mass and force in physics could first be introduced to the child at a practical, enactive level using objects of different weights on a slope. These concepts would then be returned to at a later stage and explored in greater depth. Bruner referred to this idea as the **spiral curriculum**, the idea that concepts should be grasped intuitively then revisited.

The teacher's role is to provide guidance and accelerate the child's learning. An important concept in Bruner's theory was the idea of **contingency**. He believed that effective teaching/instruction should be dependent on the behaviour of the child. He also emphasised the importance of scaffolding or supporting children's thinking attempts.

In *The Process of Education*, Bruner set out his ideas about teaching. These included:

▨ The importance of structure in learning and teaching: by structure, Bruner was referring to the ways in which ideas are related to each other. He argued that children learn structure unconsciously to start with – in a similar way to that in which they develop language – but he thought that they should be taught the fundamental principles of a subject in order to understand it and to be able to structure their knowledge.

▨ The importance of intuitive thinking: Bruner saw intuition as a way of grasping a problem or concept without using analysis or logic, and he proposed several ideas to encourage intuitive thinking. These included modelling of intuitive thinking by teachers and encouraging pupils to guess before looking at the plausibility of their guesses. This idea underlies 'thought shower' or brainstorm approaches.

▨ The importance of motivation: Bruner believed that learning should be a voyage of discovery and enquiry. Teaching methods should encourage children to engage with subject materials.

Another of Bruner's key ideas is that of **cognitive acceleration**, the idea that children's development can be speeded up through the teaching of thinking skills. Projects such as Cognitive Acceleration through Science Education (CASE) have shown how it is possible to accelerate cognitive development in Year 7 and Year 8 pupils using scaffolding and

Cognition

▨ Key terms

Spiral curriculum: the idea that the same area may be revisited in different ways as the child's thinking becomes more complex.

Contingency: the idea that effective instruction depends on the child's preceding behaviour.

Cognitive acceleration: speeding up cognition by teaching thinking skills.

AQA Examiner's tip

It is useful to develop your comparative skills. You may wish to construct a table of similarities and differences between the three theories covered here and consider the implications of the differences you identify.

■ Take it further

You can read about the application of Bruner's theory to education by going to the General Teaching Council website at www.gtce.org.uk.

encouraging pupils to work together to solve problems. Studies have found that CASE produced an overall increase in children getting grade C or above in GCSE Science in 1996. Adey *et al.* (2002) found that the same techniques could be used to improve teaching outcomes in Year 1 pupils from London primary schools. As you can see, Bruner's ideas about education are currently generating considerable interest.

Key points

- Piaget argued that cognitive development takes place in four stages loosely linked to age. Thinking is qualitatively different in each stage.

- These stages are sensory motor, pre-operational, concrete operations and formal operations.

- Piaget may have underestimated children's cognitive abilities as some of his tasks lacked human sense.

- Vygotsky suggested that cognitive development was the product of language, context and culture. Interaction and communication enables the internalisation of thinking skills.

- The zone of proximal development is an important concept in Vygotsky's theory. In the ZPD, the child works beyond their current ability with the help of an expert. The process of helping is referred to as scaffolding.

- Bruner identified three modes of representations of thought: enactive, iconic and symbolic.

- Piaget's theory influenced educational policy in the Plowden report, 1967 and stressed the importance of readiness and discovery learning.

- Vygotsky's theory emphasised the importance of instruction, scaffolding and peer tutoring.

- Bruner's theory emphasises the importance of structure and the spiral curriculum. Evidence suggests that cognitive acceleration based on Bruner's theory can improve performance.

Summary questions

1. Explain what Piaget meant by assimilation, accommodation and equilibrium.

2. Discuss two criticisms which have been made of Piaget's research methods.

3. Explain what is meant by the ZPD and scaffolding.

4. Explain one application of each theory of cognitive development to teaching or learning.

5. Discuss similarities and differences between the three accounts of cognitive development. Which account do you consider the most useful and why?

23 Development of moral understanding

Theories of moral understanding

Key terms

Moral understanding: the process by which people tell the difference between right and wrong.

Cognitive developmental perspective: sees development as primarily caused by the child's thinking.

Pro-social reasoning: how children think about helpful behaviours.

Fig. 1 *Jean Piaget*

Link

Kohlberg was also interested in the development of gender understanding in children. You can read more about his ideas by looking at pages 215–17.

Moral understanding: distinguishing right and wrong

In this chapter we are going to look at a specific area of children's thinking known as **moral understanding**. Moral understanding relates to the process by which people decide if an action is right or wrong. Clearly, small children are not born with ideas of right and wrong. Their understanding develops as they are socialised within the family, school and wider cultural setting and there are considerable individual differences in views about right and wrong. Although philosophers have been interested in moral understanding for hundreds of years, formal psychological theory about moral understanding began with publication of Piaget's 1932 book *The Moral Judgement of the Child*. Since then, this area has been dominated by psychologists working within the **cognitive developmental perspective**.

We will start by briefly considering Piaget's theory, which sees moral understanding developing in stages, loosely linked to age. We will then consider an alternative stage theory offered by Laurence Kohlberg which has generated considerable research and dominated the field for many years. Finally we shall move on to consider a specific area of children's cognition known as **pro-social reasoning**.

Investigating moral understanding: Piaget

We noted in Chapter 22, Development of thinking, that Piaget believed that cognitive development took place in stages which were loosely linked to age. Piaget applied the same 'stage' approach in relation to moral understanding. Again he worked from the premise that children are active and construct their understanding of the world through exploration. Piaget argued that moral development took place in a series of stages, with the child's thinking being qualitatively different at each stage.

We also noted that Piaget investigated children's understanding in innovative and unusual ways, devising tasks in order to tap into their thoughts and beliefs. This was also true in relation to moral understanding. Initially Piaget investigated this by considering children's understanding of rules of common games such as marbles. He chose the game of marbles because there are few real rules and because the game is usually played between children with minimal adult intervention. Piaget watched young children playing and asked them questions such as what were the rules, where did they come from and could they be changed. Piaget found that very young children believed that the rules originated from adults, children in the past or even from God! Under the age of about five, children showed no evidence of playing by rules at all. By the time they reached the age of about five, children would observe the rules rigidly and treat them as 'set in stone' and unbreakable. At this age there was often argument about cheating and rule breaking. Older children

Key terms

Vignettes: short descriptions of events, behaviour or people, which can be used in an experimental setting.

Amoral stage: the child is unaware of moral rules.

Heteronomous stage: moral rules are set by those external to the child such as parents or teachers.

Autonomous stage: the child internalises moral rules and makes decisions themselves.

of around nine or 10 realised that rules existed for the convenience of players and could be changed or manipulated as long as all players agreed.

In order to further investigate moral understanding, Piaget devised stories or **vignettes** which presented children with moral dilemmas and choices. In these, typically two children were compared: one who had deliberately broken a rule and another who had accidentally done so. Piaget asked young children to explain who was naughtiest and why. The following is an example of Piaget's stories:

> A little boy called John is in his room. He is called to dinner. He goes into the dining room. But behind the door there was a chair, and on the chair there was a tray with fifteen cups on it. John couldn't have known that there was all this behind the door. He goes in, the door knocks against the tray, bang go the fifteen cups and they all get broken!
>
> Once there was a little boy whose name was Henry. One day when his mother was out he tried to get some jam out of the cupboard. He climbed up onto a chair and stretched out his arm. But the jam was too high and he couldn't reach it and have any. But while he was trying to get it he knocked over a cup. The cup fell down and broke.

Piaget, 1932 (page 117)

Piaget found that younger children tended to judge John as naughtier than Henry. This was because they based their judgements on the amount of damage created (15 cups compared to one cup) rather than the intention or motive behind the child's behaviour.

Stages of development

Piaget argued that children develop moral understanding in three stages linked to age. The first of these is the **amoral stage**. At this age, Piaget believed that children had little understanding of moral rules, and behaviour was regulated entirely by adults. At around age five, Piaget argued that children become aware of rules about right and wrong, such as the idea that it is wrong to tell lies. Moral rules are imposed by grown-ups who tell children what they can and cannot do (does this sound familiar to you?) and the child interprets them from their own egocentric viewpoint. As Piaget noted, 'Right is to obey the will of the adult. Wrong is to have a

Table 1 *Piaget's stage of moral development*

Stage	Age	Description
The amoral stage: no rules	Under 5 years old	The young child is largely oblivious to ideas about right and wrong. Their behaviour is regulated by outside influences and adults/older children. Naughty is simply what will be punished
Heteronomous stage: others' rules	5–10	The child becomes aware that moral rules exist. They are imposed externally by adults. Rules are seen as rigid and unbreakable. The child interprets them from their own egocentric viewpoint
Autonomous stage: own rules	10+	Children see that rules exist for convenience. They may challenge rules which appear to be unfairly applied, such as adults telling them not to do things which they themselves are doing

will of one's own' (Durkin, 1995: 472). At around the age of 10, children develop autonomous morality: at this stage they begin to question rules and decide for themselves what they believe to be right or wrong. This age also coincides with the growing influence of peers on young pre-adolescents who help them to question parental rules. Piaget therefore saw moral development as related to the shift in social relationships from 'adult commanded to peer negotiated' (Durkin, 1995: 473).

Commentary on Piaget's contribution

We have already noted that Piaget's research methods have attracted a good deal of discussion from other researchers in the field. Durkin (1995) has argued that Piaget's 'imaginative empirical strategies' provided a base for many others to investigate moral development in young children. However, others have criticised Piaget's use of the game of marbles as a way of assessing moral understanding, arguing that the situation of an adult asking questions about rules does not provide a realistic understanding of children's beliefs. Wainryb and Turiel (1993) criticised Piaget's use of games arguing that many games follow social conventions rather than moral rules, a point we shall consider in some depth below.

Another set of criticisms have related to Piaget's use of vignettes which may have been rather complicated for young children to understand. In the examples you read above, you may have noticed that there were two independent variables: the amount of damage created (lots or little) and the intention of the child (naughty or otherwise). It is possible that these may have confounded each other. In order for this to have constituted a true experiment, four vignettes/conditions were needed. This demonstrates a lack of tight experimental design in Piaget's approach which we drew attention to in Chapter 22, Development of thinking. The use of stories may have also been relevant here: when Chandler (1973) changed the medium of Piaget's story to present it in video format, he found that six-year-olds could recognise intentions and produce more sophisticated moral judgements. Donaldson's criticisms about human sense considered in Chapter 22, Development of thinking, may also apply here. Piaget's stories did not always make it clear what the intentions were. It has been argued that even three-year-olds could consider intentions when making judgements about simple stories.

Piaget linked moral development to children's general cognitive development, and his cognitive developmental perspective has continued to dominate the study of moral development. Durkin (1995: 471) argued that Piaget's contribution 'remains a source of inspiration for many contemporary investigators'. Piaget believed that children's moral thinking develops gradually over stages, although many critics believe that he underestimated the age at which children reach the different stages of development. Despite arguments about specific ages, there is general agreement that moral thinking develops in a stage-like process. Kohlberg's stage theory presents a more detailed consideration of moral development which continues into adulthood.

▨ Kohlberg's theory of moral development

The study of moral development was left largely untouched after Piaget's early work (Durkin, 1995) until it was revisited by the American psychologist, Laurence Kohlberg, in the 1960s. Kohlberg agreed with Piaget that moral understanding developed in stages and he also believed that the sequence of stages was invariant so that children progressed

▨ **Take it further**

You might like to think about how the stages of moral understanding relate to Piaget's general stages of cognitive development described in Chapter 22, Development of thinking.

Cognition

▨ Link

To refresh your memory about independent, dependent and confounding variables, see page 521.

Key terms

Moral dilemmas: hypothetical situations which present the individual with a series of choices.

Qualitative data: non-numerical data often in the form of words taken from interviews.

through the stages in a logical order. However, Kohlberg believed that Piaget's method of investigating moral understanding lacked scientific rigour, so he devised an alternative to Piaget in which he developed a series of **moral dilemmas**. These consisted of short scenarios which laid out a set of moral choices of action. The child was asked to make a decision based on the behaviour of the character in the scenario and then explain the basis for their decision. This **qualitative data** was then read carefully and coded in order to classify the types of response children made.

Research study: Kohlberg (1963)

In 1963, Kohlberg investigated moral understanding using a cross-section of American boys aged seven, 10, 13 and 16 years old. Each child took part in a moral judgement interview (MJI) which lasted approximately two hours. The child was asked to consider 10 moral dilemmas. One of these is shown below so that you can get a feel for Kohlberg's methods:

> Two young men, brothers, had got into serious trouble. They were secretly leaving town in a hurry and needed money. Karl, the older one, broke into a store and stole a thousand dollars. Bob, the younger one, went to a retired old man who was known to help people in town. He told the man that he was very sick and that he needed a thousand dollars to pay for an operation. Bob asked the old man to lend him the money and promised that he would pay him back when he recovered. Really Bob wasn't sick at all, and he had no intention of paying the man back. Although the old man didn't know Bob very well, he lent him the money. So Bob and Karl skipped town, each with a thousand dollars.

www.haverford.edu/psych/ddavis/p109g/kohlberg.dilemmas.html

After each dilemma, the child was asked to comment on the actions taken by the characters in the drama, in this case Bob and Karl. They were also asked to explain and justify their answers, for example if they felt that Bob was 'worse' than Karl. Kohlberg carefully read and re-read each set of responses then classified the types of moral reasoning shown into three levels which formed the basis of his theory. Young children tended to give answers characteristic of Level 1, for example saying that Karl's actions were wrong as he might go to prison. Older children's answers were characteristic of Level 2, for example noting that Karl had broken the law whereas Bob had not. Those few individuals who reached the highest level of moral development would argue that both Karl and Bob were equally immoral as lying and breaking trust violates moral, rather than legal principles.

Kohlberg calculated the percentage of boys showing each type of response and found support for his stage theory. The children demonstrated progression through the levels as the theory predicted.

Methodological issues

Kohlberg's use of moral dilemmas has been criticised. The use of verbal data of this nature means that responses must be coded and classified in order to be compared. This process can be seen as rather subjective and researchers have pointed to the possibility of investigator bias and the subjective nature of coding. Inter-rater reliability is an important aspect of research of this nature.

Kohlberg's MJI is an example of a 'production test' in which participants are asked to produce responses to moral dilemmas which are then scored. Other researchers, such as Rest, Thoma and Edwards (1997) have devised 'recognition tests' in which individuals choose pre-scored answers from a range of statements rather than producing their own. This removes the need for coding of responses but produces data which is less rich and detailed. It is also likely to reflect the expectations of the researcher who has devised the statements.

Ethical issues

Parental consent is an important ethical principle in research involving children and young people. Parents should also be free to withdraw their children from the research at any point.

From his research, Kohlberg identified three levels of moral reasoning, which he called pre-conventional, conventional and post-conventional morality. Each level was further divided into two sub-stages giving a total of six stages in all. Children are seen to move from a state in which moral rules are simply imposed by grown-ups (pre-conventional) to a position in which they internalise the rules of their social group (conventional morality). The third level, post-conventional morality, takes place when individuals use their own values and principles to make moral judgements. Subsequent research showed that this level was not universal and in fact was rarely achieved. Kohlberg argued that children within a stage presented similar answers to different moral dilemmas, indicating a consistency to their thinking. He also argued that levels of moral reasoning were universal and seen across different cultures, a point that is examined in detail below. A summary of Kohlberg's theory is shown in Table 2.

■ **Link**

You can read more about the coding and classification of qualitative data in the section on psychological research and scientific method starting on pages 543–4.

■ **Take it further**

You can find out about a famous dilemma created by Kohlberg called the Dilemma of Heinz by going to http://psychology.about.com/od/developmentalpsychology/a/kohlberg.htm.

Table 2 *Kohlberg's levels of moral development*

Level 1: Pre-conventional Moral rules are imposed by adults such as parents and teachers	Stage 1: Punishment and obedience orientation	Behaviour is based on the authority of parents and teacher. If a behaviour is punished it is seen as wrong
	Stage 2: Individualism, instrumental purpose and exchange	The child begins to do things which are rewarded and avoids those which are punished
Level 2: Conventional The moral rules of the social group (family/religious/ethnic, etc.) are internalised and accepted. These rules are not questioned or analysed	Stage 3: Mutual interpersonal expectations (the good boy/nice girl stage)	The child internalises ideas of wrong and right from their social group Good behaviour is what pleases other people
	Stage 4: Law and order orientation	Emphasis is on doing one's duty and respecting authority. Following rules and laws
Level 3: Post-conventional The individual makes their own moral judgement and choices according to their own values	Stage 5: Social contract orientation	Laws and rules are still important, but the individual can see that sometimes they need to be changed or should be ignored as they do not apply
	Stage 6: Universal ethical principles	The individual follows self-chosen ethical principles. When their principles conflict with existing moral standards, they follow their own views regardless of majority opinion

■ Key terms

Longitudinal study: form of research that is often used in 'developmental areas' where a group of participants are studied for extended periods of time.

Meta-analysis: the combination and review of the data from many studies which have used similar methodology to investigate the same subject.

■ Link

Approaches, issues and debates

Kohlberg's theory has been criticised for gender bias. His original research was carried out with males and generalised to females, which can be considered andocentric.

■ Link

Approaches, issues and debates

Researchers such as Carol Gilligan have argued that men and women have different moral voices, with women responding to an ethic of care rather than justice. This important debate has reflected the need for research that is gender fair, which identifies and accepts differences.

Support for Kohlberg's theory

Ann Colby, a colleague of Kohlberg's followed up a sample of Kohlberg's participants in a **longitudinal study** re-interviewing them every three years over a period of 20 years (Colby *et al.*, 1983). Most of the boys reached stage 2 of moral understanding by around the age of 10. By age 22, most of the participants had reached stage 3 or 4. When the study concluded, some participants were 36 years old. However, most had remained at stage 4, with only a few progressing to stage 5.

Kohlberg (1969) carried out a cross-cultural study comparing moral development in the UK, Turkey, Taiwan, Mexico, Yucatan and the US and found a similar sequence of stages. In agreement, Snarey (1985) carried out a **meta-analysis** of 45 cross-cultural studies using 27 different countries which had used the MJI. He identified a basic stage trend supporting Kohlberg's theory. However, like Colby *et al.* (1983), Snarey's study found that the highest level – post-conventional – was largely achieved in industrialised societies and generally in relatively few individuals. Gibbs *et al.* (2007) have recently supported this further using 75 cross-cultural studies conducted in 23 different countries.

Is Kohlberg's theory gender biased?

An important criticism which has been levelled at Kohlberg's theory is that the model is gender biased. You will recall that Kohlberg's research study in 1963 used a sample comprised of young American boys to develop his model. When Kohlberg later tested girls and women, he found that they achieved a lower level of moral development on his model than boys, typically attaining stage 3 rather than stage 4. This led Kohlberg to conclude that females were less morally developed than males.

Carol Gilligan (1982), a former student of Kohlberg, has argued persuasively that women may reason differently to men about moral issues, but they are not less morally developed. They only appear to be, because the tool used to measure moral development by Kohlberg (the MJI) is inherently biased towards males and fails to measure female moral thinking.

In order to investigate moral reasoning specifically in women, Gilligan (1994) interviewed 29 American women aged between 15 and 33 facing a real-life moral decision: whether to carry on with a pregnancy or to have an abortion. The women had been referred to the research project through a counselling agency. Gilligan identified three levels of women's moral understanding from the interviews:

- Level 1: self-interest. At this level women referred to their own needs and interests in their decision to go ahead or end the pregnancy, for example having a baby might restrict their career.
- Level 2: self-sacrifice. At this level women referred to the needs and feelings of others around them, for example if their partner wanted them to end the pregnancy or if their own parents wanted to be grandparents.
- Level 3: care as a universal obligation. At this level, women attempted to strike a balance between caring for the feelings of others and their own choice and well-being.

According to Gilligan, women's moral reasoning uses a 'different voice' to men. Gilligan argues that there are two kinds of moral orientations:

- justice: doing what is fair
- caring: looking after someone in need.

Gilligan claims that socialisation emphasises different qualities for boys and girls. Boys are socialised towards independence and achievement and girls towards nurturing others and responsibility. This means that males tend to be classified in stage 4 of Kohlberg's model as they emphasise fairness and maintaining social order. Girls, in contrast, are classified at stage 3 as they are sensitised to the expectations, feelings and needs of those around them. Gilligan has argued that Kohlberg's model would classify responses referring to care as a specific obligation as conventional morality, but women making these responses are referring to the 'care' moral orientation. As Durkin (1995: 491) puts it, 'Kohlberg's schema fails to hear this care oriented voice'.

Walker (1984) has carried out a critical review of 41 studies which looked for gender differences in moral development using Kohlberg's MJI. Of these, 85 per cent found no differences at all and the remaining 15 per cent found only small differences. Silberman and Snarey (1993) added another dimension to the gender debate. They note that there are differences between males and females in emotional and physical maturity in early adolescence with girls being, on average, about two years ahead of boys in both emotional and physical types of maturity. Silberman and Snarey studied 190 American adolescents aged between eleven-and-a-half and 14 from a range of ethnic backgrounds. Whilst most students were in stages 2 or 3 (as is consistent with Kohlberg's model) girls tended to score higher than boys at this age. These findings pose questions for Gilligan's criticisms and imply that we need to consider gender differences in maturity as well as possible differences in moral levels.

Commentary – cognitive developmental theories of moral understanding

We can see that Kohlberg's theory overlaps with Piaget's but considers development to continue throughout adolescence and adulthood, therefore going further than Piaget's original model. Kohlberg and Piaget share a theoretical perspective, seeing the development of moral understanding as a cognitive process. Where they differ is in the origins of understanding: Piaget argued that this was based in the social relations and the shift from adult to peer influence. In contrast, Kohlberg suggested that moral understanding was independent of social relations and was due to the solving of cognitive conflicts.

The theories of both Piaget and Kohlberg take the view that young, pre-school children are 'amoral' and have little sense of right or wrong beyond punishment. Evidence suggests that this view may underestimate young children. For example, Constanza *et al.* (1973) redesigned Piaget's vignettes to create four conditions in which the intentions of the child (good/bad) and the outcomes of the actions (positive/negative) were systematically varied. When pre-school children were tested using these, Constanza *et al.* found that they did consider intentions, especially when the outcome of the action was positive, implying that young children are not as 'amoral' as Piaget and Kohlberg thought.

A persuasive critique of stage theories in general has been presented by Turiel (1983) who argues that children do not show general moral thinking in which all problems are addressed with the same level of reasoning. Instead, Turiel argues that we can distinguish two types of moral understanding which he refers to as **domains**. The **moral domain** relates to ideas about individual rights and how people should be treated, whereas the **social conventional domain** considers rules related to

Link

You can read more about different kinds of gender socialisation by looking at Chapter 17, Social contexts of gender roles.

Cognition

Key terms

Domains: different areas of moral reasoning, relating to individuals and social rules.

Moral domain: accepted rules relating to individual rights.

Social conventional domain: rules relating to society.

Key terms

Alpha bias: occurs when researchers assume that there are differences between men and women and one sex is seen to be inferior or lacking.

Beta bias: occurs when differences between males and females are overlooked.

Link

You may wish to refresh your memory about gender bias by looking at the Introductory chapter on approaches, issues and debates, page xiii.

living within a social community. Turiel argues that young children separate these two types of moral understanding and are able to see moral transgressions (e.g. hurting other people) as wrong, whilst seeing that others (e.g. chewing gum at school) simply convene social rules. This view challenges the claim that moral thinking occurs in a similar way across different types of moral problem.

We have seen in this chapter that Kohlberg's theory has been criticised for gender bias. In the Introductory chapter on approaches, issues and debates we distinguished two kinds of gender bias: **alpha bias** and **beta bias**. Kohlberg's original research was carried out with males only, which can be considered andocentric. His model was then constructed on the basis of this research and applied to both males and females, who typically scored less well than males on the stages of moral development. This is an example of beta bias: results of research with males have simply been generalised to females without being studied. In contrast, Gilligan's model claims that men and women have different moral voices; however, she proposes that the morality of women is different but not inferior.

Key points

- Piaget believed that moral understanding developed in three stages: the amoral stage, the heteronomous stage and the autonomous morality stage.

- Piaget used a range of methods including observation of children playing marbles and vignettes.

- Kohlberg created a three-level model of moral development based on research using moral dilemmas with a large number of American boys. The levels are pre-conventional, conventional and post-conventional morality.

- Kohlberg's model has been widely accepted and has support for the principles behind it. Cross-cultural studies have suggested that moral development follows the stages he outlined, although the higher level of post-conventional morality is rarely attained.

- Kohlberg's theory has been criticised for gender bias by Carol Gilligan (1982). Gilligan argues that women base moral decisions on the ethic of care rather than justice. Their moral reasoning is different not inferior.

Summary questions

1. Outline the stage approaches to moral understanding given by Piaget and Kohlberg.

2. Explain some of the difficulties of assessing moral understanding.

3. Discuss the claim that Kohlberg's theory is gender and culture biased.

Theories of pro-social reasoning

Learning objectives:

- explain what is meant by pro-social reasoning

- describe research into pro-social reasoning

- explain how pro-social reasoning develops.

Key terms

Pro-social actions: those actions which help other people.

Eisenberg's theory of pro-social reasoning

You may have noticed that Piaget and Kohlberg focused their research on how children think about morally wrong actions: in the dilemmas and vignettes we have considered, the child is asked about behaviours such as lying or stealing. Research using these methods does not help us to understand why a child might choose to act pro-socially. Nancy Eisenberg (1987) wished to investigate the other side of the moral development issue – what children think about the right or good thing to do and how and why they may decide to carry out **pro-social actions**.

Eisenberg developed a series of dilemmas aimed at young children in which there is a choice between helping someone in need – often at a personal cost – or pursuing self-interest. The examples that she used were everyday situations, such as helping a child who was being bullied, or giving up the opportunity to win a swimming competition to help disabled children. One of the most famous of these is shown below:

> One day a girl called Mary was going to a friend's birthday party. On her way she saw a girl who had fallen down and hurt her leg. The girl asked Mary to go to her house and get her parents so the parents could come and take her to a doctor. But if Mary did run and get the parents she would be late to the party and miss the ice cream, cake and all the games. What should Mary do? Why?

Eisenberg and Hand, 1979

In an initial study (Eisenberg and Hand, 1979), four sets of dilemmas including the above were given to a sample of 35 young children and their answers were assessed and coded. From these Eisenberg, Lennon and Roth devised the model of pro-social reasoning (1983) shown in Table 3.

Table 3 *Eisenberg et al.'s model of pro-social reasoning*

Stage 1	Hedonistic reasoning	The child is concerned with potential gain for themselves ('I would miss the cake')
Stage 2	Needs orientation	The child thinks about the needs of the character and helps in response to these needs ('They would feel sad')
Stage 3	Approval and interpersonal orientation and stereotyped orientation	The child helps to gain the approval of other people and in response to stereotypes of nice girl/boy ('It is better to help')
Stage 4a	Self-reflective empathetic orientation	Child refers to empathising with the other's feelings ('If I were in that situation I would feel …')
Stage 4b	Transitional stage	The child is moving from stage 4 to stage 5 reasoning and shows characteristics of both
Stage 5	Strongly internalised orientation	Child refers to internal moral principles ('You should help someone who is less fortunate than you are. It is important in a civilised society ')

Cognition

Eisenberg *et al.* suggested that children go through stages of pro-social reasoning, in which they move from *hedonistic* reasoning, where behaviour is self-oriented, to *needs-oriented* reasoning or helping because they understand how the other child feels. Finally, children help because they have internalised social values and moral principles relating to responsibility. You can see a summary of these stages in Table 3.

■ Research study: Eisenberg *et al.* (1987 and 1991)

Eisenberg, working with a variety of colleagues, carried out a longitudinal study in which children were asked to respond to a set of pro-social dilemmas over a period of 11 years, throughout childhood and adolescence. A sample of boys and girls were studied initially at age four, then again at age 5–6, 7–8 and 9–10.

In the follow-up study, the same group were re-interviewed when aged between 13 and 14 and again between 15 and 16. At this age, the dilemmas were altered to represent situations which would engage teenagers (the birthday party became a party) and an additional dilemma of donating blood in an emergency but missing school/exams was added.

As well as ages and stages, Eisenberg was interested to see if there were gender differences as Kohlberg had suggested.

Eisenberg *et al.* found that:

■ Hedonistic reasoning was common in the very young children. This decreased rapidly around the age of 7–8.

■ Needs-oriented reasoning peaked in middle childhood at age 7–8 and then levelled out.

■ More sophisticated forms of reasoning (stage 3, approval-oriented reasoning) did not appear much before 9–10 and then declined in mid-adolescence.

Consistent with the ideas of Kohlberg and Gilligan, gender differences in reasoning began to emerge only in adolescence, with girls appearing to be a couple of years ahead of boys, who caught up in mid-adolescence.

Methodological issues

Longitudinal studies of this nature enable the researcher to see the development of moral reasoning within a group of young people across time. In contrast to cross-sectional studies, each child's response can be compared with data from the previous study, removing the impact of individual differences.

As we discussed above in relation to Kohlberg's moral dilemmas, the coding of qualitative data is a subjective process which requires rigorous training and the need for inter-rater reliability.

Ethical issues

In this study, interviews of the youngest children took place in their home or at the university with their mothers present. Older children were interviewed at school. Both of these procedures limit the possibility of stress, which is to be commended. Older children in the study were paid for their participation in line with studies using adult participants.

Commentary on Eisenberg's theory

As you have probably noted, Eisenberg *et al.*'s model is similar to Kohlberg's theory of moral understanding. In both of these children move from being largely self-centred to seeking social approval before they develop their own individual views of what should be done. This is also broadly similar to Gilligan's theory of moral reasoning in women. Bee (1995: 363) argues that Eisenberg *et al.*'s model 'helps to broaden Kohlberg's original conception without changing the fundamental argument'.

Eisenberg *et al.* have carried out research to test their own model cross-culturally and found support. However, cultural differences are seen once again as kibbutz reared Israeli children show little evidence of needs-oriented reasoning, implying that socialisation and upbringing are important in the development of pro-social reasoning as well as moral understanding.

Key points

- Pro-social reasoning refers to how children think about helpful, pro-social behaviour.

- Eisenberg *et al.* used pro-social dilemmas to investigate children's pro-social reasoning.

- Eisenberg *et al.*'s model sees pro-social reasoning developing in three main stages: hedonistic, needs-oriented and approval-oriented. Later stages may not be reached.

Summary questions

4 What different perspective did Nancy Eisenberg bring to the study of moral understanding?

5 How might pro-social reasoning be important in terms of showing the extent of development of moral understanding of the child?

6 How might both the work of Piaget and Kohlberg be criticised by Eisenberg *et al.*?

Development of the child's sense of self and theory of mind

Cognition

Introduction

What is social cognition? Through your AS studies you will be familiar with *cognitive* psychology and the study of memory. As its name implies, social cognition takes the study of cognitive processes further by focusing on how children think about their social world and their interactions and relationships with other people. How do young children process the social information surrounding them? Social information can come through other people's facial expressions, non-verbal communications and words. For most people social relationships with others are hugely important. We can show affection and fear, manipulate, deceive, or act altruistically or aggressively in our interactions with others. But to cope with social interactions successfully, most of all we need to *understand and predict* what other people may be thinking or feeling.

Developmental social psychologists are interested in the following questions:

- What are the cognitive processes that allow us to understand other people?

- How and when do these processes develop in most children?

- What can we learn about social cognition from the experiences and perspectives of people with autism and Asperger's syndrome?

Self-recognition

Most babies are born into a social world, surrounded by other people. Before they can interact with others, they have to develop a sense of themselves as separate from other people. At birth there are some early signs of this: the baby roots (turns its head) more in response to another person touching their cheek than if their own hand is used to do it. At three months they prefer to look at video images of themselves seen from another's perspective rather than from their own (Berk, 2006), indicating that they can distinguish the two perspectives. Importantly, by four months they prefer to look at videos of other people rather than pictures of themselves. This interest in others indicates that they are beginning to develop a sense of 'self' that is distinct from other people (Rochat and Striano, 2002), and an interest in others.

In an interesting study, Lewis and Brooks-Gunn (1979) asked mothers to put red dye on their baby's nose while pretending to clean their face. When placed in front of a mirror, nine-month-old infants touched and played with the mirror, showing no awareness that the reflection was 'them'. By 15 months, however, the baby tried to rub the red mark off, using the reflection in the mirror. This indicated that they realised the reflection was 'them', and they had a sense of 'self-awareness' (note that the mirror test is used to show higher cognitive abilities in some non-human primates; see page 250). By two years old, the child can point to themselves in photographs, and usually use their name or 'me' to describe it.

In parallel with their developing sense of self, the baby is also engaging with the social world. At birth they will imitate a parent sticking their tongue out, showing an innate ability to imitate (also found in non-human primates, incidentally), and they will gaze longer at faces gazing directly at them as opposed to those that are gazing away from them. They are also sensitive to facial expressions and tone of voice (Striano and Reid, 2006). This shows that the newborn is sensitive to the social world around them. Social cognition then develops rapidly (Striano and Reid, 2006; Berk, 2006):

- 6–10 weeks: the baby is distressed by a 'still' face, not expressing any emotion or animation. This shows that they are becoming accustomed to faces communicating information.
- 3 months: regular eye-to-eye contact emerges.
- 4–9 months: eye gaze cueing and joint (shared) attention develops; the parent's gaze is used by the baby to switch attention to another toy.
- 12–15 months: protoimperative pointing (to indicate 'I want') and protodeclarative pointing (to indicate 'there is something interesting over there') emerge.
- 18 months: pretend play emerges, e.g. the baby understands that mum can pretend the banana is a telephone. This is a vital stage, as it indicates that the baby can decentre; it is beginning to see that other people can have different beliefs and perspectives about the world. They can now differentiate themselves from others (Lewis and Brooks-Gunn, 1979) and use appropriate pronouns, e.g. that is 'my' toy, that is 'me', that is 'she' (Clarke-Stewart *et al.*, 1985).
- By two years old the child has a developed sense of self. They know they are their own person and can influence other people.

Theory of mind

The expression 'theory of mind' (ToM) was first used by Premack and Woodruff (1978) in relation to the abilities of chimpanzees to deceive their keepers. Theory of mind refers to the ability to understand or read the minds of other people. An everyday example of this would be your ability to understand that your friend who is waiting to sit an exam is feeling nervous, even though you are not. Everyday life relies on the ability to explain and predict other people's behaviour, thoughts and feelings. How do we do this? Most people develop the ability to put themselves in other people's shoes and to 'take their perspective'. We imagine what we would do or how we would think and feel in their situation, and in this way we can understand them.

ToM is a complex cognitive ability which allows an individual to predict other people's behaviour. ToM allows us to understand the links between beliefs and behaviour, and the fact that even if some beliefs are false, people may still act on them. Development of ToM is seen as crucial to normal social behaviour, and its development has been a main theme of research into childhood. **False belief tasks** have played an important role in helping us to understand when children develop a theory of mind.

False belief tasks

False belief tasks are used to assess whether or not a young child understands that other people hold different beliefs to themselves, beliefs that can be wrong. An early example of this was the '**unexpected transfer task**' introduced by Wimmer and Perner (1983). In their original study, children aged four and five were shown two dolls, Maxi and his mother.

Link

Approaches, issues and debates

The early development of social behaviour is an excellent opportunity to demonstrate the nature–nurture debate in psychology. Social development is influenced by both innate factors and social experiences. Remember, there may be no simple answer to questions of this nature. Make sure that you show you are aware of the complexity of this issue and the way in which nature and nurture are likely to work together in early social development.

Link

For more on theory of mind (ToM) see pages 249–50.

Key terms

False belief tasks: tasks that allow the investigator to analyse the cognitive processing of the child by seeing whether they can recognise that others can have beliefs about the world that are wrong.

Unexpected transfer task: this takes place when one object is unexpectedly swapped for another without a person being aware of it.

Cognition

Maxi took some chocolate and put it into a blue cupboard before going out to play. Whilst he was out, his mother moved the chocolate into a green cupboard. Wimmer and Perner asked the sample of children: 'Where will Maxi look for the chocolate?'

In order to give the correct answer to this question, the child needs to put themself in Maxi's position. If they are able to do this, they will reason that Maxi would look in the blue (wrong) cupboard where the chocolate was last seen. This ability demonstrates theory of mind as the child understands that Maxi holds a false belief which is different to their own knowledge.

Wimmer and Perner found distinct differences between children aged around four and under. Those under four would typically say that Maxi would look in the green cupboard where they themselves knew the chocolate to be. Children over that age would typically answer that Maxi would look in the blue cupboard where he had last seen it. This demonstrates the ability in older children to see that other people think and believe something different to themselves, the basis of theory of mind.

A slightly different type of false belief problem is the 'appearance reality' task. A popular example is the Smarties task, developed by Perner, Leeham and Wimmer (1987). Children were shown a Smarties tube and asked to say what they thought was in it. Not surprisingly most replied 'Smarties'. The researchers then opened the tube to reveal a set of coloured pencils! Each child was then asked what another child – who was out of the room – would think was in the tube. In agreement with the Maxi study, children aged around four would answer correctly that they would think the tube had Smarties in it, whereas three-year-olds would typically give the answer of 'pencils', showing an inability to distinguish what they believed from another person's beliefs.

Perhaps the most well-known false belief problem is the Sally–Ann task devised by Baron-Cohen, Leslie and Frith (1985) (see the research study below). Baron-Cohen *et al.* showed that while over 80 per cent of normally developing children and children with Down's syndrome passed this test, only 20 per cent of children with autism passed it. This suggests that autism is linked to a failure to develop an effective theory of mind.

Research study: Baron-Cohen *et al.* (1985)

The procedure used in this study was similar to Wimmer and Perner's in 1983. However, Baron-Cohen *et al.* extended this research by using both typically and atypically developing children who were carefully matched for mental age and cognitive ability. A total of 61 children were used, comprised of three groups:

- 20 autistic children aged on average 11 years 11 months
- 14 children with Down's syndrome aged 10 years and 11 months
- 27 normally developing children aged 4 years and 5 months.

The children were told a simple story about two dolls called Sally and Ann. They were asked to name them to check that they understood who was who, then they were told that Sally placed a marble into her basket and left. While Sally was away, Ann moved the marble from the basket to a box. When Sally returned the children were asked three questions:

1 Where will Sally look for her marble? (The *belief* question.)
2 Where is the marble really? (The *reality* question.)
3 Where was the marble at the beginning? (The *memory* question.)

Baron-Cohen *et al.* reasoned that if the child has theory of mind, they will report that Sally would look for the marble in the basket where she last saw it. A child who had not yet developed theory of mind would say that Sally would look in the box where they themselves knew the marble to be. They found that all of the participants in all three groups answered the 'reality' and 'memory' questions correctly. The 'belief' question was correctly answered by 86 per cent of the Down's syndrome children and 85 per cent of the typically developing children. However, only 20 per cent of the autistic group were able to answer this correctly, suggesting that they had not yet developed a theory of mind. This led Baron-Cohen *et al.* to conclude that autistic children have difficulties in putting themselves in someone else's shoes and taking the perspective of the other.

Methodological issues

▦ This was a carefully controlled study in which Baron-Cohen *et al.* selected children with matched mental ages in the three conditions. This was to ensure that any deficits found did not relate to the children's general intelligence or level of understanding, but to their lack of social understanding.

▦ Language: it has been shown that the way questions are asked can influence results on false belief tasks. Slight changes in phrasing may have altered the results. In addition, 20 per cent of children with autism did pass the task in Baron-Cohen *et al.*'s study. How are these different? It has been shown (Frith, 2001) that performance in false belief tasks is strongly related to language development in both normal children and those with autism, and this relationship has not been fully explored.

▦ Baron-Cohen *et al.*'s research has laid the foundation for the further analysis of these issues. Baron-Cohen is a director of the Autism Research Centre, a group that actively research autism. Their work has generated many practical applications, e.g. in teacher training programmes, teachers can be made aware of the problems that children with autism can have with social interaction.

Ethical issues

▦ Parental consent is an important aspect in all research involving children. This would be extremely important in a study of this nature which used two groups of atypically developing children.

▦ Researchers in this area also need to balance the demands of the research programme with the needs of both the children and their parents.

> ▦ **Hint**
>
> **How science works**
>
> Ethical issues are a key issue in work with children, as they cannot give informed consent. They are even more important when the research involves atypically developing children, such as those with autism and Down's syndrome. Parents need to be fully informed of the nature of the research and the procedures involved, and the children treated with extreme sensitivity. (J)

Evaluation of research into theory of mind

The evidence that children younger than four consistently fail the false belief task has led researchers like Wimmer and Perner (1983) to the conclusion that young children have some form of conceptual deficit resulting in them not being able to understand false belief tasks. Such a view is controversial, not least because some researchers believe that young children's problems are a result of poor methodology rather than the child's cognitive underdevelopment. For example, Siegal and Beattie (1991) argue that the standard test questions are too complex for the young child. For example, the question 'Where will Maxi look for the chocolate?' could mean 'Where should he look to find the chocolate?' or 'Where will he look and find the chocolate?' The role of language and language development in theory of mind is not yet clearly understood.

A similar issue arises with the appearance reality tasks. When Saltmarsh, Mitchell and Robinson (1995) performed the Smarties task upon three-year-olds, performance improved when the children actually watched the typical content (e.g. the Smarties) being exchanged for the new content (e.g. the pencils). When asked to judge an ignorant doll's false belief on this, most three-year-olds could answer the question correctly. This shows that the visual and verbal presentation of the problem influences the child's understanding.

However, there is no doubt that false belief and appearance reality tasks have demonstrated a developmental progression in theory of mind. Charman *et al.* (2000) investigated the early cognitive predictors of performance on ToM tasks at 44 months. They found that shared attention at 20 months, shown by eye gaze cueing (see page 299) and protodeclarative pointing, was correlated with ToM performance at 44 months. It has also been proposed (Leslie, 1994) that early pretend play is an important part of the later development of ToM. The child is developing a 'shared social-communicative' system which will eventually allow him or her to interact effectively with their social world.

Autism

Autism was first described by Leo Kanner, working in America, and Hans Asperger, working in Austria, in the 1940s. They identified the key symptoms (Kanner, 1943):

- social withdrawal and problems with social communication
- obsession with consistency and 'sameness'; problems in dealing with change
- good at rote learning (e.g. lists of words or objects)
- minimal language
- skills with objects.

Later research by the English psychologists Wing and Gould systematically divided the symptoms of autism into three categories, known as Wing's Triad (Wing and Gould, 1979):

- Social: bizarre, minimal and severely delayed social development.
- Language and communication: impaired and deviant communication, both verbal and non-verbal.
- Thought and behaviour: rigid and inflexible thought; ritualistic behaviour and heavy dependence on repetitive routines; little or no imaginative or pretend play.

Symptoms of autism can vary in severity. At one extreme it is a serious and disabling developmental disorder, associated with slow intellectual development and low scores on IQ tests. At the other end of the autistic spectrum symptoms do not prevent people living normal lives; language and intellectual development are in the normal range, and autistic symptoms are more like eccentricities in communication and behaviour. Asperger identified these 'high-functioning' autistics, and the syndrome is usually referred to as Asperger's syndrome rather than autism.

Although not common, some autistics can show extraordinary talent in some cognitive areas, especially mathematics and calculation, and in drawing and painting. These are known as 'autistic savants', and they are

Cognition

AQA **Examiner's tip**

Various experimental techniques have had to be developed to work with young children. In your answer be ready to discuss particular problems with this area of research, for example how questions have to be carefully phrased, or the value of longitudinal studies.

of considerable interest to researchers into the functional organisation of the brain.

There have been many theories about the causes of autism since Kanner and Asperger's first descriptions. One of the most influential is related to the ToM. Developed by Baron-Cohen, Leslie and Frith (1985), this theory proposes that in autism theory of mind or 'mentalising' fails to develop. Normally developing children develop a theory of mind, and this enables them to understand their own thoughts and feelings, and the thoughts, feelings and the behaviours of others. This ability to 'mind read' is what allows us to communicate effectively and interact with other people. We observe other people's actions and interpret them according to our ToM; it is the basis of normal social communication. Now imagine a child of five who has not developed a theory of mind. What would the implications be?

- Minimal social communication and interaction. Other people are not seen as independent agents with their own thoughts and feelings.

- A lack of imaginative play – as children grow, their play becomes based on imagination and role-playing, requiring them to use their theory of mind and understanding of others.

- Delayed language development. We use language to help understand the intentions and beliefs of others and to communicate our own intentions. A theory of mind provides the background and context for language development. In turn, language development is crucial to the development of theory of mind.

We have already seen (pages 299–300) that false belief tasks are an effective way of assessing the development of theory of mind. In the Baron-Cohen *et al.* (1985) key study above, we saw that children with autism performed significantly worse on the Sally–Ann task than normal children and children with Down's syndrome. Subsequent studies have confirmed that children with autism have big problems with false belief tasks. So another major contribution of work on ToM is to provide an explanation for this serious developmental disorder.

Stages of the development of perspective taking

The psychoanalyst Robert Selman investigated stages in the development of perspective taking. Selman (Selman and Byrne, 1974) believed that young children do not really understand the feelings and experiences of others until they have those feelings and experiences themselves. Perspective taking is a skill that takes time to fully develop. Note that perspective taking is closely linked to the theory of mind discussed above. It requires the child to develop an understanding of the world as seen from the perspective of other people. This is a basic element of ToM.

Based upon a short scenario, we can look at the different stages of development and skills required for each stage.

Emily is nine years old. She loves to skateboard. She can perform dangerous tricks on the skateboard and impresses people with her skill. One day she falls from her skateboard. She does not hurt herself badly, but her mum sees her fall and tells her not to skateboard because next time she might be hurt much more seriously.

Later that day, Emily and her friends meet James. James has been pushed to the ground by a group of kids who stole his mobile phone. Emily sees them ahead, and realises that she can catch them up using her skateboard. But then she remembers what her mum said. Will Emily chase the children? Do you think Emily's mum will tell her off?

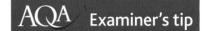

AQA Examiner's tip

Autism is not on the Specification and you cannot be asked a question directly about autism. However, research into autism is closely related to theory of mind and it provides research evidence that helps us to evaluate the contribution of ToM to psychology.

Cognition

Take it further

Simon Baron-Cohen has been a key figure in research into ToM, and in particular the relationship between ToM and autism. Visit the Autism Research Centre website at www.autismresearchcentre.com where you can read papers on many issues to do with ToM and the brain, gender differences and autism.

Cognition

Table 1 *Selman's stages of perspective taking*

Stage	Age	Stage name	Stage description	Scenario response
1	3–6 years	Undifferentiated perspective taking	The child can recognise that the self and 'others' are different and can have different thoughts and feelings. It is common for the child at this stage to confuse the two	The child says that Emily will get the mobile phone back using her skateboard because she wants to make James happy. Emily's mum will be happy because Emily has helped James and made him happy
2	5–9 years	Social informational perspective taking	The child begins to understand that different people may have different perspectives since they have access to different information about the situation	If the child was asked 'How would Emily's mum react if she found out she had been skateboarding again?' the child might say 'If she did not know anything about the stolen mobile phone then she would be angry. But if Emily showed her mum the stolen mobile phone and explained what she had done, then Emily's mum might change her mind and not be angry'
3	7–12 years	Self-reflective perspective taking	The child develops the ability to see things from another's point of view. This includes seeing their own thoughts, feelings and behaviour from another's perspective	If a child reading the scenario was asked 'Would Emily get punished?' a child would commonly report 'No, Emily's mum will understand the reason why Emily used her skateboard'. The crucial point to note here is that the child understands that Emily's action of using the skateboard is influenced by her knowing that her mum will be able to understand why she did it. The child reading this scenario must have the ability to understand that the mum could see Emily's action from Emily's point of view
4	10–15 years	Third-party perspective taking	The child is able to step outside a normal two-person situation and imagine how they and others are viewed, e.g. imagine having a fight with another person. You will have your view; your opponent will have his view. But imagine what a bystander might be witnessing. At this stage you are able to take that bystander's position	If a child reading the scenario was asked 'Would Emily get punished?' the child would report that Emily should not get punished as Emily thought it was important to help James and get the mobile phone back by using her skateboard. Crucially at this stage the child might also report that Emily should not get punished as she can make her mum understand why she used the skateboard. This kind of response requires the child to become a third party, seeing Emily and her mum as an independent observer might
5	14 years–adult	Societal perspective taking	This is a broader perspective where the child understands that a view held by a third party can be influenced by a variety of different forces, e.g. cultural norms/values, religion, etc.	In the scenario, when the child is asked 'Should Emily get punished?' they will say no, since the action of the other group of children, stealing James' mobile phone, was morally wrong. This wider view justifies Emily disobeying her mother

Evaluating Selman's stages

Positive points:

▥ There are a number of studies such as Gurucharri, Phelps and Selman (1984) that provide clear support for Selman's stages, emphasising the developmental nature and increasing complexity and sophistication of perspective-taking abilities.

▥ Applications of research: O'Keefe and Johnston (1989) researched perspective taking and teacher effectiveness. They emphasise that a crucial component to this developmental process is teacher responsiveness to the child, which in turn is influenced by an understanding of the stage of perspective taking that the child has reached.

Negative points:

▥ Children's social world: there is a great need for research to link the different aspects of the child's social world together and to understand the role of perspective taking in parent–child and peer relationships generally (Fitzgerald et al., 2003).

▥ Longitudinal research: Kurdek (1977) suggests that perspective taking is a complex social cognitive skill. To understand it fully requires a broader approach than simply describing the stages, in particular *longitudinal* studies. The process of perspective taking is far more complicated than current models suggest.

▥ Digital world: in an age when many children have internet email accounts and a presence on social networking sites, Selman's stages of development seem a little outdated given that forms of communication are changing so rapidly. Methods of social interaction are not as personal as they used to be. For example, in education, web-based discussions are a common occurrence. Since the dynamics of communication have changed, it is possible that the development of social cognition, including perspective taking, have changed as well (Jarvela and Hakkinen, 2003).

Key points

▥ Social cognition is essential to our ability to understand and predict the behaviour of other people.

▥ The development of social cognition begins at birth, with the newborn showing some awareness of other people.

▥ By 18 months the child has a developing sense of their own identity and sense of self.

▥ Theory of mind is the ability to understand the thoughts and actions of other people by 'taking their perspective'. It develops at around four years of age. In autism, development of theory of mind is severely impaired.

▥ Selman's stages describe the development of perspective taking in children. Although this has proved useful, the model is culturally highly specific and may be less applicable in an era of increasingly electronic social communication.

▥ Link

Approaches, issues and debates

Selman's views are of a white, middle-class, Western researcher who has been researching white, middle-class groups of children (Weiner et al., 2003). Quintana, Castaneda-English and Ybarra (1999) argue that this approach has ignored the development of perspective taking and socialisation in minority ethnic communities and cross-culturally.

■ Summary questions

1 Babies show an awareness of others from a very early age. Discuss whether this is likely to be due to innate factors or whether it depends on experience.

2 What is theory of mind? What has research told us about the development of theory of mind?

3 Outline and evaluate Selman's stages of the development of perspective taking. Include a brief assessment of the relationship between perspective taking and theory of mind.

Cognition

Biological explanations of social cognition

Cognition

Learning objectives:

- outline key brain areas involved in social cognition and evaluate relevant research evidence

- understand the possible role of mirror neurons in our feelings of empathy for other people

- evaluate research evidence on the role of mirror neurons in the human brain.

Link

Approaches, issues and debates

Although brain scanning can provide a huge amount of information on the brain systems involved in social cognition, there is a great danger of *reductionism*. Social cognition involves complicated cognitive, social, and emotional behaviours *between* people, and if we do not study these and rely only on the biological approach we will never develop a full understanding of social cognition.

Introduction

As we have seen, social cognition involves a broad set of abilities. Think of social interaction. We need to *perceive* people and situations, perhaps *remember* previous encounters. We need to apply our mentalising abilities to *interpret* actions of others, and there will almost always be an *emotional* aspect to situations and people we encounter. Perception, memory, interpretation and emotion involve many interconnected structures and pathways in the brain, so there is no simple answer to the question of the biological basis of social cognition.

Evidence from studies with 'neurotypicals'

The introduction of brain-scanning techniques over the last 15 years has allowed the brain mechanisms of social cognition to be studied in normal human participants, or 'neurotypicals'. The result, reviewed in Adolphs (2003), is a complex network of structures and pathways involved in various aspects of social cognition. Some key areas include:

- The amygdala: a structure buried within the temporal lobe of the brain that is important in recognising and interpreting facial emotions in others. It is also involved in organising our emotional responses.

- The parietal cortex: part of the forebrain, this area is important in our ability to distinguish ourselves from other people; the *self–other* distinction.

- The frontal cortex: the main part of the human forebrain, this area is vital in bringing together information from other parts of the brain to build an integrated picture of our social environment. Therefore, it is also the area involved in social decision making, planning and reasoning.

- Motor-related areas: these are parts of the cortex involved in the control of movement as well as other functions. Important in social cognition are the premotor cortex in the frontal lobe, and areas in the lower part of the parietal cortex.

Evidence from people with autism

There is evidence, outlined above, that in autism theory of mind does not develop. This has drastic effects on social cognition. Many aspects of theory of mind overlap with what we would include as social cognition, such as the self–other distinction, and interpreting social situations. Therefore, we can look at the abnormal development of the autistic brain for clues as to what structures are involved in social cognition.

Unfortunately autism is usually associated with low IQ, delayed intellectual development and a high frequency of other developmental disorders such as epilepsy (Happe, 1994). So, even though many abnormalities have been found, they tend to be inconsistent across different studies. However, areas often found to be abnormal in autism include (Frith, 2001):

- the amygdala
- the frontal cortex
- the junction between the temporal and parietal lobes of the brain.

Note that these areas coincide with areas identified in studies with normally developing children as involved in social cognition. It provides strong evidence that social cognition problems seen in autism are a result of abnormal development of structures that are part of the brain network controlling social cognition in the normal brain.

It is also significant that autism involves a significant genetic factor. Concordance rates for monozygotic twins (see page 259) range between 36 per cent and 90 per cent, far higher than the concordance rate for dizygotic twins. We saw above that newborn infants can already imitate simple actions, such as a parent sticking their tongue out, but this early development of imitation is absent in children who go on to develop autism (Ramachandran and Oberman, 2006). In normal infants there must be an innate or *hardwired* ability to map the mother's facial expression onto its own brain centres controlling facial movement. This innate ability is missing in autism, and it may be part of a genetically controlled abnormality in development. Note that this simple form of imitation probably reflects the first stages in developing a theory of mind.

▨ Evidence from psychopathy

The psychopath dramatised on TV and in the media is usually an aggressive serial killer. In fact psychopathy is described in terms of a range of features that revolve around social cognition. The psychopath manipulates and uses people for their own ends, apparently without any conscience or guilt. A core symptom is their lack of *empathy*. Empathy refers to our ability not just to recognise the feelings of other people, but to experience emotions of sympathy and compassion in response to those feelings. If we see someone in pain, we recognise how distressed they must feel and we also *experience* sympathy. These feelings of empathy lead us to help people in trouble, but they can also prevent us doing things that hurt others. We can predict how they will feel, so we do not do it.

People with high levels of psychopathy show reduced reactions to facial expressions of fear and distress. When given moral dilemmas to solve, they tend to choose practical solutions rather than morally correct ones (Blair, 2003) and they score lower on tests of empathy. Empathy is an aspect of social cognition that requires the ability to mentalise using our theory of mind. Psychopaths do not lack a theory of mind; in fact, they are skilled at manipulating others, and can be superficially charming friends. They do appear to lack the link between mentalising and empathising. They can identify the emotions of others, but this does not lead to the feelings of sympathy and compassion that are fundamental to social cognition. It has been proposed that this emotional impairment interferes with the normal socialisation of the child (Blair, 2003).

Psychopathy is not related to major abnormalities in brain function in the way that autism seems to be. However, a number of studies, in particular brain scanning, have identified two key structures that seem to function abnormally in psychopathy. These are the amygdala and one part of the frontal cortex, the orbitofrontal area.

▨ **Link**

Approaches, issues and debates

There is evidence for a significant genetic factor in autism. Therefore this condition represents an example of the nature–nurture debate in psychology. It may be that children with autism inherit a brain dysfunction that prevents the normal development of social cognition. Opponents of this *nature* argument believe that environmental stimulation can help reduce autistic symptoms; this would be evidence for the *nurture* side of the argument.

Cognition

Key terms

Neuron: the brain is made up of around 100 billion neurons. Neurons are specialised to transmit electrical activity and are connected to each other by synapses. The electrical activity codes information in the brain.

Electroencephalograph (EEG): a recording of the electrical activity of the brain. Electrodes on the scalp pick up electrical activity from the millions of neurons in the brain. Different patterns of EEG activity can reflect different brain states, such as arousal and the stages of sleep.

Link

See Chapter 2, Sleep states, page 15 for a description of the use of the EEG in sleep research.

Link

Approaches, issues and debates

Our knowledge of the mirror neuron system is based largely on studies with non-human animals. Although scientifically rigorous, this raises problems of generalising from animals to humans, and ethical issues of working with animals. These are excellent areas for evaluation and commentary.

Evidence from mirror neurons

Mirror neurons are seen as one of the most exciting developments in brain research over the last 15 years, particularly in relation to social cognition.

The hundred billion or so cells that make up the human brain are called **neurons**. They transmit information throughout the brain using electrical impulses. We can record this electrical activity from single neurons (called single-cell or single-unit recording), or we can record the activity of millions of neurons using the **electroencephalograph (EEG)**. These recordings can help to unravel the function of neurons in different parts of the brain.

Systematic single-cell recording can only be done in non-human animals as it involves implanting thin electrodes into the brain so that they contact individual neurons. In the early 1990s a research group at the University of Parma were recording from neurons in the part of the macaque monkey brain that controlled motor behaviour (movement). When the monkey reached for a peanut the neurons fired, as they were part of the brain's systems for controlling voluntary movement. Then, in an accidental observation, they noticed that the same neurons fired when the monkey *observed* another monkey making the same movement, while they themselves did nothing. They followed up this accidental finding by systematically studying this effect. Their findings were as follows (Di Pellegrino *et al.*, 1992; Rizzolatti *et al.*, 1996):

- A class of neurons in the motor cortex of the monkey brain fire when the monkey makes a simple goal-directed movement (e.g. reaching for a peanut), but also when the monkey observes another monkey making the same movement. As the neurons in the observer's brain seem to be imitating or mirroring the activity of the neurons in the observed monkey's brain, they were called mirror neurons.

- Mirror neurons also fire if the monkey sees a human making the same goal-directed movement.

- Mirror neurons only fire if there is an interaction between the movement and an object. They do not fire if random movements with no target are observed. There has to be some *meaning* to the movement.

- The observer monkey does not have to *see* the movement. Mirror neurons that fire when another monkey reaches for a peanut and eats it, will fire if they *hear* a peanut shell being cracked open, i.e. they are responding to the meaning. Mirror neuron activity reflects knowledge and understanding of the movement.

Since the first studies many others have expanded our knowledge of the mirror neuron system (MNS). Mirror neurons are found in many parts of the brain that overlap with the social cognition network outlined above, especially the motor-related areas. This gives a clue to its possible function. For example, mirror neurons fire to facial expressions. It seems that if we see a particular expression, we automatically imitate it in terms of our own facial muscles and this triggers activity in our mirror neurons. This pattern of brain activation then gives rise to the feelings associated with that facial expression. In this way, the MNS allows us to feel the same emotions as the person we are observing.

This could be the foundation of empathy and understanding of others. Scanning studies have also shown that observing someone in pain activates the same brain systems that are activated when you feel pain yourself (Rizzolatti *et al.*, 2006). So we directly experience the same sensations as the other person, which is the foundation of empathy.

In fact it has been found that the mirror neuron system in humans is less activated in people who score low on empathy scales (Gazzola, Aziz-Zadeh and Keysers, 2006) and in participants with autism (Oberman *et al.*, 2003). Hadjikhani *et al.* (2006) studied participants with autism and found less cortical matter in areas associated with the mirror neuron system. A defective mirror neuron system may therefore be the basis of autistic problems with social communication and interaction.

Evaluation of the biological explanations of social cognition

At present we are just beginning to study the brain mechanisms of social cognition, and many problems remain:

- Social cognition is a broad area and many of the concepts are poorly defined. It involves perception of social signals, socialisation, theory of mind and mentalising, and emotion. It will be very difficult to unravel the precise brain mechanisms underlying all of these different aspects and how they interact.

- The approach is reductionist, like all biological explanations. It is important not to let a focus on the brain divert us from the study of the development of social cognition at behavioural, family and social levels.

- The mirror neuron system is seen as a potential basis for social cognition. However, it has one central problem. Single-cell activity can only be recorded in non-human primates such as monkeys. There is no *direct* evidence for mirror neurons in humans. Human studies can only use *indirect* methods, such as subtle changes in the EEG or changes in general brain activity in areas that are thought (from monkey studies) to be part of the mirror neuron system.

- Finally, the mirror neuron system is not enough in itself for complex social cognition. Monkeys have an MNS, but only limited social cognition in areas such as deception. The human brain mechanisms underlying social cognition have evolved way beyond the mirror system identified in monkeys.

Key points

- Social cognition involves perception, memory, interpretation, theory of mind and emotion. It is therefore likely to involve many brain areas and pathways.

- Work with normal participants ('neurotypicals'), people with autism and those with high levels of psychopathy has identified key brain areas for social cognition. These include the parietal cortex, the frontal cortex, motor-related areas and the amygdala.

- Mirror neurons fire when we make a movement or when we see another person make the movement. They are sensitive to 'intentionality', and do not fire to random movements.

- They have been used to explain empathy responses to other people, especially in relation to facial expressions.

- However, the direct study of mirror neurons has been done on non-human primates. They can only be studied indirectly in humans, and we have to be cautious in generalising from animals to humans.

Summary questions

4 'Social cognition' is a broad term. Outline and discuss some of the cognitive and emotional processes that contribute to social cognition, and the implications of this complexity for the study of the biology of social cognition.

5 Outline and evaluate research into mirror neurons. Explain briefly the role they may play in human empathy.

Cognition

Cognition and development end of topic

How science works: practical activity

In this section of the course, we have seen that psychologists have used a variety of methods to investigate children's cognitive and moral development. Many of these have been based upon the use of vignettes or scenarios. You can carry out an investigation yourself to assess if there are gender differences in moral reasoning in early adulthood as Kohlberg claimed. In order to do this, you will need to reread some of the vignettes used by Kohlberg which have been designed for adolescents. You may decide to construct your own similar dilemma for the purposes of this research or to use one of Kohlberg's original dilemmas which you can find at www.haverford.edu/ (search for 'dilemmas').

When you have constructed/selected the dilemma you intend to use, you should ask a small number of 17–18-year-olds, both male and female, for their informed consent to participate in your study. Your participants will need to respond to your chosen dilemma by writing answers to your question(s). The data you obtain here will be qualitative in nature and you will need to decide how to code the responses and put them at the different levels of Kohlberg's stages of moral reasoning. You can then compare the responses given by males and females to see if there are differences in line with Kohlberg's claims. In order to generate sufficient data to test using inferential statistics (the chi-squared test) you could work as a group. If you do this, you will need to use the same dilemma and ensure reliability by using the same coding system.

Take it further

You could also try this task with Selman's stages, using the text as a guide to categorising responses.

Further reading and weblinks

Goswami, U. (1998) *Cognition in Children*. Hove: Psychology Press.

This is an excellent overview of critical thinking about cognitive development.

Wood, D. (1988) *How Children Think and Learn*. Oxford: Blackwell.

This is a really excellent text which considers the applications of Piaget, Vygotsky and Bruner to education.

http://psychology.about.com/library/quiz/bl_piaget_quiz.htm

This is an example of some of the useful quizzes to test your knowledge of Piaget's theory.

www.gtce.org.uk/research/romtopics/rom_teachingandlearning/bruner_may06/

You can read about the application of Bruner's theory to education on the General Teaching Council website.

www.infed.org/thinkers/bruner.htm

This article explores the work of Bruner and has some important lessons for informal educators and those concerned with the practice of lifelong learning.

http://psychology.about.com/od/developmentalpsychology/a/kohlberg.htm

Find out about a famous dilemma created by Kohlberg called the 'Dilemma of Heinz'.

www.psychology.nottingham.ac.uk/staff/plm/c81ind/Lecture6.pdf

If you search the internet for information on theory of mind you will find some very good academic websites run by university departments covering the Sally–Ann test and other methods of assessing social understanding.

www.nas.org.uk/autism

You can read more about the difficulties with social cognition experienced by people with autism by going to the National Autistic Society's website.

You may wish to watch the film *Rainman* directed by Barry Levinson (1988). This film tells the story of a road trip taken by a man (Tom Cruise) and his autistic savant brother (Dustin Hoffman).

AQA Examination-style questions

Remember for all questions that assess analysis and evaluation there is a need to include reference to relevant approaches, issues and debates. Overall, in a question there will be roughly a third of the marks for showing knowledge and understanding of relevant theories, concepts and studies, and two-thirds for demonstrating effective, well-structured analysis and commentary/evaluation. Look in the Examination skills section at the end of the book for further help on how to approach the exam.

Biological rhythms and sleep

1   Outline and evaluate evolutionary explanations of the function of sleep.   *(25 marks)*

2   Discuss the consequences of disrupting biological rhythms (e.g. shift work, jet lag).   *(25 marks)*

3   **(a)**   Outline **one or more** consequences of disrupting biological rhythms.   *(5 marks)*

      (b)   Outline and evaluate explanations of narcolepsy.   *(20 marks)*

Question 1 requires focus on explanations of the functions of sleep – why we sleep. Candidates should be careful not to get sidetracked into focusing on the nature of sleep.

Question 2 is an example of a question that gives examples, but you must remember that these are provided purely for guidance. There is no stipulation that the candidate must write about shift work and jet lag. However, as these have both been heavily researched, it is likely that such material would form the basis of an answer, but any other material relevant to the question would also be perfectly allowable.

Question 3(a) is worth 5 marks and so answers should be tailored to provide an outline that is sufficient to attain that level of credit. Writing too much will not gain any extra credit and it may reduce the time available to answer 3(b) which is worth 20 marks of which 4 marks will be for description of the explanation and 16 for the evaluation.

Perception

1   Describe and evaluate Gregory's top-down/indirect theory of perception.   *(25 marks)*

2   Discuss research into the development of perceptual abilities.   *(25 marks)*

3   **(a)**   Outline the development of perceptual abilities.   *(9 marks)*

      (b)   Evaluate explanations of prosopagnosia.   *(16 marks)*

Question 1 names a particular theory, in this case Gregory's top-down theory of perception. This means that the candidate must orientate their answer around this theory, although other theories could provide evaluative material as comparison and contrast. Any theory that is specifically identified on the specification can have a question asked about it.

In Question 3(a) the stipulation is to outline, therefore evaluative comments will not receive credit. The situation is reversed with Question 3(b) as the stipulation here is to evaluate, therefore any descriptions of explanations here will not receive credit.

▓ Relationships

1	Discuss the relationship between sexual selection and human reproductive behaviour.	*(25 marks)*
2	**(a)** Outline the influence of childhood experiences on adult relationships.	*(5 marks)*
	(b) Outline and evaluate evolutionary explanations of parental investment.	*(20 marks)*
3	Nazma and Andrew are from different cultural backgrounds; Nazma is from an Asian family background whilst Andrew is from a traditional white English background. They met at university and have been married for three years. Recently problems have emerged in the relationship and the marriage has broken down.	
	(a) Suggest how psychological research can help us to understand the breakdown of relationships such as that of Nazma and Andrew.	*(21 marks)*
	(b) Explain **one** methodological difficulty of researching into relationships.	*(4 marks)*

Question 2 is a 'parted' question whereby part (a) only requires an outline, but part (b) requires both an outline and an evaluation. Therefore any evaluative material offered in part (a) will not receive credit, whilst any answer to part (b) that only focuses on an outline or an evaluation will not gain full access to all 20 of the marks. Of the 20, 4 marks will be for description of the explanation and 16 for the evaluation.

Question 3 is a 'stem' question where the information in the stem brings together two subsections of the relationships topic – breakdown of relationships and the nature of relationships in different cultures. Therefore, candidates should use relevant material from both of these subsections in order to formulate answers.

▓ Aggression

1	Compare social and biological approaches to explaining aggression.	*(25 marks)*
2	**(a)** Outline **one or more** evolutionary explanations of human aggression.	*(9 marks)*
	(b) Evaluate one of the explanations offered in **(a)**.	*(16 marks)*
3	Discuss the role of neural and hormonal mechanisms in aggression.	*(25 marks)*

Question 1 is an example of a question that brings together two subsections of the aggression topic – social psychological and biological theories of aggression. A good way to set about this would be to provide an outline of the main features of each and then to identify and discuss ways in which they differ, such as the amount and robustness of the research evidence, similarities and differences relating to assumptions, research methods, position relating to debates in psychology.

In Question 2(b) candidates need to make it absolutely clear which of the explanations described in part (a) is being evaluated. Eating behaviour examination-style questions.

1	**(a)** Outline **one** psychological explanation of one eating disorder.	*(9 marks)*
	(b) Evaluate the explanation offered in **(a)**.	*(16 marks)*
2	**(a)** Outline the role of the neural mechanisms involved in controlling eating and satiation.	*(5 marks)*
	(b) Outline and evaluate evolutionary explanations of food preference.	*(20 marks)*
3	**(a)** Outline **one or more** explanations for the success or failure of dieting.	*(9 marks)*
	(b) Evaluate evolutionary theories of food preference.	*(16 marks)*

In Question 1(a) make it clear which eating disorder is being explained.

For Question 2(b), of the 20 marks for this part, 4 marks will be for description of the explanations and 16 for the evaluation.

Question 3 is divided into two parts and each part has different requirements. Part (a) requires an outline of one or more explanations for the success or failure of dieting, therefore any evaluation of explanations will not gain any extra credit and will merely waste valuable writing time. If you choose to outline more than one explanation, one could be for success and the other for failure. Part (b) requires an evaluation of evolutionary theories of food preference. This is drawn from a different subsection of the eating disorders topic and any description here of evolutionary theories will not receive credit.

Gender

1   (a) Outline the role of hormones in gender development.   *(5 marks)*
     (b) Discuss the role of genes in gender development.   *(20 marks)*
2   Describe and evaluate research studies into psychological androgyny and/or gender
     dysphoria.   *(25 marks)*
3   Compare the gender schema theory and the biosocial approach to gender development.   *(25 marks)*

Question 1 has a 5-mark and 20-mark split. The 5 marks in (a) are for purely outlining the role of hormones in gender development. Any evaluation here would not accrue credit. Part (b) has 4 marks for outlining the role of genes in gender development. The additional 16 marks are for the commentary on /evaluation of the role of genes in gender development.

Question 3 brings together material from two sections of this topic. The simplest way to set about this would be to provide an outline of the main features of each approach and then to identify and discuss ways in which they differ, such as the amount and robustness of the research evidence, similarities and differences relating to assumptions, research methods or position relating to debates in psychology.

Intelligence and learning

1   (a) Outline the nature of simple learning (classical and operant conditioning).   *(9 marks)*
     (b) Evaluate the role of conditioning in the behaviour of non-human animals.   *(16 marks)*
2   (a) Outline evolutionary factors in the development of human intelligence.   *(5 marks)*
     (b) Discuss the role of environmental factors associated with intelligence test
          performance.   *(20 marks)*
3   (a) Outline Gardner's theory of multiple intelligences.   *(9 marks)*
     (b) Evaluate the role of environmental factors in intelligence test performance.   *(16 marks)*

Question 2 is divided into two parts. Part (a) is quite straightforward, you are required to outline Gardner's theory – but remember, no evaluation of the theory is required. The stipulation in part (b) is to discuss the role of environmental factors associated with intelligence test performance. 'Discuss' involves providing a brief outline of relevant environmental factors, worth 4 marks, and an evaluation of these factors, worth 16 marks. Relevant issues, debates and approaches should also be included in the answer to part (b), for example the nature–nurture debate and ethical factors involved in researching intelligence test performance.

Cognition and development

1   Discuss the development of the child's sense of self.   *(25 marks)*
2   (a) Describe **one** theory of cognitive development.   *(9 marks)*
     (b) Evaluate the theory offered in (a) in terms of its applications to education.   *(16 marks)*
3   Outline and evaluate one theory of cognitive development and one theory of moral
     understanding.   *(25 marks)*

Question 2 is an example of a question that is specifically orientated on a particular area. This occurs in part (b) of the question where the candidate is required to evaluate the theory of cognitive development offered in part (a), but purely in terms of the theory's applications to education.

Question 3 is not a parted question, but it requires candidates to outline and evaluate two theories from different subsections of the cognition and development topic. Nine marks would be available for the outlining of the theories and 16 marks would be available for their evaluation, therefore the emphasis should be more on the evaluation than on the description of the theories.

Psychopathology

Introduction

Psychopathology is the scientific study of abnormal behaviour. As you have already seen at AS, there are various ways of defining abnormality and no single definition is completely adequate. Therefore, it is not surprising to find that the field of psychopathology addresses a wide range of mental, emotional and behavioural problems and encompasses research into many different aspects, e.g. classification, diagnosis, **aetiology**, prevention and treatment.

Most people working within the field of psychopathology adopt a particular model or paradigm. It is important to understand that the paradigm within which psychologists and doctors work determines the ways they explain and investigate mental illness, and the treatments they favour. A psychodynamic theorist, for example, would be interested in exploring childhood experiences for clues about the origins of adult mental illness, whereas a biologist would be more interested in looking for genetic markers. Similarly, they would differ in their methods of investigation, with the former using psychoanalytic techniques and the latter using controlled experiments. No single **paradigm** is 'correct' and there is a tendency amongst modern practitioners to adopt an **eclectic approach**, particularly as far as treatment is concerned. In this topic, we will be looking at some of the major types of mental disorder and considering causal explanations from a number of different models. Chapter 25, Explanations, diagnosis and treatment, explores common issues of explanations and diagnosis, and the following chapters in the section provide more specific information.

Mental illnesses like schizophrenia and depression differ from physical illnesses in a number of significant ways. There are no physical tests, for example X-rays or blood and urine tests, that will confirm a diagnosis of schizophrenia. However, mental illnesses like depression exist on a continuum – most people are a bit down or sad sometimes, but it is not always clear when this 'normal' emotion becomes 'abnormal'. Classification systems have been developed to help clinicians make more accurate diagnoses of mental disorders. The two major classification systems are the *DSM-IV* and the *ICD-10* and we will consider them in more detail in this topic.

One of the main reasons for classifying and diagnosing mental disorders is to make sure that the most appropriate therapy is provided. For example, a technique such as systematic desensitisation is often the therapy of choice in treating phobias, but it is of little use in treating schizophrenia. Each model of psychopathology gives rise to its own range of therapies and we shall look at their appropriateness and effectiveness.

The classification manuals list hundreds of disorders and the AQA Specification focuses on three. You must choose to study one of them in detail. They have been selected because they are relatively common disorders and have been well researched. We will be looking at issues relating to the classification and diagnosis of these disorders and also considering their major clinical characteristics. We shall then look at various psychological and biological explanations of these disorders and at the therapies associated with these explanations.

Key terms

Aetiology: the cause of a disease, condition or mental disorder.

Paradigm: a shared set of assumptions, methods, and terminology about what should be studied and why and how.

Eclectic approach: where therapists dip into various treatments and approaches and combine aspects of each.

Hint

The information in Chapter 25 is relevant to ALL of those that follow in the psychopathology topic so be sure to read it.

Copyright © AQA, 2009. Please refer to the current version of the specification on AQA's website at www.aqa.org.uk/qual/gce.php

Psychopathology

Psychopathology

25 Explanations, diagnosis and treatment – an overview

Explanations and treatments

Learning objectives:

- understand common elements of explanations of psychopathology and therapies

- evaluate explanations and treatments of psychopathology.

Link

See pages 236–47 in the *AQA Psychology A AS* student book for an account of the biological and psychological approaches and pages 256–67 for an account of the therapies.

Hint

This chapter contains elements which are relevant to ALL of those which follow in the Psychopathology section and so should be read by all students.

Link

Approaches, issues and debates

Different approaches, such as the biological and behavioural, can be evaluated in terms of issues and debates. These can include, for instance, how they stand in relation to reductionism, free will versus determinism, or the nature–nurture debate.

As you will have realised from your AS studies, there is no single explanatory approach in psychology. Psychology is a broad-ranging discipline that encompasses many different theoretical perspectives or paradigms.

This is certainly true in the field of psychopathology, where several different models are used to explain the origins of mental disorders and to suggest methods of treatment. These models can be split into two major categories:

- The medical (biological) model views mental disorder as an illness caused by underlying biological factors (it is sometimes called the 'disease model').

- Psychological models view mental disorder as the result of psychological dysfunction.

You first met these approaches in the *AQA Psychology A AS* student book and they are discussed in more detail in the Introductory chapter on approaches, issues and debates in this book. We will look at them in more detail in the context of the specific disorders in the three chapters that follow, so the main features are simply summarised here.

Main theoretical approaches in psychopathology

Evaluating explanations

As you can see from Table 1 (overleaf), all of the major theoretical perspectives have an explanation for mental disorders. Some of these are more appropriate for explaining certain disorders rather than others. For example, behaviourist theory offers a reasonable account of phobic disorders, but it is much less convincing in explaining the origins of schizophrenia. For this reason, you need to think very carefully about each explanation in the context of the particular disorder you are studying. You need to consider factors such as the quality of the supporting evidence, and we will look at this in more detail in the relevant sections. The most important thing for you to understand is that no single explanation accounts for all of the complex and diverse aspects of particular mental disorders. Most researchers and clinicians working within the field of psychopathology accept that mental disorders arise from a complex interaction of biological, psychological and environmental factors.

Evaluating therapies

As you can see from Table 1, each of the major models not only attempts to explain the disorders but also offers ways of treating them. The AQA Specification requires you to consider the appropriateness and effectiveness of therapies for your chosen disorder. You will find that some therapies are more suited to particular disorders than others, and we will consider this in more detail in the following chapters. Researchers use various methods to investigate the effectiveness of therapies, but

Table 1 *Summary of the main theoretical perspectives in psychopathology*

Model	Biological (medical)	Behavioural	Cognitive	Psychodynamic
Key concepts	Behaviour is determined by genetic, physiological and neurochemical processes. The nervous system, especially the brain, is the focus for biological psychologists	Behaviour is shaped by the environment and consists of a set of learned responses to external stimuli. Behaviour is learnt through processes of conditioning and imitation	The human mind is conceived as a sort of information processor that sifts incoming information, manipulates it so that it can be stored effectively and accessed when needed. Human behaviour is heavily influenced by schemas (ways of thinking about the self and the world)	Behaviour is the product of complex interactions between conscious and unconscious processes, many of which have their origins in childhood
Assumptions about normal behaviour	The nervous system is functioning normally	The individual has learned a wide range of adaptive behaviours which allow him/her to function adequately in everyday life	The individual has realistic and positive schemas and can use their cognitive process effectively to monitor and control behaviour	The three parts of the personality – id, ego and superego – are balanced. There is always some degree of intra-psychic conflict present, but defence mechanisms are employed effectively to protect the individual
Assumptions about abnormal behaviour	There is some change in either the structure or function of the brain/ nervous system. This can take the form of a brain injury, genetic disorder or chemical imbalance	The individual has either failed to learn sufficient appropriate adaptive responses or has learned maladaptive responses	Negative schemas lead to negative thoughts. These thoughts are irrational and impair the ability to use cognitive processes effectively. The individual no longer feels in control	Emotional disturbance, particularly excessive anxiety, arises as a result of unresolved conflicts and/or fixation at one of the psychosexual stages of development
Preferred methods of study	Mainly experimental. Advances in scanning techniques have revolutionised research into the structure and function of living brains	Mainly experimental. In the past many experiments were based on non-human animals	Mainly experimental	Case study using psychoanalytic techniques such as dream work, free association and projective tests
Preferred methods of treatment	Physical treatments such as drug therapy, ECT (electro-convulsive therapy) and psychosurgery	There are various types of behavioural therapy based on different types of learning: ■ systematic desensitisation, flooding and aversion therapy (classical conditioning) ■ behaviour shaping and token economy (operant conditioning) ■ modelling (SLT)	There are various cognitive-based therapies. The most widely used are CBT (cognitive-behavioural therapy) and RET (rational emotive therapy)	Insight-oriented psychotherapy using methods such as dream analysis, free association and transference
Aims of treatment	To alleviate/eliminate symptoms and/or rectify the underlying cause of the disorder	To get rid of maladaptive responses and to learn new, adaptive ones	To challenge irrational patterns of thinking and dysfunctional thought processes so that the individual can regain control and use cognitive processes effectively	To uncover and work through unconscious conflicts and to bring them to conscious awareness. To restore a reasonable balance between the id, ego and superego

results can be difficult to interpret because of methodological, practical and ethical issues. You can show that you have an understanding of how science works if you consider some of the following general questions concerning such research:

▓ *Does the research compare like with like?* In order to investigate the effectiveness of therapies, investigators often compare one group of people who receive the therapy against a group who do not (a control group) or against a group who are receiving another type of therapy. However, as you will see, the diagnostic criteria for many mental disorders are broad and have also changed significantly over the last 50 years. This means that people diagnosed with, for example, schizophrenia might be quite different from each other. This makes it very difficult to compare the effectiveness and/or appropriateness of treatments unless the researcher has selected the sample very carefully according to the same diagnostic criteria.

▓ *Does the investigator have an effect?* It has been shown that the effectiveness of therapies, particularly psychological therapies, can be due to a combination of factors including characteristics of the therapist. The researchers who carry out clinical trials into therapies are often highly skilled in the particular therapeutic technique and are committed to demonstrating its worth. Therefore, it is sometimes the case that treatments that seem to be very effective in clinical trials do not work as well outside the research study when they are delivered by other practitioners.

▓ *Does previous treatment have an effect?* By the time patients have been recruited for a research programme, they have often already started conventional treatments for their particular disorder. It is important for researchers to be sure that the effects of the original treatment do not confound the results of the research into the new treatment. Ideally, patients on a research programme should stop any other treatments some time before the research programme begins. However, for obvious ethical and practical reasons this often does not happen.

▓ *Are improvement effects really due to the therapy?* A related problem is that of the **placebo effect**. This refers to a fairly common phenomenon where patients recover or show improvement in their symptoms simply because they are receiving attention from a therapist and because they expect the therapy to do them some good. In other words, a successful outcome has nothing to do with the treatment itself. One way of dealing with this problem in research trials is to include a control group who do not have the treatment but who are treated exactly the same in every other respect. For example, in research into the effectiveness of a new drug, the control group would be given a tablet that looks the same as the real drug but which does not contain the active ingredients. An additional control is to carry out the study as a **double-blind** design. This means that neither the participants nor the researcher know who is taking the real drug and who is taking the placebo until the study is completed. If, then, the people who have taken the drug show significantly greater improvement than the placebo group, the researchers can be fairly confident about concluding that the drug is effective. However, if you think about psychological therapies, which depend on direct communication with the patient, it is almost impossible to have a placebo group or to conduct the study as a double-blind. Control groups for this kind of research are often told they have been allocated to a 'waiting list' group – in other words, they are effectively denied treatment during the course of the research programme. This raises obvious ethical and practical problems.

▓ Key terms

Placebo effect: a participant showing improvement purely from believing they are receiving treatment.

Double-blind: neither researcher nor participant know which condition the participant is assigned to (e.g. placebo or real drug) until study is completed.

Psychopathology

How do we measure effectiveness? It is sometimes difficult to interpret the results of research studies because it is not clear what we mean by the term 'cure'. For example, is a person with major depressive disorder 'cured' if the main symptoms are kept under control by drugs even though they return if the drugs are discontinued? Is someone with a bird phobia only 'cured' if they take up bird-watching as a hobby, or is it enough for them to show less anxiety about birds than they did before? In disorders such as schizophrenia, there are many different types of symptom and not all of these respond to the same therapy. For example, positive symptoms can be reduced by drugs whereas negative symptoms usually cannot (see page 336). It is important for researchers to define their measures of effectiveness clearly so that accurate conclusions can be drawn. Another problem for establishing effectiveness is the effect of the passage of time. Some therapies take considerably longer than others to take effect. At what point in time should the measure of effectiveness or improvement take place?

Classification and diagnosis

The dominant approach to psychopathology is the biological model. It uses the model of physical illness and applies it to psychological disorders. It makes the following assumptions:

- The individual with a mental disorder is seen as passive and is referred to as 'the patient'.
- Mental abnormality manifests itself in certain signs and symptoms.
- Signs and symptoms regularly occur together in clusters called 'syndromes'.
- Syndromes represent distinctive disorders that can be considered independently of one another.
- Explanations and remedies can be found for each of these separate disorders.

Central to these assumptions is the idea that mental disorders can be classified and diagnosed. A diagnostic system is a set of possible types of abnormality and the rules for recognising them. An ideal diagnostic system has certain characteristics:

- The categories are mutually exclusive – categories do not overlap – an entry in one category cannot simultaneously belong to another category.
- The categories are jointly exhaustive – they cover the whole range of possible categories so that nothing is left over that does not fit neatly into one of the categories.
- Features of a disorder must be either present or absent – we must be able to make either/or decisions from the category description.
- It should be reliable and valid (see below).

Advantages of classification/diagnosis

Classification and diagnosis have several benefits:

- Communication shorthand: a patient with a mental disorder often has numerous symptoms. It is much simpler to incorporate these symptoms into a single diagnosis and this makes communication between mental health professionals much easier.
- Aetiology: there is no obvious single cause for most mental disorders, but certain disorders are more reliably associated with particular causes or aetiologies. Knowing the diagnosis can aid research in investigating the underlying cause.

- Treatment: treatments are often specific to certain disorders. Symptoms of schizophrenia, for example, respond well to certain anti-psychotic drugs but not to anti-anxiety drugs. A reliable diagnosis can point to a therapy that will alleviate symptoms.

- Prognosis: an accurate diagnosis can provide valuable information about the likely course of a disorder. This information can be very helpful in planning the treatment and management of mental disorders.

Disadvantages of classification/diagnosis

- Misdiagnosis: one of the most obvious problems associated with diagnosis is when it goes wrong and individuals are given inappropriate therapy or even, in extreme cases, wrongly institutionalised.

- Assumption of separate categories: any diagnostic systems assume that there is a discontinuity between 'normal' and 'abnormal' states. In other words, you either have the disorder or you do not – there are no grey areas. While this is often the case, there are also many people who are somewhat depressed or slightly anxious.

- Labelling: diagnosis leads to labelling. While this can be helpful in terms of providing the appropriate treatment, it can be stigmatising and can lead to a self-fulfilling prophecy.

- Historical and cultural context: disorders included in the diagnostic manuals sometimes reflect social/political attitudes at the time. For example, homosexuality was included in the early manuals as an example of a mental disorder. The implication of culture and its relation to diagnosis is acknowledged in the *DSM-IV* as follows: 'A clinician who is unfamiliar with the nuances of an individual's cultural frame of reference may incorrectly judge as psychopathology those normal variations in behaviour, belief, or experience that are particular to the individual's culture.'

Reliability and validity

A classification system can only be useful if those applying it are in agreement about a particular diagnosis. In physical medicine, a diagnosis can usually be verified by some sort of laboratory test (e.g. blood and urine tests, X-rays). For abnormal behaviour, there is no objective test and the only means of assessing reliablility is to see whether diagnosticians agree with one another. There were huge problems of reliability associated with early diagnostic manuals. These have been addressed by later versions but still not completely overcome. Low reliability can undermine validity. Descriptive validity refers to the ability of diagnostic systems to describe syndromes accurately and differentiate between categories. Predictive validity refers to the ability of the systems to predict the course of the disorder and the outcome of any treatment. It seems that both descriptive and predictive validity are high for certain disorders but not for others.

The classification systems

There are two widely used systems in psychiatry for defining and classifying mental disorders. The *International Classification System for Diseases (ICD)* was developed by the World Health Organization (WHO), and the *Diagnostic and Statistical Manual of Mental Disorders (DSM)* was developed by the American Psychiatric Association (APA). Both systems categorise disorders on the basis of signs and symptoms and do not contain causal explanations. The manuals are frequently revised to reflect changing views in psychiatric practice.

Take it further

You might like to find out about a study by Rosenhan (1973) where healthy volunteers were diagnosed with schizophrenia on the basis of a single symptom. Once admitted to mental hospitals, 'normal' behaviour such as writing notes was interpreted by staff as further evidence of their disorder. Note that there were flaws in this study and it was conducted more than 30 years ago when diagnostic practice was very different.

Link

Approaches, issues and debates

The study of classification and diagnosis is an example of *socially sensitive research*. Diagnosing people and labelling them with a psychopathology such as schizophrenia can have drastic effects on their lives, as other people are often suspicious of such labels. It is also an area that can be criticised as *culturally biased*. We usually assume that systems such as *DSM* and *ICD*, developed in the West, apply across all cultures. In fact, research shows that there can be significant cultural influences on psychopathology (see page 323).

Psychopathology

ICD

The main function of the *ICD* is to facilitate the collection of general health statistics. Mental disorders were first included on the list in 1952 and form only one small section of the manual. The *ICD* has been revised a number of times and is currently in its tenth edition (*ICD-10*); version *ICD-11* is planned for 2011. The APA and WHO are working together to bring the relevant sections of *DSM* and *ICD* into line with one another so there is greater consistency. It identifies 11 general categories of mental disorder.

DSM

The first two versions (1952 and 1968) reflected the dominance of the psychodynamic approach in contemporary psychiatry. In response to a need to make the *DSM* more consistent with the *ICD*, to improve the reliability and to facilitate research, *DSM-III* was published in 1980. *DSM-IV* was published in 1994 and this was further revised in 2000 as *DSM-IV-TR*. The *DSM-V* is tentatively scheduled for publication in 2011.

The *DSM* is used by mental-health professionals mainly to make diagnoses and it is also used for research purposes. Studies investigating specific disorders often recruit patients whose symptoms match the criteria listed in the *DSM* for that disease. The current *DSM* is a categorical classification system. The categories consist of groups of symptoms, and a patient with a close approximation to the prototype is said to have that disorder. For nearly half of the disorders, symptoms must be sufficient to cause 'clinically significant distress or impairment in social, occupational, or other important areas of functioning'. In contrast, *ICD-10* criteria do not include the social consequences of the disorder.

One important difference between the *DSM* and *ICD* is that the *DSM-IV-TR* organises each psychiatric diagnosis into five levels (axes) relating to different aspects of disorder or disability:

- Axis I: clinical disorders, including major mental disorders, as well as developmental and learning disorders (these include depression, anxiety disorders and schizophrenia).
- Axis II: underlying pervasive or personality conditions, as well as mental retardation (e.g. antisocial personality disorder and problems of intellectual development).
- Axis III: Acute medical conditions and physical disorders. (This includes medical problems that could lead to or exacerbate mental disorders, e.g. brain injuries.)
- Axis IV: psychosocial and environmental factors contributing to the disorder.
- Axis V: Global Assessment of Functioning or Children's Global Assessment Scale for children under the age of 18 (on a scale from 100 to 0). This scale is used to rate the ability to function socially, psychologically and at work. A score above 90 indicates superior functioning, while a score below 30 indicates serious impairment.

The clinician is required to make a thorough examination of the individual and to consider his/her symptoms and behaviour in the light of all five axes. This is an attempt to improve the accuracy and reliability of diagnosis.

Early versions of the manuals were not very reliable. Reliability in this context means the likelihood of different clinicians using the same system to arrive at the same diagnosis for a particular patient. There were several reasons for the low reliability. One problem was that key terms were not clearly defined and another was that clinicians used different techniques when interviewing and assessing patients. These two problems have since been addressed and more detailed, operational definitions have been included in later versions of the manuals. Most psychiatrists now also use standardised interview schedules when assessing patients and taking their clinical history, for example the Present State Examination (PSE), developed by Wing *et al.* (1974). Wing and colleagues have also developed computer programs such as CATEGO which generate a diagnosis based on a rating of the symptoms. This eliminates any personal bias on the part of the clinician.

Cultural issues

The widespread international acceptance of the *ICD* and *DSM* has meant that other diagnostic systems are no longer in frequent use. However, it is worth mentioning that psychiatrists in countries such as Pakistan, India and China think that the classifications developed in the West place too much emphasis on the separation of mind and body. The Chinese classification of mental disorders, second edition (*CCMD-2-R*), although largely based on *ICD-10*, excludes certain categories and includes a category called neurasthenia. This is defined as a 'weakness of the nerves' and is one of the most frequent diagnoses made in China and in other far-eastern countries. It is listed in *ICD-10*, but only because this is an international classification system. In the *DSM*, the term has been dropped, but it is listed in an appendix of culture-bound syndromes. It is worth noting here because the diagnosis is sometimes made in far-eastern countries as a 'cover' for the more serious disorders of schizophrenia and depression as a way of avoiding the stigma associated with those disorders. However, it does have implications for treatment.

Key points

- Psychology is a broad-ranging discipline that encompasses many different theoretical perspectives (or paradigms). In the field of psychopathology, several different models are used to explain the origins of mental disorders and to suggest methods of treatment. These models can be split into two major categories: biological and psychological.

- While all of the models offer explanations for mental disorder and suggest treatment methods, some of these are more appropriate to certain disorders than others.

- Therapies have been suggested by all of the models. It is important to make sure that the most appropriate and effective therapy is chosen for each individual patient. The effectiveness of therapy is assessed by research studies. It is important to be aware of some of the methodological and ethical issues that surround such research because these issues can affect the accuracy of conclusions.

- Classification systems have been developed to make the process of research and diagnosis simpler. The major systems in use across the world today are DSM-IV-TR and ICD-10. They have been revised many times and are now very similar to each other.

- There are several issues surrounding the classification and diagnosis of mental disorders which need to be considered. One major issue concerns the reliability and validity of diagnostic categories.

Link

Approaches, issues and debates

The research evidence for cultural differences in the classification and diagnosis of psychopathology means that *cultural bias* can be used as an effective evaluation of our current *ICD* and *DSM* systems.

Psychopathology

Summary questions

1 What are the major theoretical perspectives in psychopathology?

2 What is meant by the 'placebo effect' and how does it affect research studies into the effectiveness of therapies?

3 Give a brief outline of *DSM-IV-TR* and *ICD-10*.

4 One criticism of classification and diagnostic systems is that they lead to stigmatisation. Why do you think that there might be greater stigma attached to diagnoses such as schizophrenia and depression in Eastern as opposed to Western countries?

Classification and explanations of schizophrenia

Learning objectives:

- describe the clinical characteristics of schizophrenia
- understand issues surrounding the classification and diagnosis of schizophrenia
- describe and evaluate psychological explanations of schizophrenia.

Key terms

Psychotic disorders: a traditional way to classify mental disorders was to designate them as either neurotic or psychotic. Although *DSM-IV-TR* and *ICD-10* no longer use these terms, they are frequently used by clinicians and researchers in the field of abnormal psychology. In psychosis, the individual loses touch with reality.

Neologisms: literally 'new words'. Refers to spoken nonsense words which can be the result of brain damage or other conditions.

Catatonic behaviour: debilitating physical effects of (usually) a psychological condition such as schizophrenia. A marked motor abnormality, usually rigidity of limbs but can be other negative effects.

Clinical characteristics

Schizophrenia is a disorder characterised by distorted thinking, impaired emotional responses, poor interpersonal skills and a distortion of reality. The term 'schizophrenia' comes from the Greek words for split mind. Bleuler, who first coined the term, wanted to convey the fragmented nature of thinking that occurs in people with schizophrenia. The disorder has nothing to do with the quite distinct diagnosis of multiple personality disorder (split personality).

It is the most common and best known of the **psychotic disorders**. In most countries around the world, the prevalence of schizophrenia is about 1 per cent in the population aged over 18.

The diagnostic criteria for schizophrenia are very similar in the *ICD* and *DSM*. The major difference is that the *DSM* specifies that signs of disturbance must be present for at least six months, while the *ICD* requires that important symptoms are present for only one month.

Diagnostic criteria for schizophrenia

This is the definition:

At least one symptom listed under (1) or at least two under (2). Symptoms should be present for most of the time lasting for at least one month at some time during most days.

(1) (a) Thought echo, insertion, withdrawal or broadcast
    (b) Delusions of control, influence or passivity; delusional perceptions
    (c) Hallucinatory voices: running commentary, discussion of patients, or coming from another part of the body
    (d) Persistent delusions that are culturally inappropriate or impossible

(2) (a) Persistent hallucinations in any modality accompanied by half-formed delusions or overvalued ideas
    (b) **Neologisms**, breaks in the train of thought, resulting in incoherence or irrelevant speech
    (c) **Catatonic behaviour**
    (d) Negative symptoms – apathy, paucity of speech, blunting or incongruity of emotional response

Exclusion clauses:

- If patient also meets criteria for manic episode or depressive episode, the criteria listed above must be met before the mood disturbance developed.
- The disorder is not attributable to organic brain disease or alcohol/drug-related intoxication, dependence or withdrawal.

Adapted from ICD-10

Some researchers, notably Crow (1980) in the UK, have found it useful to distinguish between so-called positive and negative symptoms. Positive symptoms are those which are an addition to the individual's behaviour (e.g. hallucinations, delusions, disorganised speech). Negative symptoms involve losses of emotion, interests, pleasure, etc. They are associated with social withdrawal, apathy and indifference to personal welfare and hygiene.

Course of the disorder

The disorder generally develops in early adult life and although men and women are pretty equally affected, peak age of onset in women is 5–10 years later than in men. This appears to be a genuine difference and has not yet been adequately explained. Childhood schizophrenia is occasionally diagnosed but it is rare.

It is an episodic illness in which periods of psychotic disturbance are usually interspersed with more normal periods of functioning. The emergence of psychotic symptoms usually occurs after a prodromal period of a few weeks or months in which changes in mood and behaviour are evident to people close to the sufferer but specific symptoms have not yet appeared. During this period, individuals often suffer from low mood and anxiety and experience difficulties in social relationships and in concentrating on work or study. The active phase of the disorder follows and a psychotic episode may last from one to six months but can extend to a year. Inter-episode functioning varies greatly between individuals – better inter-episode functioning is associated with better prognosis.

There is a lack of general agreement about the outcome for people diagnosed with schizophrenia. Early clinicians like Kraepelin believed that recovery from schizophrenia was impossible. However, more recent, well-designed longitudinal studies have shown that approximately two-thirds of people diagnosed with schizophrenia will make a substantial recovery (for a review see Johnstone, 1991). Outcome is affected by a number of biological, psychological and social factors. Depression quite frequently occurs co-morbidly with schizophrenia and, sadly, between 10 and 15 per cent of people diagnosed with schizophrenia commit suicide (Birchwood and Iqbal, 1998).

▓ Issues surrounding classification and diagnosis

▓ The diagnosis of schizophrenia has been very widely used in the past, and prior to the 1970s there was a significant difference in the prevalence rates of schizophrenia in different countries. In America, particularly, the diagnosis was used liberally in comparison to other countries because their classification systems used broader definitions. In the US 20 per cent of patients were diagnosed with schizophrenia in the 1930s but this rose to 80 per cent in the 1950s. At the Maudsley Hospital in London, the diagnosis rate of 20 per cent remained constant throughout this same period (Cooper *et al.*, 1972). In order to eliminate these diagnostic differences, attempts were made to bring the various classifications systems more into line with one another, and the two major classification systems (the *ICD* and *DSM*) are now very similar.

▓ However, there are several other diagnostic tools in addition to the *DSM* and *ICD* that have been developed specifically to help clinicians diagnose schizophrenia (e.g. Schneider Criteria, Research Diagnostic Criteria, St. Louis Criteria, etc.) and which are still used by clinicians. The use of such criteria can actually improve the reliability of diagnosis. For example, Farmer *et al.* (1988) found high levels of reliability using the standard interviewing technique known as PSE (Present State Examination). Reliability in this sense means that different clinicians using the same criteria arrive at the same diagnosis. However, the fact that different criteria have been used to diagnose schizophrenia makes it difficult to research studies. In studies of treatment outcomes, for example, it is difficult to compare data based on individuals who have been diagnosed with schizophrenia using different criteria.

- It is confusing to have several alternative sets of diagnostic criteria for schizophrenia for the reasons explained above. The fact that it is so difficult for clinicians to agree precisely what they mean by the diagnosis of schizophrenia emphasises the point that all definitions are fairly arbitrary and liable to be modified or superseded.

- Szasz (1979) has questioned the whole concept of mental illness and has suggested that the process of diagnosis is just a form of politically sanctioned social control.

- Other critics of diagnosis have suggested that it is stigmatising to attach a 'label' of schizophrenia to an individual. Scheff (1966) believed that people labelled with a diagnosis will conform to the label and it therefore becomes a self-fulfilling prophecy. While this is clearly an inadequate explanation for a serious disorder like schizophrenia, it is nonetheless true that mental illness labels stick, and they can be used to describe the person rather than the disorder.

- More recently, Boyle (1990) and Bentall (1988), while accepting the general idea of mental illness, have suggested that the concept of schizophrenia is neither reliable nor valid and so the diagnosis is not clinically or scientifically useful.

- In clinical practice, it is often difficult to define the boundaries between schizophrenia and other disorders, e.g. mood disorders, personality disorders and development disorders such as autism. It is sometimes possible to use additional tests to make the distinction. For example, drug-induced psychosis can be differentiated by carrying out extended observations and toxicology tests. However, particularly in the case of mood disorders, it is more difficult. Depression is frequently co-morbid with schizophrenia.

- The *ICD* and *DSM* have tried to address the problem of symptom overlap by proposing mixed disorder categories such as schizo-affective disorder or post-psychotic depression, but the validity of such categories has been questioned.

- There is a marked variability among people with schizophrenia in terms of symptoms, course, treatment response and possible causal factors. This has led people to suggest that schizophrenia is not a single disorder and various sub-types have been suggested (see Table 1). However, the validity of these sub-types has been questioned. Many people diagnosed with undifferentiated schizophrenia are later recategorised when other symptoms develop. In practice, most British psychiatrists prefer to use the overarching diagnosis of schizophrenia and only use the sub-categories in the minority of cases where there is very close correspondence to the criteria.

- A valid classification system should be able to predict outcome and response to treatment. However, it has proved very difficult to predict either of these with accuracy and there are wide individual variations.

- There is now evidence that early diagnosis and prompt assignment to treatment is associated with a better long-term outcome for people with schizophrenia (Jackson and Birchwood, 1996). This demonstrates how important it is to get the diagnosis right.

Hint

How science works

Sciences such as chemistry and biology have complex classification systems, e.g. for different types of compounds or for different types of animal or plants. Classification systems in psychopathology are similar in that they are trying to bring organisation to a complicated area. However, this chapter demonstrates how difficult it can be to develop a reliable classification system for human behaviour. It will sometimes be relevant for you to compare psychology as a science with biology and chemistry.

Table 1 *Sub-types of schizophrenia*

Sub-type	Characteristics
Paranoid	Characterised by delusions (particularly of persecution) and hallucinations – symptoms such as disorganised speech and flat **affect** are usually absent
Catatonic	Characterised by unusual motor activity – either marked agitation or complete immobility, often accompanied by extreme negativism and peculiar posturing. This disorder is very rare
Hebephrenic (ICD) or disorganised (DSM)	Often begins at an early age – characterised by incoherent and disorganised speech, flat and/or inappropriate affect and bizarre behaviour. Hallucinations and delusions, but not as structured as in paranoid schizophrenia
Undifferentiated	Diagnosed when an individual is clearly showing schizophrenic symptoms that do not fit neatly into one of the other categories. Sometimes it is later seen as the early signs of one of the other sub-types
Residual	At least one episode of schizophrenia experienced in the past but no longer exhibiting prominent signs of the disorder

Key terms

Affect: in a psychological context this refers to feelings and emotions.

Take it further

Why do you think that depression often occurs alongside schizophrenia?

Key points

- Schizophrenia is a serious mental disorder which affects about 1 per cent of the population.

- It is characterised by positive symptoms (which include various thought disturbances, delusions and hallucinations) and negative symptoms (which include social withdrawal, apathy and inappropriate emotional responses).

- There have been serious issues concerning the reliability and validity of the diagnosis and classification of schizophrenia. This has improved over recent years with the standardisation of the major classification systems.

- People with schizophrenia present with a wide range of symptoms and this has led clinicians to believe that there are several sub-types of the disorder. However, the validity of some of these sub-types has been questioned.

- It is important to diagnose schizophrenia correctly in order to provide the most appropriate form of treatment.

Summary questions

1. Give a brief explanation of what is meant by the term 'schizophrenia'.
2. Briefly outline the main diagnostic criteria for schizophrenia.
3. Explain three issues surrounding the classification and diagnosis of schizophrenia.

Psychopathology

Explanations of schizophrenia

Learning objectives:

■ describe and evaluate biological explanations of schizophrenia.

Key terms

Monozygotic (MZ) twins: twins born from the same fertilised egg. Also known as identical twins, they have exactly the same genetic make-up.

Dizygotic (DZ) twins: twins who develop from two separate fertilised eggs and have no more in common genetically than any other siblings – on average, having about 50 per cent of the same genes. Also known as fraternal twins.

Concordance rate: this is the extent to which twins are similar, i.e. if one twin has the disorder, it shows the likelihood of the other having the same disorder.

Link

Approaches, issues and debates

The relative influence of genetic and non-genetic factors in schizophrenia is an excellent example of the nature–nurture debate in psychology. Don't forget that if you discuss this in your answer, you do not have to say that one or other is more important. Most behaviour represents an interaction between nature and nurture.

Biological explanations of schizophrenia

Genetic hypothesis

Schizophrenia appears to run in families, and controlled genetic studies (e.g. Gottesman, 1991) have shown that the risk for a particular individual developing schizophrenia is proportional to the amount of genes they share:

■ For **monozygotic (MZ) twins** the risk is 48 per cent.

■ For children of two affected parents the risk is 46 per cent.

■ For **dizygotic (DZ) twins** or children with one affected parent the risk is 17 per cent.

■ For grandchildren the risk is 5 per cent.

■ For the general population the risk is 1 per cent.

However, it is also clear that, even when the relative is genetically identical (i.e. a monozygotic twin), the chance of developing schizophrenia is well below 100 per cent. This suggests that other factors play an important part and two main methods have been used in an attempt to disentangle genetic and environmental factors: twin studies and adoption studies.

Twin studies

The assumption underlying this research is that monozygotic twins will show a greater **concordance rate** than dizygotic twins. This is because, although both types of twin probably share the same environment, they vary in their genetic similarity. MZ twins are genetically identical to one another whereas approximately 50 per cent of the genes of dizygotic twins are the same, as in normal siblings.

A number of twin studies have been conducted and most of these have demonstrated much higher concordance rates for monozygotic twins than for dizygotic twins. For example, Gottesman (1991) reported on several studies carried out since 1966 which all show this trend. A study reported by Cardno *et al.* (2002) based on the Maudsley Twin Register which used strict diagnostic criteria, showed a concordance rate of 26.5 per cent for monozygotic twins and 0 per cent for dizygotic twins. While this provides strong evidence for a genetic component, there are problems with this kind of research:

■ Monozygotic twins are relatively rare in the population and, of these, only 1 per cent would be expected to have schizophrenia, so sample sizes in these studies are usually small.

■ Twin studies do not all use the same diagnostic criteria so comparisons cannot always be made. Different definitions produce different concordance rates (McGuffin *et al.*, 1984).

■ With advances in genetic research techniques, it is now easier to assess zygosity accurately. However, in many of the reported twin studies, different criteria were used to distinguish between dizygotic and monozygotic twins.

■ Concordance rates can also be calculated in different ways and vary widely depending on the method used.

Concordance rate appears to be related to the scientific rigour of the studies. For example, studies that have used 'blind' interviewers (i.e. people who are not aware of the diagnosis of the patients) have found lower rates of concordance than other studies. Marshall (1990) has suggested that the better controlled the study, the lower the concordance rate.

Adoption studies

It is difficult with twin studies to separate the effects of heredity from the effects of environment because twins are usually raised together. Adoption studies allow researchers to look at people who were born to schizophrenic mothers but brought up by adoptive parents with no history of the disorder. Kety (1994), for example, found high rates of schizophrenia in individuals whose biological parents had the disorder but who had been adopted by psychologically healthy parents. Tienari (1991), in the Finnish Adoption Study, identified 155 adopted children whose biological mothers had been diagnosed with schizophrenia. He compared them with a matched group of adopted children who had no family history of schizophrenia. He found that about 10 per cent of the adopted group whose mothers had schizophrenia developed schizophrenia compared to only 1 per cent of the second group. Studies such as these provide strong evidence for a genetic component in the development of schizophrenia. However, as with twin research, there are methodological problems with some of the reported adoption studies which affect the validity of the findings.

It does seem likely that there is a genetic component in schizophrenia, but that any pattern of inheritance is likely to be complex.

Biochemical factors

Genetic factors operate through brain mechanisms, and either biochemistry or neuroanatomy could provide vehicles for genetic transmission. The brain is composed of millions of neurons which make up the main anatomical structures of the brain. Neurotransmitters are the chemical messengers that transmit impulses across the synapses between neurons. Several neurotransmitters have been implicated in schizophrenia but the most promising line of research has focused on dopamine. According to the dopamine hypothesis, schizophrenia results from an excess of dopamine activity at certain synaptic sites. This could be caused either by the release of excess dopamine by presynaptic neurons, an excess of dopamine receptors or over-sensitivity of dopamine receptors. Support for the dopamine hypothesis comes from various sources:

- Phenothiazines (drugs which act by blocking dopamine at the synapse) are effective in alleviating some of the major symptoms of schizophrenia.

- Clozapine, a drug that is one of the most clinically effective treatments for schizophrenia, was once thought to be weak at blocking dopamine receptors. However, positron emission tomography (PET) scans have now shown that it occupies dopamine receptor sites to the same extent as other **neuroleptic drugs** (Farde *et al.*, 1992).

- L-dopa (a drug used to treat Parkinson's disease) acts by increasing dopamine levels. It can produce symptoms of schizophrenia in previously unaffected individuals.

- Amphetamines (stimulant drugs that act by increasing the availability of dopamine and noradrenaline in the brain) can induce symptoms of acute paranoid schizophrenia in previously unaffected individuals and increase the severity of symptoms in previously diagnosed cases of schizophrenia.

Fig. 1 *MZ twin studies have been used for investigating the genetic basis of anxiety disorders and other characteristics*

Take it further

With the development of the field of molecular genetics, there has been some progress in identifying gene markers associated with schizophrenia. You might like to research this a little further. If you are not daunted by biological jargon, a good starting point is Biology Online (www.biology-online.org) – search for 'molecular genetics of schizophrenia' and click on the link to the study of that name.

Psychopathology

Key terms

Neuroleptic drugs: a class of drugs sometimes called major tranquillisers. They are used mainly to treat patients with psychotic conditions such as schizophrenia. They include the phenothiazines.

Post-mortem examinations of people with schizophrenia have shown an increase of dopamine in parts of the brain. For example, Seeman (1987) reviewed a number of studies which found increases in dopamine receptor density between 60 and 110 per cent compared to controls.

PET scans have allowed the investigation of live brains. Wong *et al.* (1986) found a two-fold increase in the density of dopamine receptor sites in schizophrenic patients who had never been treated with drugs compared to patients who had been treated with drugs and to a control group.

Issues with the dopamine hypothesis include the following:

Phenothiazines do not work for everyone diagnosed with schizophrenia. They also tend only to alleviate the positive symptoms and not the negative symptoms. However, as noted above, there are different types of schizophrenia and these might have different underlying causes.

Similarly, L-dopa and amphetamines do not worsen symptoms in all people diagnosed with schizophrenia.

Post-mortem examinations have usually been carried out on people who have taken neuroleptic drugs for years. Therefore, it is difficult to tell whether increased dopamine levels are the result of drug therapy rather than the cause of schizophrenia.

Later PET scan studies (e.g. Farde *et al.*, 1990) have not replicated Wong's results.

It is likely that dopamine is implicated in causing schizophrenia, but this is an oversimplified explanation on its own.

Neuroanatomical factors

There is growing evidence that people with schizophrenia may have abnormalities in the structure of the brain. For example, the frontal lobes, which are known to have an important role in higher intellectual functioning and fluent expression, are smaller than in controls. Buchsbaum (1990) has used PET scans to reveal reduced cerebral blood flow in these regions. This also fits with symptoms of schizophrenia such as altered gait and posture and abnormal eye movements which are known to arise from frontal lobe dysfunction. Szesko *et al.* (1995) have shown that the asymmetry found in normal brains in the prefrontal cortex is absent in people with schizophrenia.

Ventricles are fluid-filled cavities in the brain and numerous studies have shown that these are larger in people with schizophrenia, particularly on the left side. Andreasen *et al.* (1990) conducted a very well-controlled CT scan study and found significant enlargement of the ventricles in schizophrenic patients compared to controls. Interestingly, this was only the case for men and not for women.

Abnormalities have also been found in the limbic system (e.g. Jernigan *et al.*, 1991), which has a role in the regulation of emotion, and in the corpus callosum, which connects the two hemispheres of the brain.

Although abnormalities have been found in schizophrenic brains, much of the research is difficult to interpret and there have been contradictory findings. It can also be difficult to disentangle cause and effect because many of the individuals who are investigated in this type of research have suffered symptoms of schizophrenia for years and have been taking long-term medication. One of the major problems is that these abnormalities are not found in all people with schizophrenia. This has led researchers such as Crow (1985) to suggest two different types of schizophrenia with different underlying pathology:

Link

For more information on positive and negative symptoms, see page 325.

▓ Type 1 schizophrenia: a genetically inherited disorder associated with dopamine dysfunction and characterised by positive symptoms (e.g. hallucinations, delusions). This type has acute onset, responds well to antipsychotic medication and has good inter-episodic functioning.

▓ Type 2 schizophrenia: a neurodevelopmental disorder arising from **prenatal insults** or **perinatal insults** and characterised by negative symptoms (e.g. apathy, social withdrawal). This type develops over a period of time, is characterised by poor pre-morbid functioning and follows a chronic course. It is marked by neuropsychological deficits and does not respond well to antipsychotic drugs.

While this so-called 'two-syndrome hypothesis' accounts for many of the apparent contradictions of the available research data, it is something of an oversimplification since many diagnosed cases of schizophrenia show aspects of both types, and acute schizophrenia often develops into the more chronic form.

Summary

Research evidence seems to suggest that schizophrenia is a brain disorder, but the critical underlying structures and neuropathological processes have not yet been clearly identified. The disorder runs in families and twin/adoption studies have suggested that genetic factors are important. However, as Gottesman has shown, 63 per cent of people diagnosed with schizophrenia have no family history of the disorder at all. We have also seen that no study has demonstrated a 100 per cent concordance rate in identical twins. This means that other factors must be important. Biochemical and neuroanatomical factors also clearly play a role and they may be the means by which genetics exert their influence. Another strand of biological research has investigated possible neurodevelopmental factors in the origins of schizophrenia, e.g. prenatal and perinatal complications that give rise to brain abnormalities.

Given that no biological explanation accounts for all cases of schizophrenia or even for all aspects of the disorder within an individual, it seems likely that social and psychological factors play a part, and that is what we shall consider next.

▓ Key terms

Prenatal insults: factors that might have an effect on the baby while it is still in the womb, e.g. maternal flu virus.

Perinatal insults: problems that could occur around the time of birth such as obstetric complications.

Psychopathology

AQA Examiner's tip

In the exam, do not fall into the trap of criticising biological explanations because they fail to take into account environmental factors. Biologists accept that disorders such as schizophrenia arise through an interaction between biological and environmental factors.

▓ Psychological explanations of schizophrenia

It is clear that biological factors alone cannot account for the origin and maintenance of schizophrenia and we need to look for other contributory factors.

While all of the major psychological perspectives have provided explanations, not all of them are convincing for this particular disorder. According to one psychodynamic view, for example, schizophrenia arises from the inability to test reality (i.e. to draw logical conclusions and to distinguish between the internal and external world). Although psychoanalysts do not deny the impact of genetic vulnerability, the root of the difficulties is traced back to childhood experiences. The primary caregiver is crucial in helping the infant to overcome its anxieties, to deal with its emotions and to enable it to distinguish between the internal and external world. If the care is inadequate, the child will not develop a proper sense of self. During the transitional and sometimes turbulent period of adolescence, when threats to their fragile sense of self occur, the symptoms of schizophrenia start to emerge. However, there is little evidence to support the psychodynamic view. Similarly, the behavioural approach has failed to provide an explanation that accounts for the complexity and diversity of the schizophrenic syndrome. According to behaviourists, children learn to behave in odd, bizarre ways and repeat these behaviours because they are rewarded by attention and sympathy. This is a highly unlikely mechanism for the acquisition of the extraordinary range of behaviours characteristic of schizophrenia.

More convincing explanations are found in family and cognitive models.

Family models

Early theories were based largely on clinical observations and were not well supported by empirical research. According to the double-bind theory (Bateson, 1956) for example, a child has repeated experiences with one or more family members in which he/she receives contradictory messages. For example, a parent might say, 'You look sleepy and you need to go to bed now'. This suggests concern for the child's welfare, but the tone of voice and the body language might suggest hostility and the desire to get the child out of the way. Repeated exposure to such contradictory messages causes the child to resort to self-deception and to develop a false concept of reality and an inability to communicate effectively. Research conducted before the mid-1970s generally supported the view that schizophrenia was most commonly found in dysfunctional families. However, family interactions were only studied after the schizophrenia was diagnosed and studies rarely involved proper control groups.

More recent research and therapeutic work has centred on the concept of expressed emotion (EE). This was originally based on work by Brown (1972) which showed that patients with schizophrenia were more likely to relapse if they returned to homes characterised by high levels of expressed emotion (high EE), e.g. hostility, criticism and over-concern, than to homes characterised by low levels of expressed emotion (low EE). EE is assessed by taping an interview with a relative of someone with schizophrenia and rating the following:

- the frequency of critical comments made by the relative
- the number of statements of dislike/resentment towards to patient
- a rating of statements reflecting emotional over-involvement with, or over-protectiveness of, the patient.

Subsequent research has consistently shown that there is a strong relationship between relapse and living with a high EE relative (e.g. Tarrier *et al.*, 1988). The EE concept certainly seems to be a strong predictor of the course of the disorder.

However, the studies of EE are correlational and may reflect the consequences of living with a severely disturbed individual rather than having any causal significance. High EE patterns have also been found in the families of patients with other disorders such as depression and eating disorders (Kavanagh, 1992) so it is not a defining characteristic of families with a schizophrenic member. There have also been some concerns about the way in which EE is measured – assessment requires only one observation or interview and this might not be sufficient to give an accurate picture of family dynamics.

In spite of some of these reservations, it seems clear that the family environment has a role in the onset and, more particularly, the course of schizophrenia. Several **prospective studies** have been conducted which have found that high-risk children who go on to develop schizophrenia, in contrast to those who do not, are more likely to come from families

Key terms

Prospective studies: in the context of schizophrenia research, this refers to a study which involves a large group of children who are monitored over a period of years to see the differences between those who develop schizophrenia and those who do not.

characterised by negative relationships. For example, the Israeli **high-risk study** found that, among the high-risk group, none of those who had received 'good parenting' from a parent with schizophrenia went on to develop schizophrenia or a related disorder. It is thought that bad parenting and dysfunctional patterns of communication alone do not cause the disorder. Rather, it is believed that an underlying vulnerability in certain individuals interacts with environmental stressors to give rise to the onset of schizophrenia. (See the diathesis–stress model on page 334).

Cognitive models

Cognitive theories have focused on the impaired thought processes that characterise schizophrenia. Cognitive deficit theories explain schizophrenia in terms of attentional impairment. We are normally able to use selective attention mechanisms to filter incoming stimuli and process them to extract meaning. It is thought that these filtering and processing systems are defective in the brains of people with schizophrenia and that they become overwhelmed with sensory information that they are unable to interpret. This idea is supported by the finding that people with schizophrenia perform poorly on various information processing tasks such as reaction time, visual tracking, short-term memory, size estimation and categorisation. Cognitive theories simply describe symptoms of schizophrenia in cognitive terms rather than explaining how the symptoms originate. In order to explain the cause of these cognitive deficits, cognitive theorists assume underlying physiological abnormalities. Models that integrate neurological and cognitive explanations are called neuropsychological models. Two of the best known of these theories are those proposed by Frith (1992) and Helmsley (1993).

Frith's model

Frith has suggested that people with schizophrenia cannot distinguish between actions that are driven by external forces and those driven by internal intention. He distinguishes between conscious and preconscious processing. Conscious processing is where the highest level of cognitive functioning takes place in full subjective awareness. We have limited capacity to deal with such higher-order processes and this means that we can usually only carry out these tasks one at a time. In contrast, preconscious processes occur without awareness – they are automatic and many operations can be performed simultaneously. If the filter between the two types of processing breaks down, inconsequential information could be passed into conscious awareness. Because it is usually only important information that arrives into conscious awareness, this unimportant information is misinterpreted and seen as something significant that needs to be acted on. Frith believes that this is how delusions are experienced. He seeks to explain auditory hallucinations in a similar way. We are constantly bombarded with sounds, both verbal and non-verbal, and it is likely that preconscious mechanisms test various hypotheses before the final interpretation is passed on to conscious awareness. If the preconscious/conscious filter is defective, it is possible that erroneous early interpretations of non-speech sounds as speech seep into consciousness and are then experienced as voices. Frith believes that this faulty filter is underpinned by an irregularity of the neuronal pathways connecting the hippocampus to the pre-frontal cortex which is linked to faulty regulation of dopamine in this part of the brain. Frith has provided some evidence for his hypothesis by demonstrating changes in cerebral blood flow in the brains of people with schizophrenia

Key terms

High-risk study: the prevalence of schizophrenia in the general population is 1 per cent, which means that an impractically large group of children would have to be studied to find some who go on to develop schizophrenia. Instead, participants are chosen from 'high-risk' populations, i.e. children who have a parent with schizophrenia, and these are studied alongside a control group.

Take it further

Find out more about prospective, high-risk studies. One important example is the so-called Israeli high-risk study (Marcus, 1987). Also, Bebbington and Kuipers (1994) have reported a meta-analysis of prospective studies investigating the role of EE as a factor in relapse.

Psychopathology

Hint

How science works

Theories or models (terms which are roughly equivalent: see Hint, page 76) are used to describe and explain behaviour. The best theories do both, but some, such as the cognitive model of schizophrenia, simply describe the symptoms in terms of deficits in cognitive processes. It does not *explain* where these deficits come from, so it is not a complete model of the disorder.

Hint

How science works

When you are evaluating explanations, one basic assumption of scientific theory is that it should always adopt the simplest explanation possible as long as it can account for all of the known data. This is known as the principle of parsimony.

while engaged on specific cognitive tasks. However, there has not been universal support for this theory and it has been criticised for failing to take sufficient account of environmental factors.

Helmsley's model

Helmsley (1993) believes that some of the psychotic symptoms of schizophrenia arise from a disconnection between stored knowledge and current sensory input. Cognitive psychologists refer to stored knowledge as schemas. We have schemas for various events and activities, e.g. a schema for shopping in the supermarket or for filling the car with petrol. This means we know what to expect when we revisit these activities and can therefore decide, rapidly and automatically, which aspects of the scene we need to pay attention to and which we can take for granted. In people with schizophrenia, this differentiation between schemas and new situations does not occur and they do not know which stimuli to attend to and which to ignore. Internal events are misinterpreted as sensations caused by external stimuli and can result in the experience of hallucinations. Helmsley believes that this is caused by abnormalities in the hippocampus. As with Frith's model, however, there is as yet no unequivocal evidence to support Helmsley's theory.

Diathesis–stress model

Schizophrenia is a complex disorder or set of disorders and it is unlikely that a single cause will be identified. Most researchers now accept an integrative approach that acknowledges the contribution of a number of different factors to its origin. Zubin and Spring (1977) were the first to put forward the idea that stressful life events could trigger psychotic symptoms in individuals with an underlying biological predisposition to schizophrenia. Theories such as these are called diathesis–stress models. Genetic factors or adverse conditions in the womb can lead to a biological vulnerability and this can take the form of biochemical or neuroanatomical abnormalities. The biological vulnerability can lead to psychological vulnerability such as an inability to process information appropriately. These cognitive processing deficits, in turn, can lead to cognitive distortions, misattributions and hyperarousal. If the individual is exposed to stressful life events, a family environment which is high EE or an environment which is over-stimulating, these cognitive difficulties can become exacerbated and go on to produce some of the psychotic symptoms of schizophrenia such as delusions and hallucinations. However, the individual will probably not experience psychotic episodes if he or she has good coping skills and/or lives within in a warm, supportive family with good social support.

The diathesis–stress model is helpful in drawing together biological and psychological factors. It also has implications for therapy, suggesting that treatment programmes should combine a variety of biological, behavioural and family interventions. We will look at treatments for schizophrenia in the next section.

■ **Link**

Approaches, issues and debates

The diathesis-stress model is popular in many areas of psychology and is a key part of the nature–nurture debate. If you introduce the debate into your discussion and cannot decide whether nature or nurture is more important, then an interaction between the two is often a sensible conclusion. Diathesis–stress represents such an interaction between nature (genetics) and nurture (environment).

Key points

- There appears to be a strong biological underpinning for schizophrenia. A number of twin, family and adoption studies have shown that there is likely to be a strong genetic component. However, genetics alone cannot explain the origins of the disorder.

- Biochemical factors seem to make an important contribution. According to the dopamine hypothesis, schizophrenia results from an excess of dopamine activity at certain synaptic sites. This idea is supported by a body of research evidence, but it is unlikely that dopamine dysfunction on its own is sufficient explanation.

- New techniques such as PET and MRI scans have made it possible to look at living brains, and some neuroanatomical damage has been found in people with schizophrenia. It is not entirely clear whether this damage is the result of the disorder or whether it contributes to its cause.

- Given that no single biological explanation can account for schizophrenia, it seems likely that there is an interaction of biological and psychological/ environmental factors.

- Family models have looked at the dynamics of family relationships. The most promising approach is one that has identified the role of high expressed emotion (EE) as a factor in maintaining schizophrenia.

- Cognitive models have focused on the impaired thought processes which are characteristic of schizophrenia.

- The diathesis–stress model draws together biological and psychosocial explanations. This suggests that an underlying vulnerability to develop schizophrenia is only activated if the individual is exposed to certain psychological/environmental triggers.

Summary questions

4 How do researchers investigate genetic factors in the origins of schizophrenia?

5 Briefly outline the dopamine hypothesis.

6 Why do you think the psychoanalytic and the behavioural approaches offer inadequate explanations for schizophrenia?

7 Explain how EE in a family can affect the course of schizophrenia in a family member.

8 100 per cent concordance for schizophrenia has never been demonstrated in MZ twins. Use the diathesis–stress model to explain why this is the case.

Therapies for schizophrenia

Learning objectives:

- describe and evaluate biological therapies for schizophrenia

- describe and evaluate psychological therapies for schizophrenia.

Link

For more information about the use of ECT to treat depression, see pages 356–7.

AQA Examiner's tip

Do not dismiss psychosurgery and ECT as barbaric. Modern, sophisticated techniques have made both procedures considerably less drastic and they are now used only sparingly. The key evaluative point is that these treatments are not appropriate or effective for people suffering from schizophrenia.

Biological therapies

Until the 1950s, the treatment of schizophrenia was fairly primitive. Severely disturbed individuals were institutionalised in grim, unstimulating and often overcrowded environments. They were frequently restrained using straitjackets and, in some cases, subjected to a surgical procedure called the prefrontal lobotomy, in which the frontal lobes were disconnected from the rest of the brain. Moniz (1936), the originator of this technique, claimed a high success rate and thousands of operations were carried out in Europe and the USA over the next 20 years. There is no evidence that such treatment alleviated symptoms of schizophrenia and in many cases it produced severe cognitive and emotional impairment. In the same period, electro-convulsive therapy (ECT) was also used extensively, but this too has proved to be ineffective and has been abandoned in the treatment of schizophrenia (although it is still considered an effective treatment for profoundly depressed people).

Drug therapy (chemotherapy)

The introduction of drugs called antipsychotic drugs (also referred to as neuroleptics) has revolutionised the treatment of schizophrenia. Chlorpromazine, a derivative of phenothiazine, was found to tranquillise surgical patients without sedating them. This finding led French psychiatrists, Delay and Deniker in 1952 to discover that this drug had a therapeutic effect on schizophrenic patients and alleviated psychotic symptoms of hallucinations and delusions. Fifty years later the phenothiazines are still widely regarded as the most effective treatment for schizophrenia. The drugs appear to work by binding to dopamine receptors in the brain and thus preventing dopamine itself from binding to the receptors. By blocking dopamine, the positive symptoms of schizophrenia seem to be contained and there is marked cognitive and behavioural improvement as well.

Numerous studies have shown that the neuroleptics are effective in controlling positive symptoms and have allowed people with schizophrenia to live outside institutional care (Julien, 2005). Continued use of the drugs at a low dosage has also been helpful in preventing relapse. Hailed as 'wonder drugs' in the 1950s, the neuroleptics have unfortunately not entirely lived up to this early promise for various reasons.

Commentary

- The most widely used drugs do not seem effective against the negative symptoms (e.g. apathy, social withdrawal, impaired personal hygiene).

- They usually reduce the symptoms of schizophrenia within six months, but symptoms often return if medication is then stopped (Rzewuska, 2002).

- They are not effective for everyone diagnosed with schizophrenia. About 30 per cent of patients either do not respond to antipsychotic drugs or are intolerant to them. Clozapine (see point below) can sometimes be effective with these treatment-resistant patients, but only about half of such patients respond favourably (Wahlbeck *et al.*, 1999). This means that a minority of people with chronic schizophrenia cannot be helped with antipsychotic medication.

- They produce some distressing and sometimes irreversible side effects. Relatively minor side effects include drowsiness, visual disturbance, dryness of the mouth, changes in weight and depression. More seriously, they can induce a disorder called tardive dyskinesia which is irreversible and involves uncontrollable lip and tongue movements and facial tics. Approximately 24 per cent of people develop this after taking neuroleptics for seven years.

- Adverse effects sometimes cause patients to stop taking their medication. This leads to the so-called 'revolving door phenomenon' whereby patients relapse and have to return to hospital. To combat this, patients are sometimes given injections (depots) of long-lasting neuroleptics which takes away their option to 'stop taking the tablets'. However, this can be criticised for removing control from the individual.

- A new range of atypical neuroleptics has been introduced which avoid some of the problems of the older drugs. Clozapine, for example, appears to be effective in controlling positive symptoms particularly in those who have proved resistant to other neuroleptics (Meltzer, 1999) and does not give rise to the side effects mentioned above. However, it can produce a condition in which the immune system is damaged. This can be counteracted by the use of other drugs and by regular blood monitoring. However, this makes the treatment expensive and time-consuming.

- Regulation and monitoring of antipsychotic drugs is very important. It has been found that doses of antipsychotic medication are sometimes too high because they have not been reduced to a maintenance level after the acute stage is over. This exposes patients unnecessarily to risks of side effects. However, it is sometimes difficult for clinicians to gauge the appropriate dosage. Some patients do not require maintenance medication after the acute stage, while others quickly relapse without it.

Psychological therapies

It is clear that biological therapies alone cannot cure schizophrenia and many clinicians would agree that the most beneficial treatment combines antipsychotic medication with a psychological intervention. Patients who have been treated with biological therapy in hospitals are often discharged from this protective environment into stressful home and social situations. They then find that medication is not sufficient to help them function in their natural environment and a relapse becomes inevitable. Psychological interventions appear to be a useful supplement to stop this pattern of re-hospitalisation. It is important to understand that most individuals assigned to psychological interventions are also simultaneously taking neuroleptic drugs. We will now consider some of the available psychological treatments.

Psychodynamic therapy

Many psychoanalysts (including Freud) have agreed that it is impossible to establish an appropriate therapeutic relationship with psychotic patients, and the nature of some of their symptoms (e.g. disordered language or communication) makes them less susceptible to psychoanalytic techniques. Psychoanalysts such as Fromm-Reichmann (1948) and

Hint

How science works

In science, a theory leads to predictions. For instance, the theory that schizophrenia is related to raised levels of brain dopamine leads to the prediction that drugs decreasing levels should be effective, as indeed they can be. So the effectiveness of treatments can help support a particular model, although don't forget that drugs do not work for all people with schizophrenia. For each disorder you study, think about the relative effectiveness of therapies and what this might say about the possible causes. (E)

AQA **Examiner's tip**

Remember to consider ethical issues when evaluating therapies. Should patients have the right to refuse medication that could bring about long-term, irreversible side effects?

Rosen (1947) pioneered the use of modified psychoanalytic therapy to treat schizophrenia, but there is no evidence of its effectiveness. Tarrier (1990) has even suggested that the over-stimulation provided by such therapy can promote relapse. It has been found that patients exposed to psychoanalytic therapy may need longer hospitalisation, develop worse symptoms and are more likely to refuse further treatment (Drake and Sederer, 1986).

Social interventions

Social interventions often make use of behavioural techniques. There is considerable evidence that social factors affect the course of schizophrenia. It therefore makes sense to assume that some kind of social intervention might have a therapeutic effect on people diagnosed with schizophrenia. In a classic study, Wing and Brown (1970) compared female in-patients on a range of positive and negative symptoms and behavioural ratings. They found marked differences in negative symptoms between those women from wards which were stimulating and those which were not. After social changes were introduced at the less-stimulating hospitals, significant improvements were observed in about a third of the patients. This kind of finding has been replicated in a number of studies and has influenced policy in providing hospital and day-care environments that promote self-esteem and personal control.

Milieu therapy is a similar idea used while the individual is still in institutional care or in day-care centres. It aims to include the patients in decision-making and in managing wards. Social learning programmes focus on improving self-care routines, conversational skills and job-role skills. Milieu therapy can include a token economy system where patients earn privileges by conforming to expected norms, e.g. staying out of bed during the day, refraining from bizarre behaviour. Rewards for appropriate behaviour can take the form of having visitors, going out for the weekend, seeing a particular TV programme, etc. Although this kind of approach has been criticised for being too controlling, it has been shown to be effective in helping patients to achieve independent living.

Social skills training (SST) programmes have been developed to help modify or improve the social behaviour of people diagnosed with schizophrenia. Social skills training is an active therapy that uses various behavioural techniques such as modelling, reinforcement, role-playing and practice in real-life situations to enable individuals to acquire appropriate verbal and non-verbal skills. Halford and Hayes (1992) have produced a training programme comprising a number of different modules. These include conversation skills, assertion and conflict management, medication self-management, time use, survival skills and employment skills.

Commentary

Critics of this kind of therapy suggested that the training did not generalise to real-life situations, but as the training programmes improved and developed, this criticism became less valid. Birchwood and Spencer (1999) have reviewed research into SST and found that such programmes are generally beneficial in increasing the individual's competence and assertiveness in social situations. However, it appears that some kind of active intervention needs to be maintained otherwise social skills will start to deteriorate again.

Key terms

Milieu therapy: a type of social skills training programme used to support patients in institutional care.

AQA Examiner's tip

This kind of therapy is aimed at helping people with schizophrenia to adapt to everyday functioning. It is not intended as a 'cure' for schizophrenia and you should bear this in mind when you are evaluating it for appropriateness/ effectiveness.

Cognitive-behavioural therapy (CBT)

Tarrier

Tarrier (1987), using detailed interview techniques, found that people with schizophrenia can often identify triggers or precursors to the onset of their psychotic symptoms and that they develop their own methods of coping with the distress caused by hallucinations and delusions. Cognitive strategies included the use of distraction, concentrating on a specific task and positive self-talk. Behavioural strategies involved initiation of social contact or withdrawal from social contact. They also used relaxation techniques, breathing exercises or ways of drowning out the hallucinatory voices by shouting or turning up the volume of the TV. At least 73 per cent of his sample reported that these strategies were successful in managing their symptoms. On the basis of this kind of study, a therapeutic approach called Coping Strategy Enhancement (CSE) was developed. This aims to teach individuals to develop and apply effective coping strategies which will reduce the frequency, intensity and duration of psychotic symptoms and alleviate the accompanying distress. There are two components:

- Education and rapport training: therapist and client work together to improve the effectiveness of the client's own coping strategies and develop new ones.

- Symptom targeting: a specific symptom is selected for which a particular coping strategy can be devised.

The strategy is practised within a session and the client is helped through any problems in applying it. The individual is then given homework tasks to make sure that the strategy is practised and they are asked to keep a record of how it has worked. The aim of CSE is to ensure the adoption of at least two appropriate strategies per distressing symptom.

Commentary

A controlled trial carried out on people diagnosed with schizophrenia by Tarrier et al. (1993), found a significant alleviation of positive symptoms in a CSE group as opposed to a non-treatment group held on a waiting list, and a significant improvement in the effective use of coping skills. This kind of research study is encouraging and suggests that CSE provides an effective way of helping people with the disorder to control their symptoms.

Beck and Ellis

Another form of cognitive therapy is based on the work of Beck and Ellis. According to this approach, irrational beliefs about the self and about the significance of events are directly responsible for causing distress or other negative emotions. The goal of therapy is to challenge these negative beliefs and put them to a reality test. The therapist asks for the evidence that supports a particular delusion and then encourages the client to generate alternative, more plausible explanations. This is sometimes achieved by setting up an experiment to test the validity of the belief. For example, Chadwick et al. (1996) reported a case of an individual who believed he could make things happen simply by thinking them. He was shown paused video recordings and asked to say what would happen next. In over 50 trials, he did not get a single prediction correct and was able to understand that he did not have the power to influence the events after all.

Hint

Have you noticed that the term 'patient' is used in the context of biological therapies but 'client' is used in the context of psychological therapies? Think about why these different terms are used.

AQA Examiner's tip

Evaluation does not have to be 'black' or 'white'. This kind of therapy does not offer a cure for schizophrenia and does not claim to do so. However, it does seem to offer an effective means of alleviating the distress associated with the more florid symptoms and this is very positive.

Hint

How science works

Tarrier's 1993 study was well-controlled. However, out of an initial sample of 49 people, 45 per cent refused to cooperate or dropped out during the trial. This is a frequent problem of **outcome research** in schizophrenia and is a useful point to bear in mind when you are evaluating the effectiveness of therapies. Dropping out causes the loss of valuable data. (F)

Key terms

Outcome research: research studies which compare the outcome of different therapeutic techniques.

Link

For a fuller explanation of Beck and Ellis' therapies, particularly in relation to depression, see pages 357–8.

Psychopathology

Commentary

Research studies investigating the effectiveness of this kind of therapy have shown that it can bring about significant reduction in the severity of delusional symptoms (Kuipers *et al.*, 1997).

Yet another form of cognitive behavioural treatment called Integrated Psychological Therapy (IPT) has also been found to be effective in improving attention and concept formation. IPT aims to identify the specific cognitive deficits shown in schizophrenia and to remedy them. For example, clients are taught to recognise and respond appropriately to social cues and to understand and evaluate verbal statements accurately. Studies (e.g. Brenner *et al.*, 1992) have shown that people treated with this therapy show lower hospitalisation rates and decreased scores on psychopathology than control groups. However, while it leads to modest improvements in how the individual thinks, it does not eliminate schizophrenic patterns of thinking.

Family intervention

Research on expressed emotion (EE) has shown that certain aspects of family life can affect the course of schizophrenia. This has led to the development of various family intervention programmes. Central to these programmes is the emphasis on inclusion and sharing information. Sessions aim, at the beginning, to develop a cooperative and trusting relationship with the family group and the contributions of all family members are valued. The therapist provides information about the cause, course and symptoms of schizophrenia, while family members, including the individual with schizophrenia, bring to the group their own experiences of the disorder. The goal of the sessions is to provide the whole family with practical coping skills that enable them to manage the everyday difficulties arising as a consequence of having schizophrenia in the family. Family members learn more constructive ways of interaction and communication and are encouraged to concentrate on any good things that happen rather than on the bad things. It is accepted that the family might sometimes feel angry and impatient and ways are discussed of expressing these feelings without resorting to high EE patterns of behaviour. The family and the individual with schizophrenia are also trained to recognise the early signs of relapse so that they can respond rapidly and reduce its severity.

Commentary

Several studies have been conducted in the UK and other countries to compare high EE families who are then randomly assigned either to family intervention, routine treatment or a control treatment. There has been overwhelming support for the effects of family intervention. It has been shown not only to reduce the rate of relapse significantly, but also to improve compliance with medication and to reduce ratings for EE within the family.

Summary

It is important to consider the whole picture when prescribing treatment for people with schizophrenia. In the first stages after diagnosis, drugs are usually the most important treatment option. They can reduce severe symptoms within a few months. However, it is the nature of the disorder that patients frequently have poor social skills and problems with everyday living. Psychological therapies and family intervention programmes can help people to develop the skills and the confidence to live normally in the community.

Key points

■ Various therapies are used in the treatment of schizophrenia. In most cases, the first line of treatment is to use drugs. Phenothiazines, whose antipsychotic properties were discovered in the 1950s, are still widely used today.

■ Antipsychotic medication has been shown to be very effective in reducing the positive, psychotic symptoms of schizophrenia. The typical drugs are less good at addressing the negative symptoms. Newer, atypical drugs such as clozapine seem more effective at targeting both negative and positive symptoms. However, all of the drugs can have serious side-effects and they do not help everyone with schizophrenia.

■ Psychological and psychosocial therapies are used mainly to supplement medication and are not usually effective on their own. While drugs tend to target the psychotic symptoms of schizophrenia, psychological interventions are intended to help people with schizophrenia to cope with the problems of everyday living. They often involve other family members as well because schizophrenia can have devastating effects on the whole family.

Summary questions

9 What are phenothiazines and how do they work to reduce the symptoms of schizophrenia?

10 What are the advantages and disadvantages of newer neuroleptic drugs such as clozapine?

11 People with schizophrenia do not always comply with their drug treatment. Why do you think this is the case?

12 Why are therapies based on talking inappropriate for people with schizophrenia in the early stages after diagnosis?

13 How can CBT be used to help people with schizophrenia?

14 In the absence of any effective treatment, people with schizophrenia were often heavily sedated and physically restrained in the past. In the 1950s, the phenothiazine drugs were hailed as a miracle cure. However, critics of drug therapy say that drugs are nothing more than a 'chemical straitjacket'. What do you think they mean by this and is their argument justified?

Classification and explanations of depression

Learning objectives:

- describe the clinical characteristics of depression
- understand issues surrounding the classification and diagnosis of depression.

Key terms

Mood: the sustained internal emotional state of an individual.

Affective: the external expression of the current emotional state.

Major depressive disorder: this applies to individuals who only experience depressive episodes, and it is sometimes referred to as unipolar disorder (although this is not a *DSM* term).

Bipolar I disorder: this applies to individuals who experience both depressed mood and manic episodes, including delusions and hallucinations.

Take it further

For the purposes of preparing for the exam you only need to know about unipolar depression. However, if you are interested in finding out more about bipolar disorder, you will find lots of relevant material on the internet.

Clinical characteristics

The term 'depression' is used in everyday speech to cover a range of experiences. We sometimes use the term to convey a mood state in which we feel upset over the break-up of a relationship or the loss of a job. This is a normal reaction to a distressing event and is usually temporary. Clinical depression, on the other hand, is a collection of physical, mental, emotional and behavioural experiences that are more prolonged, severe and damaging. Depression is one of several disorders generically called **mood** (or **affective**) disorders.

The two major mood disorders recognised in the *DSM-IV* are **major depressive disorder** and **bipolar I disorder**.

The disorder included in the Specification is depression. This term is usually interpreted as either major depressive disorder, dysthymic disorder or minor depressive disorder – in other words, a disorder in which the individual only experiences depressed moods. Bipolar I disorder is only diagnosed in people who have cycles of both depression and mania or hypomania. The two broad types of mood disorder are considered to have a different aetiology. They also have a different course and require different treatment.

In this chapter we shall be concentrating on unipolar disorder and, in particular, on major depressive disorder (MDD). The diagnostic criteria for MDD are very similar in the *DSM-IV* and *ICD-10*. The symptoms have to be present for at least two weeks but may often have been present for considerably longer before the patient consults a doctor.

Diagnostic criteria for major depressive disorder

This is the definition according to the *DSM-IV*:

Five (or more) of the following symptoms have been present for the same two-week period and represent a change from previous functioning; at least one of the first two symptoms (depressed mood or loss of interest or pleasure) is included in these:

- Depressed mood most of the day, nearly every day (as indicated by either subjective report or observation by others). In children and adolescents, this can be irritable mood.
- Markedly diminished interest or pleasure in all (or almost all) activities most of the day, nearly every day (as indicated by either subjective report or observation by others).
- Significant weight loss when not dieting, or weight gain (e.g. a change of more than 5 per cent of body weight in a month), or decrease or increase in appetite nearly every day. In children, consider failure to make expected weight gains.
- Insomnia (not being able to sleep) or hypersomnia (sleeping too much) nearly every day.

- Psychomotor agitation or retardation nearly every day (observable by others not merely subjective feelings of restlessness or being slowed down).

- Fatigue or loss of energy nearly every day.

- Feelings of worthlessness or excessive or inappropriate guilt (which may be delusional) nearly every day (not merely self-reproach or guilt about being sick).

- Diminished ability to think or concentrate, or indecisiveness, nearly every day (either by subjective account or as observed by others).

- Recurrent thoughts of death (not just fear of dying) recurrent suicidal ideation without a specific plan or a suicide attempt or a specific plan for committing suicide.

- In addition, the symptoms:
  - cause clinically significant distress or impairment in social, occupational, or other important areas of functioning
  - are not due to the direct physiological effects of a substance or a general medical condition
  - are not better accounted for by bereavement.

American Psychiatric Association

The *DSM-IV* includes a category of mood disorder called dysthymic disorder (dysthymia in the *ICD-10*) where fewer and, usually, milder depressive symptoms are present for over two years. As well as the symptoms of major depression, there are symptoms of pessimism, low self-esteem, low energy, irritability and decreased productivity. There is also a category of 'depressive disorder not otherwise specified', which includes:

- Premenstrual dysphoric disorder – depressive symptoms occur regularly towards the end of the menstrual cycle – symptoms are severe enough to interfere with work, school or other usual activities.

- Minor depressive disorder – episodes of at least two weeks of depressive symptoms, but with fewer than five of the items required for MDD.

- Recurrent brief depressive disorder – episodes lasting from two days to two weeks and occurring at least once a month for a year (but *not* associated with menstrual cycle).

Course of the disorder

MDD is a universal disorder and is found with similar frequency in all of the countries sampled in a review by Smith and Weissman (1992). According to this review, the rates of depression in Europe range from between 4.6 per cent to 7.4 per cent, while a US survey (Blazer *et al.*, 1994) found the rate in the US to be 4.9 per cent. If people diagnosed with dysthymic disorder are also taken into account, it is estimated that a further 2–4 per cent of the population might be affected. These figures show that depression is the most common mental disorder.

Depression used to be considered a disorder of middle or old age. However, it now seems clear that the most common age of onset is in late adolescence or early adulthood. It also seems from various research studies that depression is on the increase in young people, although it is not clear why this should be so.

One striking statistic is that depression is more common in women than men at a ratio of about 2:1. It is not entirely clear why this is the case, but various biological and psychosocial reasons have been suggested.

Take it further

Findings from surveys showing an increase in depression in young people has led some people, e.g. Martin Seligman and Oliver James, to speculate about whether we live in 'An age of melancholy'. James has claimed that depression is related to 'affluenza'. You can find out more about these ideas by going to www. guardian.co.uk/lifeandstyle/2006/jan/01/healthandwellbeing.features. What do you think might account for this trend? What psychosocial factors might be responsible according to James and Seligman?

Key terms

Relapse: when symptoms get worse during a period of incomplete or brief recovery.

Recurrence: a new episode of depressive symptoms following a period of recovery of more than two months.

Major depressions have to last at least two weeks to meet the diagnostic criteria, but beyond this minimum there is considerable variation in the length of depressive episodes. An interesting and consistent finding from various longitudinal studies (e.g. Coryell *et al.*, 1994) indicates that most major depressions disappear eventually, whether they are treated or not, and that most individuals recover within a period of 4–6 months. However, **relapse** and **recurrence** are fairly common.

Ongoing behavioural problems arising from the disorder may be fairly substantial. A long-term follow-up study carried out by the World Health Organization (Thornicroft and Sartorius, 1993) assessed functioning over a 10-year period and found that only a third of their sample showed normal functioning over that period. Research has shown three main areas where depression causes impaired functioning: work; parent/child relationships; and marital relationships. It is significant that even relatively mild depression can interfere with normal functioning. Depression is also one of the few psychological disorders that can be said to be potentially fatal. It has been estimated that approximately 10–15 per cent of individuals with a diagnosis of major depressive disorder eventually kill themselves (Clark and Fawcett, 1992). However, depression is also associated with increased mortality because of accidents or other medical problems. This could be because depressed individuals are less likely to seek treatment or because depressive symptoms make them more accident prone. It has also been suggested that depression might affect the body's immune system (Evans *et al.*, 1992).

Issues surrounding classification and diagnosis

There is a view that depression should not be 'medicalised'. The argument goes that all humans have mood levels – it is a natural phenomenon and it is wrong to classify it as an example of pathology. However, supporters of the medical model would say that mood can show extreme manifestations, like other natural biological phenomena such as the level of blood pressure or blood sugar, and can cause illness in the people who experience them. If blood sugar levels rise and we develop symptoms of diabetes or blood pressure rises to the extent that it puts us at risk of heart failure, it would be accepted as an illness which requires treatment. No one would dismiss it as a phenomenon 'within the range of normality'. It is a question of degree – we all experience sadness from time to time but a diagnosis of depression would only be made where the depressed mood causes serious impairment of functioning.

The symptoms of depression as outlined in the *DSM* criteria could be experienced by a range of people in unhappy situations or with abnormal personalities. A minimum of five symptoms from the *DSM* criteria (the *ICD-10* is very similar) are required for a diagnosis. This is a relatively undemanding requirement and, as you can see from the list of diagnostic criteria at the start of this chapter, two individuals could score their five symptoms from a completely different set of alternatives. This is a problem for the diagnosis and classification of mood disorders.

As we have seen above, there are various types of depression in the classification manuals and it can sometimes be difficult for clinicians to make the distinction. One clear distinction would seem to be between unipolar and bipolar disorder, but even this is not straightforward. Coryell *et al.* (1995) have shown that about 10 per cent of people diagnosed with major depressive disorder go on to develop bipolar episodes. Similarly, someone with dysthymic disorder can have a major depressive episode as well. This is called 'double depression' and was observed in about 25 per cent of depressed patients in a large study conducted by the National Institute of Mental Health (NIMH) (Keller *et al.*, 1983).

Some of the other diagnostic categories mentioned above are used mainly as research criteria and have not all been validated. The criteria for premenstrual dysphoric disorder, for example, are included in the appendix of the *DSM-IV* to help researchers and clinicians evaluate the validity of the diagnosis. Whether this is a genuine syndrome in its own right remains a controversial issue.

Mood has a seasonal variation within the normal population and the term 'SAD' (seasonal affective disorder) has come to be used for depressive disorder that occurs only or mainly in the winter. This is recognised in the *DSM* as 'mood disorder with seasonal pattern', but the idea that it is a valid separate syndrome has been questioned. A specific form of bright-light therapy has been developed to treat it, but this is controversial and research on effectiveness has been inconclusive. Many clinicians prefer to treat it like MDD, using conventional antidepressant therapies.

In addition to the formal diagnostic sub-types recognised in the diagnostic manuals, clinicians have also considered other distinctions. One idea is that there are *endogenous* depressions (arising from internal, biological factors) and *non-endogenous* or reactive depressions (arising from environmental stressors). There is little conclusive evidence to support this distinction in terms of the causes of depression (Hammen, 1995), but there do seem to be two fairly reliable different symptom clusters with the so-called 'melancholic' (this term is now preferred to 'endogenous') depression characterised by more severe symptoms and a greater likelihood of suicide. It might simply be that the two types exist along a continuum and that melancholic depression is simply at the most severe end. However, it does seem to have implications for therapy, with melancholic depression responding more positively to ECT and to certain antidepressant medications.

> **Link**
>
> See pages 356–7 for more information about ECT and pages 355–6 for more information about antidepressant medication for melancholic depression.

You might have noticed in the list of diagnostic criteria that notes about diagnosis in children have been included. Essential features of depression are similar in adults and children but depression can remain undetected in children. This is partly because children often have coexisting disorders involving conduct problems and disruptive behaviour so that depression is overlooked as a diagnosis. It is also partly due to the fact that certain depressive symptoms are more likely to be found in children than in adults, e.g. irritability rather than obviously depressed mood.

It can be difficult to determine whether mood disorder symptoms in a patient who has another medical condition (e.g. dementia, cancer, thyroid disorders) are secondary to the effects on the brain of the medical condition (classified as a mood disorder caused by general medical condition); secondary to the effects on the brain of drugs used to treat the medical condition (classified as a substance-induced mood disorder), or reflective of a primary mood disorder unrelated to the medical condition (e.g. MDD). It is important to make the correct diagnosis in order to select the most appropriate and effective therapy.

A related problem is that of co-morbidity. In other words, depression frequently occurs alongside other disorders such as substance abuse, alcoholism, eating disorders and schizophrenia, and it can be difficult for clinicians to decide which is the primary disorder. Anxiety so

> **Link**
>
> **Approaches, issues and debates**
>
> Classification and diagnostic systems for psychopathology have been developed in Western societies, and can be criticised for ignoring the influence of cultural factors. Note also that the greater frequency of depression diagnosed in women may represent a real gender difference; alternatively, the fact that psychiatrists may be more inclined to diagnose women with depression would represent a gender bias.

Psychopathology

frequently coexists with depression that a new category has appeared in the *DSM* of 'anxiety not otherwise specified' that is a mixture of anxiety/depression symptoms.

■ While psychiatrists are the doctors who specialise in mental disorders, the GP is usually the first point of reference for someone suffering the symptoms of depression. It is estimated that about 3 per cent of the general population in the UK are treated by their GP for depression. However, it has also been suggested that approximately half of the people who go to their GP with depressive symptoms are not recognised as having depression (Goldberg and Huxley, 1992).

■ It is also important for a clinician to take into account an individual patient's cultural background before making a diagnosis. While depression is a universal disorder and symptoms are similar around the world, there are some cultural differences, the most pronounced being between Western and non-Western cultures. One difference is that people from non-Western cultures often present with more bodily complaints than subjective distress. This could be misinterpreted if only Western-based diagnostic tools are used.

■ As noted above, depression occurs twice as frequently in women as in men. Some people have suggested that this is simply an artefact of the process of assessment and diagnosis. Men may be less likely to admit to symptoms of depression and more likely to forget previous symptoms. However, there does seem to be a genuine difference that could be accounted for by certain psychological and biological attributes of women. See page 349 for a further discussion of this.

Key points

■ Depression is a mood disorder which is found with similar frequency all over the world. It is probably the most common mental disorder.

■ Major depressive disorder (MDD) is characterised by sadness and lack of interest or pleasure in everyday activities. Individuals have to show a range of symptoms for a prolonged period in order to meet the criteria for MDD.

■ It can affect all ages, but there is evidence that it is on the increase in young people.

■ A number of issues surround the classification and diagnosis of depression. For example, there is overlap with some other disorders and it is also likely that there are different sub-types of depression, but not all of these are seen as valid. There are slight cultural and gender differences in presentation and these can get in the way of accurate diagnosis.

See page 349 for a further discussion of this.

AQA Examiner's tip

Try not to 'compartmentalise' information – it is important to see links. For example, the issues surrounding classification and diagnosis could also be used in an essay evaluating explanations (e.g. are there different explanations for different sub-types?) or in an essay on therapies (are the individuals included in the outcome research all suffering from the same symptoms?).

Summary questions

1. What is meant by the term 'unipolar disorder'?

2. Briefly outline the main clinical characteristics of major depressive disorder.

3. Why can depression be seen as a potentially fatal disorder?

4. Identify three issues that surround the classification and diagnosis of depression.

5. Depression is a very common disorder and can be quite mild. It is self-limiting in that the symptoms usually disappear even if not treated (although they tend to recur at a later point). If this is the case, why do you think that it is important to classify and diagnose depression?

Explanations of depression

Learning objectives:

- describe and evaluate biological explanations of depression
- describe and evaluate psychological explanations of depression.

Link

Approaches, issues and debates

For most disorders there is evidence from MZ/DZ twin studies for the involvement of genetic factors. However concordance rates are never 100 per cent, and often very much lower. This means that twin studies also provide evidence for *non-genetic* factors in disorders such as depression and schizophrenia. It suggests that they are a mixture of nature and nurture.

Key terms

Concordance rate: the extent to which twins are similar, i.e. if one twin has the disorder, it shows the likelihood of the other having the same disorder.

Monozygotic (MZ) twins: twins born from the same fertilised egg. Also known as identical twins, they have exactly the same genetic make-up.

Dizygotic (DZ) twins: twins who develop from two separate fertilised eggs and have no more in common genetically than any other siblings – on average, having about 50 per cent of the same genes. Also known as fraternal twins.

It is important to find the causes of depression in order to establish the most effective form of therapy. Individual cases of unipolar disorder are frequently preceded by life events or difficulties. The failure to cope with these events seems to be linked to vulnerability factors. These could be genetic or the result of adverse early experiences.

Biological explanations of depression

There are several reasons why biological factors are strongly implicated in the origins of depression:

- The symptoms of depression usually include physical changes (weight gain/loss, fatigue, sleep disturbance, etc.).
- Depression runs in families.
- Biological therapies such as the use of antidepressant drugs are helpful in alleviating symptoms of depression.
- Certain drugs used in the treatment of other medical conditions can induce symptoms of depression in non-depressed individuals. Similarly, certain head injuries and other illnesses can give rise to depression.

Genetic factors

Since it is known that depression tends to run in families, researchers have been interested in the role of genetic factors. One way of investigating this is to use twin pairs where one twin has depressive disorder, and then to determine the likelihood of the other twin having the same disorder (the **concordance rate**).

The genetic basis is strongest for bipolar disorder where almost 60 per cent of **monozygotic (MZ) twins** will develop the same bipolar disorder as their co-twin. Research has been less consistent for unipolar disorder but, using the Maudsley Hospital Twin Register, concordance rates of 46 per cent were found in MZ twins and 20 per cent in **dizygotic (DZ) twins** (McGuffin *et al.*, 1996). Both of these rates are considerably higher than for the lifetime risk of developing depression that apply to the general population. However, the concordance rates are never 100 per cent and twins usually share very similar psychosocial experiences, so genetics cannot offer a complete explanation.

There appears to be strong evidence that a predisposition to mood disorders is genetically transmitted (Andrew *et al.*, 1998), but it is not clear exactly what is genetically transmitted and by what mechanisms.

The diathesis–stress model suggests that certain individuals have a genetic predisposition which makes them more susceptible to developing depression when they are exposed to environmental stressors. Kendler *et al.* (1995) provided support for this model in their Virginia twin study. They found that women who were genetically predisposed to depression (i.e. they had a twin already diagnosed with the disorder) were far more likely to develop depressive symptoms when faced with negative life events than women who were at less risk of depression (i.e. they had a twin who did not have the disorder.)

Psychopathology

Biochemical factors

Amine hypothesis

It has been suggested that depression is caused by low activity of certain monoamine neurotransmitters – particularly noradrenaline, serotonin and, to a lesser extent, dopamine. These neurotransmitters act like chemical messengers in the nervous system and are known to be particularly active in parts of the brain associated with reward and punishment. They help to regulate the hypothalamus, which is a crucial link between the nervous system and the endocrine system and is involved in sleep, appetite, sexuality and physical movement – some of the key areas affected in depressive disorders.

Support for this idea has come from drug therapy:

▨ Antidepressant drugs such as tricyclics and **MAOIs**, which work by increasing the available amount of noradrenaline and **5HT** in the brain, were found to be effective in alleviating the symptoms of depression.

▨ Conversely, depression is an unwanted side-effect of reserpine, a drug used to treat high blood pressure, which acts by depleting levels of noradrenaline. Similarly, antidepressant drugs like Prozac, which are effective in producing relief from symptoms of depression, work by increasing the availability of serotonin (but have negligible effects on noradrenaline).

Such findings led originally to the idea that depression is simply caused by a depletion of the amines, primarily noradrenaline and serotonin, while mania is caused by an overabundance of these amines. However, it now seems that the mechanism is more complex than that. One problem for the original theory is that antidepressant drugs do not simply target these particular neurotransmitter levels – they have other effects in the brain as well. This means that we cannot be sure that it is the change in neurotransmitter levels that accounts for the effectiveness of the drug. It follows that we cannot conclude that these neurotransmitters cause the depression in the first place.

Another problem is that they exert an immediate effect on neurotransmitter levels but take several weeks to have an effect on the mood symptoms of depression. It is also the case that newer, equally effective antidepressant medications do not work by increasing neurotransmitter availability in the same way as the first generation of drugs.

These problems with the simple, basic theory have led researchers to suggest that depression arises from a much more complex interaction of neurochemical factors. Research into the amine hypothesis continues, but the precise link to depression is not yet clear. It could even be the case that the dysregulation of the amine system is the *result* of depression rather than the *cause*.

Neuroendocrine factors

You will recall from your AS studies that the hypothalamic-pituitary-adrenal (HPA) axis is important in our reaction to stress. A consistent finding when comparing depressed and non-depressed individuals shows differences in the functioning of the HPA. A stress reaction leads to the production of cortisol, a key hormone in arousal. In normal people, a homeostatic mechanism prevents excessive or prolonged arousal in response to a stressor. Cortisol levels are often found to be elevated in people with depression and levels drop again once the depressive episode is over. This might be linked to the amine hypothesis – when noradrenaline

Psychopathology

■ **Link**

For more information about tricyclics and MAOIs, see page 355.

To revise how the synapses work, look at the *AQA Psychology A AS* student book, page 140.

levels are low, the hypothalamus loses its ability to regulate cortisol levels. When noradrenaline levels rise again (i.e. when the depressive episode is over), the hypothalamus can again start to control cortisol levels. However, high levels of cortisol are not specific to depression as they are also found in people with anxiety disorders. It is not clear whether raised levels of cortisol are an effect of depression or a contributory factor.

Neuroanatomical factors

It has been observed that people who have head injuries or strokes in the frontal parts of the brain have a strong likelihood of developing depression. Post-stroke depression is associated particularly with lesions in the left frontal region (Starkstein and Robinson, 1991). The frontal lobes have an important role in planning and judgement as well as being involved in emotion and motivation. Starkstein and Robinson have suggested that stroke-induced damage to the amine pathways which connect the frontal lobes to the limbic system might be responsible for the depressive symptoms. These findings in stroke patients have led to speculation that there might be similar brain abnormalities in other depressed patients. Some evidence to support this has been found from neuro-imaging studies and from electro-physiological recording (EEG). Powell and Miklowitz reviewed some of these studies (1994) which found evidence of structural abnormalities in the frontal lobes of patients with unipolar disorder, but they cautioned against assuming that there is a direct causal connection.

The role of female hormones

We have noted that women are twice as likely as men to be diagnosed with depression. The occurrence of depressive symptoms in some women in the premenstrual phase and after giving birth (postpartum) have led to speculation that ovarian hormones might play a role. It is important to note that only about 10–15 per cent of women meet the criteria for major depressive disorder (MDD) after child birth, so this is clearly not an inevitable reaction to hormonal fluctuations. It has also been found that women who do experience postpartum depression are usually also experiencing psychosocial difficulties and have had prior episodes of depression (Gotlib *et al.*, 1991). Research into the effects of female hormones on depression has produced inconsistent findings and is beset with methodological problems. Nolen-Hoeksema (1990) reviewed a number of studies and found no convincing link between adult depression and the levels of hormones.

Psychological explanations of depression

Psychoanalytic theories

There have been several psychoanalytic theories of depression, so there is no single unitary view. Central to all of these viewpoints is the idea that unconscious forces and experiences during early childhood contribute to the development of depression in adult life. We will look first at Freud's original view set out in his 1917 essay 'Mourning and Melancholia'. Freud related the origins back to the **oral stage** of development.

Individuals whose needs are not met by parents during this stage become fixated and are inclined to be excessively dependent on other people. This dependent personality style makes them particularly vulnerable to depression. They spend much of their time and energy on seeking the love and approval of others, often at considerable personal cost. They also become angry when their needs are not met, but this anger is turned

Key terms

Oral stage: according to Freud, this is the first of several psychosexual stages through which human infants develop towards maturity. It is characterised by dependency on the caregiver. It is possible to become fixated (stuck) at any one of these stages and this has consequences for later development. Fixation can occur as the result of either over- or under-gratification.

Hint

Try to make links with other parts of the Specification when you can. Remember the views of another psychoanalyst (Bowlby) on the importance of secure attachment? He believed that insecure parent–child attachments or separations could lead to later depression. There is some evidence to support this view from studies of depressed adolescents (Hammen et al., 1995).

Hint

How science works

The scientific method emphasises theory construction leading to hypotheses that can be tested in controlled conditions. A key problem with Freud's ideas is that many of the concepts are not defined well enough ('operationalised') for clear-cut hypotheses to be formulated and tested. It does not necessarily mean that Freud's ideas are wrong, only that they cannot be rigorously tested. (A)

Hint

How science works

When you are evaluating explanations, one basic assumption of scientific theory is that it should always adopt the simplest explanation possible as long as it can account for all of the known data. This is known as the principle of parsimony.

inwards. This is an unconscious process and the individual does not recognise the emotion as anger and certainly does not connect it with anger towards the parents. If an actual loss occurs in later life, e.g. the death of a loved one, or a symbolic loss such as being made redundant from a job, the individual feels the loss more acutely than other people and may regress to the oral stage. The individual feels anger at being deserted, but turns the anger inwards because the outer expression of anger is unacceptable to the superego.

Bibring's psychodynamic theory (1965) held that depression was the result of low self-esteem brought about by harsh and critical or perfectionist parenting. This produces a wide discrepancy between the child's self as it really is and the ideal self, and the individual constantly fails to live up to his/her unrealistic ego-ideal. There is some support for the idea that low self-esteem precedes and accompanies depression and that this low self-esteem is sometimes associated with a history of harsh or critical parenting (Blatt and Zuroff, 1992).

Freud's theory was important for stressing the role of early experience in creating a vulnerability to depression and this idea is central to other psychodynamic and cognitive theories.

There is also some evidence for the idea that a set of dependent personality traits characterise people with depression. However, these traits appear to fluctuate with the level of depression so they might be an effect of the disorder rather than a causal factor.

There is also some support for the idea that the loss of a parent to death or divorce can be linked to later depression (Bifulco et al., 1987).

There have also been studies which have shown that depressed people show more anger than controls who are not experiencing depression, but this is overt anger rather than anger turned inward as predicted by psychoanalytic theory.

On the whole, the evidence for psychodynamic theories is not strong and it is difficult to disentangle the effects of having depression from the underlying causes.

Behavioural theory (learning theory)

Lewinsohn (1974) proposed that depression arises from a lack of positive reinforcement. This can be because the individual never enters into social situations or because the individual's behaviour in social situations is such that it does not elicit a rewarding response from other people. Some people who are depressed do indeed seem to lack the social skills that enable them to get along with others. It has been suggested that depressed individuals make their problem worse by alienating others and Coyne (1985) has shown that people often react with anger or annoyance at those who are depressed, and they try to break off any interaction as soon as possible. If they persevere with the interaction, they could become depressed themselves – being around people with depression can, in itself, be depressing. This might be one reason why depression occurs in families.

This model does not account for why the depression arose in the first place – it could be that depression leads to lack of social skills rather than the other way round.

Cognitive-behavioural theories

The idea of learned helplessness was embedded originally in learning theory and was formulated to explain the behaviour of animals in response to inescapable painful stimuli. Maier *et al.* (1969) found that dogs which were subjected to inescapable electric shocks, later made no attempt to escape when they were placed in situations where the shock was avoidable. They just tended to lie down in a corner and whine. In further studies, it was found that levels of the neurotransmitters noradrenaline and serotonin were reduced in the animals in which this learned helplessness had been induced. It is known that low levels of these neurochemicals are associated with depression. Later studies showed that learned helplessness could be induced in the laboratory in humans as well as animals. For example, humans subjected to inescapable noise or asked to solve impossible cognitive problems failed later to escape noise or to solve simple problems (Hiroto and Seligman, 1975). Such research led Seligman to propose that 'learned helplessness' might be an appropriate model of human depression. He saw some similarities between the characteristics of learned helplessness and the symptoms of depression, e.g. passivity, cognitive deficits, sadness, anxiety, loss of appetite and reduction in norepinephrine and serotonin. Although it was possible to induce learned helplessness in the laboratory, it soon became clear that for depression to develop, cognitive factors also had a role. Abramson *et al.* (1978) reformulated the theory to include a cognitive level of explanation. Attribution is the key concept in this reformulated theory and a maladaptive **attributional style** is considered to be a prerequisite for depression. When an individual experiences failure, he or she tries to attribute the failure to some underlying reason. Attributions can come under the following headings:

⬛ internal/external

⬛ stable/unstable

⬛ global/specific.

Individuals with a maladaptive attributional style blame negative events on internal, stable and global factors and positive events on external, unstable and specific factors. These people are thought to be more vulnerable to depression.

Table 1 is an example of how people can make different attributions for the same event. Imagine, for example, that you fail an exam.

⬛ Key terms

Attributional style: an individual's way of explaining events that happen to them and others.

Table 1 *An example of attribution*

Response	'I am not clever enough'	Response	'This was a really difficult exam that everyone found hard'
Internal	Cleverness is a personal ability	External	Someone else devised an exam paper that was too hard for the people it was aimed at
Stable	Cleverness is not likely to change much over time	Unstable	Another exam paper might be less challenging
Global	Cleverness affects pretty much everything you are expected to do	Specific	The difficulty only applies to this exam – not to other aspects of your life

There is some evidence to support the model. Therapies aimed at changing explanatory styles have been effective in alleviating symptoms of depression (see the Therapies section on pages 357–8). However, learned helplessness cannot offer a complete explanation for depression:

It does not, for example, account for suicidal thoughts or behaviour. Learned helplessness is characterised by passivity and not an active wish to die.

It cannot adequately account for the gender differences in depression as there is no evidence that suggests women are more vulnerable to learned helplessness than men.

Similarly, it does not really account for the different types of depression. The symptoms of helplessness are most like those of endogenous depression and yet endogenous depression has traditionally been thought of as a disorder stemming primarily from biological causes.

While it has been demonstrated that the explanatory style associated with learned helplessness is often found in people with depression, it might just help to maintain the disorder rather than being a causal factor.

Beck's cognitive theory

Beck (1967, 1976) believes that depression is a disorder of thought rather than of mood – the depressed individual thinks about themselves, the environment and the future in pessimistic terms. Beck originally trained as a psychoanalyst and believes that the foundations for depression are often laid in childhood. As a result of early traumas and unhappy experiences, the individual develops negative schemas or core beliefs that lead to negative automatic thoughts. These are habitual ways of thinking which arise spontaneously without deliberate choice and are constantly critical and derogatory.

When faced with stresses, such individuals tend to apply faulty logic to their interpretation of events. Beck calls these errors of logic cognitive distortions or biases.

Table 2 *Beck's cognitive biases*

Cognitive distortion	Examples
Selective abstraction	A tendency to focus on small, usually negative, aspects of a situation and ignore the wider picture, e.g. 'One person at the dinner table left a bit on his plate so I must be a terrible cook'
All or nothing thinking	A tendency to see things in black and white and ignore the middle ground, e.g. 'I am a success' or 'I am a failure'
Overgeneralisation	A tendency to make a general conclusion based on one event, e.g. 'He did not smile at me – he must hate me'
Personalisation	The attribution of the negative feelings of others to the self, e.g. 'My teacher looks angry – I must have done something to upset her'
Magnification	The tendency to exaggerate the significance of an event, e.g. 'I could not park my car in a very narrow space so I must be a terrible driver'
Minimisation	The tendency to underplay a positive event, e.g. 'I did well in that exam – it must have been a fluke'

Certain stressful situations tend to trigger memories in the individual of the circumstances which first led them to acquire negative schemas. For example, a child who was frequently criticised and corrected for making mistakes might develop a schema about being incompetent. If in later life the individual's performance at work is criticised, this schema is reactivated – he/she is reminded of past failures and now expects only failure in the future too.

Beck (1983) has modified his theory over the years and he now believes there are two types of negative schema that characterise depression:

- Sociotropy: this relates to interpersonal relationships, and individuals with this type of negative schema perceive themselves as failing at relationships. Their core belief could be something like: 'If I am not liked by everyone, I am worthless'.
- Autonomy: this relates to personal achievement, and individuals with this type of negative schema perceive themselves as failing to achieve work- or study-related goals. Their core belief could be something like: 'If I am not successful and in control, I am worthless.'

Cognitive theories of depression have been extremely influential and have stimulated huge amounts of research that have contributed to our understanding of the disorder and how to treat it. They have given rise to a range of therapies and, on the whole, these seem to have been very helpful for people with depression.

Beck's later idea that individual personality differences can predict the type of event that triggers depression could be used to explain some of the different symptom sub-types.

However, it is difficult to determine the extent to which distorted cognitive patterns cause depression. Numerous studies (see Gotlib and Hammen (1992) for a review) have shown that depressed people do indeed show more negative thinking than the controls. However, as yet there is no convincing evidence that such thinking precedes a depressive episode. It seems likely that negative thinking is a consequence of depression and that it might well serve to maintain the disorder rather than explain its origins.

Stressful life events

Major life events such as bereavement, unemployment, divorce, etc. may be precipitating factors in depression. Brown and Harris (1989), in a review of several studies, reported that about 55 per cent of depressed patients had at least one severe life event in the months before diagnosis. However, information about life events is collected retrospectively and may not be accurately recalled. It is also difficult to quantify the impact of a life event. For example, job loss could have more serious consequences for some individuals than for others. It is also hard to explain why many patients do not report life events in the run-up to their diagnosis and many other people who are affected by serious psychosocial stressors do not develop depression. The diathesis–stress model could provide the answer, i.e. life events trigger depression in individuals who already have an underlying genetic predisposition, personality type or adverse early experience.

Take it further

There is a consistent finding that depression is more common in women than in men. One suggestion is that women experience greater stress than men (e.g. Kendler *et al.*, 1993) and that they have less adequate coping mechanisms (e.g. Nolen-Hoeksema, 2002). Find out a bit more about some of these suggestions.

Key points

- There are several biological explanations for depression.

- There is some evidence of a genetic influence, although it is not yet known how this influence is exerted.

- Since a direct genetic link cannot account for all cases of depression, a diathesis–stress model has been suggested which proposes that a genetic vulnerability to depression is only activated in the face of particular psychological/social triggers.

- Possible biochemical factors include dysfunction of certain neurotransmitter systems (mainly serotonin and noradrenaline) and elevated levels of the hormone cortisol. However, it is not clear whether these irregularities are a cause or an effect of the disorder.

- Similarly, brain abnormalities have been found in some people with depression, but it is not clear whether there is a direct causal connection.

- There are also several psychological explanations for depression.

- Psychoanalytic theories focus on loss and/or poor parenting in childhood, but there is no strong supportive evidence for this. Similarly there is little support for traditional behavioural theory that attributes depression to lack of positive reinforcement. Later, cognitive-behavioural theories such as the learned helplessness model have more support.

- Cognitive-behavioural theories link depression to irrational thinking processes. There is considerable evidence that depressed people show negative thinking, but it is likely that this cognitive style maintains the disorder rather than causes it in the first place.

- Social factors may also have a role. Major life events could precipitate depressive episodes. This links to the diathesis–stress model.

- There is no single explanation for depression that accounts for all of the data. It is likely that different factors interact to bring about the disorder.

Summary questions

6 Why are biological factors strongly implicated in causing depression?

7 How can twin studies be used to investigate possible genetic factors?

8 Briefly outline the amine hypothesis.

9 What is meant by the diathesis–stress model?

10 Outline the learned helplessness model of depression.

11 With many of the explanations of depression, it can be difficult to disentangle cause and effect. Explain why this is the case.

Therapies for depression

Learning objectives:

■ describe and evaluate biological therapies for depression

■ describe and evaluate psychological therapies for depression.

AQA Examiner's tip

Bear in mind when you are evaluating therapies that depression covers a wide range of symptoms and possible underlying causal factors. Certain therapies may be effective in alleviating some symptoms but not others.

Hint

While you are reading the biological therapies section, think about the ethical issue of informed consent. Given what you now know about the symptoms of severe depression, think about how much patients genuinely understand about their treatment options.

Key terms

Monoamine-oxidase inhibitors (MAOIs): a class of antidepressant drugs that raise levels of serotonin and noradrenaline in the brain.

Tricyclic antidepressants: these raise levels of serotonin and noradrenaline in the brain.

Selective serotonin reuptake inhibitors (SSRIs): these are a newer form of antidepressant drug which act specifically to raise levels of serotonin in the brain.

Link

Look back at Chapter 25, Explanation, diagnosis and treatment, for more on the criteria for evaluating therapies.

Clinicians often take an integrative approach to treating depression. We have seen in the previous section that many factors contribute to the origins of depression and that these factors interact. It is not surprising, therefore, that effective treatment programmes often include a mixture of biological and psychological therapies.

Biological therapies

The most widely used treatment for depression is chemotherapy, i.e. the use of antidepressant drugs. Effective drug treatments for depression developed rapidly in the 1960s with the introduction of two groups of drugs:

■ **Monoamine-oxidase inhibitors (MAOIs).** They are effective in treating the symptoms of depression but they do cause unwanted side-effects that can, in extreme cases, be life-threatening. People prescribed MAOIs need to restrict their diets to exclude foods which react adversely with the drug. For these reasons, MAOIs are usually only prescribed when other medications have proved ineffective for the particular patient.

■ **Tricyclic antidepressants.** This group of drugs basically work by raising levels of serotonin and noradrenaline in the brain, although the specific effects depend on the mechanisms targeted. They have been shown to be quite effective in alleviating symptoms of depression and have fewer side-effects than MAOIs.

Later, a new class of drug was discovered, called **selective serotonin reuptake inhibitors (SSRIs)**. These drugs, which include the well-known brand Prozac, were originally thought to be free of side-effects and were prescribed extensively. However, after a few years, doubts were raised about their safety and, in particular, there were reports about Prozac being linked to suicidal behaviour. This remains unresolved although research has suggested that, in most cases where patients on Prozac have attempted suicide, there has been a prior history of suicidal thinking.

Commentary

All of these drugs have the potential to cause unwanted side-effects and clinicians need to make careful judgements about which drug is the most appropriate treatment choice. It can be difficult to predict treatment response and drugs that work with one individual may not be effective for another. There is no evidence that depressions apparently caused by psychological factors are less responsive to drugs than more biologically determined depressions. Clinicians need to consider the individual patients and their circumstances – some of the drugs cause drowsiness, for example, while others do not, and some are lethal if taken in overdose and so are not suitable for people with suicidal tendencies.

Take it further

Some interesting research has investigated the sociotropic/autonomic personality types and found that individuals who score high on measures of autonomy respond significantly better to medication than people who score high on sociotropy (Peselow *et al.*, 1992). Why do you think this might be the case?

Hint

One less obvious issue is non-compliance. Many patients either stop taking their prescribed drugs or fail to follow dosage instructions accurately. This is a factor to bear in mind when evaluating the effectiveness of drug therapy.

Hint

Just because antidepressant drugs that increase levels of serotonin and noradrenaline reduce the symptoms of depression, it is tempting to assume that depression is caused by a lack of these neurotransmitters. This is faulty logic and is known as the **treatment aetiology fallacy**. It could be that the drop in amine levels is the result of the depression.

Key terms

Treatment aetiology fallacy: an example of faulty logic in drawing conclusions about the causes of mental disorders. Just because a particular drug provides relief from symptoms does not mean that a lack of that drug is the underlying cause. Aspirin can remove the pain of a headache, but headaches are not caused by lack of aspirin in the nervous system.

Fig. 1 *Patient being prepared for electro-convulsive therapy (ECT). The treatment entails passing a current through the brain causing a convulsion in the patient. It is used to treat severe cases of depression and occasionally for schizophrenia and mania. It is not known how it works and its effectiveness as a treatment is debated*

Drug therapies, particularly the tricyclics and the MAOIs, have an almost immediate effect on levels of neurotransmitters in the brain but do not bring about any therapeutic effect for a couple of weeks. This suggests that the causal link between low levels of monoamines in the brain and depression depend on complex mechanisms.

It can be difficult to assess the effectiveness and appropriateness of antidepressants. A number of studies have reported a much higher rate of reduction of symptoms when medication is used as opposed to placebos (Thase and Kupfer, 1996). However, as noted above, depression covers a wide range of symptoms which may respond differentially to different treatments.

The drugs do not provide a complete cure from depression. There is some evidence that symptoms return when the drugs are no longer taken. Depressed individuals usually have to continue to take drugs for some time after they have shown an improvement. Studies have shown (Kessler *et al.*, 2002) that this so-called 'maintenance therapy' significantly reduces the risk of relapse. For this reason, doctors often keep patients on the antidepressant drugs indefinitely.

In any case, the notion of a 'cure' is difficult to define. When do you assess this, i.e. at what point in the course of treatment? How do you assess it – what measure do you use to ascertain whether someone has recovered or not?

It seems clear that very few, if any, depressions arise solely from biological factors in the absence of environmental stressors. Antidepressants seem to be quite effective in reducing some of the symptoms of depression, but they can have no effect on the life circumstances of the individual. For this reason, drug therapy is often combined with various psychological interventions.

Electro-convulsive therapy (ECT)

ECT was first introduced as a therapeutic technique in the 1930s. It was frequently misused and caused physical and emotional damage to many patients. However, its use today is highly controlled and it is administered under considerably safer conditions. Patients are first given sedatives and muscle relaxants. Electrodes are attached to the scalp and a small electric current is passed through the brain for a fraction of a second inducing a convulsion that lasts for approximately one minute. When the patient comes round from the anaesthetic, they will normally have no recollection of the treatment. Clinicians differ in the precise way that they administer the procedure. For example, it is not clear exactly how much current should be passed through the brain or whether the treatment is effective when electrodes are only placed on one side of the head instead of both. Similarly there is variability in the number and regularity of treatments offered within a course. A double-blind study (Lerer *et al.*, 1995) comparing the efficacy of the treatment when given twice or three times weekly found little difference in clinical outcomes, but there were fewer cognitive side-effects in the twice-weekly programme.

It is thought that ECT increases the availability of monoamines and that it reduces blood flow in the frontal temporal regions, but the precise mechanisms are unclear. It is extremely effective in cases of severe depression particularly where there are psychotic features or suicidal intent (Sackheim and Rush, 1995) so that it has become the treatment of choice for those patients.

Commentary

ECT remains a slightly controversial treatment because it is an invasive assault on the brain and no one is entirely clear how it works.

Although modern techniques have eliminated some of the more serious side-effects associated with ECT, there is some evidence that it causes short-term memory loss. However, in a review of research in this area, Devanand *et al.* (1994) found no convincing evidence that ECT causes long-term memory deficits or that it causes any structural brain damage.

There are also ethical considerations with the use of ECT. Although informed consent should be given before this treatment is carried out, it is questionable whether severely depressed people really understand the procedures or the implications of the treatment.

Other biological therapies

There are a few other biological therapies for depression including light therapy for people with SAD. These particular patients do not seem to respond well to antidepressants, but their depression has sometimes been reduced by sessions of daily exposure to a source of bright light. The precise reasons for this are not fully understood.

Some of the treatments outlined above are invasive and have to be prescribed and supervised by suitably qualified medical practitioners, thus taking control away from the patient. One method that does not have these limitations is physical exercise. Studies of depressed patients have shown that exercise can help to reduce symptoms. There is no suggestion that this constitutes a complete treatment programme or that it could be substituted for drug or psychotherapy, but it does seem that it could be a useful additional tool in the treatment of depression.

Psychological therapies

There are several psychological interventions that have been used to help people with depression. The most widely used is some form of cognitive-behavioural therapy.

Cognitive-behavioural therapy (CBT)

This therapy was developed by Beck and is based on his theory of depression. The therapy aims to identify and alter negative beliefs and expectations (cognitive element) and to alter dysfunctional behaviours that are contributing to or maintaining the depression (behavioural element). The therapy is intended to be relatively brief consisting of about 20 sessions over 16 weeks. It is an active, directive therapy which focuses on the here and now although, in the initial session, the therapist often asks for background information about the past to throw some light on current circumstances. There are several aspects to the therapy including behavioural activation, graded homework assignments, thought-catching, cognitive restructuring and problem solving.

Behavioural activation is a technique for encouraging the client to identify pleasurable activities and to overcome obstacles in carrying them out.

Graded homework assignments are given to allow the client to experiment with the activity and to engage in progressively more rewarding activities.

Thought catching is a technique that encourages the client to record their own thoughts and feelings and, with the help of the therapist,

Take it further

Another therapy based on cognitive-behavioural principles was developed by Albert Ellis and is now called rational emotive behavioural therapy (REBT). Find out a bit more about this and you could use it as an example of a psychological intervention, although it is not usually the treatment of choice for people with depression.

Link

See pages 352–3 for more on Beck's theory of depression.

Table 3 *Example of challenging negative thoughts*

Emotion-arousing events	Automatic negative thoughts	Challenges to maladaptive thinking
I had a bad day, felt fed up, and went shopping. As I walked along, I saw someone from work but he ignored me	He does not like me. I feel sad and rejected. I feel sick. I just want to go home	He looked quite preoccupied – he might have had something on his mind. He did not actually see me

to challenge these thoughts when they are unhelpful. The client keeps a written record usually divided into three columns and the therapist teaches techniques for challenging the negative thoughts, e.g. 'What is the evidence?'; 'Is there another way to interpret the situation?'; 'What is the worst thing that could happen?'

Once the therapist has addressed the 'surface' negative thought, he or she will start to challenge deeper core beliefs, e.g. 'If people ignore me or do not like me, it means that I am worthless'. Where appropriate, the therapist will also teach practical techniques such as improved conversational skills.

Commentary

There have been numerous studies that have shown that CBT is effective in reducing symptoms of depression and in preventing relapse (Kuyken *et al.*, 2007). A number of studies have also compared the effectiveness of CBT with antidepressants and other types of psychotherapy. Findings are not conclusive and studies have been beset by methodological and sampling problems. However, CBT appears to be as effective as medication in reducing symptoms of depression in the acute phase and some research (e.g. Fava *et al.*, 1994) has shown that CBT is superior to drug therapy in treating the residual symptoms, i.e. the symptoms that remain after a medication programme. CBT is often used effectively in conjunction with antidepressant medication. For example, in a large comparison study, Keller *et al.* (2000) found that recovery rates were 55 per cent using the drugs alone, 52 per cent using CBT alone, but 85 per cent when the two therapies were used in combination.

It is difficult to predict which clients will respond well to CBT. Research is inconclusive, but it appears to be suitable for both severe and milder forms of depression. Simons *et al.* (1995) found that CBT is not effective for people who have very rigid attitudes and are resistant to change, or for people who have high stress levels in response to genuinely difficult life circumstances that brief therapy cannot resolve.

The client undergoing CBT is a more active participant than is possible with biological treatments and the therapy is not physically invasive. The client is provided with techniques to help themselves. However, clients do sometimes become dependent on their therapist and the effectiveness of the therapy depends on client cooperation.

Psychoanalytic therapy

The goal of classical psychoanalysis is to allow the client to work through their intensive depressive and angry feelings and to find more realistic standards for self-evaluation. It also allows them to develop more appropriate internal working models for relationships. This is achieved through a process called transference in which self-directed hostility and criticism and ideas of abandonment and loss of autonomy are projected

Hint

How science works

In science, a theory leads to predictions. For instance, the theory that depression is related to low brain serotonin levels leads to the prediction that drugs increasing levels should be effective, as indeed they can be. So the effectiveness of treatments can help support a particular model. However, as CBT can also work with depression, this would support cognitive theories of depression. For each disorder you study, think about the relative effectiveness of therapies and what this might say about the possible causes. (E)

onto the therapist. The therapist helps the client to interpret this transference by pointing out the similarities between the patient–parent relationship and the patient–analyst relationship.

There is some evidence from controlled trials that brief psychodynamic psychotherapy is an effective treatment for people with depression (Holmes, 1999) but it is not appropriate for everyone.

Interpersonal psychotherapy (IPT) is based on the interpersonal therapy model of Harry Stack Sullivan, who, although coming from a psychodynamic background, was strongly influenced by ideas in social psychology. He believed that depression can arise from and lead to interpersonal relationship difficulties. IPT was developed in the 1970s and 1980s as an out-patient treatment for adults who were diagnosed with moderate or severe non-delusional clinical depression. It attempts to improve interpersonal functioning and so alleviate some of the symptoms of depression. IPT takes its structure from psychodynamic psychotherapy, but also from contemporary cognitive behavioural approaches in that it is time limited (approximately 12–16 weeks) and employs homework, structured interviews and other assessment tools and focuses on the here and now. The therapy consists of a number of stages:

- First stage: identification of the client's major problem areas, and creation of a treatment contract.
- Intermediate stages: working through the identified problems with the therapist. These can include grief (a delayed/distorted grief reaction to a loss), role dispute (difficulties in establishing appropriate and reciprocated expectations within a relationship), role transition (giving up an old role and taking on a new one, e.g. retiring or being made redundant from work) and interpersonal deficits (poor social skills or patterns of communication and difficulties in forming friendships).
- Termination stages: consolidation of what has been learned and looking forward to how the techniques learned in therapy can be applied in the future.

Commentary

A number of studies have demonstrated the efficacy of IPT in the treatment of depression. For example, in one of the largest clinical samples of depressed patients in the US, the National Institute of Mental Health Treatment of Depression Collaborative Research Program, Elkin *et al.* (1989) found that IPT was as effective as cognitive therapy and drug therapy in the reduction of depressive symptoms and that it produced more rapid gains in interpersonal functioning. Its use has been extended to adolescent and geriatric depressed patients and the results are promising. However, it has not been as extensively researched as cognitive therapy and it is not clear yet for which groups of depressed patients it is likely to be most effective (for a recent overview, see Joiner *et al.*, 2006).

Summary

Depression seems to respond to a number of different therapies and studies have shown that cognitive, interpersonal and biological therapies can all be effective (DeRubeis *et al.*, 2005). Most clinicians now recommend a combination of different types of therapy since this might be more effective than any individual therapy alone.

Key points

■ There are a range of therapies available for the treatment of depression.

■ Biological therapies include the use of antidepressant drugs and ECT. Both types of therapy have been shown in studies to be effective, but they do not offer a complete cure. When medication stops, relapse is quite common.

■ Psychological therapies are also available and the most widely used are CBT and IPT. There is a considerable body of evidence that has shown both of these methods to be effective.

■ Clinicians often choose to offer a combination of different therapies. There is some evidence to suggest that some form of psychotherapy alongside antidepressant drugs is the most effective form of treatment.

Summary questions

12 What are some of the problems associated with drug therapy?

13 Give a brief outline of the procedures used in ECT.

14 What is the goal of CBT and how is it achieved?

15 What is the evidence that IPT can be a useful therapy for depression?

16 It can be very difficult to assess the effectiveness of therapies. Explain some of the methodological and ethical problems that occur in treatment outcome research for depression.

28 Anxiety disorders

Information relevant to both OCD and phobias

Learning objectives:

- understand what is meant by the classification 'anxiety disorders'
- understand issues surrounding the classification and diagnosis of anxiety disorders.

AQA Examiner's tip

For the exam, you need to concentrate on one type of anxiety disorder and you can choose from phobic disorders or obsessive-compulsive disorders. However, you will also find it useful to read about anxiety disorders in general as this provides important information that can be relevant for either disorder.

Link

Our reaction to fear and anxiety is similar to the stress response that you learned about at AS. See page 138 in the *AQA Psychology A AS* student book.

Introduction

Everyone experiences anxiety at times in their life and it is a normal reaction that alerts us to impending threat. Its purpose seems to be to warn us of a potential danger and to allow us to take measures to deal with it. The threat can be external (e.g. a physical threat – a car that pulls out suddenly in front of us) or internal (e.g. an emotional threat – we are worried that we will not get the grades we need to go to university). In either case, we can carry out certain behaviours to avoid the danger (e.g. swerving to avoid the car or working hard to revise for our exams). Anxiety is a basic, fundamental emotion that is found across ages, cultures, races and species and is vital to survival. It can also be a factor in determining success on various tasks. Classic laboratory studies have shown that moderate levels of anxiety can lead to optimum performance on a task, while either too much or too little anxiety leads to impaired performance (Yerks and Dodson, 1908). However, when anxiety becomes excessive, prolonged and out of all proportion to the threat posed, it can become a destructive disorder. Like depression, anxiety exists on a scale of severity from normal, adaptive levels to levels that cause severe disruption to the ability to function normally in everyday life.

Categorisation

The *ICD-10* and *DSM-IV* differ slightly in the way that they list them, but both make distinctions between a variety of different anxiety disorders. The main anxiety disorders are as follows:

- separation anxiety
- phobias
- generalised anxiety disorder
- panic disorder
- post-traumatic stress disorder
- obsessive-compulsive disorder.

Anxiety disorders are thought to represent the single largest mental-health problem in America and in the UK. A British survey has found that 16 per cent of the population suffer from some form of pathological anxiety (Hale, 1997) and a more recent survey in America (Kessler *et al.*, 2005) found prevalence rates of 18 per cent. Given that people troubled by anxiety states are sometimes reluctant to come forward for diagnosis and treatment, the actual numbers could be higher than this.

Clinicians have tried to make a distinction between the terms 'fear' and 'anxiety'. Both refer to a complex set of reactions in response to a threat, but the crucial difference is that we are anxious when the source of danger is unclear or diffuse, and frightened in the face of specific objects or situations. In practice, it can be difficult to distinguish between them and, in emotional, physiological and behavioural terms, the two are pretty much the same (see Table 1 overleaf).

Table 1 *Common fear/anxiety components*

Emotional response	Cognitive response	Physiological response	Behavioural response
We feel a sensation of alarm, dread or panic If the fear is prolonged we also feel drained and overwhelmed	We have specific thoughts about the awful consequences which might occur. For example, if we are in a car that is being driven at speed along the motorway, we might think about the possibility of crashing, and we can envisage a scene of devastation and the noise of breaking glass and squealing of tyres	Our heart beats faster and our muscles tense. Our mouth feels dry and we sometimes feel as though we are going to faint. We often have a strong urge to urinate. These and other physiological responses are part of the body's 'fight or flight' response	There is a tendency either to freeze or to run away from what has frightened us. Similarly, we might show either aggressive or avoidance behaviour. An individual who is afraid can show all of these behaviours, often in rapid succession

Key terms

Somatoform disorders: these are distinguished by physical symptoms which cannot be fully explained by a medical condition or by substance abuse.

Neurosis: an old psychological term which refers to a state of excessive anxiety associated with self-defeating tendencies. It has come to be associated mainly with Freud, who believed that neurosis occurs when an individual tries to keep emotional problems hidden from conscious awareness.

Issues surrounding classification and diagnosis

- The disorder of anxiety appeared for the first time in the seventh revision of the *ICD* in 1957 and its categorisation was influenced by theoretical conceptions of anxiety at the time. The current *ICD-10* lists anxiety disorders under the general heading of 'anxiety states' and they are grouped with stress-related and **somatoform disorders** because of their historical association with the concept of **neurosis**.

- Anxiety disorders have probably been the class of disorders most affected by changes in the *DSM-IV*. Increasing knowledge over the last 20 years about the possible biological factors underlying anxiety has changed the concepts of these disorders by shifting the diagnostic bases from the psychodynamic formulation as neuroses to much more valid, reliable and recognisable criteria (they vary for each of the anxiety disorders and are described in the relevant sections below). They are now very similar to the categories in the *ICD-10*.

- In spite of these changes, there is still a problem for clinicians in distinguishing between normal and pathological anxiety. Normal anxiety can be an advantageous response to a potentially dangerous or threatening situation. Pathological anxiety, on the other hand, because of its intensity, duration and inappropriateness, is a maladaptive response. A clinical diagnosis of anxiety is only made if the anxiety is prolonged, it is perceived by the sufferer as being out of his or her control and it significantly impairs normal everyday functioning.

- However, even with more precise criteria, anxiety is difficult to define and the precise combination of emotions/symptoms varies from individual to individual and from situation to situation. This can make diagnosis difficult.

- Anxiety can be a symptom of many medical conditions as well as other mental disorders, especially depressive disorders. It is sometimes difficult for clinicians to decide which is the primary disorder. For example, excessive alcohol consumption can be an inappropriate coping response to anxiety states. However, it is also known that excessive drinking can make individuals more susceptible to anxiety. In schizophrenia, anxiety is a frequent result of delusional thinking – in this case, schizophrenia is clearly the primary disorder.

- The coexistence of depression and anxiety is very common – as many as two-thirds of depressed people also have prominent anxiety symptoms and it can be difficult to identify the primary disorder. Following the lead of the *ICD-10*, the *DSM-IV* now includes a mixed anxiety-depressive disorder in the appendix as an example of an 'anxiety disorder not otherwise specified'. This describes a syndrome in which the symptoms do not meet the criteria for either an anxiety disorder or a depressive disorder alone, but where the combination of symptoms causes significantly impaired functioning. One criticism of this diagnostic category is that it can discourage clinicians from taking the time to complete a thorough clinical history and assessment in order to differentiate true depressive orders from true anxiety disorders.

- Many people diagnosed with one anxiety disorder also show signs of another anxiety disorder. This raises issues about the validity of some of the categories as distinct syndromes.

- It is important to get the diagnosis correct as this has implications for therapy.

- As noted above, it is difficult to estimate the exact number of people suffering from anxiety disorders because people are often unwilling to admit to their difficulties and so do not go for help. This means that anxiety disorders probably frequently go undiagnosed.

- There is some evidence that anxiety disorders can present differently in different cultures. For example, Neal and Turner (1991) reported that anxiety disorder among urban African Americans involves suspiciousness as a key sign whereas this is not usual in European Americans. It is not entirely clear why these differences exist, but it is a factor to be taken into account when making a diagnosis. In several cultures, the presenting symptoms are physical rather than psychological. In fact, there is no word for anxiety in certain African and oriental languages and a physical term is preferred. For example in Yoruba, an African language, the phrase used is 'the heart is not at rest'.

Key points

- Whilst mild anxiety can improve performance, moderate to severe anxiety can disrupt everyday functioning.

- Anxiety disorders are very common mental-health problems.

- Anxiety disorders can be difficult to define and distinguish as symptoms vary from person to person.

- It can also be difficult to distinguish between normal and pathological anxiety.

- Anxiety disorders may present differently in different cultures.

Summary questions

1. Explain the difference between fear and anxiety.
2. Outline the four components of anxiety.
3. Discuss difficulties in distinguishing between normal and pathological anxiety.

Classification and explanation of phobic disorders

Learning objectives:

- describe the clinical characteristics of phobic disorders

- describe and evaluate biological explanations of phobic disorders

- describe and evaluate psychological explanations of phobic disorders.

Clinical characteristics

Phobic disorders are a group of disorders in which anxiety occurs only, or mainly, in clearly defined situations which are not actually dangerous. It is acceptable, and even sensible, to show a fear reaction in a threatening or startling situation. Certain mild fears such as fear of heights, darkness, rats, spiders, etc. are often quite normal within particular cultures and they do not usually lead to total avoidance or to a disruption of everyday functioning. The following are necessary in order for a clinical diagnosis of a phobia to be made:

- There must be a marked and persistent fear out of all proportion to the actual danger posed by the situation.
- There must be an immediate anxiety response or panic attack provoked by exposure to the feared stimulus.
- The sufferer must recognise that the fear is unreasonable and excessive.
- The sufferer must recognise that the reaction is beyond voluntary control.
- The sufferer avoids or endures the phobic situation with extreme anxiety or distress.
- The avoidance or anticipation interferes significantly with the person's normal routine.
- In individuals under the age of 18 years, the duration must be at least six months (according to the *DSM-IV* only).

Phobic disorders have the same basic symptoms as generalised anxiety disorders. The difference between them is that in phobic disorders the symptoms only appear in response to particular situations and circumstances. When such situations occur, the individual experiences the following symptoms:

- Anticipatory fear, irritability, poor concentration, restlessness and sensitivity to noise.
- Increases in autonomic arousal lead to a dry mouth, difficulty in swallowing, excessive wind and frequent-urgent bowel movements and urination.
- The individual often experiences difficulties breathing and feels palpitations and chest pains. Hyperventilation (over-breathing) can lead to feelings of dizziness and tingling in the hands and feet.
- Increased muscle tension leads to the experience of headaches, tremor and general aches and pains.
- In social phobia, blushing and trembling are frequently reported.
- Sleep is often disturbed and the individual frequently reports night terror.

Phobias are probably the single most common mental disorders in the UK and USA where approximately 5–10 per cent of people have some form of phobia. Given that the disorder often goes unreported, it is likely that the actual rate is even higher. Most phobias fall into the category of specific phobia, but the major classification systems differentiate between three types of phobia:

- specific phobia
- social phobia
- agoraphobia.

Specific phobia

People with a specific phobia are inappropriately anxious in the presence of a particular object or in a specific situation. The individual tries to avoid exposure to the feared stimulus or to escape from it if it is encountered. The *DSM-IV* lists some distinctive types of phobia:

- animal type (e.g. rats, spiders, snakes, dogs)
- natural environment type (e.g. heights, storms, water)
- blood-injection type (the sight of blood or injury or the prospect of having an injection cause heightened anxiety. This is slightly different from the other phobias in that it has slightly different physiological effects and it is particularly likely to affect many members and generations of a family)
- situational type (e.g. planes, lifts, enclosed places)
- other type (these are specific phobias that do not fit neatly into the other categories. The *DSM* gives some examples – fear of choking/vomiting or contracting an illness; in children, avoidance of loud noises or costumed characters).

The age of onset for most specific phobias is in childhood and, in many cases, the phobias have disappeared by adolescence. It is not entirely clear why some phobias persist into adulthood, but it seems that the most severe phobias are the ones that last the longest.

Social phobia

Social phobias occur in about 3–7 per cent of the population. They usually begin in adolescence and are almost equally frequent in males and females. The first episode usually occurs in a public place, often with no apparent triggering reason. The individual experiences inappropriate anxiety in social situations (e.g. in restaurants, seminars, board meetings, etc.). Socially phobic people try to avoid these situations, and even the thought of going into such a situation provokes anxiety. They experience many of the general anxiety symptoms (see previous page) but they also commonly report uncontrollable blushing and trembling.

Agoraphobia

People with agoraphobia are anxious when they are away from home, in crowds or in any situation which they cannot easily leave. They avoid these situations and feel very anxious when anticipating them. Most cases begin in the early or mid-twenties and the first episode typically occurs without warning in a public place (e.g. a supermarket queue, on a bus, etc.). The individual experiences extreme anxiety, feels faint and has palpitations. They rush away from the place to go home where recovery is usually rapid. The sequence of anxiety and avoidance occurs frequently over the next weeks and months and the panic attacks occur in more and more places. This leads to an increasing habit of avoidance of public places.

Take it further

You might like to look at the *ICD-10* and *DSM-IV* criteria for the various phobias. You can find them on the internet.

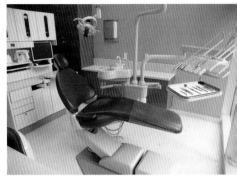

Fig. 1 *Going to the dentist can cause sufferers of the blood-injection type of phobia acute anxiety*

Psychopathology

■ Link

Look back at pages 362–3 for the issues surrounding anxiety disorders in general as these are also relevant for phobias.

■ Issues surrounding classification and diagnosis

■ Fear is a normal adaptive response. Phobias should only be diagnosed in people who meet the stringent requirements of the *DSM* or *ICD* criteria.

■ Similarly, shyness can be a normal, acceptable personality trait. The diagnostic criteria for social phobia are set at a level of severity to exclude people who are simply very shy.

■ Diagnosis of specific phobias is not usually difficult although they often co-occur with depression. People with OCD sometimes present with a specific fear and avoidance behaviour, but careful clinical assessment will reveal the associated obsessional thoughts that are absent in specific phobias. For example, someone with OCD might avoid knives because they worry that they will kill someone. However, people with a knife phobia avoid knives because they are frightened of cutting themselves.

■ There are some similarities between people with specific illness phobias and people with hypochondriasis (a disorder in which people mistakenly believe that minor changes in their physical functioning indicate that they have a serious illness). However, someone with an illness phobia fears that they might contract a particular serious disease (usually cancer or Aids) even though they recognise that their fears are irrational.

■ Social phobias can occur with agoraphobia and/or panic disorder. Both diagnoses can be made, but most clinicians prefer to identify a primary disorder because this has implications for treatment.

■ There are some similarities between social phobia and avoidant personality disorder. In theory, social phobia has a recognisable onset and a shorter duration, but in practice it can be difficult to differentiate. Many people demonstrate characteristics that meet the criteria for both diagnoses (Schneier *et al.*, 1992).

■ The *DSM-IV* and *ICD-10* are broadly similar and they both differentiate specific phobia, social phobia and agoraphobia. They differ slightly in how they deal with agoraphobia in that the *DSM*, but not the *ICD*, classifies agoraphobia in which panic attacks are prominent as 'panic disorder'. There are also slight differences in the criteria for social phobia, with the *ICD-10* placing greater emphasis on symptoms of anxiety.

■ There are some cultural differences in phobias. For example, an incapacitating fear of offending other people through one's own social awkwardness is diagnosed in Japan (*taijin kyofusho*) but not in the West. It differs from social phobia in that the fear is of doing harm to others, not of the social situation per se. This is an exaggerated form of the type of modesty and regard for other people which is a cultural norm in Japan.

■ Link

Approaches, issues and debates

This is an example of the nature–nurture debate in psychology. Biological researchers stress the importance of innate factors in determining mental disorder whereas many psychologists believe that mental disorders arise from environmental influences. Most people now adopt an interactionist view where they acknowledge the contribution of both factors. In the case of phobias, the weight of evidence seems to suggest that environmental influences are paramount.

■ Biological explanations

Genetic factors

As you will see in the section on psychological explanations below, phobias are generally thought to occur as a result of some form of learning. However, it is difficult to explain why some people develop these crippling fears while others, exposed to very similar environmental influences, do not. This has led researchers to look at possible genetic factors in the transmission of phobic disorders.

There is some evidence from twin and family studies that there is a genetic component in phobic disorders. Skre *et al.* (2000), for example, found a higher **concordance rate** for phobias in MZ than in DZ twins. In a study of about 1,200 male twin pairs, Kendler *et al.* (2001) found evidence for some genetic influence in all types of phobic disorder. Fyer *et al.* (1993) found that social phobias are considerably more common in the relatives of social phobics than in the general population. Blood and injection phobia seems to have a particularly strong familial element. The prevalence of this type of phobia in the general population is about 3 per cent. However, Ost (1992) found that 64 per cent of individuals with blood/injection phobia have a first-degree relative with the same disorder.

Even if genetics do contribute to the origins of phobic disorders, it is not clear exactly what is passed on in the genes. One suggestion is that people at high risk of developing phobias inherit a genetic over-sensitivity of the sympathetic nervous system (see the chapter on stress in the *AQA Psychology A AS* student book, page 138). Lacey (1967) identified a dimension of autonomic activity which he called stability-lability. People who are classified at the labile end of the dimension are particularly edgy or jumpy and have autonomic arousal systems which are particularly sensitive to a range of stimuli. This so-called autonomic lability is thought to be at least partly determined by genetics and may well contribute to the origins of phobic disorders.

Another suggestion is that people who develop phobic disorders have a particular kind of temperament which might have been inherited. Kagan (1997) has looked at the trait of shyness in very young children. He found that some infants as young as four months old show heightened anxiety and agitation in response to certain stimuli. He also found that children defined as behaviourally inhibited at 21 months were at greater risk of developing a phobia at the age of seven or eight years than uninhibited children (32 per cent versus 5 per cent).

Evaluative commentary

There have been relatively few family and twin studies looking specifically at phobic disorders and some of the evidence has been contradictory.

The finding that phobias run in families could be accounted for in behavioural terms through modelling (see page 371). Families not only share genes, they have considerable opportunity to observe and influence one another as well.

Even if genetics do play a role, it is not clear exactly what is passed on genetically.

GABA hypothesis

This hypothesis has been proposed specifically to account for phobic disorders and generalised anxiety (Bernstein, 1994). Anxiety is thought to develop from a dysfunction of neurons that normally produce gamma aminobutyric acid (GABA). In normal functioning, GABA is released automatically in response to a high arousal level. It binds to GABA receptors on excited neurons thereby causing them to be inhibited. This results in a reduction in arousal and, accordingly, a reduction in the experience of anxiety.

Commentary

Support for this theory comes from the finding that treatments using anti-anxiety drugs called benzodiazepines (e.g. Valium or Diazepam)

Psychopathology

Key terms

Concordance rate: the extent to which twins are similar, i.e. if one twin has the disorder, it shows the likelihood of the other having the same disorder.

work by binding to the GABA neuro-receptors and thus reducing feelings of anxiety. Benzodiazepines only seem to have a temporary therapeutic effect and symptoms come back when medication ceases.

Neuroanatomy

There is some evidence from PET scans that people with phobias have increased blood flow in the amygdala compared to controls when they experience anticipatory anxiety.

Commentary

Successful treatment with the drug Citalopram or with cognitive behaviour therapy has been shown to decrease blood flow in this region (Furmark *et al.*, 2002). However, not all people with phobias show these blood-flow abnormalities and it is, in any case, not clear whether they are a causal factor or a result of phobic disorder.

■ Psychological explanations

Psychodynamic explanations

According to Freud (1906), phobias are a defence against the anxiety experienced when unpleasant impulses have been repressed. The repressed feelings are displaced on to an object or situation with which they are symbolically associated. These objects/situations become phobic stimuli and can be avoided. In this way the individual is also able to avoid dealing with the repressed conflict. Freud believed that these repressed conflicts occurred in childhood and he reported a famous case study to illustrate his explanation.

Little Hans was a five-year-old boy who developed a fear of horses and would not go out for fear of being bitten. He also developed a more particular fear of the blinkers and muzzles associated with horses. Freud interpreted this fear in terms of the Oedipus complex in which young boys develop an intense, unconscious fear of their fathers. He proposed that Little Hans had transferred this unacceptable fear of his father to a more appropriate fear object, i.e. horses (the muzzles and blinkers were thought to be related to his father's glasses and moustache).

Commentary

There is little evidence to support Freud's theory of phobia acquisition. It is based almost entirely on case study evidence and there is no compelling independent support for the theory. In the case of Little Hans, he had actually had the frightening experience of witnessing a horse falling over in front of him on the street. This means that his fear could be explained more simply by the behavioural account (see below).

Learning theory

Early behavioural theories considered phobias to be the result of classical conditioning. Once a phobic response has been established, the individual tries to avoid the object or the situation in the future. This means that the individual never experiences the feared stimulus in safe, harmless conditions and so the original fear is never extinguished. The avoidance behaviour produces feelings of relief, in other words it is rewarding and so the behaviour is maintained (operant conditioning).

We can look at Little Hans' experience from a behavioural perspective. Hans himself reported that his fear of horses started when he saw an accident with a horse. The horse (a neutral stimulus) falls down in front

■ **Link**

The case study method is explained in the section on psychological research and scientific method, on page 517.

■ **Link**

You can read more about the Oedipus complex in the *AQA Psychology A AS* book, page 240.

■ **Hint**

How science works

When you are evaluating explanations, one basic assumption of scientific theory is that it should always adopt the simplest explanation possible as long as it can account for all of the known data. This is known as the principle of parsimony.

■ **Link**

See your *AQA Psychology A AS* student book, pages 241–2 for more information about classical conditioning.

of him thrashing about and making a lot of noise. Noise and danger constitute an unconditioned stimulus (UCS) which automatically produces an unconditioned response (UCR) – a fear reaction. The UCS (noise and danger) is associated with the horse which has now become a conditioned stimulus (CS) producing the conditioned response (CR) of fear. Hans now stays at home to avoid seeing horses so he is never able to subject his fear to a reality test, i.e. to see horses and find that they are not always frightening.

Commentary

This is a simple theory and might explain some cases of phobic disorder. It has given rise to several therapies which have proved effective in treating phobias (see below). However, it cannot account for all of the available data. For example:

- Many people with a phobia have no memory of a traumatic conditioning incident.
- Many people who do experience a traumatic event do not go on to develop a phobia.
- Many common phobias are of objects rarely if ever actually encountered in real life, e.g. snakes.
- Rates of phobic response to frequently encountered dangerous/ frightening stimuli, e.g. guns, knives, traffic, are quite low.
- Phobias tend to run in families – this is better explained either by genetic factors or by vicarious learning.

Such problems with the basic learning theory account have led researchers to propose other processes.

Learned preparedness model

Seligman (1971) has proposed the preparedness theory in response to some of the criticisms of the basic conditioning theory. It seems clear from experimental studies that we acquire phobic reactions to certain stimuli more easily than to others. Seligman believed that, in our evolutionary history, it would have been beneficial for our survival to have a fear of potentially dangerous stimuli such as spiders and snakes. As a result, he proposed that we are biologically prepared to react anxiously to stimuli that were threatening to our prehistoric ancestors. Note that this does not mean we have an innate fear of spiders, snakes, etc. but rather that following some sort of conditioning experience, we are much more likely to develop a phobia of these kinds of stimuli rather than to stimuli which have no such significance.

Commentary

There is a considerable body of evidence that supports this theory. For example, Merckelback and de Jong (1999) found that the most common phobias are to stimuli that were present and dangerous in the prehistoric world. Marks (1977) has also demonstrated that fear is more easily acquired to primitive stimuli than to others. He reports a case of a woman who was involved in a car accident when she was looking at a picture of a snake. She subsequently developed a phobia of snakes but not of cars.

■ Hint

How science works

In science, a theory leads to predictions. For instance, the theory that phobias are related to early learning experiences leads to the prediction that behavioural therapies should be effective, as indeed they can be. So the effectiveness of treatments can help support a particular model. For each disorder you study, think about the relative effectiveness of therapies and what this might say about the possible causes. (E)

Psychopathology

Research study: Öhman *et al.* (1975)

In a series of experiments, Öhman *et al.* (1975) showed that, once acquired, a conditioned response to primitive stimuli takes much longer to extinguish than a conditioned response to other stimuli. They used classical conditioning to produce a fear response in a group of volunteers who had no existing phobic disorders. The experimenters presented various stimuli that were classified as either fear-relevant (e.g. pictures of snakes and spiders) or fear-irrelevant (e.g. pictures of flowers and mushrooms). As each picture was presented (CS), the participant received a brief electric shock (UCS). The pictures were later re-presented, but this time without the accompanying shock. Anxiety levels were tested by measuring skin conductance levels.

Fear conditioning occurred very quickly and easily in the fear-relevant condition. It only required one pairing with the electric shock. It took on average five pairings of the picture with the electric shock to condition a fear response to the fear-irrelevant stimuli.

People are more likely to learn a fear response to stimuli that have the potential to be dangerous or threatening than to stimuli which are completely harmless.

Methodological issues

Öhman's studies were carefully conducted under controlled laboratory conditions. This means that they have good internal validity and can be replicated. He used the findings from the original study to suggest hypotheses for further study.

Ethical issues

The participants were subjected to electric shocks in this study. While not dangerous, the intensity of the shock level was individualised for each participant before the start of the study to make sure that the shock was uncomfortable but not painful. This was necessary to make sure that it acted as a genuinely aversive stimulus, but it does mean that participants were subjected to some slight physical discomfort. Participants were all volunteers and were told in advance that they would receive small electric shocks.

None of the participants had phobic reactions before the study. It is possible that the exposure to the fear-relevant stimuli triggered a lasting fear in them.

Variations on the study

Öhman and his colleagues conducted several variations of this study and discovered the following:

- The fear conditioned by the neutral stimuli soon extinguished, whereas the fear to the fear-relevant stimuli remained. In other words, once the pairing with an electric shock stopped, the fear response to the fear-irrelevant stimuli disappeared. The fear response to the fear-relevant stimuli, on the other hand, persisted in the absence of further shocks.

- Once the fear response to the fear-relevant stimuli had been conditioned, it could be triggered by subliminal exposure to the phobic stimulus (i.e. when the presentation of the picture stimulus was so brief that it was not consciously perceived). Öhman and his colleagues have suggested that this finding helps to explain some of the irrationality of phobic responses: it could be that people with phobias are not able to control their fear because it arises from cognitive processes that are out of conscious control.

There is also supporting evidence from animal studies. Cook and Mineka (1990) found that monkeys can be rapidly conditioned to fear toy snakes and toy crocodiles, but not fear-irrelevant stimuli such as flowers or toy rabbits. The laboratory-reared monkeys had no previous experience of either the fear-relevant or fear-irrelevant stimuli before the experiment so this is strong support for the preparedness theory which suggests that evolutionary factors are responsible for selective fear response.

Modelling

One very simple behavioural account of phobia acquisition is modelling. This is the idea that we learn phobic responses through imitating the behaviour of others. This is known as **vicarious conditioning**. The clearest demonstration of modelling was shown by Mineka *et al.* (1984). They reared rhesus monkeys with parents who had an intense fear of snakes. The young monkeys observed their parents interacting fearfully with various real and artificial snakes and non-fearfully with other, neutral stimuli. After only six sessions, the fear of the young monkeys was indistinguishable from that of the parents and was still evident at a three-month follow-up.

Commentary

This is a very simple explanation and has been supported in animal experiments (see above) and in human studies (e.g. Bandura and Rosenthal, 1966). However, many people seeking treatment for phobias have no recollection of becoming fearful after watching the distress of another person. Similarly, many people witness the distress of others but do not go on to develop phobias themselves.

Cognitive-behavioural model

Davey (1997) has modified the basic behavioural model by including some cognitive factors that might influence the acquisition of phobias:

▨ Familiarity with the feared stimulus: if an individual has experienced numerous trauma-free encounters with a particular stimulus, he or she is less likely to acquire a phobia in response to a single traumatic exposure. On the other hand, if the individual has encountered a particular stimulus on previous occasions in rather negative circumstances, he or she is more likely to develop a phobia after a traumatic encounter.

▨ Learning from others: a phobic reaction can be learned through information provided by other people or by observation of someone else.

▨ Previous negative beliefs and expectations about particular stimuli can influence the reaction to a traumatic event involving that stimulus, making it more likely that a phobia will develop.

Once acquired, the phobia can then be maintained through cognitive rehearsal of fear. Many people with phobias think about the feared stimulus in its absence and ruminate about the possible dreadful outcomes that will occur if they encounter the actual stimulus. The more they do this, the greater the phobic reaction if they come face to face with the feared stimulus.

Hint

The study by Cook and Mineka provides really strong support for the preparedness theory. Why is it useful to use animals in this kind of study and what are some of the disadvantages?

Key terms

Vicarious conditioning: learning through observing the behaviour of others and the consequences of their actions.

Psychopathology

Commentary

This offers a more detailed explanation than the basic behavioural model but it still depends on a direct conditioning experience and, as noted above, this is not always the case for people with phobias. There is some evidence (Davey, 1997) that a therapy derived from his theory called 'threat devaluation' can reduce the impact of the fear response, and so provides support for the premise of this explanation.

Key points

- Phobias are characterised by a persistent fear of an object or situation which most people do not perceive as fearful.

- Phobic objects and situations produce extreme anxiety which interferes with everyday functioning.

- 5–10 per cent of people experience some type of phobia.

- Classification systems distinguish between specific phobias, social phobias and agoraphobia.

- Family and twin studies suggest that there may be a genetic basis to some phobias, although the precise mechanisms are not yet understood. Psychodynamic explanations focus on repressed impulses but have received minimal support.

- Behavioural explanations suggest that phobias result from a traumatic incident in which fear is rapidly associated with an object or situation. However, many phobias cannot be traced back to a traumatic incident, and some people experience trauma (e.g. a car crash) but do not develop a phobia.

- According to the behavioural model, phobias may also be learned via observation and modelling.

- Seligman's preparedness theory suggests that we are 'prepared' to develop phobias of objects which posed a threat in the evolutionary past such as poisonous spiders or snakes. Considerable evidence supports this claim.

- Cognitive factors such as negative beliefs and expectations may also play a role in the development of phobias.

◼ **Summary questions**

4 Outline the characteristics of specific phobias, social phobias and agoraphobia.

5 Explain one piece of evidence which shows that biological factors may play a role in phobias.

6 Discuss the view that phobias can be explained by the behavioural approach.

Therapies for phobias

Learning objectives:

- describe and evaluate biological therapies for phobic disorders

- describe and evaluate psychological therapies for phobic disorders.

Biological therapies

Many clinicians feel that drugs are of little benefit to people with phobias, particularly specific phobias. Anti-anxiety drugs such as benzodiazepines have been used, but results on effectiveness have not been conclusive. Perhaps surprisingly, antidepressant drugs have been found to be helpful for some people with social phobias. In particular, specific serotonin re-uptake inhibitors (SSRIs) are sometimes used to help people with social phobias and agoraphobia and there is some evidence that these can relieve symptoms. This is possibly because people with social phobia and agoraphobia often have depressive symptoms as well.

Commentary

Long-term medication with benzodiazepines can lead to tolerance and dependence (Roy-Byrne and Cowley, 1998), and for this reason their use is recommended only for short-term relief of symptoms while other treatments take effect. In the few research studies with children, benzodiazepines have worked only marginally better than placebos. SSRIs, which work by increasing the availability of serotonin in the brain, have been shown to be effective for social phobias and for some cases of agoraphobia and, unlike the anti-anxiety drugs, they are not addictive. However, they take up to six weeks to have a therapeutic effect and need to be continued for at least nine months (Davidson *et al.*, 2004). If SSRIs fail to have any effect, clinicians sometimes prescribe another type of antidepressant called monoamine oxidase inhibitors (MAOIs), but these are more likely to have unpleasant side-effects. This, in turn, leads to non-compliance, i.e. many people with phobias stop taking the medication because they do not want to experience the side-effects.

Psychological therapies

Psychodynamic therapy

The intention of psychodynamic therapy is to uncover the repressed conflicts that are thought to underlie the fear reaction. The phobia is thought of as a symptom of the underlying conflict and is not, therefore, tackled by the therapist directly. Therapists use psychoanalytic techniques such as free association and dream analysis as a way of uncovering the repressed feelings and dealing with them.

Commentary

Psychodynamic therapy can be time-consuming and expensive. There is no convincing evidence that it is effective in reducing or removing phobic responses.

Behavioural therapies

Every theoretical model has its own approach to treating phobias, but behavioural techniques are by far the most widely used. The choice of technique depends on the type of phobia. For specific phobias, there are three main methods:

- desensitisation

Psychopathology

▦ flooding

▦ modelling.

↱ Systematic desensitisation was developed by Joseph Wolpe (1958). Clients are taught relaxation techniques on the basis that relaxation and fear cannot coexist. Once they are in a state of deep muscle relaxation, they work with the therapist to develop a so-called hierarchy of fear. They think about their feared object/situation and create a list of scenes involving the phobic object in ascending order of fear. For example, someone with a fear of spiders might put 'hearing the word spider' at the bottom of the list and 'having a real spider on the table right in front of me' at the top. With the aid of the therapist, and in a state of relaxation, they start to think about the situations on their list. They begin with the least feared situation and are either presented with the situation for real (*in vivo* desensitisation) or it is imagined (covert desensitisation). Over a period of several sessions, the client is gradually taken through the list, pairing each of the scenes on the list with the new response of deep relaxation. The goal of therapy is to reach the top item in the list and so to overcome the one that frightens them the most.

Flooding forces clients to face their feared objects/situations with no gradual build-up and with no means of escape. It is, of course, vital that the client consents to this frightening treatment. For example, a person with claustrophobia (fear of enclosed places) might be put in a large cupboard for several hours. The rationale for this treatment is that it allows the phobic person to stay in the feared situation for long enough to realise that nothing dreadful happens to them. As with systematic desensitisation, exposure can be *in vivo* or covert.

Modelling (vicarious conditioning) allows the client to watch another person (who is not phobic) confronting the feared object/situation. The model is sometimes the therapist but can be someone who is similar to the client in a variety of ways. The therapist then gradually involves the client in the exercises. The client might first be asked to describe how the therapist deals with the object/situation, then to approach the object/situation themselves and finally to touch the object or confront the situation.

Many behavioural therapists combine features of each of these exposure techniques depending on the nature of the phobia. They are also increasingly using virtual reality techniques to simulate real-world objects and situations.

Social skills training is another behavioural technique used mainly with people who have social phobias. Clients role-play new, more appropriate behaviours with their therapist who provides feedback and praises (reinforces) effective behaviours. This kind of training often takes place in groups because it seems that reinforcement from people with similar social difficulties is more powerful than reinforcement from the therapist alone.

Commentary

In a number of studies behavioural exposure techniques have been found to be effective in the treatment of specific phobias. The typical figure given for improvement is about 80 per cent of clients presenting for treatment (Marks, 1990). Such treatment programmes can bring about significant clinical improvement in a relatively short period of time. In fact, it has been shown that improvement can occur after a single three-hour session (Hellstrom *et al.*, 1996). These therapies require the participation and commitment of the client and, because they can be challenging and fear-inducing in themselves, a large number of clients drop out of treatment. Relaxation techniques also have to be practised regularly between sessions and some clients lack the motivation for this.

Social skills training has been shown to help people cope better with social situations, but on its own it does not eradicate the social phobia completely (Rodebaugh *et al.*, 2004). It seems to work best in conjunction with other therapies.

Cognitive-behavioural therapies

This type of therapy has been shown to be particularly helpful in treating the anxiety disorder of PTSD (post-traumatic stress disorder), but it has been less widely used for phobias. When it is applied to phobic disorders it is normally used in conjunction with behavioural exposure techniques. Cognitive-behavioural therapy is based on the idea that anxiety arises from and is maintained by irrational beliefs. The goal of therapy is to challenge these beliefs. For example, in phobias, many people engage in cognitive rehearsal of the fear. They focus on, rehearse and overestimate the possible unpleasant outcomes that might occur if the phobic object is encountered. The more they do this, the greater the fear reaction tends to be. One type of cognitive therapy developed by Davey (1995) aims to help people to develop coping strategies to downplay their fears. Davey (1999) has identified various cognitive processes which can be applied:

- Downward comparison: 'Other people are having a worse time than me'.
- Denial: 'This has not happened to me'.
- Cognitive disengagement: 'This is not important enough to get myself into an anxious state about'.
- Faith in social support: 'I have family and friends who can help me to get through this'.

Commentary

Cognitive therapies have been used fairly successfully with social phobias by reducing social fears (Rodebaugh *et al.*, 2004), but CBT on its own does not completely eliminate social phobias. It has also been useful in helping people with agoraphobia to deal with their panic attacks. The therapy is less successful with specific phobias, possibly because sufferers are already fully aware that their phobia is irrational and excessive.

Summary

There is no single therapy that seems to be effective for all types of phobia. Biological therapies can be useful in the short term while an individual is waiting or preparing for a behavioural treatment programme. Exposure therapy is the treatment of choice, but research indicates that a combination of different approaches is the most effective in reducing symptoms. The crucial aspect of any therapy seems to be actual contact with the feared stimulus (van Hout and Emmelkamp, 2002). Even Freud (1919) stated that psychoanalysis alone could not deal with a phobia: 'One succeeds only when one can induce them to go about alone and to struggle with their anxiety while they make the attempt.'

Key points

- Biological treatments such as drugs have had limited success in treating phobias and may lead to issues of dependency and tolerance.

- There is little evidence to suggest that psychodynamic therapies are effective in treating phobias.

- Some behavioural therapies such as desensitisation and flooding are based on exposure to the feared object. Other behavioural therapies include modelling and social skills training.

- Exposure therapies help about 80 per cent of phobic patients in a short period of time.

- Cognitive therapies target the irrational beliefs which often accompany phobias. These focus on downplaying fears (Davey, 1995).

- Cognitive therapies are more useful with social phobias than specific phobias.

- No single treatment is effective for all types of phobia. A combination of different approaches is likely to be most effective.

Summary questions

7 Explain what is meant by exposure therapies.

8 Explain one example of a cognitive treatment for phobias.

9 It is claimed that no single therapy is effective for all types of phobia. Why do you think this is?

Classification and explanation of obsessive-compulsive disorder (OCD)

Learning objectives:

- describe the clinical characteristics of OCD

- describe and evaluate biological explanations of OCD

- describe and evaluate psychological explanations of OCD.

■ Clinical characteristics

OCD is an anxiety disorder that is thought to affect between 1 and 3 per cent of the population, although the precise extent is not known. Most people with OCD have both obsessions and compulsions. We probably all have intrusive or repetitive thoughts from time to time that can be irritating, e.g. an advertising jingle that we cannot get out of our head. Obsessions, on the other hand, are ugly and alien thoughts, e.g. that you might kill a friend or blurt out a blasphemous remark at a religious service. Similarly, people (particularly children) often carry out little ritualistic behaviours like avoiding the cracks in the pavement. However, compulsions are highly distressing, involuntary behaviours that produce marked distress and interfere with everyday life.

■ Obsessions are recurrent, intrusive thoughts, ideas, images or impulses. Individuals experiencing them find them distressing and, sometimes, even abhorrent or morally repugnant. Obsessions often have sexual, blasphemous or aggressive themes. The individual tries to deal with these intrusive thoughts, either by ignoring them or by 'neutralising' them with some other thought or action.

Compulsions are irresistible, repetitive physical or mental actions that people feel compelled to carry out. They are often performed in a stereotypical way according to a set of rigid rules. Individuals with OCD recognise that these actions are unreasonable and excessive, but they cannot stop themselves. They believe that by carrying out this ritualistic behaviour they can prevent some dreadful consequences and can reduce their distress. Their performance is never directly pleasurable, but it can relieve some of the tension and anxiety. The most common examples of compulsive behaviour are checking and washing. For some people, the obsession with cleanliness leads to washing hands regularly with bleach or disinfectant and making the skin raw.

The disorder can frequently have a negative effect on family and social relationships as the behaviour of the individual with OCD can cause irritation and resentment in others. This can heighten feelings of anxiety and depression in the sufferer and leads to further deterioration in relationships. OCD seems to occur equally among men and women and the onset of the disorder is usually in adolescence or adulthood, although it can begin in childhood. Some people with OCD develop symptoms fairly suddenly and these symptoms often emerge after a stressful event, e.g. a pregnancy or a bereavement, although approximately 30 per cent of cases have no clear triggers. Many people keep their condition secret, so there can be a considerable delay in accessing treatment. The symptoms of about 30 per cent of patients improve considerably in response to some form of therapy, about 40 per cent show moderate improvement and about 30 per cent do not significantly recover. About 30 per cent of OCD patients also have depression and suicide can be a risk. The *ICD-10* and *DSM-IV* have similar diagnostic criteria for OCD.

Fig. 2 *Excessive hand washing is the most common manifestation of OCD*

Diagnostic criteria for OCD (adapted from the *ICD-10*)

1 Either obsessions or compulsions (or both) are present on most days for a period of at least two weeks. Obsessions and compulsions share the following features, all of which must be present:

- They are acknowledged as originating in the mind of the patient and are not imposed by outside persons or influences.
- They are repetitive and unpleasant, and at least one obsession or compulsion that is acknowledged as excessive or unreasonable must be present.
- The patient tries to resist them. At least one obsession or compulsion that is unsuccessfully resisted must be present.
- Experiencing the obsessive thought or carrying out the compulsive act is not in itself pleasurable (this is to be distinguished from the temporary relief of tension or anxiety).

2 The obsessions or compulsions cause distress or interfere with the patient's social or individual functioning, usually by wasting time.

3 The obsessions or compulsions are not the result of other mental disorders or mood disorders.

Issues surrounding classification and diagnosis

It has been estimated that 75 per cent of normal adults have fleeting unwanted thoughts and engage in mild checking behaviour. Therefore, obsessive-compulsive behaviours are probably within the spectrum of normal behaviour. As with many other anxiety states, it is a matter of degree – OCD is only diagnosed when the obsessive thoughts and/ or compulsions are so excessive, distressing and time-consuming that they seriously interfere with everyday living.

- Although case studies have been described for hundreds of years, it was thought until recently that OCD was relatively uncommon, affecting only 0.05 per cent of the population. However, careful, well-controlled community studies have shown that the rate is much higher – around 3 per cent (Kessler *et al.*, 2005). This is probably because people with OCD are often secretive about their disorder and manage to conceal it for years.

- OCD frequently occurs with depression and it can be difficult to disentangle the two disorders.

- OCD symptoms can resemble schizophrenia when the nature of the obsessional thoughts is particularly bizarre. However, provided that the clinician makes a careful assessment of the patient and their other symptoms, the two disorders are usually readily distinguishable.

- OCD is not confined to Western cultures and has been reported in countries such as India, Taiwan and Israel (Yaryura-Tobias and Neziroglu, 1997). The basic features of the disorder seem to be the same in all cultures where it has been found.

- There has been a tendency to assume that OCD is a single category. Researchers (e.g. Jakes, 1996) have suggested that there are sub-groups of patients who differ in the nature of their compulsions, e.g. some have mainly checking compulsions while others engage mainly in cleaning rituals. It might be the case that these sub-types have different origins and might respond to different treatments.

■ Biological explanations

Genetic factors

OCD is thought to run in families and it is assumed that this might reflect genetic factors. Studies of family history are sparse, but it seems that relatives of OCD sufferers have a greater tendency to suffer from other anxiety disorders than the general population (Black *et al.*, 1992). However, this study found that only 2.5 per cent of relatives actually had OCD – a figure similar to the prevalence rate in the general population. Other studies (e.g. Pauls *et al.*, 1995) have found higher rates but only when they included people who have some symptoms of OCD but not the full-blown diagnosis. A review of 14 published twin studies found that of 80 MZ twin pairs, 54 were concordant for OCD and in 29 DZ twins only nine were concordant for OCD (Billett *et al.*, 1998).

Exactly how genetic factors contribute to the disorder is unknown, but it is thought that they might operate by influencing brain structure which, in turn, then impacts on the individual's ability to perform mental tasks.

So far, no specific gene has been identified, but some interesting recent research has implicated a gene called sapap3. This is expressed in a part of the brain, the striatum, that controls processes such as planning and initiating appropriate action, and it has been implicated in human OCD. Feng *et al.* (2007) have demonstrated that mice lacking this gene show high levels of anxiety and spend excessive amounts of time on grooming behaviour to the extent that they have pulled out their own fur. When given extra sapap3 protein, the abnormal behaviour disappeared.

Commentary

There have not been many large, systematic and well-controlled twin studies looking specifically at OCD, although there is evidence for a slightly higher concordance rate in MZ rather than DZ twins. Family studies have also supported the idea of some genetic contribution to

OCD. Even if genes do have a role in the origins of OCD, it is not clear exactly what is passed on. Gene research is relatively new and has not yet been replicated by others. It is also difficult to generalise from animals like mice to human beings. Nevertheless, it is a promising area of research which might tell us more about the origins of OCD.

Biochemical factors

A deficiency in the neurotransmitter serotonin could be a causal factor. Serotonin and other neurotransmitters travel from nerve cell to nerve cell across fluid-filled gaps called synapses. When serotonin is released by one cell, it enters another cell through a special area of the cell membrane called a receptor.

In OCD, it is thought that certain receptors block serotonin from entering the cell. This leads to a deficiency of the neurotransmitter in key areas of the brain. The main evidence in support of this hypothesis comes from the finding that certain drugs called SSRIs provide some relief from symptoms in OCD. This type of drug works by preventing nerve cells that have just released serotonin from absorbing it back into the cell. This makes it readily available at synapses for other neurons. This family of drugs is now a major focus for new treatments and there is considerable evidence that it can reduce symptoms of OCD in adults and children (see page 384).

Commentary

Although the finding that SSRIs provide considerable relief from the symptoms of OCD suggests that low levels of serotonin are a causal factor, it now seems that the link is not that straightforward. SSRIs take about 6–12 weeks to bring about any therapeutic change and it is known that long-term administration of these drugs affects serotonin function but does not increase availability. In any case, these drugs provide only partial relief from symptoms and most studies have been able to demonstrate only a 50 per cent improvement (Insel, 1991), with some patients deriving no benefit at all. It now seems clear that although serotonin is implicated in OCD, serotonin dysfunction alone cannot explain this complex disorder.

Neuroanatomical factors

As suggested above, genetic factors might work by influencing the brain's structure. Various areas of the brain have been implicated in OCD.

One suggestion is that there is some abnormality in the basal ganglia. There is a considerable body of evidence that links OCD to impaired functioning of the basal ganglia. OCD is often found in cases of Huntington's chorea, Parkinson's disease and Tourette's syndrome, which are all disorders in which the basal ganglia are implicated (Wise and Rapoport, 1989). It has also been demonstrated that basal ganglia damage resulting from a head injury can give rise to OCD (Max et al., 1994) and that surgery which disconnects the basal ganglia from the frontal cortex can reduce symptoms in severe OCD (Rapoport et al., 1995). However, results using neuro-imaging techniques have been rather inconclusive and basal ganglia impairment has not always been found in OCD patients when compared to controls (Aylward et al., 1996).

Another structure in the brain that might underpin OCD is a circuit involving three anatomical brain regions. These are:

▨ the orbital-frontal cortex (OFC)

▨ the caudate nucleus

▨ the thalamus.

Link

See your *AQA Psychology A AS* student book pages 139–41 for an explanation of receptors and synapses.

Hint

How science works

In science, a theory leads to predictions. For instance, the theory that OCD is related to low levels of brain serotonin leads to the prediction that drugs increasing levels, such as clomipramine, should be effective, as indeed they can be. So the effectiveness of treatments can help support a particular model, although don't forget that drugs do not work for all people with OCD. For each disorder you study, think about the relative effectiveness of therapies and what this might say about the possible causes. (E)

Psychopathology

The OFC is the part of the brain that becomes aware if something seems wrong. For example, when the OFC registers that there is dirt nearby, it sends a signal to the thalamus. The thalamus directs signals from many parts of the brain to places that can interpret them – in this case back to the OFC. These nerve-cell connections form a loop in the brain. The caudate nucleus lies between the OFC and the thalamus and regulates signals sent between them. When the thalamus receives a 'worry' signal, it becomes excited and sends strong signals back through the loop to the OFC, which interprets them. Normally, the head of the caudate nucleus acts like the brake pedal on a car, suppressing the original 'worry' signals sent by the OFC to the thalamus. This prevents the thalamus from becoming hyperactive. But in OCD, the caudate nucleus is thought to be damaged, so it cannot suppress signals from the OFC, allowing the thalamus to become over-excited.

If this occurs, the thalamus sends strong signals back to the OFC, which responds by increasing compulsive behaviour and anxiety. This could explain the repetitive and seemingly senseless rituals performed by obsessive-compulsives. There is some support for this idea from drug research that shows SSRI medication to be effective for OCD. One of its modes of operation is to increase stimulation of serotonin receptors in the OFC and thereby to inhibit its overactivity.

Key terms

MRI: magnetic resonance imaging.

Research study: Menzies *et al.* (2007)

Another interesting line of research used **MRI** scans to look at the brains of 31 people suffering from OCD, 31 of their healthy close relatives (i.e. siblings, parents, children) and a group of 31 unrelated controls with no family history of OCD. In addition they measured their ability to stop repetitive behaviours by giving them a simple quick response task which they had to stop at the sound of an electronic beep.

It was found that the OCD patients and their healthy relatives both scored lower on the stop-response task than the controls. In other words, they seemed less able to stop repetitive behaviours. They also showed abnormalities in brain structure compared to controls. In particular they had larger amounts of grey matter in the cingulated, parietal and striatal regions and lower amounts of grey matter in the OFC and the right frontal regions of the brain. These are parts of the brain known to have a regulatory role and so it makes sense for them to be involved in OCD.

Methodological issues

It is often difficult to know whether brain abnormalities *cause* a disorder or result from *having* the disorder. This research is useful because it uses MRI technology to show the abnormalities in the brains of healthy individuals who have relatives with OCD.

Ethical issues

MRI scans are not invasive and cause no long-term damage. However, the procedure could be uncomfortable for some people and the researchers needed to make sure that they had fully informed consent from all of the participants before the study began and that participants were aware of their right to withdraw at any time.

Commentary

The biological explanations, although promising, cannot yet offer a complete explanation of OCD. Biochemical explanations owe most of their support to the fact that medication that increases serotonin availability appears to work. However, it does not work for everyone with OCD and symptoms recur when medication stops. It is also risky to infer the cause of a disorder from a therapeutic effect (**treatment aetiology fallacy**).

Another problem for the serotonin hypothesis is that studies have failed to provide evidence that OCD patients differ in their serotonin levels either from people with other types of anxiety disorder or from controls. For example, in assessments of serotonin levels in cerebro-spinal fluid Pigott *et al.* (1996) found no differences between OCD patients and controls. There is more convincing evidence about impairments in certain brain structures but findings have not been consistent. One of the major challenges for biological theories is that certain psychological interventions appear to have a strong therapeutic effect on OCD and yet do not rely on drug therapy or other physical interventions. For these reasons, we will now turn to psychological explanations.

Psychological explanations

Psychodynamic explanations

Freud believed that OCD was the consequence of problems with toilet training. According to Freud, we develop through a series of psychosexual stages. During the anal stage, young children become angry when their parents try to make them use the toilet in an appropriate way. They are not powerful enough to resist their parents and so their anger is **repressed**.

In later life, these repressed aggressive thoughts sometimes try to find expression, but this is disturbing to the individual and causes anxiety. As a way of reducing this anxiety, the aggressive impulses are displaced and substituted by more acceptable thoughts and impulses. However, if these thoughts intrude into consciousness, they appear alien and frightening. This anxiety is managed by carrying out compulsive rituals to cancel out the undesirable impulse.

Commentary

There is little evidence for this explanation. In particular, Milby and Weber (1991) have found no greater incidence of parent–child toilet-training conflicts in people with OCD compared to controls.

Given the relationship to the anal stage, it has also been suggested that OCD occurs in people with a so-called anal or obsessive personality (characterised by perfectionism, neatness, meticulousness, etc.). However, the evidence for a relationship between this personality type and OCD is not strong – it is difficult to assess personality reliably, particularly the personality before the onset of the disorder (Rachman and Hodgson, 1980). On the whole, clinical data shows that some people who develop OCD do have the anal personality traits before the onset of the disorder. However, many OCD sufferers do not show these personality characteristics and many people who do have them do not go on to develop the disorder.

Key terms

Treatment aetiology fallacy: an example of faulty logic in drawing conclusions about the causes of mental disorders. Just because a particular drug provides relief from symptoms does not mean that a lack of that drug is the underlying cause. Aspirin can remove the pain of a headache, but headaches are not caused by lack of aspirin in the nervous system.

Repressed: pushed out of conscious awareness into the unconscious mind. This usually happens to traumatic memories or thoughts and protects the individual from anxiety.

Link

See your *AQA Psychology A AS* student book pages 240–41 for details about the stages of psychosexual development.

Psychopathology

Behavioural theory

Behaviourists have concentrated on explaining compulsions rather than obsessions. They suggest that in a fearful situation people might by chance act in a certain way, e.g. wash their hands. When the threatening situation goes away, the individual associates the action (classical conditioning) with the removal of the threat and so they perform the action again in similar situations because they have learned that this reduces anxiety (operant conditioning). However, this simply serves to maintain longer-term anxiety because they never learn that no harm will occur if they do not carry out ritualistic behaviours.

Commentary

This idea has led to a reasonably effective therapy, exposure and response prevention (ERP; see page 385), but the theory does not explain obsessive thoughts and it does not effectively explain why the compulsions start in the first place. At most, it simply explains why the compulsive behaviours are maintained.

Cognitive-behavioural theory of OCD

This theory was formulated by Rachman and Hodgson (1980). Their starting point was that we all experience intrusive thoughts occasionally. However, in most cases we are not made anxious by them and we are able to dismiss them fairly easily or distract ourselves from them. Individuals with OCD, on the other hand, are not able to dismiss these thoughts so easily. Rachman and Hodges also believe that we are less able to dismiss unwanted thoughts if we are feeling anxious, stressed or depressed. We know that depression is common in people with OCD. This means that this kind of individual will find it particularly difficult to get rid of obsessive thoughts. Rachman (1997) has further suggested that obsessions are caused when an individual catastrophically misinterprets the significance of the intrusive thoughts. He gives an example of a young man who has recurrent thoughts and images about causing physical harm to the young child of a friend. Instead of being able to dismiss these thoughts, the young man interprets them as revealing him to be a potential murderer and a completely worthless human being. Beliefs such as these lead to a state of anxiety and distress which the individual tries to reduce by suppressing the thoughts. Unfortunately, this seems to make the intrusive thoughts even worse.

Commentary

There is some support for this explanation. Salkovskis and Kirk (1997) asked people with OCD to keep a daily diary in which they recorded the frequency of their obsessional thoughts. They were instructed to try to suppress these thoughts on some days and to allow them in on other days. The number of intrusive thoughts was significantly higher on the days when they deliberately tried to suppress them.

Since it is very hard for people with OCD to suppress their intrusive thoughts, they engage instead in a series of 'safety behaviours' to try to reduce the possible negative outcomes of their impulses. These safety behaviours can take several forms:

- cleaning/checking rituals, etc.
- neutralising the thought by substituting a repeated phrase, e.g. 'Jesus loves me', etc.
- seeking reassurance from others.

■ Hint

This finding seems counter-intuitive, but just stop reading for a moment and try to follow this instruction:

- In the next five minutes, DO NOT THINK ABOUT POLAR BEARS.

You will probably find it very hard to comply with this instruction.

■ Hint

How science works

When you are evaluating explanations, one basic assumption of scientific theory is that it should always adopt the simplest explanation possible as long as it can account for all of the known data. This is known as the principle of parsimony.

Such strategies provide temporary relief from anxiety, but, as in the simple learning theory (see pages 239–44), the individual never learns that no harm will occur if they do not carry out these behaviours.

Key points

■ OCD usually starts in adolescence or early adulthood.

■ Obsessions are recurring thoughts or images, for example of dirt and contamination. Compulsions are repeated actions which people carry out to relieve the anxiety of the obsession thoughts, such as hand washing.

■ Symptoms should be present for at least two weeks in order for OCD to be diagnosed.

■ Many people experience recurring thoughts without them becoming pathological.

■ Biological explanations focus on genetics, brain structures and neurotransmitters.

■ Family history and twin studies suggest that there may be a genetic component to OCD, but the precise mechanisms remain unclear.

■ Dysfunction in the serotonin system and brain structures, including the basal ganglia and the cortico-striatal circuit, have been implicated in OCD.

■ The psychodynamic approach views OCD as originating in problems with toilet training. This explanation has received little empirical support.

■ The behavioural approach focuses on explaining compulsions (behaviours) rather than obsessions (thoughts).

■ Cognitive-behavioural explanations note that most people experience intrusive thoughts. It is when these are interpreted in catastrophic ways and suppressed that OCD occurs.

Summary questions

10 Outline the clinical characteristics of OCD.

11 Summarise the behavioural and cognitive explanations of OCD.

12 What evidence is there that OCD may have biological origins? What does this approach fail to explain about OCD?

Psychopathology

Therapies for OCD

Learning objectives:

■ describe and evaluate biological therapies for OCD

■ describe and evaluate psychological therapies for OCD.

There is a growing belief that OCD has its origins mainly in biological factors, and this has had implications for treatment over recent years. The main treatments of choice are drug therapy and/or some form of cognitive-behavioural therapy. The chronic nature and fluctuating course of OCD means that long-term supportive psychotherapy is often required.

■ Biological therapies

The biological treatment of choice is drug therapy. The standard approach is to use antidepressant drugs, particularly those which have a specific effect on the neurotransmitter serotonin.

SSRIs such as Prozac have been shown to be effective in reducing symptoms of OCD in both children and adults (Rauch and Jenike, 1998). Another type of drug called Clomipramine, which also works by increasing the availability of serotonin, is also effective. It was not initially clear whether these antidepressant drugs were simply alleviating depressive symptoms that often occur in OCD rather than obsessive symptoms. However, Thoren *et al.* (1980) found that Clomipramine was significantly superior to placebo in relieving obsessional symptoms. The therapeutic effect was not related to the presence or absence of depressive symptoms in the patient. It has also been found that antidepressant drugs which affect neurotransmitters other than serotonin do not have a therapeutic effect in OCD.

However, all of these drugs cause side-effects and there is a strong risk of relapse when coming off medication. Foa *et al.* (2005) found that although Clomipramine was more effective than placebo, it was less effective than ERP (see below).

Psychosurgery is sometimes used in the case of treatment-resistant OCD. However, it should be noted that such therapy is considered only as a last resort if all other treatment options have failed to work. Surgery involves the use of radio-frequency waves to destroy a small amount of brain tissue which then disrupts a specific circuit in the brain implicated in OCD. This is the cortico-striatal circuit which includes the orbital-frontal cortex, the caudate nucleus and the thalamus (see pages 379–80). Various techniques are used, but the safest appears to be the anterior cingulotomy. There are some slightly less permanent, brain-based techniques such as vagus nerve stimulation and transcranial magnetic stimulation (TMS). Though in its early stages of research, TMS has shown promising results. The magnetic pulses are focused on the brain's supplementary motor area (SMA) which plays a role in filtering out extraneous internal stimuli such as ruminations, obsessions and tics. The TMS treatment is an attempt to normalise the SMA's activity so that it properly filters out thoughts and behaviours associated with OCD.

Commentary

The evidence about the efficacy of psychosurgery is inconsistent, although it has been estimated that long-term effectiveness in alleviating symptoms is somewhere between 25 and 70 per cent depending on the criteria used for assessing success. However, all of these techniques are drastic and irreversible and can cause seizures. They also raise ethical issues in terms of informed consent – patients who are disturbed enough to warrant consideration for psychosurgery might well not have the insight to understand the implications of such therapies.

■ Psychological therapies

Psychoanalytic therapy aims to uncover the unconscious conflicts that the individual has repressed. Traditional psychoanalysis uses a variety of techniques including free association and dream analysis. However, there has been no controlled study of its effectiveness with OCD and it is not generally thought to be appropriate for people with OCD.

■ Behavioural therapy
Modelling

This is a straightforward behavioural technique in which the therapist demonstrates 'fearless' behaviour. For example, the therapist might

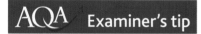

handle an object which the patient regards as contaminated. In later sessions, the client is asked to handle the object.

Response prevention

People with OCD carry out compulsions in order to relieve their anxiety. However, observation has shown that for many people, the carrying out of rituals actually has the reverse effect, i.e. it increases anxiety. The idea of this therapy, often called exposure and response prevention (ERP) is to stop the ritualistic behaviour.

The client is gradually exposed to the fear stimulus and then helped to avoid their normal 'safety' rituals. Relaxation is taught in order to help clients cope with the high levels of physiological arousal associated with their fear. Techniques include verbal persuasion, continuous monitoring and engaging in alternative behaviour. Deliberate forceful intervention is not helpful and simply leads to non-cooperation by the client. Other family members are often involved in helping to stop the ritualistic behaviour.

Cognitive approaches

These have built on behavioural techniques and use a number of additional cognitive strategies including:

- Challenging inappropriate thoughts (testing the reality of their negative expectations).
- Thought stopping: distracting the client from inappropriate thoughts by literally shouting 'Stop!' and asking them to switch their thinking to a pre-prepared image or thought. The client gradually develops the skill of stopping their own thoughts when they threaten to overwhelm.

Commentary

Salkovskis and Kirk (1997) reported moderate success for ERP although complete removal of symptoms occurred in less than half of the participants and it is quite common for patients to drop out of therapy or to refuse to cooperate.

Behavioural and cognitive-behavioural therapies take a relatively short time (approximately 3–8 weeks) and do not have side-effects like drugs.

It seems that pure cognitive interventions are not as effective as ERP, but in combination they are more effective than either on its own (van Oppen *et al.*, 1995).

Key points

- Antidepressant drugs such as SSRIs which work on serotonin have had some success in treating OCD, supporting a biological explanation. However, the treatment aetiology fallacy may be at work here.

- Recent research has begun to explore the use of radio waves targeted at the cortico-striatal circuit.

- Behavioural treatments such as exposure and response prevention (ERP) have shown moderate success.

- Cognitive-behavioural treatments involve thought stopping and challenging negative thoughts.

Psychopathology

Hint

Try to think why people might drop out of this kind of therapy. Do you think people might prefer to take drugs. Why do you think this might be so?

Summary questions

13 Outline the biological treatment options available for OCD.

14 How do exposure and response prevention treatments target OCD?

15 Discuss the claim that the effectiveness of treatments tells us important things about the cause of OCD.

Psychopathology end of topic

How science works: practical activity

For ethical reasons it is very difficult for A Level students to carry out research projects in the field of psychopathology. However, you might like to carry out a survey about attitudes of people to mental illness. There are many popular myths about mental illness (e.g. 'Schizophrenia is a split personality'; 'Mentally ill people are violent'; 'Depressed people should pull themselves together', etc.). It is important to try to dispel such untruths and to make people better-informed about mental illness. The Department of Health regularly carries out surveys to assess public awareness. You might like to look at the results of a recent survey. Search for 'attitudes to mental illness in England 2007' on the Department of Health website www.dh.gov.uk.

In your class, you could draw up your own attitude questionnaire and gather data from other students and people that you know. Use the Department of Health survey to help you decide on the questions. The simplest method is to generate a set of statements and ask people to indicate their level of agreement using a five-point scale (where 5 = strongly agree and 1 = strongly disagree). Your aim is to find out what potentially negative attitudes exist and perhaps suggest ways of informing people better to address this and so reduce prejudices.

Make sure that you have a mixture of positive and negative statements, e.g. positive: 'People with a mental health problem should have the same right to a job as anyone else' and negative: 'People with mental illness do not deserve our sympathy.' If you do not do this, there is a danger of people falling into a response set, i.e. not really reading the questions properly and always ticking, for example, the 'agree' box. Make sure that you have enough questions to provide you with interesting data, but not so many that people will get bored or fatigued by answering them.

Before finalising the items, work out how each is going to be analysed or scored. You may want to do a small pilot trial to test the questions.

Pool all of the data that your classmates have gathered and then draw bar charts to describe the results. You could include some more personal questions at the end, e.g. 'Have you consulted a GP in the past 12 months about any personal, mental or emotional problems?'; 'Has anyone in your family or close circle of friends been diagnosed with a mental illness?' When you analyse your results, you could then compare people who answered 'Yes' to either of these two questions with people who have had no personal experience, and see if their answers to earlier questions differ in any way. You could also compare answers from people of different age groups to see if there are any differences.

There are important ethical considerations to take into account before you carry out this kind of survey. You must tell people in advance that the questions concern attitudes to mental illness and make it clear that they can withdraw at any time if they feel the questions are intrusive. You must also assure all of the participants that the data will be kept anonymous and confidential. It is obviously not your intention to confirm prejudices in people, so you might like to prepare a short information sheet that explodes some of the myths about mental illness and give it to the participants after they have filled in the questionnaire.

Link

You can refresh your memory about questionnaires by looking at page 517 and about bar charts by looking at page 533.

Further reading and weblinks

www.guardian.co.uk

www.timesonline.co.uk

www.independent.co.uk

It is useful to look at the online pages of some of the major UK newspapers. They often contain interesting news and feature articles on mental disorders and these can provide an excellent basis for class discussions.

www.bbc.co.uk/science/humanbody

You can find some good interactive activities on the BBC website. These change from time to time, but there are sometimes activities related to mental disorders.

www.mind.org.uk

It is also useful to look at the website for Mind, the leading mental health charity in England and Wales. It contains helpful information about various mental disorders.

Davison, G., Neale, J.M. and Kring, A.M. (2003) *Abnormal Psychology* (9th edn). New York: Wiley.

This is a good example of a book on abnormal psychology. There are a huge number of books available which deal with mental disorders. Many of these are highly specialised and provide a much deeper and more complex level of detail than can be reasonably expected at A Level. If you want to find out more about psychopathology, the most accessible sources are general textbooks on abnormal psychology. These are often aimed at undergraduate students but are generally written in an accessible style with good illustrations and feature articles that make them suitable for interested A Level readers.

Media psychology

Introduction

Key terms

Media: different means of communicating ideas and images to a large audience. Television, films, radio, newspapers and the internet are different examples of media. The term is also used to refer to 'the press' in general or news reporting agencies.

Antisocial behaviour: a general term which relates to behaviours which are considered disruptive or harmful.

Aggressive behaviour: behaviour that is carried out with an intention of causing harm to another person.

Pro-social behaviour: actions which aim to help others.

For the last 50 years or so, people have been exposed to an increasing amount and range of broadcast **media**. The first real 'medium' of communicating images and ideas was through films, and in the UK in 1951 a staggering 1.4 billion visits were made to the cinema! The 1960s saw the increasing availability of television in people's own homes, and in the 1990s there was a rapid expansion from four 'terrestrial' channels to multi-channel cable and satellite television, available 24 hours a day.

Terrestrial television is regulated by the 'watershed', which states that certain sorts of image, mostly those depicting particular levels of sex or violence, should not be shown until after 9.00pm. However, cable and satellite channels are not regulated in the same way, nor is the internet. In the last couple of years websites such as YouTube have provided a forum in which ordinary people can transmit ideas, music and images to potentially vast, worldwide audiences. Of course, websites are used for many useful and pro-social reasons; however, they have also been used by individuals to transmit disturbing ideas and images. For example, in November 2007, the Finnish teenager Pekka-Eric Auvinen posted a video on YouTube entitled 'Jokela High School Massacre' before carrying out his threats.

In this section of the course, we shall consider the impact of media on persuasion including the psychology of advertising. We will then go on to examine the potential impact of images shown in the mass media (including television, films and computer games) on **antisocial behaviour**, **aggressive behaviour** and **pro-social behaviour**. Finally, we shall consider how parasocial relationships (those with people we see on television and celebrities) might be understood and the functions they might serve.

Cortes (2005) argues that 'the mass media teach whether or not media makers intend to or realize it'. Cortes identifies five ways in which the mass media may influence: presenting information, organising ideas, disseminating values, creating and reinforcing expectations and providing models for behaviour. Interestingly it is the last of these – providing models for behaviour – which has led to the most substantial body of research work over the last 50 years and which started with the work of Bandura in 1961.

Media psychology

29

Persuasion, attitude and change

Persuasion and attitude change

Media psychology

Learning objectives:

- explain what is meant by the terms 'attitude' and 'persuasion'

- describe explanations of persuasion including the Hovland-Yale model and the elaboration likelihood model

- understand criticisms of models of persuasion.

Key terms

Attitude: a predisposition to be a certain way to an object, person or situation that involves feeling, thinking and knowing.

Persuasion: a deliberate attempt to change another person's attitude.

Three components: this relates to models which see attitudes as having feelings, beliefs and behaviours.

Two-component models: these view attitudes as a mental readiness to act associated with evaluations.

Hint

You can easily remember the three-component model of attitudes as the components conveniently start with the first three letters of the alphabet – ABC! To remember both models, make a mnemonic for yourself using the letters ABCRE (Affective, Behavioural, Cognitive, Readiness, Evaluation).

Introduction

The word **attitude** is used extensively in everyday life. How many times have you heard it said that 'X has an attitude problem'! Considerable time and effort have gone into researching why people have the attitudes they do and how attitudes can be changed. **Persuasion** often takes place by way of advertising or propaganda. This chapter starts by considering how psychologists define attitudes and goes on to look at two different approaches to explain persuasion – the Hovland-Yale model and dual-process approaches. Before you begin reading this chapter, list the number of attempts that have been made to change your attitude or act in a certain way so far today. Scary, isn't it!

What are attitudes?

The word 'attitude' comes from the Latin word *aptus* which literally means 'ready for action'. Attitudes are hypothetical constructs – things in people's heads which cannot be seen directly. Traditional approaches saw attitudes as having **three components**:

- The affective component refers to the 'feelings' or emotions associated with the attitude.

- The behavioural component refers to a tendency to act in a certain way.

- The cognitive component refers to the beliefs and thoughts about the attitude object.

For example, if Sam has a positive attitude to sport, he or she experiences positive *feelings* when watching or playing sport, engages in sporting *activities* and *believes* sport is part of a healthy lifestyle.

In contrast, **two-component models** of attitudes argue that attitudes involve a readiness to act in a certain kind of way which influences our judgements. They see attitudes as 'lasting, general evaluations of people (including oneself) objects, or issues' (Petty and Cacioppo, 1986 cited in Hogg and Vaughan, 2005). In both of these models, attitudes are seen as being relatively permanent, lasting across time and different situations. This claim has been disputed recently by discursive psychologists and we will examine this critique later in the chapter.

How are attitudes changed?

The Hovland-Yale model

We have already noted that research does not take place in a vacuum but relates to a specific social context and time. Research into attitudes and persuasion thrived in the period towards the end of the Second World War. At that time, many governments were interested in the ways in which groups of people in Europe had embraced political ideologies such as Fascism and Communism. Carl Hovland was employed during this period by the US War Department who were particularly interested in propaganda, an interest which continued during the Cold War of the 1950s. Hovland moved from his post with the War Department to Yale University where he carried out considerable research into the psychology of attitudes and persuasion.

Hovland argued that we can understand attitude change by considering it as a **sequential process**. The first stage in the sequence is attention – in order to be persuaded, an individual must notice the attempt to persuade them. Every day people are bombarded with hundreds of persuasive messages and adverts and many of these will simply not be noticed. The second stage is comprehension – the recipient must understand what is being said to them. It may be that they are not persuaded if the advert or message goes straight over their heads. The message followed by advertisers is to keep it simple! The third stage is reactance – the individual will react to the message, either with broad agreement or they may dispute it as a load of rubbish. Following this is acceptance – the message will only be accepted if it is believed.

Fig. 1 *The sequence of attitude change*

The Hovland-Yale model (Hovland, Janis and Kelley, 1953) argued that persuasion was dependent on several factors, the **source**, the **message**, the **medium**, the **target** and the situation, which could be neatly summarised as 'who says what to whom'. Hovland emphasised that rather than being separate, these three factors interacted with each other, so for example a different type of message would be needed for an educated audience compared to a less informed audience.

The Hovland-Yale model dominated our understanding of persuasion for 30 years or more and led to a huge amount of research into the factors which make communication persuasive. We do not have the space to cover this research in detail here, but you can get a flavour of the type of method used by reading the featured research study below. A summary of research findings is shown in Table 1.

■ **Key terms**

Sequential process: the idea that attitude change takes place in a series of stages.

Source: who is doing the persuading.

Message: the content of what is said.

Medium: how it is put across.

Target: the person who is being persuaded.

■ Link

You can see how this sequence works in television advertising by looking at pages 399–401.

■ Media psychology

Table 1 *Research into the Hovland-Yale model*

Source factors	■ Credibility – people are more likely to be persuaded by a credible or expert source (Hovland and Weiss, 1952). ■ Physical appearance – physically attractive sources are more persuasive than less attractive sources (Kiesler and Kiesler, 1969). ■ Speed of speech – rapid speakers are more persuasive than slow speakers (Miller *et al.*, 1976).
Message factors	■ Content – messages which are not deliberately targeted at us are more persuasive (Walster and Festinger, 1962). ■ Fear – persuasion can be increased by fearful messages (Meyerowitz and Chaiken, 1987) but a large amount of fear can lead people to switch off.
Medium factors	■ Audio-visual messages are more persuasive than written messages (Chaiken and Eagly, 1983) especially if the message is simple. Written messages are better if processing effort is required.
Target factors	■ Self-esteem – people with lower self-esteem are easier to persuade than those with higher self-esteem (Janis, 1954).
Source X target	■ We are more likely to be persuaded by someone who is similar to us, for example from the same ethnic background (Qualls and Moore, 1990).

■ Research study: Meyerowitz and Chaiken (1987)

Meyerowitz and Chaiken (1987) looked at the role of fear in message content. They studied female university students who were randomly allocated to one of three conditions and given a leaflet relating to breast self-examination:

- The *loss condition* pamphlet emphasised the dangers of failing to self-examine.
- The *gain condition* pamphlet emphasised the positive consequences of self-examination in terms of early detection and treatment.
- The *neutral condition (control)* pamphlet contained neither type of information, but gave basic facts about breast cancer.

The students were re-interviewed after four months and asked about their attitude to self-examination and how often they had carried it out. The loss group who had been exposed to most fear were the only group to change their behaviour (they self-examined more) and change their attitude towards self-examination.

Methodological issues

This study demonstrates clearly the highly controlled experimental approach to studying attitudes that was widely used to test the Hovland-Yale model. Participants were exposed to a message and some aspect of the source, medium, message content or target was varied. Attitudes were measured before and after the persuasive attempt to assess the degree of change.

In this study, follow-up took place after four months. This is commendable as it ensures that attitude and behaviour change are relatively permanent.

Ethical issues

These study participants were exposed to potentially fearful messages relating to their health. This was likely to have been a stressful experience. It is unlikely that fully informed consent was gained as this may have confounded the findings. Debriefing is used in situations when information has been withheld.

■ Take it further

You might like to watch a range of television adverts and identify which of the principles above are being used to persuade. Make a grid and record how many adverts use fear, credible/expert sources, etc. You could develop this idea further and collect some qualitative data by asking a sample of people which is their favourite television advert and why.

■ Key terms

Cognitive misers: the idea that people take shortcuts and jump to conclusions when processing social information.

The Hovland-Yale model saw people as largely rational, dealing with and weighing up a huge amount of information in a series of carefully thought-out sequences. This approach was therefore cognitively expensive as it assumed that people always think carefully. More recently, social psychologists have pointed to evidence which suggests that people do not always consider information as thoroughly as this model suggests. In effect, most of the time we are **cognitive misers**: we take shortcuts and jump to conclusions on the basis of very limited information.

For this reason, more recent approaches to persuasion have been termed parallel or 'dual-process' models. This is because they distinguish between two types of persuasion – those which involve careful and rational consideration of the arguments (as in the Hovland-Yale model) and those in which minds are made up on the basis of very limited information. Either of these two, parallel processes can operate when exposed to a persuasive argument.

Dual-process models of attitude change

Dual-process models are based on the underlying assumption that people are not always willing or able to think systematically about the arguments when exposed to a persuasive attempt. Two important dual-process models are the elaboration likelihood model proposed by Petty and Cacioppo (1986) and Chaiken's systematic and heuristic processing model (1980). As we can see from the name 'dual process', these models agree that there are two ways in which people process persuasive messages.

The elaboration likelihood model (ELM)

Petty and Cacioppo (1986) agreed that when an attempt is made to persuade someone, they consider the argument. However, they viewed people as cognitive misers who do not always think deeply or take into account all of the information, for example, about the sender/source of the message. The elaboration likelihood model argued that there are two specific 'routes' to attitude change:

- The central route – this involves a great deal of thought and cognitive effort. The person follows the arguments closely and carefully and may consider counter arguments. Whether or not they are persuaded depends on the quality of the argument. Attitude change is likely to be permanent.

- The peripheral route – in contrast the peripheral route involves minimal cognitive effort. The person does not pay much attention or give much thought to the message they are presented with. They are likely to respond to cues and to use shortcuts to make their decisions as to whether or not to change their views. Attitude change is likely to be temporary.

An important concept in the ELM is the **need for cognition** (or NC). Petty and Cacioppo (1986) have argued that people who are 'high in need for cognition' are more likely to use central processing. Research evidence such as the study by Vidrine, Simmons and Brandon (2007) below, has supported this claim.

Tesser and Shaffer (1990) have further argued that factors including personal relevance and direct experience influence whether or not a person will engage in central processing. If the message presented has little relevance to us or we have no direct experience of it, we are likely to resort to peripheral processing.

Research study: Vidrine, Simmons and Brandon (2007)

One attempt to assess the importance of NC in smokers was carried out by Vidrine, Simmons and Brandon. They used 227 student smokers who were measured to assess their NC then exposed to one of three conditions:

- a fact-based leaflet emphasising smoking risks
- an emotion-based leaflet emphasising smoking risks
- a control condition.

In accordance with the ELM model, the researchers found that those with a high NC responded better to the fact-based leaflet suggesting that they had read and considered the arguments. In contrast, those with low NC responded better to the emotion-based leaflet implying that they were using peripheral processing.

Key terms

Dual-process models: these distinguish between two types of processing involving more or less cognitive effort.

Need for cognition: the view that some people have a stronger need to know than others and like to get to grips with arguments. Someone with a high need for cognition is likely to agree with statements such as, 'I like to solve problems and puzzles'.

Link

Approaches, issues and debates

Dual-process models of persuasion take the view that individuals choose one of two routes when exposed to persuasive messages, suggesting some degree of control and autonomy or an element of free will.

Media psychology

Methodological issues

This study is an example of a highly controlled laboratory experiment. However, as participants know they are taking part in a study they may give socially desirable answers. The short nature of the study means that we cannot be sure if attitude change is temporary or more lasting.

Ethical issues

As with any study using potentially fearful messages to influence attitudes, participants were exposed to some psychological stress. Informed consent is an important principle of research of this nature, along with debriefing.

Systematic versus heuristic processing

An alternative dual-process model is presented by Shelly Chaiken (1980). The systematic/heuristic model agrees with the ELM that there are two types of processing which loosely correspond to the central and peripheral routes. When using **heuristic processing**, we take shortcuts to make up our mind and over-simplify. With heuristic processing, the message context (where and how it is said) is more important than the content (what is said). When using **systematic processing** we consider the arguments carefully. The decision to use one or the other of these strategies is said to depend on how important the issue is. So, for example, if you were choosing a university to study at or buying a car you may well use systematic processing; less-important decisions such as which pizza to choose may use heuristic processing.

Research study: Ito (2002)

Ito looked at the effects of heuristic and systematic processing using a sample of Japanese University students. Ito varied the strength of a persuasive message (strong or weak) and the delivery by a high- or low-credibility source giving four conditions:

- Strong message – high credibility source.
- Weak message – high credibility source.
- Strong message – low credibility source.
- Weak message – low credibility source.

When participants were involved/interested in the issue at stake, Ito found that they were influenced by the strength of arguments, but the source had little impact. This implies that they were using systematic processing. In contrast, those with low interest in the issue were influenced by the credibility of the source rather than strength of argument, implying that they were using heuristic processing. This study demonstrates neatly the two types of processing suggested by Chaiken's model.

Methodological issues

Ito's study demonstrates clearly the experimental approach to studying attitude change. Experimentation of this nature allows manipulation of one or more independent variables (in this case credibility of source and strength of message) and tight control of outside factors which may influence the outcome. However, the measurement of attitude change immediately afterwards is short term and does not allow us to assess if changes are relatively permanent.

Key terms

Heuristic processing: taking mental shortcuts to simplify.

Systematic processing: carefully considering the available arguments.

Link

Approaches, issues and debates

Research into attitudes and persuasion takes a cognitive-social approach to social psychology, seeing people as 'thinkers' within a social environment. The cognitive-social approach sees attitudes as relatively consistent entities, existing in people's heads, guiding behaviour and decision-making. This view of attitudes is challenged by discursive social psychologists who argue that attitudes are contradictory rather than consistent.

Ethical issues

This study required information to be withheld from participants to prevent social desirability effects. This can be justified if the deception is mild and participants are fully debriefed afterwards.

The models we have looked at so far have seen attitudes as 'belonging' to individuals. However, some attitudes are widespread and shared by many members of a community – often, sadly, those involving racial and other prejudices. Potter (1996) has argued that traditional approaches to understanding attitudes have failed to consider the importance of **collective attitudes** like these. Social representations theory (Moscovici, 1984) has presented a valuable contribution to understanding such attitudes, arguing they originate in conversations and are circulated as people talk to each other and via the mass media.

The models that we have examined so far take a 'cognitive social approach' to understanding attitudes. By this we mean that they view people as thinkers, processing information given by others within a social setting. In contrast, **discursive psychologists** have criticised the idea that attitudes are consistent and measurable. By studying the ways in which people express their attitudes in everyday talk, they point to the view that attitudes shift and are often contradictory even within the same sentence. So the same person may express both positive and negative views of something within a single sentence! Discursive psychologists suggest that we should view attitudes not as measurable entities but as 'resources' – people use them in conversation to persuade other people of their viewpoint. For this reason they choose to study discourse.

Key points

- Attitudes can be seen as having two or three components.

- Sequential models of attitude change describe four stages – attention, comprehension, reactance, change.

- The Hovland-Yale model looked at factors in terms of source, message and recipient and interactions between the factors.

- This model generated considerable research into persuasion.

- Dual-process models argue that people are cognitive misers who do not always pay attention to arguments.

- The ELM model distinguishes between central and peripheral processing.

- Chaiken's model distinguishes systematic and heuristic processing.

- Dual approaches have received research support.

- The cognitive social approach to attitudes has been criticised by discursive psychologists who argue with the claim that attitudes are consistent and measurable.

- It has also been criticised for ignoring widely held 'social' attitudes.

Link

This study uses an independent measures design. You can remind yourself about different types of experimental design by looking at Chapter 38, Designing psychological investigations, page 515.

Key terms

Collective attitudes: attitudes that are widespread, shared by large numbers of people and circulated via newspapers and other media. They are also known as social representations.

Discursive psychologists: psychologists who study discourse or talk and examine how language is used in everyday settings.

AQA Examiner's tip

Make sure that you can explain the differences between the Hovland-Yale model and dual-process approaches to persuasion.

Summary questions

1. Explain what is meant by the term 'attitude' and refer to two-component and three-component models.

2. Outline the main features of the Hovland-Yale model of attitude change.

3. Explain how two-component models differ from the Hovland-Yale model.

4. Discuss the view that people are 'cognitive misers'.

Media psychology

The influence of attitudes on decision-making

Learning objectives:

- describe the importance of consistency between sets of attitudes

- explain how attitudes influence decisions and decisions can influence attitudes

- understand the challenge made by Bem's self-perception theory to dissonance theory.

Key terms

Consistency theory: a theory which argues that attitudes fit together, and conflict between related attitudes leads to discomfort.

Cognitive dissonance: discomfort which is experienced when two cognitions or attitudes clash. Dissonance motivates us to change attitudes.

The role of cognitive consistency

In this section of the chapter, we are going to examine how the attitudes we hold influence the behaviours we choose to carry out. Each day, most of us make many different sorts of decisions, from the trivial choice of what to eat in the canteen, to more serious or potentially life-changing decisions such as choosing a university or degree course. How do these decisions relate to our attitudes?

Some theorists have argued that a major 'driver' of decision-making is the need for consistency between attitudes. You may have noticed that attitudes do not exist separately from each other but fit together and interrelate with each other. So, for example, if your friend holds strong attitudes against cruelty to animals, they are also likely to hold negative attitudes relating to testing of cosmetics on animals and battery farming. Here we are going to examine the influential explanation put forward by cognitive dissonance theory which is an example of a **consistency theory**. We will then consider the alternative approach suggested by Bem's self-perception theory.

Dissonance theory

Dissonance theory (Festinger, 1957) was based on earlier consistency theories such as Heider's balance theory (Heider, 1946 and 1958). Originally proposed in the 1950s, dissonance theory was substantially revised and updated in the 1990s. According to this approach, an important influence on our decisions is the need for consistency between attitudes and cognitions (beliefs) especially when cognitions are related to each other. Festinger believed that pairs of cognitions could have three possible relationships:

- Consonant cognitions fit easily together: I am against cruelty to animals and I do not eat meat.
- Dissonant cognitions are pairs which clash with each other: I am against cruelty to animals but I really want to buy that suede jacket/ those leather boots.
- Irrelevant cognitions which have no relationship: I am against cruelty to animals and plan to study history at university.

Festinger believed that when two related cognitions clashed or were inconsistent with each other, we experience **cognitive dissonance**. This is an uncomfortable feeling which we are motivated to reduce. Dissonance can be reduced by changing one of the cognitions. Festinger's theory was neatly demonstrated by forced compliance studies like the one featured below. As you read it, note how social psychological research has changed over the last 50 years.

Research study: Festinger and Carlsmith (1959)

Male students were asked to participate in an extremely dull, repetitive task and then told to inform other students who were waiting to take part that the task was exciting and fun – clearly an outright lie! Half were paid $1 and the others $20.

Festinger measured their attitude to the task at the end and found that those paid the measly $1 rated it as worthwhile whilst those paid $20 still rated it as dull and boring. Why? According to Festinger:

▥ The $20 group experienced consonant cognitions: they could tell themselves that they had told a lie but had been paid handsomely for it.

▥ The $1 group in contrast experienced dissonant cognitions. They could not justify their behaviour in the same way so to reduce the dissonance (I lied and was paid peanuts to do so!) they changed their attitude to the task.

Methodological issues

The use of male students in this experiment is likely to produce sample bias. The sample was both androcentric and ethnocentric, making it very difficult to generalise from these results.

Ethical issues

This study shows how research was carried out before the establishment of ethical guidelines and principles. Students were misled as to the nature of the task, and did not give their fully informed consent. They were also subjected to psychological stress by being pressurised to lie to others. Research of this nature is very unlikely to be approved by today's ethics committees.

Post-decisional dissonance

Festinger also applied his theory to explain dissonance which takes place following decisions. Imagine that you have to choose between two equally attractive university offers. You visit both universities and like them equally, but you are forced to choose one and reject the other in order to have a lower 'insurance' offer. Eventually you accept University A. This is likely to produce dissonance due to the co-existence of the cognitions 'I really like University B' and 'I have rejected University B'. The most sensible thing to do to reduce the dissonance is to find good reasons to shore up and support your choice by looking for advantages of University A over B and by emphasising the negative aspects of University B.

This was shown to happen in a study by Knox and Inkster (1968) who used punters in a betting shop. The punters were asked how sure they were that a particular horse was going to win a race before they had put money on it and again after they had placed their bet for it to win. Knox and Inkster found that the punter became much more certain after the bet that their chosen horse would win, showing how they changed their attitudes post decision.

The **selective exposure hypothesis** further argued that after a decision is made, people actively seek information which supports their choice and avoid information which contradicts it to prevent further dissonance.

Since its original formulation, dissonance theory has been substantially revised. Cooper and Fazio (1984) argued that the amount of dissonance depended on two conditions:

▥ There should be unpleasant consequences arising from one of the cognitions.

▥ The individual must feel a sense of personal responsibility for their decisions and behaviour.

▥ Key terms

Selective exposure hypothesis: the idea that we actively seek information which supports the decisions we have made.

Steele (1998) added another point to make dissonance theory work, suggesting that situations involving dissonance often involve fairly unpleasant behaviours. If the choice is between changing the view we have of ourselves (our self-concept) and changing our attitudes, we will change the attitude every time.

Self-perception theory

One of the first major challenges to dissonance theory was made by Darryl Bem (1967 and 1972) who took a different approach to understanding attitudes. He argued that, quite a lot of the time, people are unaware of exactly what their attitudes are or what they think about particular issues (does this sound familiar to you?). Bem argued that we approach our own attitudes in a similar way to that in which we approach other people's. So, for example, you may not have had a discussion about your pal's attitude to going to university, but you deduce from their behaviour – refusing to go out/revising/cutting down hours at work – that their grades and educational future are pretty important to them. According to Bem, exactly the same process is used to arrive at our own attitudes. We look at what we do (behaviour) and then fill in or infer what our attitudes must be on the basis of our actions. This does not apply to all attitudes but simply to those where we do not really know what we think and the 'internal cues' to our behaviour are weak or ambiguous. So, in Knox and Inkster's study, Bem would argue that the punters were not really sure which horse would win, but when they saw they had put money on it, they could infer their attitude from the action.

The battle between dissonance and self-perception theory raged throughout social psychology in the 1970s with each producing different interpretations of the same findings. Finally in 1977, Fazio, Zanna and Cooper announced that both theories were right, putting an end to the argument.

Bem's theory was right in explaining ordinary situations where attitudes and behaviour differ, where we do not hold strong attitudes about an issue. However, Festinger's theory was right in situations where there was an extreme difference between behaviour and underlying cognitions.

Deaux, Dane and Wrightsman (1993) argued that dissonance theory has provided the best example of what happens to attitudes and why they change following our decisions. This theory can be applied to almost any situation where an individual makes an important choice or decision.

One problem with consistency theories in general is that although we know that attitudes fit together, there has been little theoretical explanation of why this should be (Potter, 1996).

Summary questions

5 Explain what is meant by the term 'cognitive dissonance'.

6 Describe a situation which could lead to post-decisional dissonance.

7 Explain how self-perception theory would interpret studies of cognitive dissonance.

Key points

- Attitudes tend to fit together in consistent patterns.

- When attitudes or cognitions clash, we can experience cognitive dissonance.

- Dissonance was demonstrated originally using forced compliance studies.

- Post-decisional dissonance takes place following a decision.

- Self-perception theory argued that people often do not know what attitudes they hold but infer them from behaviour.

- Both theories are probably right in different situations.

The influence of television on persuasion

Learning objectives:

- describe the different ways television is used to persuade
- understand the psychological principles used in television advertising and persuasion.

Link

You can refresh your memory about sequential models by looking back at page 391.

Introduction

Television is perhaps the most obvious medium through which persuasive messages are presented. You are likely to be exposed to a range of attempts to change your attitudes and behaviour each time you turn on the television. The amount of money allocated to television advertising implies that it is highly effective and studies have supported this claim. Oskamp (1988) argued that television adverts are a powerful influence on attitudes and Taras *et al.* (1989) noted that children's requests for certain foods correlate strongly with the amount of television advertising the product is receiving. In this part of the chapter we are going to consider how television advertisers use the psychological principles behind persuasion to change our views and influence our behaviour.

Some of the more obvious attempts at persuasion on TV include:

- Adverts – these aim to create a favourable view of a product and to influence you to buy or use the product.
- Political messages – party political broadcasts are often used before elections to persuade voters to choose a candidate or a party.
- Attitude campaigns – these are used to attempt to influence attitudes and therefore change some aspect of behaviour. One example of this is the annual drink-drive campaign which aims to dissuade drivers from drinking at Christmas.
- Television appeals – for example Children in Need and Comic Relief aim to encourage watchers to donate money.

How does television persuade us?

We saw at the start of this chapter that sequential models argue that persuasion takes place in stages. We are going to look at each of these in sequence.

Principle one – capture their attention

As we have seen, the first stage of attitude change relates to attention. In order for adverts, campaigns or party political broadcasts to work, they have to grab our attention. For this reason, adverts and campaigns often start with eye-catching or iconic images which 'grab' the idle watcher. A recent example of this is the much-loved 'drumming gorilla' advertising Cadbury's chocolate. The importance of attention was demonstrated by Olney, Holbrook and Batra (1991) who measured 'channel hopping' during adverts and found that unique, eye-catching adverts captured watchers' attention. In the extract below, Mark Sweney writing in the *Guardian* reflects on the eye-catching properties of successful adverts:

> With hundreds of TV channels and the likes of Facebook and Bebo competing ever more furiously for our attention, it is no surprise that advertisers are arguably becoming increasingly controversial ... it's a deliberate marketing tactic.
>
> As they reach for another cigarette from a carton emblazoned with the word 'Smoking Kills' the notion that lighting up is bad for you isn't going to be breaking news to very many smokers.

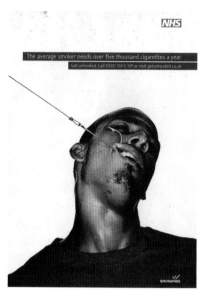

Fig. 2 *Why do you think this advert attracted so many complaints?*

Media psychology

Take it further

You could find out about the attention-grabbing advertising campaigns created by Toscani for Benetton during the 1990s. These used images of bloodstained newborn babies, and Aids victims, and were widely criticised for lacking taste.

Key terms

Classical conditioning: learning by association. A neutral stimulus (toilet roll) is paired with an unconditioned stimulus (fluffy puppy) which produces an unconditioned response. After repeated pairings, the neutral stimulus becomes a conditioned stimulus and produces a conditioned response.

Mere exposure hypothesis: the idea that the more we are exposed to something, the more we will like it.

So for the Department of Health's anti-smoking campaign to have any point at all it is going to have to be especially arresting – hence the controversial fish hook campaign ...

'Feel good' adverts such as Cadbury's Gorilla or Sony's Balls scoop truckloads of awards and critical acclaim ... But ad agencies scramble over one another to handle serious work by clients such as the NSPCC ... it is often the most annoying adverts on TV that prove to be the most effective and memorable ... 'Annoying adverts like Cillit Bang can have that way of worming their way into your head', said Saatchi and Saatchi strategy director, Richard Huntington.

The Guardian, *30 April 2008*
(see *www.guardian.co.uk/media/2008/apr/30/advertising.television1*
for the full article)

Principle two – comprehension

Comprehension is extremely important in relation to attitude change in political and health campaigns but much less important in terms of advertising of products. This demonstrates neatly the distinction made earlier between systematic and heuristic processing. Many television adverts encourage heuristic processing and the main message is obscure (sometimes deliberately) and has to be worked out. After all, adverts are meant to entertain as well as persuade. In political campaigns, evidence suggests that messages should be presented clearly and simply. For complex messages, written forms are much more effective than television.

Principle three – create a favourable association

This is based on the stage of reactance. Once an advert has been noticed, the aim is to create a favourable evaluation of the product you are selling, and this is done by association. So, drinks adverts play on association with laid back, relaxed, sunny afternoons. The method by which this is done involves **classical conditioning**. In classical conditioning, a positive image is associated with the attitude object so that the attitude object comes to produce the same response as the image. In the advertisements for Andrex toilet tissue, the cute, fluffy Labrador puppy is associated with the product just as the Dulux dog is associated with paint. It can also help to create a favourable evaluation of the advert. If people like an advert and talk about it in the pub, this provides valuable reinforcement or repetition (see principle four).

Another way in which classical conditioning works is through the use of music. This was neatly shown in the film *Jaws* (Spielberg, 1977) where a high-pitched sound was used to signify impending shark attack! If you think about your all-time favourite adverts, they often involve distinctive music – sometimes you know what the advert is before it starts just as a result of the music. This approach has been used to good effect in television campaigns for political parties, for example the use of 'things can only get better' in the general election of 1997. Smith and Mackie (2000) argue that 'classical conditioning is the backbone of the emotional appeal'.

Principle four – make it memorable!

Another important principle in TV advertising is repetition. This idea is based on the early work of Zajonc (1968) who found that familiarity is an important part of liking, and devised from this the **mere exposure hypothesis**. The advertising industry argues that message needs to be repeated if it is to work (Ray, 1988). Tellis (1987) argued that adverts should be repeated two or three times a week if possible. An alternative approach to this is to maximise coverage and split adverts, giving a very short clip before and after a break in a film.

Key points

- Television adverts can be used to persuade people to buy or use products. Television is also used for attitude change, campaigns in health, and politics.

- Television advertisers primarily follow the four stages in sequential models of persuasion.

- It is important to capture the viewer's attention in successful advertising.

- Comprehension is less important as advertisers encourage heuristic rather than systematic processing.

- Adverts use classical conditioning to associate positive images and emotions with products.

- The most successful adverts are often the most irritating or offensive!

AQA Examiner's tip

Make sure that you can explain the psychological principles used by advertisers and relate them back to models of persuasion.

Take it further

Use the internet to explore examples of subliminal advertising. Do you think the evidence shows that subliminal messages can persuade?

Summary questions

8 Explain how classical conditioning and familiarity/mere exposure are used in advertising.

9 Discuss the importance of systematic and heuristic processing in television advertising.

10 Discuss the view that successful adverts can be loathed as well as liked!

11 For each explanation of persuasion and attitude change in this chapter write a brief statement about how it would explain the effectiveness of television in persuasion.

Media psychology

30

Media influences on social behaviour

Explanation of media influences on social behaviour

Media psychology

Learning objectives:

- explain what is meant by aggression, antisocial behaviour and pro-social behaviour

- describe the short- and long-term effects of watching violence on anti-social and aggressive behaviours

- describe the effects of the media on pro-social behaviour

- understand explanations of these effects.

Introduction

In this section of the course, we are going to examine a debate which you may already be familiar with. This debate concerns whether or not exposure to violent images in the media (notably television, films and computer games) produces psychological effects and how these effects can be explained. You are undoubtedly aware that this debate resurfaces at regular intervals – often after high-profile cases where individuals have committed acts of violence which bear a strong resemblance to those shown on films. But this is often over-simplified into a discussion of whether watching violence leads to violent behaviour. As we will see in this chapter, the effects of watching violence are more complex and subtle than simple imitation. We will start by establishing these effects – both short and long term – and consider psychological explanations of them. It is important to note that opinions on this topic have been varied, not just amongst lay people but also amongst psychologists, as you will see!

What kind of programmes show pro- and antisocial behaviours?

Watching television and DVDs is one of the most popular and time-consuming leisure activities. In 2005, time spent watching averaged around 160 minutes a day for men and 145 minutes for women (Office for National Statistics, 2006). Antisocial behaviours appear in many different types of programmes including children's cartoons, news broadcasts, films and daytime 'reality' shows. Pro-social behaviours are shown in a similar range of programmes as well as on children's television and in fundraising events such as *Comic Relief*. Soap operas such as *Hollyoaks* and *EastEnders* are rich sources of both pro- and antisocial behaviours.

In 1989, Heymann carried out some research which found that children watched on average 3.5 hours of television a day. At that time, evening television showed five violent acts per hour and cartoons showed a staggering 20 per hour! Smith *et al.* (2006) carried out a content analysis of 2,227 US television programmes from 18 channels. Seventy-three per cent of the programmes showed some form of helping with 2.92 acts of helping per hour which rose to 4.02 acts in children's television.

Influences on physiological responses

If you are a regular watcher of horror films and violence, you may remember that when you first started watching them your heart would beat faster at particularly spooky or gruesome scenes. This is called **increased arousal** and it is part of your stress response.

Physiological arousal has been used to explain why watching violence might increase the tendency to behave aggressively. Zillman's excitation transfer theory (1979) argues that the arousal produced by watching

Key terms

Increased arousal: the increased heart rate and sweating which is often a reaction to watching violence.

is transferred to real-life situations which involve conflict. So, if an individual who has watched violence is provoked by someone else, their already high level of arousal is misinterpreted as coming from the provocation and an aggressive response may be produced. Alternatively, the level of arousal produced by watching may increase to such a point that it cannot be controlled by the usual methods (Berkowitz, 1993).

With regular watching, arousal tends to reduce and may even disappear altogether so that many people become less likely to have a reaction each time they watch. This is known as **desensitisation**, literally becoming less sensitive and responsive to violence, and it also takes place when people play violent computer games (Bartholow, 2006). Huesmann *et al.* (2003) have used the idea of desensitisation to explain why some watchers of violence may act aggressively. When faced with a violent act, non-watchers experience a strong stress response, but regular watchers may be able to act aggressively as they have lost the natural reactions that may deter them from carrying out such behaviours.

Explanations based on arousal can help to explain aggressive behaviour which occurs immediately after watching violent television. However, they struggle to explain violence which occurs some time after watching. They also overlook the importance of factors such as self-control and moral restraint which prevent most people from acting aggressively most of the time.

Influences on cognitions

Cognitive priming refers to the idea that watching violence leads people to store memories or **scripts** of violent acts. These scripts are then retrieved and activated in real-life, similar situations and may 'prime' watchers to respond in a similar way to the script. Put simply, watching television or a film puts us into a state where we react similarly to something which happens in the real world.

Huesmann *et al.* (2003) have argued that the learning of aggressive scripts can also help us understand why some people may go on to behave aggressively. Once a child has learned a script, it is used to define situations and to guide how to behave if similar situations arise. Violent scripts are accessible because they are seen so often on television.

Recently advances in brain scanning have supported the idea that scripts are stored in long-term memory. Murray *et al.* (2007) used functional magnetic resonance imaging (fMRI) to compare the brain areas which were active when a sample of eight children watched both violent and non-violent television programmes. In both conditions, the regions which process visual motion were active as would be expected. However, when the children watched the violent film, a network of right-hemisphere regions was activated. These included the posterior cingulate, the amygdala, the interior parietal and the pre-frontal and motor cortices, a network of brain regions which regulate emotion, arousal and attention. As well as this the areas of the brain responsible for storing **episodic memories** were active, implying that the acts seen may be stored as aggressive scripts for later use.

Influences on aggressive behaviour

The issue of possible imitation of aggressive behaviour has produced the fiercest debate between researchers. In order for you to gain a flavour of this debate, studies by Huesmann *et al.* (2003) and Gunter *et al.* (2002) are included here in some detail.

Key terms

Desensitisation: a reduction in physiological arousal and emotional responses to violence.

Cognitive priming: the storing of aggressive ideas/scenes which may be activated later in similar situations.

Scripts: stored ways of behaving in social situations which may include roles and plans of action.

Episodic memories: long-term memories for events which are stored in the hypothalamus.

Media psychology

▥ Research study: Huesmann *et al.* (2003)

Huesmann *et al.* carried out a longitudinal study of 557 boys and girls in Chicago. Children were studied in 1977 when they were aged 5–8 and asked about their favourite programmes and television characters. Popular shows in the 1970s included *Starsky and Hutch*, *The Six Million Dollar Man* and *The Bionic Woman*. The children were asked which characters they most identified with.

In 1991, 398 were followed up in their early twenties. They were asked to identify their three favourite television programmes and to say how often they watched them. They were also asked to name three people who knew them well and the researchers carried out a face-to-face or phone interview with one of those people. The 'friend' was asked to comment on how often the participant lost their temper and whether or not they grabbed, hit or shoved other people. Finally, Huesmann *et al.* examined official records to assess which of the sample had been involved in crimes of all kinds.

Huesmann *et al.* found that:

▥ The viewing of violent television shows when children were between six and nine years of age correlated significantly with measures of adult aggression in both men and women 15 years later.

▥ This correlation was significant for physical aggression in both men and women and for 'indirect' aggression in women only.

▥ The more a child had identified with same-sex violent models, the more likely they were to be aggressive in later life.

▥ Those men classed as high-violence viewers in boyhood had three times the crime conviction rate of low-violence viewers.

Methodological issues

▥ Longitudinal studies of this nature are to be commended for the lengthy follow-up into adulthood, although participant drop-out is often an issue. The use of a wide range of methods to assess aggressive behaviour in adulthood is also to be commended. Particularly notable is the use of interviews with named individuals close to the participant.

Ethical issues

▥ As a correlation study, this avoids many of the ethical issues associated with experimentation in this area.

Fig. 1 The A-Team: *does this kind of programme need a health warning?*

▥ Research study: Gunter *et al.* (2002)

Gunter *et al.* studied the impact of the introduction of television to the geographically remote community of St Helena, a British colony in the South Atlantic with a population of 6,000. In 1993, two years before the introduction of television, Gunter *et al.* studied the children to provide a baseline measure of aggressive behaviour. Twenty-three boys and 24 girls aged 3–4 were sampled (the total number of children this age on the island) and their teachers were asked to comment on the levels of antisocial behaviour using a pre-school behaviour checklist. At this point, the incidence of antisocial behaviour was very low – in fact, St Helena's children were described as 'the best behaved in the world'.

In 1995 television was introduced to St Helena in the form of CNN, which broadcast news reports. Cartoon Network was added in 1996 and in 1998 the island began to receive Movie Magic, the BBC, Discovery and Supersport. Gunter *et al.* returned to St Helena in 1998 and asked the children to keep a three-day diary in which they recorded all of the programmes they had watched. From this it was possible to assess the amount of violence each child had been exposed to. They were again assessed by teachers, this time using Rutter's Behaviour Questionnaire as a post-television antisocial behaviour measure.

- Gunter *et al.* found that the average amount of television watched during the three-day period was three hours and 10 minutes and children had viewed an average of around 95 acts of violence during that period. Boys had seen more acts of violence on average than girls and they displayed more antisocial behaviour than girls at this second assessment.

- Although there was no overall increase in aggressive behaviour post television, specific relationships existed between programme content and antisocial behaviour, and this was more noticeable when a large number of cartoons were watched.

- Children with higher antisocial behaviour scores before television was introduced were most likely to watch a large number of cartoons, implying that children with an interest in violence may select programmes with that sort of content.

Methodological issues

This is an example of a natural experiment in which the independent variable (exposure to television) occurred without intervention from the researcher. The assessment of antisocial behaviour before and after the introduction of television allows proper comparisons to be made.

However, teachers' ratings of behaviours may have been influenced by their own views relating to the impact of television.

Ethical issues

As a natural experiment, with no direct manipulation of the TV, there are few ethical issues here. Parental consent and debriefing are essential principles in research of this nature.

Huesmann *et al.*'s study indicated that children do copy aggressive and violent behaviour and that this continues into ongoing aggressive behaviour patterns in adulthood even linking to involvement in crime. However, Gunter's natural experiment has demonstrated the importance of social context and cultural factors on media influence and has shown that it is important not to over-generalise findings of research into the media violence link.

However, large-scale **meta-analyses** have supported Huesmann *et al.*'s findings. Anderson and Bushman (2002) reviewed a series of studies using different quantitative methodologies with over 48,000 participants in total and calculated the overall **effect size**. In this substantial review, watching violence had a significant effect on later aggressive behaviour across all the four types of study. The effect was strongest in laboratory experiments as we would expect, but there was still a substantial effect in field and longitudinal studies.

Media psychology

Key terms

Meta-analyses: the analysis of the findings of a large number of studies which have used similar methodology.

Effect size: a measurement of how much effect the independent variable has on the dependent variable on a scale of 0 (no effect) to 1.0.

Table 1 *Results of Anderson and Bushman's meta-analysis*

	Number of studies	Effect size
Cross-sectional studies	86	0.18
Longitudinal studies	42	0.17
Laboratory experiments	124	0.23
Field experiments	28	0.19

Take it further

Carry out a content analysis of British television and compare the amount of violent acts shown on television in St Helena (see Gunter *et al.*'s study) with the figures for British television. Do you think the two are comparable?

Hint

You can remember the names of the four main media effects on antisocial behaviour using the mnemonic PAID (Priming/Arousal/Imitation/Desensitisation).

Anderson and Bushman (2002) argued that the link between watching violence and acting aggressively can be understood by using the analogy of smoking and lung cancer:

- Some smokers get lung cancer, but some do not. Some watchers end up acting violently, but others do not.
- People differ in how susceptible they are to smoking-induced cancer. People differ in how susceptible they are to film and television violence.
- Researchers knew that smoking caused cancer long before they understood the precise mechanisms involved. Researchers know that watching violence 'causes' violence although they have not entirely teased out the mechanisms!

Effects of watching pro-social behaviour

Not surprisingly, the study of pro-social behaviour has attracted rather less debate and research attention than the possible link with antisocial behaviour! Despite this, some researchers such as Hearold (1986) have claimed that pro-social television has a greater effect on behaviour than antisocial television does.

A number of studies have used the method of exposing children to pro-social television and observing their behaviour for short periods afterwards. Using this approach, Rushton (1975) found that when young children were shown pro-social programmes, their attitudes towards pro-social behaviour improved. However, changes in actual behaviour were short lived and lasted only a couple of weeks. Van Evra (1990) found that watching pro-social programmes seemed to be associated with increases in sharing and cooperation in young children.

More recently, researchers have pointed to the importance of the child's level of cognitive development in relation to gains from watching pro-social behaviours. Rosenkoetter (1999) examined the role of sitcoms using a sample of children from the USA aged five, seven and nine. The children watched an episode of *The Cosby Show* or *Full House* and then took part in an interview to see if they had grasped the moral principle behind the episode. Rosenkoetter found that about a third of year ones and about a half of year threes had grasped the moral idea behind the story, suggesting that children's ability to benefit from such programmes depends on their understanding of the message behind the story. Rosenkoetter also correlated the child's watching of sitcoms as reported by parents with the amount of helpful and pro-social behaviour they showed and found a significant correlation. This research implies that regular watching of programmes with pro-social content does influence how helpful children are. This view is supported by research carried out by Fogel (2007) which also points to the importance of adults watching with children and discussing what is seen.

Fig. 2 The Cosby Show, *an example of a pro-social television programme*

Research study: Fogel (2007)

Fogel examined the effects that watching pro-social sitcoms had on children aged between eight and 12 living in California. Children completed a questionnaire about their normal television-watching habits and were allocated randomly to one of two conditions:

- The experimental group watched a 30-minute episode of *Hang Time* and then took part in a 15-minute discussion about it with an adult.
- The control group watched the same episode of the programme but did not discuss it.

The study found that those in the experimental group who had experienced adult mediation showed improved scores over the control group in measures of pro-social behaviours including tolerance and friendship. The researchers conclude that watching and discussion with an adult is valuable in order for children to benefit most from pro-social programmes.

Methodological issues

This study uses real television programmes giving it a high level of validity. However, as children know their behaviours are being observed, they are likely to respond to demand characteristics and may give socially desirable answers.

Ethical issues

As with all studies involving children, parental consent is an important principle here. Fogel's study has powerful implications for ensuring that children gain maximum benefit from watching pro-social programmes.

Explaining influences on behaviour

The studies above have shown that watching violence in childhood links to aggressive behaviour in adulthood and that watching pro-social programmes has an effect – although possibly short term – on pro-social behaviours. Here, we are going to examine two explanations of how these behavioural effects might take place. Rather than being seen as separate, competing explanations, social cognitive learning theory can be seen as a development of **social learning theory**, which addresses the limitations of the earlier approach. Comstock and Paik's 'third variable' theory (1991) provides an alternative explanation to social learning approaches.

Social learning theory

Social learning theory was based on research carried out by Bandura, Ross and Ross in a series of experimental studies in the 1960s (Bandura, Ross and Ross, 1963). These rather contrived studies involved showing groups of young children violence using real life or filmed adult models and observing their play immediately afterwards. It was consistently found that children exposed to a violent adult model would play more aggressively than a non-exposed group. Imitation was found to be more likely if the violent model received a reward for their actions rather than being punished.

Key terms

Social learning theory: the idea that behaviours are learned through observation of role models and imitation of their actions.

Media psychology

Key terms

Vicarious experience: learning through observation of another person's actions rather than through direct experience.

Link

You can read more about Skinner's theory of operant conditioning by looking at pages 241–2.

Link

Approaches, issues and debates

Social learning and social cognitive learning theory take the view that watching violence can influence cognitions, although there is less agreement as to the effects on aggressive behaviour. This view can be seen as somewhat deterministic as it assumes that individuals have little ability to resist media influences.

Link

Approaches, issues and debates

Social learning approaches can be seen as reductionist as they take the view that aggressive behaviour can be explained solely through role models and learning experiences ignoring the role of biological factors.

Social learning theory argues that children learn behaviours through two mechanisms:

- Learning via direct experience – this is based on Skinner's principle of operant conditioning. If a child acts aggressively (for example pushing another child to get a toy at playgroup) and receives a reward, the behaviour is likely to be repeated. If the child is reinforced for helpful behaviour they will repeat this.
- Learning via **vicarious experience** – this involves learning through observation and imitation of role models. If a child sees a role model act aggressively or pro-socially and gain a reward, they may copy the behaviour.

Of course, children and adults are exposed to a range of media role models who may act aggressively or pro-socially including television characters, celebrities and sporting figures. Social learning theory acknowledges that children do not passively imitate any role model they see but are highly selective, choosing dominant and powerful individuals as models (Bussey and Bandura, 1984). Whether or not an individual behaves aggressively or pro-socially in a specific situation depends on their previous experiences, for example if they have been rewarded in the past for such actions. It also depends on the likelihood of the behaviour being rewarded or indeed punished in the current situation. Therefore, social learning theory helps us to understand how children acquire behaviours in the first place and how and why they might use them and continue to act aggressively (Hogg and Vaughan, 2005).

Bandura *et al.*'s studies, whilst helpful in opening up debate into media effects, clearly suffered from a range of methodological problems. Critics pointed out that the young children involved were likely to respond to demand characteristics within the situation, as one was heard to say, 'That's the doll we are supposed to hit', and that rough play with an inanimate toy is very different to real-life aggression against another living being.

Social learning theory saw children as relatively passive observers and imitators of the behaviours they saw around them. Bandura *et al.* were forced to extend their theory to acknowledge the importance of cognitive factors in order to explain how the child responded to watching violence. For example, in order for a child to imitate the behaviour of a role model, they must pay attention to the behaviour and store a representation of it in their memory. In order to repeat the behaviour, the child should be capable and motivated to reproduce the behaviour.

Social cognitive observational learning theory

Social cognitive observational learning theory is a development of social learning theory which takes into account the above criticisms and acknowledges the importance of cognitive factors in the development of aggressive behaviours. Children are not seen as simply learning behaviours, but also developing ways of thinking and beliefs about violence from the programmes they see. According to social cognitive observational learning theory, children have an inborn tendency to imitate the behaviours which they see around them, as learning via observation is much safer than learning from experience (Butterworth, 1999). Therefore, young children will tend to copy both pro-social and antisocial behaviours from models including family, peers, friends and television.

However, children who are exposed to violent models are said to develop three types of social cognitive structure which influence their behaviours:

- **Schemas** – those who view violent television often hold the view that the world is a dangerous and hostile place.
- Scripts – watchers of violence may develop aggressive scripts in which aggression is used as a way of solving interpersonal problems and conflicts.
- **Normative beliefs** – people who watch violence often see aggressive and violent behaviour as normal and a part of everyday life.

As the child grows up, scripts become more complex and automatic. Children exposed to violent media may begin to see other people as hostile and the world as a dangerous place.

Social cognitive observational learning theory is a powerful theory which acknowledges the importance of observational learning of behaviours and of schemas relating to violence. It is currently generating considerable research into the effects of cognitive structures on aggressive behaviour.

Considerable evidence has supported the claim that children develop scripts and normative beliefs from watching violent programmes. For example, Gerbner *et al.* (1994) found that children who watch violence are more likely to interpret other people's behaviour as hostile and Guerra, Huesmann and Hanish (1995) have shown that children's normative beliefs are related to what they watch on television.

Comstock and Paik (1991) have put forward a different argument to account for the 'watching–acting' link known as **third variable theory**. They argue that although there is a link between watching and acting aggressively, the two factors correlate rather than one (watching violence) causing the other (acting aggressively). Comstock and Paik note that a fairly large number of characteristics relating to family background and personality also correlate with watching violence and acting aggressively. So, for example, children from lower socio-economic classes tend to watch more television as do children with lower levels of measured intelligence. This may be due to a number of different reasons, such as the dislike of alternative, more cognitively demanding activities or the cost of alternative forms of entertainment for example. According to this approach, the 'link' that can be seen between watching violence and acting aggressively can be explained through one of these 'third' underlying variables which 'causes' more watching and more imitations of aggression.

Key points

- Television and films show a range of pro-social and antisocial behaviours.
- Watching violence leads to initial arousal followed by desensitisation.
- Watching violence can lead to aggressive scripts which may be recalled in real-life situations.
- There has been considerable debate about the effects of watching violence on later aggressive behaviour.
- Meta-analyses show that watching violence in childhood has an effect on aggressive behaviour in adulthood.
- Children who watch pro-social behaviour act more helpfully, although the effects may be short lived.
- Media influences have been explained by social learning theory using concepts of observation and modelling.
- Social cognitive observational learning theory argues that children also learn scripts, schemas and normative beliefs which influence behaviour.

Key terms

Schemas: sets of ideas about an object or activity which come from past experience and may be taken in from the wider culture. A gender schema refers to the set of ideas about what activities, toys and behaviours are appropriate for a particular sex – boy or girl.

Normative beliefs: ideas of what is normal and acceptable.

Third variable theory: the idea that the link between watching and acting aggressively is purely correlational and both factors are caused by another variable.

Link

You can read more about correlation by referring to Chapter 39, Data analysis and reporting on investigations, page 515.

Media psychology

Summary questions

1. Explain what is meant by desensitisation, scripts and cognitive priming.

2. Summarise findings of research into the effects of television on pro-social and antisocial behaviours.

3. Contrast the explanations given by social learning theory and social cognitive observational learning theory for aggressive behaviour. Which do you find the most convincing and why?

4. How does third variable theory explain the link between watching violence and acting aggressively?

The effects of video games and computers on young people

Learning objectives:

- explain the differences between gaming and watching violence
- describe research into the main effects of playing computer games
- understand explanations of gaming effects including the general aggression model.

Further reading and weblinks

You can read an article about the classification of *Manhunt 2* at www.guardian.co.uk/technology/2008/mar/15/games.

Introduction

More recently, research has turned to consider the potential impact of playing computer games. These differ from television and films as the player takes an active role in carrying out violence rather than simply watching. Improvements in computer graphics have meant that depictions of violence are becoming more and more realistic. Content analyses of computer games have noted that the main content is violent. Dietz (1998) examined 33 popular games made by Nintendo and Sega and found that 80 per cent contained some form of aggression. Half contained violence towards another person and in 21 per cent the violence was directed at women. In a more recent study, Haninger and Thomson (2004) examined 80 computer games aimed at teenagers and found that 94 per cent contained some sort of violence.

In June 2007, *Manhunt 2* was the first game in a decade to be banned by the British Board of Film Classification (BBFC) for its violent content. In *Manhunt 2*, the player takes the role of a scientist who has been forced to take part in a series of terrifying experiments before escaping from an asylum. The player's job is to help him in his fight for freedom. The game was described by the BBFC as containing gratuitous violence and being 'sadistic, brutal and bleak', as the *Guardian* summarised:

> Manhunt 2 was finally cleared for adult use only in March 2008. Growing concern about the potential impact of computer games such as Manhunt 2 has led the government to commission a review in 2008 of their impact, overseen by Tanya Byron, a 'television psychologist'.
>
> The Guardian, *15 March 2008*

The effects of playing violent computer games

As with research into the effects of television and film, studies using computer games have identified a range of effects. Guo (2007) identified the main effects of playing violent games as increasing physiological arousal, decreased helping behaviours and increased aggressive behaviours, feelings and cognitions. Research has also drawn attention to the desensitising effects of computer games to both gaming and real-life violence. As we noted above in relation to television violence, most debate centres on the issue of whether or not aggressive behaviour is increased by playing. It is also important to note that, given the relatively recent development of computer games, long-term studies of their impact do not yet exist.

Increased physiological arousal

As with watching violence, playing violent games leads to an increase in physiological arousal as shown by heart rate and blood pressure. Music is an important factor in increasing arousal. During game playing, Tafalla (2007) examined the effects of music on using the game *Doom* and found that both men and women showed increased arousal (higher blood pressure/heart rate) when the music was playing.

Reduced helping behaviours

Sheese and Graziano (2005) studied the relationship between playing violent games and later helpful, cooperative behaviours. Forty-eight participants played either a violent or doctored, non-violent version of the game *Doom* in

Media psychology

pairs. They were then given the option of cooperating with or exploiting each other or withdrawing from the game. Sheese and Graziano found that those who had played the violent version were more likely to choose to exploit than cooperate, and they argue from this that playing violent games may well undermine cooperative and pro-social behaviours.

Increased aggressive behaviour, cognitions and feelings

In contrast to research on watching violence, research into the effects of playing computer games has implied that they probably do not increase aggressive behaviour in most people! Sherry (2001) has argued that the relationship between playing violent games and aggressive behaviour is weaker than the relationship between watching violent television and aggressive behaviour. Unsworth, Devilly and Ward (2007) have disputed the view that there is a link between playing computer games and aggressive behaviour in most people. Unsworth *et al.* measured players for aggressive feelings before, during and after playing *Quake II* and found that the feelings did not change in most players – only those who were already aggressive before the game became more angry after playing. In another study, Van Schie and Wiegman (1997) studied 346 children and found no relationship between times spent playing games and levels of aggression. However, time spent playing was correlated positively with the child's level of intelligence.

Desensitisation to violence

Advances in technology have also led to an increased ability to study brain responses to gaming. Bartholow (2006) compared the brain responses of habitual players with those who do not play violent games choosing to focus on the P300 component of the 'event-related brain potential'. He found reduced brain response (i.e. desensitisation) in those used to game violence and argued that this study is the first to link violent game playing to brain processes. More worryingly, Carnagey, Anderson and Bushman (2007) have suggested that gaming leads to desensitisation to real-life violence.

AQA Examiner's tip

Make sure that you can describe the main effects of playing games and give supporting evidence for these effects.

█ Research study: Carnagey, Anderson and Bushman (2007)

Carnagey *et al.* examined the effect of playing violent computer games on later responses to real-life violence. A sample of participants were asked about their normal playing habits and were then randomly allocated to one of two conditions:

- █ Playing a randomly selected violent game for 20 minutes.
- █ Playing a non-violent game for 20 minutes.

Following this, all participants watched a film which depicted real-life violence whilst wired to measure their physiological response including heart rate (HR) and galvanic skin response (GSR). Those who had played the violent game had lower HR and GSR, implying that they had a reduced physiological response to real violence.

Methodological issues

This study is a good example of a tightly controlled laboratory experiment which enables cause and effect to be established. The dependent variables here (HR and GSR) are largely free from participant reactivity, providing a high level of validity.

The use of filmed violence here is essential for experimental control. However, it is likely that response to genuine real-life violence would have been greater than to filmed violence.

As with other studies the measurement of the dependent variable has taken place here almost immediately after playing the game.

Ethical issues

As with all media effects research, there are important issues relating to informed consent here. The impact of playing violent games would require careful debriefing.

Explaining the effects – the general aggression model

The general aggression model (GAM) (Anderson and Gill, 2000/Anderson and Bushman, 2002) argues that input variables (including individual factors such as personality and gender) and situational factors (such as provocation) influence or mediate an individual's reaction to playing violent computer games. Therefore the GAM helps to explain the differences in vulnerability to playing violent computer games. Exposure to games is said to increase aggression through three possible pathways:

- Arousal: playing violent games increases the level of physiological arousal shown in heart rate and blood pressure. A higher level of physiological arousal may lead to aggressive behaviour if the opportunity arises.
- Cognitions: playing violent computer games may lead to priming of aggressive thoughts.
- Affective: playing computer games may increase aggressive or hostile feelings.

A study by Bushman and Anderson (2002) confirmed that playing games leads to expectancy that other people will react in a hostile way. Two hundred and forty-four participants played either a violent or a non-violent game and were then given short stories to complete in which characters encountered an interpersonal problem. Those who had played the violent game completed the stories with more aggressive endings, suggesting that they had developed 'hostile expectancy biases'.

Research into input variables has been relatively limited (Arriaga et al., 2006) but studies carried out by Guimetti and Markey (2007) and Unsworth (2007) support the claim that variables such as mood and personality influence response to games. Guimetti and Markey (2007) tested the claim that personality traits such as an aggressive disposition are important in mediating people's responses to playing computer games. They used 79 female and 88 male US students. All were initially assessed for anger then assigned either to play a violent game or a non-violent action-packed game. After this, they were asked to complete a series of stories which were assessed for aggressive content. Guimetti and Markey found that only those who were assessed at the start as 'angry' became more aggressive after playing a violent game. Those who were not already angry showed little effect, supporting the suggestion made by the GAM.

Link

Approaches, issues and debates

The general aggression model acknowledges that input variables mediate the influence of computer games, implying some role for choice and autonomy. It also acknowledges the contribution of factors other than experience and can be seen as less reductionist than other approaches.

Summary questions

5 Outline three effects of playing computer games.

6 Describe research into one of these effects.

7 Discuss the difficulties in carrying out research in this area.

Key points

- Many computer games contain violent content.
- Games differ from watching filmed violence as they ask the player to take an active role.
- Computer games have been shown to increase arousal, decrease helping behaviour and lead to desensitisation to game and real-life violence.
- The evidence surrounding imitation of aggressive behaviour from computer games is weak.
- Most studies focus on short-term effects and use experimental methodologies which may lack validity.
- The general aggression model argues that input variables influence the individual's reaction to game playing.

31

The psychology of celebrity

The attraction of celebrity

Learning objectives:

■ explain what is meant by parasocial relationships, celebrity worship and stalking

■ understand social psychological explanations of parasocial relationships including attachment theory and the absorption addiction model

■ understand the possible evolutionary origins of parasocial relationships

■ describe research studies into intense fandom, celebrity worship and stalking.

Key terms

Parasocial relationships: one-sided relationships in which one person is unaware of the existence of the other.

Stalking: the repeated following and harassing of another person that threatens their safety.

Likert scale: a way of measuring attitudes towards something such as tendency to contact a favourite celebrity. There are usually five levels of agreement (strongly agree, agree, do not know, disagree and strongly disagree) scored from 1 to 5.

Introduction

Celebrities – it seems you cannot open the newspaper or browse the internet without having another instalment in the colourful life of Pete Doherty, Amy Winehouse or Britney Spears. Turn on the television and you are likely to find a range of celebrity-based programmes, head down to the newsagents and you will find a variety of magazines catering to the celebrity watcher. It seems that we live in a celebrity-obsessed culture in which many people have a strong desire to find out more about the lives of their favourites.

This chapter considers explanations of why people form 'relationships' with celebrities. These are unlike real relationships as they are entirely one-sided. For this reason, psychologists term them **parasocial relationships**. Most parasocial relationships are likely to be relatively harmless, but a small number develop into stalking. **Stalking** has been defined by the British Crime Survey as 'a course of conduct involving two or more events of harassment causing alarm, fear or distress' (Walby and Allen, 2004). Most stalking takes place between two people known to each other, but there have been many examples in which celebrities such as Madonna and Steven Spielberg have been stalked by obsessed fans. We will consider explanations of why a small number of people may go on to this much more serious behaviour. What divides the casual from the hardcore fan, who queues all night for a sight of their idol and ends up hanging around outside their door?

Measuring attraction to celebrities

One way in which we can measure attraction to celebrities is the Celebrity Attitude Scale devised by McCutcheon (2002). The scale consists of 23 items scored on a **Likert scale** which are answered using a score of 1–5. The CAS consists of three sub-scales which measure different aspects of celebrity worship. These are:

■ The Entertainment/Social sub-scale. This 10-item scale measures the social aspects associated with the celebrity worship such as discussions with friends and shared experiences. An example item could be, 'My friends and I like to discuss what X has done'.

■ The Intense Personal sub-scale. This nine-item scale measures the intensity of the person's feelings towards the celebrity along with obsessional tendencies. Sample items include, 'I consider X to be my soul mate'.

■ The Borderline Pathological sub-scale. This four-item scale measures potentially harmful aspects of feelings towards the celebrity, for example, 'If X asked me to do something illegal as a favour I probably would'.

■ Key terms

Vignettes: short written descriptions of events, behaviour or people, which can be used in an experimental setting. Researchers can vary some aspects of them to investigate an independent variable.

Pathological view: the pathological view of parasocial relationships argues that they are formed due to poor psychological adjustment.

Positive/active view: the positive/ active view of parasocial relationships argues that they are healthy and fulfil important social functions.

Absorption-addiction model: this argues that people with poor real relationships seek parasocial relationships.

■ Link

You may wish to refresh your memory about attachment theory by reading pages 101–5 of Chapter 9, Effects of early experience and culture on adult relationships.

■ Measuring stalking

The issue of stalking poses methodological problems for the psychologist. Whilst high-profile case studies exist (such as the case of Mark Chapman who stalked and shot John Lennon), these are clearly extreme one-offs and we cannot generalise from them. A methodological problem is that people define stalking differently. What one person may see as reasonable behaviour, such as an ex-girlfriend or ex-boyfriend hanging around outside someone's house every night for a week, another might see as threatening and unacceptable. For these reasons, psychologists often use scenarios or **vignettes** to investigate beliefs about stalking. For example, Dennison and Thomson (2002) gave four-page scenarios to a sample of Australian adults and Sheridan (2003) gave UK students single-paragraph vignettes to investigate definitions of stalking. Whilst vignettes have the advantages of allowing researchers to control and manipulate aspects of a situation, they lack validity.

■ Three levels of parasocial relationship

McCutcheon *et al.* (2004) argue that using the CAS allows us to identify three levels of parasocial relationship, from the fairly harmless to the serious. These may also be seen as stages and below we will examine explanations of why someone might move from harmless to obsessional celebrity worship:

■ Level one: the entertainment/social level – the person is attracted to the celebrity because of the entertainment they provide. They are a source of fun and enjoyment.

■ Level two: the intense personal level – a small number of fans become intensely engaged with their chosen celebrity.

■ Level three: the borderline pathological – an even smaller number engage in behaviours that may be seen as obsessional and pathological, such as following the celebrity home and writing to them. At this stage, celebrity worship can be seen as having got out of hand and become the much more serious stalking.

■ Are parasocial relationships acceptable?

Maltby *et al.* (2001) argued that there are two views of parasocial relationships which see them very differently. The **pathological view** argues that those who attach themselves strongly to celebrities generally have poor adjustment and mental health and may lack social skills and the ability to make real and fulfilling social relationships. This view is taken by the absorption-addiction model (McCutcheon *et al.*, 2002) and by attachment theorists who argue that the need to form parasocial relationships originates in early insecure attachments between children and their parents.

In contrast, the **positive/active view** (Jenkins, 1992; Jenson, 1992) argues that celebrity worship fulfils important social functions. Here we shall examine each of these explanations and consider how far evidence supports these views.

The absorption-addiction model

The **absorption-addiction model** (McCutcheon *et al.*, 2002) argues that people pursue parasocial relationships due to deficits or lacks within their real life. Relationships with celebrities are seen as an attempt to cope with or escape from reality. People may follow celebrities to gain a sense of personal identity and to achieve a sense of fulfilment. The absorption-addiction model is closely tied to the three levels of celebrity worship. Whilst most fans stay at the fairly harmless level one stage, those who have a weaker sense of personal identity or poorer psychological adjustment may go beyond this and 'absorb' themselves in a celebrity's life to gain a sense of stronger identity. A personal crisis may also lead an individual to move from one stage to the next. Parasocial relationships are seen as being addictive so the individual needs to feel an increasingly stronger sense of involvement with their celebrity. Stalking is the third stage reached by a few people who have the poorest mental health and adjustment. This model therefore predicts an association between poorer psychological health and the strength or level of parasocial relationships.

The positive/active view

An alternative, positive view of parasocial relationships was presented by Jenkins (1992) and Jenson (1992). Jenkins and Jenson argue that parasocial relationships serve important functions and enable fans to enhance their lives through taking an active and positive role. They may help to create social networks with other fans (through fan clubs and 'fanzines' (fan magazines)) and allow fans to develop their sense of appreciation of other people's talents.

Attachment theory

A third explanation of parasocial relationships is based on attachment theory (Keinlen, 1998; McCann, 2001). You met this theory at AS level in developmental psychology and you may have rediscovered it in the topic on relationships earlier in this book. According to this approach, the tendency to form parasocial relationships originates in early childhood relationships between young children and their primary caregivers. This theory argues that those with **insecure attachment types** as adults are more likely to become strongly attracted to celebrities than those with secure adult attachment types. Parasocial relationships are seen as being attractive to *insecurely attached* people because they make no demands and the fan does not run the risk of criticism, disappointment or rejection that is part of real relationships. According to this approach, those with an anxious-ambivalent attachment style are likely to be needy and clingy in their real face-to-face relationships, which makes parasocial relationships attractive to them.

Attachment explanations have also been applied to help understand extreme celebrity worship including stalking. Keinlen (1998) and McCann (2001) have suggested that stalking behaviour in adolescence and adulthood is directly related to insecure attachment patterns. They argue that those with an anxious-ambivalent adult attachment type seek the approval of their attachment person and may try to contact or meet their idol. In contrast, the insecure-avoidant types prefer to keep a distance in relationships but may pursue their attachment object to retaliate against a perceived wrongdoing.

Testing these explanations

These explanations have different views of the mental health and adjustment of those who engage in parasocial relationships. The absorption-addiction model argues that those with poorer adjustment are likely to seek parasocial relationships to make up for deficits within their own lives, whereas the positive/active view argues that they enable fans to tap into social networks with other fans and to enhance their social lives. These opposing views make very different predictions about the psychological well-being and adjustment of people who engage in

■ Link

Approaches, issues and debates

Attachment theory see the origin of celebrity worship lying in insecure childhood relationships. This view can be seen as relatively deterministic.

■ Key terms

Insecure attachment types: these are divided into two types. Anxious ambivalent types alternate between closeness and wanting distance, whereas insecure avoidant types keep a distance and avoid closeness in their relationships.

■ Link

For more information about attachment theory, see Chapter 4, Attachment in everyday life, in the *AQA Psychology A AS* student book.

AQA Examiner's tip

Ensure that you can distinguish between the three psychological models of celebrity worship.

Media psychology

parasocial relationships. However, it is equally possible that there is no simple relationship or possibly no relationship at all between psychological adjustment and parasocial relationships (Maltby *et al.*, 2001).

Research study: Maltby *et al.* (2001)

Maltby *et al.* (2001) set out to look for possible links between poorer mental health and celebrity worship. They used a sample of UK students (126 male and 181 female) living in South Yorkshire who were asked to complete two psychological measurements:

- A 23-item CAS (celebrity attitude scale) based on a Likert measurement.
- A general health questionnaire (GHQ28) devised by Goldberg and Williams (1991) which measured symptoms of depression, anxiety and social dysfunction.

Maltby *et al.* found that individuals who had reached the first level of celebrity worship had some degree of social dysfunction. They often lacked social relationships in their real life, experienced loneliness and used the celebrity relationship to 'soothe the empty self'. Those who had reached the second level scored highly on anxiety and depression. Maltby *et al.* were unable to test the third level as the GHQ does not include items to measure serious problems with adjustment. However, this study provided clear support for the pathological view of celebrity worship.

Methodological issues

This study uses a correlational method, therefore it is important to note that cause cannot be established. Whilst there is an association between poorer mental health and degrees of celebrity worship, it cannot be concluded that one causes the other.

Ethical issues

In any study which measures aspects of psychological functioning, there are potentially serious ethical issues. Although this study uses a non-clinical population (students), researchers would need to ensure that those students who were identified as having some degree of social dysfunction or symptoms such as anxiety/depression were made aware of sources of help and support available.

Others have set out to compare the predictions made by the attachment theory and the absorption-addiction model. As we noted above, attachment explanations locate the need for celebrity relationships within insecure childhood attachments. This view has been tested by a variety of researchers including McCutcheon *et al.* (2006) and Roberts (2007).

Research study: McCutcheon *et al.* (2006)

McCutcheon *et al.* set out to test if there is a link between insecure attachments, mild celebrity following and approval of stalking behaviours. In this study a number of hypotheses were tested including:

1 If adults with an insecure adult attachment type were more likely to become 'attached' to celebrities than those with a secure adult attachment type.

2 If adults with an insecure adult attachment type were more likely to agree with/condone stalking and obsessive behaviours towards their celebrity figure than securely attached adults.

3 If there was a correlation between stalking tendency and pathological attachment to celebrities.

McCutcheon asked 299 students, male and female aged 16–42, to complete four measurements. These were:

- McCutcheon's (2004) 23-item celebrity attitude scale.

- An unpublished celebrity stalking scale consisting of 11 items such as, 'A fan managed to get hold of the personal number of their favourite celebrity and rang them 4 times in 2 days making obscene comments'. Participants were asked to use a Likert scale to rate how appropriate the behaviours were.

- A relationship questionnaire devised by Bartholomew and Horowitz (1991) to measure adult attachment type.

- A parental bonding scale which asked participants to recall their early relationships with both of their parents up to the age of 16.

McCutcheon found no support for hypothesis 1 above. There was no relationship between insecure attachment and the tendency to form parasocial relationships with celebrities. However, the second and third hypotheses were supported. Those with insecure attachment styles were more likely to think that stalking was acceptable, and there was a relationship between pathological attachment and the tendency to stalk.

Methodological issues

This study involved a range of measurements and scales. Note how the researchers used counterbalancing to control for potential order effects.

Ethical issues

As with Maltby's study, there is a need for sensitivity and careful debriefing after research of this nature. Participants should be directed to appropriate sources of support and help if they request this.

Link

You can read more about counterbalancing in the *AQA Psychology A AS* student book on page 110.

Whilst McCutcheon's study suggests that attachment style is not related to mild celebrity worship, it does offer support for the attachment explanation of stalking. This was further supported by Roberts (2007). A mixed-sex sample of 200 students completed an attachment questionnaire and a scale which measured attempts to contact celebrities. Roberts found that there was a significant correlation between a preoccupied attachment style and attempts to contact celebrities. These findings imply that more serious aspects of stalking/fan behaviour may indeed be related to insecure attachment styles.

Evolutionary explanations of celebrity worship

Evolutionary explanations look for how behaviours seen today (such as celebrity worship) may have conveyed survival advantages in our evolutionary past. Evolutionary psychologists argue that the tendency to look up to and imitate others could have had powerful advantages in the past. Kate Douglas (2003) writing in the *New Scientist* claimed that

Link

Approaches, issues and debates

Evolutionary explanations of celebrity worship argue that such behaviours have evolved via natural selection for their survival value. This explanation may be seen as reductionistic as it focuses on the past as an important factor in behaviour, but ignores current issues within the individual's life which may also play an important role.

'far from being a form of madness, paying special attention to successful individuals is amongst the cleverest things our big-brained species does'. Learning by trial and error can be expensive in evolutionary terms, for example eating a new food source which turns out to be poisonous. In contrast, **observational learning** and imitation of others is much less risky. However, imitation will only bring benefits if successful individuals are imitated. The ability to copy others who show successful behaviour allows us to gain some of the advantages possessed by them.

The prestige hypothesis

Henrich and Gil-White (2001) argue that social learners would benefit most if they copied individuals who were highly successful or 'prestigious' – the **prestige hypothesis**. Because it might have been difficult to assess exactly which aspects or traits made an individual successful in the past, the most sensible option would be to copy them all, which is termed 'general copying'. Followers may also benefit from protection or additional resources if they stay physically close to successful individuals.

This approach therefore argues that the genetic predisposition to copy successful individuals is in the gene pool today because it enabled our ancestors to be more successful. General copying (for example dressing like a celebrity) was useful when it was unclear which aspects of their behaviour led to success.

Evaluation of the hypothesis

- Some have disagreed with this explanation. For example, Dunbar (cited in Douglas, 2003) argues that our attraction for celebrities comes from the need to monitor and prevent social free loaders and to ensure that those who have social power give something back.
- Evolutionary explanations such as the prestige hypothesis are extremely difficult to test as we cannot go back to hunter-gatherer days to observe behaviour.
- Although celebrity worship exists in some people today, persuasive evidence points to the importance of experiences – early attachments and searches for identity – in the development of these behaviours.

Key points

- Parasocial relationships are those where one person is unaware of the existence of the other.
- Attitudes to celebrities can be measured using the celebrity attitude scale.
- The CAS identifies three levels of celebrity worship.
- Pathological explanations argue that those with poorer adjustment are likely to form parasocial relationships.
- Positive models argue that parasocial relationships fulfil important social functions.
- Evidence has supported the pathological view.
- Evolutionary explanations such as the prestige hypothesis argue that imitation and copying of prestigious individuals conveyed survival advantages in the past.

Key terms

Observational learning: this refers to learning through observation of another person's actions rather than through direct experience.

Prestige hypothesis: this refers to the tendency to imitate members of a social group who have prestige or power. Prestigious individuals in the past were likely to have been good hunters or those with special survival skills.

Summary questions

1. Explain what is meant by parasocial relationships and stalking.

2. Outline two social psychological explanations of parasocial relationships.

3. Discuss evidence for the pathological view of parasocial relationships.

4. Discuss the view that evolutionary explanations are difficult to test.

Media psychology end of topic

How science works: practical activity

You can investigate possible links between watching television or playing violent games and aggressive cognitions using the method of correlation. You may like to start by reflecting a little on the ethical advantages of correlational methods over experimentation in this area.

In order to assess a possible relationship, you will need to devise two measurements:

- A questionnaire which measures the exposure participants have had to watching violent media such as television or playing computer games. You will need to think about the number of questions to use and how they might be scored.
- A measurement of their response to one or several hypothetical scenarios using vignettes. For example, you could present a situation in which someone spills beer over you in a bar with three possible 'response options' giving differing levels of aggressive response.

Both of these measurements should be capable of producing a score as you will need to correlate the results using an appropriate statistical test such as Spearman's rank order correlation coefficient.

You will need to think carefully about the order in which you ask your participants to carry out the tasks in order to minimise demand characteristics. You will also need to consider whether to provide full information before the study or whether to withhold some information which you then provide when you are debriefing the participants.

Link

You can refresh your memory about correlational statistical tests and find the formula by looking at Chapter 39, Data analysis and reporting on investigations, pages 532–42.

Further reading and weblinks

There are lots of websites where you can find out more about the St Helena study, e.g. www.studentpsychology.com/common/supplementary/1841692514/125,126.pdf.

You can find out more about the government-commissioned review of media violence by going to www.news.bbc.co.uk (search for the article 'Video games ratings face overhaul'). The final review can be accessed at www.dcsf.gov.uk/byronreview.

You can explore the world of subliminal advertising (and Derren Brown) by going to www.youtube.com and searching for 'Derren makes a subliminal ad'.

You can find out more about the need for cognition and complete a scale yourself by going to www.prenhall.com/divisions/hss/app/social/chap7_2.html.

The psychology of
addictive behaviour

Introduction

People have become addicted to various substances for centuries. Alcohol was discovered early in human civilisation and although most people use it only recreationally there have always been some vulnerable to addiction. However, over the last 50 years, addiction to so-called drugs of abuse has become a major social problem. Drugs such as heroin and cocaine and milder ones such as cannabis are widely available. They not only affect individuals and their families but are the basis of a criminal industry and the source of widespread antisocial behaviour. Legal drugs such as alcohol and nicotine can also lead to addiction, which in terms of social consequences can be as damaging as illegal drugs; because of the numbers involved the social and health costs of smoking and drinking are enormous. Besides drugs, people can become addicted to other behaviours, such as gambling. Again, the effects on individuals and their families can be drastic.

Are different forms of addiction similar in their characteristics? Can they be explained using the same psychological models? Are both biological and psychological mechanisms involved? Are the different stages of addiction – initiation, maintenance, cessation, relapse – affected by the same factors? To what extent do we understand how to prevent addiction, or to intervene to help people fight their addiction?

In the two chapters that follow we explore these questions. In the first we look at biological, cognitive and learning models of addiction, with an emphasis on smoking and gambling. In the second we begin by covering some of the factors thought to be involved in vulnerability to addiction, and in particular the role of the media. Then there is a review of models of prevention, and finally a detailed look at types of intervention and their effectiveness in reducing addictive behaviour. These include biological and psychological methods, and public health campaigns.

Biological, cognitive and learning models of addiction

Addictive behaviour

Learning objectives:

- describe and evaluate biological, learning and cognitive models of addiction

- understand the reasons for initiation, maintenance and relapse of addictive behaviours.

What is addictive behaviour?

In the past, definitions used to focus on substance misuse. For example:

> Addiction is a state of periodic or chronic intoxication produced by repeated consumption of a drug, natural or synthetic.

World Health Organization, 1957

However, there is now a growing movement which views a number of other behaviours (i.e. ones that do not involve taking drugs) as potentially addictive, e.g. gambling, overeating, sex, exercise, playing computer games and even wealth acquisition.

A later definition of addictive behaviour by Marlatt *et al.* (1988) reflects this broader concept of addictive behaviour:

> a repetitive habit pattern that increases the risk of disease and/or associated personal and social problems. Addictive behaviours are often experienced subjectively as 'loss of control' – the behaviour contrives to occur despite volitional attempts to abstain or moderate use. These habit patterns are typically characterized by immediate gratification (short term reward), often coupled with delayed deleterious effects (long term costs). Attempts to change an addictive behaviour (via treatment or self initiation) are typically marked with high relapse rates.

Marlatt et al., 1988

Different types of addictive behaviour arise from different factors. However, certain elements of addiction seem to be shared across different substances and behaviour. For example, all addictions seem to be characterised by self-indulgent behaviour which provides short-term pleasure in spite of an awareness of the long-term damaging consequences. Addiction provides a powerful and rapid means of changing mood and sensations. In most addictive behaviours, the rate of **relapse** after a period of abstinence is high and the factors that contribute to relapse are similar for most addictions.

Given these similarities, there are models which provide a general account of addiction and we will look at the following:

- biological
- cognitive
- learning.

Serious, disabling addictions are regarded as mental disorders and they are described in the current versions of the major classification systems, the *ICD-10* and *DSM-IV-TR*.

Key terms

Relapse: the return of signs and symptoms of a disorder (in this case, addictive behaviour) after the individual has enjoyed a remission, i.e. a period without any signs or symptoms.

Link

See pages 321–3 for a fuller description of the *ICD-10* and *DSM-IV-TR* classification systems.

In clinical settings the World Health Organization (WHO) now prefers the term 'dependence' to 'addiction'. Dependence, is characterised by a continuous or intermittent craving for the substance to avoid a **dysphoric** state. Individuals have a strong desire to take the substance and show progressive neglect of other forms of satisfaction. They frequently develop **tolerance** and experience withdrawal symptoms if they stop taking the substance.

Dependence is differentiated from the terms 'abuse' (*DSM*) or 'harmful use' (*ICD*) which are used to describe a maladaptive pattern of substance use leading to impairment of general health. Some individuals meet the criteria for substance abuse but do not meet the criteria for dependence.

The AQA Specification requires you to look particularly at gambling and smoking addiction. These two types of addictive behaviour are regarded rather differently in the classification systems. Smoking addiction is included in a class of disorders called 'substance-related disorders' and reflects the WHO definition of addiction given at the beginning of this chapter. In other words, it is seen as a form of intoxication produced by repeated consumption of a drug (in this case **nicotine**). Gambling addiction, on the other hand, does not involve taking in substances, and is classified in the *DSM-IV-TR* as an impulse-control disorder (in the *ICD-10* it is classified as habit and impulse disorder), but in behavioural terms it is considered an addiction. Smoking and gambling are considered in more detail on pages 431–7.

Models of addictive behaviour

General models of addiction originated mainly to explain addiction in the sense of substance dependence/abuse. However, they can be applied to other forms of addictive behaviour such as gambling.

Each of the models offers an explanation for initiation, maintenance and relapse of addictive behaviours and also some suggestions for treatment:

- Initiation refers to the process where individuals start to become addicted.
- Maintenance is the process whereby people continue to behave addictively even in the face of adverse consequences.

Key terms

Dysphoric: a state of mind characterised by depression, anxiety and guilt.

Tolerance: this occurs when a drug produces a decreased effect after repeated administrations, or increasing doses are required to produce the same effect. Drug tolerance can involve both psychological and physiological factors.

Nicotine: a chemical compound found naturally in plants of the nightshade family including tobacco. It is highly addictive and is one of the main factors responsible for the dependence-forming properties of tobacco smoking.

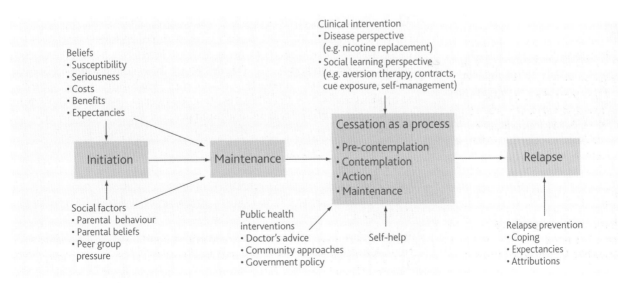

Fig. 1 *The stages of substance abuse*

■ Relapse is the process whereby individuals who have managed to give up their addictive habits start to show signs and symptoms of the behaviour again.

Biological models

Biological models are sometimes referred to as 'disease models'. They share the following assumptions:

■ Addiction is a specific diagnosis, i.e. you are either an addict or you are not – you cannot be 'slightly addicted'.

■ Addiction is an illness.

■ The problem lies in the individual.

■ The addiction is irreversible.

■ There is an emphasis on treatment.

Some biologists believe that people who show addictive behaviour have an underlying physiological abnormality which predisposes them to addiction. **Alcoholics Anonymous** (AA), for example, take the view that alcohol addiction is an allergic response.

There is little evidence for this view, but there is some support for the idea that genetics might play a role. It is unlikely that a single gene is responsible for addictive behaviour. It is more likely that multiple genes are involved and that different genes underlie different addictions. For example, there seems to be a link between tobacco smoking and genes involved in dopamine regulation (Lerman *et al.*, 1999) whereas research into cannabis, cocaine and heroin addiction has found links to a gene in a different brain system (Comings *et al.*, 1997).

Much of the research into genetic vulnerability has been conducted in the context of alcohol addiction, but it seems likely that other forms of addiction might follow the same pattern (see also the sections on smoking and gambling below).

Researchers often carry out family studies to investigate the possibility of genetic transmission. Family studies of alcohol-use disorders have shown high rates amongst relatives. For example, Merikangas *et al.* (1998) found that 36 per cent of the relatives of the individuals with an alcohol disorder had also been diagnosed with an alcohol-use disorder. While there are several studies showing similar results, it is impossible to separate out the effects of genetic and environmental influences. However, some adoption studies (i.e. where children are not brought up by their biological parents) also lend support to the idea of a genetic contribution to addiction, e.g. Heath (2000). Twin studies offer additional support for a genetic component (heritability). For example, heritability of nicotine dependence has been estimated at between 60 and 70 per cent (e.g. Kendler *et al.*, 1999) and of alcohol dependence at 39–60 per cent (Heath and Martin, 1993).

Commentary

Even if we could confirm a genetic component in addictive behaviour, it would still be necessary to find the mechanism by which the genetic influence takes effect. The effect could be:

■ biochemical, i.e. in terms of how various addictive substances are metabolised in the brain (see below)

■ psychological, i.e. in terms of how psychological factors such as personality determine behaviour.

■ **Key terms**

Alcoholics Anonymous: a self-supporting, self-help agency which aims to support alcoholics who want to stop drinking.

■ **Link**

For more about the nature–nurture debate see pages 59–62.

■ **Hint**

No study has demonstrated 100 per cent heritability, so genetic factors cannot possibly be solely responsible for the development of addictive behaviours.

Addictive behaviour

Whatever the precise mechanism, it is important to understand that a predisposition to become dependent on alcohol, cannabis, nicotine, etc. will only express itself if the individual consumes large amounts of the substance. In other words, someone with a genetic vulnerability to alcohol addiction will not become an alcoholic if he or she never drinks alcohol. The trigger to start drinking (or smoking, using cannabis, etc.) in the first place probably results from environmental factors.

Biochemical factors

Different substances have different effects on the brain and nervous system, but two major pathways have been identified as being important in the development of substance addiction:

- the dopamine reward system
- the endogenous opioid system.

Neurotransmitters are brain chemicals necessary for the transfer of information within the nervous system. One neurotransmitter – dopamine – has received special attention from researchers into addiction because of its apparent role in the regulation of mood and emotion and in motivation and reward processes. Although there are several dopamine systems in the brain, the mesolimbic dopamine system appears to be the most important for motivational processes. In normal dopamine activity, cells in the mesolimbic dopamine system are spontaneously active, releasing small amounts of dopamine into the synaptic cleft. The levels of dopamine produced when the cells are active at this low rate may be responsible for maintaining relatively stable mood states. Research suggests that both alcohol and nicotine affect the nervous system by increasing dopamine levels (Altman *et al.*, 1996). It has been suggested that people who are susceptible to addictions might have inherited a rather more sensitive mesolimbic dopamine pathway (Liebman and Cooper, 1989).

Link

Approaches, issues and debates

There has been a long running debate as to whether people can control their addictive behaviour, and explanations of addiction can be evaluated in terms of free will and determinism. If biochemical/ biological factors cause addictive behaviour, this would be a highly deterministic explanation with little room for free will. Learning, cognitive and social approaches allow more room for free will and choice.

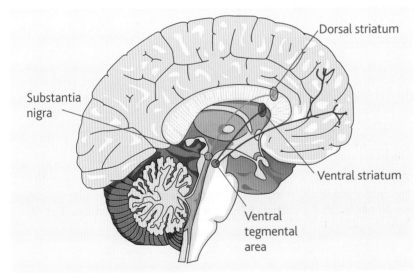

Fig. 2 *Mesolimbic pathway*

Most of the time, humans seem able to exercise some sort of choice over whether or not to engage in behaviours, and we try to maintain a balance so that we do not become addicted. We may sometimes overeat or over-indulge in alcohol at a party, but we are quickly able to revert to our everyday, more moderate pattern of food and alcohol consumption. This is

Addictive behaviour

■ Link

See Chapter 15, Eating disorders, for a discussion of bulimia, and Chapter 28, Anxiety disorders, for a discussion of obsessive compulsive behaviour.

■ Key terms

Enkephalin: an opiate neurotransmitter in the brain. The release of enkephalin is associated with feelings of pleasure and euphoria.

Endorphins: opiate neurotransmitters such as enkephalin and beta-endorphin.

Opioid systems: neurotransmitter pathways in the brain using opioid (or opiate) neurotransmitters such as endorphin and enkephalin. They are involved in states of reward and pleasure, including addictive behaviours.

Psychoactive drugs: substances which act primarily on the central nervous system (CNS) where they alter brain function and result in temporary or sometimes longer-lasting changes in perception, mood, consciousness and behaviour. These drugs can be used recreationally to deliberately alter conscious experience, or therapeutically as medication.

Withdrawal symptoms: these occur when an individual stops an addictive behaviour such as smoking, gambling, taking psychoactive drugs. Certain drugs cause neuroadaptive changes in the brain, which means that tissues have to readjust when the drugs are stopped. This readjustment phase takes time, during which the individual suffers withdrawal symptoms. These can be psychological as well as physical.

because we have the ability to balance two competing neurochemical systems – the reward reinforcement system which finds the eating and drinking pleasurable and therefore reinforcing, and a control system which tells us when we have had enough. It appears that serotonin, another neurotransmitter, plays an important role in this control. Serotonin levels are lower in people who are impulsive. Patients who attempt compulsive suicides and impulsive homicidal behaviour, and those with severe early-onset alcoholism as well as bulimia, all have low levels of serotonin (Oldham, Hallander and Skodal, 1990). It has also been observed that patients who are obsessive (i.e. those who reflect excessively prior to performing a behaviour) are characterised by high metabolic rates in the frontal areas of their brain and by high levels of serotonin.

There is increasing evidence to suggest that the brain's opioid system may also play an important part in addiction. Opioid neurotransmitters in the brain include **enkephalin** and the **endorphins**. The **opioid systems** are activated in states of pleasure, and can be directly stimulated by addictive drugs such as heroin, alcohol and nicotine. The drug Naltrexone is sometimes used in the treatment of alcohol addiction. It works by blocking opioid receptors in the brain and so prevents the rewarding effects of alcohol. Similarly, long-term tobacco smoking has been shown to disrupt the opioid system (Krishnan-Sarin, Rosen and O'Malley, 1999).

Neuroadaptation

One theory of drug dependence is based on the idea of neuroadaptation (Koob and LeMoal, 1997). In other words, changes occur in brain chemistry as a result of taking **psychoactive drugs**. If drug use is stopped, the adaptations are no longer needed so they disrupt the brain's homeostasis. This explains why people develop tolerance to drugs and need to take higher and higher doses to gain the same effects and also why they develop **withdrawal symptoms** if they stop. The unpleasant withdrawal symptoms makes people want to start taking the addictive substance again and so the addiction is maintained.

Commentary

It seems highly likely that brain mechanisms play an important role in addictive behaviour. This is becoming increasingly clear from research studies into alcohol, nicotine and opiate drug addictions. It also seems likely that biological factors operate in other types of addiction where no chemical substance is involved, e.g. gambling. However, much of the research produces correlational data and it is therefore difficult to draw conclusions about cause and effect.

More research also needs to be carried out that will help us to explain why many people drink alcohol, dabble in gambling and smoke cigarettes but do not become addicted. This may reflect a genetic vulnerability in some people.

As we have noted in other parts of this chapter, addictive behaviour results from a combination of factors – biological, social and psychological. Biological accounts alone cannot offer a complete explanation for such complex behaviour as addiction.

Learning (behavioural) models

Since the 1970s there has been a shift away from seeing excessive smoking, drinking, drug-taking, etc. as illnesses and instead it is seen as part of an individual's general behavioural repertoire. Learning (behavioural) models are part of the learning approach that sees addictive behaviours as:

- acquired habits which are learned according to the principles of social learning theory
- things that can be unlearned
- not 'all or nothing' categories. In other words, there are degrees of smoking (drinking, drug-taking, etc.) behaviour
- no different from any other behaviours.

Learning can take place in a number of different ways:

- classical conditioning
- operant conditioning
- observational processes.

Classical conditioning

Classical conditioning is the process where an unconditioned stimulus (US) (e.g. sitting with a group of friends) spontaneously produces an unconditioned response (UR) (e.g. feeling relaxed). If the US is frequently associated with a conditioned stimulus (CS) (e.g. smoking a cigarette), this CS will come to produce the conditioned response (CR) of feeling relaxed. In this way, the individual has learned that smoking can provide the same rewards as the original US.

In this model, the unconditioned stimulus can be external (e.g. being with friends) or internal (e.g. mood).

The relevance of classical conditioning to addiction was first formally suggested by Wikler (1948), an American doctor, in the context of people addicted to opiate drugs. He noticed that patients who had been treated for drug addiction experienced uncomfortable withdrawal-like symptoms if they returned to places associated with their former drug use. He explained this as follows: withdrawal symptoms occur as an unavoidable physiological response in drug takers who do not get their regular 'fix'. Most addicts experience withdrawal symptoms from time to time if they have a delay in finding a supply. Withdrawal symptoms can, therefore, be seen as a UCR. The addict reacts to the withdrawal symptoms by seeking out their next dose – this exposes them to a whole range of environmental cues (e.g. places where drugs are available, needle and syringes, etc.). These cues then become CSs which produce the CR of withdrawal-like symptoms.

If this theory is correct, it has implications for treatment programmes (see pages 446–51).

A later elaboration called 'cue exposure theory' (Heather and Greeley, 1990) suggests that this could explain the strong cravings that people often experience once they have been weaned off their addictive substance.

Operant conditioning

Operant conditioning is a rather different process that depends on the consequences of actions. Behaviours are likely to be repeated if they are rewarded in some way. The reward can take two forms:

- positive reinforcement where the reward is a desirable consequence, e.g. feeling relaxed or confident, gaining the approval of friends
- negative reinforcement where the reward is the removal of an unpleasant consequence, e.g. the relief from withdrawal symptoms if smoking/drug-taking, etc. continues.

 Link

For more on conditioning see Chapter 20, Animal learning and intelligence.

 Link

Approaches, issues and debates

Reductionism is usually associated with the biological approach to behaviour. However, explaining addiction using classical conditioning is another form of reductionism, claiming that addictive behaviour is due to simple associations between stimuli and responses. This ignores social and cultural factors in addiction.

Addictive behaviour

In the case of addictive behaviour, the rewards will vary depending on the substance and on the individual and their own needs, past experience, personality and current life circumstances. Another principle of operant conditioning is that specific behaviours are more rewarding in some contexts than others. For example, Peter has learned that taking an illegal drug is more rewarding when he is in a low mood so, in his case, depression could be a trigger for drug use (depression has become a 'discriminative stimulus'). Lisa, on the other hand, only finds it exciting to take drugs when she is with a group of friends rather than on her own. For her, being with friends is the discriminative stimulus.

Social learning theory (SLT)

This has developed out of traditional learning theories but, unlike them, it is not rooted in observations of non-human animal behaviour. Instead, it takes into account some of the more complex perceptual and reasoning skills of humans. According to SLT, we do not need to experience directly the consequences of a given behaviour but, instead, can learn through observing what other people do or say. For example, by observing significant people in our lives, e.g. parents, friends, we learn that smoking, drinking alcohol, taking drugs, gambling etc. can be attractive and rewarding.

The social learning model also incorporates some cognitive-behavioural models such as the labelling model and the outcome expectancy model. These approaches emphasise factors like expectancy, attributions, imitation and self-efficacy in the regulation of addictive behaviours:

- Cognitive labelling model: according to this theory, an emotional experience is the result of an interaction between physiological arousal and its cognitive interpretation (the cognitive label). The intensity of the emotion is determined by the strength of the physiological arousal. For example, imagine that someone who is addicted to alcohol passes a pub with an open door. This cue associated with drinking provokes a physiological response (e.g. increase in heart rate) and also activates mental processes (e.g. memories of drinking alcohol). The person interprets the physiological reactions as a need for drink (I feel physically aroused. I am somewhere associated with drinking alcohol. So, this physical feeling must mean that I need a drink).

- Outcome expectancy model: according to this theory, someone with addictive behaviour has particular expectations when confronted with cues for the addictive substance. For example, seeing a group of people drinking at a party might trigger the following thoughts: I can see how much they are enjoying drinking. That makes me realise how much I enjoy drinking. I would like to experience those effects again now.

Commentary

Theories based on classical and operant conditioning can probably account for some aspects of addictive behaviour, although they do not take sufficient account of the fact that humans are thinking beings and do not respond in simple stimulus-response fashion to environmental triggers. Social learning theory, on the other hand, acknowledges the importance of cognitive factors and so this theory links traditional behaviourism to more cognitive approaches. The theories of cognitive labelling and outcome expectancy are rather simplistic and research into their validity as explanations has been inconclusive (Tiffany, 1999).

However, the central idea of SLT that stresses the importance of role models in shaping behaviour is able to explain how media representations of drinking, smoking, gambling, etc. behaviour can influence people to initiate or to maintain addictive behaviours.

Cognitive models

Cognitive approaches emphasise the processes that control mental functions such as communication, learning, problem-solving, planning, remembering, etc. (See also the theories of reasoned action and of planned behaviour on pages 443–4.) Self-regulation is thought to be a key factor in the development of addiction problems. Self-regulation involves weighing up the relative importance of social and physical factors as well as one's own personal goals when planning behaviour. Addictive behaviours are thought to occur more frequently in people who place excessive reliance on external structures (e.g. excessive reliance on drugs or alcohol) in order to maintain a balance between their physical and psychological needs.

A similar idea is that people who engage in potentially self-destructive activities such as addictive behaviours have impaired control over their own actions. They often want to stop or reduce their drug-taking, smoking, etc. but seem unable to do so. For example, someone might decide to give up smoking but then they accept a cigarette from a friend at a party. One reason why apparently rational people behave in this way is that they have faulty ways of thinking when they are weighing up the consequences of an action. Ainslie (1992) has suggested that people are perfectly able to consider present and future consequences, but that they attach different weightings to them, with greater weight being given to the present. So, they attach too much weight to the immediate rewards of, for example, a cigarette, and at that moment they are unable to appreciate the longer-term benefits of refusing. This preference for immediate gratification over future benefits of, for instance, not smoking has been called 'cognitive myopia' (short-sightedness) (Herrnstein and Prelec, 1992).

Beck *et al.* (1993) suggested that addictive beliefs play an important part in the development of addictive behaviours. At first, the individual thinks it would be fun/exciting/daring to drink, smoke, gamble, etc. As the individual gradually comes to rely on the addictive substance, the thinking changes to ideas such as: I need a drink/smoke to get through this meeting. These individuals often also have a very negative view of themselves and may suffer from depression and anxiety.

The cognitive processing model

When we walk home, talk to friends, make a cup of coffee, etc. we pay little attention to exactly what we need to do in order to carry out these functions. In other words, they have become so practised that we perform them automatically. Tiffany (1990) suggests that addictive behaviours are regulated by automatic processing. The cognitive processing model suggests that drinking (and smoking, drug-taking, etc.) behaviours over a period of time become automatic. It is difficult to stop doing things that have become automatic. Think about watching a French film with subtitles – you really want to see if you can understand the spoken French, but you find it impossible to ignore the subtitles because reading is such an automatic process for most of us. Similarly, for an addict who wants to give up the addictive behaviour, it is very difficult. Every day they are faced with situations that trigger automatic responses

Link

Approaches, issues and debates

The cognitive approach believes that addictive behaviour is based on false beliefs. By correcting these beliefs people can exercise their free will and remove their addictive behaviour. So we can see this approach as trying to move the emphasis from behaviour that is *determined* to behaviour that is the product of *free will*.

Addictive behaviour

■ **Link**

Approaches, issues and debates

Remember in your evaluation that no single explanation can account for all aspects of addictive behaviour. Since the 1980s there has been a move away from reductionist thinking towards a more integrative approach. Addiction is thought to involve an interaction of psychological, environmental and physiological factors. This way of looking at addiction is consistent with the biopsychosocial approach to health and illness.

(e.g. passing a pub on the way home, opening the fridge where beer/wine is usually kept, meeting a friend after work, etc.). Resisting these automatic responses requires considerable mental effort. This might be just about possible as long as everything else in their life is on an even keel. However, if there are stresses at work or in relationships, the individual often finds it easier to give in to the craving and have a drink, smoke, etc. rather than struggle with the craving as well as other personal problems.

Commentary

Cognitive theories are useful in describing the thinking processes of people who become addicted to certain behaviours. It has also provided the basis for some helpful therapies for people who want to give up these behaviours. Models such as the cognitive processing model can also offer plausible explanations of why relapse occurs. However, it does not offer very convincing explanations of why people take up these potentially self-destructive habits in the first place. As is the case with all of the models described above, the cognitive explanation is useful as part of a broader explanation that includes biological and learning factors as well.

Key points

■ People can become addicted to a wide range of substances and activities.

■ Particular addictive behaviours can be explained in slightly different ways, but there are broad biological, learning and cognitive models which can be applied to all types of addiction.

■ There is some evidence for a genetic vulnerability to addictive behaviours, but it is difficult to disentangle biological influences from environmental influences.

■ It seems clear that the mesolimbic dopamine system is active in addictive behaviours, but it might not be the underlying cause.

■ According to the behavioural model, addictive behaviours are acquired in the same way as any other behaviours, through a process of classical and operant conditioning and modelling.

■ Cognitive models focus on the faulty thinking patterns that underlie addictive behaviours.

■ No single model can account for all of the complex features of addictive behaviour and it is likely that a mixture of biological, learning and cognitive factors contribute.

■ **Summary questions**

1 What is meant by the term 'addictive behaviour'?

2 Outline some of the assumptions of the biological model of addiction.

3 What evidence is there for the genetic transmission of addictive behaviour?

4 How might behaviourists explain the maintenance of addictive behaviours?

5 Why do you think many people can drink alcohol regularly in social settings without becoming addicted?

Explanations for specific addictions

Learning objectives:

- understand and evaluate explanations for smoking

- understand and evaluate explanations for gambling.

Hint

Can you see why some of the side-effects of withdrawal might reduce the motivation of smokers to stop the habit?

Smoking

Cigarette smoking is legal, widespread and, until recently, relatively socially acceptable. The WHO estimates that there are 1.1 billion smokers worldwide and, between them, they smoke 6 trillion cigarettes a year. The WHO also estimates that tobacco kills about 4 million people a year. There is now a considerable body of evidence that links smoking to high blood pressure, coronary heart disease, lung disease, cancer and strokes. Pregnant women who smoke are more likely to deliver premature and underweight babies. There is also some suggestion that smoking can increase rather than decrease levels of stress (Parrott, 2000). The fact that people continue to smoke in the face of such statistics is a measure of how powerful nicotine is as an addictive drug.

There are about 3,000 chemical components in cigarette smoke, but it is thought that nicotine is the active and addictive ingredient. Tobacco companies have often tried to deny the addictive quality of nicotine, but a considerable body of scientific evidence suggests otherwise. Hilts (1994) compared nicotine to five other psychoactive drugs – heroin, cocaine, alcohol, caffeine and marijuana. He ranked nicotine lowest in terms of intoxication effect but highest in terms of dependence. Smokers who try to give up have a relapse rate of 70 per cent in the first three months after stopping. One of the problems of stopping is that the individual experiences withdrawal effects which can be very unpleasant and last for a few weeks. A common problem associated with stopping smoking is increased appetite and weight gain.

A one-pack-per-day smoker administers about 200 puffs of nicotine to themselves daily (about 70,000 doses of nicotine a year). A major difference between cigarette smoking and other drugs such as cocaine or alcohol is that chronic use of nicotine does not seem to result in major impairment of mental functioning. It is classed as a psychoactive drug, but its effects on the brain and behaviour seem to be rather more subtle than other drugs.

Tobacco is the most common form of nicotine and it is usually smoked in cigarettes, cigars and pipes. Nicotine affects the central nervous system (CNS) and it is estimated that 25 per cent of the nicotine inhaled in smoking reaches the brain in less than 10 seconds – faster than if it had been injected directly into the bloodstream. Nicotine can have both a stimulant and depressant effect on the nervous system and smokers report that they enjoy smoking because of both its arousing and relaxing properties. Nicotine is thought to produce its positively reinforcing and addictive properties by activating the mesolimbic pathway. This is the same system affected by cocaine and amphetamines. Nicotine also works by increasing the concentrations of noradrenaline and adrenaline circulating in the nervous system and by increasing the release of vasopressin, endorphins, ACTH and cortisol.

Explanations of smoking

There are many reasons why people smoke and it is not possible to isolate a single factor.

Addictive behaviour

Biological factors

There is some evidence of a genetic factor in smoking behaviour. An early study (Shields, 1962) looked at 42 twin pairs who had been reared apart. They were chosen to try to separate out the effects of genetics from family influence. Only nine pairs were discordant for smoking behaviour (i.e. where one twin was a smoker and the other was a non-smoker), suggesting that genes might play a part.

Social factors

Most smokers begin the habit in childhood or adolescence, so much research has focused on factors which make children vulnerable to smoking behaviour. Traditional learning theory can explain smoking initiation in terms of operant conditioning: the child starts to smoke to obtain the powerful reinforcement of peer approval. However, it is nearly always the case that the first experience of smoking is very unpleasant in physical terms. Operant conditioning cannot adequately explain why children persist in the face of this quite powerful punishment. SLT can provide a more convincing explanation of why children become smokers. According to SLT, children imitate the behaviour of role models. Role models are more likely to exercise an influence if they are of the same sex, age or ethnic background as the observer. It is also the case that people with higher status, whether from within the individual's own circle (e.g. parents, teachers, etc.) or from a wider sphere (e.g. sports or media celebrities) exert a stronger influence than low-status individuals (Winett *et al.*, 1989). Children observe role models smoking and clearly finding it an enjoyable and rewarding experience. Even though the children originally find their own smoking aversive, they persevere because their observation of others leads them to expect future enjoyment for themselves (i.e. they observe others and form behavioural plans on the basis of future outcome expectations).

One of the main influences on smoking in children is parents' attitudes to smoking: children are twice as likely to smoke if their parents are smokers (Lader and Matheson, 1991). In contrast, if parental attitudes are firmly against smoking the child is seven times less likely to start smoking (Murray *et al.*, 1984).

Peer pressure is also thought to be an important influence, although the way in which peers exert the influence is probably quite complex. It has been suggested that children can be coerced into smoking by peers who bully, tease or reject them for not smoking. On the basis of a large-scale study in Scotland, Michell and West (1996) suggested that adolescents are considerably less susceptible to this kind of pressure. They have proposed the idea that some young people show a 'readiness' for smoking and that it is only in this group that peer pressure has an effect. Young people who have decided they do not want to smoke tend to adopt strategies for avoiding contexts in which smoking might be expected and in choosing friends who think in the same way. If this is the case, it has implications for health campaigns. They are less likely to be effective if they focus on resistance to bullying/peer pressure. Instead, they need to make smoking seem 'uncool' so that young people do not choose to start smoking in the first place (see pages 440–1).

Individual differences

Studies in the USA have shown strong links between smoking and certain other characteristics, e.g. poor performance at school, low self-esteem, minimal engagement in sport, evidence of other risk-taking behaviour such as drinking alcohol and taking illegal drugs (Mosbach and Lenenthal, 1988).

▮ Hint

How science works

Scientific studies have shown that parental attitudes and smoking behaviour play an important part in whether children begin smoking. So an intervention based on these findings would target parental behaviour as a method of reducing smoking in young children. In this way science can inform government and health campaigns aimed at improving health-related behaviour in society. (I)

Cognitive factors

There are various cognition models that offer explanations for smoking behaviours. These include the theory of reasoned action (TRA) and the theory of planned behaviour (TPB) (see pages 443–4). Conner *et al.* (2006) investigated the role of planned behaviour in smoking initiation in 11–12-year-olds. They tested 675 non-smoking adolescents with various baseline measures including TPB, and nine months later they checked whether any of the adolescents had taken up smoking. They used a carbon-monoxide breath monitor to assess this to avoid subjective judgement and they found that behavioural intentions were generally a good predictor of later smoking behaviour.

It is estimated that one-third of the world's smokers live in China, so identification of people likely to start smoking is important in developing prevention campaigns. Guo *et al.* (2007) tested more than 14,000 Chinese schoolchildren with TRA and TPB measures and found that both were useful predictors of later smoking behaviour.

Problem gambling

There is some confusion about terms used to describe addictive gambling. 'Pathological gambling' is the term generally used to describe a diagnosable psychiatric disorder and is reserved for the extreme end of the continuum of gambling behaviour. 'Problem gambling' is the term used to describe mild to moderate problems associated with gambling and as a general overarching term for all levels of potentially harmful gambling behaviours.

There is no single, clear-cut definition of what gambling is, but it is widely agreed that it is an activity in which two or more people agree to take part – usually the operator and the person or persons who wish to gamble. The stake (normally money) is paid by the loser to the winner. The outcome is uncertain but it is usually due to chance.

According to the *DSM-IV-TR*, to be diagnosed with pathological gambling the individual must show at least five of the following characteristics:

- preoccupation with gambling
- need to gamble with increasing amounts of money in order to achieve the desired excitement
- repeated unsuccessful efforts to control, cut back or stop gambling
- restlessness or irritability when trying to cut down on gambling
- use of gambling as a means of escaping from problems or relieving dysphoric mood states (e.g. feelings of helplessness, guilt, anxiety and depression)
- return to gambling even after losing money, in the hope of winning it back
- lying to family members, therapists or others to conceal the extent of gambling
- committing illegal acts such as forgery, fraud or theft to finance gambling
- jeopardising or losing significant relationships/jobs/educational opportunities as a result of gambling
- reliance on others to provide money to relieve a desperate situation caused by gambling.

The *ICD-10* has similar but less-detailed criteria.

Problem gambling usually starts in adolescence for men and later in adulthood for women. It is often a fairly gradual process with individuals progressing from social to frequent, problem and finally pathological gambling.

A recent survey carried out in 2007 by the National Centre for Social Research at the request of the Gambling Commission provided some interesting statistics about gambling in Britain. For example, 68 per cent of the population, that is about 32 million adults, had participated in some form of gambling activity within the past year. For around 10 million people, their only gambling activity in the past year had been participating in a National Lottery draw. Only a small proportion of people engaged in the new forms of gambling available in Great Britain. For example, only 6 per cent of people used the internet to gamble (3 per cent did online gaming such as playing poker or casino games and 4 per cent placed bets with a bookmaker). The survey measured the levels of problem gambling using two internationally recognised scales, the *DSM-IV* and the Canadian Problem Gambling Severity Index (PGSI) developed in 2001. The *DSM-IV* screen found that the rates of problem gambling in the adult population were about 0.6 per cent, which equates to about 284,000 adults. This emphasises the fact that for most people who dabble in gambling, it does not become an addictive problem.

Explanations of problem gambling

Biological factors

There is evidence from twin studies to support the idea of a genetic vulnerability to pathological gambling (e.g. Eisen, Lin and Lyons, 1999). It is not clear how genetic transmission works, but Comings *et al.* (2001) have suggested the possibility that the genetic process involves the genes controlling the activity of the brain neurotransmitters dopamine, serotonin and norepinephrine.

One of the factors that seems to motivate gamblers is the 'high' or 'buzz' they experience when they seem close to winning. It has been found that certain neurotransmitter levels rise in gamblers after a winning streak (Shinohara, Yanagisawa and Kagota, 1999). Neurotransmitters are chemical substances which act like messengers in the nervous system. Raised levels of both dopamine and noradrenaline have been found in people after episodes of gambling and, in pathological gamblers, they have been found in the anticipatory stage before the gambling actually begins. Meyer *et al.* (2004) compared a group of problem gamblers while they were engaged in gambling and during a control condition when they were playing cards, but not for money. They found increased secretion of cortisol and increased heart rate in the gambling condition compared to the control condition. Both increased heart rate and increased secretion of cortisol are linked to an acute stress reaction.

Stopping gambling seems to result in the same kind of withdrawal symptoms associated with stopping drugs. Rosenthal and Lesieur (1992) found that over 60 per cent of pathological gamblers reported physical side-effects during withdrawal (e.g. insomnia, loss of appetite, muscle weakness and aches, breathing difficulties and chills), and that these were sometimes more severe than those reported by a comparison group during withdrawal from drugs.

In addition to biochemical changes, several studies have indicated other potential brain abnormalities. A number of studies have found a link between frontal lobe dysfunction and problem gambling (Cavedini *et al.*, 2002) and have also demonstrated high rates of EEG abnormalities (Regard *et al.*, 2003).

Take it further

You can find the report on gambling in Britain at www.gamblingcommission.gov.uk. It provides some interesting data and also it is a good example of a survey. It provides comparison data from a similar survey in 1999 which shows how gambling patterns have changed.

Link

See pages 138–42 in the *AQA Psychology A AS* student book for information about the physiological stress response.

Sociocultural factors

Not surprisingly it has been found that people who have greater access to gambling opportunities are more likely to become social and problem gamblers. Ladouceur *et al.* (1999) looked at gambling patterns in a number of different countries and found that pathological gambling rates increased as the availability of gambling increased. However, a national study in Australia (1999) found slightly different results. In spite of significant differences in access to gambling across the various Australian states and territories, there were few overall differences in problem gambling. However there was one interesting exception in that problem gambling using gaming machines was related to increased availability of these machines.

There was some concern in the UK that the introduction of the National Lottery in 1994 would lead to widespread gambling problems. There is no evidence to suggest that this is the case. A survey carried out by GamCare in 1998 found that only 65 per cent of the UK population had played the National Lottery in the previous year compared to 90 per cent of adults in Sweden and New Zealand. Interestingly, the more recent UK survey (see page 434) found that the number of adults playing the National Lottery had dropped to 57 per cent.

It has been suggested that alcohol consumption increases gambling behaviours, particularly in problem gamblers. However, the evidence on this is not entirely consistent. Young game-machine players have been shown to persist much longer after initial losses when they have been drinking alcohol than when they have not (Pols and Hawks, 1991). However, while they are gambling, regular casino gamblers actually seem to drink less than they usually consume.

Psychological factors

One risk factor for pathological gambling is a high level of impulsivity in childhood. A disorder that is characterised by this is attention-deficit/hyperactivity disorder (ADHD). It has been found (Carlton and Manowicz, 1994) that there is a higher rate of childhood ADHD reported in adult pathological gamblers than in the general population. Krueger, Schedlowski and Meyer (2005) found that people who scored high on impulsivity measures showed significantly higher heart rate levels during gambling behaviour than people with low impulsivity scores. It was also found that higher impulsivity ratings correlated significantly with the severity of the problem gambling.

As described in the section on general models of addiction, operant conditioning (see pages 427–8) is also thought to play a part in the origins and maintenance of problem gambling. The idea is that gambling behaviour is reinforced when gambling is successful, both by the tangible reward of money and by the biological 'buzz' explained above. People continue gambling in order to re-experience this reinforcement. The fact that they do not win every time and yet continue to play is explained by the notion of variable reinforcement schedules. It is a well-established finding that variable or intermittent reinforcement leads to a more rapid, longer-lasting acquisition of behaviour and that, once acquired in this way, the behaviour is much more difficult to extinguish. However, this model does not adequately account for the fact that pathological gamblers continue to gamble in the face of continual, sustained and heavy financial losses.

Cognitive processes also seem to be important in the origin and maintenance of problem gambling behaviour. For example:

Take it further

These studies are correlational (see page 515). Why is it not possible to make conclusions about cause and effect from this kind of data?

Hint

Studies such as these have implications for public intervention programmes. See pages 451–2.

Addictive behaviour

It has been found (Oei and Raylu, 2004) that children's attitudes to gambling are influenced by the attitudes of their parents, particularly their fathers.

It has also been suggested that gamblers engage in a form of irrational self-talk while gambling. Delfabbro and Winefield (1999) found that 75 per cent of game-related thoughts during gambling were irrational and encouraged further risk-taking. This kind of irrational cognition might well maintain arousal during gambling episodes. Sharpe, Tarrier and Schotte (1995) demonstrated a relationship between the frequency of irrational verbalisations and arousal levels.

Mood state seems to contribute to the likelihood of gambling and problem gamblers often report that they gamble to escape being depressed or they gamble after a frustrating day.

Commentary

Gambling activities vary considerably and not just in terms of the probability of winning or the potential size of the win. There are varying degrees of gambler involvement, amount of skill required and the interval between placing a stake and knowing the outcome. For people who play fruit machines, it has been suggested that even the colours of the screens and the sound effects might affect the likelihood and strength of the addiction (Parke and Griffiths, 2006).

Because of these numerous variations, it seems unlikely that a single explanation can account for gambling behaviour. Sharpe (2002) has proposed a biopsychosocial model which incorporates an interaction of factors. She suggests three main early contributory factors:

biological vulnerability involving the brain's reward systems

family attitudes that support gambling

high levels of impulsivity.

Her idea is that these factors make it more likely that a young person will start to experiment with gambling and will then become socialised into a gambling culture. Some early wins may reinforce gambling behaviour through a process of operant conditioning. Cognitive influences then come into play and the individual selectively focuses on the experience of winning rather than on the times when losses occur, thereby distorting beliefs about gambling and the likelihood of winning. At the same time, the individual experiences pleasant physiological responses that give them a 'high'. A combination of these factors leads to the maintenance of a gambling pattern and the individual increasingly turns to it in order to avoid stress and increase arousal.

A slightly different biopsychosocial model has been proposed by Blaszczynski and Nower (2002). Their pathway model suggests that there are three distinct routes to problem gambling:

'Behaviourally conditioned': people on this pathway are not pathologically disturbed. Instead, they gamble excessively because of poor decision-making strategies and bad judgement. Any additional problems such as depression, other substance abuse, anxiety, etc. are the result rather than the cause of the excessive gambling.

'Emotionally vulnerable gamblers': people on this pathway have a predisposition to emotional susceptibility. They use gambling as a way of modifying mood states. They usually display high levels of depression, anxiety and substance dependence and they show poor stress-coping mechanisms. They tend to engage in avoidant or passive-aggressive behaviour and use gambling as a means of emotional relief.

Link

Approaches, issues and debates

Remember that often no single approach or explanation can explain a particular behaviour. Biopsychosocial models are complicated, but take a realistic view that gambling involves the interaction of different factors operating at different levels.

Addictive behaviour

■ 'Anti-social, impulsive problem gamblers': people on this pathway have an underlying biological dysfunction and are characterised by antisocial personality disorder, high levels of impulsivity or attention deficit disorders. They often have a range of problems which are independent of the gambling behaviour, e.g. substance abuse, low boredom threshold, a craving for sensation, criminal activity, poor relationships, etc.

AQA Examiner's tip

You can also use the more general explanations given in the previous sections to explain why people smoke and gamble.

Key points

■ Tobacco smoking is a highly addictive habit.

■ There is some evidence of a genetic vulnerability to becoming addicted to smoking.

■ Smoking is strongly influenced by family and peer behaviour.

■ Other factors such as low self-esteem and poor school performance also seem to be important factors.

■ Problem gambling usually starts in late adolescence/early adulthood.

■ The same kind of brain reward systems appear to be involved in gambling as in other addictive behaviours.

■ High levels of impulsivity are associated with problem gambling.

■ Biopsychosocial models integrate biological, cultural and psychological factors into a more holistic explanation.

Summary questions

6 Briefly outline the SLT explanation of smoking.

7 What is meant by the term 'problem gambling'?

8 How might biochemical factors be linked to gambling?

9 Explain why no single explanation can adequately account for problem gambling.

Addictive behaviour

Vulnerability to addiction and reducing addictive behaviour

Vulnerability to addiction

Learning objectives:

■ understand factors that may contribute to vulnerability to addictive behaviour

■ understand and evaluate relevant research findings

■ understand and evaluate research into the role of the media in addictive behaviour.

It is important to remember that drug-taking and other addictive behaviours always take place in a society with particular social and cultural norms, attitudes and values. Attitudes to alcohol provide a good example of the variations between cultural groups. In some societies, for example in countries such as Saudi Arabia, alcohol is banned for religious reasons and it is expected that no one should drink alcohol. In some European countries, for example France, it is the cultural norm for people to drink alcohol, particularly wine and it is considered odd if people completely abstain (Heath, 2000). Different cultures have different expectations as to the level of alcohol intake that is deemed acceptable and, as part of government health campaigns, many countries issue guidelines.

■ Vulnerability factors

Self-esteem

It seems that people with low self-esteem can be more vulnerable to addictive behaviour than others. Certainly, in the case of adolescent gamblers, low self-esteem and higher rates of depression including a heightened risk of suicide attempts have been demonstrated (Deverensky *et al.*, 2003).

Attributions

Cognitive biases can play a part in addictive behaviour. Young male problem gamblers sometimes have unrealistic ideas about their chances of winning and of their ability to influence outcomes (Moore and Ohtsuka, 1999). However, these cognitive distortions are evident in many people who gamble and so do not explain why some individuals gamble to excess.

People with addictive behaviour often have an external locus of control and a poor sense of self-efficacy.

Personality

Some psychologists believe that there is a so-called addictive personality. For example, Hans Eysenck (1997) has proposed a psychological resource model, i.e. the individual develops an addictive habit because it fulfils a certain purpose related to the personality type of the individual. Eysenck believes there are three major personality dimensions which are passed on genetically:

■ P (psychoticism): some of the characteristics of this dimension are aggression, coldness, impulsivity and egocentricity.

■ N (neuroticism): the characteristics of this dimension include moodiness, irritability and anxiety.

■ E (extraversion): some of the characteristics of this dimension are sociability, liveliness and optimism.

■ **Link**

Locus of control is explained in your *AQA Psychology A AS* student book, page 219.

There has been research into the possible relationship between drug dependence and Eysenck's personality dimensions. There is little evidence to support a relationship between E and drug dependence, but there is more convincing evidence of a link between dependence on alcohol, heroin, benzodiazepines and nicotine and higher-than-normal scores in N and P (Francis, 1996). In other words, people who are more moody, irritable and anxious (high N) and those who are more impulsive and aggressive (high P) are more likely to have problems with substance dependence.

However, this is correlational research and it is difficult to make statements about the causal relationship. It may be that people who have a drug problem become more moody, anxious, aggressive, etc.

There has also been substantial research into the link between alcohol addiction and personality disorders. These are a group of mental disorders characterised by distinctive, maladaptive personality traits. There is a strong link between alcoholism and antisocial personality disorder (also known as sociopathy) (Rounsaville et al., 1998) and with conduct disorder (e.g. attention deficit disorder) (Slutsky et al., 1998). However, this research is correlational and it is not clear whether there is a causal link. Nevertheless, clinicians need to be aware that substance addiction frequently coexists with other mental disorders as this has implications for successful treatment.

Gender

There are some gender differences in addictive behaviour, but these seem to operate differently depending on the addictive substance. In tobacco use, for example, there appears to be an increase in female smoking in the US and the UK, whereas male smoking rates have remained stable or even shown a slight decline. One suggested reason for this finding is that smoking is perceived to control weight. Smokers weigh on average 7 lb less than non-smokers, and people who quit smoking often show weight gains of about 6 lb. Ogden and Fox (1994) found that female dieters used cigarette smoking as a weight maintenance strategy.

In gambling, on the other hand, boys are more regular gamblers than girls. Jacobs (2000) has summarised differences as follows: young males spend more money on gambling, start gambling earlier, enjoy more skill-based games and gamble on a greater number and variety of games.

Social context of addiction

Drinking alcohol and, to a lesser extent, smoking cigarettes are seen as socially acceptable behaviours. In fact drinking alcohol is often seen in Western cultures as marking a transition from childhood to adulthood. This seems to be happening at an early age in the UK. About a third of British 13–14-year-olds report having been drunk on more than one occasion (Sutherland and Wilner, 1998).

It seems that people with antisocial behaviour are more likely to develop substance-use problems. It has been shown that adolescents with conduct disorders are more likely to develop problems than people without such disorders (Cicchetti and Rogosch, 1999). The same researchers have also reported that children with anxiety or depressive symptoms begin substance use at an earlier stage and are more likely to develop problems with that use.

Family influence

Children and adolescents often model their behaviour on parents and older siblings (see social learning theory, page 428). Parents' drug use has been linked to the onset and frequency of alcohol and cannabis use in adolescents. Older brothers' drug use and attitudes towards drug use have been shown to influence younger brothers' drug use.

It has also been shown that parents with permissive attitudes towards drug use have children who are more likely to start taking drugs. Risk of substance misuse is also higher if there is family discord or inconsistent parenting, or low levels of bonding within the family.

Adolescent problem gambling has been shown to be strongly related to parental attitudes. Youth problem gamblers are more likely to have a mother or father with gambling problems and many parents of young gamblers are unconcerned about their children's gambling (Fisher, 1999).

Sociocultural background is also a factor in predicting later substance misuse. Hall *et al.* (1990) found that people from lower socio-economic backgrounds are more likely to develop problem substance use. The same applies to those who grow up in areas where there are high rates of crimes. Similarly, people who have completed fewer years of education and have performed poorly at school show a greater vulnerability. Adolescent problem gamblers show a wide range of school-related difficulties. For example, they have been found more likely to truant from school, to argue, lie and steal in order to finance their gambling (Fisher, 1999). There seems to be a link between alcohol abuse and problem gambling, particularly in males (Vitaro *et al.*, 2001).

The role of the media in addictive behaviour

The media in its various forms has an important role to play in shaping and reflecting human behaviour. It seems likely that the way in which habits such as smoking, gambling and drinking alcohol are portrayed in the media could have an effect on people's attitudes and behaviour in relation to these habits. We tend to think mainly of television in this context, but cinema, films, radio, newspapers, magazines and the internet all can have an influence.

Advertising is one obvious way in which the media is used to manipulate opinion and behaviour, but other devices such as product placing in television and cinema drama and the portrayal of attractive role models can also have an effect. Popular game shows such as *Who wants to be a millionaire?* and *Deal or no deal* have clear elements of gambling in them and promise huge rewards in return for a certain degree of risk-taking. Such shows make gambling seem acceptable, harmless and potentially very rewarding.

Advertising

Advertising has been used in two ways:

- to encourage the sales of tobacco, alcoholic drinks, lottery cards, etc.
- to promote government health campaigns such as anti-smoking, drink-driving crusades.

Advertising may be an important factor that influences the initial decision of some people to start gambling. Lotteries, which are seen by many people as a soft form of gambling, are widely advertised across Europe including the UK on billboards, in newspapers and magazines and on TV.

Link

For more on media psychology, see pages 388–419.

The availability of lottery cards in shops and garages also makes them more accessible/acceptable. A televised draw for the National Lottery focuses on the attractiveness of winning but does not show the huge number of people watching who do not win. The advertising slogan 'It could be you' seems designed to emphasise the chance of winning rather than the huge odds against a win (14 million to one for the jackpot prize).

Advertising of alcohol and cigarettes does seem to increase awareness of these products and shape attitudes, particularly in young people. For example, Chapman and Fitzgerald (1982) found that under-age smokers reported a preference for heavily advertised brands, and Atkin *et al.* (1984) found that 12–17-year-olds who had been exposed to higher levels of advertising were more likely to approve of under-age drinking and drunkenness.

The effects of advertising on alcohol and cigarette consumption and on gambling behaviour are hard to measure. However, the influence is thought to be sufficiently strong and legislation has been introduced in the UK to ban cigarette advertising and to restrict alcohol advertising (see Chapter 34, Reducing addictive behaviour, page 452). There have also been calls to ban or restrict gambling advertising, but this has not been endorsed by the government.

Models in the media

Behaviours such as drinking alcohol have been widely portrayed on television as acceptable social activities and effective strategies for problem-solving (Hansen, 1986). Smoking was similarly portrayed as socially acceptable and even sophisticated, although this has changed over recent years. Social learning theory suggests that we can learn behaviour through a process of observation and vicarious reinforcement. This means that it is likely that characters seen on TV might act as powerful role models. These models can demonstrate positive or negative images. For example, a BBC TV comedy drama series screened in October 2008 called *Sunshine* was described in a BBC press release as follows:

> Sunshine is a bittersweet story of three generations of the Crosby family. Bob (Bing) Crosby grew up to be one of the most likeable people around, and his natural wit and optimism were infectious to those around him. The only negative trait in Bing's life was his inability to resist gambling a few quid on the occasional bet.
>
> Bernadette, his childhood sweetheart and mother of their son, Joe, loves Bing for the person she's known all her life and, although she doesn't approve of and is often infuriated by his casual betting, she always reluctantly forgives him.

The British Comedy Guide, *www.comedy.org.uk/guide/tv/sunshine/*

This show presents the image of a 'loveable rogue' even though he has a gambling habit that threatens to destroy himself and his family.

At the same time, on the long-running radio show *The Archers*, a story line concerning a central character showed the damaging effects of gambling. The local vet was depicted as having a gambling addiction that threatened to destroy his career, family and social/financial standing. He was 'saved' from this disastrous decline by attending Gamblers Anonymous and there were regular references to his GA sessions on the programme.

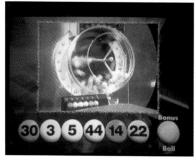

Fig. 1 *The very first national lottery draw in Great Britain took place in 1994*

Hint

How science works

If studies show that advertising significantly affects the smoking and drinking habits of children and adults, then government bans on advertising cigarettes, for instance, would have a sound scientific basis and would be likely to be effective. (I)

Take it further

You might like to carry out a small-scale content analysis of UK television programmes to find out how often characters in dramas/ soaps, situation comedies, etc. are seen smoking, drinking alcohol or gambling. See page 455 for more details of how to carry out a content analysis.

Key points

■ Factors such as self-esteem, cognitive distortions, neuroticism and psychoticism have been shown to be related to addictive behaviour.

■ There are gender differences in addiction, with more females than males smoking, but with gambling more common in males.

■ The family and parental attitudes are key factors in alcohol and drug use, and in problem gambling.

■ The media can influence addictive behaviours both positively and negatively, especially through advertising and role models. Many of these effects can be explained through social learning theory.

Summary questions

1 Outline and evaluate research into at least two factors that may contribute to vulnerability to addiction.

2 Discuss ways in which the media can have both positive and negative effects on addictive behaviours.

3 Adolescent problem gamblers have been shown to have more school-related difficulties. Why should these two observations be correlated?

Reducing addictive behaviour

Learning objectives

- understand how the theory of reasoned action and the theory of planned behaviour can be used to explain the prevention and reduction of addictive behaviours

- understand the relationship between the theory of reasoned action and the theory of planned behaviour.

Link

See the section on public health interventions and legislation, pages 451–3.

Take it further

An article in the *Times* in September 2007 suggested that the new Gambling Act 2005 would cause unforeseen problems:

'The authors of an official report into problem gambling have warned that the number of "casualties" will inevitably increase following the liberalisation of laws.

Under the new Gambling Act, which came into force yesterday, bookmakers, casinos and internet gambling firms will be allowed to advertise on television for the first time.

The legislation also paves the way for 16 new casinos – all bigger than existing establishments – although plans for a Las Vegas-style gambling Mecca in Manchester appear to have been shelved by Gordon Brown.'

Try to track down this article (search for 'Leap in gambling addiction' at www.timesonline.co.uk) and find out a bit more about the Gambling Act 2005. Do you think it will lead to more problem gambling?

It is clear from what we have seen so far in this section that addictive behaviours can seriously damage the health and well-being of the individual and their family. The consequences of addiction also have implications beyond those of the individual addict. National costs in terms of health bills, social security benefits and lost working days are enormous. It is therefore important to find ways of reducing addictive behaviour. This is not a straightforward task. Many people with addictions would like to give them up, but it is the nature of addictions that giving up can be difficult if not impossible.

Models of prevention

It is possible to be a social gambler, drinker or smoker without becoming addicted. However, certainly in the case of smoking, nicotine appears to be a powerfully addictive drug and, once hooked, smokers find it very difficult to give up. It is probably better not to start smoking at all and this is what many prevention campaigns aim to achieve.

There are two possible approaches when trying to prevent people from becoming addicted:

- education – to provide information and guidance and to heighten awareness of the possible consequences of excessive smoking, drinking, gambling, etc.
- introduction of social change – by putting up the price of alcoholic drinks, cigarettes, etc.; controlling advertising for cigarettes, alcohol and gambling; controlling sales.

Theory of reasoned action (TRA)

Health psychology is a growing branch of psychology that aims to understand what causes illness, how it should be treated and what the relationship is between health and illness. One area of research interest is the way in which health beliefs lead to health behaviours. A number of theories have been developed to try to explain the links between perceptions and behaviour. The theory of reasoned action (TRA) was proposed by Fishbein and Ajzen (1975, 1980) and consists of three general components:

- attitude
- subjective norm
- behavioural intention.

This theory offers a way of understanding the factors involved in how people decide on their actions (e.g. to start smoking in the first place or to give up smoking). The basic idea is that a person's voluntary behaviour is predicted by an interaction between the individual's attitude towards that behaviour and how they think other people will view that behaviour. Attitudes and norms are not always equally weighted and this will depend both on the individual's personality and on situational factors. For example, if you are someone who does not really care what other people think about you, you are less likely to attach much weight to social norms.

For example, imagine you are thinking about giving up smoking:

- Attitudes: you believe that giving up smoking will improve your health, that it will save you money, that it will be difficult to do, that you will suffer unpleasant withdrawal symptoms and that you will put on weight. Each of these beliefs can be weighted, e.g. you might feel that not putting on weight is more important to you than saving money.

- Subjective norms: most of your friends have given up smoking and would be supportive, your flatmate still smokes and makes fun of people who try to give up. These norms are weighted depending on the importance that you attach to the opinions of others.

- Behavioural intention: your attitudes towards giving up smoking combined with your subjective norms about it will influence your intentions (to give up smoking or not) and this will lead to your actual behaviour.

The theory of planned behaviour (TPB)

The TRA was refined and developed by Ajzen and others (Ajzen, 1985) into the theory of planned behaviour (TPB). The extended theory contained an additional component of 'perceived behavioural control', which is similar to the idea of 'self-efficacy' (Bandura, 1977). Self-efficacy relates to the belief that the individual can successfully carry out a behaviour to achieve a desired outcome, e.g. 'I am sure I will be able to give up smoking'.

According to the TPB, behavioural intentions are the outcome of the following beliefs:

- Attitude: this can be a positive or negative evaluation of the behaviour combined with beliefs about the outcome (e.g. giving up smoking is a challenge and it will improve my health).

- Subjective norm: perception of social norms/pressures to perform the behaviour, and an evaluation of whether the individual is motivated to comply with this pressure (e.g. my friends will approve of my attempt to give up smoking and I want their approval).

- Perceived behavioural control: a belief that the individual can carry out a particular behaviour based on a consideration of internal control factors (e.g. skill, abilities, information) and external control factors (e.g. obstacles, opportunities). These are weighed up in the light of past behaviours.

These three factors interact to form a behavioural intention which then leads to the actual behaviour.

Hint

How science works

Addiction is a major social problem. Successful interventions would therefore make a significant contribution to reducing the personal and social costs of addictive behaviours. Science can make a major contribution by showing through controlled studies that some forms of intervention are more effective than others. (I)

Gambling prevention

There is currently little research into the effectiveness of attempts to prevent problem gambling. Since cognitive factors are known to play an important part in the development and maintenance of problem gambling behaviours, prevention programmes have been largely based on changing faulty thinking and providing accurate information about gambling. One early prevention programme was trialled by Gaboury and LaDouceur (1993) in a classroom setting with high-school students in Canada. It consisted of general information about gambling, its possible negative consequences and strategies to control gambling behaviour. While the programme significantly improved knowledge about gambling in the experimental group both immediately after the sessions and at six-month follow-up, no influence was demonstrated on actual gambling behaviour.

Key points

- The main approaches to preventing addictive behaviours involve either education or social change.

- The theory of reasoned action consists of three main components – attitudes, subjective norms and behavioural intention. These interact in determining whether an individual may decide to give up smoking or gambling for example.

- The theory of planned behaviour introduces a further element – perceived behavioural control. This is similar to Bandura's concept of self-efficacy.

Summary questions

4 Outline the theory of reasoned action.

5 Outline the theory of planned behaviour. How does it differ from the theory of reasoned action?

6 Explain why perceived behavioural control is a critical factor in the theory of planned behaviour.

Types of intervention

Learning objectives:

- ◼ understand psychological interventions for addictive behaviours and evaluate their effectiveness

- ◼ understand biological interventions for addictive behaviours and evaluate their effectiveness

- ◼ understand the role of public health interventions and legislation in reducing addictive behaviours.

There are many different reasons for developing addictive habits and it is likely that people will not all respond in the same way to treatment programmes. Therefore, the most successful interventions are multicomponent programmes that can be tailored to individual needs. It is also important to understand that some therapies are specific to the particular addictive substance (e.g. alcohol, nicotine) or behaviour (e.g. gambling).

Any successful intervention depends on the motivation of the individual to change. This is a major stumbling block in the case of people with addictive behaviours because they often refuse to admit that they have a problem. If and when people with addictive problems (e.g. with drug-taking, smoking, alcohol, gambling, etc.) come forward for help, the intervention offered will depend on the stage they have reached in their addictive cycle.

Prochaska and DiClemente (1983) put forward their stages-of-change model to describe the processes involved in overcoming addiction:

- ◼ pre-contemplation
- ◼ contemplation
- ◼ preparation
- ◼ action
- ◼ maintenance.

According to this model, progress across the stages is not straightforward and individuals can switch backwards and forwards. They call this the 'revolving door phenomenon'. DiClemente *et al.* (1991) found that people in the preparation stage were much more likely to have made an attempt to give up smoking at one- and six-month follow-up than people in the contemplation stage.

◼ Psychological interventions

These are primarily behavioural and cognitive. According to learning theory, we can unlearn inappropriate behaviours such as addictions by using various learning-based techniques:

- ◼ aversion therapy
- ◼ contingency contracting
- ◼ cue exposure
- ◼ self-management techniques.

Aversion therapy

This is based on the idea of punishment rather than reward and has been used to treat smoking and alcohol addiction. Early programmes which administered mild electric shocks every time the individual took a sip of alcohol or a puff on a cigarette were not successful. One of the reasons was that the effects did not last outside the clinic setting. To avoid this problem, alcoholics have been given the drug Antabuse which makes them sick every time they consume alcohol and so establishes a link between alcohol in drinks and vomiting. This has been shown to be effective (Lang and Martlatt, 1982) but it has two major limitations:

it requires the person with the alcohol problem to take the drug in the first place and they might not be willing to comply

it ignores the reasons that led to the alcoholism in the first place.

For smoking, a form of aversion therapy called rapid smoking has had some success. The individual is required to sit in a closed room and take puffs on a cigarette every six seconds, which is much faster than normal. This rapid inhalation leads to feelings of nausea and makes the individual feel quite ill. The idea underlying this therapy is that the smoker will associate unpleasant feelings with smoking and so they will develop an aversion to cigarettes (Spiegler and Guevremont, 2003).

There is some evidence to suggest that this technique can help people to give up smoking, particularly when it is used as part of a multicomponent programme. However, results have not been consistent across studies and there is also a slight risk associated with this treatment for people who have cardiopulmonary disorders. Another problem for behaviour-based therapies is that they focus on the act of smoking rather than tackling the underlying addiction.

Aversion therapy has also been used to stop people drinking alcohol, but such attempts have not been effective long term and have been questioned on ethical grounds.

Take it further

Why do you think aversion therapy might raise ethical issues?

Contingency contracting

This approach requires the individual to identify the environmental factors that are associated with smoking/drinking. For example, if an individual always smokes in the garden, the garden will become a strong external cue for smoking. The therapist aims to gradually expose the client to different cues and helps them to develop coping strategies to deal with the cues without resorting to smoking/drinking. This is a more effective approach than cue avoidance in which alcoholics, for example, are kept in hospital to detoxify. Cue avoidance reduces the patient's physical dependence on alcohol, but it does not teach them to deal with cues when they return to everyday life.

Cue exposure

Addictive behaviours are often aroused in the presence of various stimuli, or cues. For instance, smoking is often associated with drinking, so alcohol becomes a 'cue' that stimulates smoking. Cue exposure involves presenting the cue to the individual and helping them to control their reaction to it, i.e. to develop coping strategies. In this way the response of 'smoking' in the presence of alcohol fades away or extinguishes. This is thought to be more effective than simply trying to avoid the cues, for example never drinking.

Self-management techniques

This approach involves a variety of behavioural techniques that the individual can use on their own although the programme is usually monitored by a therapist. The individual is asked to keep a daily record of smoking/drinking habits and is encouraged to try to become aware of the things that make them want to smoke/drink (e.g. Where do I smoke? What have I been doing that makes me need a drink?) and to question the effects of smoking/drinking (e.g. Do I feel better after a drink? What do I expect will happen after I have smoked a cigarette?). Such techniques can be useful as part of a broader treatment programme, but they do not seem to be particularly effective on their own (Hall *et al.*, 1990).

Addictive behaviour

Commentary

While these behaviour-based therapies can be effective, they all share the problem that they do not really address the underlying reasons why people have become addicted in the first place and so treatment benefits are often short-lived. A method that is more effective than using any of these techniques on their own is to combine them in an integrated, multi-perspective cessation programme. These programmes often incorporate biological methods such as nicotine replacement (see page 449).

Cognitive therapy

Cognitive psychologists have identified three 'stages of change' relevant to stopping smoking:

- Contemplation and commitment: many smokers are ambivalent about giving up smoking and often try to reassure themselves that they do not have a problem. They need help to develop their commitment and motivation to give up. Once the individual has made the commitment, a plan can be worked out to start the process.
- Action: a specific plan for giving up is agreed and put into action (e.g. nicotine substitutes, engaging the help of friends, family and colleagues).
- Maintenance: stopping smoking can take a long time and there is always the danger of relapse. The individual needs to develop self-monitoring strategies to prevent a relapse occurring.

There is some evidence to suggest that smokers do not necessarily need professional help to guide them through these stages. For many people, self-help approaches can be effective (Curry, 1993).

Cognitive-behavioural therapy (CBT)

CBT often involves training in social skills and strategies for preventing relapse as well as traditional cognitive techniques of challenging faulty thinking patterns. Because relapse is frequently associated with marital problems, particularly in alcohol addiction, CBT programmes often include the problem drinker's spouse or partner whenever possible and this helps them to improve their communication and problem-solving skills.

CBT has been shown to be a reasonably effective therapy, but it is often more effective when used in combination with medication. For example, in a study of people with alcohol-related problems Feeney et al. (2002) reported 14 per cent abstention rates in a group who had received CBT alone compared with 38 per cent in a group who had received both CBT and medication.

Motivational interviewing (MI)

This is a relatively new form of brief cognitive therapy which focuses on trying to help people with addictive behaviours to develop the motivation to change their habits. They are encouraged to review their addictive habits and to weigh up the positive and negative effects that the addiction has on their lives. This is a non-directive intervention where the therapist aims to get the client to argue his or her own case for changing their habits. As yet, there has not been much research into the long-term benefits of this approach. However, Dunn, Deroo and Rivara (2001) found that it was effective in helping clients with substance addictions, particularly as a way of encouraging them to progress on to more intensive treatment programmes. In a meta-analysis, Burke *et al.* (2003) found that MI had led to a 56 per cent reduction in alcohol consumption in the people who had been offered this treatment.

Commentary

There is research that supports the effectiveness of many of these psychological interventions. An interesting finding from a large-scale alcohol treatment trial comparing three different types of psychological therapy found no significant overall differences in their effectiveness either at one-year or three-year follow-up. However, it was found that certain types of client fared better with one treatment as opposed to another (Project MATCH Research Group, 1998). For example, people with lower levels of dependence responded most favourably to CBT. This finding has important implications for the choice of therapy for individual clients.

Biological interventions

Biological therapies are based on the idea of addiction as a disease and usually involve the use of medication. They normally aim for complete abstinence, i.e. for a situation where the individual no longer drinks, smokes, takes drugs, etc. at all. If an individual abstains from a previously addictive behaviour, it is almost inevitable that they will develop withdrawal symptoms. Therefore, it is an important part of any treatment programme to manage these symptoms when they occur. They can be very severe (e.g. seizures and delirium), particularly in the case of alcohol and illegal drugs, and often require the individual to stay in hospital to ensure adequate supervision.

Biological interventions have been widely used to help people give up smoking. Currently, three classes of medications have been approved for smoking cessation:

- nicotine replacement products (patch, gum, spray, inhaler and lozenge)
- bupropion
- varenicline (the most recent approval).

All of these drugs have been shown to be effective in controlled clinical trials in comparison to placebo treatment.

Nicotine replacement therapy (NRT)

Nicotine medications such as nicotine gum, patches and nasal sprays, mimic or replace the effects of nicotine derived from tobacco. They help people to stop smoking in several ways:

- Even in relatively low doses, they help to relieve withdrawal symptoms when a person stops using tobacco.
- They provide positive reinforcement, particularly because of their arousal and stress-relieving effects. Positive reinforcement is most likely in response to rapid-delivery formulations, such as nicotine nasal spray and, to a lesser extent, nicotine gum. The use of these products allows smokers to self-administer nicotine when they have the urge to smoke cigarettes. Nicotine patches, on the other hand, deliver nicotine gradually and result in sustained nicotine levels throughout the day, thus not providing much positive reinforcement.
- They seem to desensitise nicotine receptors in the brain. This means that if the person lapses and smokes a cigarette while on nicotine replacement therapy, the cigarette will appear less satisfying.

Link

Approaches, issues and debates

Biological interventions assume that addiction is a disease process involving biological changes in the brain. This takes responsibility away from the person concerned, but also takes away the idea that they have free will and could actually change their addictive habits without the help of drugs. It is a highly deterministic approach, but equally there is good evidence that some addictions, such as smoking, do involve chemical changes in the brain.

Addictive behaviour

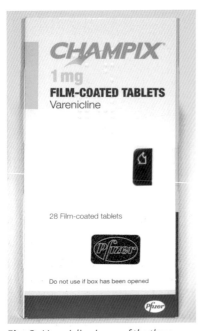

Fig. 2 *Varenicline is one of the three approved forms of treatment to cease smoking*

Bupropion

The antidepressant drug buproprion has also been used as a treatment for smoking. It works by increasing brain levels of dopamine and norepinephrine, simulating the effects of nicotine on these neurotransmitters. As one effect of bupropion seems to be to block the nicotine receptor, so, as with the nicotine replacement therapies, it could reduce the positive reinforcement from a cigarette in the case of a lapse. It has been shown to be reasonably successful in treating cigarette smoking (Watts *et al.*, 2002).

Varenicline

Varenicline is a drug that causes dopamine release in the brain. It also blocks the effects of any nicotine added to the system. Clinical trials have found that varenicline is superior to bupropion in helping people to stop smoking. It has also been shown to reduce relapse in smokers who had been abstinent 12 weeks after initial therapy.

Nicotine vaccines

At time of going to print these were undergoing clinical trials. Acute immunisation is performed so as to develop antibodies to nicotine. The antibody binds to the nicotine and slows its entry into the brain, thereby reducing the reinforcing effects of cigarette smoking. If it proves effective, the nicotine vaccine will be a logical approach to preventing relapse.

Commentary on nicotine interventions

The currently available nicotine replacement therapies deliver nicotine into the bloodstream much more slowly than cigarette smoking does. So for most smokers nicotine medications are not perceived as being as satisfying as smoking a cigarette, and some will give up the therapy and relapse.

Meta-analyses of the effectiveness of nicotine patches have provided considerable support for the view that it is the nicotine rather than other components in cigarettes that underlies addiction and maintains cigarette smoking, it is sensible to consider nicotine maintenance as an alternative to tobacco use for smokers who find it impossible to give up. While this does not get rid of the nicotine addiction, it does avoid the ingestion of some of the other harmful components of cigarettes. However, there are some concerns involving the safety of nicotine per se, including cardiovascular disease, cancer, reproductive disorders and delayed wound healing.

Nicotine increases the heart rate, constricts cutaneous and coronary blood vessels and temporarily increases blood pressure. Nicotine also reduces sensitivity to insulin and may aggravate or precipitate diabetes. It is not a direct carcinogen, but there are concerns arising from animal studies that it may be a tumour promoter. Nicotine can have adverse effects on foetuses and, in general, it is not desirable to use nicotine during pregnancy. However, if the alternative is cigarette smoking, then nicotine is undoubtedly less harmful.

In summary, while nicotine is not entirely without harmful effects, the benefit of nicotine maintenance therapy to avoid smoking appears to far outweigh the risks.

Commentary on biological interventions

Biological approaches to treatment can be very helpful in reducing addictive behaviour particularly in people who are very dependent. However, critics argue that it takes away the responsibility of the individual and categorises addictive behaviour as a disease. As we have noted above, addictive behaviours involve a complex combination of factors and no single type of treatment intervention can work alone.

Public health interventions and legislation

Doctors' advice

Doctors are seen by many people as authoritative and credible sources of information about health issues. So they have a clear role to play in advising people about the dangers of excessive smoking and drinking. It is thought that about 70 per cent of smokers in the UK consult their GP each year. A study carried out across five London GP practices compared results where patients were given varying degrees of assistance:

- Given follow-up only: 0.3 per cent had given up smoking at 12 months.
- Filled in a questionnaire about their smoking habits and then given follow-up: 1.6 per cent had given up smoking at 12 months.
- Advised by the doctor to give up smoking, filled in a questionnaire on their habits and given follow-up: 3.3 per cent had given up smoking at 12 months.
- Advised by the doctor to give up, given a leaflet with tips for giving up and given follow-up: 5.1 per cent had given up smoking at 12 months.

These look like very small changes, but if all GPs advised their smoker patients to give up and provided them with some tips on how to do this, it would produce half a million ex-smokers within a year in the UK (Ogden, 2007).

Doctors are also well placed to provide early treatment for alcohol problems. They are likely to know the patient and their family quite well and can give advice and information at an early stage when safer drinking levels rather than complete abstention might be appropriate. Such brief interventions can be successful in people with mild alcohol problems but not for those who have become alcohol dependent (Room *et al.*, 2005).

Workplace intervention

Over recent years, more and more businesses and other workplaces have adopted strategies for discouraging smoking. These attempts have now been enforced by government legislation.

Legislation

One way of discouraging smoking or excessive alcohol intake is via government legislation or guidelines. This can take various forms:

- restrictions or a ban on advertising
- increasing the cost
- controls on sales
- reducing the harmful components in cigarettes or drinks

Hint

How science works

Although we assume that GPs could have a major role in reducing addictive behaviours, studies such as this provide solid scientific evidence that different types of advice from doctors have different effects. These sorts of studies help us identify the most effective GP-based interventions. (I)

Addictive behaviour

■ ban on smoking or drinking in public

■ complete ban on smoking and drinking.

Restricting/banning advertising

Advertising aims to promote the idea that smoking and drinking are sophisticated, sexy things to do. Social learning theory would suggest that such advertising causes us to associate these kinds of characteristics with smoking and drinking. If this is the case, a ban on advertising should remove this source of learning. In the UK, cigarette advertising was banned in 2003 and cannot now be shown in any public form, i.e. in magazines, newspapers or in television and cinema adverts. It is still legal for alcohol to be advertised, but it is unclear what effect this has. Alcohol providers argue that advertising simply encourages existing drinkers to change brands rather than encouraging increased overall consumption. This was also the claim of tobacco companies before cigarette advertising was made illegal. However, in the UK, annual expenditure on alcohol advertising rose from £150 million to £250 million between 1989 and 2000. During that time there seemed to be a strong correlation between advertising expenditure and alcohol consumption by children aged 11–15 years (Academy of Medical Sciences, 2004). Similarly, an American study of young people aged between 15 and 26 found a strong correlation between the number of adverts for alcohol that they watched and the amount of alcohol consumed (Snyder *et al.*, 2006).

> ### Hint
>
> **How science works**
>
> These studies are useful, but they only provide correlational data, so we cannot be sure that there is a direct causal link between advertising and increased consumption. (E)

It is not easy to conduct controlled studies of the effects of restrictions on advertising, and results have often been confounded by other variables. However, studies comparing cigarette consumption before and after total bans on advertising (for example in Finland (Pekurinen, 1989)), suggest that there is a significant reduction that cannot be attributed to other measures, e.g. increased health education, tighter restrictions on sales to young people. As far as alcohol is concerned, restrictions on advertising appear to have less effect on consumption (Smart, 1988). It might be that there is less public sympathy for such restrictions because drinking alcohol is still seen as socially acceptable.

Although it is not clear that a total ban on advertising alcohol would significantly reduce consumption, there is some evidence that control over targeting audiences might have some effect. New rules came into force in the UK in 2005 which banned adverts from having a strong appeal to those under 18. In other words, they should not portray role models that would have particular relevance for young people or associate drinking with youth culture. However, adverts are still readily accessible on internet sites such as MySpace and YouTube.

Increasing the cost

One possible strategy is to substantially raise the price of cigarettes and alcoholic drinks by increasing taxes. There does seem to be a relationship between the cost of cigarettes and alcohol and the amount that is bought. By increasing the cost, it could encourage people to stop, and it might deter children from starting in the first place. In cognitive terms, this could be a powerful factor when people are weighing up the perceived costs of their behaviour against the perceived benefits. However, for political reasons increasing taxes is not as straightforward as it seems.

Controls on sales

Another preventive measure could be to control the sales of alcohol, cigarettes, lottery cards, etc. There are already restrictions in place in terms of age, but some people argue that alcohol, for example, is too widely available and easy to buy. In fact, legislation has been relaxed so that supermarkets can now sell alcoholic drinks around the clock seven days a week.

Reducing the harmful components

A proposal in the USA supported by the American Medical Association (AMA) suggested a gradual reduction in the nicotine content of cigarettes over a period of years. The idea is that smokers would be gradually weaned from nicotine addiction, and find it easier to give up cigarette smoking. One concern with this kind of strategy is that smokers would compensate for the reduced nicotine by smoking more cigarettes or smoking them more intensively. A small-scale study (Benowitz *et al.*, 2007) gave some support for the efficacy of this strategy. Twenty-five per cent of the smokers in this experiment gave up smoking spontaneously by the end of the trial and there was no evidence in any of the sample of increased smoking. Tengs *et al.* (2005) performed a computer simulation of the effects of a compulsory nicotine reduction policy. This simulation predicted that a progressive decrease in the nicotine content of cigarettes over six years would result in a decline in smoking prevalence from 23 to 5 per cent of the US population. They concluded that, in spite of any mortality increases due to compensatory smoking or the emergence of a black market, implementation of the AMA proposal would be likely to prevent the addiction of scores of new smokers and result in important gains to the nation's health.

Ban on smoking in public

Public smoking has gradually become less acceptable in the UK and legislation introduced in July 2007 means that it is now against the law to smoke in any enclosed public places in England. This followed similar bans in other countries, including Ireland, Scotland and several states in the US and Italy. Such a ban should reduce the likelihood of currently common cues to smoking (e.g. pubs, restaurants, etc.) becoming associated with smoking. One of the problems with this kind of strategy is that people might simply compensate by drinking and smoking more at home. There is also the danger that such a ban encourages a sense of group solidarity or a feeling of shared 'wickedness' among the smokers who huddle on pavements outside pubs, and simply make the habit seem more attractive.

Complete ban on cigarette smoking and alcohol drinking

It is, of course, already illegal to take certain types of drug such as cannabis, heroin and cocaine. The legal ban on the recreational use of such substances has obviously not eradicated the problem of drug addiction. In fact, some people have lobbied for the legalisation of these drugs as a way of making them more controllable. A complete ban on cigarette smoking and alcohol consumption seems to be highly unlikely for political reasons.

Take it further

You might like to look at the current UK licensing laws and see how they have changed over the years (try www.youthinformation.com). Do you think legislation should be used to control drinking and smoking? Why do you think politicians are often unwilling to support the introduction of more restrictive legislation?

Take it further

In 2007, the Chief Constable of North Wales, Richard Brunstrom, called for the legalisation and regulation of all 'harmful drugs' (*Daily Telegraph*, 16 October 2007). This is a controversial suggestion that has little backing from other police chiefs or from MPs, although he has had some support. What do you think are the advantages and disadvantages of legalising drugs?

Addictive behaviour

Key points

- Psychological interventions include behavioural strategies such as aversion therapy, contingency contracting, cue exposure and self-management techniques. These techniques do not address the underlying reasons why people become addicted in the first place.

- Cognitive therapies such as cognitive-behavioural therapy and motivational interviewing do address reasons for addiction and have been shown to be effective, especially in combination with medication.

- Biological interventions such as nicotine replacement therapy have been shown to be effective in dealing with withdrawal symptoms and so helping people to give up smoking. However, the biological approach sees addiction as a disease, and takes away individual responsibility.

- Public health interventions such as advice from doctors, workplace interventions, restricting advertising and bans on public smoking have all been shown to have some effect on the levels of smoking and drinking. However, it is difficult to assess the precise effect of a single intervention as so many factors are involved in addictive behaviours.

Summary questions

7 Outline one psychological and one biological intervention for the treatment of addictive behaviours.

8 Evaluate at least two public health interventions used to try to reduce addictive behaviours.

9 Discuss the effectiveness of psychological *and* biological interventions for the treatment of addictive behaviours.

The psychology of addictive behaviour end of topic

How science works: practical activity

The media are believed to exert an influence on our behaviour, so that addictions to alcohol and cigarettes, for instance, may develop after initial exposure to people (models) drinking and smoking in the media. We now have laws banning smoking in enclosed public spaces, but drinking is not subject to the same types of legislation. Are smoking and drinking also portrayed differently in the media, now that smoking is increasingly seen as anti-social?

Students can do a content analysis. You should choose a random selection of television programmes to be watched over, for example, two weekends. They should be taken from before and after the 9pm watershed (this would be another variable – are people shown smoking and drinking more after the watershed than before?).

You then need to decide on how to code the content of the programmes; for instance, presence of cigarettes or alcohol in the scene, people actually smoking and/or drinking, etc. Then programmes can be allocated to different students, and the results pooled. You would need to think carefully about data presentation and analysis:

1 Data presentation; would smoking/drinking acts per hour be a better measure than simple number of programmes containing smoking or drinking?

2 Would graphs or histograms be more effective at showing the results of the content analysis?

3 If you wanted to compare the frequency of drinking acts with the frequency of smoking acts, or the frequencies of either before and after the watershed, what test would you use?

4 What would your hypotheses be?

Further reading and weblinks

Further reading books and websites and the research studies for this chapter can be found at www.nelsonthornes.com/psychology_answers.

Anomalistic psychology

Introduction

Charles Fort was one of the first researchers to formalise the study of anomalous phenomena. Events like raining frogs, UFOs, the power of the mind and other issues that are on the outer fringes of conventional science are known as 'Forteana'. Fort demonstrated that conventional science ignored such happenings since there was no rational explanation for them.

What is anomalistic psychology?

A central concern of anomalistic psychology is the study of **paranormal** events, experiences and related beliefs explained through established psychological and physical factors. Anomalistic psychology differs from parapsychology, in that parapsychology is a more refined field of study which examines experiences and phenomena that can be studied under controlled conditions (e.g. **extrasensory perception (ESP)** and **psychokinesis (PK)**). Research into psychic phenomena dates back to the formation of the Psychical Research Society in 1888, although the study of such phenomena was not formally recognised as a discipline in psychology until the mid-1920s when the first parapsychology laboratory was set up at Duke University in the USA.

Anomalistic psychology cannot be treated in the same way as other topics in this textbook. The main issue for any researcher in this area is that what they are investigating most of the time seems not to physically exist or to have a rational explanation. Unlike more conventional areas of psychology, anomalistic psychology has different groups of researchers – those that fundamentally believe the phenomena exist, and others who are sceptics. This provides some interesting methodological and theoretical issues, and it is certainly an area of research that generates heated debate.

Any subject in psychology can be approached from a number of different perspectives. These theoretical foundations give a starting point for the research hypotheses. In this topic, the cognitive, personality and biological factors underlying the exceptional experiences are considered. Do you have a mascot or a routine that you think brings you luck in exams or before a public performance? Have you considered how a person's culture might sometimes dictate ritualistic action? The 'functions' of the paranormal and related beliefs are considered, including the cultural significance of such beliefs. Superstition and coincidence as well as deception and self-deception are also investigated.

Belief is at the centre of anomalistic experience. In 2002 when David Beckham broke his left foot, the psychic Uri Geller asked the British nation to touch their television screens and concentrate on mending the damage. He believed that doing this would speed up the healing of the foot by two months, which would mean that David Beckham could play in the World Cup. This topic focuses on the *belief in* 'exceptional experience' and how belief shapes people's judgements and observations of exceptional experience. Finally, research examining belief in psychic healing, out-of-body experience and psychic mediumship is considered.

Specification	Topic content	Page

Pseudoscience and scientific fraud

Learning objectives:

- understand the nature of pseudoscience and scientific fraud

- explain methodological and theoretical issues in anomalous experience

- draw conclusions from the current research into anomalous experience.

AQA Examiner's tip

In order to identify what a pseudoscience is, it is a good idea to make clear exactly what *science* is. This not only shows the examiner the breadth of your knowledge, but it also allows for good comparisons to be made between the two.

Key terms

Falsification: a term first introduced by Sir Karl Popper (1902–94) who argued that falsification related to the process of proving a hypothesis incorrect. He argued that this was the only way for scientific knowledge to be built up.

Objectivity: a term that is used to refer to views being based on observable phenomena and not on personal opinion, prejudices or emotion.

Replicability: the ability for procedures and/or findings to be reproduced or repeated.

Introduction

Anomalistic psychology examines paranormal events, experiences and related beliefs and attempts to explain these through psychological and physical factors. The study of anomalistic experience is at the edge of science; many ideals that conventional research uses and that are respected are not used in anomalistic studies. Often there is a lack of carefully controlled and thoughtfully interpreted experiments that are the basis of the natural sciences and contribute to their development.

Is anomalistic psychology a fringe science just because of its lack of methodological rigour? A look at the methods of investigation will allow us to assess this idea.

Scientific and pseudoscientific methods

Bauer (2004) noted that the boundaries between science and pseudoscience are often not clear. He comments (jokingly) that geniuses (scientists) are cranks that just happen to be right, while cranks (pseudoscientists) are geniuses that just happen to be wrong! Science and pseudoscience have developed as opposites, but a careful look at the methods and approaches of each might reveal more similarities than are immediately obvious.

What does 'being scientific' mean?

Science might be thought of as a quest for understanding that usually creates laws and principles that can be tested experimentally (Filippo, 1991).

Pseudoscientific information may be seen as a mistaken belief and not scientific due to its lack of testability and inability to stand up to critical analysis and **falsification**.

Science, meaning 'knowledge', as such refers to the obtaining of knowledge. The defining feature of the scientific approach is its method – a systematic process designed to objectively collect information and test theories. Central characteristics of this would be **objectivity**, **replicability** and the following of the philosophical doctrine of **empiricism**. Science approaches its study of any phenomena in a rational and logical manner where reasoning is based upon evidential verification and support. Karl Popper's influence on the scientific method was profound, suggesting that science should advance using the **hypothetico-deductive method**. The crucial characteristic of this approach was to suggest that it should always be possible to show that a theory is false, i.e. we should be able to falsify the theory. This emanates from the idea that a theory can never be 'proven' right, but one piece of evidence against a theory can prove it wrong.

Science and pseudoscience: a methodological comparison

Similarities

- Some areas of pseudoscientific research use similar methods to scientific research. Both gather data, both have a research question upon which hypotheses are based, the investigation tests the hypothesis, and the results are then published.
- Both scientists and pseudoscientists pick and choose their areas of study. There are cases in which pride, greed and hunger for fame have got the better of scientists and pseudoscientists and facts have been chosen selectively.
- Similar experimental methodologies are used to generate the data.
- Different research methods can be used in the acquisition of knowledge.

Differences

- The way that the results are interpreted and communicated is different. Science ensures peer review of findings, whereas often in pseudoscience there is direct communication of results to the public. This avoids the critical assessment of the research that scientists have to endure.
- While pseudoscience might pick and choose what to study, most scientists would argue that their selection of what to study is dictated by their knowledge of what areas would genuinely benefit the advancement of human understanding (Radner and Radner, 1982).
- While science formulates hypotheses and the information and then gathers the data, pseudoscience often formulates hypotheses to support the data gathered (Filippo, 1991).
- Validation of the scientific analysis of phenomena can be ensured through **methodological pluralism** ensuring that hypotheses can be rigorously assessed and if needs be **falsified**. Pseudoscience ensures that the methods used provide a means of generating data to support the stated hypotheses, which does not necessarily check the assumptions of the research.

Hint

The difference between pseudoscientific and scientific approaches can be seen in the methodology and rigour. Due to the subject matter of anomalistic psychology, there will always be a lack scientific rigour and opportunities for fraud.

Hint

How science works

You need to appreciate that scientific knowledge is based upon experimental evidence. New evidence will change scientific knowledge. It is also a requirement for scientists to communicate information and ideas in appropriate ways using appropriate terminology. In sharing their research, scientists give other researchers in the field the opportunity to replicate and test their work. The question is, to what extent can a pseudoscience such as the study of anomalistic experience match these criteria?

Key terms

Empiricism: a view that suggests that experience is central to the development and formation of knowledge, and thus central to the scientific method. Experience or evidence arises out of experiments not intuition or revelation.

Hypothetico-deductive method: the basic rule in science that you first generate a hypothesis, then create an investigation to test it and finally, having tested your hypothesis, you revisit your hypothesis to see if your original proposal was correct.

Methodological pluralism: a term that is used to describe the approach of a researcher using more than one 'method' in their analysis. Often it is the case that by using more than method (hence plural) the researcher can be sure of a more valid outcome.

Falsified: shown to be wrong.

Link

For more information on the scientific method and its philosophical underpinnings, see Chapter 37, The application of scientific methodology in psychology, pages 508–10.

AQA Examiner's tip

Comparisons show an advanced level of understanding. They show your confidence with the subject matter and allow you to highlight similarities and differences in the work you are examining, such as here between pseudoscience and natural science.

Link

For more information about the alternatives to the scientific approach, see the research methods chapters at pages 510–11.

■ Take it further

Radner and Radner (1982) identified a much longer list of how the scientific and pseudoscientific traditions differed. Investigate their work. What other comparisons did they make between science and pseudoscience? Using this information write a paragraph that compares the two approaches from the point of view of Radner and Radner.

■ Link

For more information on Popper look at Chapter 37, The application of scientific methodology in psychology, pages 508–10.

▨ Key terms

Monozygotic (MZ) twins: twins born from the same fertilised egg. Also known as identical twins, they have exactly the same genetic make-up.

Positive correlation: a link between two variables that shows that as one variable increases so does the other.

Psi phenomena: relates to the collective study of paranormal events, e.g. extrasensory perception.

■ Link

For more information about how such fraudulent research contributes to problems of validation, see Chapter 37, The application of scientific methodology in psychology, page 513.

■ Hint

The view of these psychologists is divided into either sceptic or believer. This provides good structure for your argument about research in this area and not only forces you to describe research, but it also allows you to give the alternative point of view as well.

Science and pseudoscience: 'ways of thinking' with more differences than similarities

Underlying research, there are the traditions (ways of thinking) that inform the research methods that are used. With this in mind, Radner and Radner (1982) identified several ways in which the scientific and pseudoscientific traditions differ:

▨ Anachronistic thinking: the view that pseudoscience often uses theories that are outdated, disproved or not even proven to support the research. Science has a system of continual updating of research theories.

▨ Looking for mysteries: explanations in pseudoscience often ignore disagreement with conventional scientific research, since scientific research looks at and tests phenomena that actually happen rather than things that could possibly have happened.

▨ Appeal to myths: myths are used by pseudoscience to support theories, unlike science where theories are tested by empirical research and the validation of findings.

▨ 'Grab bag' approach to evidence: quantity not quality of evidence is often used by pseudoscientists to support theoretical views. Science only accepts evidence that has been rigorously tested and shows quality of research design and investigation.

▨ Irrefutable hypotheses: pseudoscientists defy falsification, since they create theories that are hard to prove false. With science, falsification is proof of the quality of the investigation and theory based upon it.

Currently there is a divide between those who believe in the benefit of understanding anomalous experience and those who are sceptical of the explanation of anomalous experience (French and Wilson, 2006, 2005). These sceptics have good reason to be critical as throughout history there have been examples of scientific frauds that make scientists question the integrity of anomalistic psychology.

The reality of scientific fraud

If researchers followed Popper's scientific approach, situations of fraud would not arise, but they do. These cases are not just restricted to the area of anomalistic psychology. Sir Cyril Burt was a highly respected academic who had a profound influence on the content and direction of modern psychology, especially with his contribution to the understanding of the genetic basis of IQ. Burt was the first British Psychologist to be knighted and he was also the president of the British Psychological Society. In one of his studies, Burt used 53 sets of **monozygotic (MZ) twins** that were reared apart from each other, showing a +0.771 correlation between their IQs – this is a very strong **positive correlation**. Interestingly this study matched to the third decimal place his previous small study. This could have been coincidence but the BPS found him guilty of fraud with many scientists believing that he invented crucial aspects of his data to support his theory.

The views of anomalistic psychologists remain divided when evaluating the evidence of anomalistic presences and experiences. There tend to be opposites, those who are sceptics and those that value the evidence to date as providing some level of understanding. Researchers such as Dean Radin and Jessica Utts suggest that evidence for certain **psi phenomena** is reasonably well established through research that has been repeated many times. For example, Radin (1997) did a meta-analysis of psi experiments and showed that the incidence of anomalous ability was much greater than would be expected if performance was just by chance.

Broad and Wade (1982) mention a series of cases where there has been known or suspected scientific fraud, and show that it is not just confined to the study of anomalistic phenomena. However, there have been notable examples of fraudulent activity in that area, either by way of the fabrication or erroneous interpretation of data or by deliberate methodological design flaws. It has been claimed that 'fraud is perhaps the principal source of successful results in parapsychology' (Charpak *et al.*, 2004).

A look at the research of Sylvia Browne (1999), Edgar Cayce (1967), John Edward (2001), Uri Geller (2000), Ellen Greve (2000), Walter J. Levy Jr (1974), James Van Praagh (1997), Mother Shipton (1641) and S.G. Soal (1941) certainly seems consistent with this view. Therefore, we have to ask whether anomalous experience is reality or the product of fraud.

Is anomalistic experience reality or fraud?

In assessing whether reality or fraud dominates this area of research, most have focused on demonstrating the existence of ESP. Can individuals use skills not within the normal sensory range to complete tasks? Most research in this area makes use of studies to establish the presence or absence of ESP.

What is ESP?

This is a term relating to the ability to perceive outside the known sensory system. This is usually seen as a collective term for showing a range of skills such as **telepathy** (mind reading), **clairvoyance** (contact with the non-living) and **precognition** (predicting future events) (Reber and Reber, 2001). Any skills that can usually be attributed to the normal senses such as smell, sight, touch, hearing and taste are not classified as extrasensory perception.

The academic need to prove the existence of extrasensory perception skills often means that scientists will manipulate their experiment or interpret their data in a way that might support the existence of their claim. What follows is a series of well-documented cases where anomalistic experience has been investigated and deemed to exist, but the conclusions were based on fraudulent methods and data analysis.

There has been a series of well-known studies of psi phenomena that were initially very convincing. As George R. Price (1955) notes:

> Surprisingly it is not only believers who are reluctant to imagine fraud, but virtually all sceptics as well ... thus we find sceptics searching for every other conceivable sort of explanation. While the one explanation that is the simplest and most in accord with everyday experience is dismissed as inconceivable.

Price, 1955

Research study: Soal–Goldney (1938–41)

By 1939 Soal, a mathematician, had investigated a form of ESP called telepathy with some 160 participants in around 128,000 card-guessing tasks. Initially the results looked disappointing. But then a closer statistical analysis was performed on the data revealing that some individuals had performed better than others. Experiments into telepathy require a sender, an agent and of course the experimenter. The sender is the person who 'sends' the

Take it further

While a selection of this research is examined in this chapter, you can expand your knowledge by conducting an investigative analysis on the remaining researchers. You could structure your notes along the lines of (a) who did the study, (b) what it was about, and (c) whether it was a fraud and why.

Key terms

Telepathy: commonly seen as a means of communication between minds through non-conventional means.

Clairvoyance: the power to perceive objects, persons or events not accessible by way of the normal senses.

Precognition: knowledge of something before it actually occurs.

information by extra sensory means to the 'agent' (i.e. the receiver). In the 1939 sample two participants had statistically significant results ('Mrs Stewart' and 'Shackleton'). In 1941 Shackleton was tested further by Soal and Goldney. The protocols were put in place to give the impression to the outside observer that methodologically the experiment was sound, and there was good protection from cheating (by either the participant or the experimenter). Soal and Goldney even invited academics from other institutions and countries to be present at the investigations, although no magicians or conjurors were present (the presence of magicians/conjurors is often used in psi research to verify scientifically that no magic techniques were used to influence the results). So what was so fraudulent? The basic procedure was mainly carried out in Shackleton's own photographic studio, while several other replications were done in Soal's offices. The sender was in one room, with an experimenter sitting across from them. In front of the sender there was a screen with a square hole cut out. The cards used for this study had pictures of animals on one side (elephant, giraffe, lion, pelican and zebra). The aim was for Shackleton (the receiver) to guess what card the sender in the adjoining room was looking at. The experimenter told Shackleton when to make a guess. With each trial the cards were shuffled by either an experimenter or an independent observer. No one else apart from the sender could see the cards. The experimenter told the sender which card to pick up by signalling 1, 2, 3, 4 or 5 to them. Shackleton recorded his answers on a scoring sheet. This happened 50 times. Shackleton's success rate was unusually good. This suggests that the cause was well beyond that of simple chance.

Methodological issues

When the results were first published, the Soal–Goldney research was thought to be sound and to demonstrate extra sensory perception. The fraud was so good that highly esteemed writers and commentators, and people with a distinguished scientific background, noted the research:

> Dr Soal's results are outstanding. The precautions taken to avoid deliberate fraud or the unwitting conveyance of information by normal means are described in detail, and seem to be absolutely water-tight.
>
> *Broad in* **Hansel**, *1989*

> Soal's work was conducted with every precaution that it was possible to devise.
>
> **Hutchinson**, *1989*

Soal's *apparent* attention to possibilities for cheating allowed a very effective fraud. The last of Soal's experiments was conducted in 1943, but it was not until the 1970s (Scott *et al.*, 1974 and Marwick, 1978) that the first questions were asked about his data. For example, if you examine the number (between 1 and 5) that the experimenter showed to the agent to signal which card to pick up, this might not have been chosen randomly. Hansel (1989) notes that the list was 'kept under lock and key until brought to the sitting in a suitcase that was never out of his [the experimenter's] sight'. Soal claimed that this list was random, but no one observed him creating it. In theory, Soal could have produced a list where the number was often 1, and 1 could easily be changed to a 4 or adapted to a 5 later. One of Soal's 'agents' (Mrs Albert) stated that she had witnessed Soal changing the 1 on a score sheet to a 4 or a 5 on a number of occasions (Scott *et al.*, 1974; Alcock, 1981).

This research remains notorious. The impression that Soal gave of experimental meticulousness had a serious adverse effect on the credibility of anomalistic research (Alcock, 1981).

Ethical issues

- The extent to which Soal went to provide the appearance of scientific rigour emphasises his deceptive nature.
- Under current ethical guidelines, there is an expectation that colleagues are used to ensure the ethical nature of the enquiry. But if Soal is not honest with his own colleagues as to the nature and content of his enquiry, it seems hard for his colleagues to provide suitable peer review of the content of the study.

There were wider theoretical issues that arose out of this research. Soal needed to show that there really were psi phenomena in some selected individuals. This *personal pressure to succeed* interfered with his professionalism. The need to succeed in being one of the first to scientifically prove psi phenomena would be an honour – but it was an honour that eventually cost him his scientific respect, rigour and reputation.

Research study: Walter J. Levy Jr (1974)

Levy Jr investigated the precognitive ability of rats to create physical changes using will-power (psychokinesis). He implanted electrodes into the brains of rats. According to previous research, electrical stimulation (shock) of the pleasure centres of the brain would cause them immense pleasure. Shocks were delivered by a computer at random intervals linked to the decay of atoms in a sample of radioactive strontium 90. With no human interference the computer would shock the rats' pleasure regions 50 per cent of the time. Levy Jr hoped to show that if the rats could anticipate the computer by using ESP or influence the decay of the radioactive source by psychokinesis, their pleasure score would exceed 50 per cent.

Levy Jr claimed that the pleasure score rating of the rats was 54 per cent, showing that the rats had some anomalous ability. The pleasure scoring was measured, quantitatively, by the number of shocks received.

Methodological issues

Investigation by his own research assistants proved that the results were due to Levy Jr tampering with the experimental apparatus. Another set of apparatus installed without Levy Jr's knowledge confirmed the suspicions since the levels recorded were lower than those recorded by Levy Jr. Asher (1975) notes how the person who challenged Levy Jr's results 'on more than one occasion witnessed Levy pulling a plug from the back of the random generator, causing the equipment to only record "hits" for a period of time' (*Time*, 26 August 1974). Levy Jr admitted his fraud and resigned from his post.

Hint

How science works

Scientists have to evaluate methodology, the evidence and data. In the case of the Soal–Goldney research the data appeared out of the ordinary compared to what would be expected. Science has a role to play in ensuring that the research conducted is robust. In this case experiments must be designed adequately to test predictions. Soal–Goldney's research gave the impression of being methodologically robust, but closer examination of the procedures allows us to see the many flaws that meant fraudulent behaviour was possible.

Furthermore, the use of animals in research is always questionable, not least because it is very difficult to generalise from animals to humans in a meaningful way. This means that even if psi skills were identified, it does not necessarily mean that humans share these skills.

Ethical issues

Animal research is an emotive and controversial area which is strictly controlled today. In the years of research surrounding Walter J. Levy Jr this was not the case. It is possible in the process of preparing the rats for use and in the subsequent experiment that the rats used might well have been subjected to a certain level of pain given that they underwent surgery to insert the electrodes and they were given electric shocks.

Dr Joseph Rhine, Levy's mentor and a distinguished researcher in anomalous research, published an article in 1974 called Security versus deception, in which he admitted that the length of time it has taken to accept anomalistic experience as a 'reputable scientific study area' has mainly been due to 'suspicions surrounding the honesty of the investigators themselves'.

This study shows again that once researchers have publicised their findings, any fraudulent activity can usually be identified and results can be checked by repeating the study. The ability to prove something wrong is a central characteristic of science. Walter J. Levy Jr admitted to friends that there was an implicit pressure upon him to replicate his earlier research findings. A pressure that forced him to act fraudulently.

Psychic powers and Sylvia Browne

Many people claim to have psychic powers. We will look at one more closely here. Sylvia Browne is a well-known American psychic, TV host, and police department and FBI assistant. She claims that her psychic abilities are innate, and that she can see a wider range of **vibrational frequencies** than the normal human being. The accuracy of Browne's predictions have been questioned, e.g. she predicted that Bill Clinton would be falsely accused in the Lewinsky scandal, and that Osama Bin Laden and Saddam Hussein were hiding in caves and Bin Laden had died (proved by the CIA to be incorrect). In her predictions in 2000, she did not predict the 9/11 twin towers attack, although she reportedly said in the week *after* the attacks that she had a lot of dreams involving fire in the week leading up to the attacks. She has had numerous feuds with sceptics such as James Randi, but one of the most striking examples of her fraudulent claims is the Sago Mine controversy. Browne was making an appearance on a radio show, giving predictions for the following year. During the programme a piece of unconfirmed news was broadcast suggesting that 12 out of 13 trapped miners had been found alive. Browne said that she knew this would be the case. It later emerged that only one of the miners was alive; Browne's response was:

> Yeah, I don't think there's, I don't think there's, I don't really think there is anyone alive. If there is, I think there may be only one ... I just don't believe that there's ... I haven't heard anything because I've been with you, but I don't just think they are alive.

Coast to Coast *radio programme, 3 January 2006,*
presented by George Noory

Key terms

Vibrational frequencies: a term specific to many mediums' claims. It is used to assert that 'the other side' (what we might call Heaven) exists but cannot be seen, and that the medium's special ability to recognise these frequencies justifies their position as a medium.

In 1992, Browne and her husband were convicted of fraud and grand theft.

Sylvia Browne's predictions are usually no better than chance. While she has made some correct predictions, this has to be understood in the wider context of the number of predictions that she has got incorrect. As far as anomalistic psychology is concerned, actions of individuals such as Browne provide sceptics with ample evidence that anomalistic powers do not exist, and they detract from the rigour of those researchers that are determined to test for the existence of it. If anything, individuals such as Browne cause *more* questions to be raised in the minds of many scientists regarding whether there are any anomalistic forces at work at all.

Hint

Using examples such as Sylvia Browne, you can argue that there is increasing evidence to disprove the so-called abilities of mediums.

Summary

The claims of individuals such as Sylvia Browne reinforce the need to scientifically study this area to assess the genuineness of such powers and to establish the anomalistic ability of individuals, especially in ESP and psychokinesis. Whilst identifying fraudulent research is one thing, it is more important to have precautions against cheating in the first place. Bearing this in mind, the following section examines the controversies surrounding research into ESP and psychokinesis.

Key points

- The boundaries between science and pseudoscience are not clear.

- Some authorities would view anomalistic psychology as a fringe science because of its lack of methodological rigour.

- There are some similarities, but there are greater differences between science and pseudoscience. Radner and Radner (1982) reinforce this point with their four identified differences between the two.

- The fraudulent activities of a few researchers in this area puts even more pressure on those academics seriously trying to establish anomalistic ability.

- Fraudulent research in most cases has encouraged serious researchers of the topic to create research programmes that are so tightly controlled that the opportunity for fraud is drastically reduced.

Summary questions

1. What is the difference between anomalistic psychology and parapsychology?

2. What is the difference between science and pseudoscience?

3. Outline and evaluate research into the claims of some anomalistic researchers that psychic abilities exist and can be studied.

Ganzfeld studies of ESP and studies of psychokinesis

Learning objectives:

▪ understand what research using the ganzfeld technique of ESP is

▪ describe the controversy surrounding the ganzfeld studies of ESP

▪ understand the nature of research into psychokinesis

▪ describe the controversies surrounding research into psychokinesis.

Fig. 1 *Zener cards*

Key terms

Quasi-scientific: the term quasi means that it is 'not strictly' scientific.

Ganzfeld: German word meaning 'total field', and the name of the method used by anomalistic psychologists to examine ESP.

White noise: a type of noise that is created by combining all forms of human sound together, usually all of different frequencies.

Pink noise: white noise but with the high frequencies left out.

Ganzfeld chamber: an enclosed environmentally controlled room.

Free associate: verbalise thoughts that come into your head, literally anything that comes into your mind at that time.

What is ESP?

ESP relates to abilities beyond the understanding of science where the perception of phenomena is possible outside of the normal five senses. These abilities are usually categorised into: telepathy, psychokinesis, clairvoyance and precognition. ESP is a term that was introduced by J.B. Rhine at Duke University in the US. His early experiments used Zener cards and had some influence in establishing the plausibility of anomalistic phenomena in a **quasi-scientific** manner. The Zener cards used to research telepathy (see Figure 1) are made up of five cards that show either a circle, a cross, wavy lines, a square or a star. Rhine would shuffle these (later they were shuffled by a machine). The cards would be laid out in a line, the sender would view them and 'transmit' them to the agent (the receiver).

What are ganzfeld studies?

The earliest forms of **ganzfeld** experiments were designed to ensure that signals received by participants were coming from their own mind, not an audible or visible stimulus. To achieve this, the participant's eyes were covered up with half ping-pong balls so that the visual field was completely white, and the participant wore headphones playing either **white noise** or **pink noise**. A red light was shone on the face of the participant (receiver), and often a relaxation tape (e.g. of the sound of the sea) was played to the participant through headphones to ensure they were in a relaxed state of mind. Before being isolated in the **ganzfeld chamber**, the receiver was asked to **free associate** for about 20 minutes. Once the participant was isolated, the experimenter could hear what the participant was saying and could communicate with them.

Another individual performed the role of the sender. This person was placed in another room (for the purposes of scientific rigour, the further away the better). The sender had a selection of non-transparent packets, each containing a set of slides or pictures (with later experiments, this included video footage). There was no link between the images, and ideally the target image was chosen randomly. The sender concentrated and tried to use mental intention to telepathically communicate information about the image to the receiver. A single ganzfeld session can last between 15 and 30 minutes. The receiver has his or her eyes uncovered and headphones removed. The receiver is presented with a set of images (usually four) and asked to what degree they think each stimulus was the target image. If the highest rating is awarded to the target it is recorded as a hit. Using this method, the expected hit rate just by chance will be 25 per cent.

So there are three parts to the ganzfeld experimental procedure:

▪ preparing the receiver and the sender

▪ sending the target information

▪ judging the outcome.

Commentators such as Radin (1997) and Carroll (2007) observe that ganzfeld experiments were and still are common means of investigating ESP. There are two forms of ganzfeld experiments: early studies (1974–81), such as those outlined above, and later studies (1983–89). Between

1981 and 1983 studies were still conducted, but during this time autoganzfeld studies were created and initially run. Autoganzfeld studies were originally created by Berger (1983). They were called autoganzfeld studies because the researcher, sender and receiver were all separate from each other. Furthermore, the researcher was isolated from the selection of the material that would be used by the sender. The material was selected automatically by a computer. So advances in computer technology meant that improvements in security and preciseness could be achieved.

Research study: Sargent et al. (1979)

Sargent et al.'s research is a good example of a rigorous attempt to study ESP.

Each participant arrived at the laboratory and was greeted by Sargent and his colleagues. Drinks were offered and music was playing to keep the atmosphere informal and relaxed. When the participant was ready to start the experiment, they were given a short pre-session questionnaire to complete. The participant was then asked to lie on a mattress, half ping-pong balls and cotton wool were placed over their eyes and taped on, and headphones playing white noise at a comfortable level were put over their ears. A red light was shone onto the ping-pong balls, and the participant was then shut in the room.

The sender (whom Sargent calls the agent) went to Sargent's office and selected the 'target' (the image to be sent). The agent was usually either the experimenter, a friend of the experimenter, or a student. In the office there were 27 different sets of four pictures labelled A, B, C and D. These images were chosen by the experimenter so that there were no links between them. There were two copies of each set, one for the agent to take away and one for the receiver to pick from later. The sender (agent) selected four envelopes containing the letters A to D and this determined which image would be the 'target'.

Randomisation of choice of targets was complicated. The 27 sets of four pictures were each numbered 01 to 12 and 14 to 28. The agent chose one of these by selecting an arbitrary starting point in a random number table, and taking the first number near to that point between 01 and 28 (excluding 13). This dictated which set of pictures was used. The pictures in each set had a label, A, B, C or D. In this experiment there was a pile of 20 small brown sealed envelopes, each one containing a letter (A, B, C or D). There were five of each letter in the pile. The agent opened a book of random digits and, starting from any location, selected a number between 0 and 20 that was nearest that point (for example the number 11). The agent then counted that number down in the pile of 20 envelopes (in our example, 11), and cut the pack. He then looked at the next number in the random number table between 0 and 20 (e.g. 3) and counted down the remaining pile by that number (in our case, 3). The agent took out the selected envelope. The letter in this envelope determined the image to be 'sent'.

At the end of the ganzfeld session, the experimenter went into the room where the participant was, and removed the headphones and ping-pong balls. The participant walked to Sargent's office and was asked to score (on a scale of 1–100) all four pictures, the higher scores being given to pictures that the receiver thought they had been sent. The agent was then asked to come back into the

Anomalistic psychology

receiver's room and disclose what the target was. A hit was identified by the participant giving the target image the highest score.

Of the 12 sessions conducted, six were direct hits. This rate of 50 per cent was much higher than the 25 per cent (one in four) which would be expected by chance alone.

Methodological issues

- Opportunities for cheating were not minimised, e.g. Blackmore (1987) reports that in her observations of Sargent's research, between session 8 and session 9 (of the 12 in the experiment) two sets of envelopes disappeared from the drawer of the office.

- During session 9, Sargent came into the receiver's room during the judging. He was not officially taking part, but insisted he should come in and help since the participant was saying very little. Interestingly, on the same trial Sargent made an arithmetic 'mistake', meaning that the session was recorded as a direct hit when in fact it should not have been.

Ethical issues

- While Sargent may have consulted his colleagues over potential ethical issues in the study as he is required to do under ethical guidelines, his fraudulent behaviour undermines this.

- The ganzfeld materials used in studies are somewhat different to what a normal lay person might be used to experiencing. While it is clear that Sargent did protect the participants physically, arguably they might have experienced marginal distress given the extreme novelty of the situation.

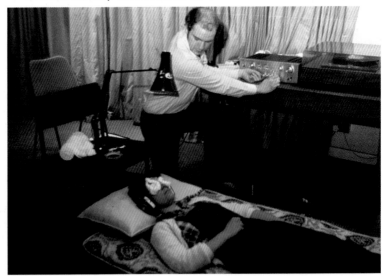

Fig. 2 *Ganzfeld experimenter Carl Sargent adjusts sound and lighting for subject on floor. Cambridge, 1981*

There are broader theoretical issues with this research. Since Sargent's studies are a fairly substantial part of the collection of ganzfeld experiments, it is not surprising that many academics question the value of the early research and results showing evidence of psi. If Sargent's research is removed, this weakens the argument for there being evidence for psi. Blackmore says:

Sargent's studies form a considerable proportion of the [earlier] total ganzfeld database. In view of Sargent's unwillingness to explain errors found, or to make his data available to other researchers, I suggest that these results be viewed with caution.

Blackmore, 1987

Ganzfeld studies: criticisms and controversy

The validity of theories produced by anomalistic psychologists is only as strong as the methods they use when conducting research. With many of the earlier studies, there were problems of sensory leakage (i.e. other means by which information could have been indicated to the receiver) and randomisation anomalies. From 1989 onwards this criticism was tackled by the use of automated slides – part of what was known as the autoganzfeld method. Magicians are sometimes employed as consultants to ensure that protocols are followed and that inadvertent sensory leakage does not occur (Bern, 1994).

Problems of randomisation can be seen in the research done by Sargent. In the early 1980s, Hyman conducted a meta-analysis of 42 pieces of research. As a result of this, he argued that there was insufficient evidence to prove the existence of psi because of the flaws in the ESP research. He suggested three areas where there were flaws:

- security
- statistical analysis
- procedure.

His meta-analysis used 48 per cent of the ganzfeld database, suggesting that more methodologically rigorous studies need to be conducted before any conclusions are drawn from the body of research. In evaluating the ganzfeld database, Harris and Rosenthal (1988) comment that for every study showing a significant effect, there is at least one critical commentary of it. Hyman (1996), known as a sceptic of psi research, states that the later ganzfeld studies were no better methodologically than the earlier studies and 'constitute neither a successful replication of the original ganzfeld experiments nor a sufficient body of data to conclude that ESP has finally been demonstrated'. The strongest sceptics of psi phenomena are often psychologists.

Milton and Wiseman (1999) conducted a meta-analysis and concluded that investigating the effect of ESP through ganzfeld techniques is methodologically flawed because replication is practically impossible. To show the strength of ESP in the laboratory, other psychologists have re-analysed the same data and come to different conclusions. For example Bem, Broughton and Palmer (2001) conducted their own meta-analysis of the same data used in the Milton and Wiseman (1999) study. Bem and his colleagues drew a more positive conclusion. They found that the 'hit rate' for all such experiments was around 30 per cent as opposed to the 25 per cent expected by chance.

Radin and Schlitz (2002) further conducted a meta-analysis of ganzfeld studies and concluded that the 'hit rate' in many of the ganzfeld studies was so strong that the odds of chance being the causal factor was around a trillion to one! Radin and Schlitz felt quite confident that they had surveyed all known studies, a point that is disputed by Harris and Rosenthal, who studied double the number of sessions studied by Radin and Schlitz and found an average hit rate of 28 per cent. Endersby makes a point that students of anomalistic psychology need to heed:

AQA Examiner's tip

Knowledge of meta-analysis research shows your awareness of methodological issues and it also shows how you can evaluate the area with research that has tried to bring a wide variety of studies together. However, be aware that the meta-analysis research has its own pitfalls.

Anomalistic psychology

■ Key terms

File drawer effect: selective reporting of previous research. Information that is used regularly is easily accessed, whereas information that is hardly ever referred to gradually gets lost.

Sheep-goat effect: the suggestion that the attitude of the participant (whether they believe in ESP or not) can affect ESP scores.

Macro PK: a form of psychokinesis that focuses on clearly observable effects (e.g. scissors being levitated between two hands).

Micro PK: a form of psychokinesis with weaker effects that are not always noticeable to the naked eye and often require statistical evaluation.

'There is no doubt that figures can be tweaked up or down by ruling in or out certain experiments'. This is known as the **file drawer effect**. We should be sceptical about all meta-analyses since they seldom seem to report the large number of studies that showed no ESP effect. One methodological conclusion that can be drawn here would be that meta-analyses are of only limited worth in an area that is known to have questionable methodology and limited success with replicability.

> The best way to resolve this controversy … is to await the outcome of future Ganzfeld experiments. These experiments ideally, will be carried out in such a way as to circumvent the file drawer problem, problems of multiple analysis, and the various defects in randomisation, statistical application, and documentation.
>
> *Hyman and Honorton, 1985*

Ganzfeld research has been further undermined by the suggestion that it could be influenced by the experiment effect. Rosenthal and Harris (1988) thought that the expectations and attitudes of the experimenters might influence the results. To illustrate this, a comparison was made where the atmosphere at the ganzfeld study was either welcoming or cold and abrupt. The results showed that ESP scores for participants who were treated warmly were higher than for those treated abruptly.

Other psychologists (Schmeidler and Edge, 1999) question the strength and validity of the ganzfeld research since it could be subject to the **sheep-goat effect**. Over a nine-year period, Gertrude Schmeidler split her participants into 'sheep' (those that believed in ESP) and 'goats' (those who did not). Her results (which have been successfully replicated) show that there was an above average hit rate for those that believed in ESP and a lower than average hit rate for those that did not, since here it clearly seems that belief in anomalistic powers shapes experience of it.

■ Studies of psychokinesis: criticisms and controversies

> Perhaps in fifty years we will be using psychokinesis to open our garage doors by the mind only, without making any physical contact.
>
> *Radin, 1997*

Psychokinesis (PK) has been defined by Jean Moisset (2000) as 'an action of the mind on animate matter, as well as physical energy, able to provoke the deformation or displacement of an object (telekinesis)'. It has only been a fairly recent phenomenon for anomalistic psychologists to try to reproduce this in controlled laboratory surroundings. J.B. Rhine was again an early pioneer in this area. As early as the 1930s, Rhine was investigating psychokinesis using the basic method of dice throwing. Before the dice were thrown, the participant had to state the numbers that would come face-up when they landed. Results were 'encouraging' but not as strong as the research findings into ESP. Rhine did conclude that some similarity existed between psychokinesis and ESP, since one was a central part to the other. PK relies on the processes of ESP. From Rhine's work on PK, the study of PK can be split into two distinct areas – **macro PK** and **micro PK**. There has been a greater research focus on micro PK than on macro PK.

Schmidt's electronic coin flipper

In the 1960s came the development of a new means of testing, the 'electronic coin flipper' (Schmidt, 1969). This system worked on the random decay of radioactive particles. As they decay, rays are given out that are not affected by temperature, air pressure, electrostatic forces, magnetism or chemical change. In these experiments Schmidt asked his subjects to influence the falling of a coin (either heads or tails). This is a system that makes fraud almost impossible. Schmidt was applauded by other members of the scientific community who had previously ridiculed a lot of parapsychological research on the basis that it was full of methodological flaws. Schmidt had revolutionised the methodology with which parapsychological study could be performed. His results showed that when the participants were asked to send their mental energies towards the coin, making it flip, a significant statistical deviation from chance was witnessed.

From a critical viewpoint, the fact that not all participants achieved the task suggests that psychokinetic abilities and the methods for testing them are not foolproof or accurate. The main benefit of this research is that later random-event generators and computerised techniques of randomisation were based on the electronic coin flipper.

Uri Geller

Uri Geller is possibly the most well-known person with apparent psychokinetic abilities. He focuses much of his attention on macro PK. Geller was studied at the Stanford Research Institute in the 1970s by Targ and Puthoff (1976) who thought that he was so gifted they invented the term 'Geller effect' to describe his powers. Since then Geller has performed in front of thousands of people all over the world. He has demonstrated his ability to use ESP, and psychokinetic energy to bend spoons, metal bars and metallic objects and stop the movement of clocks. However, in a series of demonstrations the fraudulent nature of some of Geller's work was seen. One of the most notable examples was Geller's appearance on Jimmy Carson's *Tonight* show. On the recommendation of James Randi (a well-known magician), the programme presented Uri Geller with various materials such as drawings that were sealed in envelopes (he was asked to describe the drawing); a set of non-transparent beakers (Geller was asked which ones had water in them); and some spoons (he was asked to bend them in public). It is important to say that neither Uri nor his staff had any prior contact with these materials. In front of millions of viewers Uri could not complete the tasks given to him, stating he 'did not feel strong' and he 'needed more time'. As far as Randi was concerned, this was definitive evidence that Uri was a fraud – after all, if his abilities were exceptional then he should be able to perform them regardless of situation or context.

James Randi notes: 'if Uri Geller bends spoons with divine powers then he's doing it the hard way' (Randi, 1995). Other critical accounts of Geller's actions came from his friend Itzhaak Saban, who was often used as a confederate in the audience. The psychic power that Geller claims seems to be increasingly questionable, although his website suggests that he has been employed by oil companies to help them find oil, for example in 1976 Pemex (a small Mexican Oil company) employed him to dowse for oil.

Nina Kulagina

Another famous example of PK ability comes from the Soviet Union. Nina Kulagina was a housewife who demonstrated her abilities to

Fig. 3 *Helmut Schmidt and his electronic coin flipper*

▇ Hint

Trying to make the whole study of anomalistic psychology such as psychokinesis more scientific meant that it was easier to rule out other confounding variables (explanations) for the abilities witnessed. Schmidt's coin flipper was an early attempt to make the study of this area more scientific and less open to criticism from sceptics and scientists alike.

Fig. 4 *Uri Geller*

Fig. 5 *Nina Kulagina*

Western scientists. She could make a range of objects move, alter the course of a moving object, make a frog's heart beat faster and slower, she could even apparently make it stop.

Kulagina has been photographed levitating items. In video footage she is seen to move items that are in a plastic box. It emerged later that often items were attached by a thread to her leg. When she was studied, it was often at her home or in hotel rooms, thus stringent experimental controls were not applied. This was apparently due to the fact that each session would take several hours of 'preparation' (Kulagina called this 'concentration time'). It is possible that many of her apparent abilities could be explained in terms of simple conjuring techniques. For example, she claimed to control a compass, but a magnet held behind her (out of view of the witnesses) would achieve this. She claimed to move items across a table, but thread or even hair could be used to achieve this. Her claims cannot be entirely falsified since no magician was present at her demonstrations. If a magician had been present, the abilities of Nina Kulagina might have been more rigorously assessed.

It is likely that the controversy over the psychic powers of ESP and psychokinesis will continue for some time. Anomalistic psychology is known for random results, uncoordinated observations (even over the same experimental data), inconsistent findings from experiments, and a lack of defined concepts. Anomalistic psychology is waiting for an Einstein to revolutionise the area of study.

Key points

- ESP has its origins far back in history and these are well documented, for example, in ancient Greek literature (e.g. the Oracle of Delphi).

- Ganzfeld studies can be divided into the early studies (1974–81) and the later studies (1983–89). The main difference is the degree of technical assistance used. The later studies making use of the autoganzfeld technique – due to lack of technological advancement this would not have been widely available in the earlier studies.

- Methodological rigour dogs most of the psi research in this area. Methodological weaknesses mean that the potential for other influence over behaviour is far greater and less controlled.

- Uri Geller and Nina Kulagina are good examples of individuals that would seem to have psychokinetic powers – although questions have been raised in both cases about the exact causes of the skills they show.

- There are many controversies surrounding research into psychic ability such as ESP and psychokinesis. Fraudulent activity by a minority of researchers has influenced opinion about the worth of research in the area as a whole.

- Criticism and controversy surround ESP and psychokinesis research centres regarding the methodology used, and how secure it is in ensuring that no other form of sensory communication reveals the answers. Only when all of the other possible variables are controlled and the results can be replicated will extrasensory research be given scientific credibility.

Take it further

Can you bend a spoon or fork? Do you think there is any value or truth in psychokinetic ability? Outline the reasons for your answer and justify your reasoning with research.

Summary questions

4 What are ganzfeld studies and how might ganzfeld research be criticised?

5 What is psychokinesis? In what way might scientific fraud explain the findings of research in this area?

6 To what extent does anomalistic research into ESP or psychokinesis provide support for the claim that psychic power is the genuine power of a few chosen individuals?

Factors underlying anomalous experience

Cognitive, personality and biological factors

Learning objectives:

- understand the cognitive factors underlying anomalous experience

- understand how a person's personality traits can impinge upon anomalous experience

- describe the biological underpinnings of anomalous experience

- draw reasoned conclusions from the different factors that underlie the anomalous experience.

Hint

How science works

Chapter 34, Theoretical and methodological issues in the study of anomalous experience, looked at types of anomalistic experience and the study of it by psychologists. Belief in such abilities might be underpinned by various factors such as cognitive, personality or biological influences.

Key terms

Scholastic Aptitude Test (SAT): in the USA these are used as the basis for university course offers.

Introduction

The phenomenon of anomalistic experience can be understood simply as a psychic skill, such as in the claims of Uri Geller or Nina Kulagina. Yet there could be other factors that influence our understanding of anomalistic experience. For example, Wiseman and Watt (2006) note that people who believe in psychic abilities are often those individuals who are most likely to misinterpret a normal explanation for a behaviour with a paranormal cause. In this chapter we examine the potential influence of cognitive and personality factors as underlying dispositional (as opposed to situational) influences on psi ability. Persinger and Koren (2001) encourage us not just to restrict our focus on anomalistic ability to psychological factors, since 'to date there has not been a single type of paranormal experience that is not understandable in terms of known brain function'. With this in mind, we also examine the potential biological influences upon anomalistic ability and the effect on psychic ability.

Cognitive factors

Various cognitive factors are considered by research in this area. These include the idea that anomalistic belief develops:

- because people have psychological characteristics that make them more likely to misconstrue normal experiences as paranormal ones

- partly because it gives the believer some control, or because it is central to religious or philosophical beliefs (Irwin, 1992 and Lawrence *et al.*, 1995).

- as the result of genuine experience of anomalistic phenomena.

The misattribution hypothesis

Alcock (1981) and Blackmore (1992) have argued that the belief in anomalous phenomena comes about when people think that events were caused by supernatural powers rather than normal, everyday occurrences. According to the cognitive approach, there are several explanations as to how this misattribution occurs. Below are some types of explanation with accompanying examples of how they might affect belief in psychic ability, and an evaluation of each.

Poor cognitive abilities

The suggestion by some psychologists (e.g. Pasachoff, Cohen and Pasachoff, 1970; Ottis and Alcock, 1982; Gray, 1987; Messer and Griggs, 1989; Musch and Ehrenberg, 2002) is that believers in psychic abilities tend to have *lower intellect*. Studies in America have aimed to establish that belief in psychic ability is directly linked to cognitive ability/IQ. These studies often took course grades, performance on the **Scholastic Aptitude Test (SAT)**, exam performance and the highest level of educational attainment and compared them with the level of belief in psychic ability. Generally those with a lower level of achievement had a heightened belief.

A more consistent set of results has come from research examining belief in psychic ability and performance on **syllogistic reasoning tasks**. In this task, non-believers seem to perform better (Polzella, Popp and Hinsman, 1975; Wiseman and Watt, 2006). Wiseman and Watt (2006) say that with 'the exception of the relationship between belief in psychic ability and performance on syllogistic reasoning tasks, the existing literature does not support the notion that believers and disbelievers in psychic ability differ in their levels of general cognitive function'. Winkelman (2001), an anthropological parapsychologist from the USA, observed children in a remote Mexican village and found that formal education tends to reduce the effects of ESP. Again this strengthens the argument that belief is often related to educational level and cognitive ability.

Evaluation

Thalbourne and Nofi (1997) note that the results are *inconsistent*, with many researchers not able to replicate their findings. Some researchers have drawn the opposite conclusion (e.g. Emmons *et al.*, 1981) that research is consistent. Similar conflicting results have been found from the research of psychologists examining psychic belief and IQ scores (Caldwell and Lundeen, 1932; Emme, 1940; Killeen, Wildman; Wildman, 1974).

In anomalistic studies, most of the participants are university students, so the samples and the results are not representative of the wider population. Interestingly there seem to be differences between university courses let alone the wider population. As Happs (1987) and Otis and Alcock (1982) show, anomalistic belief is discipline dependent. For example, those doing a scientific course tend to show lower levels of belief that those on a humanities course (although this is not always the case).

Probability misjudgement

Wiseman and Watt (2006) suggest that another potential cognitive factor affecting performance is probability misjudgement. For example, if you randomly think about a friend that you have not heard from for a long time and then he or she suddenly phones you, you might think that this has a psychic basis rather than it happened by chance.

Evaluation

Blackmore and Troscianko (1985) argued that individuals who made poor probability judgements were more likely to suggest that their experiences were psychic. However, Musch and Ehrenberg (2002) urge caution since this could also be explained by poor cognitive ability.

The tendency to find links in distantly related material

Morris (1986) suggested that it is possible to argue that individuals who believe that they have had a psychic experience think this because there appears to be an inexplicable association between their thoughts and events in the real world.

Evaluation

Brugger and Graves (1997) and Houran and Lange (1998) suggest that this ability to find links is plausible. They did research where participants were presented with random dot pattern images and asked to identify the images within them. Blackmore and Moore (1994) found that believers were more able than non-believers to identify the non-existent images.

Syllogistic reasoning tasks:
participants are given a pair of statements and then a conclusion; they have to decide whether the conclusion can be derived from the statements.

AQA Examiner's tip

Research from an anthropological source can still be valid, even though this is a psychology essay. The anthropological research often informs and provides depth to current psychological issues.

AQA Examiner's tip

Terms such as 'syllogistic reasoning tasks' seem complicated. But from the examiner's point of view this shows your engagement with technical terminology.

Fantasy proneness

Fantasy proneness

Lynn and Rhue (1988) give a different explanation, suggesting that the apparent psychic experience of some individuals is due to fantasy proneness. This is the idea that the individual finds it difficult to separate their experiences of reality from fantasy.

Evaluation

Marks (1988) asserted that fantasy-prone people were more likely to report having unusual perceptual experiences such as visions, hearing voices or seeing apparitions. Research in the 1980s and 1990s found a link between psychic ability and the ability to be hypnotised (Palmer and Van Der Veldon, 1983; Pekala, Kumar and Marcano, 1995). However, results in this area have been difficult to replicate.

Spontaneous paranormal experiences

Between 1973 and 2007 Rex Stanford was the President of the Parapsychological Association. He introduced the psi mediated instrumental response (PMIR) model. This is based on the idea that sets of spontaneous paranormal experiences may give an incorrect perspective of the workings of psi in natural situations. This is because these experiences tend to feature items suggesting a 'perceptual-cognitive model of psi, since such psychic experiences seem to come in the form of thoughts, feelings and mental images albeit degraded ones' (Watt, 2000) that somehow provide information to the experiment. Nagtegaal (2000) argues that Stanford's analysis may have ignored another form of spontaneous psi experiences, 'odd coincidences'. It could be argued that lucky coincidences are in a sense a direct effect of non-intentional psi. Nagtegaal suggests this could be connected with a belief in good luck. After all, Smith, Wiseman and Harris (1997a) reviewed research into the phenomenon of luck and psi ability and highlighted the work of Smith *et al.* (1997b). In this research, participants were categorised as lucky, unlucky or uncertain and then their success on a laboratory psi task based on guessing the outcome of pseudo-RNG (random number generator) coin flips was monitored. Lucky participants were more confident of success than unlucky participants (although the difference was not statistically significant). This finding could be seen to reflect the sheep-goat effect – a term used to explain the difference between those that believe (and follow like sheep) and those that do not (the goat).

The use of Stanford's PMIR model is further criticised by Watt and Ravenscroft (2000) who examined the direct relationship between PMIR and luck. Making use of Smith *et al.*'s (1997b) luckiness questionnaire, they derived no results that showed a direct link between luckiness and non-intentional psi. Their study involved using a **reciprocal helping design** in which each participant had the opportunity to make use of their psychic ability non-intentionally to help the other participant avoid a negative situation. Some conditions and factors were varied. They concluded that 'the design might be more apt for studying "**altruistic psi**" than the kind of self-benefiting, non-intentional psi that might characterise luck in action' (Nagtegaal, 2000).

Stanford accepted the criticisms and abandoned his model in favour of a new approach that he called conformance behaviour of psi, stating that his previous PMIR model of psi was 'too psychobiological or cybernetic' (1973). In the new model, Stanford changed his academic thinking about psi. He accepts that communication of information is not across

Key terms

Reciprocal helping design: a design of study used by Watt *et al.* (2000) in which non-intentional psychic ability was observed to aid another participant.

Altruistic psi: a form of psychic ability that has no personal gain to the person using their ability.

AQA Examiner's tip

Remember, criticising the methodology of a study is a valid means of evaluating. It also shows your grasp of research methodology.

Take it further

- Using your internet skills, investigate the range of luck questionnaires that are available. Search for Smith *et al.*'s (1997b) study. See if you can find a copy of the original luck questionnaire that they used.

- Now look at the types of questions used in the questionnaire. Critically analyse the questionnaire. Can you identify any pitfalls relating to the styles of questions, the format or even the method itself?

- Present your findings in a report. You might have a copy of the questionnaire, followed by your critical analysis of it.

channels, but more importantly he sees psi as a character disposition like creativity and personality.

Creativity

Relatively few studies have tried to demonstrate a link between creativity and intelligence and psi ability, but little significant evidence has been found. Holt (2007) sought to establish the strength of the link between artistic creativity and psi. Previous research dating back to the 1960s (e.g. Moss, 1969) showed that a link was plausible. However, Holt identified methodological issues with the research and conclusions, noting that 'the overall outcome of the study was perceived to be such that the methodology warrants further research, although a number of pitfalls were identified, psi-performance was at levels commensurate with the performance of artists in previous free-response ESP research' (Holt, 2007). Creativity is a factor that crosses the boundaries of cognitive and personality factors, and is considered below.

Personality factors

There has been considerable empirical interest in determining the personality correlates of ESP.

Irwin, 2004

As far back as the 1940s there were studies that tried to demonstrate a link between personality or attitudinal traits and ESP performance. Ramakrishna (2001) tested a group of early adolescent high-school students in India for a correlation between personality traits and performance on ESP tasks. He used the terms 'psi hitters' and 'psi missers' to describe those with good or bad performance. Table 1 gives a summary of the work; adjectives are used to describe enduring qualities of individuals in each category.

The research of Palmer (1978) agreed with these earlier findings. In his studies, Palmer observed that neurotic subjects tended to score at chance level or below on ESP tasks, whereas well-adjusted and stable

Table 1 *Personality traits and ESP performance (Ramakrishna, 2001)*

Psi hitters: positive ESP scores	Psi missers: negative ESP scores
Warm, sociable	Tense
Good natured, easygoing	Excitable
Assertive, self-assured	Frustrated
Tough	Demanding
Enthusiastic	Impatient
Talkative	Dependent
Cheerful	Sensitive
Quick, alert	Timid
Adventuresome, impulsive	Threat-sensitive
Emotional	Shy
Carefree	Withdrawn
Realistic, practical	Submissive
Relaxed	Suspicious
Composed	Depression prone

Source: www.williamjames.com

individuals were more likely to score a higher-than-chance hit rate on ESP tasks. As always, there are methodological issues with this finding. For example, if ESP tests are given to a group of people at once, the effect noted above (Palmer, 1978) does not seem to happen. This might be due to the **deindividuation** of the neurotic individual, which results in lower levels of anxiety being experienced and therefore has an effect on ESP performance. This supports the point raised in Chapter 34, Theoretical and methodological issues in the study of anomalous experience, that anomalistic research is prone to confounding variables that need to be controlled before firm conclusions can be drawn.

Honorton, Ferrari and Bern (1998) were particularly interested in extroversion as a personality trait, noting how in many previous studies extroverts tended to score better on ESP tasks than introverts (e.g. Palmer 1978; Palmer and Carpenter, 1998). Influenced by the work of psychologists such as Ramakrishna, John Palmer and Carl Sargent, Honorton *et al.* (1998) conducted a meta-analysis of 38 experiments examining ESP performance and personality assessment of introversion and extroversion. In their assessment they noted that extroverts scored higher than introverts in 77 per cent of the experiments. Whilst this shows moderate support for a link between personality type and ESP performance, there are questions about the degree to which the results can be generalised to the real world. Since the experimental situation is very artificial, the mundane realism is low. Extroversion and introversion might not be the only variable that has a causal effect. It is possible that individuals who take part in experiments are those who show 'super social adjustment', i.e. they readily adapt to new social situations such as an unknown laboratory. Therefore, we could suggest that anyone who is comfortable and relaxed in a social situation should be able to do the ESP tasks. When **spontaneous ESP tasks** are given, the effects of personality profiles (introversion/extroversion) are not seen (Haight, 1979). Ross and Joshi (1992) have argued that it is not so much introversion/extroversion that is the causal factor affecting anomalistic experience, but how prone the individual is to psychosis.

Biological factors

Researchers looking at physiological psychology report abnormalities in the temporal lobe function of those individuals reporting good psi ability (e.g. Neppe, 1983; Persinger, 1984; Makarec and Persinger, 1987; Persinger and Valliant, 1985). Persinger and Koren (2001) stated that all anomalistic experience could be explained through physiological brain function as a result of these temporal lobe abnormalities.

Thinking about this critically, Persinger and Koren's physiological emphasis might be overstated since there is little experimental data apart from his own which backs up his claims. An examination of the **EEG** measurements of participants during an ESP task shows that the level of **alpha waves** recorded could be linked to performance, but it appears to be the case only if the participant commented about being in an altered state of consciousness whilst doing the task (Irwin, 2004).

Other research has contradictory findings. Using a single participant, McDonough, Don and Warren (2005) found a link between performance on ESP tasks and **delta waves** and **theta waves**. With this evidence, it is possible that low cortical arousal could be a factor in success in anomalous tasks. However, this conclusion did not hold up when the same study was conducted with a larger group of participants (Irwin, 2004). Instead, alpha waves and **beta waves** were found to have more

Link

For more information on deindividuation, see Chapter 10, Social psychological approaches to explaining aggression, pages 117–19.

Key terms

Deindividuation: a state of lowered self-awareness. This might be the result of becoming part of a group and may result in a loss of personal identity albeit temporarily.

Spontaneous ESP tasks: ESP performed outside the laboratory in a more naturalistic context.

EEG: a diagnostic test of brainwave activity.

Alpha waves: measuring 8–12 Hz – this is borderline brainwave activity usually seen in relaxed states.

Delta waves: seen in the EEG of a person in the deeper stages of NREM, these have a large amplitude and a frequency of about 1–4 Hz.

Theta waves: 4–7 Hz – a brainwave pattern that occurs when you are drowsy.

Beta waves: 14–30 Hz – a normal state of brain activity.

AQA Examiner's tip

Biological explanations are complicated, but your knowledge of these will provide good evaluation material for the failings of psychological explanations (cognitive and personality). Remember that good evaluation can also be achieved by comparing the explanations. The focus of one approach will be the failing of another.

Anomalistic psychology

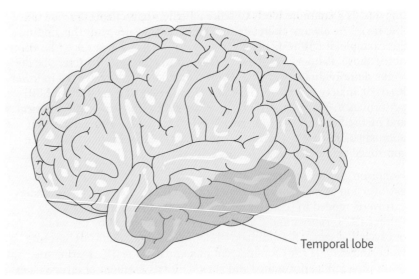

Fig. 1 *The temporal lobe*

Link

For more information about the different types of brainwave patterns see Chapter 2, Sleep states, pages 15–18.

influence. It is possible that the physiological factors being considered here are too simple and that there might be a relationship between ESP performance and EEG wave level, or other cognitive factors might influence performance. There might also be different levels of information processing that affect performance.

Research into the physiology of anomalistic experience has also looked at the possible effect of the brain hemispheres. Some researchers have suggested that ESP tasks are processed by the right hemisphere. However, other researchers have attempted to assert that it is not the right hemisphere but the left hemisphere that is the critical vehicle for psi ability and performance (e.g. Broughton, 1976; Broughton and Millar, 1977; Maher, Peratsakis and Schmeidler 1979; Maher and Schmeidler, 1977). Such studies involved a group of volunteer participants taking part in a forced-choice ESP task. This was created to activate one hemisphere, so they were simultaneously given a distracting task designed to engage the other hemisphere. The conclusion was that right hemisphere activation was dominant.

In a much more scientific study, again by Broughton and his colleagues (1991), it was found that high scores on ESP tasks are more likely with parent–child pairs and sibling pairs, whereas spouse pairs score at the same level as chance. Broughton thinks that this finding needs further research, particularly in relation to the nature–nurture debate, because the crucial variables are not easily separated. Is the cause psychological, i.e. due to the emotional closeness of the pairs, or is it biological, i.e. genetic?

Research into the physiological factors that underlie anomalistic experiences continues. In the 1970s, the focus was generally on trying to demonstrate that the right hemisphere of the brain was associated with psi abilities. In the mid-1980s this expanded to include understanding the neurophysiological basis for anomalistic experiences. Gordon (1986) introduced a new methodology called cognitive laterality battery (CLB) to try to prove single hemisphere activation and control. CLB is a measure of hemispherical differences prior to a psi task being done. CLB consists of eight sub-tests that measure specific cognitive functions that are known to be controlled by either the right or left hemisphere of the brain. Using CLB, Alexander *et al.* (2001) correlated ESP scores with cerebral hemisphere dominance and found no significant effect.

The focus on factors underlying anomalistic experience has shown that there is a link between all of the factors, with one affecting another. It therefore seems artificial to separate out the factors when they all form part of a process that helps to explain the anomalistic experiences of individuals. This detailed level of analysis of anomalistic experience ignores the larger, societal influences that shape anomalistic belief and experience. We must be aware that generalisations are not representative of cultural differences (an imposed etic). Often, the cultural background of an individual dictates their attitudes and philosophies, which might include a belief in anomalistic experience.

Link

For more information about imposed etic see Chapter 10, Social psychological approaches to explaining aggression, page 117.

Key points

- Research into psychic ability has identified a number of key factors that seem to be associated with psi ability, especially in the areas of cognitive, personality and biological influences.

- Cognitive influences might explain apparent psi ability as being down to (a) misconstruing normal situations as paranormal ones; (b) the influence of religion or philosophy on the believer; or (c) the result of some genuine anomalistic phenomena.

- Personality factors have been advanced as an alternative explanation for the psi abilities seen by some participants in studies. Research by Ramakrishna identifies a range of personality traits that are characteristic of the people he calls 'psi hitters' compared to those that do not perform as well on ESP tasks.

- Biological influences must not be ignored. As Persinger (2001) noted: 'to date there has not been a single paranormal experience that is not understandable in terms of known brain function', although debates continue over exactly what biological processes are involved.

Summary questions

1. What cognitive factors have been identified as influencing psychic ability?

2. In what way can personality influence psychic ability? Can cognitive and personality influences be seen as separate influences on psychic ability? Explain your answer.

3. Outline and evaluate research into cognitive, personality and biological influences on psychic ability.

Functions of paranormal and related beliefs

- understand the function of paranormal belief

- provide a critical analysis of the function of paranormal and related beliefs

- describe examples of paranormal and related beliefs explaining how these are often culturally significant.

Function

Belief in the paranormal is not uncommon. The Koestler Parapsychology Unit (part of the University of Edinburgh) reports independent polls suggesting that approximately 50 per cent of the British population have some belief in one or more paranormal experiences and general paranormal phenomena. How might such a level of belief be explained, and what is the primary function of belief? The underlying factors of cognition, personality and biology have been examined above. Other psychological perspectives would simply argue that the function is one of fulfilling one's psychodynamic needs. The psychodynamic functions hypothesis would suggest that the function of belief in anomalistic powers is centrally 'needs serving'. Researchers such as Irwin (1990) and Lawrence *et al.* (1995) suggest that paranormal belief comes from the fantasy proneness of those that state they have had paranormal experiences. From a psychodynamic perspective it is possible that fantasy proneness and the subsequent belief in paranormal experiences arise from the need to deal with traumatic or abusive childhoods. Irwin (1990) notes: 'fantasy proneness seems to emerge partly as a result of physical abuse and other traumatising childhood events … it is possible therefore that childhood trauma is an important factor in explaining [the function and] the individual's fundamental openness to paranormal belief'. Lawrence *et al.* (1995) refer to this as a means of gaining control over troublesome, quarrelsome, chaotic and traumatic home environments. Watt, Watson and Wilson (2007) ask us to view the overall social picture within which paranormal and anomalistic experience is often reported. Due to the continued rise in the rate of divorce and the lack of job security, which requires parents to continuously move to find work, children now lack the stability and security that they possibly enjoyed in previous centuries. Paranormal beliefs, therefore, arise out of a child's lack of control over the familial situation and direction. Paranormal belief provides structure, order and familiarity. Wiseman and Watt (2006) refer to paranormal belief as providing an illusory sense of control when all else is out of control. Of course belief in the paranormal can perform a self-asserting function whereby unconfident individuals are able to become more self-confident. Irwin (1992) showed that believers in the paranormal were often also those that when judged by independent reviewers were seen to be more controlling and assertive towards others. It was as if the belief gave structure, purpose and strength to the unstructured and weak individual.

The function that belief in anomalistic phenomena performs is only as important as its ability to provide explanation. Often those individuals that *come to believe* only do so because the anomalistic force provides a way of explaining something that cannot be explained by other means. To this extent belief in anomalistic ability performs a stabilising function alongside socialisation. After all, if you are brought up believing in a greater power or good, you are less likely to question the inequality of the present situation that you may find yourself in. This certainly seems to be the neutralising effect that religions have on their generally dwindling masses. Maybe belief in anomalistic ability is a replacement for religion. It could be said that the central religious faiths are losing their strength to govern and counsel their congregations, and in a world that is becoming ever more secularised, the function that a belief in anomalistic ability performs might simply be replacing religion. Karl Peltzer (2002), in looking at black South African students and their paranormal belief, noted that these beliefs are strong motivators and organisers shaping individual and collective behaviour. For example, such belief can shape behaviour and understanding often in times when all else seems oppressive and against you (as it was under apartheid). Keinan (2002) suggested that the function of belief in the paranormal is governed by the stress of the situation that you find yourself in. When your situation in life appears to be more or less out of control, belief in paranormal and anomalistic forces increases. What we see here is a dual function. Firstly it provides explanation for the situation and secondly it provides the illusion of self-control. Empirical research supports this view. Blackmore and Troscianko (1985) split participants into two groups: believers and non-believers. Their experiment centred around participants playing a computer game. The aim was to try to control whether a coin landed as heads or as tails. The control of this would be via a push button. In half of the trials the button did influence the outcome. In the other half of trials it did not. Despite both groups having the same restricted amount of control, it was the 'believers' that consistently said they had the most control over the task presented to them.

▪ Cultural significance

Blaisdell and Denniston (2002), using the Human Relations Area File (HRAF), investigated 122 world cultures as well as the extensive previous research by Murdock (1967). The analysis clearly showed that paranormal belief was inherently bound up with culture. In these investigations, clear cultural differences were seen in the process and passage to the afterlife. For example, violent or premature death was associated with vengeance in the afterlife (by ghosts/ghouls). Interestingly those societies that were characterised by a stratified (but not egalitarian) social experience emphasised the central importance of family and kin relations in the afterlife. Warring or clan-based cultures often spoke of their belief in vengeance themes when speaking about the afterlife. Vengeance themes were also apparent in cultures where animal husbandry was practised, but not in agriculture-based cultural contexts or hunter-gatherer societies. In societies where there were large populations the consistent belief was the centrality that kinship plays in the afterlife. In the broader sense of the word, culture can include religions. Mencken, Bader and Stark (2008) note that often the religious denomination you adhere to shapes your belief in anomalous experience. For example, they note that Catholics are far more likely to have a high score in relation to belief in the paranormal. In Catholicism events surrounding the Virgin Mary are central to belief. Yet with other religions, such as Evangelicalism, this strength of belief is in fact discouraged.

In his research on Hindu death rituals, Bailey (1996) shows how clearly culture shapes attitudinal belief in the paranormal. Dharma embodies a set of spiritual ideals that should be aspired to. Good acts in the present life will be rewarded through reincarnation into a better position and ultimately to Heaven. The paranormal belief in the need for the dead person to be reborn dictates the ceremonial death ritual. Centrally though, this example shows how paranormal belief and its cultural significance are inextricably linked. One dictates the other.

But for psychic ability to work, and for those that profess the skills to practise their abilities, there will still be an element of deception and

▪ Link

This experiment shows the practical illustration of a term described earlier – the sheep-goat effect. See page 470 for more information.

AQA Examiner's tip

Cultural awareness is always handy – especially for evaluation. Never assume what is experienced in one particular culture is the same for all. A common criticism of most psi research is that it is culturally relativist, i.e. it is specific to the culture in which it has been studied.

Anomalistic psychology

self-deception inherently bound up in the process. It is to this issue that we now turn, examining the related issues of superstition and coincidence that so readily shape our everyday human behaviour. After all, when was the last time you walked under a ladder?

Conclusions

From the observations in this section it seems to be the case that anomalistic experience can be explained beyond the simple level of psychic skill and can be assumed to have potential cognitive, personality and biological influences. While research seems to support multiple influence, it would seem wise to assume that the composite effect of all influences together seems to allow some individuals to perform psychic tasks accurately. Such psychic abilities perform socially ingrained functions, and sociologists would be the first to see the belief in an afterlife or some anomalistic power as the basis for control and stability in an often very unfair society. It must be noted though, that such belief in, and the nature of, the anomalistic skill or phenomenon is culturally specific and often highly integrated into the order and structure of the society from which it emanated (Bailey, 1996). In assessing the impact of anomalistic phenomena we must be aware of the nature of our own beliefs, seeing ourselves influenced by the perceptions of others, and deceiving ourselves into false beliefs (self-deception).

Key points

- Belief in the paranormal is very common, although the exact shape, form and content of paranormal belief is subject to cultural differences.

- Researchers like Lawrence *et al.* (1995) suggest that paranormal belief is simply the result of the 'fantasy proneness' of individuals. Some psychodynamic theorists would argue that this might be the result of traumatic early childhood experiences. The issue of childhood experience is also stressed in the more contemporary work of Watt *et al.* (2007).

- Culture has an impact on paranormal belief. Blaisdell and Denniston (2002), in their extensive research using HRAF, identified that belief in an afterlife had profound effects for many on their current existence and daily social behaviours. Bailey (1996) reinforces this point in his cross-cultural analysis of Hindu and English funeral rites and belief in the afterlife.

- Belief in the paranormal is a natural extension of superstition – the belief in something that cannot be explained by normal means. Superstition affects behaviour in many more ways than we would care to admit.

Summary questions

4 According to the Koestler Institute what function does belief in the paranormal perform? Can you give a personal example of this? What benefit did it give you?

5 Wiseman and Watt (2006) refer to paranormal belief as providing an illusory sense of control when all else is out of control. What do they mean?

6 Outline and evaluate the statement that belief in the paranormal is culturally specific.

Deception, self-deception, superstition and coincidence

Take it further

Looking at the extracts above, what do you notice about them? What do they have in common? Now think of five examples where you might deceive yourself into believing something that is clearly not true.

The difference between deception and self-deception

Self-deception is a less-familiar term, so we will look at that first. Consider the following extracts:

> Eighty-five percent of medical students think it is improper for politicians to accept gifts from lobbyists. Only 46% think it's improper for physicians to accept gifts from drug companies.
>
> *Adapted from* **Wanzana**, *2000*

> A 2001 study of medical residents found 84% thought that their colleagues were influenced by gifts from pharmaceutical companies. But only 16% thought that they would be similarly influenced.
>
> **Gilbert**, *2006*

Self-deception relates to a process of misleading ourselves to accept as true or correct that which is clearly not true (Carroll, 2005). It is a means of getting ourselves to believe in something that is clearly false. The above extracts, taken from a medical journal and a US newspaper, are simple examples of this everyday occurrence. Let us consider the example of a student revising for their A Level psychology exam. As we all know, revision is a mundane but necessary process. The student might do some revision and justify a break to themselves because they have 'worked hard' so far, even though the quality of their revision is far from perfect. So the action of having a break despite poor revision is justified through a process of self-deception. Other typical examples can be seen in social situations. The person who is a smoker but is trying to quit, and states to themselves that just one more will cause no harm. Or the individual with a new hairstyle who justifies to themselves that the change of style suits them, even when it clearly does not.

Fig. 2 *Self-deception and deception*

Deception is the simple misrepresentation of information, a process in which you might convince another that the information you present is true when it is clearly not. Hyman (1989) stated that deception is something that

> implies that an agent acts or speaks so as to induce false belief in a target or victim ... including practical jokes, forgery, imposture, conjuring, confidence games, consumer and health fraud, military and strategic deception, white lies, feints and ploys in games and sports, gambling scams psychic hoaxes and much more.

Hyman, 1989

Psychological explanations

If we accept for the moment that self-deception is the process of misleading ourselves, eventually leading us to accept something that is incorrect, how might psychology explain this? Let us use an example. Think about a teacher who was bad at their job but convinced themselves that they were good at it. This is paradoxical. Psychology therefore is trying to explain how one's knowledge system can allow a glaringly obvious contradiction to take place. Why did the teacher not realise that they were bad at their job?

Clinical psychology, psychiatry, and cognitive psychology certainly pose questions:

- How is self-deception to be understood in terms of how we organise our knowledge?
- What is the function of self-deception?
- How common is self-deception?
- How can self-deception be identified and studied through research?

Evolutionary psychology

Evolutionary psychologists have argued that there are adaptive advantages to deception and the relationship between deception and self-deception in Darwinian terms of survival. Lockard (1980) and Trivers (1985) argued that by subconsciously deceiving themselves, a person might be better at deceiving others. Such behaviour has developed through a process of natural selection. Ethologists and evolutionary psychologists would argue that this would provide an 'evolutionary advantage' in animal interactions (Trivers, 1985). Trivers' view was that if the animal deceived itself, it might actually become a better deceiver of others – and in so doing ensure its survival and the passing on of its genes to the next generation. Think about the situation of a fight. If the opponents believe that they are invincible (even if they are not) they have the correct psychology to give the fight their best shot. However, Moomal and Henzi (2000) suggested that whilst in the short term deception was favourable, in the long term it is counterproductive. Deception, from an evolutionary perspective, does not seem to pay.

Psychoanalysis

Psychoanalysis certainly provides an account of deception and self-deception. Freud's writings shine some light on this area. Renowned for his work on the unconscious influences behind behaviour, Freud raises an interesting issue. The effect of the ego can be seen consciously, that is the behaviour you show. But Freud commented that often the route of self-deception involves the deception being used consciously with the ego, therefore in turn influencing behaviour, but such thought was not in the

■ Link

Approaches, issues and debates

Evolutionary psychology is often at odds with the philosophy of scientific research. When it comes to the work of evolutionary psychologists, their research is *post hoc* – after the event.

■ Link

Approaches, issues and debates

Evolutionary psychologists have a very particular perspective on human behaviour, which commonly centres around notions of survival value. But the evolutionary perspective is often at odds with the more scientific thinkers within psychology. The question is: where are the boundaries of scientific study? Can psychological focus on anomalistic experience ever be a science?

ego's consciousness, and hence the paradox. In other words, this level of thinking was not a conscious thought. Psychoanalytic accounts tend to be theory laden, and often they are more about providing an account than about defending cognitive threats.

Warner (1980) is a psychoanalyst who argues that clinical psychologists and psychiatrists view self-deception as performing a dual role. Primarily, it has the function of self-protection from painful knowledge (Murphy, 1975; Sackheim and Gur, 1978). However, rather like a **shaman** who uses trickery to impress patients, the psychiatrist also deceives themself into thinking that the psychotherapeutic techniques used have healing potential even when scientific evidence suggests the opposite. The nature of the self-deception is potentially shaped by the culture in which it takes place.

Cognitivism

Cognitivism provides logic to this easily confusing area. Gur *et al.* (1979) used a voice recognition task and asked participants to record their voice onto tape. The tapes were played back and the participants were asked to identify their voice. They were also monitored using a skin-conductive response, intended to be a measure of unconscious recognition. A **skin-conductive response** was shown when the participant heard their own voice but they could not verbally identify it, and this was self-deception. This suggests that the recognition behaviour was initiated by the individuals, but it is a behaviour that does not always work within the realms of conscious cognition.

Of course Gur *et al.* recognise that some aspects of self-deception occur very consciously – not least the example of impression management. Gur *et al.* showed that 'impression management' (how you want others to view/see/know you) is the outcome of the conscious deception of others.

Ray Hyman is a professional researcher, but in his youth he read palms. From this he was aware that clients were usually happy with what they were told. He decided to conduct an experiment where he told the client the exact opposite of what the reading actually said and, to his astonishment, found that the readings were even more of a success. This process is known as self-validation – clients want the reading to be accurate and therefore convince themselves that the person doing the reading has great insight (*NOVA* on PBS Television). Hyman (1972) produced a classic work on water dowsing where he showed that it does not work, but noted 'most people are convinced that it does because of natural psychological biases and social processes'. Hyman puts dowsing skills (as shown in experimental studies) down to a **clever Hans effect**.

Cognitive psychologists have struggled with the contradiction between knowledge of reality and belief in yourself. Mele (1997) used cognitive bias studies (often making use of paradigmatic cases) to try to resolve the paradox of self-deception. He concluded from the analysis of several previous investigations (all using broadly similar methodology) that 'self-deception is neither irresolvably paradoxical nor mysterious, and it is explicable without the assistance of mental exotica [fantasy]'. Mele is saying that the cause of self-deception can be seen more clearly by considering one's own thoughts and feelings. The cause of self-deception is not a paradox, but simply our capacity to acquire and use views that affect our motivation.

Shaman: an individual in tribal societies that would often be a link between the visible world and the afterlife, and could be seen to be endowed with special powers that enabled them to cure the sick by supernatural means.

Skin-conductive response: a means of quantifying bodily reaction that can be used to indicate reaction at an unconscious level.

Symbolic interactionist: a major sociological view that suggests that people behave in a way that is influenced by their interaction with and interpretation of others.

Clever Hans effect: based upon the 1907 study by Fungst and Stumpf of a so-called 'clever horse' that could perform basic forms of interaction such as calculation, etc. It turned out to be the result of unconscious cues given by the owner that indicated when Hans should start and stop his behaviours. In short, unconscious behaviours in the actions or statements of a researcher can indicate to the participant what they should do.

Take it further

The work of Gur *et al.* investigates issues very similar to a well-known sociologist Erving Goffman, who wrote prolifically about impression management from his theoretical view as a '**symbolic interactionist**'. Investigate the work of Erving Goffman and his writings on impression management. To what extent can Goffman's explanation provide an account for the process of deception and self-deception?

Take it further

Think of an example of where you have clearly deceived yourself, for example by thinking you are attractive or handsome when you might not be. Using this section of the book and your wider reading, consider how evolutionary psychology, psychoanalysis and cognitivism might explain your distorted view.

Fig. 3 Olympic diver Tom Daley has a toy monkey that is present at all competitions and sits on his bag where 'he can see Tom'

Take it further

What superstitions do you have, e.g. do you do anything in particular before sitting an important exam? Create a set of interview questions that seek to identify a range of respondent views of superstitions. There are various factors that you might need to take into account. For example, how does this belief vary between different religions, age groups and nationalities?

Superstition

The word 'superstition' refers to the subjective belief that a behaviour will have an effect on another area, either positively or negatively. It is often applied to practices surrounding luck, spirituality or prophecy. Superstition can be seen in many areas of everyday life, e.g. theatre, magic, even sport. The 2008 Olympic Games held in Beijing, People's Republic of China, started at *eight* minutes past *eight* on the *eighth* of August (which is the *eighth* month) 2008. In China, the number 8 sounds like the word for fortune, prosperity and good health.

Some of the athletes competing in the Beijing Olympic Games have superstitions of their own, for example:

- Tom Daley (diver) has a toy monkey that is present at all competitions and sits on his bag where 'he can see Tom'.
- Cassie Pattern (swimmer) does not leave home until her teddy bear and toy clown are tucked up in bed.

Other Olympic athletes have other rituals:

- James DeGale (boxer), before a fight, always puts his left sock and shoe on before his right one.
- Tom Parsons (high jumper) always wears Aston Villa socks.
- Helen Reeves (canoeist) listens to the same three music tracks in a particular order: Dolly Parton *9 to 5*; Neil Diamond *Forever in Blue Jeans*; White Stripes *Seven Nations Army*.
- Amir Khan (boxer) finds a quiet spot to pray before a fight.
- Sally Gunnell (the retired hurdler) kept a bag of lucky stones in her kit bag, and a Chinese number 7 in her spikes bag.

Skinner (1948) looks at superstition in animals, describing some lesser-known findings from his research with pigeons. He shows how several pigeons demonstrated what could be called superstitious behaviour in the expectation that food would come from the dispenser in the cage, e.g. turning around, moving of the head like the pendulum of a clock. Even though this had no effect on the frequency with which the food was dispensed, the pigeons continued the behaviour. Skinner believed that the same process is involved in superstition in humans. Staddon and Simmelhag (1971) challenged Skinner's views and gave other reasons for the behaviour of the pigeons, but Skinner's explanation does give a reason as to why superstitions are so persistent. The behaviour is not rewarded every time it occurs, but there is enough of a link in the mind of the animal/individual that they continue the behaviour thinking that it is affecting the outcome. For example, the Olympic diver Tom Daley once put his toy monkey on top of his bag when he went to compete. In that instance, he dived better than normal. In another competition, he did not put his toy monkey on top of his bag and in that instance he only gave an average performance. Reference can be made here to the frequency with which we observe, in everyday life, various prevention rituals – for example not walking under ladders or not putting new shoes on the surface of a table. This reinforcement effect seems to be true regardless of culture.

Coincidence

The term 'coincidence' describes the odd experiences that we all have, e.g. you are talking about a certain person with your best friend, and the person you have been talking about comes over to say hello. There is a question about whether coincidence shows some form of psychic ability or is simply a result of chance. Marks and Kammann (1980) investigated this. They conclude that we should view psychical phenomena realistically, that when two random events happen with a link, it is difficult not to believe that this link is meaningful. Marks suggests that other factors play a part. Our memories are fallible and therefore often significant memories remain whilst insignificant memories fade. In the continual reconstruction of memories, we often add other memories, emotions and even fantasies. From this research at least it would appear that unless we keep an exact written log of all that we see and do, we cannot be completely sure that coincidences could not have occurred by chance.

Concluding thoughts on the factors underlying anomalous experience

Could the effect of anomalistic behaviours simply be the product of our own self-deception – our failure to look at a situation rationally and scientifically? When we steer clear of cracks in paving slabs or avoid walking under a ladder or placing new shoes on a table we are, in a sense, confirming our own semi-conscious belief in the power of superstition, which is a natural extension of anomalistic experience in everyday life.

Key points

- Self-deception is a term that is not commonly used, and for that matter not commonly understood. Yet the effects of this are readily available for the psychologist to observe in most social situations.

- Clinical psychology, psychiatry, evolutionary psychology, psychoanalysis and cognitivism all advanced potential explanations for the purpose of deception and self-deception.

- Ray Hyman, using palm reading as an example, furthers this psychological analysis to suggest that through self-validation (individuals often want the reading to be right) people will convince themselves that the reading is correct even when it clearly is not!

- Superstition is an anomalistic power that exerts great influence over daily behaviour.

- Research into coincidence is still developing, but the research by Marks and Kammann (1980) suggests that coincidence could simply be put down to fallibility of memory and confabulation.

Summary questions

7 What is the difference between deception and self-deception?

8 To what extent does Skinner's reasoning explain superstitious behaviour in humans?

9 How might personality, cognitive and biological factors explain belief in psychic personalities such as Uri Geller?

Anomalistic psychology

Psychic healing

Learning objectives:

- define what exceptional experience is
- define what psychic healing is
- describe the process of psychic healing
- examine the effect of belief on the working of psychic healing
- evaluate research and draw conclusions on the research conducted into belief in psychic healing.

What is exceptional experience?

Exceptional human experience is an umbrella term for many types of experience generally considered to be psychic, mystical, encounter type experiences, death related experiences and experiences at the upper end of the normal range, such as creative inspiration [and the like].

Rhea White, 1994

In this section we examine belief in psychic healing, near-death and out-of-body experience and psychic mediumship. All are exceptional experiences that can have a profound and long-lasting effect on individuals.

A leap of faith

Fig. 1 *A psychic healer 'cures' a patient*

What is psychic healing?

As far as the medical establishment is concerned, psychic healing is a new and alternative form of treatment. However, the origins of this therapy pre-date most medical techniques and interventions, and can be found in every culture around the world (Benor, 2001). There are several names for the practice: psychic healing (in the USA); faith healing (so called by the media and religious groups); paranormal healing (in Europe); and mental healing (as referred to in **Index Medicus**).

There are two ways to administer psychic healing:

- the laying on of hands
- distant healing.

AQA Examiner's tip

By showing your knowledge of the different forms of psychic healing, you are showing a high degree of accuracy in your work and the depth of your knowledge.

Key terms

Index Medicus: a comprehensive index of medical journal articles between 1879 and 2004.

Most media reports about faith healing deal with instantaneous cures, but it is more common for results to be seen gradually, where treatment is given over several weeks or months. There are various approaches to psychic healing, the most well known being the **therapeutic touch**. Other approaches include **reiki** and **shamanism**. The latter has been practised for thousands of years, but there has been little research into the therapy and it is not clear if there is any therapeutic advantage or whether the results seen are simply due to culturally defined placebos.

Research into psychic healing

Krieger (2000) conducted one of the earliest studies into the healing effects of psi (the paranormal). He thought that healers somehow increased the **vitality** of the patients. Krieger took blood samples from patients before and after the healing session to observe if there had been any fluctuation in red blood cell **haemoglobin** levels. The healer placed one or both hands on the patient and went into a state of visualisation where he or she saw positive energy around the patient's body. Forty-nine patients were treated by the healer. As a control, a further 29 people with comparable conditions were not treated by the healer. The blood samples from the two groups were then analysed. It was found that the patients who were treated by the healer had higher haemoglobin levels in their blood, and generally felt better than those in the control group. What was particularly interesting was that this effect appeared to last for a long period of time. In a follow-up study a year later, the haemoglobin levels of the 'treatment' group were still significantly higher than in the control group.

Benor (1992, 2000) identified 197 studies of psychic healing, showing significantly positive results for humans (as well as plants, animals, even bacteria, yeasts and cells in laboratory cultures).

Research study: Keller and Bzdek (1986)

Keller and Bzdek looked at the effect of therapeutic touch on tension headache pain. There were 60 participants, ranging in age from 18 to 59 with a mean age of 30. In order to take part in the research, they had to be suffering from a clear definition of tension headaches, i.e. a dull, persistent head pain, usually bilateral (affecting both sides of the head), with feelings of heaviness, pressure or tightness which did not have a known medical cause, and they must not have taken headache medication in the previous four hours.

The participants were randomly assigned to the therapeutic touch or control group. Both groups were 'blind' (i.e. they were not aware which group they had been allocated to). The severity of the headache was measured using part of the **MMPQ**, which was completed immediately before and five minutes after the treatment.

In both the experimental and the control group, the participants were asked to sit quietly for the five-minute duration of the procedure. The healer positioned herself by the participant and placed her hands 6–12 inches away from the participant's skin without touching them. In the experimental group, the healer assessed the energy field and redirected areas of accumulated tension out of the field, then rested her hands around the head or solar plexus in areas of imbalance or deficit in order to direct life energy to the participant. In the control group, the healer focused on subtracting 7s from 100 (the aim here was to focus the participant's

Key terms

Therapeutic touch: a controversial method of healing in which the patient is 'treated' by the psychic healer. The hands of the healer never touch the patient, remaining 4–6 inches above the skin, touching and changing the area of energy surrounding the body but not coming into contact with the body itself.

Reiki: a method of hand healing whereby the practitioner places their hands on the subject. It originated in Japan's Taisho Period (1912–26).

Shamanism: a form of tribal religion that relies on the acceptance of an individual as a shaman – a religious leader, healer and worker of magic – who through special powers can contact and communicate with the spirit world.

Vitality: liveliness, ability to fight off infection. This has links to the metabolism and so oxygen consumption, and the ability to carry oxygen in the blood can be objectively measured through haemoglobin levels.

Haemoglobin: the part of the body's red blood cells that carries oxygen.

MMPQ: the McGill-Melzack Pain Questionnaire. This is a tool designed specifically to quantify subjective pain for analysis.

Take it further

Produce a fact pack about psychic healing for a layperson to read. This should include:

- what psychic healing is
- the different forms available and an explanation of them
- a summary of evidence supporting the case *for* psychic healing
- a summary of the research evidence *against* psychic healing.

mind away from the healing process). The same healer performed in both of the groups, the only difference was what they were thinking during the process.

Before the procedure, the severity of the headache as rated by the participants in both groups was equivalent. This was assessed by the use of the MMPQ. Following the procedure, 90 per cent of the participants of the treatment group reported lower levels of headache pain. This was assessed five minutes after the treatment and again four hours after it. A statistical analysis of the results found them to be at a very high level of significance ($P < 0.0001$).

Methodological issues

- The detailed definition of a tension headache ensures consistency between participants.
- However, the assessment of whether or not they met the definition was a subjective one on the part of the patient and researcher.
- The sample size, whilst demonstrating a trend, is not large enough to ensure generalisability to the larger population.
- Volunteer sampling, as used in this study, is the least representative sample type as participants choose to be in the study.
- Expectancy effects were ruled out by designing the experiment so that all participants went through the same process and were not aware whether or not they were receiving the therapeutic treatment.
- There might be a psychosomatic effect to the procedure. The participants *think* they will get better and do regardless of the thoughts of the 'healer' during the treatment. This placebo effect is known to be a powerful one, and ultimately this is what the power of the therapy is being tested against.

Ethical issues

- In order that the results of the study were not influenced by the effect of demand characteristics, participants were not told which group they were in.
- The psychologist has a duty of care to protect the participant both mentally and physically. While it is clear that the participants experienced no physical harm, for those that had never experienced a process of psychic healing before, there may have been a degree of apprehension.

Link

For more information about significance levels see pages 529–30.

AQA Examiner's tip

While this study places a heavy emphasis on psychic healing as a phenomenon rather than the belief in it, the study raises interesting issues of how science works. For example, in this case the experimenters carried out their study using appropriate apparatus and every attempt was made to take accurate measurements in a methodical way that maximised the design and minimised risk to the participants, researchers and others.

Christianity (catholicism, Christian Science, pentecostalism/charismaticism, etc.) as well as spiritualism has a history of belief in healing powers. Vicars or priests may lay hands on individuals, or pray, and will that 'with the power of the holy spirit' they may get better. In Christian Science members *believe* that healing occurs through prayer. In pentecostalism or charismaticism belief in divine healing can also be seen. In spiritualism there is a combined approach between faith healing and traditional medical therapy. Kenyon-Jones (1948), a spiritualist writer, noted that the spirit world is asked to relieve the body of its ills and through faith, confidence and belief, sometimes combined with medicine if needed, the ills of the body go. Religions can provide a belief system that gives structure and meaning to life at times when all else seems lost.

Underlying this form of healing is the fact that the patient and, one assumes, the therapist, believe that the healing will work. This emphasises the importance of 'belief' in the working of the healing process. The healer must be competent and believe in their powers. Some of the literature surrounding the teaching of psychic healing is vague about the process involved:

> The way to learn psychic healing is to just do it, and have faith that it will work if success is in the subject's and your best interests ... you will be able to do it by a mystical process you will probably never understand. I know I don't understand it.

> *Hewitt, 1996*

The idea that some people are just 'born' with these special powers goes against scientific thinking. Katra (1999) noted that although she has been practising psychic healing for over 20 years, she cannot explain the process. In MacMillan's book *The Reluctant Healer* (1952), she says that she does not understand her abilities and cannot explain why she has them and others do not. Yet both fundamentally talk about the belief they have in their abilities to heal others, and the belief that their participants have in them to make them better.

Katra offers an explanation for the ability of psychic healers. She was once a sceptic. Disbelief in the process of psychic healing raises our 'psychic shields' with the result that there cannot be communication between the healer and the patient. In order for the process to work, the healer and the patient must believe in the benefit it will have. Furthermore, the length of time given to healing seems to have an influence. Katra notes that this is 'sometimes ten minutes, and at other times forty-five minutes ... [I] don't know why a certain length of time is required for that spiritual healing thing.' (Katra, 1999). Taking the sceptical view, experiments still have many variables that could affect their success, and therefore any research into psychic powers is going to have methodological flaws. However, Targ (1998) shows that despite sceptical views, belief in psychic healing or its effectiveness constitutes at least in part a logical explanation for its effectiveness. He gives three potential explanations:

- The healer's presence: the fact that the healer is present with them in his/her capacity as 'the healer' distracts the patient's attention away from the pain or problem, increasing the patient's sense of relaxation.
- Connection with the healer: this connection by distance or by presence activates natural body systems of self-healing through psychological and mental means, such as the **endocrine system** and associated **neurotransmitters**.
- ESP: the healer uses ESP in the form of psychokinesis, directly interacting with the patient's body. A link between the healer's mind and the patient's body is formalised.

A *belief* in any one or all three of these things ensures that the psychic healing experience has potentially positive effects.

A study conducted by Lyvers, Barling and Harding-Clark (2006) on the healing abilities of a well-known psychic who claimed that he can heal people from looking at and manipulating their photographs, showed that the man's claims were false. This was a **double-blind study**. Lyvers *et al.* noted that belief in, rather than the actual abilities of, a psychic is central to effectiveness of psychic healing and other similar non-medical treatments, since the belief would seem to temporarily alleviate pain maybe by using one's own internal pain response systems.

Key terms

Endocrine system: the system of glands in the body that secrete hormones directly into the circulatory system.

Neurotransmitters: chemicals in the brain that are important in transmitting information across the synapse. Therefore they are vital to the brain's normal functioning. Examples include serotonin and dopamine. The neurotransmitters are generally thought to be responsible for factors such as feelings, emotions, actions and behaviours.

Double-blind study: a method in which neither the researcher involved in the conducting of the experiment nor the participant knows what issue is being examined or what the expected outcome is. This is mainly to reduce the overall effect of expectation on the researcher's interpretation of the results and the participant's behaviour. This method shows how research into anomalistic experience is striving for scientific rigour by ruling out extraneous variables affecting behaviour.

Take it further

Targ provides this explanation as a way of understanding the process of psychic healing. Using the internet and key words such as 'Russell Targ and Spiritual Healing' see if you can find further evidence supporting his understanding of psychic healing.

AQA Examiner's tip

When you make statements about what researchers have said, it is good to back up their claims with those of other researchers. You will then be assessing the validity of the research and not just describing it.

The power of belief

The debate about the psychological underpinnings of psychic healing continues. It is not clear whether there are any scientifically proven systems in the process, or whether healing occurs as a result of the participants' belief that it will happen. Belief certainly shapes the positive experience of psychic healing, and for those who claim to deliver it psychic healing is a real process and therefore one that warrants further investigation.

Key points

- Psychic healing is known under different names in certain areas of the world or in different disciplines.

- There are different forms of psychic healing. Therapeutic touch is the most common in the Western world. Central to every version is the need for belief in the system in order for it to be effective.

- The main problem with any research in this area is that it is difficult to create investigations where there are directly observable results that are objective and can be replicated to assess the validity of the research. In areas such as this, reliance on self-reporting techniques of data collection means that levels of belief and their links to treatments are difficult to judge and establish.

- Keller and Bzdek (1986) investigated the effect of the therapeutic touch technique on headache pain. Their research showed that the group that experienced the healing therapy reported lower levels of pain than the control group. Such a study, while looking primarily at the phenomenon of psychic healing, does illustrate how a scientific approach can be taken in the examination of a pseudoscientific topic such as psychic healing.

- Targ (1998) shows that belief in the process of psychic healing has a moderating effect. She gives three potential explanations (the healer's presence, connection with the healer and ESP).

Summary questions

1. What does psychic healing involve?
2. Describe and evaluate one study that examines psychic healing.
3. To what extent does research evidence substantiate the view that belief in psychic healing is central to its effectiveness?

Out-of-body and near-death experience

Learning objectives:

- define what out-of-body and near-death experiences are

- explain how belief in out-of-body and near-death experiences shapes incidence of it

- examine the effect of belief in near-death and out-of-body experiences

- evaluate and draw conclusions about the importance of belief through research into out-of-body and near-death experiences.

Introduction

> Admittedly I was very ill, I had anorexia. I laid on my bed and went to sleep. I then felt a positive sensation, and I realised that I was above my body. I could see my body, I was laying in a foetal position. I could see everything in the room, I must have been about 8–9 ft above myself. I felt great; I had no pain, and had an immense sense of positivity. I just knew I would beat my illness! Everything about my experience I remember, the room, the colours the bright light in the distance, everything!

Bailey, 2008

Death, as a subject in both psychology and sociology, is an area that needs researching but because of its dark and 'final' nature it has only had substantial investigation over the last 50 years. Elisabeth Kubler Ross has been very active in this area, but her analysis has focused on death itself. There was little if any reference in her work to out-of-body or near-death experience despite reported cases pre-dating her research. This area is not considered by many researchers because belief in exceptional experience throws up difficult methodological problems and the claims are difficult to substantiate objectively. The investigation of experiences of such exceptional phenomena does not fit neatly into the usual psychological methodology.

Out-of-body experience is argued by researchers to refer to a feeling of being able to view yourself and the world from out of your own body (Blackmore, 1982). Typically this sensation has been reported as being experienced with dreams and day-dreams (Peterson, 1997). Some researchers have suggested that this is a state that can be induced by giving anaesthetic (Woerlee, 2008). Through electrical stimulation of the brain, others (e.g. Glannon, 2007) have identified research that implicates specific areas of the brain in the phenomenon. The juncture of the right **temporal lobe** and **parietal lobe**, as well as an area called the right **angular gyrus**, have shown that when stimulated (as a treatment for epilepsy), subjects commonly reported an out-of-body experience.

The term 'near-death experience' was introduced by Moody (1975). He defines a near-death experience as 'a distinctive subjective experience that people sometimes report after a near-death episode'. By 'near-death episode', we mean a situation where a person might be clinically dead, near to death or very likely to die. People who have reported near-death experiences have often been involved in serious accidents or have been injured as a result of military combat.

Near-death experience

Belief and near-death experience

Many authors in this area emphasise the unique nature of the experience (Blackmore, 1982), although it can broadly be categorised as 'pleasant' or 'disturbing'. According to IANDS (International Association for Near Death Studies), common features of near-death experiences include:

Key terms

Temporal lobe: the part of each hemisphere of the brain that is centrally responsible for hearing and auditory memory. It is found at the front of the head below the frontal lobe.

Parietal lobe: a part of the brain that is centrally responsible for the perception of sensory signals such as pain and touch.

Angular gyrus: a location in the brain that is at the junction between the temporal and parietal lobes.

- intense emotion
- seeing one's body from above (out-of-body experience)
- movement through darkness towards 'light'
- encounters with dead loved ones
- a life review
- for some, a decision to return to their body.

The individual's belief about these events is what gives them their significance. A major contributor to research into near-death and out-of-body experiences is Atwater. She notes that for pleasant near-death experiences there is often a sensation of floating out of one's body; passing through a long black tunnel and the subsequent ascension towards light; friendly greetings from familiar and unfamiliar voices; the realisation that time does not exist; disappointment at being revived (Atwater, 2007). A disturbing near-death experience will often cause the person involved to look for meaning in it. Changes in behaviour are possible as a result of the experience; an increase in religious practice is often one outcome. A person's beliefs or cultural background will influence how they interpret an experience. The individual's interpretation of the experience could therefore shape their wider spiritual or religious beliefs.

Evidence challenging belief in near-death experience

Accounts of near-death and out-of-body experiences are not uncommon, and reports appear in both psychological and medical literature (Barrett, 1926; Osis and Haroldson, 1977; MacMillan and Brown, 1971). With the use of a dichotomy of research summarised by Blackmore (1982) it is possible that the belief in the importance of near-death experience might be challenged by simple biological and medical phenomena. Look at Table 1 below. Rather than simple belief in an 'exceptional and meaningful experience' Blackmore suggests that near-death experience might be explained by a variety causes. No 'belief needed here', just simple biological and scientific fact.

Link

The International Association for Near Death Studies (IANDS) is a good place to start when researching this area. Their website (www.iands.org) is useful as it offers a compelling research gateway into near-death experience.

Link

Biological science is at the heart of the scientific approach. Explanations that are provided from this discipline often adhere to stringent principle and methodological procedures of science. Look at pages 506–7 for the criteria of science .

Key terms

Anoxia: absence of oxygen in the brain.

Hypercarbia: a condition where an individual has an unusually high level of carbon dioxide in their blood.

Cortical disinhibition: random firing neurons that can often lead to potential hallucinogenic states.

Table 1 *Science speaks: scientific explanations for near-death experience*

Explanation	Evidence	Evaluation
Anoxia or **hypercarbia**	Anoxia is blamed by some for the experiences that people have during near-death experiences	This does not explain those people that will have a near-death experience without having anoxia or hypercarbia
	Cortical disinhibition is related to anoxia and could provide an explanation for the 'light at the end of the tunnel' descriptions that are common among people who have near-death experiences	The eye has most of its visual cells in the centre of the visual field, with fewer at the edge. If the cells are triggered randomly, as with anoxia, this will produce the effect of a bright light in the centre of the visual field and a gradual darkening at the edge (i.e. a tunnel)
		Sabom (1998) disagrees with the above explanation. His studies measured body gases in people who have had near-death experiences and found normal body gas levels (including oxygen). Not all researchers are convinced that his chosen method of taking blood samples is accurate (Gilkman and Kellehear, 1990)

Temporal lobe stimulation	Research using stimulation techniques of the temporal lobe show how participants will often report memory flashbacks and body distortions. The temporal lobe (as well as the limbic system) is central to near-death experience, but it is unclear whether this is due to anoxia. According to Saavedra-Aguilar and Gomez-Jeria (1989), a simple neurobiological explanation for near-death experiences could be abnormal neural activity within the temporal lobe	Research evidence is not clear. There is some evidence to support the assertions. However, some other researchers suggest the potential for a personality prone to near-death experience (Ring, 1984) based on the instability of their temporal lobe activity
Endorphins	This research is based on that carried out by Carr (1982). Endorphins (the body's natural narcotics manufactured in the brain to reduce sensitivity to pain and stress) are crucial in blocking out body pain, and are known to give people a sense of well-being. Endorphins can induce states of intense pleasure and acceptance, which are similar to those reported in positive near-death experiences	Investigations by Atwater (1992) and Greyson and Bush (1992) question the potential of this explanation. They argue that negative near-death experiences are increasingly common, and the endorphins account cannot explain this. Other researchers (e.g. Judson and Wiltshire, 1983) suggest that the narcotic influence of endorphins is not responsible for the near-death experience state. They suggest that the neurotransmitter serotonin is more critical (based on research by Morse, 1994). However, Jansen (1989) disputes this, suggesting that endorphins do not deliver what is needed for hallucinogenic potential. Rather, he suggests that the involvement of the NMDA receptors (n-methyl-d-aspartate) are simply part of a much more complicated process
Administered drugs	Given the high doses of drugs that are given during operations, it is not surprising that some scientists have suggested that near-death experiences are a by-product of the drugs administered. Jansen (1996) created near-death experiences using ketamine	Some patients who have had near-death experiences have not been under the influence of drugs (medical or recreational). Greyson and Stevenson (1980) show that patients who are under the influence of painkillers are less likely to report a near-death experience, and if they do it tends to be less vivid
Expectation	Near-death experiences often happen to those who think they are dying. Gabbard, Twemlow and Jones (1981) and Owens, Cook and Stevenson (1990) stress that near-death experiences are often had by those who think they are going to die but do not. According to researchers such as Osis and Haraldsson (1977), it is possible for cultural heritage and religion to inform the content or form of the near-death experience, e.g. for Christians to talk about there being a Jesus form/person in the light, whereas Hindus more commonly report seeing the messengers from Yamraj	Religious denominational differences cannot account for the similarities between near-death experiences across culture. Ring and Franklin (1981) show that someone attempting suicide does not necessarily have a horrible near-death experience; it is often similar to other reported experiences, and the near-death experience can reduce future suicide attempts
Possibility of life after death	Blackmore (1982) argues that brain and brain function is not the only cause since it cannot explain the belief in the idea that a 'soul' leaves the body, which is common in many Western and non-Western cultures	There is no scientific means of finding out if the evidence that supports it is true. There is qualitative evidence of individual cases where patients have reported being able to hear conversations or see instruments that they should not have been able to see given their state in hospital, e.g. Clark (1994) refers to the case of 'Maria' who during her near-death experience saw a shoe on an inaccessible ledge in the hospital. Later her social worker investigated this and found the shoe! The problem is that no one involved gave an independent account of the observation, so the observation is a story and not a scientific account. While proponents of the near-death experience view say this is conclusive evidence, sceptics would argue that there is no scientific basis to the claims

*Source: Based on **Blackmore** (1982)*

Out-of-body experiences

Research into out-of-body experiences

Research study: Ehrsson (2007)

A scientific attempt to examine out-of-body experience-like states

Ehrsson (2007) is sceptical about the exact nature of out-of-body experiences and has searched for a way to study this. Using an ingenious experiment, Ehrsson argued that out-of-body experiences are caused by a disconnection between the brain circuits that process visual and touch-sensory information. In his study, a total of 42 participants (individually) stood in front of a camera while wearing video-display goggles.

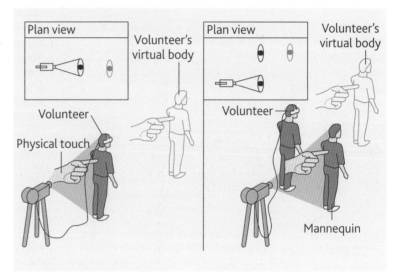

Fig. 2 *Ehrsson's experimental set-up*

Using the goggles, the participants could see their own back and a three-dimensional virtual own body that was standing in front of them. When a pen was used to stroke the back of the participant, the participant could see the back of the virtual body being stroked at the same time or with a slight time lapse.

Despite the pen being stroked along their own back, the participants commonly reported that the sensation they experienced was that of the pen being stroked along their virtual body. When a mannequin was used and stroked with the pen, the participants still perceived themselves as being stroked by the pen. Even when the equipment was turned off and taken away and the participants were asked to return to the position where the experiment had taken place, the participants overshot where they had been standing and stopped at a point in the room where the virtual body would have been positioned.

Ehrsson concluded that self-visual perspective disruption can in turn lead to the experience of a new viewpoint that might explain the accounts of those who report the extraordinary feelings and emotions associated with out-of-body experience.

Methodological issues

- The sample size was small and volunteer sampling was used, which means the results cannot be assumed to be representative of the target population.

Ethical issues

- In order to ensure that the participants did not know too much about what was being investigated, the information passed to the participants was kept to a minimum. As with other research in this area of psychology, the need to ensure that the study is methodologically secure often leads to ethical compromises. Here, fully informed consent is highly unlikely.
- Confidentiality of the participant's results was ensured through the appropriate coding of participant findings.

Arising from Ehrsson's study there is a notable theoretical issue to examine. The experimental set-up does provide means by which avenues of understanding in out-of-body experiences can be studied. Indeed, as Blackmore (2008) commented when referring to Ehrsson's findings: 'this has at least brought out-of-body experiences into the lab and tested one of the main theories of how they occur'.

Belief and out-of-body experiences

It is clear that science, through the views of many biologists, produces very convincing arguments against the notion that 'belief' is central to the workings of a near-death experience. Blanke (2004) suggested that out-of-body experiences are caused by neurological functioning. Through a series of experiments involving a small sample of female participants, he reported that if a mild electric shock is administered to the angular gyrus, an out-of-body experience occurred. One participant reported a shadowy person behind her. But the sample size of this study was small making it hard to generalise the findings. Nevertheless 'belief' in the possibility of out-of-body experience must shape the experience of the participants. Gow, Lang and Chant (2004) link belief in out-of-body experience to personality features of individuals. In a study of 167 participants who were either 'believers' or 'non-believers', participants were asked to complete a series of questionnaires. Those that had experienced out-of-body experiences from the sample were more fantasy prone, had greater belief in the paranormal and showed more **somatoform dissociation** – all of which are characteristics of 'believers'. What is the cause and what is the effect? Does the individual's personality shape their beliefs, or ultimately do their beliefs shape their personality? It may be hard to separate these.

Belief versus science

While people keep on reporting exceptional experiences, there will be continued interest in these extraordinary phenomena that are associated with the final phase of life. Science argues a good case against the importance of belief in these experiences, but it is nevertheless a causal factor in the experience of them. They provide us with meaning at a time when often our life and experiences are meaningless. Morse (1994) notes that 'just as near-death experiences (and out of body experiences) can reduce the fear of death in people who have them, so they can help all of us accept death as a positive aspect of life'.

Key terms

Somatoform dissociation: the reduction in sensorimotor integration (e.g. speaking, seeing, feeling, moving) as essential components of experience.

Key points

■ Near-death experiences are traditionally different to out-of-body experiences. Out-of-body experiences involve a person looking at their own body from above. Near-death experiences involve a variety of effects including the loss of pain, seeing bright lights and positive feelings.

■ There are various biological explanations for near-death phenomena including anoxia, hypercarbia, temporal lobe function abnormalities, endorphins and administered drugs. A psychological explanation is the expectation of life after death.

■ Ehrsson has attempted to research out-of-body experiences in a scientific study, an attempt that has been commended by Blackmore.

Summary questions

4 What is the difference between a near-death experience and an out-of-body experience?

5 What is an experimenter's greatest problem in researching this area? Explain your answer making reference to research to back up your claim.

6 Discuss the statement 'near death experiences are real psychic phenomena'.

Psychic mediumship

Learning objectives:

 define what psychic mediumship is

 describe the process of psychic mediumship and the influence of belief

 describe research examining belief and psychic mediumship

 evaluate research investigating the powers of psychic mediumship.

Key terms

Tanakh: the form of bible used in Judaism.

Cold reading: a technique that dates back to the mid-1800s that can be used to make a person think that you know more about them than you do.

Link

For comparisons between this area of pseudoscience and the criteria for scientific understanding, see pages 506–7.

What is psychic mediumship?

Mediumship has a stereotypical image, owing in part to the common portrayal of it in both television series and films. Mediumship is a practice where the medium acts as a facilitator of communication between the physical world and the spiritual world. A commonly accepted version involves the medium going into a trance so that the dead person can enter the body of the medium, or somehow communicate to them, and then relay messages from the 'other side'. According to this definition, mediums have the power to listen to the spirits and to converse with them. Once in a trance the medium will speak like the deceased, but upon exiting the trance they will have no recollection of it.

The strength of the idea of mediumship is due partly to the popularity of spiritualism in the USA. Mediumship is not a new phenomenon, there are examples going back to the time of the prophets. For example, in the story of the *Witch of Endor*, the witch raises the spirit of the deceased prophet Samuel for the Hebrew king Saul to question him about a coming battle. This is referred to in the First Book of Samuel in the **Tanakh**.

Psychic mediumship: simple belief or scientific fact?

Like most exceptional experiences, often psychic meetings can work if you want them to. People will generally come away with what they expect. Belief in the psychic medium will often blind the participant to the rather more 'worldly' and fraudulent tactics (e.g. **cold reading**) that are available in order to get details from you about the person the medium is meant to be contacting.

Psychic mediumship has not been extensively researched, partly because it does not fit into current scientific models and partly because it is difficult to research scientifically. Remember that scientific studies must be controlled and the results must be repeatable; they are usually peer reviewed and they must be open to falsification. The idea of spiritualism took hold in the Western world around 1848, and most research into this phenomenon was conducted then.

Many researchers have investigated psychic mediumship, most notably Professor Robert Hare, Sir William Crooke and Sir Oliver Lodge in the 19th and 20th centuries. These three are all well-known and respected scientists in their respective fields. Hare (1855) devised a variety of instruments to aid his investigation of the spiritual powers of mediums. After conducting his research, he concluded (contrary to his original beliefs) that spiritualism was real. After completing 20 years of research, Sir William Crooke agreed:

> I have never had any occasion to change my mind on the subject. I am perfectly satisfied with what I have said in earlier days. It is quite true that a connection has been set up between this world and the next.
>
> *Crooke, 1917*

The importance of these early contributors to this area of enquiry is that they brought with their studies a background in science, a belief in scientific rigour that was to characterise later research in the field.

Anomalistic psychology

▓ Key terms

Triple blind: in this case the medium, the researcher and the sitter will have no information about the nature of the sitting and no prior knowledge of the persons involved.

Survival of consciousness: the idea of continued existence, separate from the body, of an individual's consciousness or personality after physical death.

Super psi: skills such as very strong ESP; retrieval of information using psychic skills.

Veritas: a research programme that was developed to test the hypothesis that the consciousness of a person (be it their personality or their identity) survives physical death. This research programme closed in January 2008 broadening its focus to spiritual communication. With this change of focus came a change of name – it became the Sophia research programme.

Sophia: this project primarily investigates the claims of forms of communication involving different spiritual levels from the deceased individuals themselves to guides, angels and higher power and divinity. It is involved in healing and life advancement.

Belief in the actions of psychics seems to result in an attributable explanation for events personal to yourself. From a sceptical point of view, you could argue that if you are fantasy prone or over-willing to attribute any event to the power of exceptional experience, then you might see the psychic as having some influencing power.

Investigations by Beischel and Schwartz (2007) used a **triple blind** technique to avoid conventional methodological flaws as well as other influences such as telepathy and other forms of information reception. For this investigation, eight university students were 'sitters'. Four had experienced the death of a parent and four the death of a peer. Eight mediums were used, each of whom had shown independently a high degree of accuracy in their readings. The degree of accuracy was assessed by the completion of a series of trial runs. This is a point which Fontana (2005) stated was an obvious necessity when conducting research into psychic mediumship. In Beischel and Schwartz's study the mediums knew nothing about their sitters or about their deceased parent or peer. The results showed that certain mediums could give accurate information about the deceased. Whilst the use of a triple blind experimental design ensured that some means of communication could not interfere with the results, it is possible that other paranormal factors had an effect. Beischel and Schwartz suggested that other influences would include **survival of consciousness** or **super psi**.

Research by Russek and Schwartz (2001) suggests that highly skilled mediums can give accurate readings of people about whom they know nothing, revealing information that is so personal that the chances of guessing those details is well beyond chance. Another line of enquiry currently being examined is whether your consciousness (your identity) survives physical death. Studies into this area have been carried out by the **Veritas** project and latterly the **Sophia** project; in both projects the studies were conducted by Schwartz and his associates.

The skill of the psychic medium, at least from the sceptic's point of view – is to play on the participant's beliefs. Often *belief* that the medium can make contact shapes the whole experience. Indeed often this should be understood in the context of a paying customer who is 'willing' the medium to make contact; and often, due to their emotional state, they will interpret anything as a sign that contact has been made.

This certainly raises the issue as to whether the apparent ability of psychic mediums should be put down to the skill of cold reading. Analysis of some of the readings by mediums gives a clue. An examination of the famous psychic medium John Edward can provide an example. He might say that he could feel himself being pulled to a certain part of the audience, then he used sentences like: 'I'm getting an M name, like … Mary, Marie, Maria'. By doing this, he can pick up on clues given by the sitter, reinforce correct information and quickly gloss over wrong information. The sitter gets the impression that the medium knows a lot about them. Remember that whilst televised psychic mediums can seem very accurate, the programmes are heavily edited, which means that the actual experience is different from what is viewed.

Suggestibility also has an effect. John Edward has been criticised for targeting people when they are vulnerable (e.g. they have just lost a loved one) and are therefore more suggestible than usual. One final point to consider is that the messages sent back from beyond the grave are usually positive: X is doing well, Y is happy and at peace. Is life after death always so good? Perhaps the readings from psychic mediums match cultural beliefs that are held about the experience of life after death.

■ The problem of researching 'belief' and psychic mediumship

Sceptics of psychic mediumship have been given credibility by the uncovering of famous fraudsters such as James Van Praagh and Sylvia Browne. However, so long as people search for meaning in death and the afterlife, there will continue to be a role for psychic mediumship. Again it would seem that 'belief' is the pivotal factor in the exceptional experience of psychic mediumship.

While scientific research suggests that a well-trained psychic does have some abilities, such research still has its flaws. The problem is that the very factor that seems to influence it – belief – is the factor that current scientific methodologies find very difficult to flawlessly explore.

Key points

- Film and television coverage and storylines have a strong influence on what we think is involved in psychic mediumship.

- Like most areas of anomalistic psychology, psychic mediumship is difficult to study scientifically, especially the effect that belief has on those that visit and are influenced by the medium's comments.

- Psychic mediumship can involve many forms, but belief in them is central to all.

- Research has shown that with experienced psychic mediums the accuracy rate is high. However, even the most controlled studies cannot rule out all variables (forms of communications) that could cause the results to be significant. So while science still leaves other potential causes to account for the actual abilities of the psychic, it is belief in them that is at the heart of their varied success.

- One explanation for the apparent ability of psychic mediums is cold reading, and the uncovering of famous fraudsters has given support to sceptics. Such evidence fuels the views of sceptics, but from our point of view it suggests that the sitter's belief in the psychic has a stronger effect than actual knowledge of their abilities in the first place.

Summary questions

7 What is psychic mediumship and what does it involve?

8 Outline one study that has examined the process of psychic mediumship.

9 To what extent is belief a suitable explanation for the effect of psychic mediumship?

How science works: practical activity

Practicalities will dictate that you will not be able to recreate a ganzfeld study or scientifically validate the anomalistic powers of a medium or psychic healer. But you could establish if there is a link between the type of personality and belief in anomalistic phenomena. This area of research was investigated by Ramakrishna Rao *et al*. Your study will be a broad although not total replication of the original investigation. You should aim to assess the **temporal validity** of the original research.

For this investigation, first you need to think about the ethical and methodological issues surrounding correlational studies. What ethical issues will arise in your practical? Why not note them down in a table stating what the ethical issues are and then, in another column, how you will overcome them (see Table 1 for an example).

Table 1

Ethical issue	How I intend to overcome this issue
Deception: I will not be telling the participants everything about the investigation I am conducting since it might influence the type of response that they give, particularly if they know what I am investigating. Such demand characteristics would bias my results	To overcome the problem of not telling the participant all of the details prior to consent, I will thoroughly debrief them at the end of the investigation. This will involve an explanation of why they took part, how their results were used, why deception was necessary and the reassurance that their results will be kept confidential. Finally, I will give them a chance to ask questions about the study

Now justify the method that you have used. In a psychological write-up following an investigation the researcher will justify the choice of method. So think now about why the correlational method is the best here.

Get participants to complete an online personality questionnaire such as that found at http://similarminds.com/global-adv.html. You could also make use of the Eysenck Personality Questionnaire, which similarly has a extroversion, introversion, neuroticism and psychoticism scale. Ramakrishna Rao *et al*.'s comments suggested that those who perform better on ESP tasks tend on the whole to be the more extrovert individuals rather than the neurotic individuals who tend to be more introverted.

Once the personality test is conducted, ask the respondent if they would complete a short questionnaire about anomalistic issues. To ensure quantifiable data you will need to ensure that closed questions are asked. You might want to use the 1–5 Likert scale form of answer. Table 2 shows an example of this.

You should have at least 10 questions examining belief in anomalistic issues. The content of this might cover many of the areas that these chapters have covered so far. You now need to add up the score. Add together the scores (e.g. 5, 4, 3, 2 or 1) for each of the answers so that you have one total.

Temporal validity: the extent to which a research finding is relevant and true of the period of time in which it was conducted.

Table 2 *Likert scale*

Certain individuals have the power to move or manipulate objects using the power of their mind.				
5	4	3	2	1
Strongly agree	Agree	Neither agree nor disagree	Disagree	Strongly disagree

The correlation can now be performed between the personality score and the score of the anomalistic questionnaire. The appropriate test for statistical significance will be the Spearman's rho rank correlation.

Do your findings show similar characteristics between people who tend to 'believe' in anomalistic issues and powers? Draw similarities between your results and Ramakrishna Rao *et al.*'s study. Why do you think there are differences in the findings?

 Link

For more information about Spearman's rho rank correlation test, see pages 535–7.

 Further reading and weblinks

www.crystalinks.com/telekinesis.html

Look at this website for understandable information about telekinesis and psychokinesis, with limited technical jargon.

www.iands.org

The website for the International Association for Near-Death Studies is a good starting place to research near-death experience, and good summaries of research are available.

www.lutz-sanfilippo.com/library/general/lsfscience.html

An interesting site that offers the reader a low-level philosophical examination of what science is.

www.quackwatch.com/01QuackeryRelatedTopics/pseudo.html

This website discusses some interesting issues regarding the distinction between science and pseudoscience.

www.silvamethod.com/rp/docs/SPPH_crenshaw.pdf

For information that can support your case *for* psychic healing, the above pdf document provides enlightening reading and some real attempts to make scientific this area of pseudoscientific research.

http://skepdic.com

An absolute must for researchers in this area is The Skeptic's Dictionary.

www.sylvia.org/home/index.cfm

For information about Sylvia Browne see her official website.

http://site.uri-geller.com

Information about Uri Geller can be found on his own official website.

Psychological research and scientific method

Introduction

Psychology as a science

Psychology is described by the British Psychological Society as 'the science of people, the mind and behaviour'. You may find other definitions elsewhere which have a slightly different focus on the subject matter, but many will start 'psychology is the *science of*'. So, as well as appreciating theories and knowledge in psychology, anyone who wants to fully understand psychology needs to understand what science is and to understand the scientific process. It could be argued that an appreciation of the scientific process in psychology is more important than an understanding of theories (Dyer, 2006), as it allows you to evaluate the usefulness of theories and research and to distinguish between science and non-science (e.g. philosophy) or pseudoscience (e.g. astrology). The new knowledge gained from applying scientific methodology in psychology has to be reviewed by the scientific community to decide whether it represents a valid contribution to the subject. The application of the scientific method and the validation of new knowledge are discussed in Chapter 37, The application of scientific methodology in psychology.

The scientific process uses trustworthy methods to study people, the mind and behaviour. Without these trustworthy methods we cannot test ideas or form theories. The subject matter of psychology is vast and therefore psychologists use a wide variety of methods. In choosing an appropriate method to study the subject matter it is important to consider the reliability and validity of the data collected. Since psychology uses people (or more rarely animals) as participants in research another vital aspect in choosing and applying a research method is ethical concerns. All research must conform to the highest ethical standards. The selection and application of research methods is the subject of Chapter 38, Designing psychological investigations.

Once data has been gathered from a study it needs to be summarised and analysed carefully. This enables psychologists to understand what the data means and how to interpret it. The analysis forms the basis of the discussion of the aims and/or hypotheses. Finally, because it is important to share research findings, psychologists need to understand how to report their investigations. There are conventions relating to how research is presented to the scientific community in order for the information from the research to be understood clearly. Data analysis and reporting on investigations are discussed in Chapter 39, Data analysis and reporting on investigations.

Specification	Topic content	Page

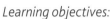
37 The application of scientific methodology in psychology

The features of science

Key terms

Objectivity: a term that is used to refer to views being based on observable phenomena and not on personal opinion, prejudices or emotion.

Empiricism: a view that suggests that experience is central to the development and formation of knowledge, and thus central to the scientific method. Experience or evidence arises out of experiments not intuition or revelation.

Replicability: the ability for procedures and/or findings to be reproduced or repeated.

Rational: based on reason.

Link

The scientific method is discussed in detail on pages 508–10.

The nature of science

The word 'science' is derived from the Latin *scientia*, meaning 'knowledge'. However, not all knowledge is scientific. For example, I know that Dickens wrote *Hard Times* and that Spain won Euro 2008, but this knowledge is not science. Science is concerned with a body of systematic knowledge that covers general truths and general principles and laws. The term 'science' is also used to refer to a system of obtaining knowledge. The general truths, principles and laws are found and tested using the 'scientific method', which in essence is a systematic process designed to obtain objective information and to test theories. The concept of **objectivity** is central to science. It is the key feature that distinguishes scientific knowledge from other sources of information. Objective knowledge is information that can be verified by measurements and is based on the philosophical doctrine of **empiricism**. Objective knowledge is therefore available to other scientists to check and verify it. This ability to check and verify information is another key feature of science, **replicability**. Scientific information is available to public scrutiny and others should be able to repeat any study and get the same information. For example, using a variety of information obtained through empirical methods, Miller (1956) claimed that the capacity of short-term memory is seven, plus or minus two items. This claim about specific objective knowledge has been tested by generations of psychology students ever since! Miller's findings are therefore replicable.

Another feature of science is that it is **rational**. Scientific explanations have to be consistent with known facts and they have to follow rules of logic. Scientists have to use an explicit process of reasoning using logical arguments and verifiable information. If, because of lack of knowledge, scientists make assumptions then these should also be made explicit. This transparency of information allows scientists to discuss and evaluate competing ideas and theories.

Science and non-science

The key features of objectivity, replicability and rationality separate scientific knowledge from other types of knowledge and information. Shaughnessy, Zechmeister and Zechmeister (2006) identify a number of key features that characterise scientific and non-scientific approaches:

■ Science is empirically based whereas non-science is frequently intuitive.

▩ The process of collecting scientific information is systematic and controlled, but non-scientific information is often gathered in a random and uncontrolled fashion. The reporting of science-based information is unbiased and objective, but it can be biased and subjective in non-science.

▩ Ideas or hypotheses in science can be tested (see page 508) but they cannot be tested in non-science.

We are exposed to different types of explanations of events and phenomena on a daily basis in newspapers, on television and in books. Many of these explanations are non-scientific, but it can be difficult to separate them from scientific ones. Bordens and Abbott (2008) and suggest there are three types of explanation of human behaviour that we should be careful to separate these from scientific explanations. They are:

- commonsense
- belief-based
- pseudoscience.

Commonsense explanations are those we develop from our experiences and from our ideas about what is true about the world. This type of explanation tends to based on a limited amount of information and to rely on intuition. It is usually accepted at face value and is rarely tested. However, scientific explanations that are based on carefully collected evidence can show that commonsense explanations are wrong. For example, if asked whether you are more likely to be helped if in distress when there is one person near you or five people, the commonsense answer is five. The intuitive commonsense explanation is that when there are five people there is a greater chance that one of them will help. Psychological research, gained from empirical evidence, has shown that in general the reverse is true – a single person is more likely to help than all five.

Some explanations of human behaviour are based on individuals' or groups' beliefs. These beliefs may be religious, political or personal in origin. Belief-based explanations tend to be accepted because they are consistent with a framework of belief. They can be based on little or no evidence and may even be claimed to be true in the face of contradictory evidence. In contrast, science attempts to present the best explanations that are available to explain the existing evidence. If further evidence shows that explanation to be false, then a new explanation is sought (see the hypothetico-deductive method on pages 458–9).

Pseudoscience is false science. Pseudoscientific explanations can be difficult to identify because they are presented as being scientific but they are not. One of the main differences is that scientific explanations are based on evidence that is replicable, whereas evidence for pseudoscientific explanations is either vague or not easily reproduced. Another is that in science any evidence that does not support an explanation is studied carefully and may lead to a change of explanation. In pseudoscience such evidence is minimised or explained away. Scientific knowledge is made public for scrutiny in publications that have been checked by other scientists (see peer review pages 512–13), but pseudoscience tends to be publicised in non-verifiable sources (e.g. on the internet).

Key points

- Science is concerned with a systematic body of knowledge that covers general truths and laws.
- Scientific knowledge is based on information that has been obtained objectively.
- Scientific knowledge is open to scrutiny and is replicable.
- Science tries to explain facts rationally using logic.
- Scientific knowledge differs from non-scientific knowledge.

Link

See *AQA Psychology A AS* student book, Chapter 11, Social influence in everyday life.

Take it further

Review some of the material you studied in Media psychology, The psychology of addictive behaviour, and Anomalistic psychology, and compare some of the scientific psychological information with information from other sources.

- Is there anything in the psychological information that is not objective, replicable or rational?
- Can you find evidence of commonsense, belief-based or pseudoscientific explanations in the other sources?

Summary questions

1 List the key features of science.

2 Use the list to compare psychology with a non-science subject such as English.
   a Do the key features apply to psychology?
   b How many of the key features apply to English?

3 One of the key features of science is objectivity. Consider whether this is possible when studying other people's behaviour (e.g. is it possible to remove personal or cultural bias from psychology?).

The scientific process

▓ Introduction

One of the defining features of science is the way in which knowledge is gathered. Over time scientists have developed a number of principles that guide the way they collect information. These principles guide the process of 'doing science'. Dyer (2006) argues it is these that 'make science most distinctive as a human activity, and differentiate it most clearly from other, non-scientific, activities'. These activities refer to both the way data is gathered and to how theories and laws are developed. We will begin this section by examining the scientific method before considering alternative views on how science progresses and how it should operate.

▓ The scientific method

Traditionally scientists have gathered data using empirical methods and then used induction or deduction to develop theories. Induction is the development of general truths, or theories, which can be used to explain the data that has been observed. However, this process is limited because it only explains existing data and makes no predictions about what might be found. Deduction is used when theories are developed about observed data which then result in specific predictions (hypotheses) which can be tested. If the predictions are right the theory is supported; if they are wrong then the theory (or the logic behind the prediction) is wrong. This traditional view of how science develops was criticised by Popper (1959). He pointed out that it is easy to find evidence for a theory and it is possible to devise test after test which all support it. However, no amount of evidence can ever 'prove' that a theory is right. In contrast it only takes one piece of evidence to disprove a theory. This is Popper's key idea behind an alternative to the traditional view of how science progresses. He illustrates it with a hypothetical scientist on an island who only ever sees black swans flying over. The scientist puts forward a hypothesis that all swans are black. Year after year this is supported (but never proved) as the black swans fly over. However, one year a white swan flies over the island and this one instance is enough to disprove the theory.

Popper proposed a different model of how science progresses based on the hypothetico-deductive method or scientific method. It is both a model of how science should be done and a theory of how science progresses. He suggests there are a number of stages in the scientific process.

1 Identify a problem. This can come from observations, previous research in the area or even a desire to question commonsense assumptions.
2 Develop a hypothesis about the problem. This should be predictive and, crucially, testable.
3 Devise a study to test the hypothesis.
4 Analyse and evaluate the results to determine whether they support the hypothesis or not.
5 Modify and repeat the process in light of stage 4.
6 Develop a theory.

Note that the process is cyclical (the research cycle) and that there are always more questions to be addressed.

The crucial element in the hypothetico-deductive method and the development of theory is **falsifiability** (hence the need for a testable hypothesis). It should always be possible to demonstrate that a theory is false – in other words, a good theory is refutable. Popper stresses that a theory has only been tested adequately if the researcher has tried to show that it is false. So rather than trying to find evidence for a theory, researchers should actively search for ways of disproving it (i.e. they should be searching for the white swans). A theory can never be proved but it is always possible to disprove it. If a researcher tries to disprove a theory but cannot, then the theory is strengthened. If the test does show the theory to be wrong then the theory is either modified or replaced by a better one. Popper suggests therefore that science progresses in a gradual and logical fashion. Theories are continually modified or replaced in light of new evidence. Choices between competing theories are made on the basis of which explain the available evidence best.

Theories that are tested over time and cannot be disproved become entrenched to become laws. Laws of science are considered to be universal and invariable (until there is some strong contradictory evidence, see science revolutions under The role of paradigms below). There are examples of laws in most sciences, such as Boyle's law in physics. There are few laws in psychology, partly because psychology is a young science (having only been a subject in its own right for around 120 years) but mostly because of the variability of the subject matter. Few aspects of human behaviour are universal and invariable. However, there are some, such as the law of effect.

The role of paradigms

Popper presents a somewhat *idealised* version of how science should progress. However, Kuhn (1996) showed that in *reality* science progresses differently. He noted that scientists tend to cling to theories even if contradictory evidence emerges. They carry on accepting the theory and look for flaws in the contradictory evidence. Kuhn calls this a period of 'normal science' when most scientists share a particular view or approach. The shared view or approach represents a **paradigm**. The accepted paradigm tends to dominate the science. It not only has a core set of ideas but also assumptions. These assumptions limit and define the types of questions that scientists ask. However, after a period of normal science, if more and more contradictory evidence appears some scientists begin to question the established, dominant paradigm. Sooner or later a very different theory or approach will be put forward. If this is accepted by the scientific community it becomes the new paradigm and it replaces the old in a scientific revolution. There is evidence of scientific revolutions or paradigm shifts in most sciences, such as the shift from Newton's to Einstein's theory in physics. Some psychologists suggest the shift from a dominant behaviourist view of psychology to a cognitive view in the 1960s was a similar revolution.

In Kuhn's view then, the progress of science is characterised by long periods of normal science using one paradigm followed by revolution when a new paradigm takes over (after a period of paradigm wars). So rather than the gradual logical development suggested by Popper, Kuhn proposed that there is resistance to change followed by sudden, and major, change. He also disagreed with Popper's view that theories are evaluated logically and objectively. He believed that new theories that do not suit the existing paradigm tend to be rejected, but existing theories that fit the paradigm are retained despite contradictory evidence. Finally Kuhn noted that scientists do not work in isolation but are part of a

Key terms

Falsifiability: the ability to show that a theory is false.

Paradigm: a shared set of assumptions about the subject matter of a discipline and the methods used to study it.

Take it further

Go back to section on operant conditioning in Chapter 20, Animal learning and intelligence, pages 241–4, and review the law of effect. Can you think of any psychological study that challenges it?

scientific community. This community accepts the dominant paradigm, trains the next generation using this paradigm and communicates in conferences and journals with the shared assumptions of the paradigm. It is therefore difficult to introduce new ideas or a new paradigm since it can be seen as an attack on the established members of the community. This is why change requires revolution.

Dyer (2006) sums up the difference between the Popper and Kuhn analyses of how science progresses. He notes that Popper focuses on the role of logic in the development of theories but tends to ignore the social context of scientific activity. Kuhn on the other hand emphasises the impact of social factors. Dyer goes on to say that both views are still very influential, but as yet neither is dominant.

■ Alternatives to the scientific approach

Towards the end of the 20th century there was an increase in the number of psychologists who questioned the use of the traditional scientific approach. Some began to reject this approach, or the conventional paradigm, for a number of reasons:

■ Advocates of alternative approaches point out that you cannot study people in the same way as physical phenomena such as electricity. Psychologists interact with people but a physicist does not interact with electricity.

■ Conventional research tended to study people in unnatural conditions (i.e. in laboratories or other university buildings). In other words, people were treated as if their behaviour can be isolated from the social context. In reality, critics claim, what is being studied is the unusual behaviour of psychology laboratories (demand characteristics).

■ The scientific approach emphasises control and therefore attempts to study one variable in isolation. In other words, one facet of behaviour is studied not the whole person. Critics suggest this is not possible. For example, how can one aspect of a person's memory be studied in isolation from their past experiences and current feelings?

■ As a result of the emphasis on control, the traditional approach tends to treat people as passive participants. The emphasis on recording one aspect of behaviour ignores the subjective experience of participants. They are not asked what else they think or feel. Any information gained from this approach is therefore likely to be superficial.

■ Critics also claim that the notion of objectivity in science is a myth. Past experiences, beliefs and ideas make it impossible to be truly objective about the data from a study. Psychologists face the additional problem of studying people and are therefore gathering information in a social context.

As a result of these criticisms alternatives to the scientific approach were suggested by a number of groups including the postmodernists and feminist psychologists. The postmodernists suggest that knowledge is a social construct that is subjective and is shaped by the language used to describe it and cultural context (a position known as social constructionism). Feminist psychologists focused on the relationship between researcher (for much of psychology's history this person was male) and researched, and called for an alternative, more collaborative approach. The alternative approach that has emerged has been called 'new paradigm research'.

■ Hint

In assessing how science progresses you will need to use your knowledge of psychology to compare the views of Popper and Kuhn.

■ Link

For more information about demand characteristics see Chapter 38, Designing psychological investigations, pages 521–2.

■ Link

Approaches, issues and debates

One of the criticisms of psychological research is that it is culturally biased or ethnocentric. Older research based on the traditional scientific approach tended to use etic analysis and assumed that findings were universal and culture free. New paradigm research recognises that human behaviour is influenced by culture and uses emic analysis.

New paradigm research tries to understand the subjective world of the participant and studies more complex data that cannot be reduced easily to numbers. Such information may come from in-depth interviews, written material such as diaries or, more recently, blogs. It focuses on the underlying meaning, values and emotion of the information and attempts to understand the experiential and cultural world of the participant. New paradigm research regards participants as active collaborators rather than passive participants obeying instructions. Research is a relationship between researcher and participant. This research is qualitative rather than quantitative. It is concerned with interpretation of the data and analysis of language rather than numbers.

The new paradigm approach has a growing following in psychology. Does this paradigm shift mean that the conventional scientific approach is being replaced? The answer is no, psychologists use the conventional and new paradigms when appropriate. For example, if you wanted to understand the reason that somebody had developed an eating disorder then a new paradigm, qualitative approach may be appropriate. However, if you are interested in the neural mechanisms that trigger eating then a conventional scientific approach would be preferred. Dyer (2006) describes modern psychology as being 'a multi-method discipline, employing a range of techniques in its quest for information that not only reflect the ... varied nature of the subject matter, but also the increasing sophistication of researchers'. Psychologists now have the tools and confidence to use whatever method seems best to study a particular problem.

Key points

- The scientific method is based on a research cycle in which theories are tested and evaluated.

- Popper stresses the need for theories to be falsifiable and that researchers should actively try to disprove theories.

- Theories are either strengthened by the failure to disprove them or have to be modified or replaced.

- Kuhn believes theories develop within a paradigm and that new types of theories are only accepted after a revolution and the acceptance of a new paradigm.

- New paradigm research offers an alternative to scientific psychology. It focuses on the subjective experience of people and is concerned with the interpretation of meaning.

- Psychology is a multi-method discipline.

Summary questions

4 Summarise the hypothetico-deductive method in your own words.

5 Compare the assumptions of the behaviourist and psychodynamic approaches to psychology.
   a Would you describe the two approaches as having similar or different assumptions?
   b Review Kuhn's description of paradigms.
   c Do the two approaches represent one paradigm or two?

6 List the criticisms of the scientific approach.

7 Contrast the features and assumptions of the scientific approach with the new paradigm approach.

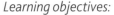
Validating new knowledge

Introduction

No matter how good or thorough research is, it is not useful to psychology or society until other people know about it. New knowledge only becomes public knowledge when it is published in a **journal** or is presented at a conference. Until research is public other psychologists cannot study the hypothesis, method, results or discussion. This means they cannot question the rationale behind the hypothesis, assess possible flaws in the method or question the results and conclusions. As Bartholomew (1982) points out: 'Until its results have gone through the painful process of publication, preferably in a refereed journal of high standards, scientific research is just play. Publication is an indispensable part of science'. Publication is the ultimate goal of any research, partly because it disseminates the findings and partly because it is the way new knowledge becomes validated.

Publishing new knowledge

The vast majority of research is first published in scientific journals. Journals therefore have a central role in the dissemination of scientific knowledge and research. Journals are periodic publications that build into yearly volumes that are kept in libraries. Therefore, the research that is published in journals becomes part of the permanent scientific record. There are a large number of journals that are devoted to psychology or that publish psychological research. Some journals are general and publish research from any branch of psychology (such as the *British Journal of Psychology*). Others are more specialised and only publish research from a specific field of psychology (for example, *Legal and Criminological Psychology* only publishes research on topics such as eyewitness testimony or offender profiling). The diversity of journals reflects the diverse nature of psychological research.

When we read the research that is published in journals how do we know if it is valid? How do we know that the research has been done well or that the results have been analysed appropriately? In extreme cases, how do we know that the research has not simply been made up? In other words what are the quality control mechanisms that regulate the introduction of new knowledge? The answer for the vast majority of work published in journals is a system of **peer review**.

When psychologists have research that they want to publish they prepare a manuscript and send it to a journal. The editor of the journal examines the topic of the manuscript and sends copies to other psychologists who are experts in that topic. These experts act as the peer reviewers. The peer reviewers read the manuscript carefully and assess all aspects of it. They then send it back to the editor with comments and a recommendation about its suitability for publication. Using these reports, the editor then has to decide whether the research should be accepted for publication, whether it should be revised or whether it should be rejected. Shaughnessy, Zechmeister and Zechmeister (2006) note that in 2003 only one in three manuscripts sent to the journals of the American Psychological Society was accepted for publication. Thus peer review acts as a control mechanism that weeds out poorer research and allows only the best to become public.

In a report on peer review by the UK Parliamentary Office of Science and Technology (2002) it was claimed that 'peer review … has become central to the process by which science is conducted'. The report points out that peer review is important and that it is a process that ensures only high-quality research is published. It is central to validating new knowledge.

Problems of validation

Although the system of peer review and publication is seen as the best method of validating new knowledge, it does have some problems. In a very small number of cases peer review has failed to detect fraudulent research. The UK Parliamentary Office of Science and Technology (2002) identify a number of different types of fraudulent research including fabrication (where data is made up), falsification (where data exists but has been altered) and plagiarism (where work has been copied from others). However, it should be stressed that cases of proven fraudulent research are very rare. Nevertheless, Bordens and Abbott (2008) identify a number of other problems relating to validating new knowledge which include:

- Consistency with previous knowledge: most findings build on previous knowledge or theory. Research that does not 'fit' with previous work is often seen as suspect and can be rejected. For example, Garcia and Koelling (1966) showed that rats could learn to avoid flavoured water even if there was a six-hour gap between tasting the water and being ill. All other work in this area (classical conditioning) had suggested that a conditioned response could not be formed if there was a gap of more than a few minutes between the conditioned stimulus and the unconditioned response. Garcia and Koelling's manuscript was rejected a number of times until other researchers began to find the same taste aversion effects. This shows that peer review can act as a conservative force that tends to maintain the status quo. In Kuhn's view of science, peer review may slow the revolution from one point of view (paradigm) to another.

- Values in science: although psychologists try to be objective, many philosophers of science suggest it is impossible to separate research from cultural, political or personal values. If the author and the reviewer share these values then they may be published as objective science. For example, Bowlby's work on maternal deprivation was seen by some later researchers to reflect the cultural values and political forces of the post-war period. It was not until some time later that others began to question his emphasis on separation from mothers rather than parents.

- Bias in peer review: like any other appraisal process, peer review is subject to bias. There are a number of ways that the review may be biased. The reviewer's theoretical view may differ from that in the manuscript (for example, if the reviewer is convinced that intelligence has a strong genetic component they might not look favourably on research that suggests that it is largely the result of upbringing). There is evidence of 'institution bias' (the tendency to favour research from prestigious institutions) and gender bias (the tendency to favour male researchers).

- File drawer phenomenon: peer review tends to favour positive results (i.e. ones where the results support the hypothesis). For this reason many negative findings (i.e. ones when the null hypothesis has been accepted) are either not published or are simply left in the researcher's file drawer. There is an obvious problem here. If 10 negative findings are sitting in file drawers but one positive finding is published, then it distorts our understanding of a topic.

Link

For an example of fraudulent research, see the controversy surrounding the work of Sir Cyril Burt in Chapter 34, Theoretical and methodological issues in the study of anomalous experience, on pages 460–1.

Link

See classical conditioning in Chapter 20, Animal learning and intelligence, on pages 239–40.

See Kuhn's view of how science progresses on pages 509–10.

Link

Approaches, issues and debates

The bias described here is based on the gender of the researcher not of the participants. It suggests that peer review has an andocentric bias.

Take it further

How does the file drawer phenomenon relate to Popper or Kuhn's view of scientific progress?

Which theory does it tend to support?

Key points

■ The goal of research is to publish the findings of new knowledge.

■ New knowledge is published in peer-reviewed journals.

■ Peer review acts as a system of quality control and ensures that the published work is high quality.

■ The process of peer review is how new knowledge becomes validated.

■ There are some potential problems of the peer-review process. It tends to be conservative, it can reflect shared values, the review may be biased and negative findings are often ignored.

Summary questions

8 Describe the process of peer review in your own words.

9 What is the purpose of peer review?

10 Briefly outline five problems of the peer-review process.

11 Consider how these problems affect the progress of science.

38 Designing psychological investigations

Research methods

Learning objectives:

▓ describe different types of research methods

▓ understand and explain the advantages of a range of research methods

▓ be able to select and apply appropriate methods.

▓ Key terms

Ecological validity: the degree to which the findings of a study can be generalised to other situations, places and conditions (e.g. the findings in one laboratory are the same as in other laboratories).

▓ Link

Review the advantages and disadvantages of laboratory, field and natural experiments that you studied for Unit 1 at AS Level.

▓ Introduction

The first stage in designing any psychological investigation is to consider what exactly you want to find and what data is needed, and then choose the appropriate method to find it. At AS Level you studied a range of methods in psychology including experimental, correlational, observational, surveys, interviews and case studies. These are reviewed below before considering which might be appropriate for a study.

▓ Review of research methods

Experimental method

Experiments are used to try to establish cause and effect relationships. This is done by manipulating the independent variable and measuring the effect, if any, on the dependent variable. A causal relationship can only be established if all other variables are controlled. Experiments can be laboratory based, when control is high, but **ecological validity** can be low. In field experiments the reverse is true. Natural experiments occur when the researcher does not directly manipulate the independent variable. These are best described as quasi-experiments. There are three basic experimental designs which can be used in any setting. They are outlined in Table 1 (overleaf).

Correlational method

Correlations are designed to investigate the strength of relationship between two variables. The strength of a correlation is expressed by the correlation coefficient. This is always between $+1$ and -1, where $+1$ represents a perfect positive correlation, 0 represents no correlation and -1 represents a perfect negative correlation. In positive correlation, as one variable increases so does the other. In a negative correlation, as one variable increases the other decreases.

▓ Advantages of the method: it allows researchers to analyse whether there is a significant relationship between two variables when the variables could not be manipulated experimentally.

▓ Disadvantages of the method: correlations do not show cause and effect, they only show that there is a relationship. A correlation does not establish whether either variable causes the other or whether a third variable influenced both. Correlations only identify linear relationships. However, relationships in psychology can be more subtle and complex. For example, the relationship between arousal and performance tends to show an inverted U relationship. When arousal increases at first so does performance, but if arousal keeps increasing eventually performance starts to decrease.

Psychological research

Table 1 *Experimental designs*

Design	Description	Advantages	Disadvantages
Repeated measure design	The same participants are used in both conditions	Participant variables are eliminated because each participant acts as their own control. Fewer participants are required	Order effects such as practice, boredom or fatigue may occur, although these can be controlled by counterbalancing. It is usually not possible to use the same materials in each condition
Independent group design	The participants are randomly allocated to different groups. The groups represent the different conditions	No order effects. The same materials can be used in both conditions	Participant variables are introduced. Differences between the conditions may be caused by the different people rather than the independent variable (IV) More participants are required
Matched pairs design	Pairs of participants are closely matched and then randomly allocated to one condition or the other	No order effects. Attempts to control participant variables	It is difficult to match everything about the participants. More participants are required

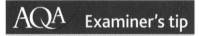

Examiner's tip

In examinations be careful to distinguish between research methods such as lab experiment and experimental design. The design refers to how you structure or organise the experiment. See Table 1 above.

Observational methods

The observational method can be used in a variety of ways ranging from controlled observations in laboratories to naturalistic observations in a natural environment. The aim of controlled observations is to control variables that might influence behaviour. Naturalistic observations aim to produce data with higher ecological validity by observing naturally occurring behaviour. Observations can also be participant or non-participant depending on whether the observer interacts with the observed or not.

Table 2 *Observational methods*

Type of observation	Advantages	Disadvantages
Naturalistic	Natural behaviour is observed. High in ecological validity	Little control over confounding variables
Controlled	Control over confounding variables	Behaviour may not be natural or normal
Participant	Easier to understand observee's behaviour. High in ecological validity	Hard to record observations (often done retrospectively and therefore unreliable). Observer can become involved with the participants and data can be subjective
Non-participant	Observations can be made as they happen and are more reliable. Lack of contact means the observer can remain objective	Behaviour may be recorded but the meaning behind it is not known

Surveys

Surveys are used to gather information about a topic from a large number of people. This information is gathered from questionnaires that might ask questions about a topic focusing on behaviour or thoughts. The questions can be open (i.e. the person can respond to the question in any way they like) or closed (i.e. the person has to choose from a limited range of responses on the questionnaire).

- Advantages: surveys gather a large amount of information efficiently. They do not require the researcher to gather the information and therefore reduce the influence of interpersonal factors.
- Disadvantages: surveys can have low response rates and this can reduce the validity of the sample. The truthfulness of the data can be influenced by social desirability. Respondents might want to present themselves positively rather than truthfully. They may even lie about sensitive issues. The method is not flexible; the researcher cannot ask supplementary questions that might arise.

Interviews

Interviews are similar to surveys because they are used to ask questions, but in interviews this is face to face. Interviews can be structured (where the questions are predetermined and often closed) or unstructured (which involves exploration of a topic or theme with more open questions). Some are semi-structured. These are based on predetermined questions but may have supplementary follow-up questions or the freedom to explore some issues in more depth.

- Advantages: interviews tend to be more flexible than surveys as researchers can interact with the participants to clarify information.
- Disadvantages: the interaction with participants may affect the data that is collected. It is a more time-consuming way of gathering data than a survey.

Case study

A case study is an in-depth study of an individual or a group. It gathers detailed information about one case. These details could come from records (medical, employment, etc.) or from studies of the case using other methods such interviews or observations. The nature of the information collected will vary from case to case and will depend on why the person or group is being studied. Case studies are idiographic.

- Advantages: a case study provides a rich source of meaningful data. Sometimes the detailed data from one individual can challenge established theories. For example, the case study of KF challenged the idea that short-term memory was a single unitary store (Shallice and Warrington, 1970). His short-term memory was damaged but the damage was selective; he found it hard to recall verbal material (letters, numbers or words) but could recall visual stimuli.
- Disadvantages: it is difficult to generalise the results, they have low population validity. It is difficult to replicate case studies so it is hard to examine the reliability of the findings.

Link

The review of research methods presented here is a summary of the knowledge you should have from your AS studies. Use your notes from Unit 1 to add details of each method.

AQA Examiner's tip

Be careful not to confuse *data collection* with a *research method*. The most common mistake is to confuse the use of observations to collect data with the observational method. However, data gathered by observation could be used for the experimental method, correlations, case studies, etc. For example, in a study of the effect of an audience on performance in sport you might use observations to get the data. However, if you manipulated whether there was an audience present or not (i.e. you used an independent variable) and the data collected by the observation was the dependent variable, then the method was an experiment.

■ Selection of research methods

The review above highlights the diversity of research methods that are used in psychology. The choice of a method is governed by what the researcher wants to find out. Borden and Abbott (2008) suggest that scientific studies tend to concentrate on one of two approaches:

■ Exploratory data collection. This is concerned with the collection of descriptive data.

■ Hypothesis testing. This is concerned with identifying links between variables. These links could be causal (in experiments) or relational (in correlations).

Figure 1 starts with the question about which of these approaches suits the aim of the research before going on to consider other questions that need to be considered.

The choice of method is just the first stage in designing the research; the important part is the detail. It is the detail that affects the reliability and validity of the data.

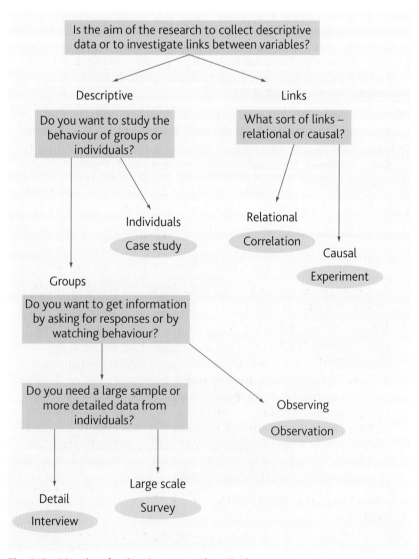

Fig. 1 *Decision chart for choosing a research method*

If the experiment method is appropriate there are a number of other factors to consider. The first is which design to use. The researcher has to weigh up whether it is more important to control participant variables or factors such as order effects and having different materials in each condition. For example, if you were studying whether more faces are recognised when they are presented upright than inverted, which method would be best? A repeated measure design would remove participant variables but would require the use of different faces in each condition. If the independent group design was used the same faces could be used for both conditions, but this method introduces participant variables. Having made the judgement about which design to use the researcher has to decide how to manipulate the IV and, crucially, how to measure the dependent variable (DV) (i.e. how the DV is **operationalised**).

There are also a number of issues to be considered if observation is the appropriate method. The first is whether to use naturalistic or controlled observation. This hinges on whether high levels of ecological validity (naturalistic) or control over confounding variables (controlled) is more important. The second is whether to use participant or non-participant observation. Here the choice is whether ecological validity is more important than reliability of the data.

The major choice when using surveys or interviews is which type of question is most useful. Closed questions provide data that can be quantified and analysed statistically. In other words, they are best for quantitative research. However, if the researcher is more interested in qualitative data or detailed information from the interviewee, then open questions are more appropriate.

The choices about what to study in a case history depend on the nature of the case and the reason the case study is being done. For example, a case study of a person with prosopagnosia would tend to focus on what the person could and could not see. The details of the person's childhood experiences, relationships with others, etc. would not be relevant to the case. However, in a case study of someone who self-harms, these types of details would be important. Their perceptual abilities would not be important.

Key points

- Psychologists use a range of research methods including experiments, correlations, observations, surveys, interviews and case studies.

- The choice of method depends on what the researcher wants to find out and can be broadly split into two categories: data collection or hypothesis testing.

- The choice of a data collection method depends on the type of information required. If the researcher wants to investigate the answers to specific questions, then interviews or surveys can be used. If the researcher wants to look at how people behave, an observation method would be used. A detailed investigation of an individual requires a case history.

- Hypothesis testing methods investigate links between variables. These links can be causal (experimental methods) or relational (correlation method).

- When a researcher has chosen a method they must then decide on the details of the design.

Key terms

Operationalised: a variable is given an operational definition (i.e. it is operationalised) when the researcher defines exactly how a concept is to be measured. For example, aggression is a concept that could be measured by the number of times a child hits other children.

Link

For more information on prosopagnosia see Chapter 6, Face recognition and visual agnosias.

Summary questions

What would be the best method for investigating the following research ideas? Briefly justify your choice.

1. An investigation of gender differences in aggression in school playgrounds.

2. A study into whether the method of loci improves long-term memory recall.

3. An examination of possible links between stress and cardiovascular disease.

4. An investigation of opinions about relationships in young adults.

5. A study of a person with multiple personalities.

6. A detailed exploration into the reasons for carrying knives at school.

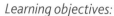

Reliability and validity

Key terms

External reliability: the ability to replicate the results of a study.

Internal reliability: consistency of a measure within a test.

Introduction

After choosing an appropriate method we have to consider how useful the data from the study is likely to be. Can we rely on the data when drawing conclusions from it? The key issues are whether the data is reliable, whether it is valid and whether there are likely to be any biases due to the sampling of the population.

Issues of reliability

The concept of reliability is linked to one of the key features of the scientific approach, replicability. In science, researchers should be able to measure or observe something time after time and get the same or similar results. Any two measurements of the same thing should be consistent with each other. If they are consistent the measure used is reliable.

Assessing reliability

For most studies the important type of reliability will be external. **External reliability** is the ability to produce the same results every time the test is carried out. It is typically assessed using the test-retest method where the test is used several times using the same or similar groups of participants. Of course few tests yield exactly the same results time after time. However, one way of getting a measure of reliability is to do a test of correlation between two sets of scores. A high-correlation coefficient indicates that the test is reliable. A low-correlation coefficient indicates poor reliability.

Internal reliability is usually associated with measures such as attitude scales or psychometric measures, for example personality tests. It is concerned with the consistency within a test. For instance, if you devised a new test of personality and in the first half participants score high on extroversion but in the second they do not, then there is no internal consistency. Internal reliability is typically assessed using the split-half method. This compares one half of the test with the other to check whether the scores of a variable (e.g. extroversion) are consistent.

Improving reliability

Reliability depends on the accuracy of any measurement. Inaccurate measurements or inaccurate data recording will inevitably reduce reliability. There are a number of ways that such inaccuracies can be reduced:

- When possible it is better to take more than one measurement from each participant. For example, if you were measuring the time it took to react to a visual stimulus you could show the stimulus three times and take an average score. This reduces the impact of any anomalous score.

- Pilot studies can be used to check that the proposed method of measurement works properly and that participants can use any apparatus successfully.

▓ When more than one investigator is used in a study the way in which they collect and record data should be standardised. For studies using observations or interviews this may require a period of training to make sure researchers are looking for, and recording, exactly the same information. This improves **inter-rater reliability**.

▓ When data is recorded or transposed it should be checked very carefully. There is no point in carefully measuring something accurately if the wrong data is then written down or entered into a computer.

▓ Issues of validity

The issue of validity raises two questions: are the conclusions drawn from data justified, and can we trust the data to represent what we intended it to? Think of validity as being the truthfulness of the measure; a valid measure is one that measures what it claims to measure. There are many types of validity but it is crucial to consider two types when designing a study. These are internal and external validity.

Internal validity

Internal validity is the ability of the study to test the hypothesis that it was designed to test. Essentially, does the DV measure what we want it to and, in an experiment, are we measuring the effects of the IV on the DV? The first of these points links to the operationalisation of variables. Most psychological constructs cannot be measured directly but are inferred indirectly from the measurements we take. For example, we cannot measure extroversion directly but we can infer that a person that strongly agrees with a number of statements such as 'I enjoy lively parties' is likely to be extrovert. However, sometimes when we operationalise variables we might choose a measure that actually does not measure what we want to. For example, I might decide to use the speed of keying a paragraph of text using a word processor as a measure of intelligence. But is this really a measure of intelligence? Does it fit with other measures of intelligence such as verbal reasoning? In this example we might be measuring the effects of other variables, such as familiarity with word-processing packages or whether the participants can touch type, rather than intelligence. These other variables are known as **confounding variables**. To improve internal validity we should try to remove all confounding variables. Removing the confounding variables is known as control. The greater the control that we have over variables the better the internal validity.

Even if we control confounding variables and have a measure that accurately reflects the variable we are studying, there are other threats to internal validity. One of these is **demand characteristics**. We may have an excellent measure of, say, extroversion, but if the participants believe the study demands they should seem introverted and they try to influence the test, the results will not be valid. Some participants may behave in the opposite way to that which they believe they should. Orne (1962) showed the effects of demand characteristics on participants' behaviour. He gave participants thousands of sheets with numbers on them. He asked them to add up the numbers on a page then tear it into pieces before going on to the next sheet. In other words, a boring repetitive task. However, because it was a psychology experiment, his participants did it for hours! Another threat to internal validity is **experimenter bias**. If, for example, we develop a good way to measure aggression but the experimenter is biased in the way this measure is

▓ Key terms

Inter-rater reliability: the degree of agreement between different observers.

Confounding variables: variables that get confused with the independent variable.

Demand characteristics: cues that lead to the tendency for participants to behave in the way they think is required of them.

Experimenter bias: the tendency of experimenters to find what they expect or want to show.

AQA Examiner's tip

There is some confusion between confounding variables and extraneous variables. Extraneous variables are variables that might affect the performance of the participant. They can be situational (lighting, time of day, etc.) or related to the participant (age, mood, etc.). Confounding variables are variables that are accidentally manipulated along with an IV and have unintended effects on the DV. For example, imagine you were measuring the effect of caffeine on reaction time and you accidentally put all of the younger participants in the caffeine group and the older participants in the control group. If the first group is faster is it due to the caffeine or their age?

recorded (e.g. tending to record one group as being more aggressive than another) then the measure is no longer valid. The final threat to internal validity in experiments comes from the design used. When the repeated measure design is used there is a danger that the results can be distorted by order effects such as practice or boredom. This can be reduced by counterbalancing. When the independent group design is used participant variables are introduced (the confounding variable of having different people in each group).

Improving internal validity

Designs that reduce demand characteristics and experimenter effects increase the internal validity. One design feature that reduces demand characteristics is known as the single-blind technique. Using this technique participants do not know what group or condition they are in and therefore cannot change their responses to suit or foil the researcher. For example, if I was interested in the influence of caffeine on reaction time I could give two groups of participants one of two strong-flavoured soft drinks, labelled either X or Y. Only I would know which contained caffeine. Since the participants would be 'blind', the group they are in does not influence their response. However, I would still know which group the participants were in.

The double-blind technique removes both demand characteristics and experimenter bias. In this case, neither the participants nor the experimenter know what each condition or group represents. Using the example above, I would give participants either X or Y but I would not know what they contained until I had collected (and preferably analysed) the data. Thus both sources of bias are removed.

Research study: Rosenthal and Fode (1963)

Rosenthal and Fode asked students to study 'dull' and 'bright' rats. The study involved finding out how quickly the rats learned to run a maze. Perhaps unsurprisingly, the bright rats were faster. However, the rats were randomly assigned, there were no bright or dull rats. Rosenthal and Fode found no evidence of any deliberate attempt by the students to distort the results and suggested it happened because of expectations. They demonstrated experimenter bias.

Methodological issues

You could question whether the study showed the effect of experimenter bias or whether it was a study of demand characteristics. Did the students (who were the real participants) do what was expected of them? Although this was a single blind study there can be cues that influence participants' behaviour.

Ethical issues

The key ethical issue is deception. Rosenthal and Fode deliberately misled the students into believing they were the experimenters.

Assessing validity

There are a variety of ways of assessing validity. The simplest is face validity. This is simply a judgement about whether a test seems to be valid and is the weakest form of validity. Criterion validity is more objective and looks at whether a test of a particular construct relates to other measures of it. There are two types of criterion validity: concurrent and predictive. A test shows concurrent validity if it shows similar findings to another existing measure. For example, if a test of neuroticism matched the judgement of experienced psychiatrists, it would have concurrent validity. Predictive validity is measured by how well a test predicts future performance. For example, if an IQ test given at the age of 14 predicts grades achieved at A Level, it would have predictive validity.

External validity

External validity is concerned with how well the results of a study can be generalised beyond the study itself. A study has external validity if the results can be extended beyond the limited sample and the setting of the study. The issue of whether we can generalise the results from the limited sample of the study is called **population validity** and this is discussed in the Issues of sampling section below. The issue of whether we can generalise the results from the setting of the study to other settings is called **ecological validity**. As psychology is concerned with human behaviour the important question is whether the results obtained in one setting can be generalised to other settings. A good example of this is Milgram's set of experiments on obedience. His demonstration of similar results at a university, a run-down office and so on showed they had ecological validity. Milgram's studies are also a good example of how to test ecological validity. Ideally a finding from one setting should be tested in other settings.

Research study: Thurston et al. (2008)

Thurston et al. have raised questions about the validity of a lot of mental-health research because of a systematic sampling error. A common practice in mental-health research is to compare a clinical group (with known disorders) with a non-clinical community group. However, Thurston and her colleagues found that in a community sample of 224 families 20 per cent of the mothers met the diagnostic criteria for one or more psychiatric disorders. This suggests that most studies are not comparing a clinical sample with a truly non-clinical sample.

Methodological issues

The inclusion criteria for the study (adolescents must have at least monthly contact with both parents) distorted the sample. More adolescents in this sample had parents who were still married than the US average (83.7 per cent compared to 64.2 per cent). Ironically, this study of population validity may have problems with population validity.

Ethical issues

The major issue of the study is whether to disclose any evidence of psychiatric disorders to the individual participants concerned. However, Thurston et al. do not discuss the issue in their report.

Ecological validity does not necessarily mean doing studies in everyday settings (these are field studies) or trying to copy real life in the laboratory (this is often an example of **mundane realism**). Researchers are more interested in **experimental realism** than mundane realism.

Key terms

Population validity: the degree to which the results can be generalised from the sample to other populations.

Ecological validity: the degree to which the findings of a study can be generalised to other situations, places and conditions (e.g. the findings in one laboratory are the same as in other laboratories).

Mundane realism: the degree to which the setting or procedure reflects that in real life.

Experimental realism: the degree to which the results reflect realistic behaviour.

AQA Examiner's tip

There is a tendency to confuse ecological validity with mundane realism. However, just mimicking real-life situations does not necessarily improve ecological validity. Sometimes mundane realism decreases validity because it increases factors such as demand characteristics.

The issue of validity is linked to reliability. Measures must be reliable if they are to be valid. For example, if we have a measure of intelligence, it cannot be valid if it shows the score to be 80 one day and 120 the next. A person cannot be both below and above average intelligence. Unreliable measures do not have internal validity. However, the reverse is not true; measures can be reliable but not valid. For example, I could test 10 people on how fast they could key a paragraph of text on a word processor and test them again a week later. I might well find that the measure is reliable but, as discussed above, it is unlikely to be a valid measure of their intelligence.

Internal versus external validity

There is a trade-off between internal and external validity and this must be considered when designing experiments. The more that confounding variables are controlled to improve internal validity the more the study becomes artificial and removed from any semblance of real-world behaviour, so external validity is reduced. Conversely, if external validity is increased by studying behaviour in natural conditions then the ability to control confounding variables is reduced and internal validity is decreased. Deciding on whether high internal or high external validity is more important depends in part on the purpose of the study. If the study is designed to test the detail of a theory then typically high internal validity would be preferred to high external validity. However, if the study is designed with the intention of applying results to the real world (e.g. the effectiveness of the cognitive interview) then it becomes more important to have high external validity.

Issues of sampling

One of the steps in designing a study is to consider who it should study or who is the target population. If you are interested in the effect of peers on gender development in primary schools then the target population will be primary-school children. However, it would be impossible to study every primary-school child in the country. Virtually every psychology study investigates a sample of the target population.

At AS Level you studied various types of samples including random, opportunity and volunteer. These are summarised in the *AQA Psychology A AS* student book.

The key issue when choosing a sample is whether it has population validity (this is part of external validity). Population validity is increased when the sample is representative of the target population. The more representative the sample the more the results can be generalised to other members of the population. Table 1 (*AQA Psychology A AS* student book, page 98) indicates that the most representative type of sample, and therefore the one that has the greatest population validity, is the random sample. However, the use of a random sample tends to be rare. A lot of psychological research has been criticised because of biases in the sampling methods. A great deal of research uses opportunity or volunteer samples rather than random. For example, Banyard and Hunt (2000) reviewed all of the studies in two UK journals over a two-year period. They found that in 71 per cent of the studies the sample was university students, a convenient opportunity sample for researchers. They note that there are many reasons that this is not a representative sample for the population as a whole. Research has consistently found that people who volunteer are not representative of the whole population (i.e. they are on average different to non-volunteers). For example, Lonnqvist *et al.* (2007) found that people who volunteer are more stable and outgoing than those that do not.

Link

Remind yourself of the types of sampling and their relative definitions, methods and population validity by looking at the *AQA Psychology A AS* student book, page 98. Alternatively the table is available at www.nelsonthornes.com/psychology_answers.

In selecting a sample there can be a conflict between the desire for good design and ethical guidelines. Population validity would be increased by having a truly random, representative sample. However, psychologists cannot force anyone to take part. Therefore there is inevitably some element of volunteer sampling.

Key points

- A measure shows external reliability if it gives the same results a number of times.
- Internal reliability is concerned with the consistency of measurements within a test.
- Internal validity is concerned with the truthfulness of the data. A measure that tests what the researcher intended has internal validity.
- Internal validity is improved by controlling confounding variables, demand characteristics and experimenter bias.
- External validity is concerned with how well the findings of any study can be generalised. Its two main components are population validity (the degree to which the findings relate to other people) and ecological validity (the degree to which the findings relate to other settings).
- There are various ways of selecting a sample from a target population. Random samples are the most representative and have the greatest population validity.

Summary questions

7 Describe one way of assessing external reliability.

8 On one side of a table list some of the threats to internal validity and on the other side indicate a way of controlling each threat.

9 Identify and describe two components of external validity.

10 Review the following studies. For each decide whether the primary concern is for internal or external validity and explain why:

  a an investigation into obedience to an authority figure

  b a study of the capacity of verbal material in short-term memory

  c an analysis of the influence of different reinforcement schedules on extinction of behaviour

  d a study into the effect of questioning styles on eyewitness accuracy.

Take it further

You can read the Banyard and Hunt report by going to the British Psychological Society website and looking for the archived articles of *The Psychologist*. The article 'Reporting research: something missing' is in Volume 13, Number 2. Use it to compile a list of reasons that students are non-representative of the population as a whole.

Psychological research

Ethical considerations in psychological research

Learning objectives:

Learning objectives:

- be familiar with the ethical principles of conducting research issued by the British Psychological Society

- understand ways that psychologists can deal with ethical issues in the design of investigations.

Introduction

It is vital that all psychological research conforms to the highest ethical standards. Psychologists study people and therefore have a duty of care. The final stage in designing psychological investigations is therefore one of the most important: making sure that the design, procedure, sample selection, data collection and storage are all done in an ethical manner. In the introduction to the 'Ethical principles for conducting research with human participants' the British Psychological Society (BPS) (1992) point out: 'In all circumstances, investigators must consider the ethical implications and psychological consequences for the participants in their research'. This section begins with a review of the BPS principles before looking at practical ways they can be addressed by researchers.

Review of BPS ethical principles

At AS Level you were introduced to the BPS guidelines for research with human participants. These are listed below.

BPS guidelines for research with human participants

The British Psychological Society code of ethics, *Ethical Principles for Conducting Research with Human Participants*, covers nine different aspects of ethics that relate to research with human participants:

- Consent: participants should give informed consent.
- Deception: participants should not be misled.
- Debriefing: following the investigation the study should be discussed with participants.
- Withdrawal from investigation: participants should feel free to leave the investigation at any time.
- Confidentiality: participants have the right to confidentiality.
- Protection of participants: this includes both physical and psychological harm.
- Observational research: the privacy of participants needs to be respected.
- Giving advice: psychologists should only give advice for which they are qualified.
- Colleagues: psychologists have a duty to make sure all research is ethical, and this includes colleagues.

Hint

Check the BPS website for the most up-to-date *Ethical Principles for Conducting Research with Human Participants* (see the link to the 'Code of Conduct and Ethical Guidelines' on 'The Society' page). If you cannot remember the details from your AS studies you should revise them now before looking at their application.

Application of BPS ethical principles

This section is concerned with the potential steps that psychologists can take when designing their studies to ensure that the BPS guidelines are followed. The key for doing so is to always bear in mind the essential principle behind the BPS guidelines which is that 'the investigation should be considered from the standpoint of all participants; foreseeable threats to their psychological well-being, health, values or dignity should be eliminated'. In other words, researchers should try to anticipate and avoid anything the might possibly upset any participant.

Most potential ethical issues can be avoided by gaining informed consent from potential participants at the outset. Researchers can get informed consent by using an information sheet and a consent form. The information sheet should explain the objectives of the study and what it will involve. Anything that might influence the participant's willingness to take part should be disclosed. The participants should also be given the opportunity to question the researcher about the information or the study. If participants do not have this full information then the study will involve some element of deception. The information sheet also provides an opportunity to stress to the participants that they can withdraw from the study at any time. All participants should be guaranteed anonymity and the information sheet should stress that data will remain confidential.

The consent form should be signed by the participant only when they have read and understood the information sheet and have had an opportunity to ask questions. Note that it is not enough for the participant to have simply *read* the information sheet, they should understand it. Thus extra safeguards should be in place if the research involves participants who may have problems understanding the information, for example children. In this case the information should be written in a clear and understandable way, and the consent form should be signed by the child and a parent or guardian.

Psychologists frequently face a dilemma; they want to give full information about a study but they do not want to cause demand characteristics. Often full disclosure would reduce internal validity. This means researchers do not give all of the details of the study and thus introduce an element of deception. The BPS recognises that it may be impossible to study some psychological phenomena without withholding some information or misleading participants. If researchers believe this is the case for their study they should first look for alternatives. When there is no alternative then they have a duty to inform participants about the true nature of the study at the earliest stage. The participant should be given the right to withdraw their data or to give retrospective informed consent. In some cases it is possible to get participants' permission to deceive them. If participants are taking part in a number of studies they can be asked in advance about the type of studies they are willing to take part in and if they would mind being deceived for the duration of the study. If they agree, they have given prior general consent.

Following any study participants should be debriefed. This serves three functions:

- It should be used to complete the participants' understanding of the study.
- It allows the researcher to monitor any unforeseen negative effects of the study.
- The debriefing should be used to find out if anything has upset or disturbed the participant.

The participant should leave in the same state as they entered. So if, for example, the study raised the anxiety levels of the participant then the debriefing should be used to lower their anxiety.

Researchers have a responsibility to protect participants from physical and mental harm. If they suspect the study is causing any harm (e.g. undue stress, anxiety or anger) then they should terminate the research even when the participant has not asked to withdraw.

█ Link

The suggested information sheet and consent form are available for owners of this book to download from www.nelsonthornes.com/ psychology_answers.

Finally, researchers should be aware that the ideas, feelings or reactions of their participants may be different from theirs. The BPS points out that researchers should 'recognise that, in our multi-cultural and multi-ethnic society and where investigations involve individuals of different ages, gender and social background, the investigators may not have sufficient knowledge of the implications of any investigation for the participants'. Researchers should consult representatives of groups that they intend to study to check for any ethical implications.

Key points

- The BPS has published a code of ethics which gives guidelines for research with human participants.

- Many ethical issues can be avoided by using a good information sheet and consent form. This allows participants to give informed consent.

- Information sheets should also inform participants about their right to withdraw at any point and of their right to confidentiality.

- Research with children requires consent from parents or guardians.

- Deception should be avoided whenever possible. When it is used researchers should seek prior general consent or retrospective informed consent.

- Participants should be debriefed after a study.

- Researchers should protect participants from physical or psychological harm throughout the study.

Summary questions

11 Two psychologists decided to investigate the influence of group size on bystander apathy. They arranged for participants to wait for a study in a waiting room. In one condition the participants each waited alone. In the other the participant believed they were waiting in a group of three, but the other two people were confederates of the researcher. After being in the waiting room for two minutes the participants saw an actor walk through the room. As soon as the actor was out of sight the participants heard a crash and a cry. The researchers recorded the number of participants who went to help in each condition and the speed of any response.

In the account above there are a number of ethical issues that have not been addressed by the psychologists.

a   Identify four of these issues.

b   Suggest how to deal with the issues.

12 The information sheet and consent form (as described on page 527) were designed for adults. What changes would you make if the participants of the study were eight-year-old children?

Probability and significance

▨ Key terms

Probability: a numerical measure of chance. It represents how likely it is that something will happen.

▨ Introduction

We use common phrases such as 'a million to one' or 'fifty-fifty' to refer to the likelihood of something happening. This type of estimate of chance is about **probability**. Science also deals with probabilities. When psychologists analyse their results they are interested in how likely it was that their results were due to chance.

▨ Probability

Probability, or p, in science is expressed as a number between 0 and 1, where 0 means an event definitely will not happen and 1 means an event definitely will happen. The reason that p is between 0 and 1 is the way probability is calculated. To calculate the probability that a particular outcome will occur, it has to be divided by the number of possible outcomes.

$$\text{probability} = \frac{\text{number of particular outcomes}}{\text{number of possible outcomes}}$$

For example, what is the probability of getting a head (one particular outcome) when you toss a coin? The result could be head or tail, giving two possible outcomes. Thus the probability of getting a head is one divided by two, which in decimals is 0.5.

Sometimes probability is expressed as a percentage not a decimal. It is easy to convert between the two. To convert a probability expressed as a decimal to a percentage, multiply it by 100. Thus 0.5 becomes 50 per cent, 0.05 becomes 5 per cent. Conversely, to convert a probability expressed as a percentage to a decimal, divide by 100. So 95 per cent is 0.95 expressed as a decimal.

Another important concept in understanding how psychologists interpret their findings is conditional probability. This is the probability of an event if something else occurs. For example, there is a particular probability of an individual from a population developing lung cancer. The probability is much greater *if* an individual smokes. This greater probability is conditional upon smoking.

▨ Statistical significance

Scientists try to generalise the findings from their sample to populations. However, as already noted, samples are prone to error. The role of statistical tests is to find out how likely it is that what we have found in our sample accurately reflects what happens in the population. For example, imagine we study aggression in a sample of 10-year-old boys. We find in our sample that there is a relationship between the amount of time spent playing aggressive video games and the level of aggression in play. But, is this true of all 10-year-old boys? We can never be certain, but statistical tests tell us how probable this is.

Key terms

Null hypothesis: there is no difference or relationship between variables in the population.

Level of significance: the level at which the null hypothesis is accepted or rejected.

Type 1 error: the error that occurs when the null hypothesis is rejected but it should have been retained.

Type 2 error: the error that occurs when the null hypothesis is retained but it is false.

Studies are designed to test hypotheses. Dancey and Reidy (2004) describe hypothesis testing as a competition between two hypotheses. These are the alternate (also called the research or experimental) hypothesis (H_1) and the **null hypothesis** (H_0). Alternate hypotheses state that there will be a relationship between variables (in correlations) or a difference between groups or conditions (in experiments). Null hypotheses state that there will be no such relationship or difference in the *population*. After doing the study we use statistical tests to calculate the probability of getting a pattern of results *if* they did not exist in the population (i.e. a conditional probability). If this probability is small enough it suggests that the pattern of findings in the sample is unlikely to be due to chance. We can infer that they are likely to reflect the pattern in the population and we can reject the null hypothesis.

This raises the question of what is a small enough probability? The level at which this is set is known as the **level of significance**. In psychology, the generally accepted level is 0.05 or 5 per cent. This is expressed as $p = 0.05$. In this context p is a conditional probability; it is the likelihood of getting the findings if the null hypothesis is true. Anything less than 0.05 is described as significant; it is unlikely that the null hypothesis is true. Anything above 0.05 is not significant as we cannot reject the null hypothesis.

Type 1 and Type 2 errors

The choice of 0.05 as the normal level of significance in psychology is not arbitrary but is designed to balance the risk of **Type 1** and **Type 2 errors**. When we do a test and find a p value that is less than our level of significance we reject the null hypothesis. We accept the alternate hypothesis that a variable had an effect on another or that there was a relationship. However, if there is actually no such effect or relationship, we have made a Type 1 error. At the 0.05 or 5 per cent level there is a one in twenty chance of making a Type 1 error. Sometimes errors are made in the other direction. When we do a test and find a p value that is greater than our level of significance we accept the null hypothesis. We reject out alternate hypothesis and suggest there is no effect of a variable or relationship between variables. However, if there is an effect or relationship, we have made a Type 2 error.

Dancey and Reidy (2004) give an example of a likely Type 1 error. In 1991 Richards and French reported an effect of anxiety on the recall of negative words. However, they failed to replicate the findings in subsequent studies. They concluded that the findings of the first study were spurious, or a Type 1 error. This emphasises the need for replication in science.

The 0.05 level of significance is regarded as the level that, for most studies, balances the risk of getting Type 1 and 2 errors. However, there are occasions when psychologists decide to use a different level of significance in their studies. Sometimes the 0.01 (or 1 per cent) level is preferred to the 0.05 level. A common reason for using 0.01 is that the findings are likely to be controversial or raise ethical dilemmas. In such studies the researcher would want to be more stringent and only present the findings as significant if there was a very small probability that the null hypothesis was true. Another reason might be that the study is theoretically very important.

Key points

- Probability is a measure of how likely it is that something will happen.

- Statistics are used to test the probability that the null hypothesis is true.

- The null hypothesis is that there is no relationship or difference between variables in the population.

- If the probability of the null hypothesis being correct is lower than the level of significance then it can be rejected.

- Type 1 errors occur when the null hypothesis is rejected but it should not have been.

- Type 2 errors occur when the null hypothesis is accepted but it should not have been.

Summary questions

1 What is the probability of getting a six when you throw a dice? Express the answer as a decimal and percentage.

2 What does $p = 0.05$ mean? Explain why the 0.05 level of significance is normally used in psychology.

3 Explain why a 0.01 level of significance may result in a Type 2 error. When would a 0.01 level of significance be used?

4 Describe one way of checking whether a Type 1 error has been made.

Dealing with quantitative data

Key terms

Descriptive statistics: techniques used to summarise data.

Inferential statistics: the use of statistical tests to draw conclusions about the populations that the samples came from.

Range: the difference between the highest and lowest score in a set of data.

Standard deviation: a measure of dispersion that indicates the 'spread' or dispersion of the data around a central value.

Link

Remind yourself of the measures of central tendency, what they are, their advantages and disadvantages by looking at the *AQA Psychology A AS* student book, page 124, Table 3. Alternatively the table is available to download from www.nelsonthornes.com/psychology_answers.

Link

Remind yourself of the measures of dispersion, when they should be used and their advantages and disadvantages by looking at the *AQA Psychology A AS* student book, page 127, Table 8. Alternatively the table is available to download from www.nelsonthornes.com/psychology_answers.

The raw data that is obtained by a study is difficult to understand and interpret without organising it in some way. Just looking at the data is not enough to determine whether two sets of scores are different (in experiments) or whether they are related in any way (in correlations). There are typically two stages of dealing with the data:

■ Summarising the data. The data needs to be summarised using measures of central tendency and measures of dispersion. Differences or relationships are often best illustrated when data is displayed graphically. The summary data that is produced is called **descriptive statistics**.

■ Analysing the data. With quantitative data this second stage requires the use of a statistical test. Researchers have to choose the right test for the study, use the test to analyse the data and then interpret the statistical findings. The analysis of data using tests is called **inferential statistics**.

Summarising data

Measures of central tendency are measures that tell us where the middle or what the most frequently occurring values are in our data. These measures are used to compare the data from two sets of scores (two groups or two conditions). The three measures of central tendency are mean, median and mode.

Measures of dispersion are used to describe the spread of scores or how much variation there is around a central score. The measures that are used in psychology are **range** and **standard deviation**.

Graphs are a very useful way of summarising data. These visual representations allow psychologists to see patterns in the data. Different types of graph are used for different types of data. The three that are most useful are the histogram, bar chart and scattergram.

A histogram is a way of showing the distribution of a whole set of data. For example, Figure 1 shows the IQ scores of a large number of students.

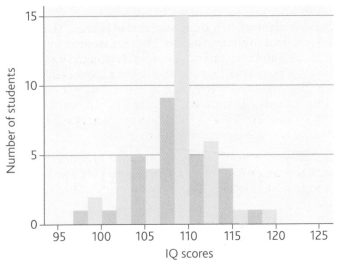

Fig. 1 *Histogram*

Note that the bars are all joined and that the width of each bar is equal. This is because they represent a continuous scale. The column area represents the frequency of the score. The greater the frequency the higher the column (in Figure 1 109 was the most common). Finally all scores should be represented even if they are empty.

Bar charts are a useful way of showing summary statistics. This could be the means or medians of groups but could also be percentages or ratios. As the scale is not continuous the bars in this type of graph should be separated. Also, not all categories need to be put onto the x-axis. You can decide the best way to show the data.

Scattergrams are used to show the relationship between two variables. On a scattergram the two variables are marked on the two axes and then each case is marked on the graph. Scattergrams are a powerful way of demonstrating both the strength and direction of correlations (see Figure 3).

Fig. 2 *Bar chart*

- The more the points cluster around a straight line the stronger the correlation.
- If the line formed by the points goes from lower left to upper right it indicates a positive correlation.
- If the line goes from upper left to lower right it indicates a negative correlation.

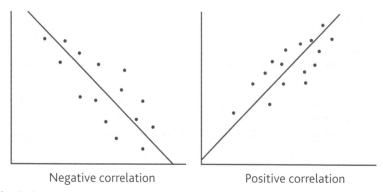

| Negative correlation | Positive correlation |

Fig. 3 *Scattergrams*

Choosing a statistical test

Statistical tests are used to calculate the probability (or how likely it is) that the results obtained in a study were due to chance. There are many statistical tests that psychologists use. They are grouped into two types: **parametric tests** and **non-parametric tests**. Parametric tests can only be used when a number of criteria about the data are fulfilled. One of the key criteria is the level of measurement of the data. Parametric tests require **interval data** or **ratio data**. Most non-parametric tests can use interval/ratio or **ordinal data** and some deal with **nominal data**. All of the tests described below are non-parametric.

The four tests needed to analyse non-parametric quantitative data are Spearman's rho, Mann-Whitney, Wilcoxon and chi-squared. How do you choose which test to use? This is based on the answers to three questions:

1 Do I want to investigate differences or relationships? If your study was an experiment then you will be investigating differences between two sets of scores. If your study was a correlation then you will be investigating relationships.

Link

Review probability and statistical significance on pages 529–30.

Key terms

Parametric tests: these can only be used when the data from a study meets a number of criteria including the level of measurement and the distribution of the data.

Non-parametric tests: these can be used when any of the criteria for a parametric test are not met.

Interval data: this is obtained when there are equal intervals on a measurement scale.

Ratio data: this is similar to interval data in that there are equal intervals across the scale but in addition there is a true zero point..

Ordinal data: this is obtained when information or scores are put in order (first, second, third, etc.). Whenever data is ranked it is ordinal.

Nominal data: this is obtained when information is put into categories or just named.

2　What sort of data do I have? Not all quantitative data is the same and research can generate different types of data. These different types of data represent different levels of measurement. Four levels of measurement are recognised:

   a　Nominal data, e.g. imagine a study of reaction time where 10 participants are classified as fast if they beat the buzzer or slow if they do not. We find that six are fast and four are slow. This data is nominal.

   b　Ordinal data, e.g. if we do the same study of reaction time but this time our 10 participants are ranked in order from fastest to slowest, we now have ordinal data. This data is more useful because we now know the relative positions of our 10 participants.

   c　Interval data, e.g. measuring temperature in degrees Celsius is a good example of an interval scale. A change of one degree is the same no matter where on the scale it occurs. The difference between 10°C and 11°C is one degree; the difference between 110°C and 111°C is also one degree. Using the interval level of measurement we can give scores rather than putting information in order. For example, if in a test of memory we found Lisa remembered 15 words, Toni remembered 12 and Kathy remembered eight, we have interval data.

   d　Ratio data, e.g. if we repeated our test of reaction times but we used an accurate way of recording time, we would have ratio data. Timing starts from zero so that a person who reacts in 400 ms (milliseconds) takes twice as long as someone who reacts in 200 ms.

For most statistical tests the difference between interval data and ratio data does not matter.

3　What type of design did I use? Was the experiment a repeated measure or independent groups design?

Use the questions on the following flow chart to guide your choice of test.

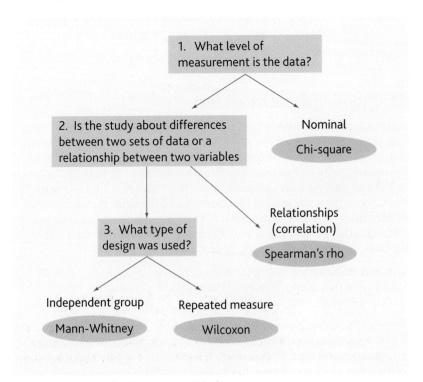

Fig. 4 *Decision chart for choosing a statistical test*

▨ Using statistical tests

One- or two-tailed

The results of tests are compared to critical values from the appropriate statistical table. These give different values depending on whether the test is a **one-tailed** or **two-tailed**. This depends on whether the hypothesis is directional or not. Directional hypotheses are one-tailed, and non-directional hypotheses are two-tailed.

It is crucial to understand whether a hypothesis is directional or not when interpreting the results of tests. For correlations this is simple: if the hypothesis predicts a positive or a negative correlation then it is directional. If it just states 'a correlation', it is non-directional. In experiments it can be more difficult as there are many ways of stating a directional hypothesis. Directional hypotheses are signalled by words and phrases such as 'more than', 'slower', 'fewer', etc. In other words, directional hypotheses give the direction of difference but non-directional hypotheses just predict a difference.

Ranking

All of the tests below, except chi-squared, require data to be ranked. This involves giving a number to each score. This is usually done in ascending order, so the lowest score is given rank 1, the next rank 2 and so on. If two scores are the same then they share two ranks and are given the average rank. The two participants with 12 in the example have ranks 3 and 4 so they are both given 3.5. Note that the next-highest score, 13, is given rank 5. Similarly, if there are three identical scores they are given the average of the three ranks they occupy. In the example three participants have 15 and they occupy rank 6, 7 and 8 so all are assigned 7.

Table 1 *Example of ranking*

Participant	Score	Rank of score
1	15	7
2	13	5
3	18	9
4	12	3.5
5	15	7
6	11	2
7	12	3.5
8	20	10
9	10	1
10	15	7

Spearman's rho

Spearman's rho (or Spearman's rank order correlation coefficient) is used to correlate pairs of scores that are at least an ordinal level of measurement (which means they can be ordinal, interval or ratio). It is based on comparing the ranks of pairs of scores. If these ranks are very similar then it indicates a positive correlation. If they are opposites then it indicates a negative correlation.

▧ **Key terms**

One-tailed test: used with a directional hypothesis that states what the direction of difference or correlation will be.

Two-tailed test: used for a non-directional hypothesis that states that there will be a difference or correlation.

AQA Examiner's tip

It is very easy to misinterpret the results of a test because of confusion over whether it is one-tailed or two-tailed. The key to understanding this is to look at whether the hypothesis is predicting a difference or correlation (two-tailed) or *the* difference or correlation (one-tailed).

■ **Hint**

There should be as many ranks as there are scores. If you are ranking a set of 20 scores there should be 20 ranks.

The formula for Spearman's rho is:

$$r_s = 1 - \frac{6\Sigma d^2}{N(N^2 - 1)}$$

Where N is the number of pairs being correlated, Σ means 'sum of' and d^2 is the square of the differences in rank. This might seem complicated, but as you can see from the example below, it is actually very easy to calculate. In the example the hypothesis was that there will be a positive correlation between test scores and the amount of time spent studying for the test.

Table 2 *Example of a Spearman's rho analysis*

Participant	Study time	Rank	Test score	Rank	d	d^2
1	100	10	60	7	3	9
2	25	2	47	4	−2	4
3	95	9	70	10	−1	1
4	60	5	53	6	−1	1
5	10	1	41	1	0	0
6	75	6	51	5	1	1
7	80	7	61	8	−1	1
8	45	3	44	2	1	1
9	55	4	45	3	−1	1
10	85	8	61	9	1	1
						$\Sigma d^2 = 20$

In the example, N (number of pairs of scores) is 10 and Σd^2 is 20.

$$r_s = 1 - \frac{6 \times 20}{10(100 - 1)}$$

$$= 1 - \frac{120}{990}$$

$$= 1 - 0.12$$

$$= 0.88$$

Calculation

Spearman's rho is calculated by using the following steps:

- Place the data into columns as in the example.
- Rank each set of scores separately. For each set give the lowest score rank 1 and work upwards (ascending order).
- Find the difference between the ranks for each pair of scores (d column).
- Square each of the d values (d^2 column).
- Add all the d^2 values to get Σd^2.
- Use the formula to calculate rho.

Interpretation

In the example the correlation coefficient was +0.88. This seems to indicate a strong positive correlation, but is it significant at the 0.05 level of significance? To establish this, the calculated value of rho has to be compared to a value from the Spearman's rho critical values table (page 569). If the observed value is equal to or more than the critical value, the null hypothesis can be rejected. When you consult the table the first step is to establish which set of values you are looking at, levels of significance for one- or two-tailed. In our example the hypothesis needs a one-tailed because it predicted the direction of the relationship. The 0.05 level of significance for a one-tailed test is shown in column 1. There were 10 pairs of scores so N = 10. The critical value of rho is therefore 0.564.

As the calculated value of rho (0.88) is higher than the critical value (0.564) the null hypothesis can be rejected. Thus we can report 'there was a significant positive correlation between study time and test results (rho = 0.88, N = 10, p <0.05, one-tailed)'.

Caution

Be aware that the accuracy of the Spearman's rho test is reduced if there are tied ranks. The presence of tied ranks could lead to errors in the interpretation of the results. However, if there are only a few tied ranks the effect is small.

Mann-Whitney

The Mann-Whitney U test is a test of difference. It can be used when the data is at least ordinal (which means the data can be ordinal, interval or ratio) and an independent group design has been used.

The formula for Mann-Whitney is:

$$U = N_1 N_2 + \frac{N_1 (N_1 + 1)}{2} - T_1$$

Where N_1 represents the number in the smallest sample and N_2 represents the number in the largest sample. The value of T is taken from the sum of the ranks of the smaller group. The value of U does depend on which T value is used; therefore, two values of U should be calculated (U and U') and the smaller one is used. The formula looks complicated but Mann-Whitney is fairly easy to calculate. In the example a teacher is looking to see if a new maths scheme has had an effect on children's maths scores. The hypothesis is that children on the new scheme will score higher than children who are not on the scheme.

Table 3

Participant (no scheme)	Maths score	Rank	Participant (new scheme)	Maths score	Rank
1	11	6.5	11	14	12
2	12	8.5	12	13	10
3	9	3.5	13	12	8.5
4	8	2	14	16	16.5
5	11	6.5	15	14	12
6	14	12	16	15	14.5
7	10	5	17	19	18
8	7	1	18	20	19
9	15	14.5	19	16	16.5
10	9	3.5			
					Σ ranks for Condition 2 = 127

Hint

Remember that Spearman's rho is used when:

▨ testing for a correlation

▨ the data is at least ordinal (i.e. it is ordinal, interval or ratio).

The accuracy of the test is reduced if there are many tied ranks.

Example of a Mann-Whitney U analysis

$$U = (9 \times 10) + \frac{9(9+1)}{2} - 127$$
$$= 90 + 45 - 127$$
$$= 8$$
$$U' = (9 \times 10) - 8$$
$$= 82$$

The smallest value is 8 so this is the U value.

Calculation

Mann-Whitney U can be found using the following steps:

- Put the data in columns as in the example.
- Rank *all* of the scores in ascending order, regardless of which group they are in.
- Sum the ranks for the smaller sample or either sample if they are equal. This value is T.
- To calculate U substitute this value of T together with N_1 and N_2 in the formula.
- Calculate U' using the formula $U' = N_1 N_2 - U$.
- Select the smaller of U or U' as your observed value of U.

Interpretation

In the example the value of U was 8. This has to be compared to a value from the Mann-Whitney critical values tables (pages 564–7). If the observed value of U is equal to or less than the critical value, the null hypothesis can be rejected. To find the correct critical value we need to know three things:

- What is the level of significance used in the study? In our example there is no need to use anything but the normal 0.05 level.
- Is the test one- or two-tailed? In our example the hypothesis was directional (children using the maths scheme would get higher scores). Knowing these two factors allows you to select the correct Mann-Whitney table (in this case, Table 2d, page 567).
- Finally, N_1 and N_2 are used to select the value from the table. In the example this was 9 and 10 so the critical value is 24.

Since the observed value is less than the critical value the null hypothesis can be rejected. We could report that children using the maths scheme had significantly higher scores than children who did not use the maths scheme ($U = 8$, $N_1 = 9$, $N_2 = 10$, $p < 0.05$, one-tailed).

Caution

Note the procedure for calculating Mann-Whitney U described here is for samples of less than 20 only. When the sample is larger a different formula is used.

Wilcoxon

The Wilcoxon matched pairs sign test is a test of difference. It can be used when the data is at least ordinal (which means it can be ordinal, interval or ratio) and a repeated measure design has been used.

In the example a researcher has investigated the recall of neutral words and emotionally threatening words. The hypothesis was that the participants will recall fewer emotionally threatening words than neutral words.

Hint

Remember that Mann-Whitney is used when:

- testing for a difference
- there is an independent group design
- the data is at least ordinal (i.e. it is ordinal, interval or ratio).

Table 4 *Example of a Wilcoxon analysis*

Participant	Neutral words	Emotionally threatening words	Difference	Rank order
1	14	15	−1	1.5
2	18	16	+2	3.5
3	19	19	0	omitted
4	20	14	+6	9
5	16	19	−3	5.5
6	15	10	+5	8
7	20	16	+4	7
8	18	15	+3	5.5
9	19	18	+1	1.5
10	20	18	+2	3.5

Sum of the ranks that correspond to the + sign:

$$3.5 + 9 + 8 + 7 + 5.5 + 1.5 + 3.5 = 38$$

Sum of the ranks that correspond to the − sign:

$$1.5 + 5.5 = 7$$

$T = 7$ (as it is the smaller value).

Calculation

- Put the data in columns as in the example.
- Calculate the difference between each set of scores. It is important to note the direction of difference.
- Rank the differences ignoring whether they are positive or negative. Zero differences are disregarded.
- Find the sum of the ranks that correspond to the positive differences.
- Find the sum of the ranks that correspond to the negative differences.
- The smaller of these is T, the notation for the Wilcoxon statistic.

Interpretation

In the example the value of T was 7. This has to be compared to a value from the Wilcoxon critical values tables (see Table 3, page 568). If the observed value of T is equal to or less than the critical value the null hypothesis can be rejected. In order to find the critical value we need to know:

- What is the level of significance used in the study? In our example there is no need to use anything but the normal 0.05 level.
- Is the test one- or two-tailed? In our example the hypothesis was directional as it was predicted that fewer emotionally threatening words would be recalled.
- The number of pairs of scores that have been ranked (N). This may not be all of the pairs in the sample since pairs that have a zero difference are not ranked. In the example the sample was 10, but one had a difference of zero so N is 9.

The critical value of T when $N = 9$ for a one-tailed test at $p = 0.05$ is 8. Since the observed value of T is less than the critical value, the null hypothesis can be rejected. Significantly fewer emotionally threatening words were recalled than neutral words ($T = 8$, $N = 9$, $p < 0.05$, one-tailed).

Hint

Remember that Wilcoxon is used when:

- testing for a difference
- there is a repeated measure design
- the data is at least ordinal (i.e. it is ordinal, interval or ratio).

Chi-squared

The chi-squared (χ^2) test is a test of association that is used when the data is nominal and is expressed as frequencies (i.e. numbers in each category). It cannot be used with percentages or averages. The frequency data must be independent so that something recorded in one category cannot appear in another. In the example below, some students are investigating the hypothesis that choice of subject is associated with personality. They have used a test of introversion and extroversion. Note that each student can only appear once. If a student studies science and is extroverted there is only one box they can be in. Chi-squared works by comparing the observed frequencies in each box with 'expected' frequencies. These are the frequencies you would have if there was no association between variables (i.e. if studying art was not associated with extroversion). The example showed here uses a 2×2 table. However χ^2 can be used for more categories. For example, we could add sports students to our study and have a 3×2 table.

The formula for χ^2 is:

$$\chi^2 = \sum \frac{(O - E)^2}{E}$$

Example of a chi-squared analysis

Table 5 *Results of the study of art and science students*

	Art students	Science students
Extroverted	19	10
Introverted	11	15

Table 6 *Row and column totals*

	Art students	Science students	Row total
Extroverted	[A] 19	[B] 10	29
Introverted	[C] 11	[D] 15	26
Column total	30	25	Grand total: 55

1 Expected frequencies for boxes A, B, C and D.

$$\text{Expected frequency (E)} = \frac{(\text{row total} \times \text{column total})}{\text{grand total}}$$

Box A
$$E = \frac{(29 \times 30)}{55}$$
$$= 15.82$$

Box B
$$E = \frac{(29 \times 25)}{55}$$
$$= 13.18$$

Box C
$$E = \frac{(26 \times 30)}{55}$$
$$= 14.18$$

Box D
$$E = \frac{(26 \times 25)}{55}$$
$$= 11.82$$

2 Calculating $\dfrac{(O - E)^2}{E}$ for each box

$$\text{Box A} = \dfrac{(19 - 15.82)^2}{15.82}$$
$$= 0.64$$

$$\text{Box B} = \dfrac{(10 - 13.18)^2}{13.18}$$
$$= 0.77$$

$$\text{Box C} = \dfrac{(11 - 14.18)^2}{14.18}$$
$$= 0.71$$

$$\text{Box D} = \dfrac{(15 - 11.82)^2}{11.82}$$
$$= 0.86$$
$$\Sigma = 0.64 + 0.77 + 0.71 + 0.86$$
$$= 2.98$$

Calculation

The stages to calculate χ^2 are:

▥ Put the frequencies in a table and calculate the row and column totals.
▥ Calculate the grand total. This is the total number of cases and is either the sum of the row totals or the column totals (but *not* both).
▥ Calculate the expected frequencies for each box in the table ((row total × column total)/grand total).
▥ Calculate $(O - E)^2/E$ for each box.
▥ Add all of the values together to give the χ^2 value. In the example it is 3.22.

Interpretation

To interpret this we have to compare our value with the value in the critical values table (Table 1, page 563). If the observed value is equal to or greater than the critical value, we can reject the null hypothesis. To find the critical value we need to know three things:

▥ Is the test is one- or two-tailed? A one-tailed test can only be used for a 2 × 1 table with a directional hypothesis. *All* others are two-tailed.
▥ The degrees of freedom and the level of significance. The degrees of freedom is calculated from the number of boxes with data in them in the table.

Degrees of freedom (df) = (number of rows – 1) (number of columns – 1)

In this case:

$$df = (2 - 1)(2 - 1) = 1$$

▥ The level of significance. As in most studies we will use the minimum level of significance of $p = 0.05$.

The critical value for χ^2 for $df = 1$ at the $p = 0.05$ (two-tailed) level of significance is 3.84. As our observed value is less than the critical value, we cannot reject the null hypothesis in this case. There is not a significant association between subject studied and personality.

Hint

Remember that chi-squared is used when:

■ the data is nominal

■ data in each frequency is independent.

The degree of freedom is determined by the number of boxes with data in them.

Most chi-squared tests are two-tailed tests.

Caution

The chi-squared result is prone to Type 1 errors when *expected* frequencies are low. There is debate about how low expected values can be. The rule of thumb is five, but Coolican (2004) suggests that it can be as low as one or two provided the total sample size is more than 20.

Key points

■ Quantitative data should be summarised using descriptive statistics such as measures of central tendency and measures of dispersion. Appropriate graphs provide a good visual summary of the data.

■ There are three key questions to be answered in choosing a statistical test:

  – What is the level of data?

  – Is the study looking for differences or relationships?

  – What type of design was used?

■ In the interpretation of the results of tests the calculated values have to be compared to critical values from tables.

■ Critical values depend on a number of factors that always include the level of significance being used and whether the test is one- or two-tailed.

Summary questions

5 In your own words explain what nominal data is.

6 In your own words explain what ordinal data is.

7 A researcher found a Spearman's correlation coefficient of 0.521 with an *N* value of 20. A positive correlation was predicted. Use Table 4, page 569 to assess whether the results were significant at the $p = 0.05$ level.

8 What statistical test would you use for the following studies?
  a An investigation of whether there is an association between extroversion/introversion in smokers and non-smokers.
  b An experiment to investigate the effect of word length on recall in short-term memory. In one condition the participants were asked to recall short words and in another long words.
  c A study of the relationship between the amount of time that students used a computer revision package and scores on a test.
  d An experiment on cognitive dissonance where participants were asked to rate how enjoyable a task was after lying about the task. Half the participants were paid £1 to lie and the others £20.

Dealing with qualitative data

Key terms

Interpretivist: the view that humans are different from other natural phenomena because of language and self-consciousness. Understanding human experience requires an understanding of the influence of these factors.

Take it further

Compare the approaches described here with the content analysis that you studied in Unit 1 (*AQA Psychology A AS* student book). Would you describe content analysis as being interpretivist?

Introduction

Qualitative research takes an **interpretivist** approach to the understanding of human behaviour. However, within that broad approach there are a variety of ways of collecting and analysing data. Silverman (2006) points out that qualitative research 'covers a wide range of different, even conflicting, activities'. Broadly speaking, it involves an in-depth analysis of people's experiences, beliefs, attitudes, etc. and involves interpretation and thematic analysis of verbal material. It is based on a different philosophy than the quantitative approach. We cannot cover all qualitative techniques here, but we will concentrate on different techniques to the one you studied at AS Level.

Gathering data

The purpose of gathering data for a qualitative study is to get 'rich' data that can be carefully analysed for meaning. This type of data is best collected by semi-structured interviews using open-ended questions, participant observation, focus group discussion or by asking for participants' diaries or notes. A variety of methods might be used in a case study. The type of method used to get the data is linked to the type of analysis and the purpose of the study. The method and purpose of sampling for qualitative research is very different to that for quantitative research. Instead of being a large sample that we are able to 'generalise' to others, qualitative samples tend to be a small, clearly defined group. The sample can involve as few as one participant. Sometimes purposive sampling is used. This involves selecting cases that illustrate some feature or purpose (Silverman, 2006). Qualitative research is about learning from the unique experiences that people have and developing insights from this.

Analysing data

Data collection and analysis are described here as separate activities for ease of description. However, in many methods the two are hard to separate. The research may involve switching from one to the other if the analysis suggests that new data is needed. In turn, more data requires more analysis, etc.

The first stage in any analysis involves organising the data. For any method that involves recording speech this means preparing a transcript. Some types of analysis require only an accurate transcription of the speech; others require details of pauses, intonation, hesitations, etc. The researcher then needs to get to know the data thoroughly. This typically requires reading the transcripts a number of times before there is any attempt at analysis. The next common step is to code the data; however, the reason for and the emphasis of the coding depends upon the type of analysis. There are a number of ways of analysing the data qualitatively including:

- interpretive phenomenological analysis
- grounded theory
- discourse analysis.

Interpretive phenomenological analysis explores how participants make sense of the world. It involves interpreting the meanings that particular events or experiences have for participants (hence phenomenological).

Grounded theory starts with coding each line of text. On further analysis the codes start to combine into larger constructs. These constructs can, in turn, be explored and links between them studied. Any theories that emerge are grounded to the data.

There are various types of discourse analysis but central to them all is the analysis of speech or written discourse. It investigates the social context of discourse and the interaction between speakers.

A common feature of these approaches to qualitative analysis is that they are inductive. Theory develops from the data during the analysis and the researchers avoid having prior assumptions. In contrast, in most quantitative research the data is analysed in terms of existing theory. Another feature is reflexivity. This is when the researcher reflects on how the research activity and the researcher shape the outcome. The researchers acknowledge the role of subjectivity both in the researcher and participant. Again, this contrasts to the assumption of quantitative researchers that it is possible to obtain objective information from participants.

Evaluation of qualitative data

Quantitative data tends to be evaluated in terms of reliability and validity. However, these concepts are difficult to apply to qualitative data. Qualitative data is based on the researcher's interpretation of the participant's subjective experience and is usually an analysis of that experience for that person, at that time in their own culture. As such, the data tends to have high external validity but low internal validity and reliability. However, the concepts of reliability and validity stem from the realist viewpoint taken by quantitative researchers. Qualitative researchers point out that these concepts do not make sense from their viewpoint and should not be used. The research is interpretive, of course other interpretations exist. Robson (2002) suggests that the concept of trustworthiness is a better way of thinking about qualitative data. One way of establishing trustworthiness is to use an external audit (Smith, 2003). This involves a check of the documentation, from transcript to final analysis, by an external party. The documentation should include notes about how any decisions or choices were made, and it acts as an audit trail. Other criteria for evaluating qualitative research might include:

- transferability (can the insights from the research be transferred to help understand similar situations or experience?)
- negative case analysis (exploring cases that do not fit the emerging concepts)
- reflexivity (Henwood and Pidgeon, 1992).

Key points

- Qualitative research stems from a different philosophical viewpoint than quantitative research.
- Qualitative research involves the collection of data that is rich in meaning from a small group of participants.
- This data is transcribed and coded before being carefully and thoroughly analysed.
- Qualitative techniques include interpretive phenomenological analysis, grounded theory and discourse analysis.
- Criteria such as transferability, negative case analysis, reflexivity and whether there is an audit trail are used to evaluate qualitative research.

Summary questions

9 Describe the type of data used in qualitative research.

10 Outline the three initial steps common to most qualitative research.

11 In your own words explain what reflexivity means.

12 Discuss how you would assess a qualitative study.

Reporting psychological investigations

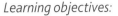

Learning objectives:

- understand the conventions of reporting psychological investigations
- understand the role of each section of psychological reports.

Sections of a report

There is no point in doing psychological research unless the findings are shared with other psychologists. As the research is published it is validated by other psychologists and becomes part of the permanent scientific record. There are conventions for reporting psychological research and these are outlined below. Harris (2008) describes psychological reports as formal documents that are composed of a series of sections. Each section is governed by conventions. Harris notes that these conventions have been developed so that information can be conveyed 'clearly, precisely, efficiently, and concisely'. Table 7 shows the different sections needed in a report. This is a general format for a quantitative report but it may vary slightly in different journals.

Table 7 *Report sections*

Section	Function
Title	To tell the reader what the report is about
Abstract	To provide the reader with a brief summary of the study
Introduction	To introduce the background and rationale of the study
Method	To describe how the study was done
Results	To summarise the findings
Discussion	To discuss the findings and their implications
References	To inform the reader about the sources of information
Appendices	Can be used for detailed information not in the report

The title

The report title is important because it will determine who reads the full report. It should be as concise as possible yet at the same time it should be informative. Anyone reading the title should know exactly what the report is about.

Abstract

The abstract of a scientific report should be a brief (150–200-word) summary of the report. If a psychologist finds a title that looks as if it may be useful, the next step is to read the abstract. The abstract should be a self-contained, clear and concise synopsis of the research question, the method used, the findings and the conclusion.

Introduction

The introduction to a report is designed to introduce the reader to the background to a study, the reasoning behind the study and finally the predictions derived from the hypothesis. The background to a study will be largely past studies and theories that are relevant to the research question. This enables readers to place the study in context. The next part of this section is used to introduce the study and to explain the ideas behind it before finally going on to specific research predictions.

Method

The method section describes how the study was conducted. It should have enough information to allow the study to be replicated. This serves two important functions. Firstly if the method cannot be replicated then the findings cannot be checked to see if they are reliable or if they have ecological validity. Secondly, disagreements amongst psychologists can be about how something has been studied. When we have precise details of the method used we can check to see if the study has internal and external validity or whether there are confounding variables, demand characteristics, sampling errors, etc.

The method section consists of a number of subsections including design, participants, apparatus and/or materials, and procedure.

The design subsection tends to be a brief outline of the method used in the study. It includes the design used (i.e. repeated measure or independent groups), the number of groups or conditions and the variables under investigation. Typically the use of control measures are mentioned here (such as counterbalancing), but the details are given in the procedure.

The participants subsection should describe key features of the participant sample (age range, gender, etc.) and how they were selected. This enables readers to gauge whether the study has population validity.

The procedure should inform the reader precisely how the study was conducted. It should include how participants were allocated, instructions, how data was collected, etc. The procedure should include any detail that might impact on internal validity.

Results

The results section should report the findings of the study clearly and accurately. Typically it is in two sections: descriptive statistics and inferential statistics. Descriptive data such as measures of central tendency and dispersion are displayed in clearly labelled tables so that any differences between groups or conditions can be seen quickly and easily. This is often enhanced with graphs. The inferential statistics are used to analyse the data. Following the analysis the null hypothesis can be rejected or accepted.

Discussion

Discussions begin with a summary of the findings of the results before going on to an exploration of the best explanation of the findings. If the null hypothesis has been rejected it may be that the best explanation is the hypothesis put forward in the introduction, but there may be other factors to consider such as problems with the method, etc. The implications of the research are discussed in the light of the information in the introduction. Harris (2008) suggests that the introduction and discussion should be seen as representing different time periods. The introduction presents the state of knowledge before the study was done and the discussion is about the change in knowledge (if any) following the findings of the study. It shows the progress of scientific knowledge.

References

All of the cited evidence in the rest of the report should appear in an alphabetical list at the end. This gives psychologists reading the report an evidence trail. It may be that some of the assumptions of the present study are based on previous work. The reference section allows them to check this.

Qualitative reports

The types of report for quantitative and qualitative research are different, particularly in the introduction, method and results section. At the end of the introduction, qualitative research does not have specific hypotheses but does have aims of the research. In qualitative research the design subsection of the method is not relevant, but a description of the analytical method is. The biggest difference is in the results section. Since qualitative research does not use numbers the results cannot include descriptive or inferential statistics. Instead the results will typically report on the analytic themes using supporting quotations.

Key points

- The reporting of psychological research is governed by conventions that ensure that information is communicated clearly and efficiently.

- Psychological reports consist of a number of sections: title, abstract, introduction, method, results, discussion and references.

- Qualitative research has different conventions, particularly in the method and results sections.

Summary questions

13 Explain why the abstract of a report is written last.

14 What is the final part of the introduction? Explain why.

15 What should descriptive statistics do? What do inferential statistics enable the researcher to do?

16 Outline three functions of the discussion and explain why these are important.

Research methods end of topic

▥ How science works: practical activities

Activity 1

There is some evidence that we recognise familiar faces from the configuration of the features (nose, eyes, mouth) rather than the shape of the head etc. Based on this, some psychologists put forward the hypothesis that famous faces should be easier to recognise when they are upright than when they are inverted, since inverted faces represent a different configuration.

▦ Select an appropriate method and design to investigate the hypothesis.

▦ How would you operationally define the IV and DV?

▦ Describe how you would address all ethical issues.

▦ What measures should be taken to improve external reliability?

▦ What measures should be taken to improve internal validity?

▦ What measures should be taken to improve external validity?

Activity 2

The data in Table 8 is from a study of the effect of face inversion on recognition of famous faces (see Activity 1). Data is from an independent group design and the researcher put forward a directional hypothesis that fewer inverted faces would be recalled.

Table 8 *Results from Activity 1*

Upright group condition	6	9	16	15	12	9	17	11	15	7
Inverted group condition	8	12	4	5	5	15	7	13	14	7

▦ Draw up a table to present a summary of appropriate descriptive statistics.

▦ Use the decision chart on page 534 to choose the appropriate statistical test.

▦ Use the step-by-step instructions to do the test.

▦ Use the appropriate critical value tables to decide whether the results are significant at the 0.05 level.

▦ Write an abstract for the study.

Further reading and weblinks

Bordens, K.S. and Abbott, B.B. (2008) *Research Design and Methods: A Processing Approach.* New York: McGraw Hill.

This book covers everything in this section in detail except for qualitative analysis.

Coolican, H. (2004) *Research Methods and Statistics in Psychology* (4th edn). London: Hodder & Stoughton.

This is a very accessible book that explains how to collect, analyse and report data for both quantitative and qualitative investigations.

Dyer, C. (2006) *Research in Psychology: A Practical Guide to Methods and Statistics.* Oxford: Blackwell.

This is a good concise guide to quantitative and qualitative research.

Harris, P. (2008) *Designing and Reporting Experiments in Psychology* (3rd edn). Maidenhead: Open University Press.

This book focuses on the design of experiments but the detailed explanation of the function of each section of the report is applicable to all quantitative research.

Smith, J.A. (2003) *Qualitative Methods in Psychology: A Practical Guide to Research Methods.* London: Sage.

This is an advanced textbook but one of the few that offers practical advice on qualitative research.

www.bps.org.uk. The website of the British Psychological Association. Check here for the latest guidelines on ethical research. You can subscribe to the BPS Research Digest from the following page: www.bps.org.uk/publications/rd/rd_home.cfm. Every two weeks you will be sent a round-up of some of the most interesting research in psychology.

www.parliament.uk./post/pn182.pdf. The Parliamentary Office of Science and Technology report on peer review. It outlines both the benefits and potential problems of the peer-review system.

www.thepsychologist.org.uk (click on the Archive link). This is the archive of *The Psychologist* published by the BPS. It deals with all aspects of psychology including research methods.

Remember, for all questions that assess analysis and evaluation there is a need to include reference to relevant approaches, issues and debates. Overall, in a question there will be roughly a third of the marks for showing knowledge and understanding of relevant theories, concepts and studies, and two-thirds for demonstrating effective, well-structured analysis and commentary/evaluation. Look in the Examination skills section at the end of the book for further help on how to approach the exam.

Psychopathology

1   **(a)** Outline clinical characteristics of schizophrenia.   *(5 marks)*

(b) 'Diagnosis is a process whereby a disease is identified and allocated to a category on the basis of signs and symptoms. Any classification system will be of little use unless practitioners can agree with each other when making a diagnosis.'
Gelder *et al.*, 1989

Discuss the reliability and validity of classification and diagnosis of schizophrenia.   *(10 marks)*

(c) Outline and evaluate **one** biological therapy for the treatment of schizophrenia. Refer to research evidence in your answer.   *(10 marks)*

2   Recent National Health Service (NHS) policy and guidelines support the increased provision of psychological therapies as treatments for anxiety disorders. However, such therapies are not without their criticisms and biological treatments have also shown themselves to have a role to play in the treatment of anxiety disorders.

Outline and evaluate psychological therapies as treatments of anxiety disorders.   *(25 marks)*

3   The biological model sees mental disorders as being physical illnesses caused by underlying physiological processes in the body. However, the perception of mental disorders as being equivalent to physical illnesses has proven very controversial.

Outline and evaluate **one or more** biological explanations for depression.
Your evaluation should refer to research evidence.   *(25 marks)*

In Question 1(b) to access the full range of marks candidates must discuss both reliability and validity. For 1(c), of the 20 marks, 4 marks will be for the outline and 16 marks for the evaluation.

The stimulus material supplied at the beginning of Question 3 is there merely to guide candidates with their answers and there is no requirement to directly address it. The actual question needs an answer that contains both an outline and an evaluation and care should be taken that both of these elements are fulfilled. It should also be kept in mind that the evaluation is worth more marks than the outline and therefore that requirement should be the main concern. A common mistake is to spend far too much time constructing an outline and then hurriedly tagging on a brief evaluation.

Psychology in action Miriam was very close to her mother Anne, but recently Ann died and Miriam has been attending a spiritualist meeting in order to try and make psychic contact with her dead mother. Friends and relatives have advised Miriam against this, as they perceive spiritualism as being pseudoscientific and having no basis in fact.

4 **(a)** With reference to the above situation describe issues of pseudoscience and scientific fraud. *(9 marks)*

(b) Evaluate research into belief in psychic mediumship. *(16 marks)*

5 **(a)** Outline **one** explanation for gambling addiction. *(5 marks)*

(b) Explain the role of the media in addictive behaviour. *(10 marks)*

(c) Outline and evaluate **one** model of prevention associated with reducing addictive behaviour. *(10 marks)*

6 Compare social psychological and evolutionary explanations for the attraction of celebrity. Refer to research evidence in your answer. *(25 marks)*

AQA Examiner's tip Question 4 is an example of a parted question. Part (a) requires just a description of issues that relate to pseudoscience and scientific fraud. Therefore any material offered as an evaluation of these issues is irrelevant, gaining no credit, and would have wasted valuable time that could have been spent on creating other creditworthy material. There is also a requirement in part (a) to make reference to the stimulus material when constructing an answer. Part (b) does require an evaluation, but this should be focused entirely on research into belief in psychic mediumship to gain credit. There is no requirement to provide an outline of research here and therefore the material offered should fit this requirement, as descriptive material will earn no credit. To gain access to the higher band of marks it is necessary in part (b) to include material on issues, debates and/or approaches.

Research methods

Many children in Scotland now have the opportunity to have all of their lessons in Gaelic from when they begin nursery education right through to the end of their primary school education. A team of researchers wanted to investigate what effect this would have on the children's learning of English. Using a school that had both nursery and primary classes and provided education in both Gaelic and English, 20 children were randomly selected from each year group, 10 of whom had all of their lessons in Gaelic and 10 of whom had all of their lessons in English. Each child was assessed in their English language ability by the use of a recognised developmental scale. Informed consent for the investigation was gained from the parents or guardians of the children as well as from the school authorities.

The researchers used a non-directional hypothesis.

Table 1 summarises the data gained from the investigation.

Table 1 *Mean scores for English language ability through nursery and primary school education*

Age	Score on English Language Scale for children taught in Gaelic	Score on English Language Scale for children taught in English
3 to 4	3	11
4 to 5	5	12
5 to 6	8	10
6 to 7	10	11
7 to 8	20	10
8 to 9	10	9
9 to 10	20	10
10 to 11	40	12
11 to 12	50	11

7   (a) Why was it not possible to gain informed consent from the children themselves?   *(2 marks)*

(b) Why did the researchers assess children who had their lessons in English as well as the children who had their lessons in Gaelic?   *(2 marks)*

(c) Write an appropriate non-directional hypothesis for this investigation.   *(2 marks)*

(d) What level of significance should the researchers use when analysing the data? Explain why this would be suitable.   *(3 marks)*

(e) (i) Explain how a random sample could have been selected for each year group.   *(1 mark)*

(ii) With reference to the above study give **one** limitation of a random sample.   *(2 marks)*

(f) With reference to the data in **Table 1** outline and discuss the findings of this investigation.   *(10 marks)*

(g) From nine years of age through to 16 years of age when they left high school, many of the children who were taught in Gaelic also learnt French. It was noted that their ability in this new language appeared to increase with age more than would normally be expected.

Design a study to investigate the **relationship** between age and ability of the Gaelic-speaking children in learning French. Sufficient detail should be given to allow replication, for example details of a hypothesis, variables, design features, procedure and sampling could be given.   *(12 marks)*

The research methods question is centred on some stimulus material, in this instance concerning language acquisition in children. Better answers will focus material onto the stimulus material and it should also be remembered to answer the question directly as any additional material that is not focused upon the demands of the question will not receive credit and wastes valuable time. For example, with Question 7(e)(ii) the answer given should be centred on a limitation of a random sample as it relates to the quoted study. Any description of what a random sample is, or how it would be constructed, would be irrelevant to the question asked.

Examination skills

Introduction

Now that the subject content is complete, your next challenge is to prepare for and sit the AQA Psychology A2 exams. In this section, we examine the skills and knowledge necessary to do well at A2 in Psychology. Knowing your subject is one thing, but being able to write concise answers to the questions set is a skill that needs to be developed through practice. Preparation is the key to your success. The more opportunities you can give yourself to become familiar with the course content and the structure of the exam, the more confident you will feel on the day. Remember the saying, 'Better the devil you know than the devil you don't'!

This chapter looks at the requirements of both A2 examinations (Unit 3 and Unit 4) and the types of question that you are likely to meet. We will consider how you should interpret and 'decode' questions on exam papers and how you should plan your answers to essays. Some of this material on essay writing may be useful to you as you are working your way through the course. However, the environment in which you write class essays is very different. For class essays, after you have written your first draft it is likely that you will return to your work, read it through, revise it and write a second version or draft. In an exam, what you write cannot be revised and redrafted. However, as you read this section, think of the process of essay writing as a skill or craft which can be developed and polished through practice.

Making the transition from AS to A2

When you took your AS exams last year, you were assessed on your ability to answer a range of questions. The questions came in a variety of formats, most of which required you to write short answers. However, you would have come across a few questions which required you to write longer, extended pieces or mini essays. These extended pieces of writing were usually marked out of 12. The main change at A2 is that you will be required to do more extended writing. In some instances you will be required to write essays worth 25 marks.

At A2, the main change to the assessment format is on PSYA3 where all of the questions will require you to write extended essays. On PSYA4, there will be one essay question in section A, but sections B and C are likely to involve shorter, parted questions. At A2 more marks are allocated for analysis, evaluation and application than for showing knowledge and understanding. However, the skills that you will be assessed on remain the same as at AS: description, evaluation and an understanding of how science works in psychology.

Table 1 *A reminder about skills*

Assessment objective	How is it assessed?
AO1: Knowledge and understanding	This is assessed through your ability to select and describe psychological theories, concepts, principles and research studies and your ability to select, organise and communicate relevant psychological information
AO2: Application of your psychological knowledge and understanding	This is assessed through your ability to analyse and evaluate theories and studies. You will need to demonstrate that you can apply your knowledge to unfamiliar situations and can assess the validity, reliability and credibility of scientific information
AO3: How science works in psychology	This is assessed through your understanding of how scientific knowledge is collected and how scientific understanding is developed in psychology. This will include your understanding of quantitative and qualitative scientific methods, ethical practices and your ability to analyse, interpret and evaluate the methodology of your own and others' psychological investigations

Key preparation: Know the enemy

The most important preparation for the examinations is to familiarise yourself with the format of the exam paper so that when you go into the exam room you know:

- how many questions you have to answer
- roughly how long you have for each question
- how many marks are available and what they are given for.

The guidelines below tell you what you need to know about each of these points. However, you will also find it useful to look at specimen papers and past papers available from the AQA website. This will help you to build up your familiarity with the format and structure of both exam papers.

The PSYA3 exam

When you sit the Unit 3 exam you will be required to answer three questions, each on a different topic taken from the eight topics in the Specification. You will have a total of one-and-a-half hours to write your answers, which means you have 30 minutes per question. Each of these three questions is marked out of 25. This is made up of nine marks for describing (AO1) and a total of 16 marks for analysis, evaluation and application (AO2 and AO3 combined). This means that you will need to do roughly twice as much evaluating as describing in your answers.

It is likely that you will have studied only three topics for this examination and will therefore have no choice of questions. As there will only be one question on each of the topics you have studied, you *must* answer the question which is set. The most important thing to note from this is that you must revise *all* of the material from each of your three topics – questions can be set on any material within the topic and can include material from different subsections. Leaving anything out of your revision could prove extremely costly. A good way to start your revision is to work with a copy of the Specification and go through your notes making sure that every section has been covered adequately. (You can download the Specification from the AQA website at www.aqa.org.uk.) If you have gaps in your notes you will need to ensure these are filled before the exam so you are not caught out!

The PSYA4 exam

The Unit 4 exam contains three sections and lasts for two hours. A total of 85 marks are available. To reflect the number of marks available for each section, you should allow about 35 minutes each for Sections A and B and about 45 minutes for Section C.

- In Section A (Psychopathology) you should answer one question which is marked out of 25. You will not have a choice but will have to answer the question set on the specific psychological disorder you have studied.

- In Section B (Psychology in Action) you will be required to answer one compulsory question worth 25 marks on the area you have studied – Addiction, Anomalistic or Media psychology. This may be broken down into two or three shorter questions with varying numbers of marks.

The assessment criteria and awarding of marks on Sections A and B is the same as for PSYA3. Nine marks overall are awarded for description and 16 marks in total are awarded for analysis, evaluation and application. Again, this means that you should spend roughly twice as much time on analysis, evaluation and application as description. Aim for a 10/25-minute split of your time.

- In Section C, there will be one compulsory question with several different parts which cover a number of aspects of psychological research and scientific method. This question is marked out of 35. Because of this you should spend a little longer, say 45 minutes, on it. Marks for this section are mostly 'how science works' (AO3).

▓ Key exam skill 1: Decode questions

Your first action when faced with any essay question should be to look very carefully at the specific wording used. The wording of the question will often put a tight 'ring fence' around what is relevant: remember that you are never going to be asked to write everything you know or have revised about a specific topic. The difference between a good answer and a mediocre one is that in a good answer the student correctly identifies what the examiner wants and provides it. How can you decide what is relevant?

Step 1: Identify the command words

Your first action when faced with a question is to identify the **command words**. These are the terms that tell you what the examiner wants you to do in the essay. Some common command words include: describe, outline and evaluate. Each of these words has a precise meaning. You should ensure that you know what each of these means as they are often misinterpreted. For example, *describe* asks you to give detail about an idea or theory or piece of research, whereas *outline* requires you to provide the basic information about the main features with less detail. You should start your approach to any exam question by identifying (and preferably underlining) the command words in the question. This will help you to plan your essay as it will tell you *how many things* the examiner wants you to do.

▓ Key terms

Command words: instructions in the question which tell you what you should do with the material. These instructions can also be called injunction words.

For example:

Outline and *evaluate* one social psychological and one biological explanation of human aggression.

In this example, the examiner expects you to present two outlines and two evaluations. You have four things to do in order to fully answer the question. If you only do two or three of these, your essay is unlikely to score a high mark.

Table 2 *Command words and what they mean*

Term	What to do
Describe	State in detail the main points of the topic being examined. This is most likely to be a theory, but it could also be a perspective or study in the context of the essay
Outline	When the question asks for an outline, the examiner is not looking for a full description but a summary of the main features of a theory or study. For an outline, try to advance the key issues, for example the main aspects of theories. 'Outline' tends to be used more often in the PSYA3 paper, given the shorter time limit for each question to be completed
Evaluate	Evaluation requires you to put a value on something. This would usually mean weighing up the theory or study being discussed in terms of its pros and cons, advantages and limitations. You should be aware that evaluation does not simply equal 'criticise' as it is important to point out strengths and positive features as well as negative ones. Where possible, try to make your comments balanced. An awareness of the positive and negative points shows the examiner that you have a broad understanding of the topic as a whole and allows you to make a judgement about the worth of the theory or study
Discuss	This term asks you to provide some description of the issue along with some analysis and evaluation, and possibly consideration of applications and implications of the topic. The evaluation may involve a consideration of strengths and weaknesses or evidence for and against. When asked to discuss a topic, there is a large amount of potential material to choose from and you should think about including some detailed material and other issues in less depth to give some 'breadth' to your essay
Consider	This is a slight variation on 'evaluate', but the requirements are largely similar. Here, again, if you are asked to 'consider the effectiveness of …' then you are being asked to write about positive and negative aspects of the topic. You should also refer to research to substantiate your assertions or conclusions based upon the considerations you have made
To what extent	'To what extent' can loosely be translated as 'how far'. When you are asked 'to what extent', the examiner is requiring you to assess what part something plays within a larger picture. For example, 'To what extent can schizophrenia be explained by biological factors?' asks to you assess how much of a role biological factors play in schizophrenia and what factors other than biological may play a part in this disorder

AQA Examiner's tip

'Discuss' is often misinterpreted by students as meaning exactly the same as describe. When you describe someone you tell us what they are like. When you discuss them, you get critical! Think of 'discuss' as 'describe *and* evaluate' and you will not go too far wrong.

Step 2: Identify the content words

Your next step in planning is to identify the **content words**, i.e. what the content material of the essay is or what the examiner wants you to describe, outline or evaluate. In the above example question about aggression, the content should include one social psychological and one biological theory of aggression. Identifying the correct material should be relatively straightforward if you have done your revision. However, it is possible to make mistakes when under pressure, so ensure that you label all of your revision notes very carefully so that you know which theories are which. It is also useful to look back at the Specification to ensure you are familiar with the terms used which may appear in essay questions. This will mean that you are not disconcerted by the words used on the exam paper. For example, a question on bodily rhythms may refer to the terms 'endogenous pacemakers and exogenous zeitgebers' as these terms are used in the Specification.

Step 3: Make a brief plan

Now that you have decoded the question you are ready to make a brief plan of your answer. Your essay plan may be very simple, but it is likely to lead you to a much better mark. You have already identified how many things you have to do from your analysis of the command words. Now you should start to generate ideas and quickly jot down your first thoughts about material which may be relevant for every task in the essay. This should only take a few minutes of your time.

Using our example essay above (see page 556), you might write down a few ideas relating to your outline of the social learning theory of aggression (Bandura: observational/vicarious learning; self-efficacy) and a handful of things relating to your evaluation (Bobo doll studies; validity; nurture; ignores nature). You should then begin to organise your ideas into a rough plan by numbering the order in which you will cover the material. You may also decide at this stage that some material is less relevant and will have to be left out.

Step 4: Refer to your plan when writing up

Although this sounds extremely obvious, you would be amazed how many students do not do this and deviate from their plan. If you keep the plan in front of you when writing, you are less likely to go off at a tangent or stray from the question. If you run out of time you can also direct the examiner to read your plan to see what else you would have covered. Although this is unlikely to lead to high marks, you will not get credit when material is in your head – only when it appears on the paper.

▮ Key exam skill 2: Learn the art of précis

On PSYA3, you will have about 10 minutes for description in your essays, increasing to just under 15 minutes in PSYA4. This means that you will need to focus on making summaries of key theories and studies to use in your exams so you do not use up too much of your precious time. Remember that only nine marks are available for description, and anything extra that you write cannot gain any more credit. When you are creating your revision materials, you should practise summarising key theories (for example, Bandura's social learning theory) with the level of detail you can produce in about 10 minutes. You may also wish to practise reducing this to a short 'outline' which can be written in about five minutes. If you look at the examination grid overleaf, you can see

▮ Key terms

Content words: these words tell you what material you should use in your essay.

AQA Examiner's tip

Look at your copy of the Specification and highlight the sections you have studied. Make sure you know the meaning and can define all of the psychological terms mentioned in the section of the Specification that you have covered. Make yourself a glossary of these terms as a revision activity.

that you need to produce summaries which are accurate and which show some evidence of breadth and depth. This means that some material will be covered in greater detail whilst other information is included in brief form.

Table 3 *AO1 mark bands*

9–8 marks Sound understanding	Your knowledge and understanding of theories and studies is accurate with a good level of detail.
	You have selected a range of relevant material to answer the question. You have balanced breadth and depth and included some material in detail and other in less detail. Your essay is clearly organised and well structured
7–5 marks Reasonable	Your knowledge and understanding of theories and studies is reasonably accurate with some detail. You have selected relevant material to answer the question: this may show depth (for example one study in detail) or breadth. Your essay is reasonably organised with some structure
4–3 marks Basic	Your knowledge and understanding of theories and/or studies is basic and in places superficial. You have selected a small amount of relevant material to address the question. The essay is likely to be disorganised
2–1 marks Rudimentary	Your knowledge and understanding are muddled and/or inaccurate.
	The material presented is brief or may be largely irrelevant
0 marks	No creditworthy material

■ Key exam skill 3: Develop your evaluation skills

There are 16 marks available for commentary and evaluation in each essay that you write for PSYA3/4. In simple terms, evaluating involves putting a value upon something or saying how good it is. In order to gain higher marks for evaluation, you will need to develop and demonstrate a range of skills and criteria. You may find it useful to look at the different components of 'evaluation' in Table 4.

For example, if you are evaluating a piece of research, you can consider it in terms of validity, reliability, bias, ethical issues and ability to generalise from the sample. It is also quite reasonable to point out the positive merits of a research study, for example to draw attention to the range of controls applied by the researchers. After all, many research psychologists do know what they are doing!

What about evaluating a theory? A relatively straightforward way to do this is to consider if there is evidence to support the theory. Of course most of the theories presented in the book have been supported by evidence at some time. You may also wish to consider whether you have met studies which contradict some of the claims of the theory. These can be powerful tools of evaluation as they show us that the theory cannot account for all of the evidence which has been collected. Other points to include might be the quality of the evidence (a judgement based on the methodology of the studies and power of the evidence), applications of the theory and the degree to which it has stimulated other research. Another effective way to evaluate can be to compare one theory or explanation with another.

AQA Examiner's tip

For higher marks, you will note that your critical commentary should include elaboration. This means an explanation of a critical point and a brief discussion of why it is important or relevant. For example, many students claim that studies lack validity or are unethical. These basic critical points should be developed (or 'coherently elaborated') in order to reach higher bands of AO2 marks.

Throughout your studies in psychology, you have been introduced to a range of approaches – different theoretical ways of studying psychology with their own assumptions and preferred research methods. You have also been introduced to a number of issues and debates which run through the topics you have studied. These can be powerful tools for evaluation and are required for access to marks in the top band. Remember that the same rules apply as for other evaluation: the points you make must be elaborated and explained. If you are going to claim that Bandura's theory overlooks the role of biological factors or nature in aggression, you should elaborate on this by identifying a strong piece of evidence which shows the role played by biology.

Table 4 *AO2/AO3 mark bands*

16–13 marks Effective commentary/ evaluation	Your commentary demonstrates analysis, evaluation and application which reflects a very good understanding of the topic. Your essay is well focused on the question and has a clear line of argument. You have elaborated and explained your critical points well and used relevant issues, debates or approaches to comment on the material. Your ideas are expressed clearly and fluently and you have used psychological language effectively
12–9 marks Reasonable commentary/ evaluation	Your evaluation demonstrates a reasonable understanding of the topic. Your essay is generally well focused on the question and has a line of argument. You have elaborated and explained your critical points reasonably and referred to some issues, debates or approaches. Your ideas are generally expressed clearly and you have used some psychological language effectively
8–5 marks Basic commentary/ evaluation	Your evaluation shows a basic, superficial understanding of the topic. Your essay is sometimes focused on the question and you have elaborated some of your critical points. You have made some reference to issues/debates/approaches, but these may not be the most relevant. Your writing and expression of ideas lacks clarity. Your use of psychological language is limited
4–1 marks Rudimentary commentary/ evaluation	Your essay demonstrates a very limited critical understanding. Your essay is weak, muddled and may be incomplete. Some of the material is irrelevant to the question. If you have made reference to issues/debates/approaches, this is muddled and inaccurate. Your essay style is confused and your ideas are hard to follow. Your essay may read as a series of unconnected points
0 marks	No creditworthy material is presented

Hint

The main approaches you have met in this course include the biological, behavioural, cognitive and psychodynamic approaches.

The main issues and debates include free will/determinism, the role of nature and nurture, ethical issues and biases in psychology and psychology as a science.

Take it further

Practise your ability to elaborate by working with another student. You should both write a list of four or five one-line criticisms of an area you are revising. For example, *Bandura's Bobo doll study was unethical*. Ask the student you are working with to elaborate on one of your criticisms starting with 'because' (e.g. *because the young children may have suffered psychological harm*). Then add another point to the argument yourself, perhaps a piece of evidence. (*Hussmann's study has shown that long-term watchers of aggression are more likely to be involved in violence at age 30*). You can make this a bit more fun by asking 'So what?' about each criticism!

Quote questions

Quote questions are more likely to appear on PSYA4 than PSYA3. There are two distinct types of quote question:

- Those where the quotation is simply there to stimulate your thinking about the topic. For example: 'Psychological research has shown that people are much more likely to experience depression now than a hundred years ago. One explanation is that modern life involves high levels of stress and psychological pressures.' Discuss the view that depression can be explained primarily by psychological factors.

▥ Those where the command in the question specifically asks you to refer to the issues raised in the quote. For example: 'The biological approach tells us all we need to know about depression.' Discuss explanations of depression with reference to the issue raised in the quotation.

In both of these questions, you should start by decoding the quote in exactly the same way that you have decoded other types of essay question. Underline the key words in the quote and translate what is being said into your own words. The quotation will generally make a claim or relate to an important debate about the question topic. In the first quotation, the key words are depression/more likely/stress and pressures. In your own words, this claim is that depression is becoming more common due to the increased stress of modern life. You can refer to this claim in your essay if you wish and it will help to create a line of argument.

In the second type of question, you will be penalised if you do not refer to the issues raised in the quotation. When you are writing your plan you should start the essay by decoding the quote, and then refer to the claim at several points in your essay, notably at the start of each paragraph to link your discussion to the quote. So for example, you might start by saying that the biological approach tells us something about depression, before outlining the biological evidence for depression. You should then refer to the quote as your argument moves on to consider the role of psychological factors by saying: 'However, the biological approach ignores the important role played by cognitive style …'.

Research method question (PSYA4 Section C)

The question on psychological research and the scientific method focuses on different assessment objectives to that of the other questions at A Level. In all other questions on PSYA3 and PSYA4 the assessment objective AO3 (How Science Works) forms a minority of the marks (4 out of 25). However, in this question AO3 accounts for 80 per cent of the 35 marks. This question is about how psychologists study human behaviour and will require you to apply your understanding of science, research methods and data analysis. For example, you may be given a description of some research and asked to explain what method was used and what the findings show and to interpret the analysis. Other questions may give you a research idea and ask you to design a study focusing on issues such as sampling, reliability, validity or ethics.

Apart from revising the research and scientific method chapters of this book there are two other ways of preparing for this question. The first is to analyse (or deconstruct) the methods and analysis used in existing psychological research. The second is to carry out a range of your own research activities that cover a variety of methods and data analysis.

Your calendar of action for effective exam preparation and completion

6 to 4 weeks before the exam	<ul><li>Start with a copy of the Specification and check that you have sufficient notes on all of the areas you have covered.</li><li>Download specimen and past papers from the AQA website and have a look at a couple of mark schemes.</li><li>Make a revision timetable. Identify the slots in the week when you plan to revise in blocks of two or so hours. Be realistic. Add the dates of the exams for your different subjects and identify what subjects will go where in the timetable. Aim to cover each topic at least twice and preferably three times.</li><li>Identify 'rewards' and put them into your timetable. These can be time off (e.g. shopping/playing computer games/a night out).</li></ul>
4 to 2 weeks before the exam	<ul><li>Make yourself a set of revision materials.</li><li>Aim to summarise your class notes using different methods, e.g. key cards/mind maps/spider diagrams, etc. Make them colourful.</li><li>Reduce each topic that you have studied down to a couple of sides of A4 writing/diagrams. These can be kept in your pocket and read on the bus/train, etc.</li></ul>
The last 2 weeks	<ul><li>Work with previous questions.</li><li>Write essay plans in five minutes firstly with your notes, then without them. Look back at your notes to see what you have forgotten to include. Using a different colour pen, add the bits you keep forgetting.</li><li>Work with a study buddy. Test each other with short questions. Practise elaboration.</li><li>Plan a treat for after the exams have finished!</li></ul>
The night before the exam	<ul><li>As a general guide, ensure that you have plenty of rest the evening before. Go to sleep early and get plenty of REM sleep to consolidate your learning!</li></ul>
The day of the exam	<ul><li>Have something to eat even if you do not usually have breakfast.</li><li>Take a bottle of water and a slow-release food like a banana into the exam.</li></ul>
And afterwards …	<ul><li>When you come out, avoid a post mortem with other people. It will almost certainly make you feel worse!</li></ul>

Doing well on the day

So, you have finally reached D-day and you know you have done quite a lot of revision – although you will also probably know that you could have done more! How can you ensure that the hard work you have done pays off on the day? It will help if you have a tactical plan to approach the paper. As you have looked at previous papers as part of your preparation, you should not be surprised by the format of the exam paper. Some students like to start by looking quickly at all of the questions to reassure themselves that there is nothing too scary in the paper. Others prefer to jump straight in with the first question. Some people like to write out all of their essay plans before starting the real work. Any of these approaches is fine but remember to stick to the three steps of planning your essays whichever approach you choose.

AQA Examiner's tip

In the PSYA3 paper you have 30 minutes per question. Make sure you take a watch into the exam, put it on the desk where you can see it and keep an eye on the time for each question. You should have a rough exam-time plan in your head (9.05am start Q1; 9.35am Q2; 10.05am Q3). Make sure you do not over-run, and be prepared to stop writing at the end of 30 minutes and start your next question. Remember that two fantastic answers scoring 20 out of 25 each but no third essay will get you a lower mark than three good enough essays which get 15 marks each!

Which order should you attempt the questions in? Some people like to start with their best essay in order to build up their confidence on the paper, moving on to the second best and ending with their least favourite topic. Others prefer to get the worst bit over with first then move on to safer ground. On PSYA4, some students argue that starting with research methods is a good way to get into the paper, as each question only carries a small number of marks. Again, all of these are perfectly acceptable strategies.

On the day you will have little time to write elaborate introductions or conclusions as you may have done in class essays. However, you might find it useful to leave a gap of about half a side at the start and end of each essay. This means that if you have spare time at the end – or if midway through another question you remember that you have missed out something really important – you can go back and add it in later.

After the exam, it is probably best to avoid analysing or talking to other people. It almost always leads to panic and a feeling that they have done better than you. When the exam is gone it is truly over. Put your notes away, cross off the date on the calendar and keep focused on the next hurdle. Good luck!

Statistical tables

Table 1 *Critical values of χ^2*

df	Level of significance for a one-tailed test					
	0.10	0.05	0.025	0.01	0.005	0.005
	Level of significance for a two-tailed test					
	0.20	0.10	0.05	0.02	0.01	0.001
1	1.64	2.71	3.84	5.41	6.64	10.83
2	3.22	4.60	5.99	7.82	9.21	13.82
3	4.64	6.25	7.82	9.84	11.34	16.27
4	5.99	7.78	9.49	11.67	13.28	18.46
5	7.29	9.24	11.07	13.39	15.09	20.52
6	8.56	10.64	12.59	15.03	16.81	22.46
7	9.80	12.02	14.07	16.62	18.48	24.32
8	11.03	13.36	15.51	18.17	20.09	26.12
9	12.24	14.68	16.92	19.68	21.67	27.88
10	13.44	15.99	18.31	21.16	23.21	29.59
11	14.63	17.28	19.68	22.62	24.72	31.26
12	15.81	18.55	21.03	24.05	26.22	32.91
13	16.98	19.81	22.36	25.47	27.69	34.53
14	18.15	21.06	23.68	26.87	29.14	36.12
15	19.31	22.31	25.00	28.26	30.58	37.70
16	20.46	23.54	26.30	29.63	32.00	39.29
17	21.62	24.77	27.59	31.00	33.41	40.75
18	22.76	25.99	28.87	32.35	34.80	42.31
19	23.90	27.20	30.14	33.69	36.19	43.82
20	25.04	28.41	31.41	35.02	37.57	45.32
21	26.17	29.62	32.67	36.34	38.93	46.80
22	27.30	30.81	33.92	37.66	40.29	48.27
23	28.43	32.01	35.17	38.97	41.64	49.73
24	29.55	33.20	36.42	40.27	42.98	51.18
25	30.68	34.38	37.65	41.57	44.31	52.62
26	31.80	35.56	38.88	42.86	45.64	54.05
27	32.91	36.74	40.11	44.14	46.96	55.48
28	34.03	37.92	41.34	45.42	48.28	56.89
29	35.14	39.09	42.69	49.69	49.59	58.30
30	36.25	40.26	43.77	47.96	50.89	59.70
32	38.47	42.59	46.19	50.49	53.49	62.49
34	40.68	44.90	48.60	53.00	56.06	65.25
36	42.88	47.21	51.00	55.49	58.62	67.99
38	45.08	49.51	53.38	57.97	61.16	70.70
40	47.27	51.81	55.76	60.44	63.69	73.40
44	51.64	56.37	60.48	65.34	68.71	78.75
48	55.99	60.91	65.17	70.20	73.68	84.04
52	60.33	65.42	69.83	75.02	78.62	89.27
56	64.66	69.92	74.47	79.82	83.51	94.46
60	68.97	74.40	79.08	84.58	88.38	99.61

*Calculated value of χ^2 must be EQUAL TO or EXCEED the table (critical) values for significance at the level shown. Abridged from **R.A.Fisher and F. Yates** (1974) Statistical Tables for Biological, Agricultural and Medical Research, (6th edn) Longman Group UK Ltd.*

Table 2a Critical values of U for a one-tailed test at 0.005; two-tailed test at 0.01* (Mann-Whitney)

n_1

n_2	1	2	3	4	5	6	7	8	9	10	11	12	13	14	15	16	17	18	19	20
1	–	–	–	–	–	–	–	–	–	–	–	–	–	–	–	–	–	–	–	–
2	–	–	–	–	–	–	–	–	–	–	–	–	–	–	–	–	–	–	0	0
3	–	–	–	–	–	–	–	–	0	0	0	1	1	1	2	2	2	2	3	3
4	–	–	–	–	–	0	0	1	1	2	2	3	3	4	5	5	6	6	7	8
5	–	–	–	–	0	1	1	2	3	4	5	6	7	7	8	9	10	11	12	13
6	–	–	–	0	1	2	3	4	5	6	7	9	10	11	12	13	15	16	17	18
7	–	–	–	0	1	3	4	6	7	9	10	12	13	15	16	18	19	21	22	24
8	–	–	–	1	2	4	6	7	9	11	13	15	17	18	20	22	24	26	28	30
9	–	–	0	1	3	5	7	9	11	13	16	18	20	22	24	27	29	31	33	36
10	–	–	0	2	4	6	9	11	13	16	18	21	24	26	29	31	34	37	39	42
11	–	–	0	2	5	7	10	13	16	18	21	24	27	30	33	36	39	42	45	48
12	–	–	1	3	6	9	12	15	18	21	24	27	31	34	37	41	44	47	51	54
13	–	–	1	3	7	10	13	17	20	24	27	31	34	38	42	45	49	53	56	60
14	–	–	1	4	7	11	15	18	22	26	30	34	38	42	46	50	54	58	63	67
15	–	–	2	5	8	12	16	20	24	29	33	37	42	46	51	55	60	64	69	73
16	–	–	2	5	9	13	18	22	27	31	36	41	45	50	55	60	65	70	74	79
17	–	–	2	6	10	15	19	24	29	34	39	44	49	54	60	65	70	75	81	86
18	–	–	2	6	11	16	21	26	31	37	42	47	53	58	64	70	75	81	87	92
19	–	0	3	7	12	17	22	28	33	39	45	51	56	63	69	74	81	87	93	99
20	–	0	3	8	13	18	24	30	36	42	48	54	60	67	73	79	86	92	99	105

*Dashes in the body of the table indicate that no decision is possible at the stated level of significance.

For any n_1 and n_2, the observed value of U is significant at a given level of significance if it is EQUAL TO or LESS THAN the critical values shown.

SOURCE: **R. Runyon and A. Haber** (1976) Fundamentals of Behavioural Statistics (3rd edn) Reading, Mass.: McGraw Hill, Inc. with kind permission of the publisher.

Table 2b *Critical values of U for a one-tailed test at 0.01; two-tailed test at 0.02* (Mann-Whitney)*

n_2 \ n_1	1	2	3	4	5	6	7	8	9	10	11	12	13	14	15	16	17	18	19	20
1	—	—	—	—	—	—	—	—	—	—	—	—	—	—	—	—	—	—	—	—
2	—	—	—	—	—	—	—	—	—	—	—	—	0	0	0	0	0	0	1	1
3	—	—	—	—	—	—	0	0	1	1	1	2	2	2	3	3	4	4	4	5
4	—	—	—	—	0	1	1	2	3	3	4	5	5	6	7	7	8	9	9	10
5	—	—	—	0	1	2	3	4	5	6	7	8	9	10	11	12	13	14	15	16
6	—	—	—	1	2	3	4	6	7	8	9	11	12	13	15	16	18	19	20	22
7	—	—	0	1	3	4	6	7	9	11	12	14	16	17	19	21	23	24	26	28
8	—	—	0	2	4	6	7	9	11	13	15	17	20	22	24	26	28	30	32	34
9	—	—	1	3	5	7	9	11	14	16	18	21	23	26	28	31	33	36	38	40
10	—	—	1	3	6	8	11	13	16	19	22	24	27	30	33	36	38	41	44	47
11	—	—	1	4	7	9	12	15	18	22	25	28	31	34	37	41	44	47	50	53
12	—	—	2	5	8	11	14	17	21	24	28	31	35	38	42	46	49	53	56	60
13	—	0	2	5	9	12	16	20	23	27	31	35	39	43	47	51	55	59	63	67
14	—	0	2	6	10	13	17	22	26	30	34	38	43	47	51	56	60	65	69	73
15	—	0	3	7	11	15	19	24	28	33	37	42	47	51	56	61	66	70	75	80
16	—	0	3	7	12	16	21	26	31	36	41	46	51	56	61	66	71	76	82	87
17	—	0	4	8	13	18	23	28	33	38	44	49	55	60	66	71	77	82	88	93
18	—	0	4	9	14	19	24	30	36	41	47	53	59	65	70	76	82	88	94	100
19	—	1	4	9	15	20	26	32	38	44	50	56	63	69	75	82	88	94	101	107
20	—	1	5	10	16	22	28	34	40	47	53	60	67	73	80	87	93	100	107	114

*Dashes in the body of the table indicate that no decision is possible at the stated level of significance.

For any n_1 and n_2, the observed value of U is significant at a given level of significance if it is EQUAL TO or LESS THAN the critical values shown.

*Source: **R. Runyon and A. Haber** (1976) Fundamentals of Behavioural Statistics (3rd edn) Reading, Mass.: McGraw Hill, Inc. with kind permission of the publisher.*

Table 2c *Critical values of U for a one-tailed test at 0.025; two-tailed test at 0.05* (Mann-Whitney)*

n_2 \ n_1	1	2	3	4	5	6	7	8	9	10	11	12	13	14	15	16	17	18	19	20
1	—	—	—	—	—	—	—	—	—	—	—	—	—	—	—	—	—	—	—	—
2	—	—	—	—	—	—	—	0	0	0	0	1	1	1	1	1	2	2	2	2
3	—	—	—	—	0	1	1	2	2	3	3	4	4	5	5	6	6	7	7	8
4	—	—	—	0	1	2	3	4	4	5	6	7	8	9	10	11	11	12	13	13
5	—	—	0	1	2	3	5	6	7	8	9	11	12	13	14	15	17	18	19	20
6	—	—	1	2	3	5	6	8	10	11	13	14	16	17	19	21	22	24	25	27
7	—	—	1	3	5	6	8	10	12	14	16	18	20	22	24	26	28	30	32	34
8	—	0	2	4	6	8	10	13	15	17	19	22	24	26	29	31	34	36	38	41
9	—	0	2	4	7	10	12	15	17	20	23	26	28	31	34	37	39	42	45	48
10	—	0	3	5	8	11	14	17	20	23	26	29	33	36	39	42	45	48	52	55
11	—	0	3	6	9	13	16	19	23	26	30	33	37	40	44	47	51	55	58	62
12	—	1	4	7	11	14	18	22	26	29	33	37	41	45	49	53	57	61	65	69
13	—	1	4	8	12	16	20	24	28	33	37	41	45	50	54	59	63	67	72	76
14	—	1	5	9	13	17	22	26	31	36	40	45	50	55	59	64	67	74	78	83
15	—	1	5	10	14	19	24	29	34	39	44	49	54	59	64	70	75	80	85	90
16	—	1	6	11	15	21	26	31	37	42	47	53	59	64	70	75	81	86	92	98
17	—	2	6	11	17	22	28	34	39	45	51	57	63	67	75	81	87	93	99	105
18	—	2	7	12	18	24	30	36	42	48	55	61	67	74	80	86	93	99	106	112
19	—	2	7	13	19	25	32	38	45	52	58	65	72	78	85	92	99	106	113	119
20	—	2	8	13	20	27	34	41	48	55	62	69	76	83	90	98	105	112	119	127

*Dashes in the body of the table indicate that no decision is possible at the stated level of significance.

For any n_1 and n_2 the observed value of U is significant at a given level of significance if it is EQUAL TO or LESS THAN the critical values shown.

Source: **R. Runyon and A. Haber** (1976) Fundamentals of Behavioural Statistics (3rd edn) Reading, Mass.: McGraw Hill, Inc. with kind permission of the publisher.

Table 2d *Critical values of U for a one-tailed test at 0.05; two-tailed test at 0.10* (Mann–Whitney)*

n_1

n_2	1	2	3	4	5	6	7	8	9	10	11	12	13	14	15	16	17	18	19	20
1	–	–	–	–	–	–	–	–	–	–	–	–	–	–	–	–	–	–	0	0
2	–	–	–	–	0	0	0	1	1	1	1	2	2	2	3	3	3	4	4	4
3	–	–	0	0	1	2	2	3	3	4	5	5	6	7	7	8	9	9	10	11
4	–	–	0	1	2	3	4	5	6	7	8	9	10	11	12	14	15	16	17	18
5	–	0	1	2	4	5	6	8	9	11	12	13	15	16	18	19	20	22	23	25
6	–	0	2	3	5	7	8	10	12	14	16	17	19	21	23	25	26	28	30	32
7	–	0	2	4	6	8	11	13	15	17	19	21	24	26	28	30	33	35	37	39
8	–	1	3	5	8	10	13	15	18	20	23	26	28	31	33	36	39	41	44	47
9	–	1	3	6	9	12	15	18	21	24	27	30	33	36	39	42	45	48	51	54
10	–	1	4	7	11	14	17	20	24	27	31	34	37	41	44	48	51	55	58	62
11	–	1	5	8	12	16	19	23	27	31	34	38	42	46	50	54	57	61	65	69
12	–	2	5	9	13	17	21	26	30	34	38	42	47	51	55	60	64	68	72	77
13	–	2	6	10	15	19	24	28	33	37	42	47	51	56	61	65	70	75	80	84
14	–	2	7	11	16	21	26	31	36	41	46	51	56	61	66	71	77	82	87	92
15	–	3	7	12	18	23	28	33	39	44	50	55	61	66	72	77	83	88	94	100
16	–	3	8	14	19	25	30	36	42	48	54	60	65	71	77	83	89	95	101	107
17	–	3	9	15	20	26	33	39	45	51	57	64	70	77	83	89	96	102	109	115
18	–	4	9	16	22	28	35	41	48	55	61	68	75	82	88	95	102	109	116	123
19	0	4	10	17	23	30	37	44	51	58	65	72	80	87	94	101	109	116	123	130
20	0	4	11	18	25	32	39	47	54	62	69	77	84	92	100	107	115	123	130	138

*Dashes in the body of the table indicate that no decision is possible at the stated level of significance.

For any n_1 and n_2, the observed value of U is significant at a given level of significance if it is EQUAL TO or LESS THAN the critical values shown.

Source: **R. Runyon and A. Haber** (1976) Fundamentals of Behavioural Statistics (3rd edn) Reading, Mass.: McGraw Hill, Inc. with kind permission of the publisher.

Table 3 *Critical values of T in the Wilcoxon signed ranks test*

	Levels of significance for a one-tailed test			
	0.05	0.025	0.01	0.001
	Levels of significance for a two-tailed test			
	0.1	0.05	0.02	0.002
Sample size				
N = 5	T ≤ 0			
6	2	0		
7	3	2	0	
8	5	3	1	
9	8	5	3	
10	11	8	5	0
11	13	10	7	1
12	17	13	9	2
13	21	17	12	4
14	25	21	15	6
15	30	25	19	8
16	35	29	23	11
17	41	34	27	14
18	47	40	32	18
19	53	46	37	21
20	60	52	43	26
21	67	58	49	30
22	75	65	55	35
23	83	73	62	40
24	91	81	69	45
25	100	89	76	51
26	110	98	84	58
27	119	107	92	64
28	130	116	101	71
30	151	137	120	86
31	163	147	130	94
32	175	159	140	103
33	187	170	151	112

Calculated T must be EQUAL TO or LESS THAN the table (critical) value for significance at the level shown.
SOURCE: *Adapted from* **R. Meddis**, *(1975)* Statistical Handbook for Non-Statisticians, *London: McGraw-Hill with the kind permission of the author and publishers.*

Table 4 *Critical values of Spearman's r_s*

	Level of significance for a one-tailed test			
	0.05	0.025	0.01	0.005
	Level of significance for a two-tailed test			
	0.10	0.05	0.02	0.01
N = 4	1.000			
5	0.900	1.000	1.000	
6	0.829	0.886	0.943	1.000
7	0.714	0.786	0.893	0.929
8	0.643	0.738	0.833	0.881
9	0.600	0.700	0.783	0.833
10	0.564	0.648	0.745	0.794
11	0.536	0.618	0.709	0.755
12	0.503	0.587	0.671	0.727
13	0.484	0.560	0.648	0.703
14	0.464	0.538	0.622	0.675
15	0.443	0.521	0.604	0.654
16	0.429	0.503	0.582	0.635
17	0.414	0.485	0.566	0.615
18	0.401	0.472	0.550	0.600
19	0.391	0.460	0.535	0.584
20	0.380	0.447	0.520	0.570
21	0.370	0.435	0.508	0.556
22	0.361	0.425	0.496	0.544
23	0.353	0.415	0.486	0.532
24	0.344	0.406	0.476	0.521
25	0.337	0.398	0.466	0.511
26	0.331	0.390	0.457	0.501
27	0.324	0.382	0.448	0.491
28	0.317	0.375	0.440	0.483
29	0.312	0.368	0.433	0.475
30	0.306	0.362	0.425	0.467

For $n > 30$, the significance of r_s can be tested by using the formula:

$$t = r_s \sqrt{\frac{n-2}{1-r_s^2}} \qquad df = n - 2$$

and checking the value of T in Table 3.

Calculated r_s must EQUAL, or EXCEED the table (critical) value for significance at the level shown.
SOURCE: **J.H. Zhar**, *Significance testing of the Spearman Rank Correlation Coefficient*, Journal of the American Statistical Association, 67, 578–80. With the kind permission of the publishers.

Index

References and other supporting documentation available online at:

www.nelsonthornes.com/psychology_answers

Acknowledgements

The authors and publishers wish to thank the following for permission to use copyright material:

page 77, Fig. 2, The British Psychological Society for V. Bruce and A. Young, 'Understanding face recognition', *The British Journal of Psychology*, 1986, Vol. 77, pages 305–27. © The British Psychological Society; pages 124–5 and page 126, The Random House Group Ltd with Philip Zimbardo for extracts from Philip Zimbardo, *The Lucifer Effect: Understanding How Good People Turn Evil*, Rider (2007); page 207, Guardian News and Media Ltd for extracts from Viv Groskop, 'The trouble with CBeebies', *The Guardian*, 2 November 2007. © Guardian News & Media Ltd 2007; page 237, Fig. 8, Palgrave Macmillan for Rosalind Searle, 'Figure 7.9' from *Selection and Recruitment* (2003), page 188; pages 342–3, American Psychiatric Association for material from *Diagnostic and Statistical Manual of Mental Disorders, Text Revision, Fourth Edition*. © APA 2000; page 423, Fig. 1, Open University Press for Jane Ogden, 'Figure 5.4 The stages of substance use', *Health Psychology: A Textbook* (2000); page 433, American Psychiatric Association for material from *Diagnostic and Statistical Manual of Mental Disorders, Text Revision, Fourth Edition*. © APA 2000; page 434, Gambling Commission for material from *British Gambling Prevalence Survey 2007*. © Gambling Commission. All rights reserved; page 483, PARS/*The New York Times* for an extract from Daniel Gilbert, 'I'm OK, You're Biased', *The New York Times*, 16 April 2008. © 2008 *The New York Times*.

Page 3, Deco/Alamy; page 24, Fig. 6, Time & Life Pictures/Getty Images; page 24, Fig.7, Time & Life Pictures/Getty Images; page 39, Fig. 1 Corbis/Louie Psihoyos/Science Faction; page 40, Fig. 2, Jupiter Images/Thinkstock/Alamy; page 83, Richard Young/Rex Features; page 85, Fig. 1, Venturelli/Romaniello/Rex Features; page 86, Fig. 2, 20th Century Fox/The Kobal Collection/Morton, Merrick; page 93, Fig. 1,

Image Source Black/Alamy; page 107, Fig. 1, R1/Alamy; page 113, Reuters/Stringer Russia; page 124, Fig. 3, Philip G. Zimbardo, Ph.D. Prof. Emeritus, Stanford University; page 129, Fig. 1, Wellcome Images/Wessex Reg. Genetics Centre; page 139, Fig. 1, iStockphoto; page 145, Fig. 2, AFP/Getty Images; page 147, Fig. 3, Amit Bhargava/Corbis; page 151, Fotolia; page 167, Fig. 1, Fotolia; page 178, Fig. 1, Ted Foxx/Alamy; page 193, Getty Images; page 194, Fig. 1, MGM/UA/The Kobal Collection; page 195, Fig. 2, Pictorial Press Ltd/Alamy; page 210, Fig. 1, Ellen McKnight/Alamy; page 213, Fig. 3, Fotolia (both); page 217, Fig. 1, HarperCollins Publishers Ltd. © 2006 Conn Iggulden and Hal Iqqulden; page 227, Rosemary Roberts/Alamy; page 231, Fig. 4, WireImage; page 232, Fig. 5, Martin Jenkinson/Alamy (left), Photo Researchers/Alamy (right); page 253, Fig. 1, David Gifford/Photo Science Library; page 269, Bubbles Photolibrary/Alamy; page 281, Fig. 4, JP Laffont/Sygma/Corbis; page 287, Fig. 1, AFP/Getty Images; page 315, Photodisc/Alamy; page 329, Fig. 1, iStockphoto; page 356, Fig. 1, Will McIntyre/Science Photo Library; page 365, Fig. 1, Fancy/Veer/Corbis; page 377, Fig. 2, John Greim/Photo Science Library; page 389, Miramax/Buena Vista/The Kobal Collection; page 400, Fig. 2, courtesy of Advertising Archives; page 404, Fig. 1, NBC/The Kobal Collection; page 406, Fig. 2, NBC/The Kobal Collection; page 421, Fotolia; page 441, Fig. 1, Matthew Polak/Sygma/Corbis; page 450, Fig. 2, Dr P. Marazzi/Photo Science Library; page 457, Charles Walker/TopFoto; page 468, Fig. 2, Fortean/Playfair/TopFoto; page 471, Fig. 3, Fortean/TopFoto; page 471, Fig. 4, Ina Fassbender/Reuters/Corbis; page 471, Fig. 5, Fortean/TopFoto; page 486, Fig. 3, Getty Images; page 488, Fig. 1, Homer Sykes/Corbis.

Every effort has been made to trace the copyright holders but if any have been inadvertently overlooked the publishers will be pleased to make the necessary arrangement at the first opportunity.